Android Apps with App Inventor

Android Apps with App Inventor

The Fast and Easy Way to Build Android Apps

Jörg H. Kloss

Addison-Wesley

Upper Saddle River, NJ • Boston • Indianapolis • San Francisco
New York • Toronto • Montreal • London • Munich • Paris • Madrid
Capetown • Sydney • Tokyo • Singapore • Mexico City

Library of Congress Cataloging-in-Publication Data

Kloss, Jörg H.
Android Apps with App inventor : the fast and easy way to build android apps / Jörg H. Kloss.
p. cm.
Includes bibliographical references and index.
ISBN 978-0-321-81270-4 (pbk. : alk. paper)
1. Application software–Development. 2. Android (Electronic resource) 3. Open source software. 4. Smartphones. 5. Mobile computing. I. Title.
QA76.76.A65K614 2012
005.3—dc23

2011047948

ISBN-13: 978-0-321-81270-4
ISBN-10: 0-321-81270-0
Text printed in the United States on recycled paper at Edwards Brothers Malloy in Ann Arbor, Michigan.
Second printing, September 2012

Editor-in-Chief
Mark Taub

Acquisitions Editor
Trina MacDonald

Development Editor
Songlin Qiu

Managing Editor
John Fuller

Project Editor
Anna Popick

Copy Editor
Jill Hobbs

Indexer
Jack Lewis

Proofreader
Lori Newhouse

Publishing Coordinator
Olivia Basegio

Cover Designer
Chuti Prasertsith

Compositor
Vicki Rowland

Translator
Almut Dworak

Contents at a Glance

Contents

Preface by Hal Abelson

Following is the original preface to this book by Dr. Hal Abelson, Professor of Electrical Engineering and Computer Science at Massachusetts Institute of Technology (Cambridge, Massachusetts), leading member of the Google App Inventor Team, and director of the new MIT Center for Mobile Learning supported by Google.

People have been doing personal computing since the 1980s. But today's mobile applications are making computing "personal" as never before. Today, we carry computers with us constantly, as smartphones and pads and the new devices that are regularly emerging. More significantly, today's personal computing is increasingly "about" us: where we live, where we work, who our friends are, what we buy, what we like, whom we talk with, and what we talk about. This personal computing is linked to global data services and information sources in a way that fundamentally transforms our experience and our perception of our world, just as television did for people beginning in the 1950s.

Television was a consumer technology. Anyone could enjoy television, but there was no way to adapt television to your personal needs, other than by selecting which program to watch from a variety of offerings from professional producers. Perhaps mobile computing will be similar, where we're all limited to choosing from among predefined applications supplied by professional developers.

When we created App Inventor at Google, we were motivated by the vision that mobile computing could be personal computing technology that you can actually personalize, by creating applications for yourself and your friends, without having to be an expert programmer. Perhaps you might create applications because you want to fulfill a special need, or learn about computing, or try your hand at distributing and selling applications, or just have fun.

App Inventor became available for general use in December 2010. It's still a beta system under development, and the Google team is working to make it more powerful and easier to use. But there is already a growing community of App Inventor users of all ages who are exploring and experiencing what it's like to make applications for themselves. Some of the things they are creating are:

- An application for sending and redeeming gift cards
- A guide to a major medical reference book
- A controller for a Lego robot
- An inventory tracker for a commercial vehicle manufacturer

- Educational programs in reading and mathematics for their kids
- Many kinds of games

You can make applications like these, too, and this book shows you how, starting with the basics of how to access the App Inventor system from the Google website and connect your mobile phone, through pointers on developing applications that use the phone's built-in accelerometer, orientation, and location sensors. Along the way, you'll get a solid introduction to creating applications with text and data and to working with images and animation. You'll learn how to control the phone's camera, how to manipulate databases on the phone and on the Web, and how to create games, send text messages and make phone calls, and manipulate maps. Each topic is accompanied by working applications and thorough explanations.

Could this be your first step toward a future in designing mobile applications? Perhaps. Even if it is not, you'll find that you can be creative and empowered with a technology that's playing an increasingly central role in your life, and the lives of us all.

—Hal Abelson
MIT Center for Mobile Learning
Google App Inventor Team
March 2011

Preface

There could not be a better time than today to start developing Android apps, for many reasons. Most importantly, developing your own apps has never before been easier than it is now with App Inventor. This development tool, which is offered by Google and Massachusetts Institute of Technology (MIT) and has been available since December 2010, is available free of charge for all to use. With App Inventor, you can develop your own apps, even if you have never programmed before, using a computer or even a smartphone. With App Inventor, you can build both small and really big apps with playful ease by assembling visual building blocks, without having to write a single line of Java code. Yet App Inventor is by no means just a toy: It is an alternative and innovative tool with which you can develop even complex and demanding apps quickly and easily, both for yourself and for other users. Take a look at the table of contents of this book, and you will be amazed to find that the early chapters of a book aimed at beginners contain instructions for developing apps in the areas of multimedia (photo, audio, video), graphics and animation, various forms of communication (speech, SMS, e-mail, web services), and even sensors (orientation, acceleration, GPS geoposition). In Figure P.1, you can see a selection of the apps you will develop in this book.

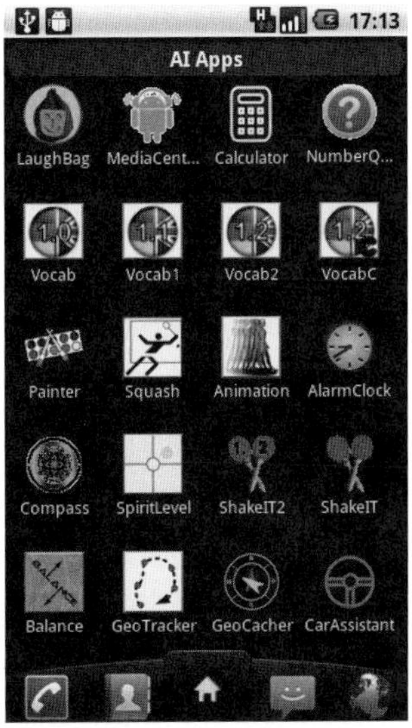

Figure P.1 Android apps developed in this book

The quick and easy start and the equally quick and intuitive development of attractive and demanding apps are the declared aims of the visual development tool App Inventor. App Inventor is aimed at a far larger target group than ordinary development tools. With App Inventor, all users of Android smartphones now have the chance to peek behind the scenes at the colorful world of apps, then have a go themselves and express their creativity by designing their own apps. Where those apps go is entirely up to the developer's individual preferences, topical emphasis, and personal motivation. You as a user can decide whether your own app is "just" a personal digital picture frame, a quiz game, a vocabulary trainer with a potentially shareable online database, or a geotracker for automatically creating a route profile while the user is hiking. The future will show to what extent the "users" of such personal apps eventually turn into "developers"—that is, whether they evolve from "passive consumers" to "active producers," thereby triggering a mini-revolution in dealing with the most modern forms of communication technology. Nevertheless, even experienced developers can profit from using App Inventor, as it enables them to produce professional prototypes and apps much more quickly and, therefore, more cost-effectively. Come and take part in these "developments" and get to know App Inventor by reading this book. You will learn to use it for your own purposes and soon appreciate its value as an immensely powerful developer tool.

Owing to its rich set of properties and features, App Inventor is in the right place at exactly the right time. Now that many billions of dollars have been invested in licenses and establishing the mobile telecommunications network infrastructure, the mobile data networks of the third generation (3G: UMTS, HSDPA) and fourth generation (4G: LTE) are available almost anywhere and at any time, with a data flat-rate tariff often being used as the basis for fast data services, mobile Internet access, and web services. In turn, the new developments by manufacturers of mobile devices keep coming in a rush. Moreover, after a deluge of new smartphones with incredible technical specifications for domestic use, the next generation of tablet PCs is being embraced by a growing number of customers who are willing to pay for them. The providers of online services and web services are also eager to make use of the new mobile possibilities and to offer the increasingly communicative Web 2.0 users mobile extensions such as location-based services and proprietary apps on the growing app market. The competition between the mobile operating systems appears almost calm and seems to be more or less settled, the "top dogs" have long since been pushed out, and, after an initial neck-and-neck race, the triumph of Android as the operating system of choice for smartphones now seems certain. With its open approach, the resulting flexibility, its free availability, and its integrative access to the entire range of features of the manifold Google Services, Android has qualities that the other mobile operating systems lack.

Despite the impressive technological advancements, users nowadays are no longer only interested in pure technical features and details. Although the Internet first started to develop thanks to just a few technologically minded enthusiasts, it has long since been transformed from a mass medium for consuming news, information, and entertainment (Web 1.0) to an active, commonplace form of communication between people (Web 2.0). Today the focus is not so much on the technology, but rather on the communication, creativity, and individuality that people can apply and express with it. This trend partly explains the increasing willingness of users to invest time and effort into creating their own profiles in social networks, to establish their own blogs, and participate in chats or online games, but also to invest money in the form of fixed and mobile telecommunications charges and the newest and most fashionable hardware. Regardless of which forms of expression users' individuality and creativity may take in the age of digital and networked communication, App Inventor offers entirely new possibilities for exercising them. Previously, users were able to move only within the predetermined limits set by the hardware manufacturer, the platform operator, and the app developer; now they can at least overcome the latter by using App Inventor, thereby gaining a piece of freedom and independence—a factor that should not be underestimated. Even if you do not have such ambitious aims, you can still have fun when developing your own apps with App Inventor. After reading this book and working your way through the many example apps, you will see the colorful app world with different eyes. And almost without noticing it, you will have become a developer of Android Apps. So, what are you waiting for?

Acknowledgments

I would like to thank everyone who has supported me during the creation of this book, directly or indirectly. This includes not least the members of the Google App Inventor Team, whose incredibly dedicated work has made such a fascinating developer tool as App Inventor and, therefore, many impressive apps—and this book—possible in the first place. I am especially grateful to Hal Abelson, Professor at the legendary MIT, central impulse giver within the Google App Inventor Team, and director of the MIT Center for Mobile Learning, for his inspiring and courageous work on this and the previous projects and for providing the preface to this book.

For the English-language revised and updated edition of this book, I would like to thank my colleagues in the German publishing house, Brigitte Bauer-Schiewek and Angelika Ritthaler, and in the United States, Jill Hobbs, Trina MacDonald, Anna Popick, and Songlin Qiu. I am particularly grateful to Almut Dworak for the excellent translation work and, beyond that, for the helpful comments and feedback on the book.

My thanks also to those who had so much patience with me while I was writing this book: my parents, my sister, Maximilian, Benedikt, and, above all, Alexandra.

—Jörg H. Kloss
January 2012

About the Author

Jörg H. Kloss has worked for many years with innovative information and communication technology, including its development, programming, and use in both private and professional areas. His private-sector beginnings with the Amstrad CPC and the programming language Basic were followed by deeper explorations at university in the area of artificial intelligence and computer linguistics, working in Pascal, C, C++, and Java, but also in specialized languages such as Lisp and Prolog. Mr. Kloss was one of the early pioneers of virtual reality (VR), augmented reality (AR), and interactive 3D worlds on the Internet. He began development work on commercial VRML-based online information systems in the mid-1990s, has worked at the renowned German VR lab of the Fraunhofer Institute for Industrial Engineering (FhG-IAO) and the American VR-Entertainer StrayLight, and was president of the European division of the VR Alliance of Students and Professionals (VRASP). In addition to numerous presentations, contributions, and other publications, Mr. Kloss has written two books that were published (in German) by Addison-Wesley: *VRML97: Der neue Standard für interaktive 3D-Welten im World Wide Web* (*VRML97: The New Standard for Interactive 3D Worlds in the World Wide Web*; 1998) and *X3D: Programmierung interaktiver 3D-Anwendungen für das Internet* (*X3D: Programming Interactive 3D Applications for the Internet*; 2010).

After developing early industrial projects based on 3D multiuser worlds for an international media house as well as for remote maintenance via the powerline of a large energy supplier, Mr. Kloss focused on telecommunications for many years, taking part in innovative projects involving multimedia data and voice technologies in the areas of fixed and mobile network communications (IP, TDM, VoIP, 3G, 4G). As these technologies have converged, Mr. Kloss has dealt increasingly with the potential of mobile data networks and services in the context of mobile augmented reality, ubiquitous computing, and contextual services. He has actively taken part in the development of Android apps with App Inventor since the early closed-beta phase.

Introduction

This book is a compendium, a practical course book, and a comprehensive tutorial in one, offering a collection of example projects for smaller and larger applications (apps) for Android devices. As a compendium, it addresses, introduces, and demonstrates more or less comprehensively every single area and almost every component of the App Inventor development tool as it was available at the time when the book was written. Consequently, this book can be used as a reference work even by experienced developers who are looking for specific instructions and information about a certain functional area. Presenting examples from a wide variety of topics, it also serves as a practical course book on the general development of apps for mobile devices with their specific multimedia, communication, and sensory properties as well as system elements that often remain uncharted territory even for the experienced PC programmer. Along with the basic aspects of application development, program structures, and functional elements, the example projects demonstrate approaches and solution strategies for the typical problems that can arise in the context of mobile applications.

As a comprehensive tutorial, this text is aimed mainly at beginners and their needs. Both the structure of this book and the development tool App Inventor are written with beginners in mind, with a clear focus on practical application. If you are a newcomer to programming in general or to app development for mobile devices in particular, specifically for Android smartphones, or if you are simply adopting the development tool App Inventor, the introductory chapters of Parts I and II of this book will provide you with the level of knowledge you need and guide you step by step through the development of Android apps with App Inventor. The many accompanying example projects and apps illustrate and extend what you have learned, invite you to experiment and try things out for yourself, and provide a starting point inspiring you to creatively develop your own apps. You will learn progressively in line with the sequential structure of the book's chapters, the topics and functional areas addressed, and the example projects we develop, all of which usually build on the knowledge gained in the preceding chapters. Along with covering the many functional areas and elements, the book also discusses basic methods of program development and explains how to use App Inventor's online resources, thereby preparing you to undertake your own development work in the future. In the process, the perspective gradually changes from the initial perspective of the beginner looking at individual components and their functions to the view of the developer focusing on the actual tasks the app performs and strategies to implement them with App Inventor.

Structure and Overview

If you take a quick look at the table of contents, you will see that this book is divided into five parts. These parts are not so much devoted to different topics, but rather reflect the intended evolution of the reader from the beginner working with App Inventor for the first time to the developer of advanced and complex apps—which we certainly hope will occur while you are reading this book and working through the chapters. This structure emphasizes the tutorial nature of this text; thus we recommend reading and working through the chapters in order. Even if you have previous knowledge of and experience with App Inventor, you should at least skim through the first few chapters to make sure you have the knowledge base that is essential for understanding the topics covered in later chapters.

Part I: Preparing Your First App

There is no way around installing the software required for App Inventor. The first chapter, "Preparation and Installation," guides you through the sometimes bumpy and not always obvious procedure of checking and setting the required system parameters on your computer, the download and installation of the App Inventor Setup Software, the obligatory registration for the online development platform, and the setup of the development parameters on your smartphone. After successful setup, you will explore the development environment of App Inventor in Chapter 2, "The Development Environment," where you learn how to use the program, explore its areas of application, and encounter its development elements in the two central AI interfaces, Designer and Editor. You will also discover how to integrate your smartphone into the development environment and what to do if you are having start-up problems. In Chapter 3, "Developing Your First App," you at last begin developing an app—that is, you design the user interface and develop the functions of your first app, "LaughBag." Once you have added a custom default icon to your app, you will discover different options for installing it on the smartphone or exporting it as APK file. This information lays the foundation for all further app projects.

Part II: Easy Projects as a Warm-Up

Before you develop your next app, Chapter 4, "Basic Terms and Central Concepts," introduces key ideas such as properties, events, and methods. Chapter 5, "The AI References," walks you through the current components, blocks, and concepts of App Inventor and those expected to included in future versions of the software. Equipped with these fundamentals, in Chapter 6, "Graphical User Interface," you use the Designer to create the UI of a demo app, becoming familiar with and actively using components such as buttons, text boxes, and check boxes. In Chapter 7, "Multimedia," you explore the topic of multimedia and its components by taking photos and looking at them in a demo app, creating a voice recording, playing audio and video files, and making the smartphone vibrate. Next, in Chapter 8, "Example Project: Creating a Media Center," you expand this demo project in the form of a media center, an optically elaborate and ergonomically designed multimedia app with multiple screens.

Part III: On the Way to Becoming an App Developer

After your quick trip through the colorful world of graphical user interfaces and multimedia functions and now that you have acquired a good sense of how easy it is to create apps with the components of App Inventor, Chapter 9, "Program Development Basics," leads you more deeply into the development of apps with blocks and block structures. A comprehensive overview provides key details about data types, data structures, and control structures, with which you can implement every conceivable functionality using App Inventor. Quick demo apps show you how to create colors; process numbers; check logic states; edit texts and strings; use variables, procedures, and lists; and control the program flow with branches and loops. Next you will find tips on program development in the discussion of App Inventor's Editor component, followed by sample projects in which you implement a traditional calculator, a number guessing game, and a vocabulary trainer as apps. Next, Chapter 10, "Storage and Databases," explains how to save data locally on your smartphone or online on a web server and how to load them from there. To practice these skills, you expand the vocabulary trainer by developing a master and a client app with a common online database and vocabulary in the cloud.

Part IV: Developing Attractive Apps

Building on the foundations of your newly acquired developer knowhow, we then turn to the really interesting apps and more challenging areas of app development. Chapter 11, "Graphics and Animation," dives straight into the topic of graphics and animation—a rather advanced topic, but one that App Inventor makes it easy to cope with. After a brief introduction to the subject area, you develop a drawing program app, in which you can draw objects on the smartphone using your finger; the app even includes an undo function. Next you learn to animate graphic objects and use collision recognition to facilitate for realistic movement simulations. To turn your new knowledge into practice, you create a 2D squash game with a scoring function and dynamic difficulty level. You also learn to use timer events for any kind of animation, develop an app for drawing keyframe animation paths with your finger and an alarm clock app that will wake you from your dreams even when it is in standby mode.

Chapter 12, "Sensors," covers a topic that is considered exotic even by experienced developers. Here, you get to know the smartphone sensors and learn about their functions and, above all, their integration into your apps. You use the orientation or position sensor and its measurements to implement a fully functioning compass app with graphical compass needle or even a graphical spirit level. You can get musical with the acceleration sensor and develop a shaker, whose sensitivity you can regulate via a slider bar, plus a balance game similar to the classical "Labyrinth." In keeping with the trend of providing location-based services, you discover ways to use the GPS sensor in your apps, by developing a geotracker for recording route profiles that you can automatically set online in real time, plus an app for geocaching complete with compass, direction, and distance indicator to the next cache.

Of course, we won't forget the almost classical area of communication—the topic of Chapter 13, "Communication." In this chapter, we work through this subject and the associated functional areas in our large and practice-oriented final project "Driver Assistance System," whose requirements and tasks we will analyze, structure, and then implement step by step in modules, following the same development path taken by professional developers. First, you are asked to integrate a module for telephone calls via speed dialing under an ergonomic interface with multiple screens. This is followed by development of a module for fully automatic receiving, processing, and answering of SMS messages; this module enables you to read incoming SMS messages aloud via a text-to-speech option and to dictate outgoing SMS messages via a voice recognition capability. Chapter 13 then introduces a central interface concept of App Inventor's Activity Starter component for calling and integrating other apps and web services, with which you can both expand the functional range of the developer language and integrate any external services into your apps. Through various modules, you learn to integrate Google Maps with your app to find the way back to where you parked your car, or Google Navigation to navigate the car driver home or to his or her workplace with one press of a button. Using a module for sending e-mails, you can inform any passengers of your current location and the time you will pick them up. Last but not least, the other central interface based on App Inventor's Web component is introduced for exchanging data with web services via their APIs. By implementing a ticker module with the latest news and stocks data, you learn how to develop information mashups based on real-time data access to the web APIs from Yahoo and Feedzilla, whereas the websites with the original full-text news can be shown directly in your app by using AI's WebViewer component. These capabilities turn your driver assistant system into a full-fledged and powerful app for serious everyday usage.

Part V: Useful Things for the Developer

Even experienced developers—among whom you can definitely count yourself after working through Chapters 1 through 13—can always learn something new and useful that they should know and keep informed about. Chapter 14, "Special Functional Areas," reveals the application-specific components of App Inventor for communicating with Twitter, for scanning barcodes, for online voting, or for using the online database of Google's Fusion Tables. This chapter also provides an overview of the dedicated component groups for developing online multiplayer games, exchanging data via Bluetooth, controlling robots from Lego Mindstorms construction sets, or even combining App Inventor with the app development in Java via the App Inventor Java Bridge.

Chapter 15, "Tips and Tools," offers helpful tips for working with the supported media formats, using the Java console, and setting up the speech module. The Appendix describes the many project, media, and APK files available on the companion website and lists further sources of information and interesting links.

Companion Website

On the companion website for this book, you can download ("Downloads") all demo and example projects from the book, as well as all media files such as the pictures or sounds needed for the projects:

`www.informit.com/title/9780321812704`

Please read the chapter "On the Companion Website" in the Appendix "Additional Resources" of this book for further details about the contents of the companion website and how to use them for your work with this book.

Requirements

One of the central characteristics of App Inventor is that you do not need to meet any special requirements to be able to develop small and large Android apps with this tool. Much like this book, App Inventor is aimed primarily at beginners in app development; no previous knowledge in programming Android smartphones, either general or specialized, is required to use this tool. If you are interested in smartphones, apps, and mobile data services, and you use them regularly to check your e-mails and update your social networks, then you should already have the prerequisites and—above all—the motivation to take the next step, have a look behind the scenes of the colorful app world, and start developing your own apps. Whether these are small helper applications or gimmicks, your own SMS manager or location-based games, or useful apps for work, everyday life, leisure time, or your club or group, with App Inventor you can turn your own ideas into apps without having to program a single line in Java. This book will show you how to do all that.

Of course, it would be a good idea if you had an Android smartphone at your disposal. From Android version 1.6 onward, you will be able to try out and use practically all of the functions described and apps developed in this book directly on your smartphone. Even if you do not yet have an Android smartphone, or if you have a smartphone running an older version of Android (prior to 1.6), you can still use App Inventor and the Android Emulator included with it to develop nearly all of the apps described in this book, test their functions, and then install them on a friend's Android smartphone. One part of the development environment for App Inventor runs on your local computer and another part on a web service, so that you need to have a PC or notebook and DSL access or a similar connection to the Internet available.

The software you need for App Inventor is available free of charge. To download and use the software, you simply need to register for the free service. This book shows you how quickly and easily all of this can be achieved and also guides you through the installation and the setup of the development environment.

Many apps—both in general and those described in this book—make intensive use of the Internet and online web services and will use your mobile data connection to do so. Do not forget that you are paying for this mobile data connection while you are testing and using your own apps. A flat-rate data plan with your cellphone provider can help you avoid unpleasant—and costly—surprises.

History

When it comes to the developer tool App Inventor and even the mobile operating system Android, it is difficult to talk about "history," given that this history is still rather young. In fact, you now stand at the forefront of this history and are driving this wave of innovation by developing apps for Android smartphones with App Inventor! Since Android was first released in October 2008, the Linux-based (and, in many respects, open) operating system for different mobile devices that was initiated by the Open Handset Alliance (OHA)—an alliance of producers, Net companies, and service providers within the telecommunications sector—and marketed by Google has developed from a niche product to a market leader. In the wake of the incredible increase in sales revenues, rapidly increasing market share, displacement of former market leaders, and practically exploding Android market, more and more producers and providers are announcing devices and services for Android, as they do not want to miss the boat.

App Inventor at Google

Good job—we now have App Inventor! With it, you may be able to actively participate in this growth process, if you have the ambition to do so. Nevertheless, it seems to be pure coincidence that free access to App Inventor was provided at the same time as the hype surrounding Android and mobile data services ramped up. When App Inventor was announced in July 2009 as an experimental teaching and learning tool for a select circle of American institutes of higher education (MIT, Harvard, and so on), the developer tool was mainly aimed at giving pupils and students easy access to programming in general and mobile devices in particular, while taking into consideration the most modern forms of information and communication technology such as social networking, location-based services, and web services within a cloud. Almost exactly one year later, App Inventor at Google was announced to the public in July 2010 and made available to interested developers as a closed beta version, albeit after they submitted an application and access was approved by the Google App Inventor Team. The period during which these would-be developers had to wait for their access being granted was marked by impatient debates in which some applicants compared the process to having to wait for Santa Claus and the long-awaited Christmas present (see Figure I.1)—an attitude that reflects the strong interest in a developer tool such as App Inventor.

Google groups

App Inventor for Android

So when can I get App Inventor?

I feel like the kid who's been watching the other kids in the block have fun
with their toys, and after some time, the kid asks Mr Clause, "Where's mine?
I've been good." And Mr. Claus says, "Don't worry. You'll get yours after
Boxing Day. Everybody will."

On Tue, Jul 20, 2010 at 10:28 PM, [redacted] <[redacted]...@gmail.com> wrote:
> I got my access yesterday. I signed up about two weeks ago.

> [redacted]

> On Jul 20, 6:20 pm, [redacted]<[redacted]...@gmail.com> wrote:
> > It seems that they are letting people in once a week. Monday me and a
> > bunch of people got access. But i also believe we all applied the
> > morning google release the beta. good luck

> > On Jul 20, 10:23 pm, [redacted] <[redacted]...@gmail.com> wrote:

> > > No one knows when you will get in.
> > > And App Inventor runs entirely in a browser. The only download is the
> > > blocks editor

> > > On Jul 20, 8:30 pm, [redacted] <[redacted]...@gmail.com> wrote:

> > > > Well, I signed up about two weeks ago and have yet to get any
> > > > response. Is there some sort of secret handshake I need to know in
> > > > order to get a download link?

> > > > Thanks

Figure I.1 Impatiently waiting to be granted access to the former closed beta version

Once access was finally granted (see Figure I.2), a new phase of intensive testing of the development environment, functions, and capacity of App Inventor began. This phase, under real conditions of use and load, was marked by adaptations, optimizations, and a vivid exchange between the Google App Inventor Team and the App Inventor closed beta users.

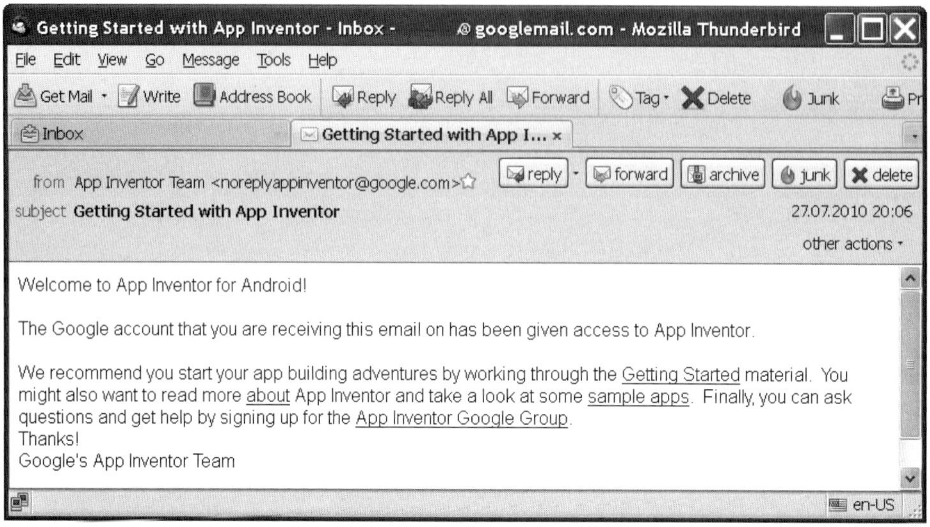

Figure I.2 Admission to former closed beta version

Over time, the development platform was tested extensively under realistic conditions, subjected to certain optimizations, and finally moved on to a stable basis version. On December 15, 2010, the Google App Inventor Team announced entry into the open beta phase and decided to open the development platform to any interested user without any access restriction (see Figure I.3).

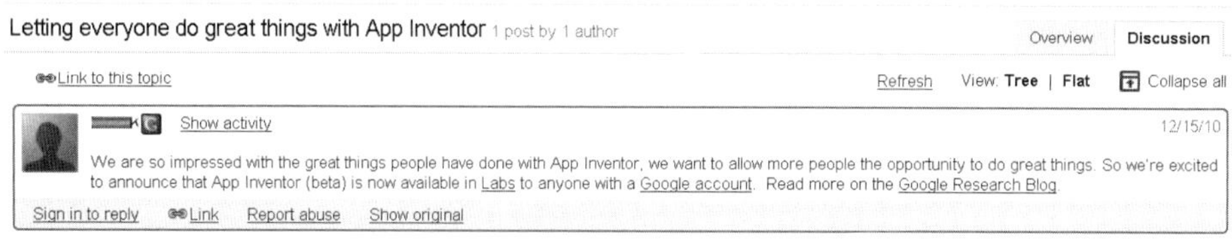

Figure I.3 Start of the open beta phase with access to anyone

Since that day, there has been even more buzz in the already turbulent Android market, and developers and users alike are feverishly working on new Android apps with App Inventor all over the world. The Google App Inventor team has been continuously expanding the developer platform and adding more and more powerful and extensive functions to App Inventor. During the year 2011, App Inventor became established as a real alternative to the Java-based Android Software Development Kit (SDK), and on the various Android markets you will find more and more apps that have been developed with App Inventor.

Open Source and App Inventor at MIT

With the year 2012, Google heralds a new era for the popular developer tool App Inventor. As with the open operating system Android itself, Google is now offering the platform for visual app development for Android as an open-source version, free of charge (see the first clause in Figure I.4). Similar to the successful concept whereby manufacturers can adapt the mobile operating system to their Android hardware, the development environment App Inventor can now also be run on different platforms by independent providers and can be adapted and developed further depending on the desired focus. For the users of App Inventor, this results in the availability of alternative platforms on which they can develop their apps depending on their personal preferences. This move will increase the multitude of options even further and ensure the development of more new features of App Inventor in the future.

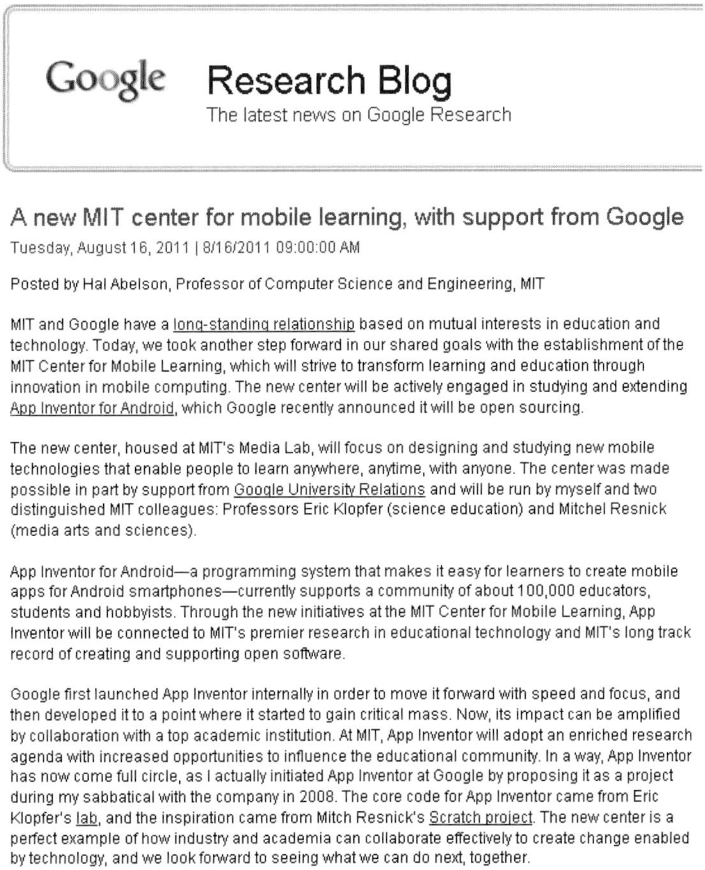
Google Research Blog
The latest news on Google Research

A new MIT center for mobile learning, with support from Google

Tuesday, August 16, 2011 | 8/16/2011 09:00:00 AM

Posted by Hal Abelson, Professor of Computer Science and Engineering, MIT

MIT and Google have a long-standing relationship based on mutual interests in education and technology. Today, we took another step forward in our shared goals with the establishment of the MIT Center for Mobile Learning, which will strive to transform learning and education through innovation in mobile computing. The new center will be actively engaged in studying and extending App Inventor for Android, which Google recently announced it will be open sourcing.

The new center, housed at MIT's Media Lab, will focus on designing and studying new mobile technologies that enable people to learn anywhere, anytime, with anyone. The center was made possible in part by support from Google University Relations and will be run by myself and two distinguished MIT colleagues: Professors Eric Klopfer (science education) and Mitchel Resnick (media arts and sciences).

App Inventor for Android—a programming system that makes it easy for learners to create mobile apps for Android smartphones—currently supports a community of about 100,000 educators, students and hobbyists. Through the new initiatives at the MIT Center for Mobile Learning, App Inventor will be connected to MIT's premier research in educational technology and MIT's long track record of creating and supporting open software.

Google first launched App Inventor internally in order to move it forward with speed and focus, and then developed it to a point where it started to gain critical mass. Now, its impact can be amplified by collaboration with a top academic institution. At MIT, App Inventor will adopt an enriched research agenda with increased opportunities to influence the educational community. In a way, App Inventor has now come full circle, as I actually initiated App Inventor at Google by proposing it as a project during my sabbatical with the company in 2008. The core code for App Inventor came from Eric Klopfer's lab, and the inspiration came from Mitch Resnick's Scratch project. The new center is a perfect example of how industry and academia can collaborate effectively to create change enabled by technology, and we look forward to seeing what we can do next, together.

Figure I.4 App Inventor with Google and MIT (http://googleresearch.blogspot.com/2011/08/new-mit-center-for-mobile-learning-with.html, as of August 17, 2011)

As one of the first providers, the Massachusetts Institute of Technology (MIT) is now making the new App Inventor available online to the public on its systems, thereby consistently continuing the tasks of the previous Google App Inventor Group (see the announcement in Figure I.4). The release process followed the original by having started with an experimental version followed by the stable public version. The cooperation between Google and MIT, which has existed since the earliest days of App Inventor, will continue in the future as well, in form of the jointly founded and financed Center for Mobile Learning (CML) at the MIT Media Lab (Figure I.5).

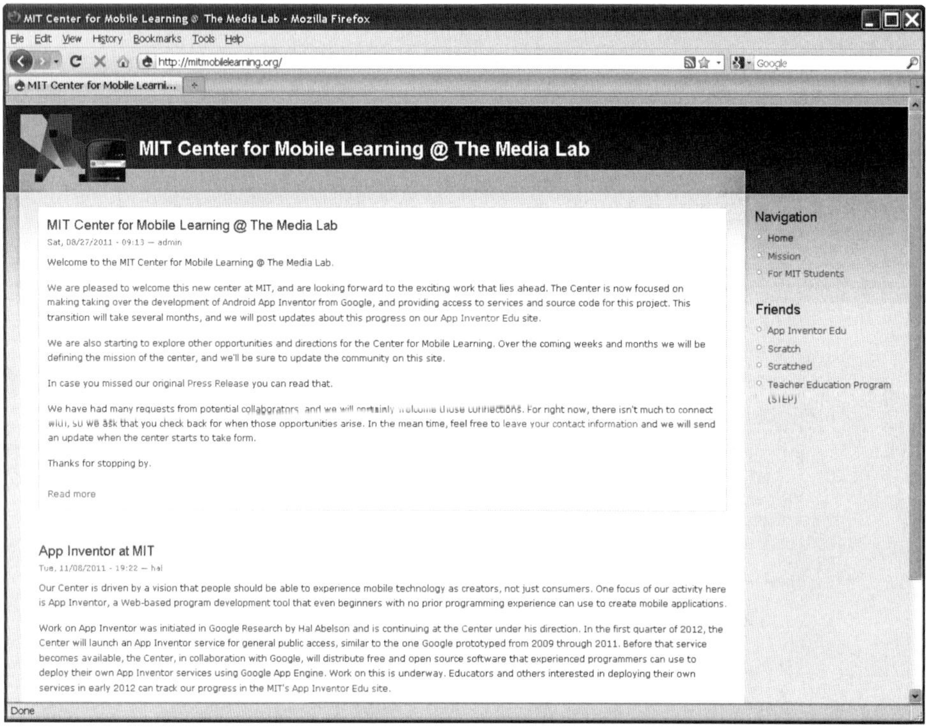

Figure I.5 App Inventor at the Center for Mobile Learning at the MIT Media Lab

This venture also provides for continuity in terms of personnel, notably Dr. Hal Abelson, who as initiator of the former Google App Inventor Group is now running the new CML, which is responsible for operating and further developing App Inventor. Figure I.6 shows the new central website for App Inventor at MIT, from where you can start to explore documentation and tutorials (Explore), special information for educators, and even curriculum materials (Teach), and—of course—also launch App Inventor (Invent).

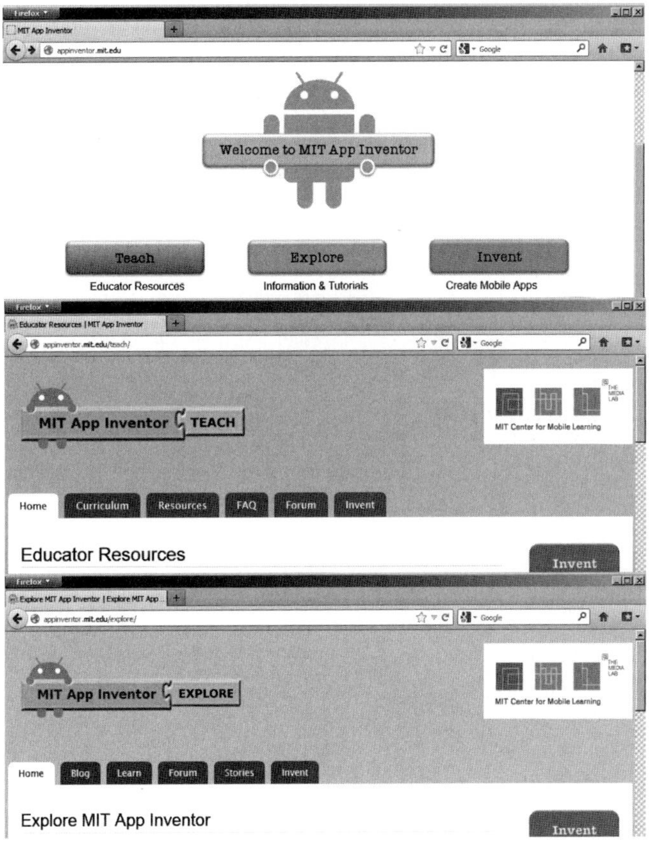

Figure I.6 Central information website for App Inventor at MIT (http://appinventor.mit.edu/)

The success story of App Inventor for visually developing Android apps continues and is expected to gain further momentum. You can become a part of this story by starting to develop apps for Android, the most widely used mobile operating system. Read this book to find out how you can use the new App Inventor to turn your ideas into reality and create your own exciting, impressive, and unique apps!

Part I

Preparing Your First App

Every beginning is hard—but not so with App Inventor (AI)! AI is aimed specifically at the needs of beginners who want to write their own app for an Android smartphone for the first time, or who have never before written a program for a digital system such as a computer or smartphone. But why "write"? With AI, you do not even have to painstakingly type complicated program code into a boring text editor, as you may have seen in some old hacker movies from the 1980s or experienced yourself in the early days of your school's or university's computer working group. With the visual development language AI, you can quickly *develop* the applications with a user interface that is as comfortable, interactive, and graphic as you would expect the final application itself to be—for example, an app for creating text, presentation slides, or balance sheets, or for editing photos. Just as you would first need to familiarize yourself with the individual functions, elements, and modules of the user interface in such applications to work with them and get the desired results, you must learn how to use the development environment of AI to develop your own apps with this tool.

Yet the basic operation of AI is remarkably simple, easily understandable, and quite often more intuitive than many software products with which you can merely write text. With AI, you can do so much more—you can turn your own ideas quickly and easily into apps for your smartphone and the smartphones of your friends, colleagues, and others. There are almost no limits to what you can do, as you can see from the vast number of apps available on Google Play (formerly known as Android Market) and elsewhere. Indeed, there are apps available for the most astonishing areas, demonstrating the enormous power of the human imagination. AI will meet you at your individual level, help you take the first steps in developing apps, and accompany you on the journey from the "clicking together" of the simplest mini-apps to the programming of more demanding and elaborate mobile applications. The entire creation process takes place within the development environment of AI, which stands ready to support you from your very first app right through your launch of a major mobile project. This great range makes it all the more important that you familiarize yourself thoroughly with AI's development environment and keep practicing how to use it and its functional elements.

This part of the book introduces the AI development environment and focuses on issues related to its access, preparation, and installation. After describing the initial setup, Part I guides you through the various development areas, introduces and demonstrates functions and elements, explains how to integrate your smartphone into the development environment, and gives you a first sense of working with AI and the challenges it presents. As this book primarily addresses the practical application of AI and the implementation of run-capable apps, this first section of the book concludes by showing you how to create a proper app "with all the trimmings" yourself. As if in passing, you will make use of all essential elements of the AI development environment during this initial project, which will prepare you in the best possible way for the many other app projects that follow.

Chapter 1

Preparation and Installation

Unlike many other books and articles, where only a short text section covers preparation and installation of the required system environment and software (if these topics are mentioned at all), this book devotes a whole chapter to this important preparatory work. There are several reasons for this emphasis.

First, AI is a development environment in a prolonged *beta phase* (the advanced test phase prior to launch of the finalized version of a software product) due to the latest updates made at the beginning of 2012. For any beta-phase product, a few particularities inevitably need to be taken into account and explained, especially regarding installation and software access. These issues are likely to be less relevant once you reach the stable final release. If you are currently using AI, you are still very close to the development processes and the developers of the AI system, who continue to diligently work on expanding and improving AI and, if necessary, fixing any bugs. You will, therefore, experience any changes or improvements more or less as they happen.

> **Current Online Information on Installation of MIT AI**
>
> To get the most up-to-date information on preparation, installation, documentation, and forums of the new and highly dynamic App Inventor at MIT please make sure you refer to MIT's websites for App Inventor.
>
> The central AI information and starting website at MIT:
>
> `http://appinventor.mit.edu`
>
> The direct links to the MIT AI system and its documentation (note that the first URL is the experimental version for the formerly closed user group, now open for all users. The second URL is currently used for the official public version):
>
> `http://experimental.appinventor.mit.edu`
>
> `http://beta.appinventor.mit.edu`
>
> You can refer to these websites to get the latest information on App Inventor in general and to find links to further sources of information.

Second, both this book and AI itself are aimed primarily at inexperienced beginners who have little or no previous experience in developing and programming software applications. Thus we can assume that at least some readers will not necessarily be familiar with independently creating a development environment and, therefore, will benefit from a step-by-step guide. In fact, the many questions posted in the AI Forum indicate that this need exists even among the early and technology-minded beta users of AI.

Main Focus Is on App Development (Not on Operating an AI Platform!)

This book is exclusively aimed at users of the AI development environment (such as that offered, for example, by Google and MIT), not at operators of the AI open-source version. All descriptions of the AI setup and similar topics refer to using the development environment and do not give any information on how to install Google's open-source system on a server or how to make it accessible to other users. If you are interested in operating your own AI platform, refer to this book's Appendix, "Running Your Own Service with App Inventor Open Source," or to the instructions at this website:

`http://appinventor.mit.edu/explore/content/running-your-own-app-inventor-service.html`

In its current beta-stage iteration, AI is not yet a well-rounded product offering a detailed product documentation and a comprehensive installation guide, or a comfortable, fully automated installation routine, as you would expect with commercially perfected software products. Nevertheless, the numerous already integrated functions are stable and are likely to remain the same or be upgraded in future versions. This chapter focuses primarily on the installation process and its documentation, which are still subject to certain dynamic changes. The dedicated AI system developers are currently seeking to further enhance the technical functionality and capacity of AI, leaving it up to other authors or their books—such as this one—to provide a guide through the occasionally still bumpy installation process.

Discrepancies in Representations

As one of the first providers, MIT makes the new App Inventor accessible to the public on the basis of Google's open-source platform on its server systems online free of charge. Similar to the MIT AI (which is almost identical to the form Google AI), other operators of the open-source platform will probably also follow the original Google AI, especially at the beginning. As it is the largest common denominator, we will therefore also follow the Google AI in terms of the tried and tested features, the operation, and the functions, as well as the setup, login, documentation, and so on. This practice is intended to ensure that this book is as universally usable as possible. The figures and individual instructions on the development environment correspond to the Google AI system and may in some cases differ from the system offered by your own provider, especially in the first part of the book. The figures may also show some links to further online information on the original domains of the Google AI systems—for example:

`http://appinventor.googlelabs.com` (The domain name before the Google Labs base platform went offline in September 2011)

`http://www.appinventorbeta.com` (The domain name before the change to the MIT platform at the beginning of 2012)

Of course, relevant information may also be found on the platform of your current AI provider, and you might want to look for appropriate information there yourself. Please do not

> panic if certain figures or representations in this book do not completely match those on your system; just adapt them to your current conditions. The highly dynamic situation of app development, on the one hand, and the changes related to App Inventor with the transition to the open-source and MIT versions, on the other hand, require a certain flexibility from AI users. Individual differences in representations and the requirements of the individual AI providers should be fairly easy to look up in the relevant documentation, probably in a subdirectory structure similar to that found in the original domains of the Google AI system (for example, `www.appinventorbeta.com/learn` is now `experimental.appinventor.mit.edu/learn` or `beta.appinventor.mit.edu/learn`).

To develop apps with AI, you will need to prepare more than one working platform, as you will be developing your projects on both the computer and the Android smartphone simultaneously.

System Requirements

Regarding system requirements for developing Android apps, we must distinguish between the two platforms involved: the computer (subsequently referred to as a PC) and the Android device (subsequently referred to as a smartphone). Although in theory you could develop apps exclusively on the PC and also test them on the computer using a cellphone simulator or the so-called emulator, the aim of developing apps is to be able to use the end product on a mobile device. For this reason, in this book, we carry out the development work directly in the smartphone wherever possible. Positioning sensors (such as GPS) and other functional elements of the mobile device then do not have to be laboriously simulated on the PC, but rather can be used directly on the smartphone during the development process. Historically, device emulators were used mostly in the early days of the open-source operating system Android for app development with the programming language Java, before Android devices became widely available. Our general recommendation, however, is to proceed in the order of the following sections during installation.

Computer Platform

The real app development with AI takes place on the PC. In this respect, the requirements of the development environment AI are no different from those of other software products. AI already offers support for the most common operating systems and computer platforms. The login screen displayed when booting your computer will usually show which operating system is installed on your machine. AI can currently run on all commercially available computers with the following operating systems:

- Windows: Windows XP, Windows Vista, and Windows 7
- Macintosh (with Intel processor): Mac OS X 10.5 and 10.6
- GNU/Linux: Ubuntu 8+ and Debian 5+

Unlike with classic local development environments, only a relatively small part of the AI software is installed directly on your PC. The largest part of the software is web based.

Thus you do the main part of your development work directly in a web browser and use this client to access the proper AI software running on a remote Google server. This approach of *cloud computing* ensures that you are always working with the most up-to-date version of AI and, in principle, can do so from any PC with Internet access that has been configured properly. Correspondingly, your app projects will no longer be saved on your local hard drive, but can instead be managed centrally on a server provided by Google. The key requirement, of course, is that you always work online while developing apps with AI and have a Google account. But do not worry: For you as user, working with AI is not much different from working with conventional local-system-based applications.

When it comes to selecting your preferred web browser, AI gives you a huge number of options. Generally, we would recommend using the most current version of your chosen browser. At the moment, you can choose from the following browsers:

- Mozilla Firefox 3.6 and higher
- Apple Safari 5.0 and higher
- Google Chrome 4.0 and higher
- Microsoft Internet Explorer 7 and higher

To find out which browser version is installed on your PC, most browsers offer information in the Help menu under the heading "About . . . ." If you select this menu option, you will see which browser version is installed on your system. Figure 1.1 shows an example of Mozilla Firefox version 3.6.8 on the operating system Windows XP.

Figure 1.1 Displaying the installed browser version

If you should discover that you have an older browser version than the one specified previously as the minimum requirement, most browsers offer a convenient update option. In Mozilla Firefox, for example, the same Help menu contains the option "Check for updates" (see Figure 1.1); if you click on this option, it checks for updates automatically. Alternatively, you can simply use your preferred search engine to find updates with an appropriate search term, such as "Firefox update."

Given that AI is a highly dynamic product that is currently subject to constant changes during the beta phase (and, therefore, while this book was being produced), the system requirements may also potentially change over time. To ensure that your version of AI is up-to-date, you as AI user should also check the online material on AI directly for updates and amendments. The usual basic rule of thumb applies: The more up-to-date your PC system environment, the more likely it is that AI will support it. The exceptions are, of course, system environments that are also in the beta stage and that have unsupported features or the all-too-common initial compatibility problems. But this exception will hardly apply for official software releases, which you as beginner will most likely be using on your system. The preceding rule of thumb similarly applies to the Android platform used.

Android Platform

The system requirements for the Android device you are using are, on the one hand, more transparent. On the other hand, they also involve more uncertainties than the requirements for established computer platforms and operating systems, due to the youth of the still-evolving Android market. The relatively short release cycles of the constantly revised and expanded Android operating system versions require corresponding adaptations of the associated software products, such as AI. Nevertheless, the Google developers have also built AI based on the principle of *downward compatibility*. This means that new Android versions should, wherever possible, also offer support for the full range of functions of older versions, so that older Android apps can run on the most modern Android devices. Downward compatibility applies in only this one direction, however; thus apps specifically developed for newer Android devices may not necessarily be supported by older Android smartphones. Before releasing an app on the market, it makes sense to test the app on different Android versions, thereby ensuring that it can run on as many devices as possible and be used by as many users as possible. Likewise, you should take into account producer-specific interfaces, such as Sense on Android devices by the manufacturer HTC, when testing your app.

The same caveat applies to the hardware of Android devices. More and more manufacturers are currently equipping their hardware with the Android operating system. In addition, the number of Android device types is growing rapidly. For example, numerous tablets run Android, as well as some netbooks and even TV systems (Google TV), and more systems have already been announced. This proliferation of Android-compatible devices opens up a wealth of possibilities for you as app developer, as you may be able to create a single app that has the potential to run on a multitude of different systems without having to make hardware-specific changes each time. Unfortunately, the reality is that apps do not always run on every Android device flawlessly today: The individual Android systems are too diverse to claim complete compatibility.

The differences are most noticeable in the technical features of the various Android devices. To use an app that offers or uses SMS or other phone functions, for example, the device must have this feature of a typical cellphone. While this capability is expected in the case of smartphones, you can currently make phone calls with only very few tablets, at least not via the classic cellphone network. The same applies to accessing the Internet via cellphone with devices that are not 3G capable. While most smartphones with a corresponding SIM combo card can make use both of cellphone services and data services, many of the current tablets have only WLAN capabilities; thus their users can access data services if they are near a hotspot.

This chain of dependencies between hardware equipment and potential app scope is repeated with a number of other hardware sensors. The increasingly important location-dependent mobile data services require a GPS receiver in the Android device, through which an app can read the current position of the smartphone and, therefore, the user seeking to use the services. Apps for navigation services require not only positioning via GPS but also an electronic compass capable of recognizing the direction in which the user is facing and adapting the display according to his or her orientation. An electronic *accelerometer* enables the app to take the user's speed of movement into account. Modern apps for *mobile augmented reality* also make use of a position sensor to recognize where the user is pointing the smartphone and what he or she is looking at through the camera display, thereby enabling the apps to accurately overlay the actual view with virtual information.

Despite the many different aspects of the Android platform that must be taken into account by apps, the selection of a suitable development platform does not bring with it any major demands. This fact, to some extent, reflects the huge success of Android itself. With the introduction of this free operating system, fully equipped smartphones began to achieve a general breakthrough at an affordable retail price. Previously, smartphones with touch screens had hardly any more features than their equivalents with keyboards, and an integrated GPS sensor was rarely affordable for the average user. Now, however, almost all Android smartphones—even those at the bottom of the price range—are equipped with the full array of sensors such as GPS, compass, accelerometer, and position sensor. Indeed, prices start at an incredibly cheap retail price of approximately $150 for a device without a SIM lock and without a cellphone contract. Of course, you would not expect the very cheapest hardware models to offer much in the way of high quality, but they basically meet all requirements for the Android apps in this book and beyond. For example, all apps in this book were developed with the HTC Android smartphone Tattoo, which can be counted among the most inexpensive entry-level smartphones. If you have a newer and more capable smartphone, you should definitely not have any hardware-related problems with our example apps.

As mentioned earlier, the functioning of apps does have a certain dependency on the Android version used, but this relationship is not usually particularly problematic for developing apps with AI due to the intended downward compatibility. If you look at the significant feature updates in the various versions up to now, they are of only minor significance for developing apps with AI because all important functions that can be addressed and used with AI are already included in Android from version 1.5 onward. The function range of AI currently focuses on the central core elements of Android apps, leaving the version-specific "subtleties" to be developed in native or Java code, which is not the subject of our book. You can see the existing and planned versions with their main new features in Table 1.1, based on the Android operating system version history on Wikipedia.

Table 1.1 **Android Versions and Their Main New Features, Based on** `http://en.wikipedia.org/wiki/Android_version_history`

Version	Release Date	Main New Features
1.1 (no longer supported)	February 10, 2009	Save MMS attachments
1.5 "Cupcake"	April 30, 2009	Automatic change between portrait and landscape, on-screen keyboard, record and play videos, connection via Bluetooth
1.6 "Donut"	September 15, 2009	VPN configurable, differentiated energy use control, text-to-speech, multiple screen resolutions, gesture recognition
2.0 "Eclair"	October 26, 2009	Digital zoom, support for Microsoft Exchange, Bluetooth 2.1
2.1 "Eclair"	January 12, 2010	Variable wallpapers, information on signal strength, Webkit upgrade
2.2 "Froyo"	May 20, 2010	New Linux kernel 2.6.32, more than 256MB main memory usage, support for OpenGL ES 2.0 and Flash, tethering
2.3 "Gingerbread"	December 6, 2010	Linux kernel 2.6.35.7, support for WebM, HTML5 audio, Google TV, NFC, more sensors (e.g., gyroscope, barometer), integrated SIP client
2.3.3 "Gingerbread"	February 23, 2011	Dual core support, optimized NFC and Bluetooth
2.3.4 "Gingerbread"	April 29, 2011	Video/voice chat, encrypted transfer of contacts and appointments
3.0 "Honeycomb"	February, 2011	Optimized support for tablet computers, Google talk with video telephony
3.1 "Honeycomb"	May 10, 2011	USB host modus
3.2 "Honeycomb"	July 16, 2011	Optimization for 7" tablet computers
4.0 "Ice Cream Sandwich"	October 19, 2011	Consolidation of development lines 2.x and 3.x and GoogleTV, unlocking by face recognition, screenshots
4.1 "Jelly Bean"	June 27, 2012	Speed optimization, Google Now integration, data exchange by NFC with Android Beam 2.0

The future will reveal to what extent the additional features and functions of future Android versions will become relevant for developing with AI. For your app development with AI, you can check the list of new Android functions when such functions are announced and released, to see if they are supported only from a particular Android version onward. For example, in this book we will develop an app with a text-to-speech component. As you can see in Table 1.1, this function is available only from Android version 1.6 onward, so your smartphone requires Android version 1.6 or higher to run this example app. The majority of the other functions to be introduced should be available from version 1.5 and, therefore, should be supported by most of the currently available Android smartphones, provided the aforementioned hardware requirements are also fulfilled.

If you are not sure which Android version is on your smartphone, you can easily find out. Go to the applications menu of your smartphone and select Settings > About Phone. This page will identify the Android version running on your phone. In Figure 1.2, the example shows an HTC Tattoo smartphone with Android version 1.6. The menu headings may occasionally vary, depending on which smartphone or operating system you are using; if necessary, check your smartphone's manual for more details.

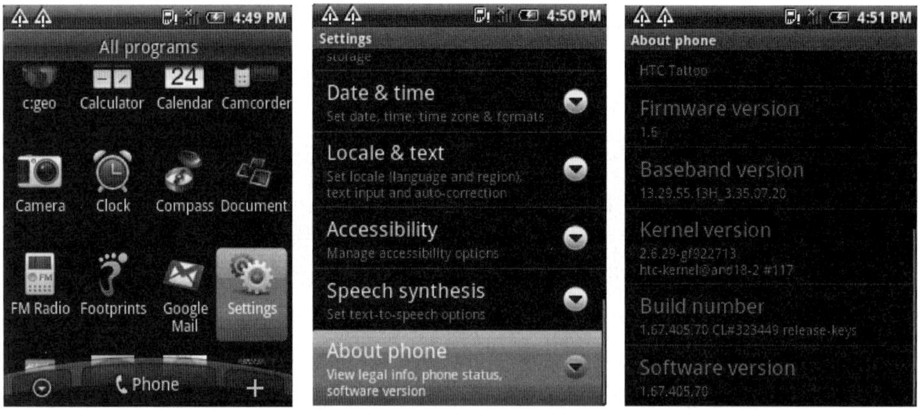

Figure 1.2 Displaying the Android version number with Settings, About Phone

If you want to update the Android operating system version on your smartphone, you can contact the smartphone manufacturer or your cellphone provider to see the available options and offers. You should think carefully about this step, however, because an update of the mobile operating system can soon become a real challenge if things go wrong unexpectedly. If you have Android 1.6, you do not need an update to work through this book and put all the example apps into practice. Even with Android 1.5, you will be able to create all of the examples, with the exception mentioned previously.

Once the aforementioned system requirements are met, there is only one other requirement to fulfill before you can begin setting up your specific AI development environment. Perhaps you are lucky and your computer already has the correct Java runtime environment installed. The next section will tell you how you can find out if it does and update it if necessary.

Java Configuration

As promised, you will not have to program your Android apps in Java. Nevertheless, a large part of the AI development environment itself has been programmed in Java, to enable AI to run on many different platforms and to make it possible to use AI from remote client computers via cloud computing. To ensure that Java programs—including AI—can be executed on your computer, a corresponding Java runtime environment (JRE) must be installed and enabled on your computer. The JRE includes, among other things, the so-called Java virtual machine (Java VM), which is kind of a uniform additional operating system capable of running on the many different operating systems of the various computers connected to the Internet. As the Java VM already contains the system-specific adaptations for the relevant computer system, Java applications such as AI no longer require them and can be run on all kinds of platforms with JRE or Java VM without further adaptation. This section describes how to check whether your PC already has the correct Java configuration, and how to configure it if not.

To work with AI, your computer needs to have Java with product number 6 or version number 1.6 or higher installed and enabled. The difference between product number and version number is not relevant for using Java, but your installation should have one of these two specified numbers. To test whether your computer system already meets this requirement, the company Oracle, which took over the original manufacturer Sun Microsystems and its rights to Java in January 2010, offers a convenient Java test web page.

> **Testing the Java Installation and Version on Your Own Computer**
>
> In your web browser, go to the Java test web page at:
> `http://www.java.com/en/download/testjava.jsp`

Once you have reached the Java test web page and can see the details of your installed Java version displayed in the middle of the page in form of a Java applet, you know that you have Java installed. Take a look at which version is displayed there. If it says "Version: Java 6" (as in Figure 1.3), your computer already has the correct Java environment. You may need to tell your firewall first that Internet access is permitted for the file `java.exe`, as shown on the right-hand side of Figure 1.3.

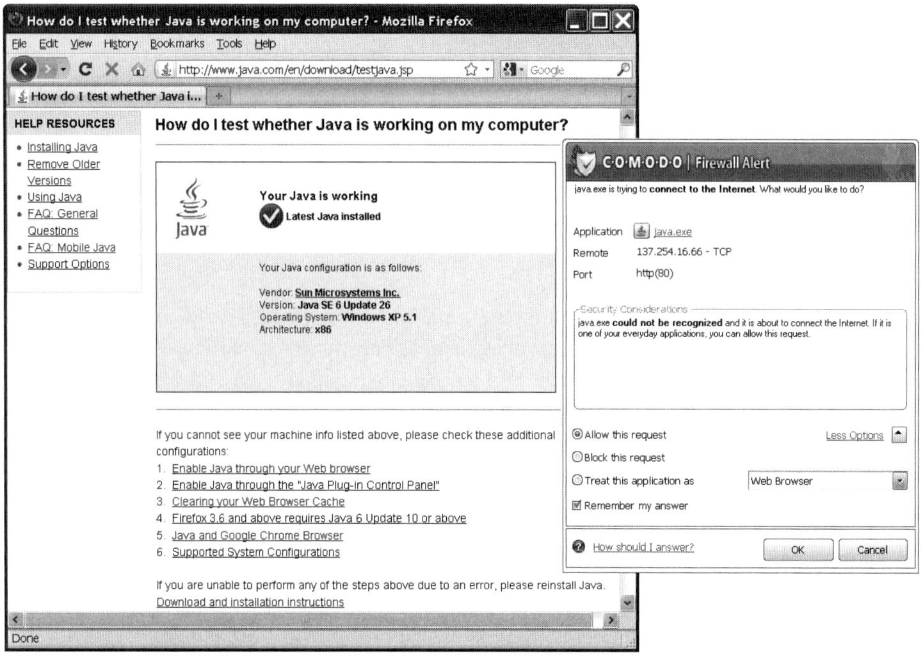

Figure 1.3 Java test web page with correct installation of Java 6

If the Java applet on the test page remains empty or displays an error message, then Java is either not enabled on your computer or not installed yet. First check your browser's Java settings by going to the Java test web page and clicking on the links below the Java applet in order, thereby enabling Java retrospectively if required. If the activation remains unsuccessful, you will have to reinstall or newly install Java on your computer. Follow the link "Download and installation instructions" on the Java test web page, or go directly to Oracle's download page.

Download and Installation of Java

Download and install the latest version of Java from the manufacturer's homepage at: `http://www.java.com/en/`

Then you can go back to the Java test web page and check that the installation was successful.

As part of the installation and activation of Java 6, *Java Web Start* should automatically be available on your computer. With Java Web Start, Java applications can be started via the Internet with one click and—unlike Java applets—can be used even without a web browser. With AI, this concept of cloud computing comes into play in connection with one of the two central interfaces—the *Blocks Editor,* which runs like a local application on your computer, but always accesses the latest version on the Google servers. Here, too, you have the option of an online function check.

Testing Java Web Start on Your Computer

Use your web browser to go to one of the Java Web Start demos at:
`http://www.oracle.com/technetwork/java/demos-nojavascript-137100.html`

To test Java Web Start, simply go to one of the Java Web Start Demos on the test page. If you can start the demo application, Java Script is installed and enabled correctly on your computer. When you first go to one of the demos, your web browser will usually ask you what you want to do with the underlying JNLP file (Java Network Launching Protocol). Select Open with > Java(TM) Web Start Launcher; if necessary, also enable "Do this automatically for files like this from now on" before clicking OK. In the future, you can then start the AI Blocks Editor with one simple click. Figure 1.4 shows as an example selecting the demo application "Draw."

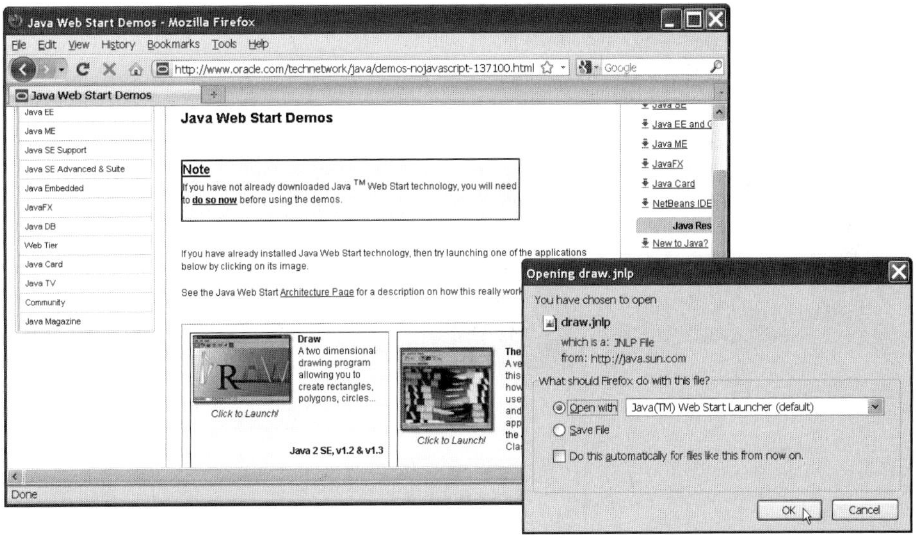

Figure 1.4 Testing Java Web Start with a demo application

The *Web Start Launcher* should then begin automatically downloading the selected application, verify it, and then start the application. Figure 1.5 shows as an example in which the user downloads and starts the demo application "Draw."

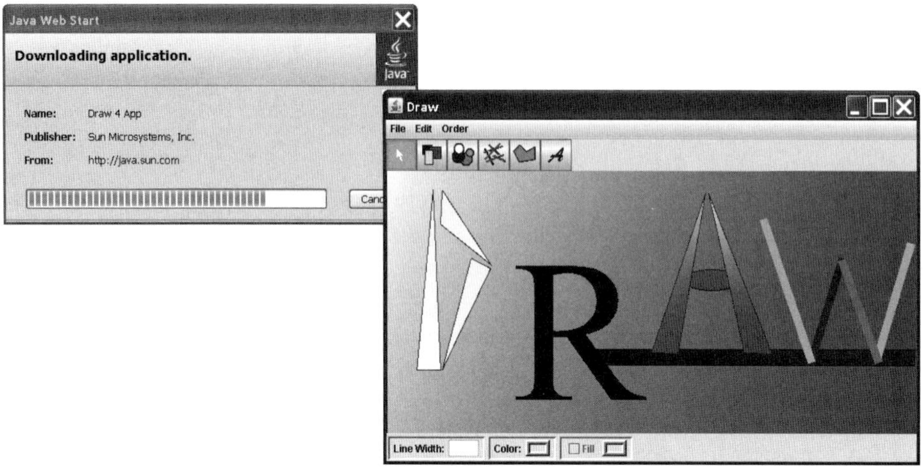

Figure 1.5 Loading and starting a demo application with Java Web Start

On the demo website, you can also find a direct link to the Java Application Manager. Clicking on this option opens the Java Control Panel; under Temporary Internet Files, you can then see the status of all the most recently opened Web Start applications in the Java Cache Viewer. In Figure 1.6, the Status column indicates with a symbol that the Java application "Draw 4 App" (the example started earlier) is currently active and connected to the server. You can also see that App Inventor for Android has been run several times in the past on this computer. If you are uncertain about the online status of AI at any stage, you can check it here. You can also use this option to remove a Web Start application in case of runtime problems by right-clicking and selecting "Delete" in the menu.

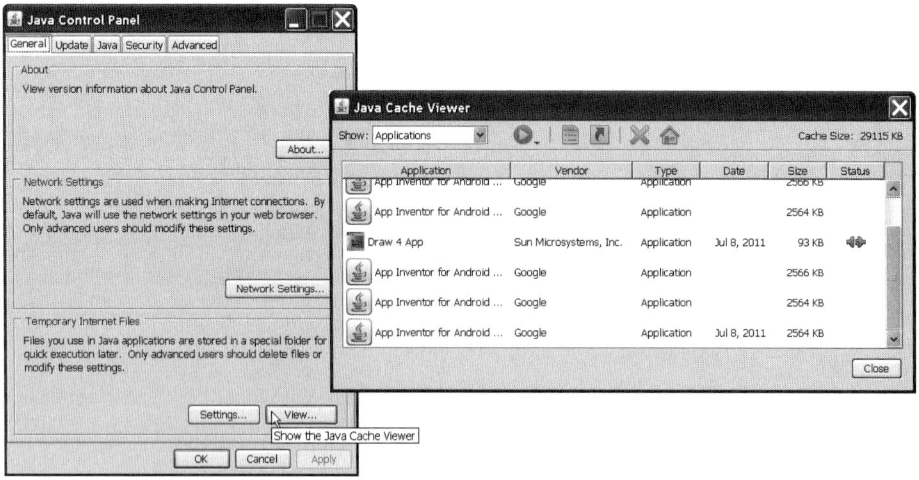

Figure 1.6 Checking the status of Java Web Start applications

If you were able to successfully start at least one of the Java Web Start demos mentioned previously *and* if the test on the Java Test website was successful, then—and only then—your system is ready to handle the installation of AI. This statement may sound rather rigid, but is based directly on the requirements established by the AI developers at Google. The aim in ruling out problems that may originate in systems other than in AI itself is to be able to concentrate fully on AI-specific topics during the beta phase, so that in case of any problems you do not have to go looking for the causes in the surrounding system environment as well. For this reason, you should try to remedy any problems that may have occurred up to now with the procedures described so far in this chapter. You will not be furthering the completion or continued development of AI in the future if you report problems in the beta group forums whose cause is ultimately an incorrect configuration of your own system environment. Further current notes on preparatory system configuration can be found in the online documentation.

Login Data for App Inventor

To use AI, you have to log in to the provider's AI platform. As you know from the section on Java configuration and in connection with the concept of cloud computing, access to AI gives you more than just a link for downloading a software package for complete installation of AI on your local computer: You also get online access to the AI platform in the most recent version of the development environment in the cloud, for which you simply need to log in each time.

To access the MIT AI system in its former experimental version (MIT App Inventor Experimental), you first needed to apply for membership to the closed testing group. If access was granted by the MIT system developers, you were able to log in to the MIT AI Experimental version by using your regular Google account data (see Figure 1.8). The current public MIT AI version is open to all users, so you do not need to apply for membership anymore. Just use your Google e-mail account login data to access the public MIT AI system. However, check the MIT website for the most up-to-date information on the login process. On the Google AI start page, you entered your complete e-mail address and the appropriate password and then clicked on the "Sign In" button to reach the development environment online. If you did not have a Google account, you were able to quickly and easily create one by clicking on the link "Create an account now" (see Figure 1.7).

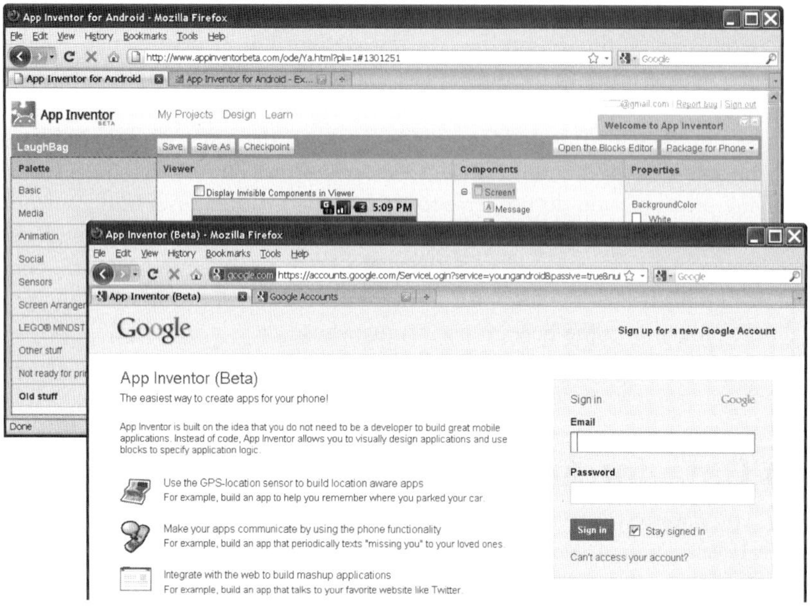

Figure 1.7 Login to the original Google AI

Please refer to the online description of the relevant providers to find out how these operators of the open-source version of AI provide access to their development platform in each individual case. To access the MIT AI system in its former experimental version (MIT App Inventor Experimental), you first needed to apply for membership to the closed testing group. If access was granted by the MIT system developers, you were able to log in to the MIT AI Experimental version by using your regular Google account data (see Figure 1.8). The current public MIT AI version is open to all users, so you do not need to apply for membership anymore. Just use your Google e-mail account login data to access the public MIT AI system. However, check the MIT website for the most up-to-date information on the login process.

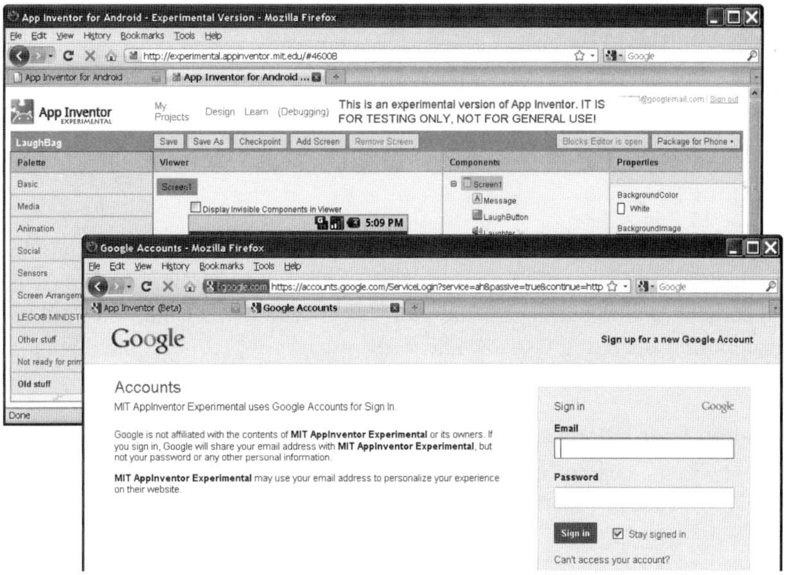

Figure 1.8 Login to the MIT AI Experimental

Access to MIT AI

For direct access to the MIT AI you can currently choose between the two links referring to the same open system platform at MIT:

`http://experimental.appinventor.mit.edu`
`http://beta.appinventor.mit.edu`

Please wait to start the development environment until you read the next chapter, because online access alone is not enough for your developer work; you need to carry out some other installations before you can use AI productively.

Installation of the App Inventor Setup Software

After the preparations in the previous sections, this next step tells you how to install the actual AI development environment on your computer. As mentioned in the context of cloud computing, only part of the development environment (the AI Setup Software) is installed locally on your hard disk and then functions in combination with web-based components on the remote servers of the AI provider. The locally installed components include system-specific drivers for connecting different Android devices to the AI software on the computer. The AI Setup Software is currently available for downloading in separate software packages for three operating systems:

- Mac OS X
- GNU/Linux
- Windows

For all three operating systems in their different versions, the online documentation offers detailed descriptions on how to install the AI Setup Software. Please refer directly to this documentation for details on the most up-to-date drivers and notes on installation and the supported operating systems. The relevant pages also contain the download link for each installation package.

> **Installation Instructions and Download Links for AI Setup Software**
>
> Please refer to the appropriate website of your AI provider (such as MIT, shown below) for the latest download and installation instructions.
>
> `http://experimental.appinventor.mit.edu/learn/setup/`

The example of a Google AI installation under Windows shown in Figure 1.9 shows how to download the associated installation file `appinventor_setup_installer_v_1_2.exe` (approximately 92MB) by clicking on the link "Download the installer." Choose the target directory on your computer and confirm the download by clicking OK.

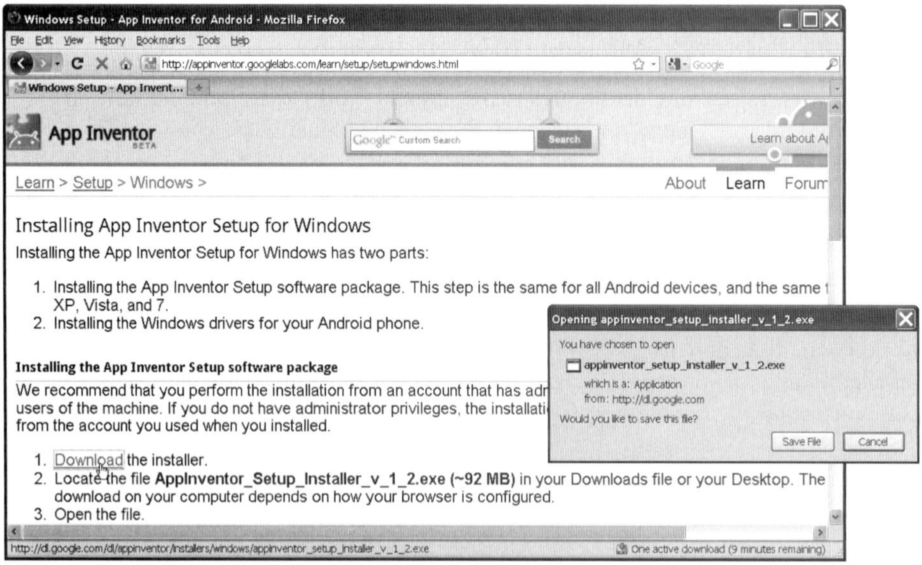

Figure 1.9 Downloading the AI installation package for Windows

Variations in Pictures Displayed

The pictures displayed on your computer may vary slightly from those shown in this book if you are using an operating system other than Windows XP. Simply select the corresponding functions on your own operating system.

Now start the downloaded setup file by double-clicking in the File Explorer. Follow the installation instructions for AI (see Figure 1.10). To install AI, you may have to confirm the security alert by clicking Run and accept the license conditions by clicking "I agree." Do not change the installation path suggested; install the program and drivers into the directory `C:\Program Files\AppInventor\commands-for-AppInventor`. After successful installation, you will find the entry "AppInventor Setup" in the Windows Start Menu as well, with the option to uninstall the program later if required.

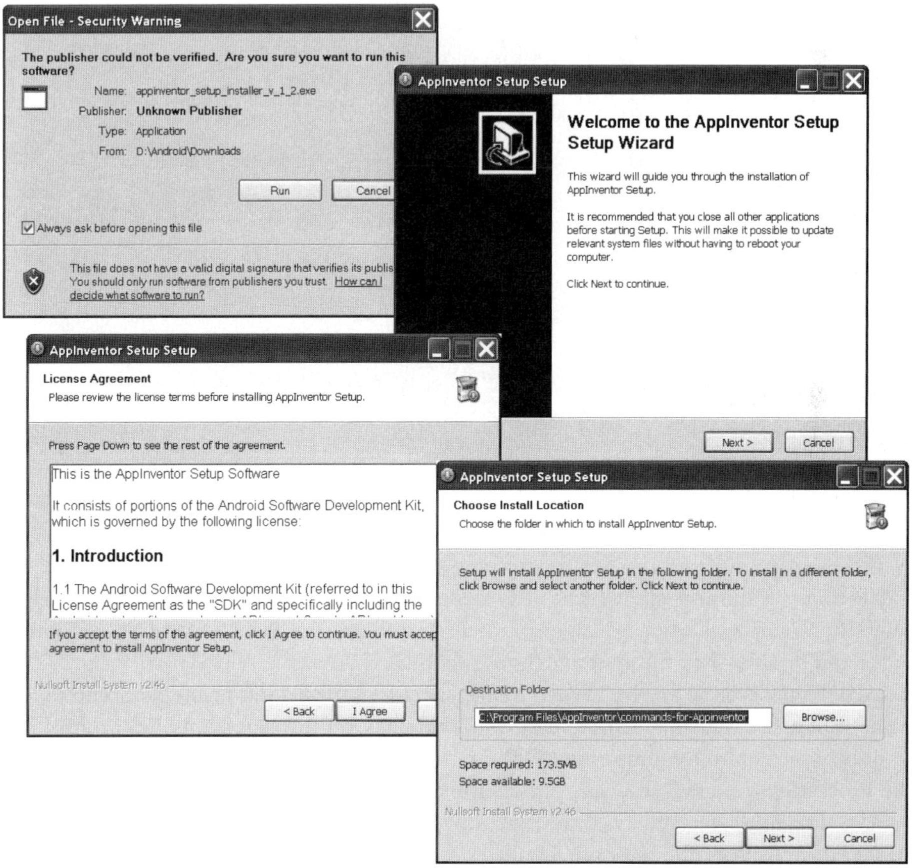

Figure 1.10 Installing AI on a Windows computer

With the installation of the AI Setup Software, USB drivers for connecting and controlling Android devices were also installed. The website mentioned previously in conjunction with the installation guideline for Windows lists only a few smartphones explicitly that are supported by the installed drivers. Nevertheless, many other smartphones are also supported. You can check whether the drivers can detect and support your own smartphone by using the ADB tool (Android Debug Bridge) included with AI. Connect your smartphone to the computer with the USB cable supplied. Go to Start > Run and open the Windows command-line window by entering the command `cmd`. Now switch to the C: drive and then to the installation directory by entering the commands `cd \` and `cd Program Files\AppInventor\commands-for-c`, followed by the command `adb devices`. You may need to grant the ADB tool access to the Internet if your firewall complains. If the List of devices attached includes an entry similar to the `HT9B2...` shown in Figure 1.11, your smartphone (`device`) was successfully detected.

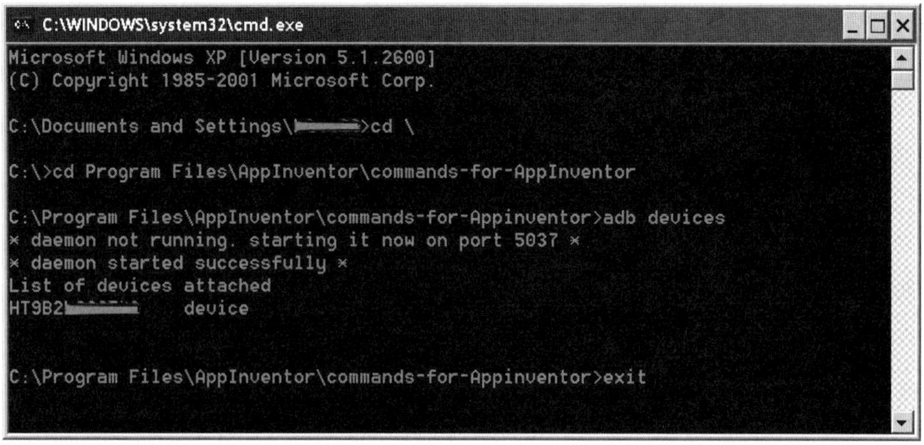

Figure 1.11 Checking computer and smartphone connectivity with ADB

If there is no such entry, your smartphone was not detected. Perhaps the AI driver installation was unsuccessful or you need a special driver for your smartphone. In both cases, the Windows Device Manager can help (see Figure 1.12). Choose Start > Control Panel and double-click on System. Choose the Hardware tab in the System Properties window and click on the Device Manager button. Now look below your computer name for an entry such as "Android Phone" and click on the plus symbol in front of it to display the Android Composite ADB Interface. Right-click on this entry and open the Properties window. Now you can see the device status under the General tab. If an error is displayed, you can try to fix it via the Troubleshoot button. If this step is unsuccessful, try to update the wrongly installed device drivers on the Drivers tab. The drivers included with AI can be found below the previously mentioned installation directory. For computers with an Intel processor, for example, they are found in the directory `C:\Program Files\AppInventor\commands-for-Appinventor\usb_driver\i386`.

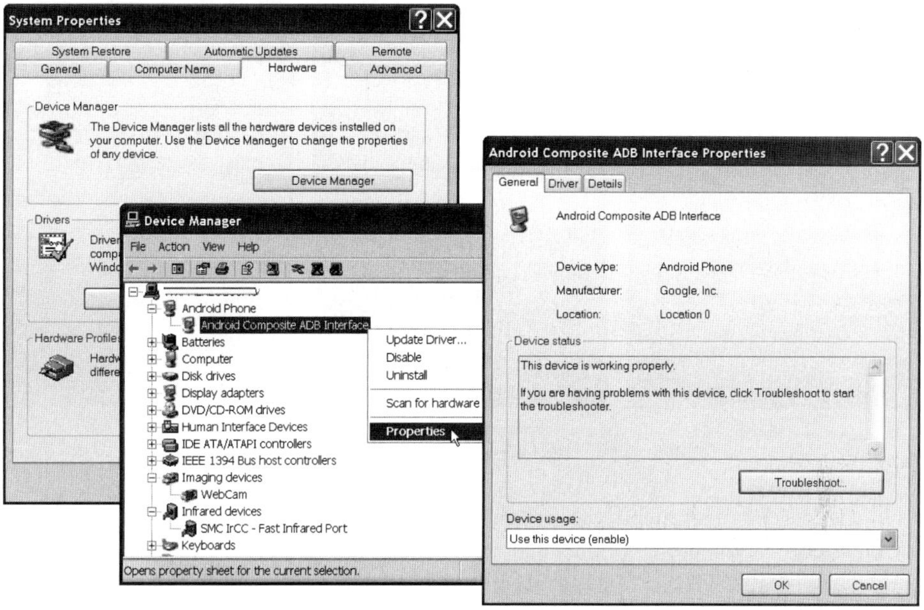

Figure 1.12 Troubleshooting during driver installation in Windows Device Manager

Android Device Settings

We want to integrate the Android device directly into the app development with AI, so that we can see and test the functions of and changes to an app in development simultaneously without needing an emulator. As part of the development environment, the smartphone must be seamlessly integrated into the development process and the technical platform. In preparation for app development, you have already installed and enabled the device driver for connecting your smartphone to the computer, as discussed in the previous section. Once the computer detects the smartphone correctly, however, you need to adapt a few settings before you can use it as part of the development environment.

The settings for development are entered in most Android smartphones in the menu of the same name. Go to your smartphone's application overview and choose Settings. In the Settings menu, choose Applications and then Development (see Figure 1.13 using the example of HTC Tattoo). The names of individual menu items may differ on your smartphone from the ones shown in Figure 1.13 under the HTC interface Sense, but the Development menu should be present on all smartphones. For more details, refer to the smartphone manufacturer's manual.

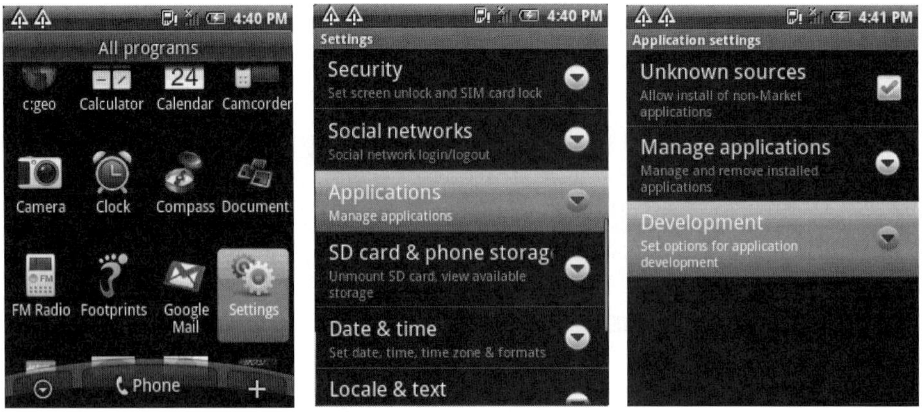

Figure 1.13 Go to the Android Development menu

In the Development menu, you will find the menu items shown in Figure 1.14. Enable the first two entries—"USB debugging" and "Stay awake"—so that they have a green check mark. "USB debugging" is required for direct communication between the AI development environment and the smartphone via USB. Enabling this option ensures that any later changes in the developed app can be directly displayed and checked in the smartphone. The "Stay awake" option prevents the smartphone's screensaver from switching on after a short period of time while you are developing the app, in which case the screensaver would stop displaying the app changes mentioned, making development much more difficult. The third item in the Development menu, "Allow mock locations," can remain disabled. This option is required when you develop an app with the emulator or on a smartphone without a GPS component when the app requires geographic location information. As no GPS data would be provided by the smartphone in these cases, they would be simulated by entering mock locations. For our purposes here, we assume that you are using an Android smartphone with GPS.

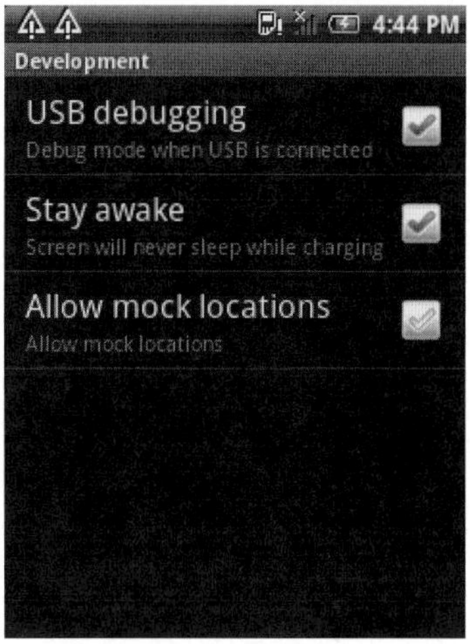

Figure 1.14 Enabling "USB debugging" and "Stay awake"

Once you have adapted the settings in the Development menu, you should make sure that the auto-rotation of your smartphone display is disabled. To do so, go back to the Settings menu and choose the menu item "Display" or "Sound & display." Disable the menu entry "Orientation" by unchecking it, as shown in Figure 1.15.

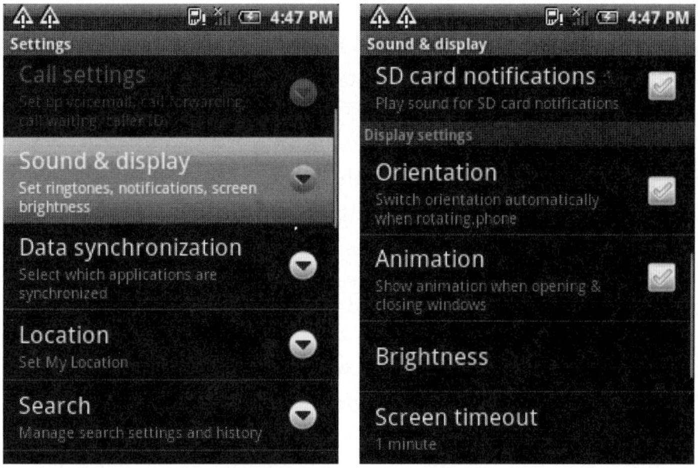

Figure 1.15 Disabling display auto-rotation under "Orientation"

AI Update of November 10, 2010

According to the AI update of November 10, 2010, deactivating the orientation is no longer necessary to prevent the app on the smartphone from crashing both in connected and nonconnected mode.

Now you have finished the few preparations that are required to use your smartphone for developing Android apps with AI. If you should decide to interrupt your development work for a while at some later stage, you may want to reset the development settings mentioned here to provide for "normal" use of your smartphone.

Disabling the Development Settings for Normal Use of the Smartphone

When you are not using your smartphone for developing apps, you should disable the setting "Stay awake" again, as the permanent display activity can use a lot of power and significantly reduces the battery life with mobile use. You can also re-enable the "Orientation" option. Before you start using AI again, you will need to change the settings as described in this section.

Allowing App Installations Without USB and from Outside Android Market

During your development work, you may sometimes want to download your own apps to your smartphone without a USB cable connection; you might also want to download apps by other developers that have not been published on Android Market. This happens via graphical QR (Quick Response) codes, which can be created with AI and read into your smartphone with a barcode scanner. To enable this function, you need to enable the item "Unknown sources" in the Applications menu (see Figure 1.13), if your smartphone offers this function. Be careful, though: There is always the potential risk of encountering malicious applications when downloading foreign apps.

You should do a final check of whether the settings on your smartphone are actually working properly. Connect the smartphone to the computer with the USB cable and unlock the display if necessary. Your smartphone should now tell you that the connection to the computer has been created and USB debugging connected. You may also be asked which type of USB connection should be created. Do not choose any Sync (synchronization) function here; instead, choose—for example—"Mount as disk drive." Your computer operating system will then search your smartphone's memory and SD card and give you the option of starting any media files found, which you should decline. The important thing is that your smartphone now has two icons in the status bar showing the connection status, as shown in Figure 1.16 on the left: the two triangles with exclamation marks in the top bar.

Figure 1.16 Displaying the connection status

Open the status bar—for example, by dragging the status bar downwards with your finger on the HTC Tattoo. The status "USB debugging connected" should appear, as shown on the right-hand side of Figure 1.16. The preceding entry, "Turn off USB storage," shows that your smartphone or the SD memory card in it has been detected and connected as an external disk drive.

SD Card: A Requirement for App Inventor

To use your smartphone with the current AI development environment, the device must have an SD memory card in it. Make sure that your smartphone meets this requirement, although practically all Android smartphones contain such a memory card.

While the presence of an SD card is a general requirement for all Android smartphones if you want to develop apps with AI, some functions of AI inevitably will not work as expected with some smartphones during the beta phase and probably in the future as well. As mentioned in the context of the Android platform, the quirks of the increasing number of new and different Android devices cannot possibly be taken into account by the AI developers. If the manufacturers deviate from the guidelines regarding implementation of the hardware interface or the Android operating system, or if inconsistencies or even errors should creep into their implementations, malfunctions cannot be ruled out. These problems typically relate to just individual partial functions, with other AI components continuing to work as expected.

Current Online Information on Preparing and Installing AI

The requirements for preparing and installing the AI development environment may change. You can always find current information on AI setup and a list of frequently asked questions (FAQ) at the website of your AI provider, such as MIT:

`http://experimental.appinventor.mit.edu/learn/setup/`

Don't be discouraged if something does not look or work exactly as shown or described in this book on your own smartphone or computer. The Android world is simply too big, too heterogeneous, too dynamic, and too open to ensure complete consistency. Instead, you should take advantage of the freedom of Android by trying it out. Do not be afraid to skip a step and find your own solutions. This pragmatic approach will be useful later, when you are developing your own creative apps.

App Inventor Forum

You are not alone with your questions, topics, and projects, but are about to become part of a worldwide and constantly growing community of Android developers using AI as a basis for their work. Get to know the projects, questions, problems, and challenges of other developers, and suggest your own topics. Become a member of the *AI Forum*:
`http://experimental.appinventor.mit.edu/forum/`

One of the five topic areas is specifically aimed at AI beginners and deals with questions and problems surrounding the installation of the setup software, the smartphone integration, and similar concerns relevant to beginners: "Getting Set Up and Connecting Your Phone to App Inventor."

Chapter 2

The Development Environment

This chapter introduces you to working with App Inventor's development environment. While becoming familiar with the individual work areas and functions of AI, you will have the opportunity to create your very first app project and be able to admire the result on your Android smartphone. In keeping with the customs of every good app development book for beginners, we will call our first project "HelloAndroidWorld," even if AI is not a programming language in the classic sense.

The design of the development environment, or integrated development environment (IDE), is crucial for a visual development language such as AI. In classic programming languages such as Java, C, and C++, the programming code can be entered with a simple text editor such as Notepad. In contrast, there is no such alternative for developing Android apps with AI—you must use the IDE offered by Google. Basic knowledge of how the AI IDE works and functions is, therefore, indispensable if you want to develop apps successfully. For that reason, this chapter introduces the details of the central interfaces *Designer* and *Blocks Editor*, explaining ways to use them, their functions and main tasks, and their interaction within the app development arena. You will also learn how to integrate your smartphone directly into the development work and environment to create visible results as quickly as possible. Of course, we will also address the potential pitfalls and occasional initial difficulties of the AI development environment, showing you efficient solutions for overcoming these problems.

Discrepancies in Representations

Please bear in mind that the figures, references, and menu structures for the AI development environment may differ depending on the provider and the version used. As it is the greatest common denominator, we use the Google AI in our figures; the systems of other providers are based on this version. For the most up-to-date information about the MIT AI, please refer to the following website:

http://appinventor.mit.edu

Welcome to App Inventor!

Before starting to create your first app project with AI, you need to have the login data for accessing the AI Online platform. If you do not yet have these data yet, return to Chapter 1 and read the section on access data to find out how to get them. Depending on the AI platform used, you may not need to have your account activated explicitly by the provider, and you can probably access the AI platform and start developing apps immediately, even without a confirmation e-mail. Its receipt was necessary for accessing Google AI when it was in its closed beta phase (see Figure 2.1), as well as for the formerly closed testing phase of the MIT AI Experimental system.

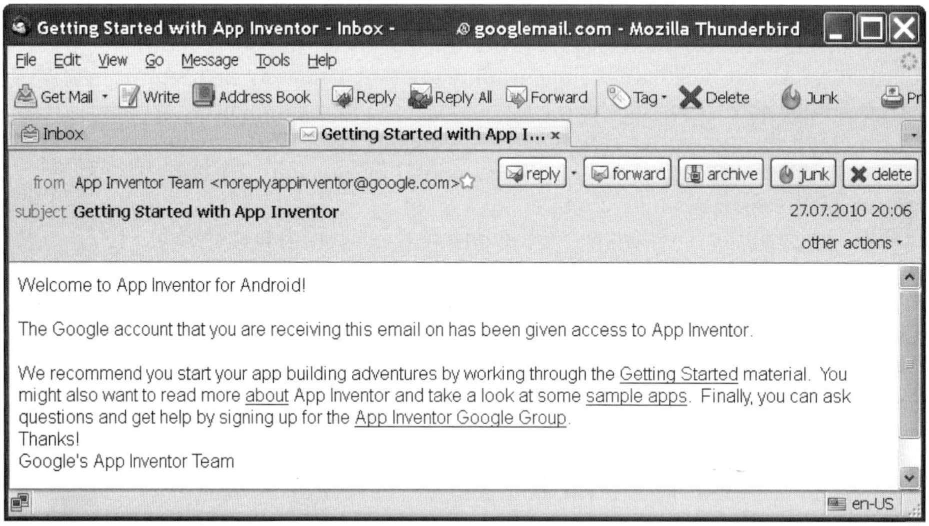

Figure 2.1 Historic activation message (no longer required!)

Of course, to successfully run AI, you also have to fulfill the system requirements described in Chapter 1, install the AI Setup Software, and enter the correct development settings on your smartphone. Connect your smartphone to your computer and confirm that it is being detected in "USB debugging" mode. Once all these requirements are met, you are ready to start the AI development environment and create your first small Android project.

App Inventor Designer

To start the AI development environment, you call the first of two central work windows, the *Designer*. In the AI Designer, you will mainly create the interface of your own apps and put them together from the functional components of AI. The AI Designer is implemented as a web application, so you load it just like a normal website into your browser by entering the appropriate web address.

> **To Start App Inventor, Type Web Address into Browser**
>
> Go the web address of your provider to start App Inventor. If necessary, refer to the provider's documentation to find the appropriate web address. The original address of the Google AI was `http://appinventorbeta.com`.
>
> The direct links to the experimental and public version of MIT AI are:
>
> `http://experimental.appinventor.mit.edu`
> `http://beta.appinventor.mit.edu`

When accessing the starting address of App Inventor, a login page encrypted via HTTPS will open (see Figure 2.2), as you already know it from the section on logging in to the Google AI system. Enter your access data and press the button to start App Inventor.

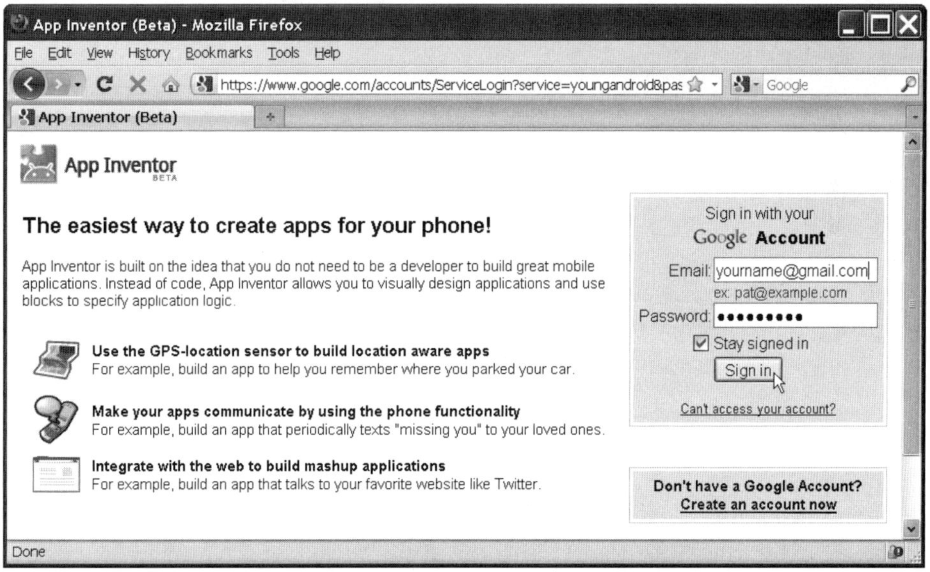

Figure 2.2 Login to start the App Inventor development environment

Once your login data is accepted, AI Designer is started in your web browser. As soon as the page has finished loading, the AI Designer start page greets you with the message "Welcome to App Inventor!" as shown in Figure 2.3. For your first visit to this site, you may have to confirm the Terms of Service and go to the start page by clicking on the link "My Projects."

Subject to Change

The images in the figures may differ slightly from those on your own computer, as there may be further changes and upgrades in the App Inventor interface design during the transition phase and beyond. You should have no trouble finding the described functions in a slightly different form or in a different place. Usually the AI Updates by the Google App Inventor Team or by other AI providers like MIT will keep you informed about such changes and upgrades.

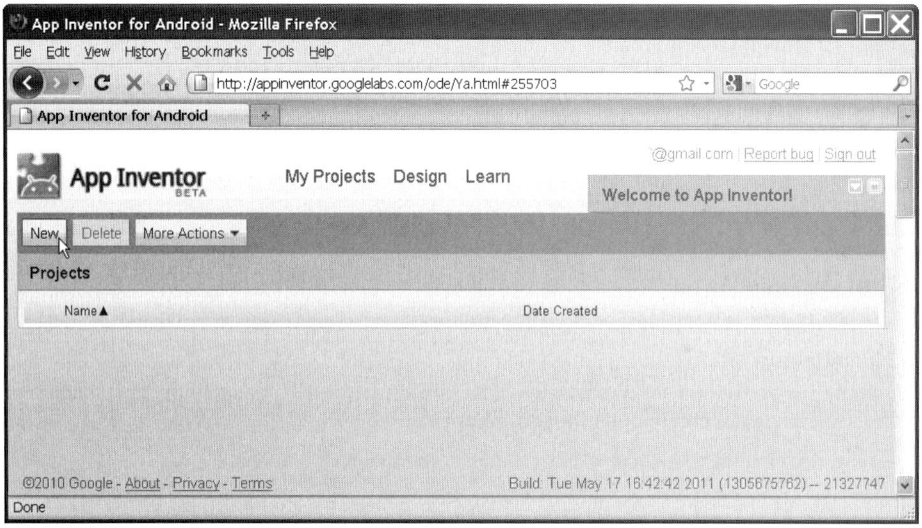

Figure 2.3 First visit to App Inventor Designer

Creating a Project in the Design Area

In the upper-left corner of AI Designer shown in Figure 2.3, you can see the App Inventor (BETA) logo. It looks like a bit like a puzzle piece and seems to symbolize the building blocks of the visual development language that you will later put together to create a fully functioning Android app. On the right next to this logo is a bar with three options: My Projects, Design, and Learn. You can use the My Projects and Design options to switch within AI Designer between an overview of your app projects and the desktop of your current app project. When first starting AI, you do not have a current app project (or any other projects), so the two menu items do not change the view at this stage.

Similarly, the *work area* in the bottom part of the window with the Projects heading and a gray background will be completely empty when you first open AI Designer, except for the information about the Google copyright, Terms of Use, and other information, plus the currently used AI version number ("Build: ..."). The Learn option permits you to navigate to the Google documentation on AI in a new browser tab.

At the upper-right corner of the window, you will see your user name in form of your Google e-mail address (see Figure 2.3). Next to it is the link "Report bug," which you can use to report any errors you might encounter during your work with AI in the beta phase. The "Sign out" option is how you log out after you are finished developing with AI, thereby closing the development environment. Below this option is a small *message area*, where the developers of Google can inform you of any updates, bugs, or other issues worth knowing about (see Figure 2.4). If there is no current information, you will see just the familiar greeting "Welcome to App Inventor!" (see Figure 2.3). The two buttons to the right of the message area are used to "expand" or "shrink" it.

In the line with the light green background below the top bar is the *function menu*, which has three buttons. Depending on what is selected in the options at the top, the function menu shows only those function buttons required for each work area. The function menu is dynamic and changes depending on the active work area; to a certain extent, this variability applies to the top bar with its options as well. For example, the current work area has no projects as yet, so the Delete button is grayed out and you cannot click on it (see Figure 2.4).

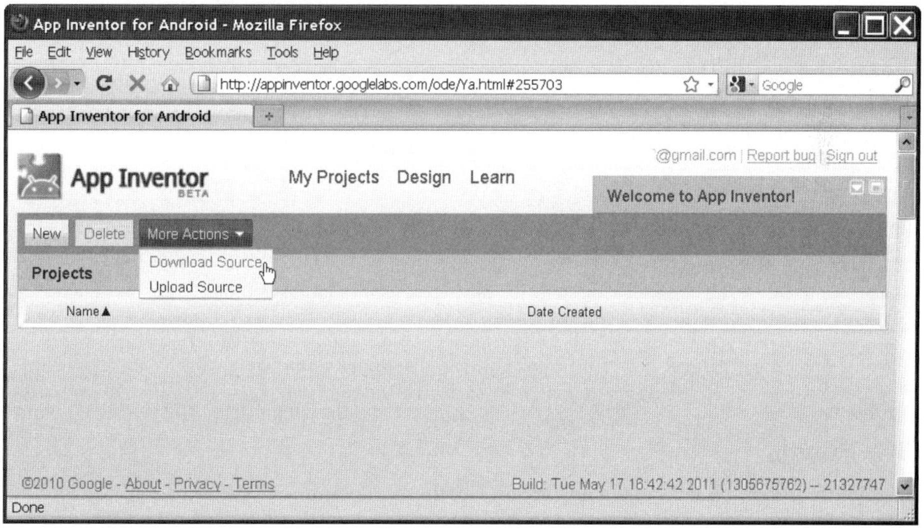

Figure 2.4 Unavailable buttons are grayed out

Similarly, the menu item "Download Sources" under "More Actions" cannot be used without an existing or selected app project; thus it is currently grayed out and not available, as shown in Figure 2.4. The menu item "More Actions" enables you to later load complete app projects to your local hard drive ("Download Source") or to upload them from the hard disk to the online AI development environment ("Upload Source"). You will get to know these functions later in more detail in connection with the security and exchange of your app projects.

Let's create an app project so that we can use the AI Designer user interface elements that require an existing project before they become available. Click on the New button to create your first app project. It opens a window "New App Inventor for Android Project ...," as shown in Figure 2.5. Enter a name for the new project in the field "Project name"; this identifier will be used as the name of the project within AI as well as the resulting Android app. In keeping with tradition, we will use the name "HelloAndroid-World". Note that the project name cannot include any blank spaces, must start with a letter, and can contain only letters, numbers, and underscores.

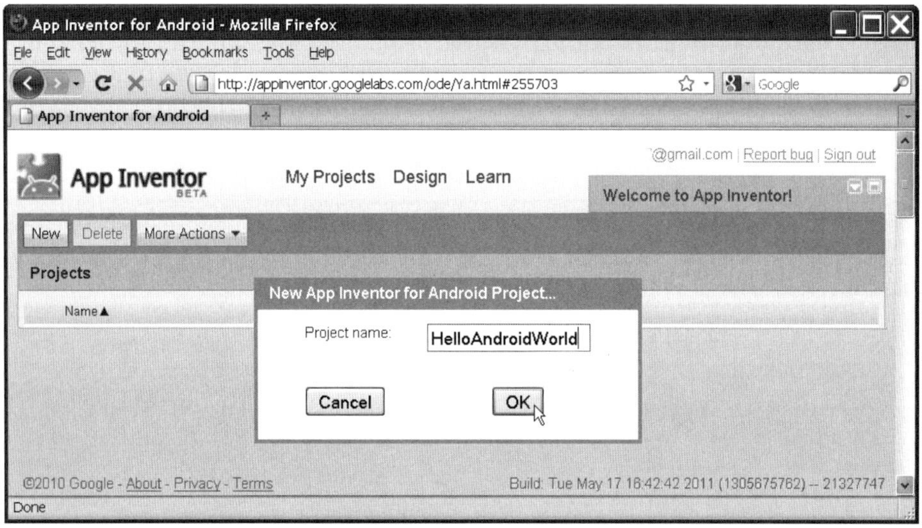

Figure 2.5 Creating a new app project in AI Designer

Five Panels

After you confirm your input by clicking OK, the comprehensive user interface of AI Designer appears after a short loading time. As shown in Figure 2.6, it contains five *panels:* Palette, Viewer, Components, Media, and Properties. In these panels, you will later create or "design" the interface of your app with the graphic and functional components of AI.

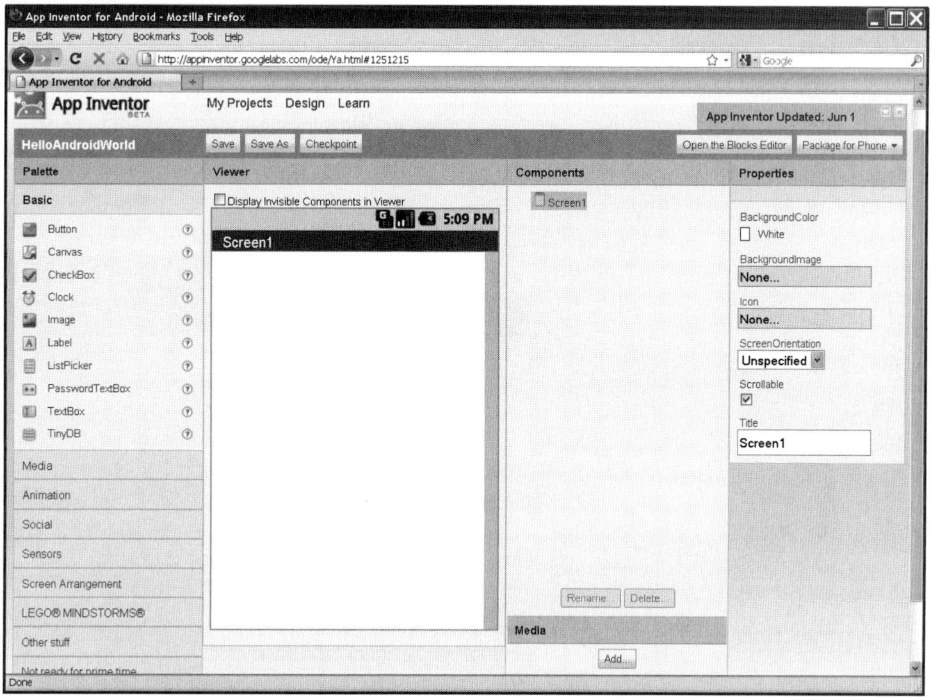

Figure 2.6 The five panels of AI Designer

Inventory of Palette Components

In the Palette panel, which is found on the left of the work area, you can find all graphic and functional *components* offered by AI for designing and developing apps. These are the building blocks or puzzle pieces you will use to put together your apps. The components are divided into different groups (sections): "Basic," "Media," "Animation," "Social," "Sensors," "Screen Arrangement," "LEGO® MINDSTORMS®," "Other stuff," "Not ready for prime time," and "Old stuff." By clicking on the group name (header) with the mouse, you can open each group and see a list of the components it contains. Figure 2.7 shows the opened group "Media" with its five components. On the right next to the component name is a question mark. Clicking on it displays a brief explanation of the component and at least one reference to further information.

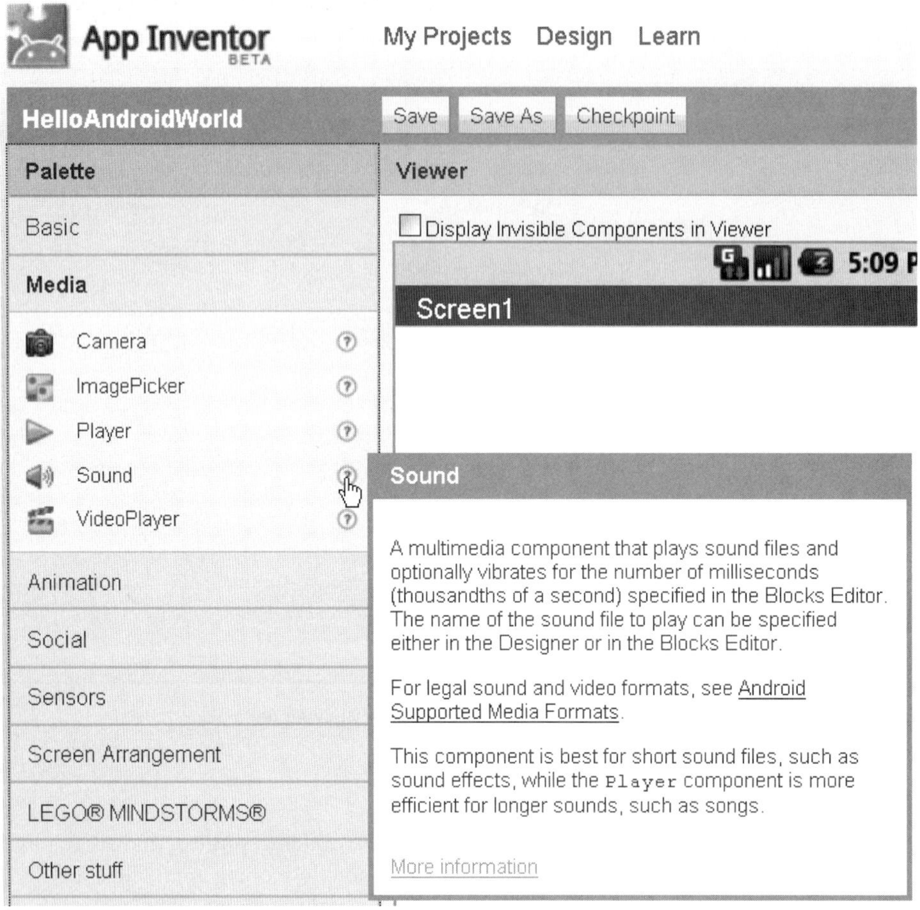

Figure 2.7 Displaying additional information on the individual components

The obligatory link "More Information" leads to the functional specification of the component in the *Component Reference*. This reference defines the use and function of each AI component and provides additional information such as methods, events, and properties, which we will encounter later in this book. Figure 2.8 shows as an example the specification of the media component "Sound," which appears in a separate tab after we click on the link "More information" shown in Figure 2.7.

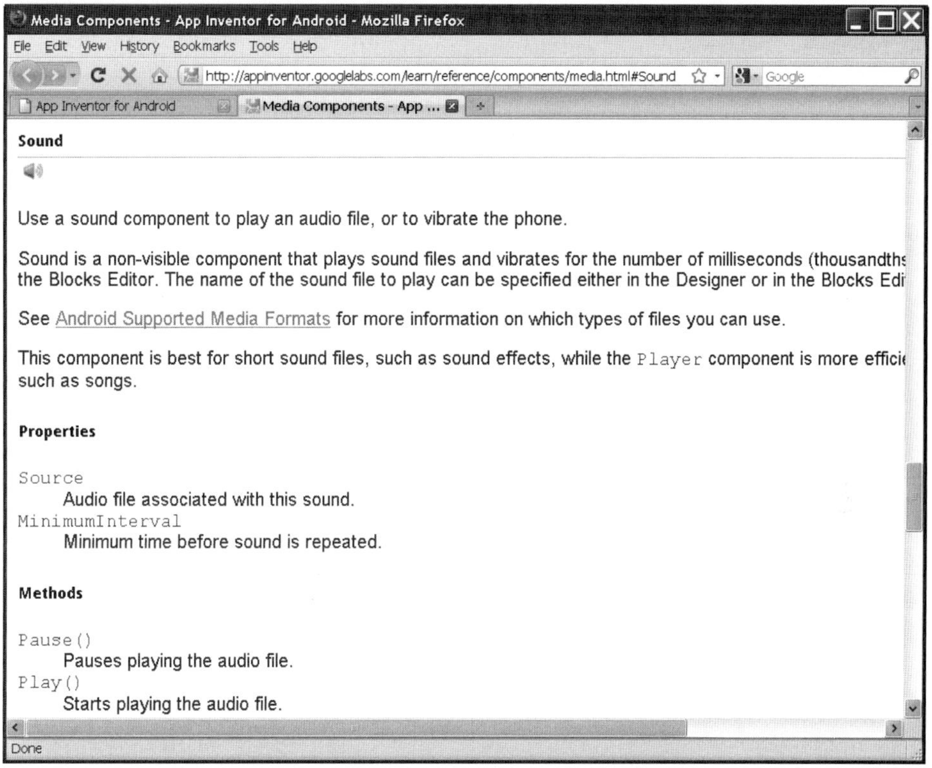

Figure 2.8 Specification of the component "Sound" in the Component Reference

The Component Reference represents a good resource for your development work later on if you need to look up details on the individual components. Use this online resource without fear; its information should always be up-to-date.

> **Note**
>
> Reference to all AI components and their functions: `http://appinventor.mit.edu/explore/content/reference-documentation.html`

Designing Apps with Component Objects in the Viewer

The Viewer panel resembles the display of a smartphone, as you can see on the left of Figure 2.9. The top line of the Viewer shows typical cellphone information such as the reception type ("G," as in GPRS), a bar indicating the signal strength, the battery state, and a clock. All of these items are actually static—that is, they are merely decorative. Below them is the design area where you will actually assemble your app's interface and functional elements interactively. To do so, you choose the desired components from the Palette by clicking on them and dragging them to the Viewer while holding the left mouse button; you can then drop the components and arrange them as you wish.

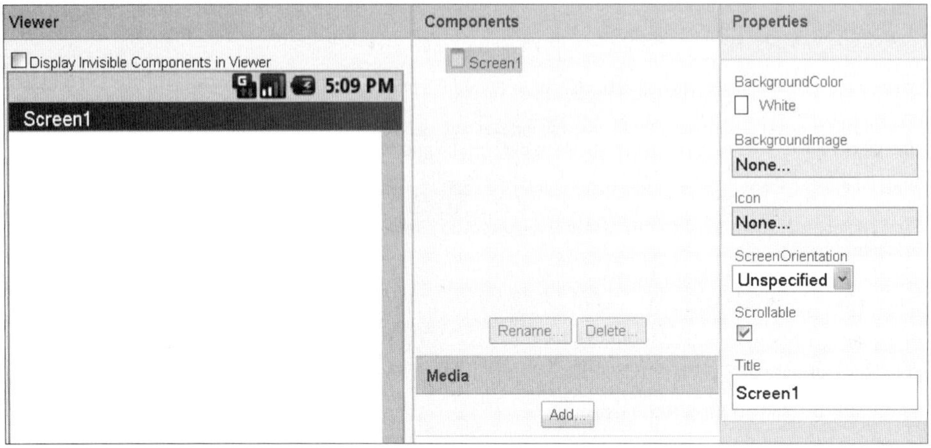

Figure 2.9 The starting component "Screen1" and its properties

A Brief Aside: The Difference Between a Component and a Component Object

When you drop a component in the Viewer, you create a corresponding *object* in the Viewer that is an analog to the selected component, but you do not actually move the component itself into the Viewer. If you look at the Palette, you will see that the component is still available there for creating the next object of the same component type. This difference is a critical one. In object-oriented programming, each object created is designated as a specific instance of its class. The individual objects of the same component type are then distinguished by assigning clear object names and (usually) by assigning different property values to the various objects. To keep things simple, we will not overemphasize the difference between the abstract component and the specific object in this book, as an exact distinction is not as relevant in developing apps with AI as it would be, for example, in object-oriented Android programming with Java. We will occasionally use the term "component object" or simply "object" when referring to a specific created object of a particular component type in AI Designer or AI Blocks Editor. Sometimes we will also designate a specific component object with its unique object name through use of a specific font.

The component objects arranged optically in the Viewer give you an approximate impression of what the app will look like on your smartphone. We say "approximate" because the representation on your smartphone can be different—for example, a line of text might break in a different place due to a different display size. You can check directly whether there is a divergence between your smartphone and the Viewer during your development work with AI, as the components you drag to the Viewer will appear almost simultaneously on the smartphone connected to the computer. Do not confuse the Viewer with the emulator mentioned in Chapter 1, however: The Viewer cannot simulate any telephone function or similar properties of your smartphone, but rather deals solely with arranging components.

Above the Viewer is the check box labeled "Display Invisible Components in Viewer." If you enable it, you can display even those components in the Viewer that you have explicitly marked as invisible previously via its initial property "Visible." That makes sense, for example, if individual components are meant to be visible only in certain situations in the finished app, but not continuously (e.g., a Stop button should become visible only if a Start button has been clicked). This check box gives you the convenient option of seeing all components while you are optically designing the app in AI Designer, so you can assess their visual appearance as a whole.

Structuring Objects Under Components and Media

In the Components panel, all component objects you dragged into the Viewer are depicted in a hierarchical tree structure. In other words, individual components are designated as subordinate to other components, forming groups with the same properties or dependencies—like leaves on branches hanging on a tree. Figure 2.9 shows only the component "Screen1," which represents your smartphone screen and forms the obligatory starting component of any app or root for all further, subordinate components. As this component is obligatory, the two buttons for renaming and deleting components are not yet activated; they apply only to other components that you add. The original Google AI supports only apps with a single screen component, so the Palette does not have a "Screen" component for selection or additions. In Google AI, apps with different screen views must be realized or improvised with different methods, as we will see later. The inclusion of the number "1" in the default name "Screen1" suggests that the Google developers did not want to completely dismiss the option of adding additional screen views in AI within an app in the future.

Another category of elements that you can add to an app are media files such as audio or video files. These items can be selected from your local hard disk by using the Add button in the Media panel and uploaded to the AI development environment. In Figure 2.9, there are not yet any media files loaded or listed, as these are also usable only in connection with appropriate components, such as those for playing audio or video files from the component group "Media."

Setting Component Properties

The Properties panel shows the properties of the component object currently selected; they appear when you click an item in the Components or Viewer panel. For now, we have only the component "Screen1" to choose from, so Properties lists its properties. The "Screen1" component has six properties: BackgroundColor, BackgroundImage, Icon (for the app's start icon), ScreenOrientation (with the options Unspecified, Portrait, and

Landscape), Scrollable (to allow the screen to scroll), and Title. You can click to select and individually change these properties.

For example, clicking on the current setting of BackgroundColor will open a color palette in which you can choose a screen background color for your app. In Figure 2.10, the color "Blue" is selected for BackgroundColor. In the "Title" field, you can change the app's title as displayed on your smartphone; for example, you can change "Screen1" to "Hello Android World!" Unlike the app's file name, the label entered in this text box can use spaces and any other symbols. The changes you make in the Properties panel are then immediately visible in the Viewer, and soon afterward in the connected smartphone.

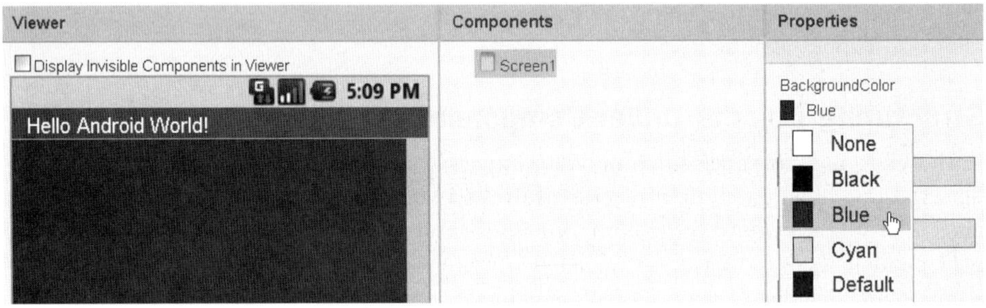

Figure 2.10 Changing component properties with the Properties panel

Managing and Saving App Projects

Now that we have investigated the panels in AI Designer that are available for creating the new project "HelloAndroidWorld," let's take another look at the two central menu bars. The top bar appears unchanged, containing three menu items: My Projects, Design, and Learn. As soon as you click on the menu item "My Projects," however, the browser view changes back to the previously empty project view "Projects" shown in Figure 2.3, but now lists the new project "HelloAndroidWorld" along with the date on which it was created, as shown in Figure 2.11.

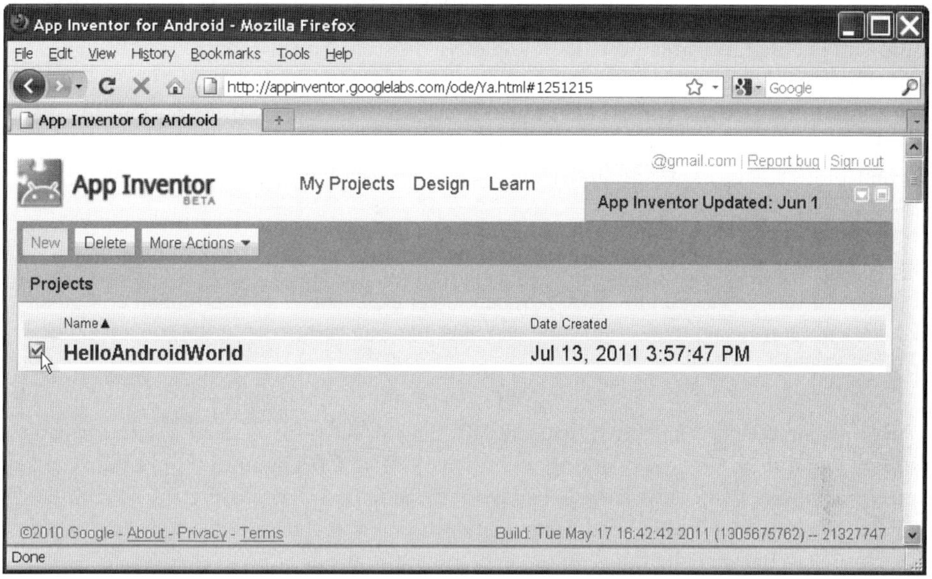

Figure 2.11 The new AI project "HelloAndroidWorld" in project view

If you highlight the project "HelloAndroidWorld" by clicking on the check box in front of the project name, the function menu offers the previously inactive functions "Delete" and "More Actions." We do not want to delete the project in this incomplete stage, nor do we want to download it to our hard disk. Instead, let's go back to the Designer view by clicking on the menu item "Design" or directly on the project name. Your project will then appear in exactly the same editing stage you left it in before (see Figure 2.12).

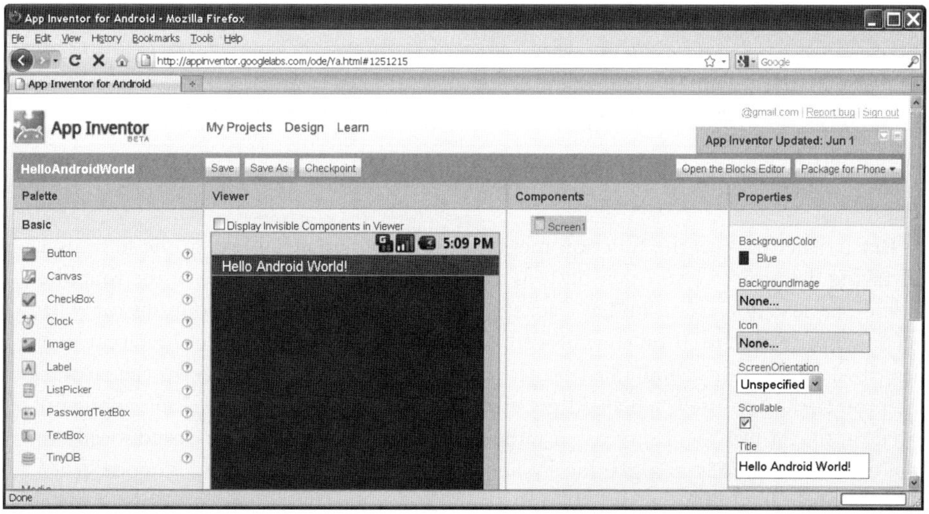

Figure 2.12 The function menu in design mode

As mentioned earlier, the function menu shows its dynamic side once we have created a project. The designer area now has completely different function buttons in the line with the light green background than we saw earlier in the project view. On the extreme left side, you can see the name of the current project, followed by three buttons for saving the current project—all on Google's AI servers. Clicking the Save button saves the current project stage explicitly under the current project name.

Regular Saving Prevents Loss of Data

Make sure that you save your current project explicitly by regularly clicking the Save button. If your connection to the AI provider server experiences an interruption or if other errors occur, you can then access the last saved project version once the connection is reestablished.

By clicking the Save As button, you can save the current project under a different name or copy it and then continue working with the copy. The Checkpoint button offers another save variant—one that comes in very handy for developing work. During app development, you may sometimes have to decide between one of several possible solutions, as if at a crossroads. Before embarking on the chosen path, you can place a "checkpoint"—a kind of marker—and save the current stage of the project. If you later decide that another solution would be better, you can go back to the previous stage of the project by selecting the checkpoint and then embark development of an alternative solution from there. AI suggests different project name endings for the various save options, such as "`_copy`" and "`_checkpoint`". The project variations you create this way are displayed in the project overview and can be selected for editing by clicking on the project name (see Figure 2.13). Of course, you can also choose your own names for the project variations you save.

Figure 2.13 Copies and checkpoints of the project "HelloAndroidWorld"

But let's get back to the function menu in the Designer area. Next to the buttons for saving the project, two other buttons appear on the right-hand side of the function menu. The selection menu under "Package for Phone" provides three options for *exporting* the app created based on the currently displayed project. Unlike the three previously described options for saving an AI project in progress, this export concerns the result of the project, the app itself, which AI generates from the project. The resulting app is not saved on the AI provider's server, but rather exported by the server and saved locally in one of three variations: as a graphically encoded download link ("Show Barcode"), as an application file (with the file extension `.apk`) on your computer ("Download to this

Computer"), or directly on your smartphone ("Download to Connected Phone") as an independent app. We will discuss these export options in more detail toward the end of this chapter. If you select one of the three export options now, an error message with a red background will appear at the top of the work area, as shown in Figure 2.14.

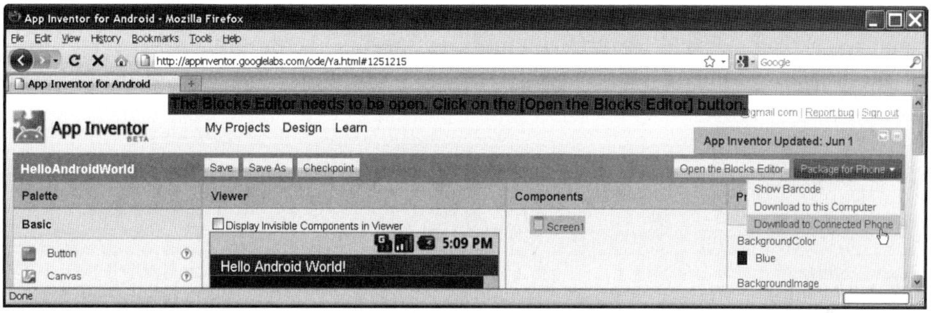

Figure 2.14 Exporting apps requires the Blocks Editor

This message points out that you first need to open another area of the AI development environment before the export function becomes available. You open it by clicking on the last remaining button on the Designer function bar, "Open the Blocks Editor."

App Inventor Blocks Editor

Apart from the Designer, the Blocks Editor forms the second central work window of the AI development environment. The Blocks Editor is where you will bring the individual components of your app to life and assign them specific tasks, which together will form the overall functionality of your app. As the AI Blocks Editor is implemented as Java Web Start application, starting it requires your computer to have the Java configuration described in Chapter 1. You start the AI Blocks Editor from the AI Designer from the function menu and by clicking the button labeled "Open the Blocks Editor," as shown in Figure 2.15.

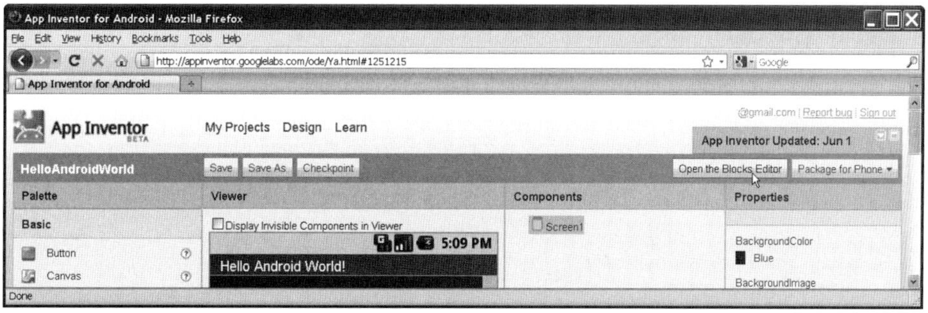

Figure 2.15 Starting the AI Blocks Editor from the function menu of AI Designer

Once you click on this button, its label changes to "Opening the Blocks Editor ... (click to cancel)," indicating that the loading process for AI Blocks Editor has begun. The web browser then asks you in a separate window what it should do with the Java Web Start application you are about to download, or rather the underlying JNLP file `AppInventorForAndroidCodeblocks.jnlp`. Proceed in the same way as in the Java Web Start demos of the previous chapter: Choose Open with > Java(TM) Web Start Launcher, perhaps activate "Do this automatically for files like this from now on" so you are not asked the same question in the future, and then confirm your choice by clicking OK, as shown in Figure 2.16.

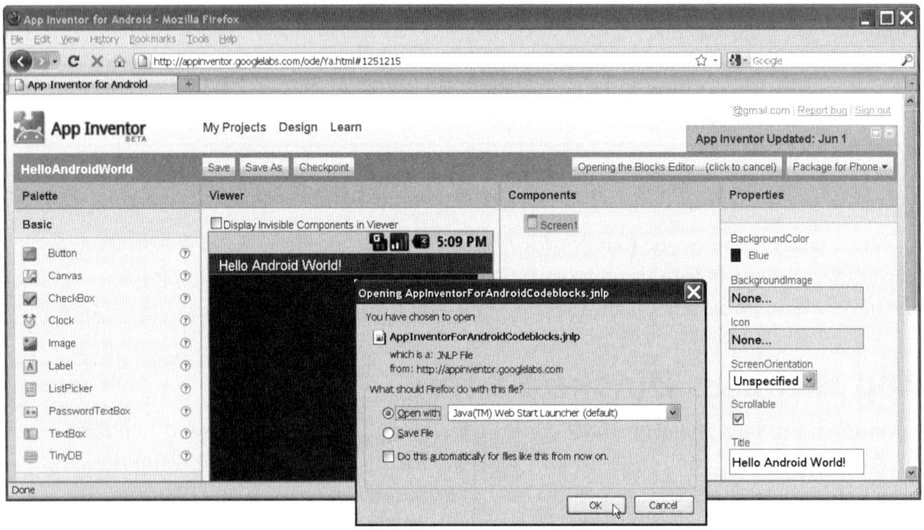

Figure 2.16 Confirm to load and start the AI Blocks Editor

The Java Web Start application AI Blocks Editor is now being loaded, as indicated by the message appearing in a separate window (see the left side of Figure 2.17). Before the fully downloaded application is executed on your computer, your operating system may first check it for a digital signature. If none is present, you have to manually confirm that you want to run the program (see the right side of Figure 2.17). Again you have the option of enabling the check box "Always trust content from this publisher"; choosing it means you will not be asked the same question again the next time you open AI Blocks Editor.

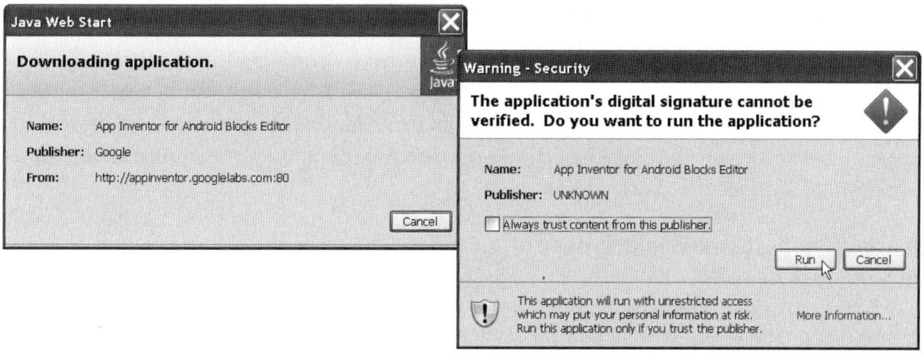

Figure 2.17 Loading AI Blocks Editor with a security check

The loading process for AI Blocks Editor can take a little while—according to Google, 30 seconds or more, depending on the Internet bandwidth you have available. After the loading and start time, a new window appears, presenting the user interface of AI Blocks Editor (see Figure 2.18). Again, it is quite empty when you first open it, but that will soon change.

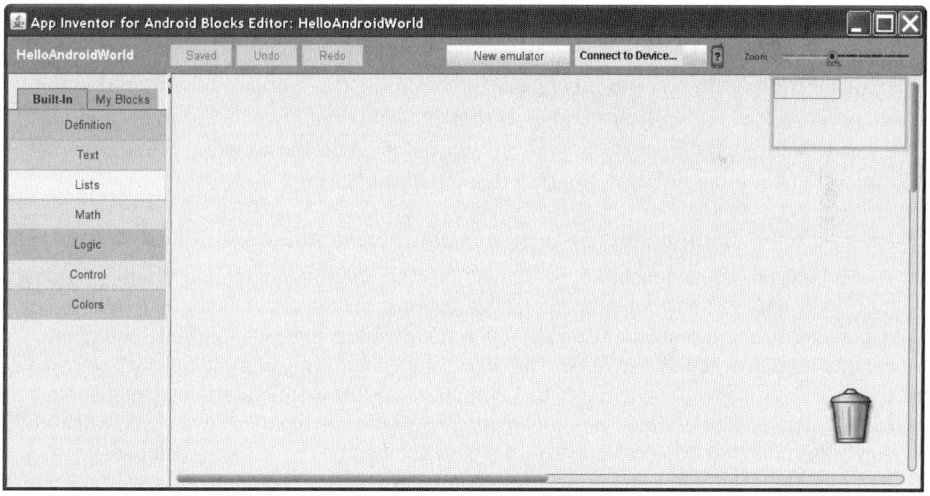

Figure 2.18 The AI Blocks Editor user interface on first start

Given that you started the AI Blocks Editor within a specific project from within the AI Designer, the initial representation of the user interface relates to the current project, "HelloAndroidWorld." The project name appears both in the window title and on the left in the green bar of the function menu shown in Figure 2.18.

Developing App Functions from Blocks

The AI Blocks Editor also presents different panels below the function menu. Similar to the AI Designer, the left column—the *block selection*—contains a list of functional groups available for selection. These groups do not contain components, but rather functional *blocks*, which make up the syntax of the visual developer language AI, similar to the command set of a classic programming language.

Commands, Blocks, and Syntax of a Developer Language

In classic programming, the individual instructions of the programming code are referred to as *commands* with which you tell the executing computer what to do if the user interacts with the program—for example, by pressing a button—or if another event occurs. The commands are listed in the program code, just as with any other language, under strict rules and combined with each other, corresponding to the *syntax* of the underlying grammar. The smallest combination of commands forms a *block*, with which you can, for example, assign text to a button (assignment block), play a media file (instruction block), or repeatedly execute a command (loop block). Within the visual developer language AI, these blocks represent the smallest units that you combine under the syntax of AI to create increasingly bigger functional units, up to the completed app.

To make it easier even for nonprogrammers to understand the role that blocks play in developing apps with AI, we can try a simple comparison of the two central work areas, Designer and Blocks Editor, plus the individual building blocks, components and blocks. Don't worry—this approach is not required for your development work with AI. After all, AI is meant to help you intuitively use and assemble the building blocks offered in your app development, without having to think too much about the application structure. Later, you will see how easily you can switch between the working environments and manage to use the different puzzle pieces in combination.

Interaction of Components in Designer and Blocks in Blocks Editor

The AI Designer is used mainly for designing the user interface of an app. For this purpose, it offers a variety of components: interactive buttons, text fields, sensors, and many other options for user input, plus text and image displays, audio and video players, and many options for output to the user. Using the AI Blocks Editor, you can systematically combine the previously isolated input and output components. Text input, selections, geographic coordinates, and other data from the input components are received, processed within the app and sometimes by accessing external data sources on the Internet, and passed on to the output component for output. The systematic interaction of the coordinated components and blocks forms the interactive app.

Generic Block Groups Under the Built-In Tab

Let's get back to selecting blocks in the AI Blocks Editor. The block selection contains two areas that you can access by clicking on the Built-In and My Blocks tabs. The Built-In tab includes seven generic block groups: Definition, Text, Lists, Math, Logic,

Control, and Colors. As the term "generic" indicates, these blocks are always generically available for app development, independent of the component objects used. To open a group, simply click on the group name. This displays the individual blocks of the group in a scrollable selection to the right of the group name. Figure 2.19 shows an extract of the available colors from the Colors group.

Blocks as Puzzle Pieces

Representing the blocks as puzzle pieces is not a random choice. A puzzle shows the correct overall picture only if all of the pieces fit together and are correctly connected. This analogy exactly applies to visual app development with AI: The app can function properly only if the correct blocks and components are connected together to form a coordinated whole. To ensure you do not make any syntax mistakes while developing your app, AI will stop you if necessary from connecting the wrong puzzle pieces.

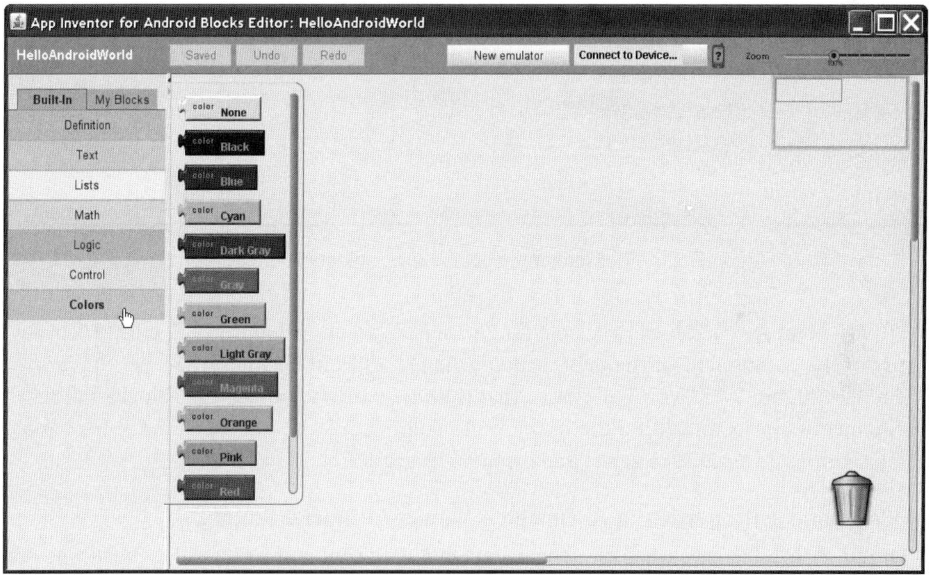

Figure 2.19 Color selection in the Colors block group

Component-Specific Blocks Under My Blocks

Things are slightly different with the block groups listed under the My Blocks tab. Here you can choose from component-specific blocks that allow you to influence the properties of those component objects that you use in the current app project. Accordingly, the block groups have the names of the corresponding component they represent in the Blocks Editor. As we are currently using the start component "Screen1" in our app

"HelloAndroidWorld," this group is the only one listed and selectable in Figure 2.20. The more components you later add in the Designer, the more groups you have available in the Blocks Editor under My Blocks.

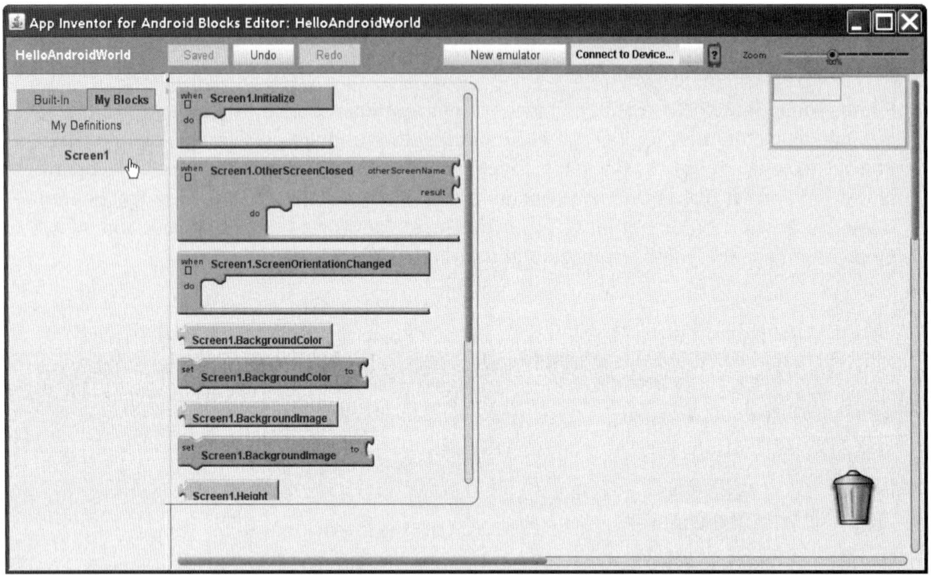

Figure 2.20 Component-specific block selection of "Screen1"

If you compare the blocks available for "Screen1" shown in Figure 2.20 with the properties of the component of the same name in AI Designer under the Properties function menu (see Figure 2.12), you will notice that they are partly identical. The Blocks Editor also contains blocks for setting the background color (`Screen1.BackgroundColor`) and the background image (`Screen1.BackgroundImage`).

Component Properties in AI Designer Versus AI Blocks Editor

If you change the properties of a component in AI Designer in the Properties menu, you are setting the *starting properties* for the app. In the AI Blocks Editor's My Blocks selection, you can change or manipulate the properties of the same component regarding the app's *runtime*. For example, if you set the background color at app start to blue, the user could click on a button with the label "Red" to change it, so long as the button is linked to a corresponding assignment block.

Implementing and Editing Apps in the Editor

To the right of the block selection, you can see the central work area of the AI Blocks Editor—the actual *editor*. The editor will be your main sphere of activity for developing the program logic that's behind the user interface of your app; it is where you will *implement* your app. In this now-empty area, you will combine the different blocks of your app so that the blocks of the input components transmit their data to the processing block structures, which then turn them into results and pass these data on to the blocks of the output components. You drag the required blocks—similar to the components in AI Designer—by holding the mouse button from the block selection of a group under Built-In or My Blocks into the editor and then assemble them like a puzzle into the desired functional *block structures* according to the AI syntax rules.

An Aside: The Distinction between an Abstract Block Type and a Specific Block Object

For the blocks in the Blocks Editor, dragging them from the block selection to the editor turns the abstract block types into specific block objects. Here, too, you have an unlimited number of blocks of the same type at your disposal. We will largely ignore this distinction between the types of blocks, however.

As the complexity and range of functions of an app increase, the number of blocks or block structures also increases, as does the display space the nascent app takes up in the editor. For that reason, the actual work area of the editor is far larger than you can see in the currently visible *main window* of the Blocks Editor. By using the scroll bars alongside the window or holding the left mouse button, you can scroll the window so that you always see the edited blocks on the screen. You can scroll even more quickly with the *scroll window* in the upper-right corner of the editor. This scroll window shows the main window as a small red rectangle within a gray rectangle, symbolizing the whole interface. By holding the mouse button and moving the red rectangle, you can scroll over the virtual workspace even more quickly (see Figure 2.21). The *zoom slider* in the function menu above the scroll window offers additional help for managing large block structures. If you slide it to the left, to a resolution of less than 100% (*Zoom Out*), you enlarge the section shown in the window, which makes the displayed blocks smaller but allows you to see more at once (see Figure 2.21). A value greater than 100% (*Zoom In*) lets you zoom into the block structure, making the section displayed smaller.

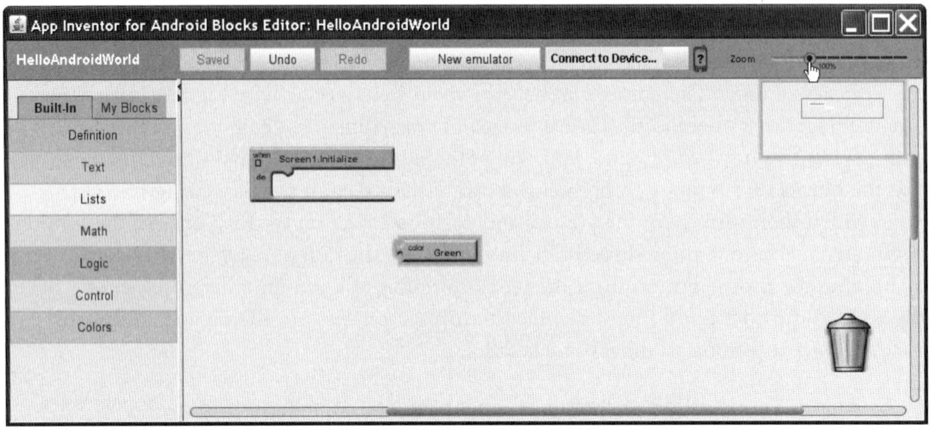

Figure 2.21 Zooming out of the partial window

Once you have arranged all components in the Blocks Editor and want to concentrate on developing the associated block structures, you can enlarge the partial window even more by hiding the block selection completely. Click on the small top triangle on the splitter bar between the editor and block selection area to collapse the latter. If necessary, you can display it again by clicking on the bottom triangle of the splitter bar, which has now moved to the left edge of the window. If the splitter bar is collapsed, you might wonder how to add to further blocks from the Built-In groups in the Blocks Editor. AI has an efficient solution, as usual. Simply left-click into a free area of the editor; all block groups from the Built-In area then appear in horizontal orientation. Click on a group to open it. You can then select the desired block and thereby create it, as shown in Figure 2.22.

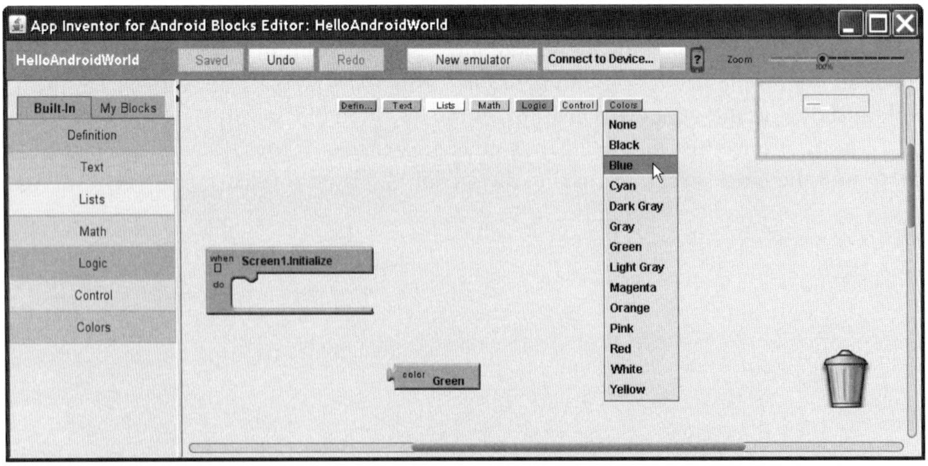

Figure 2.22 The block selection Built-In directly in the enlarged Blocks Editor

We should not forget to mention one important element within the Blocks Editor—the graphically represented *recycle bin* in the lower-right corner. As expected, it is used for deleting blocks that are no longer required in the editor. To delete a block, simply drag it to the recycle bin. This process is shown in Figure 2.23 for the assignment block for the color green.

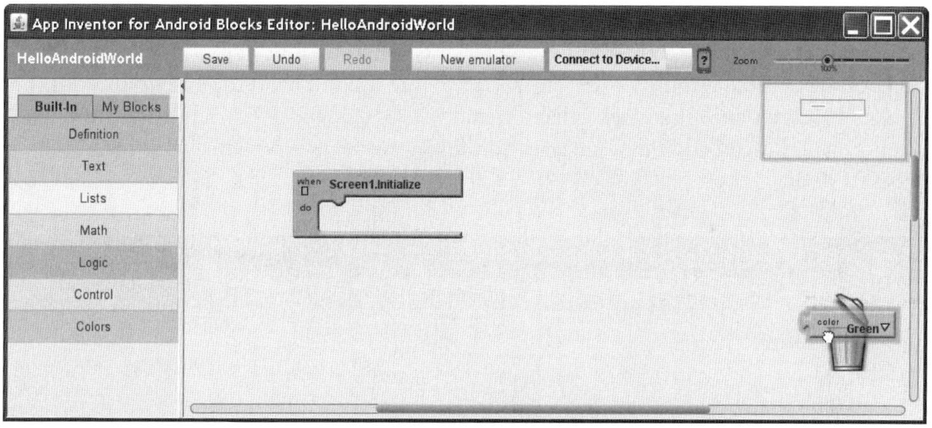

Figure 2.23 Deleting a block with the recycle bin

If, for example, you instead want to change a color from green to blue in the Blocks Editor, you do not need to delete the assignment block for green and then drag a new one for blue from the block selection to the editor. Many of the blocks have their own *property menu*, with which you can directly carry out the appropriate changes or value assignments quickly and easily. In case of the assignment block for colors, you can touch a color block with the mouse to display a small inverted triangle as symbol of an expandable menu. Click on it and you can choose from all available colors directly, as shown in Figure 2.24.

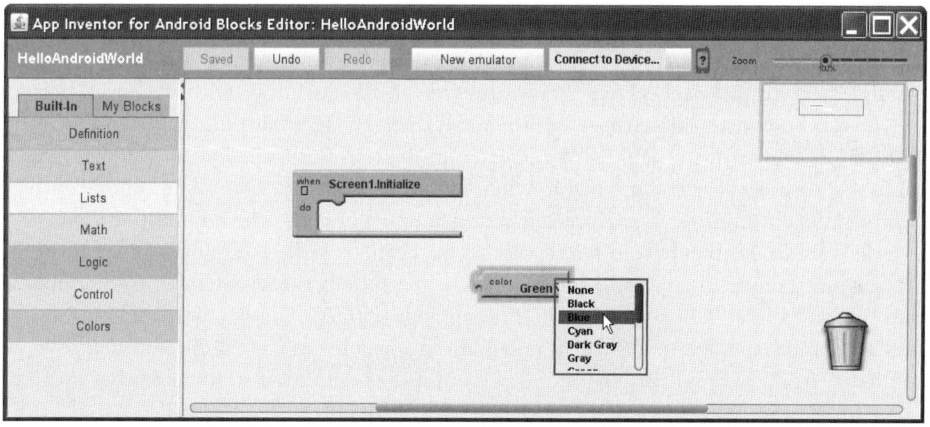

Figure 2.24 Changing a block value directly in the Blocks Editor

Setting Block Values in Blocks Editor

To set a block value, touch the block whose value you want to change with the mouse pointer. If an inverted triangle appears, click on it to choose the appropriate value from the property menu. If no triangle appears, the block does not offer options for setting properties.

Touching a block with the mouse pointer also brings up a brief explanation of the function or possible settings of the block (see Figure 2.25). This is the case with both the abstract block types in the block selection and the specific block types in the editor and often provides useful additional information during your development work in the AI Blocks Editor.

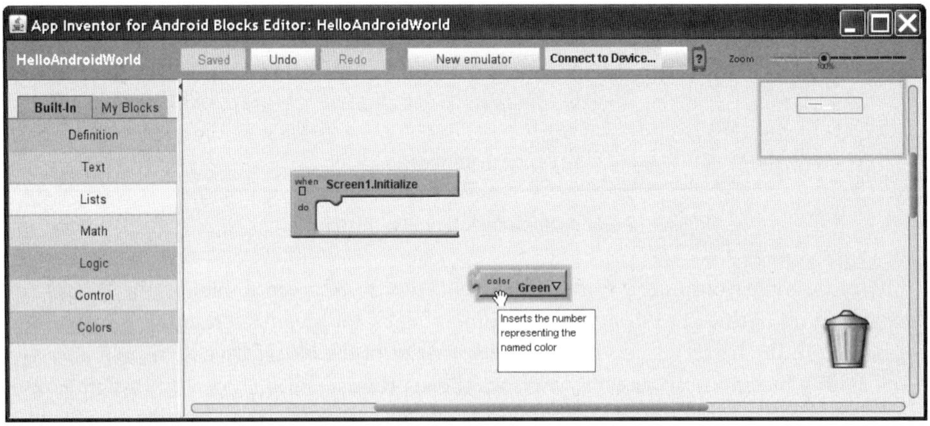

Figure 2.25 Explanatory text for blocks

Let us close out our discussion of Blocks Editor by turning back to the function menu above the editor and the block selection. Here you can see three menu items in form of the buttons Saved, Undo, and Redo, which can be used only in certain situations. For example, you can save the current block structures in Blocks Editor with the Saved button only if you have just made changes to them and these changes have not yet been automatically saved by AI on the Google servers. Only during this time does the button have the label "Save"; it is active and usable when this label is present. The Undo button enables you to undo an action—for example, inserting a new block into the editor. If you decide you do want to use the deleted block after all, you can click the Redo button to restore it.

This brings us to the last two menu items of the Blocks Editor we need to describe, as they are of decisive importance for developing apps with AI. The buttons labeled "Connect to phone" and "New Emulator" integrate the last area of the AI development environment—your Android smartphone or the emulator to simulate it, respectively. If your smartphone is not yet connected to AI, the smartphone icon next to the button shows a question mark in the display.

Before you read on, please delete any blocks you may have dragged to the Blocks Editor while experimenting and ensure that the editor is completely empty. This ensures that we avoid malfunctions on the smartphone later that could be caused by an interpretation of the randomly added and functionless blocks.

Integrate Android Phone

In addition to the AI Designer and the AI Blocks Editor, your Android smartphone forms the third area of your development environment. As described in the section on AI Designer, the Viewer panel provides only an approximate representation of the user interface of the Android app you are developing. To see how the app will really appear on your smartphone, you can integrate this device into the AI development environment. Each change in the visible components can then be immediately checked in the real Android environment of your smartphone. In addition, you can test and make immediate use of the functions modeled in the block structures behind the input and output components under real conditions and, if necessary, by using the existing smartphone hardware, such as sensors. Integrating the smartphone into your development environment clearly offers an invaluable advantage over working with the emulator, where a large part of the real operating conditions must be simulated with not-always-perfect fidelity. Of course, testing the app on your own smartphone does not yet give any reliable indication of how the app will appear and behave on other Android devices, but testing on multiple Android platforms is considered part of the advanced app development process.

To integrate the smartphone into the AI development environment, the device be physically connected to your development computer. If you have not already done so, please connect the smartphone to your computer via the USB cable supplied while you have the AI Designer and Blocks Editor open. We assume that you successfully adjusted and checked the settings as described in Chapter 1—for example, ensuring that your smartphone is correctly connected to the computer in debugging mode. Make sure your setup is correct before you continue, to rule out problems arising from incorrect smartphone settings right from the start. Unlock the display so you can follow the processes on your smartphone.

Connecting the Smartphone to Blocks Editor

If the smartphone is properly connected to the computer with a USB cable and all the settings are correct, you can now connect the phone to the AI development environment by clicking on the *connect button* ("Connect to Device") in the AI Blocks Editor; this button is found in the green function bar to the left of the smartphone icon with the question mark in the display. Clicking it opens a pop-up menu showing your smartphone with its specific device identifier (see Figure 2.26 at the back). If you have connected several smartphones via USB, all connected devices are shown here if they are detected correctly.

When you select one of the smartphones by clicking on it, the button text changes to "Connect to Device"; a pulsating yellow arrow, pointing at the smartphone icon, indicates that a connection is being established between the AI Blocks Editor and your smartphone (see Figure 2.26 at the front). If another smartphone was previously actively connected, you will first be asked if you want to end the connection to the previous device and connect to the new device.

Connect Only One Device at a Time to App Inventor

Using the pop-up menu under the connect button labeled "Connect to Device," you can integrate only one device at a time actively into the development environment. If you select a new device, the connection to the previous device is closed automatically. This restriction applies to smartphones connected via USB as well as to the emulator, which you can select just like any other physical object via the pop-up menu.

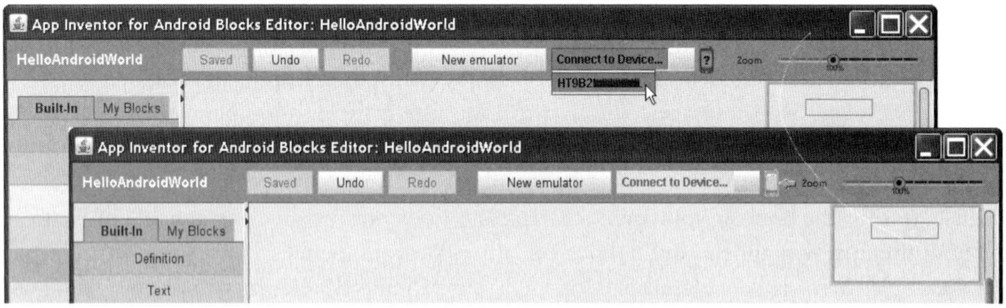

Figure 2.26 Establishing a connection between AI Blocks Editor and an Android smartphone

After some period of time, the connection is established and the display on your smartphone changes to confirm the connection (see Figure 2.27). The start screen appears, which you will recognize from when you first started the AI Designer in the Viewer panel (see Figure 2.6). Below the smartphone's status bar containing the icons for signal strength, battery charge, and time (here, these values are real), you can see the original app title of the starting component "Screen1"; below it is the app window with the default background color set to white. A message in the bottom part of the app window says "Listening to App Inventor ..." to inform you that the connection or loading process is not yet finished.

Figure 2.27 Intermediary status message on the smartphone while a connection is being established

After the basic connection between the AI Blocks Editor and your smartphone is established and the start screen described above appears on the cellphone screen, any components and blocks you may have added in the AI Designer and Blocks Editor, together with their settings, are automatically loaded and displayed, provided they are visible objects. Depending on the number of components and block structures, this loading process may take a while before the current status of your active app appears on the smartphone screen (see Figure 2.28).

Figure 2.28 Displaying the current app development stage on the smartphone

Up to now, we have not added any components and blocks to our example app. In fact, we have changed only two of the properties of the obligatory starting component "Screen1" in this chapter (see Figure 2.10): the BackgroundColor from white to blue and the app Title from "Screen1" to "Hello Android World!" Precisely these changes are now visible on the smartphone screen as well, as shown in Figure 2.28. The phone screen is now practically identical to the representation in the AI Designer's Viewer panel (see Figure 2.29).

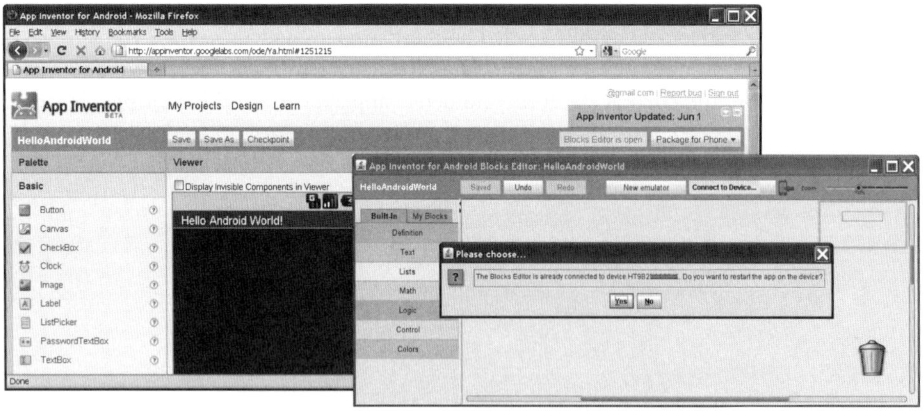

Figure 2.29 Displaying the connection status in AI Blocks Editor

Restart in Case of "Freezes"

The AI Blocks Editor now confirms that a connection to the smartphone has successfully been created by changing the symbol next to the smartphone icon in the green function menu from a question mark to a static green arrow (see Figure 2.29). The connect button now still has the label "Connect to Device." If you reselect the same smartphone from the drop-down menu, however, the window "Please choose" appears. In this window, you can restart the existing connection to the smartphone by choosing "Yes" (restart). Thus it is possible to force reloading of the currently active app on the smartphone. This step is necessary if, for example, the connection freezes and the changes are not automatically displayed on the smartphone screen.

> **If the Smartphone Freezes: Restart the App or Disconnect the USB Cable**
>
> If the app or the representation on the connected smartphone should act up, restarting the app by using the connect button and the selection window "Please choose" in the AI Blocks Editor can help. Some connection problems can also be fixed by disconnecting and then reconnecting the USB cable. Do not worry—the USB connection is rather robust and your app is also saved on your computer or the Google servers (see notes on frequently saving in this chapter).

If the connection between the smartphone and the computer should be disrupted while you are developing your app—for example, because you disconnected the USB cable—it is not a problem. Simply use the connect button and the drop-down menu to reconnect your phone.

Finishing a Session

Suppose you need to interrupt your development for a while. In that case, you have several options for terminating the connection between your smartphone and the AI Blocks Editor. You can press the Android operating system's menu key on your smartphone to show the option "Stop this application"; you can then confirm this choice with a finger touch. You also have to confirm the following security check by selecting "Stop and exit" (see Figure 2.30).

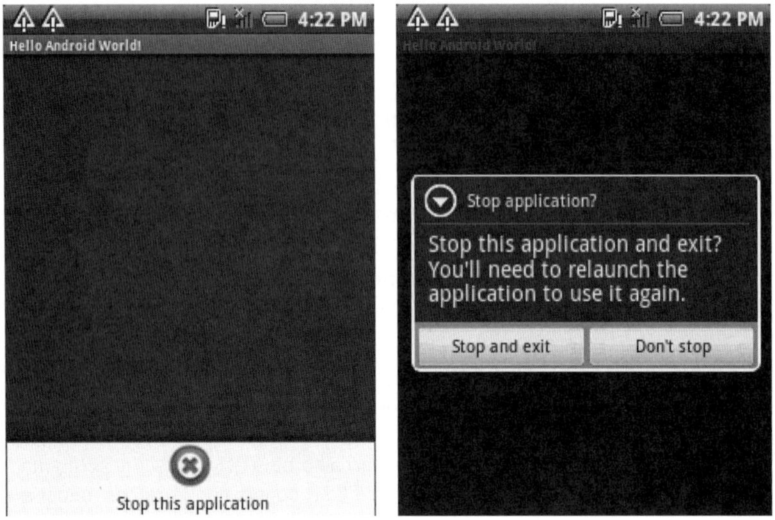

Figure 2.30 Stopping the app

Alternatively, you can simply disconnect the USB cable to safely terminate the connection between the smartphone and AI Blocks Editor. The app will be closed properly on your smartphone and can be started anew once the USB connection is restored. If you now want to stop your development work, you can simply close the Web Start application AI Blocks Editor. The button in AI Designer then changes its text back to "Open the Blocks Editor." If you want to exit AI Designer, you should click the link "Log out" at the upper-right corner of the screen, next to your login name. That way you can be sure that your project is properly closed and saved. If you are in a hurry, simply log out here even if the AI Blocks Editor is still open and connected to the smartphone and the app itself is still active on your cellphone. Both the app and the Blocks Editor are then closed automatically before AI Designer logs off, closes, and returns to the start page, ready for your next session.

With the integration of your smartphone into the Blocks Editor and Designer interfaces, you have become familiar with the AI development environment and gained a first impression of your future work as app developer. Even if the AI project "HelloAndroidWorld" is not yet a proper app, you now know the path that your app project will take—from the initial creation in AI Designer to the processes of adding components, changing properties, adding blocks in the AI Blocks Editor, integrating the smartphone, and finally viewing the app project on the smartphone. Armed with this information, you are well prepared to begin developing your first fully functioning and independent Android app for your smartphone.

Using the Emulator

As an alternative to integrating an actual smartphone into the AI IDE, you can test and simulate the look and behavior of an app you are developing by using a virtual version of a smartphone on the computer. You can access this emulator directly in AI with the menu button labeled "New emulator." An existing USB connection and any device-specific drivers are then no longer required. Be aware that the emulator offers only basic functions; telephony, SMS, GPS and other sensors can be simulated only with great difficulty, if at all. In this respect, the emulator is a suitable replacement for the smartphone only for certain aspects of testing and running apps.

Changeable Access to the Emulator

The integration of the emulator has already been subject to several changes in the still-young history of AI. Initially the emulator had to be launched as mostly independent component of the Android SDK and integrated into AI. This method is still possible and offers a high degree of flexibility in configuring the emulator. Later, you as developer had to decide straight away on starting the AI Blocks Editor whether you wanted to work with the integrated emulator or a smartphone. Currently, you can switch between smartphone(s) and emulator any time, by using the buttons labeled "New emulator" and "Connect to Device." Given the dynamic past of this feature, it would not be surprising to see further changes to starting up the emulator emerge in the future.

To integrate the emulator into the AI IDE just like a smartphone, you first need to launch it by clicking the New Emulator button in the AI Blocks Editor. This opens a window with information on the emulator, asking you to be patient while it is starting (see Figure 2.31). In fact, when you first start the emulator, it can take a minute or longer before the emulator is properly launched with the Android operating system on your computer and becomes available for use.

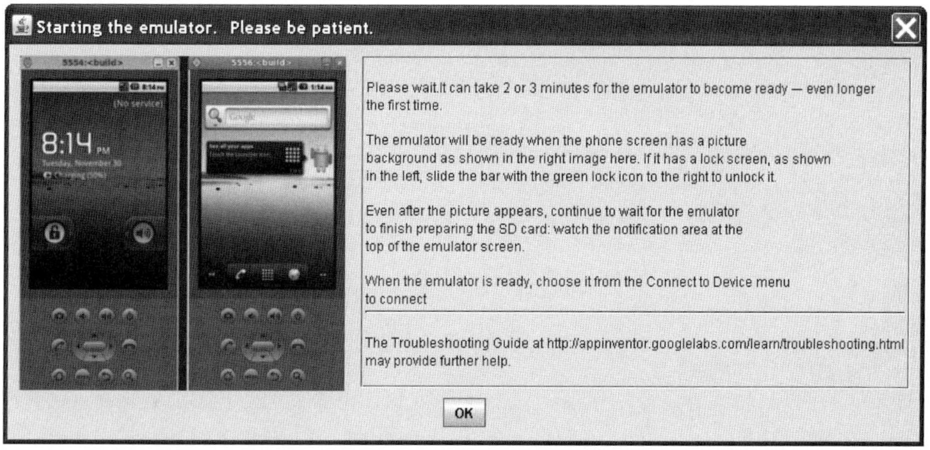

Figure 2.31 Window when starting the emulator via the New Emulator button

After a certain loading time, the emulator window opens with an identifier such as "5554:<build>" and the emulator starts to "boot" the Android operating system, as would happen when you first start your smartphone. In Figure 2.32 (far left), you can see the typical Android logo before the start image with screen lock and the display label "Android" appears (second from the left). Now you can operate the emulator in much the same way as you operate your smartphone, albeit by using the mouse pointer instead of your finger on the emulator screen. Drag the lock icon to the right with the mouse to unlock the emulator screen (second from the right). You can now access the start screen with the usual operating elements (far right).

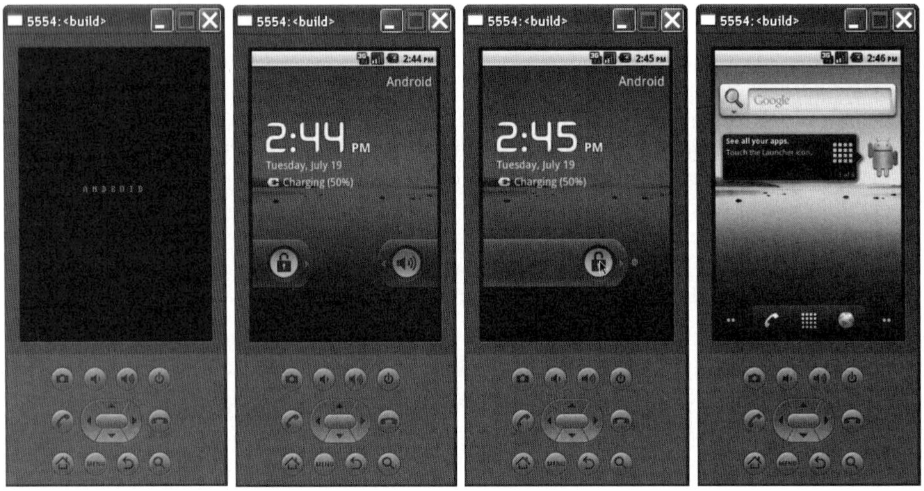

Figure 2.32 Starting and operating the emulator

Below the emulator's screen area, you can see the usual user elements that are present as physical buttons on most current Android devices. You click on these items with the mouse to go to the home screen or the menu, go back, search, move through menu items, adjust the volume, and so on. Feel free to experiment with the functions and apps already installed on the emulator—you will find almost no difference between them and your own smartphone, assuming it also has an unaltered Android interface.

To integrate the emulator into the AI development environment so you can test your apps, you proceed in the same way as when integrating your real smartphone. If you open the menu in the AI Blocks Editor under the "Connect to Device" option, you will see the emulator listed with its identifier (for example, "emulator-5554") and available for selection (see Figure 2.33). When you select it, the connection between emulator and AI IDE is created in the usual way. After a short period of time, you will see the app on the emulator.

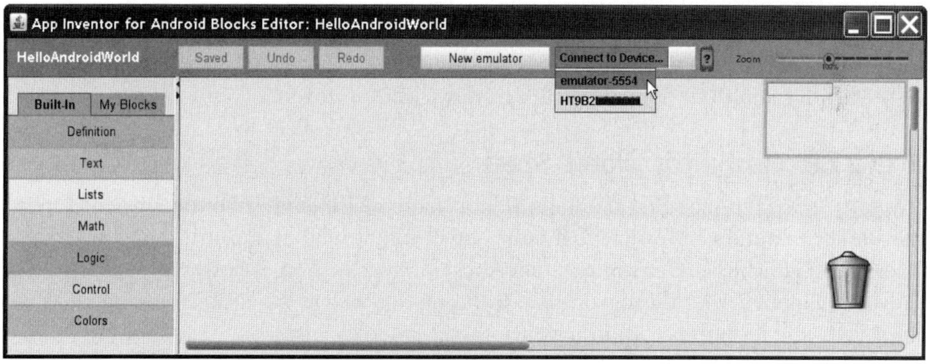

Figure 2.33 Selecting and integrating the emulator into the AI IDE

Start-Up Problems

As described in Chapter 1 in connection with the system requirements, the number of computers, smartphones, and other hardware systems on which the constantly evolving operating system Android and corresponding apps are used is steadily growing. With more and more heterogeneous system environments becoming available, there is also an increasing initial risk that these options will diverge from, and not be 100 percent compatible with, the Android specifications in their early stages of development. In turn, they may behave differently in connection with the AI development environment.

For many variations, app development with AI is still possible, even if some of the functions in your system environment behave slightly differently from the ones described here. For that reason, as we mentioned in the context of the settings for your Android device, you should not be afraid to skip a step if necessary and try to find your own solution or simply improvise. This book cannot present all existing options—let alone all future possibilities—together with workarounds, so the following variations are meant to be examples of how you can find alternative solutions for some particular cases to get closer to your aim of developing Android apps with App Inventor.

If the Blocks Editor Won't Start

If you are trying to start the AI Blocks Editor via the AI Designer button labeled "Open the Blocks Editor," it is possible that your system might neither automatically start the Web Start Launcher (and, therefore, the Blocks Editor), nor ask if you want to start it, as shown in Figure 2.16. Instead, you may be prompted to save the JNLP file locally. Do so, if possible, in a local directory near your other AI files, to ensure you can find the JNLP file easily later on. Now you can go to the directory and double-click on the JNLP file, which should download, verify, and start the Web Start application Blocks Editor, as shown in Figure 2.17.

If the Blocks Editor still does not start, and you instead see only the Java loading time and then an error message "Could not create the Java virtual machine" as shown in Figure 2.34, you can abort the starting process with by clicking OK.

Figure 2.34 Error message if starting the AI Blocks Editor fails

In this case, you can try to trick the local configuration of Java VM on your computer. The JNLP file for starting the Web Start application Blocks Editor requires a certain amount of available memory, which your local system configuration may not have. If you delete this requirement, there is a good chance that the Java applications can make do with the locally available memory space and will no longer abort the loading process. To edit the JNLP file, open a text editor such as Notepad, present on any Windows operating system. Load the JNLP file via the Notepad menu with File > Load, or simply drag the file from the File Explorer into the Notepad window. Now you can see the XML-based content of the JNLP file. Find the text section `max-heap-size="1024m"` (see Figure 2.35), and delete it completely. Then save the JNLP file under its original name `AppInventorForAndroidCodeblocks.jnlp`. Now you can double-click on the edited JNLP file and the Web Start application AI Blocks Editor should start.

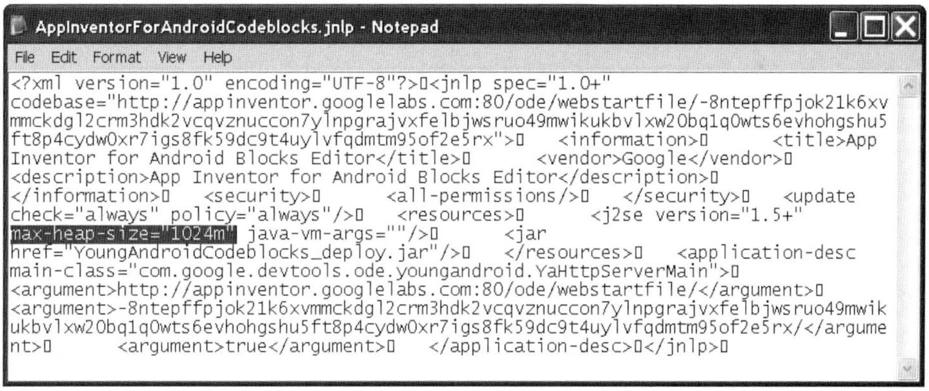

Figure 2.35 Delete the memory requirement in the JNLP file and save the new setting

If this manipulation of the JNLP file was successful, the start-up problem may still not be permanently fixed. As the AI development environment is permanently evolving, particularly in the beta phase, new versions of the JNLP file are constantly appearing. As a consequence, you may find that the file starts just fine one day, but not at all the next day. In that case, you need to download the current version of the JNLP file and manipulate it again as described previously so that you can start the AI Blocks Editor successfully. Remember that you still have to click the button "Open the Blocks Editor" in AI Designer and that you will usually be asked if you want to download the most current JNLP file. If this start-up problem occurs, you may want to make it a habit to always overwrite the old JNLP file with the new one when starting the AI Blocks Editor and then manipulate the new file as described before double-clicking on it to start the editor. Ideally, this problem will be fixed after the beta-phase AI is superseded by the final version of the program. Your usual starting procedure for the Blocks Editor could look like this:

1. In AI Designer, click the button labeled "Open the Blocks Editor."
2. Save the file `AppInventorForAndroidCodeblocks.jnlp` locally.
3. In the JNLP file, delete the text section `max-heap-size="1024"`.
4. Save the edited JNLP file and then double-click on it.

AI Updates of November 9, 2010, and February 2, 2011

In the AI update of November 9, 2010, the problematic text section `max-heap-size="1024m"` generally disappeared from the JNLP file, so these start-up problems no longer occurred. The AI update of February 2, 2011, reintroduced a default memory requirement of `"925m"`, which seems to have fixed the problem for most system environments. If you are having problems with starting the Blocks Editor, take a look at the current value listed in the JNLP file and adjust it if necessary. As you can see, this area is subject to change—so keep your eyes open for more updates.

If this measure does not fix the problem, consult the online Help for AI where you will find further information on known problems and solutions, including issues encountered during start-up of the Blocks Editor. You can find the links to the Help and Troubleshooting sites in the later section "Other Problems."

If the Connection to the Smartphone Freezes

Given that the smartphone you connect to your computer and the AI development environment is an Android device for which the dynamics and heterogeneity described previously can sometimes lead to initial incompatibilities, it also poses the greatest risk for potential problems arising. These issues are most likely to involve connection problems in various manifestations; as a result, the current app may fail to display properly on the smartphone screen. While discrepancies between the representation in the AI Designer's

Viewer panel and the smartphone are common and nothing to worry about, you will need to act if significant malfunctions occur.

First you need to ensure that your system environment and all its components fulfill the requirements for preparation and installation, as described in Chapter 1. This includes a complete and successful installation of the AI Setup Software. Installing the USB driver successfully on your computer operating system and ensuring it can detect the smartphone is vital for an error-free connection to your smartphone. You should have tested this connection with the AI Setup Software's ADB tool and fixed any problems as described in the section on installing the AI Setup Software—for example, by reinstalling manufacturer-specific drivers and the device driver. You should also have adjusted the settings of your smartphone successfully, as described in the section on Android device settings. If you have not yet met one or more of these requirements, please go back to the relevant section of this book and follow the troubleshooting measures described there.

In the early days of AI, connectivity problems with the smartphone were quite common, so the AI Google Group made repeated attempts to catalog the various smartphones and their specific problems. In addition to the smartphone and Android version used, this overview was meant to list the different components of the development environment, such as the computer hardware used and the operating system. To date, however, these efforts have not progressed beyond individual discussion threads.

Overview of AI-Supported Android Smartphones

An attempt to systematically catalog the smartphones supported by AI can be found at this thread within the AI subforum "App Inventor Coffee Shop" (previously the AI Google Group): `http://experimental.appinventor.mit.edu/forum/#!topic/appinventor/vp5pecHq8QU/discussion`

The Google App Inventor Team also addresses this problem in its many manifestations in several entries on its "Troubleshooting" website.

Help with Connection Problems on the AI Troubleshooting Website

You can find further help on connection issues on the following website (or the appropriate website of your AI provider):
`http://experimental.appinventor.mit.edu/learn/troubleshooting.html`

There is also a dedicated link to a web page titled "Work-Arounds & Solutions for Connecting Phones to the Blocks Editor" that deals exclusively with connection issues.

Specific Workarounds and Solutions for Connection Problems

You can find further information about solving connection problems on the following website (or the appropriate website of your AI provider):
`http://experimental.appinventor.mit.edu/learn/connectionissues.html`

Browse this page, and try out the solution for a system or smartphone configuration even if it does not exactly match yours. Perhaps you will be lucky and this solution will also help resolve the problem with your particular setup. If you still cannot find a solution for your connection issue here, you also have the accumulated knowledge of thousands of members of the AI Forum at your disposal. You can search the countless contributions for existing solutions or ask for assistance with your problem, as described in the next section.

If there really is no solution for your individual connection problems and the system components cannot be changed, you still have the option of carrying out your development work using the emulator as an alternative to the smartphone. Once you have developed your Android app with the AI Designer, Blocks Editor, and the emulator, you can get it to your smartphone from the AI Designer in various ways by clicking the button "Package to Phone" and the alternative menu items "Show Barcode" or "Download to this Computer." As you can see, there is (almost) always a solution!

Other Problems

If you run into any other special problems or difficulties during your development work, first confirm that all of the system requirements have really been fulfilled and that all installations and settings are working correctly and tested. Then have a look in the AI online documentation, which may describe new solutions and approaches that were not yet available at the time of printing of this book.

> **Online Documentation on Setup of the AI Development Environment, Including the Smartphone**
>
> The latest documentation on setting up the AI development environment can be found at this site (or the appropriate website of your AI provider):
> `http://experimental.appinventor.mit.edu/learn/setup/starting.html`

If you are having problems other than the ones described here, refer to the online Help on AI under "Troubleshooting." There, you will find further notes on common issues and their solutions.

> **Common Issues and Solutions on the AI Troubleshooting Website**
>
> The AI troubleshooting website contains questions and problems encountered by other AI users to which the Google developers offer solutions. Use this website (or the appropriate website of your AI provider) in case you encounter problems with other areas of AI as well, as it is a central collection of all typical issues, their answers, and constant updates:
> `http://experimental.appinventor.mit.edu/learn/troubleshooting.html`

In some cases, the problem might trace back to the provider. Please refer to the specific information sites of your AI provider to find tips, help, hints, and FAQs.

Online Help from Your AI Provider

Make use of the AI provider's website when looking for possible solutions. For the MIT AI, you can find information at:

`http://appinventor.mit.edu`

The AI Forum

If the specific problems of your individual system environment are not covered in the AI documentation and "Troubleshooting" page, you can turn to the App Inventor Forum. Here, like-minded users exchange their experiences with AI and discuss various topics on app development. Surely you will find someone here who can offer tips or even solutions for your current problem. Just as the AI IDE keeps evolving, so the AI Forum has also changed during the course of AI's beta phase. With the constantly growing number of members and their myriad contributions, the Google moderators found it increasingly more difficult to keep track of their input, structure the topics, and pass the information on for further editing in an organized way. In addition to other measures, such as introducing an Issues List (see Chapter 3), the previously centralized AI Forum "Coffee Shop" was divided into five subforums on November 17, 2010, to better organize this information:

- "AI Announcements": Official announcements by Google developers
- "Getting Set Up and Connecting Your Phone to AI": Questions and answers on problems with preparation and installation of AI IDE plus connecting smartphones (If you have questions on the topics in this chapter, this is the right place to look!)
- "Programming with AI": Questions on app development with AI (Check here if you are having problems during development with AI!)
- "AI in Education": A special forum on topics about using AI in the classroom (aimed primarily at educators, following the original intention of AI to be an entry platform for programming newbies)
- "AI Coffee Shop": General discussions on using AI, its future, and its potential as an extension of the former AI Google Group

In addition to immediately seeing the most recent three posts, as shown in Figure 2.36, you can access all posts in each forum by clicking on the forum name. To post your own contributions, you can simply register for the desired forum and submit your posts (except in the "Announcements," which are reserved for Google developers).

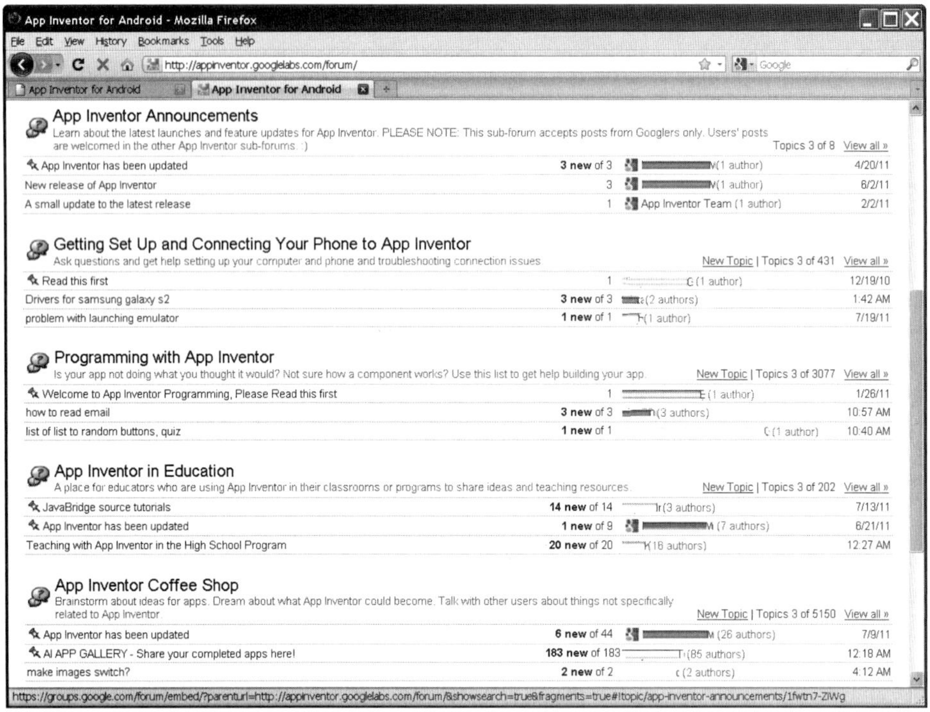

Figure 2.36 Overview of subforums within AI Forum

Above the forum overview, you can find the links to further sources of information (see the top of Figure 2.37) such as the User-FAQ, the "Troubleshooting" website, the AI documentation, and the Issues List. It's worth visiting this page regularly.

Link to New AI Forum

You can find the latest news and links to further information sources on the AI Forum: `http://experimental.appinventor.mit.edu/forum/`

Before posting a new question, you should check whether it has not already been asked, discussed, and answered. To search all the posts of the relevant subforum, enter a search term in the box above the forum posts and click the Search button (see Figure 2.37). If posts on the topic you searched for were found, the links are displayed.

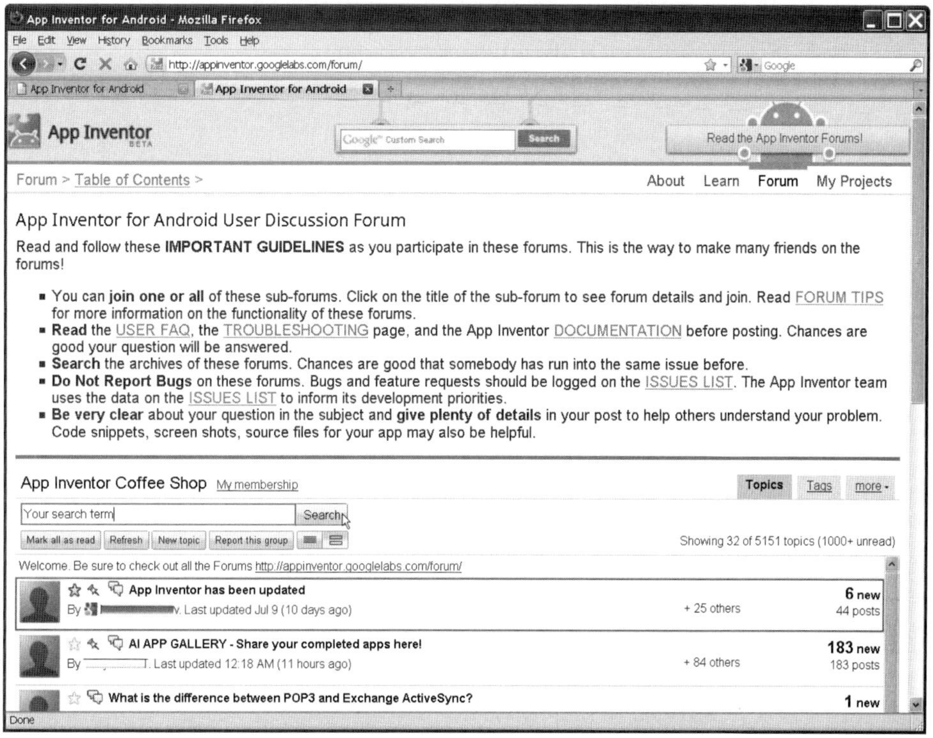

Figure 2.37 Subforum with search field and example posts

Please use appropriate search terms first to look for tips and help. Only if the problem has really not yet been discussed should you describe it in a new post and ask the other members for help with fixing it. Describe your problem as accurately as possible and submit your post. To do so, you first need to register in the relevant subforum. Then you just have to wait for an answer from the group, which usually does not take long. Together with the helpful and dedicated group members, you will certainly soon find one or more answers to your particular questions.

Chapter 3

Developing Your First App

Finally! In this chapter you will have a chance to develop your first very own Android app with App Inventor. Now that you have fulfilled all the preparation and installation requirements mentioned in the previous chapters and created your first Project "HelloAndroidWorld," all that effort is ready to pay off. And as you know, you learn best while having fun. For that reason, our first app will be all about laughter. You may remember the "laugh bag"—a popular gag toy of the 1970s that is still around today. This canvas bag contained a little plastic box inside it that would laugh like mad when you pressed on it. The kids in the 1970s had great fun with it, so why should it be any different in our age of the smartphone?

Developing the laugh bag app will introduce you to all the basic elements of app development with AI. In AI Designer, you will put together the app's graphical user interface from various components, integrate different media types, connect the components together in the AI Blocks Editor, and develop the app functions by combining the blocks to create block structures. In addition to testing the app within the AI development environment, we will prepare it as independent app so we can upload it to any Android device using a variety of export options. We will also address any problems that might crop up during app development with AI and present solutions or workarounds. By the end of the chapter, you will have taken a great step toward becoming an app developer with AI and will have acquired sufficient knowledge to be able to develop simple apps independently.

The step-by-step guide to the development process provided in this chapter reflects the most basic approach to creating an app. With simple apps, it is indeed possible to create the complete app interface in a single step and then to complete all of the block structures in a second step. For more complicated app projects, however, you will likely need to jump back and forth between the Designer and Blocks Editor and, therefore, between the individual working steps, or to run through the development cycle repeatedly for the various functional components and block structures. In the course of the book, you will become familiar with both approaches and learn to make seamless transitions between them.

Creating the Project "LaughBag"

In Chapter 2, we created our first project titled "HelloAndroidWorld." This project was automatically saved on the provider servers when you left the AI development environment. If you now reopen App Inventor with your user data, the status of your latest project is loaded and displayed automatically. Start AI by going to the start page in your web browser and sign in. It makes sense to save the web address as a bookmark in your browser to speed things up if you will be frequently developing apps with AI.

> **Sign In and Start AI Designer**
>
> Start the AI Designer by logging in to the website of your AI provider.
>
> The links to the experimental and public versions of MIT AI are:
>
> `http://experimental.appinventor.mit.edu`
>
> `http://beta.appinventor.mit.edu`

Click on the button labeled "Sign in" so the web browser begins loading AI Designer. On loading, you may briefly see the project overview before the view changes to the central interface with its five panels, into which the most recently edited project ("HelloAndroidWorld") is loaded. We recommend that you now also start the AI Blocks Editor by clicking the button labeled "Open the Blocks Editor" and connect it to your Android smartphone via the USB cable by clicking the button "Connect to phone" (see the description of this process in Chapter 2).

> **Start AI Designer, Blocks Editor, and Phone Connect Immediately**
>
> If you always start the AI Blocks Designer in addition to the AI Designer when developing apps, and you integrate your smartphone as well, you can follow all visible development steps you carry out in the Designer on the smartphone screen.

If your smartphone is connected straight away to the AI development environment, you can always see the following development steps on your smartphone screen and try them out. Alternatively, you can start the Blocks Editor and smartphone at a later stage; we will remind you of this possibility at a later point.

To create a new project in AI Designer, go to the project overview by clicking on "My Projects," where you will see the project "HelloAndroidWorld" listed. Create a new project titled "LaughBag" by clicking on the New button. Enter the project name "LaughBag" in the pop-up window and confirm by clicking OK, as shown in Figure 3.1.

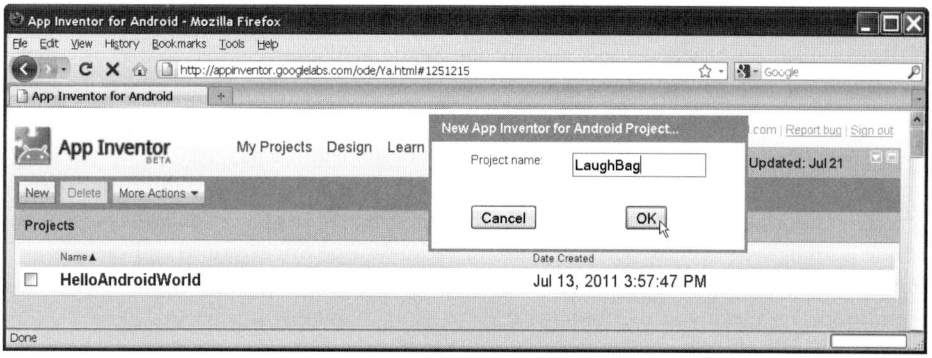

Figure 3.1 Create the new app project "LaughBag" in AI Designer

The AI Designer now creates the new project, saves the default configuration on the remote provider servers, and loads it together with the component groups into the now opening interface. The status bar at the top informs you of this process with short status messages such as "Save..." and "Load...." As our first project, LaughBag appears in the familiar default configuration. Apart from the component groups in the Palette, the Viewer shows only the starting component "Screen1," which appears as the empty screen area and is selected by default in the Properties panel.

As you can see in Figure 3.2, you can now change the app title from "Screen1" to "LaughBag" by editing the Title option accordingly. The app title will also appear on your smartphone when you use the app later. Press your computer's Enter key, and the title displayed in the Viewer also changes.

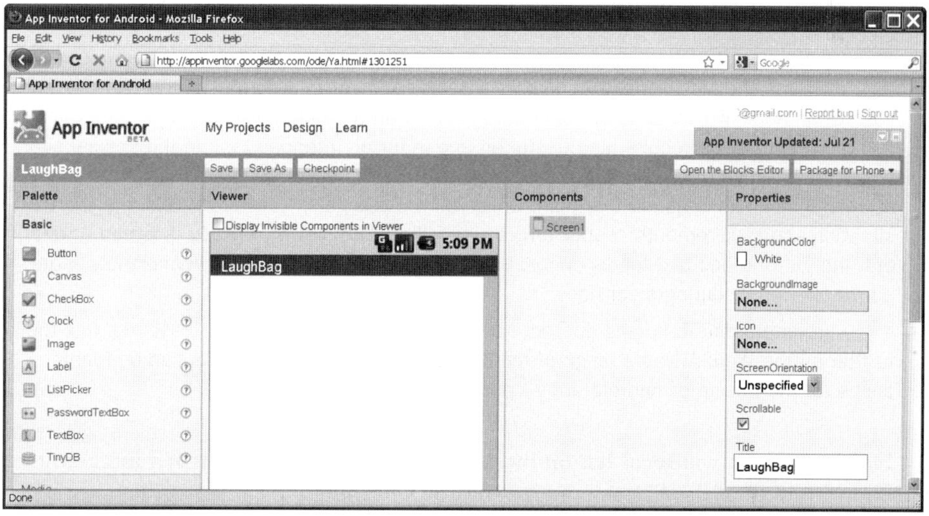

Figure 3.2 Default configuration for the project LaughBag

Checking Your Smartphone

Have you already connected your smartphone via the AI Blocks Editor? If so, you can check whether the app title has changed.

We will leave the other settings of the Screen component unchanged. The default setting "Unspecified" in the ScreenOrientation box will later automatically adapt the screen orientation horizontally or vertically depending on how the user is holding the smartphone. Setting the screen to vertical (Portrait) or horizontal orientation (Landscape) is recommended only in special situations. To make sure all user elements of the app are visible even on small screens, you should normally also leave the screen area set to "Scrollable."

Designing the User Interface

Once the project has been created and the app title changed to LaughBag, the creative part of the app development can begin. It is not a coincidence that the AI interface responsible for this task has the name Designer, because it is where you design the user interface for the future users of your app. As mentioned in Chapter 2, "The Development Environment," the user interface not only enables the user to enter input, but also provides interactive output of the relevant results to the user. The elements of the user interface are visual (e.g., text, buttons, images), of course, but also they allow for multimodal input (e.g., microphone, camera, accelerator, location sensor, GPS) and output (e.g., sound, vibrations, movies), sometimes by accessing remote sources (e.g., web services, SMS, Bluetooth). The multitude of components AI provides for this purpose has now become so great that it is difficult to categorize them comprehensively, and the Google developers are fervently doing their best to further expand the functionality of AI.

Consider Ergonomics

The significance of the design task for an app's success cannot be emphasized enough, as the user friendliness or ergonomics is a decisive factor in determining the ultimate success of an app—which, after all, is nothing more than a small mobile software program. The more intuitive, effective, and useful an app is for an intended task in the special situation of mobile use, the more the users will use the app, recommend it to other users, and download it. Try to consider this point while you are designing your apps, and imagine the situation and requirements of your target group. For example, if your app is aimed at drivers, the buttons and text labels should be big enough to read and use comfortably and—above all—safely during a car ride.

If you are interested in finding out more about app ergonomics, you can research this topic further on the Web. A whole range of recommendations and suggestions can be found online for the design of Android apps icons alone.

In this book, we will focus less on the creative or ergonomic aspects and more on the functional variety of the AI components. In turn, you should not have too high aesthetic expectations regarding our laugh bag—even the original devices from the 1970s were not very impressive in that respect.

Inserting the "Label" Component

The user interface of the LaughBag app will be fairly simple and consist of only two components, aside from the screen component. First, we want a brief text to describe how to use the app ("Please press the bag!"). Second, we want the bag itself to have several properties: It should look like a bag, and you should be able to press it to make it laugh. These properties may sound rather complicated, but they are actually just the same as for any button you know so well from a Windows or app environment. Thus the user has to be able to press or tap the button, and this button gets its individual look because you attach a text label to or image positioned on the button like a sticker.

> **"There Is More Than One Way to Skin a Cat"**
>
> Don't worry—no cats are harmed in this book. We just want you to be aware of this fact, especially as a beginner in app development. There are always multiple ways of realizing an app. Most apps fulfill a more or less useful purpose. How you achieve that goal largely depends on your creativity as a developer. AI offers a huge collection of tools that you can use to build your app. Whether you realize the laugh bag as an elaborately animated 3D graphic with haptic feedback or much more simply as a button with a picture on it is entirely up to you and your level of motivation. Both variations fulfill their primary purpose: The laugh bag laughs if you press it. If you want to demonstrate the particular capacity of your high-end smartphone with Android 2.3 or even 4.0, a 3D laugh bag will certainly more impressive than a 2D button, but the button will run without limitations even on simple smartphones with Android 1.5. You have to weigh the resources and effort involved against the desired effect.

Our modest intent is to create a manageable app for beginners that can run on as many Android devices as possible, so we use only two components in designing the visual appearance of our LaughBag app:

- *Label*: A text field that can receive any text and be placed onto the screen like a label.
- *Button*: A button that can also have a text and/or an image in addition to its switching function.

> **Further Information in the Component Reference**
>
> Further information on functions and properties of all components can be found online in the Component Reference:
>
> `http://experimental.appinventor.mit.edu/learn/reference/components/`

Together with all the other components, you will find the Label and Button in the AI toolbox—that is, in the Palette panel on the left in AI Designer. The two components are part of the "Basic" group. If it is not yet open, please click on the group name to display the components contained within it. Button is in the first position, Label in the sixth position.

We want the message "Please press the bag!" to appear in our LaughBag app, just below the title bar. We will first place the label in the Viewer, though we can move the components at a later stage if required. Grab a label in the Palette by clicking on the name or the icon of the component "Label," then hold the mouse button and drag the label into the Viewer. While you are dragging the mouse, the pointer changes from the usual mouse pointer icon to a text field—the label—containing the default text "Text for Label1," as shown in Figure 3.3.

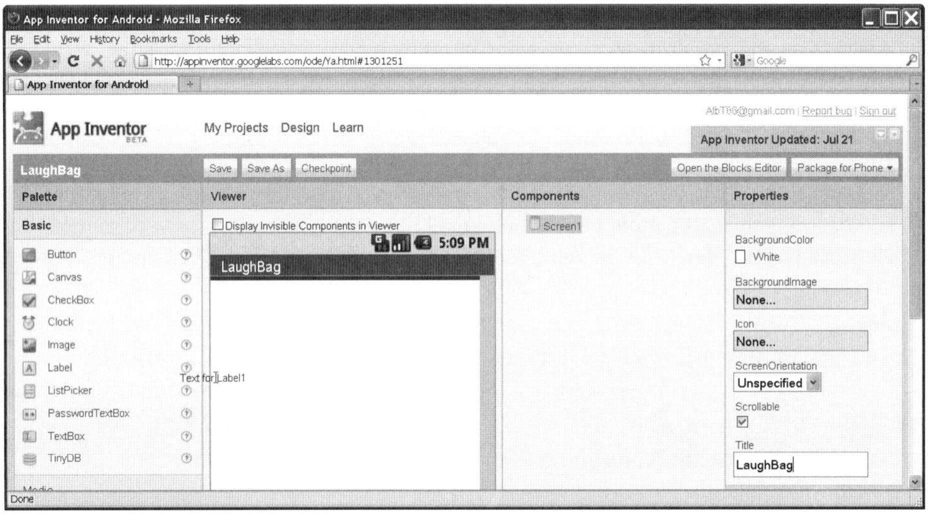

Figure 3.3 Drag a new label from the Palette to the Viewer

If you drop the label in the Viewer by releasing the mouse button, the label slots in automatically just below the title bar. Now you have created your first additional component in the LaughBag app: You have created an object of the component type "Label."

An Aside: The Distinction Between Component and Component Type

Let's remind ourselves once more of the distinction between the abstract component in the Palette and the specific object in the Viewer. If you drag a component from the Palette to the Viewer, you do not actually move this component, but rather create a specific object of the type of this component, the so-called *component object*. In theory, you can create an unlimited number of objects of the same component type and use them in your app. The distinction is similar to that between a class and an object in object-oriented programming.

Checking on Your Smartphone

If you have connected your smartphone, the new label with the default text "Text for Label1" will be visible on the screen as well. The same is true for all other visible expansions or changes you make in AI Designer, which will also become visible on the connected smartphone in debugging mode.

That is not the only reaction in the AI Designer interface, however. Once you create the label, it appears not only in the Viewer (and the connected smartphone), but also in the panels Components and Properties. As you can see in Figure 3.4, the new label appears as a component object in the Components panel, it has the name "Label1," and it is hierarchically subordinate to the central starting component "Screen1." The name and index number of "Label1" are assigned automatically by AI when a new component object is created. If you were to drag another label component into the Viewer, the newly created second label object would get the name "Label2," and so on. Feel free to try it. The second label will be positioned below the first in the Viewer, just as in the Components panel.

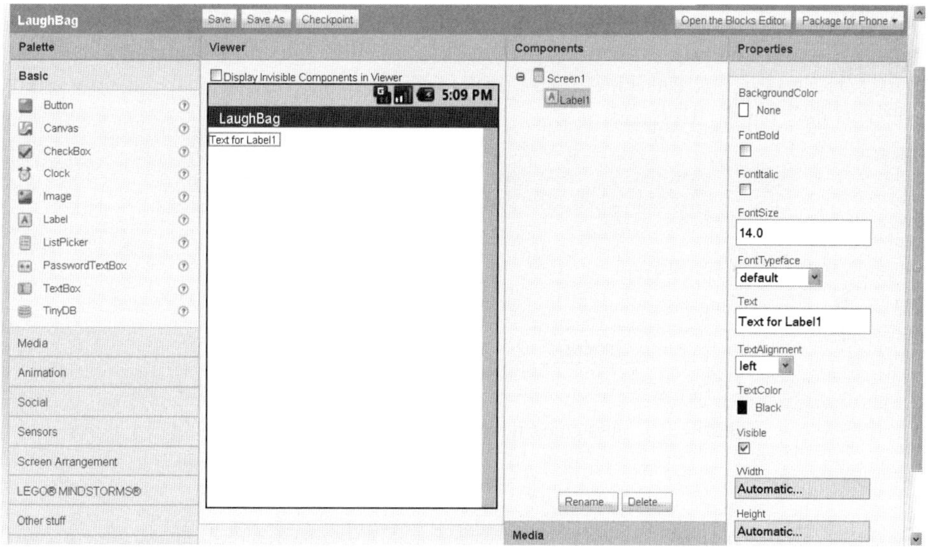

Figure 3.4 The label in the panels Viewer, Components, and Properties

At this point, you should delete all surplus labels, except for the first label. To do so, highlight them one by one by clicking on them in the Viewer or under Components and then clicking the Delete button in Components. Confirm that you really want to delete them by clicking OK. Before you continue, your workspace should once more look like that shown in Figure 3.4.

Assigning Component Names

Before we turn to the label's properties, we want to give this object a memorable name. If you assign memorable names, it becomes much easier to keep track of things when you work with the AI Blocks Editor later. If you are designing complex apps and are using many labels or other objects of the same component type that have names differing only by their index number ("Label1," "Label2," "Label3," and so on), it will be really hard to tell them all apart. It helps if the object has a name that reflects its function within the app.

> **An Aside: Assigning Names in Programming**
>
> In programming, it is common practice to assign descriptive names to objects, constants, functions, and variables, so as to make the rather abstract and cryptic program code clearer and easier to understand in case later editing becomes necessary. A good naming convention can also be an essential aspect of good and effective app development.

We want to change the name of the label from "Label1" to "Message." Click on "Label1" with the mouse to select it under Components, and then click on the Rename button. This opens a pop-up window where you can enter the "New name" and confirm it by clicking OK (see Figure 3.5). In the Components panel, the label is now listed under its new name "Message."

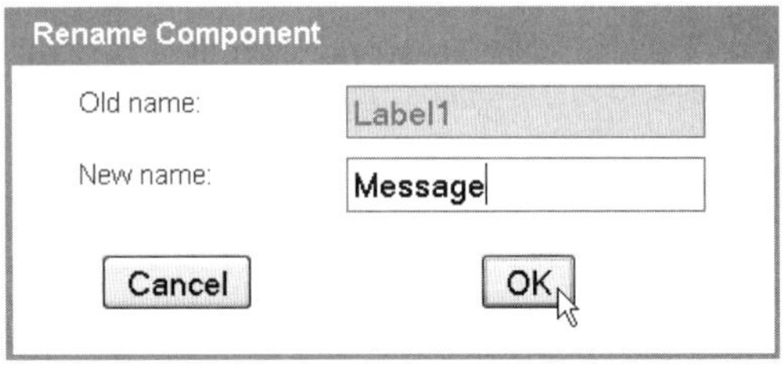

Figure 3.5 Assigning a memorable name to the new label

Setting Properties

To view and change the properties of a component, you first need to select the component by clicking on it in the Viewer or the Components panel. The selected object appears bordered in green in the Viewer and with a green background in Components. The properties of the selected component are shown in the Properties panel. Even a simple component such as the label has an impressive list of properties. For the text field, for example, you can specify or choose its Alignment, BackgroundColor, FontBold, FontItalic, FontSize, FontTypeface, and TextColor.

In addition, you can specify other properties, such as the label size, separately for the width and height of the text field. You can choose whether the label size should automatically adapt to the text dimensions (Automatic) or the dimension of the parent object "Screen1" (Fill parent) or whether the label size will be specified explicitly in pixels (Pixel). You can also choose whether the label or the text it contains should be "Visible" (or not). You might wonder what would be the point of defining a text that is then not visible. As we have already mentioned, the component properties can be changed not just during development in AI Designer, but also later during the app's execution (runtime) on a smartphone, dynamically within the program logic defined by the block structures. It is possible to not show a message in a label when the app is first run, and then display it only when a certain event occurs—for example, tapping a button.

Finally, the label also has a text field ("Text"), where you can enter the actual label text. Here you should replace the default text "Text for Label1" with our message "Please press the bag!" If you check the new message in the Viewer or on the smartphone, it will not yet look very spectacular. Feel free to set a snazzy background color, change the font color, and perhaps increase the font size. The other settings can be left with their default values. In the Viewer, your app should now resemble the one shown in Figure 3.6.

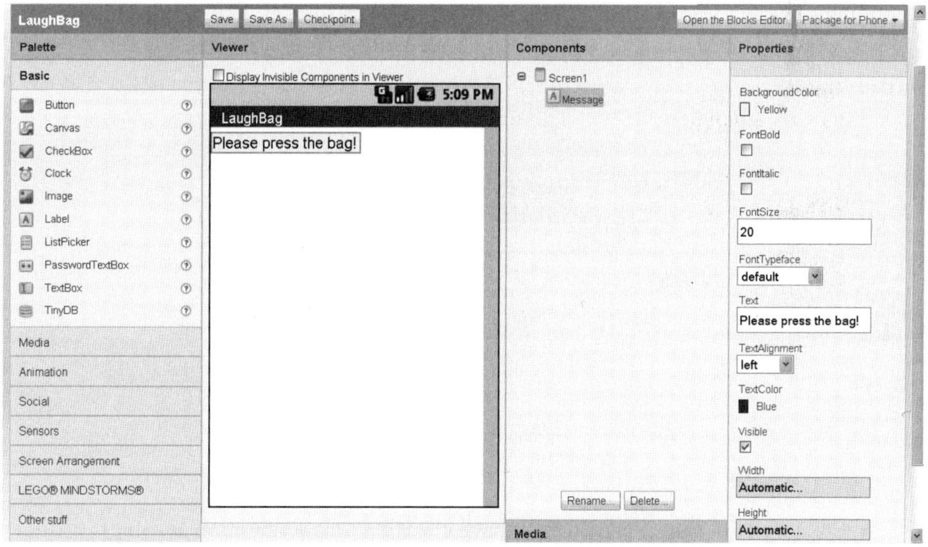

Figure 3.6 Changed properties and new design for the label "Message"

Adding the Interactive Component "Button"

Let's move on to our second component, with which we want to complete the user interface of our LaughBag app. As mentioned earlier, we want a button with a picture on it to represent the interactive laugh bag.

Interactive Components

The "Button" component is an interactive element of the user interface, unlike the label. The button receives a user action (an event), such as tapping the button, and the app processes the event and reacts with a result (laughter). In addition to the button, AI provides many other interactive components—for example, selection elements such as check boxes and lists, and sensors that react to movements by the user.

The "Button" component can also be found in the component group "Basic" in the AI Designer Palette. Grab the "Button" component and drag it to the Viewer. Again, you can see the default setting for the "Button" component while you are dragging—namely, a button with the text "Text for Button1." While you are dragging the button to the Viewer, the screen area also shows a narrow horizontal blue bar (see Figure 3.7, below the label). This bar indicates where the selected component will be placed once you drop it in the Viewer. For example, if you were to drag the component "Button" above the label, the position bar would jump above the label. If you then drop the component, it would be placed between the title bar and the label. For our app, you should drag the component below the label to place the button below it. You can grab the objects in the Viewer below the title bar later and rearrange them at will.

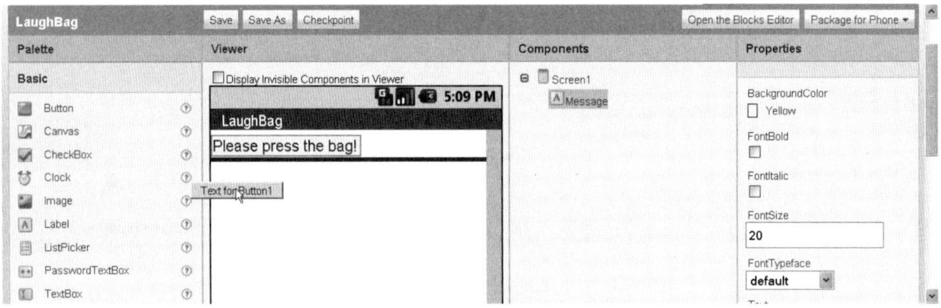

Figure 3.7 Dragging the "Button" component from the Palette to the Viewer

Just as before with the label, you now have created a second component object of the type "Button" in the Viewer. After you drop it, the button is automatically selected. The Viewer shows the graphic representation of the button with a green border, and you can also see the new button on your smartphone. Now we want to customize the button for use in our LaughBag app. First we will give it a memorable name. As shown in Figure 3.8, the button is also a child of the parent object "Screen1" in the Components panel, and again the button has a default name with an index number, "Button1." Just as before, you can click the Rename button and change the default name "Button1" to "LaughButton."

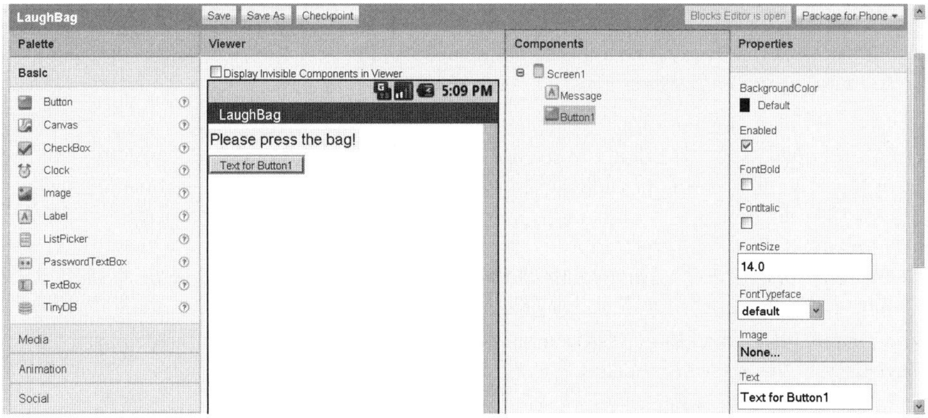

Figure 3.8 Button displayed in Viewer, Components, and Properties

In the next step, we again examine the properties of the LaughButton. They are mostly the same as those of the label. Once more, we have options for setting the text alignment, background color, bold and italic font, font size, type, and color. We can again set the button size (i.e., width and height) and decide whether to make it visible. In the text field "Text," you can change the text; let's replace the default text "Text for Button1" with "Press me!" Perhaps you would also like to edit the font and set it to bold and italics. If you wanted the button to have no text on it at all, you would need to leave the text field empty.

In addition to the familiar properties, this button has two new qualities. First, it contains an additional check box with the label "Enabled." Similar to the case with "Visible," you can use this check box to decide whether the button should be enabled when the app is run—that is, whether it should respond to being pressed. Of course, we do want the button representing the laugh bag to respond if the user taps it, so we leave the "Enabled" check box checked. The second new property is the "Image" field, whose name reminds us of our initial intention of adding an image to the button. At the moment, the field shows "None," indicating that the button does not yet have an image. Let's change that now.

Uploading and Integrating Media Files

As mentioned previously, we will design our interactive laugh bag as a button with an image of a bag on it. As the LaughButton is already positioned in the Viewer and, therefore, in the app, we now need simply choose an image for it. We need a suitable image file with the picture of a bag. If you happen to have a great photo of a pretty bag in electronic form, feel free to use it. But make sure you meet the file format requirements, so as to ensure the image file will be supported by AI and the Android devices running the app.

Image Formats

For more information on image file formats supported by Android, refer to the "Image Formats" section in Chapter 15, "Tips and Tools."

In the more likely case that you do not have a suitable image file available, you can use the image file `laughbag.jpg` located in the `/MEDIA` directory on the companion website for this book. Feel free to use it as part of this example app.

On the Companion Website: Media Files for All Example Apps in the /MEDIA directory

All audio, image, and video files used in our examples can be found on the companion website in the `/MEDIA` directory.

To place the image from the file `laughbag.jpg` onto the LaughButton, you first have to make it accessible for your development work by uploading it into the AI IDE (development environment) and the remote provider servers (Upload). Click in the LaughButton Properties on the "Image" field to open the selection list shown in Figure 3.9. As you have not yet uploaded any image files in your current app project, the list is still empty and "None" is available for selection. You need to find the desired image file on your local hard disk (previously downloaded from the companion website) by clicking the Add button. This opens the Upload File pop-up window (shown in Figure 3.9). Click the Search button, to access your local file directory—for example, via Windows Explorer. Go to the image file `laughbag.jpg` and select it by clicking the Open button. The file name and path then appear in the Upload File window, and you can confirm your choice with OK.

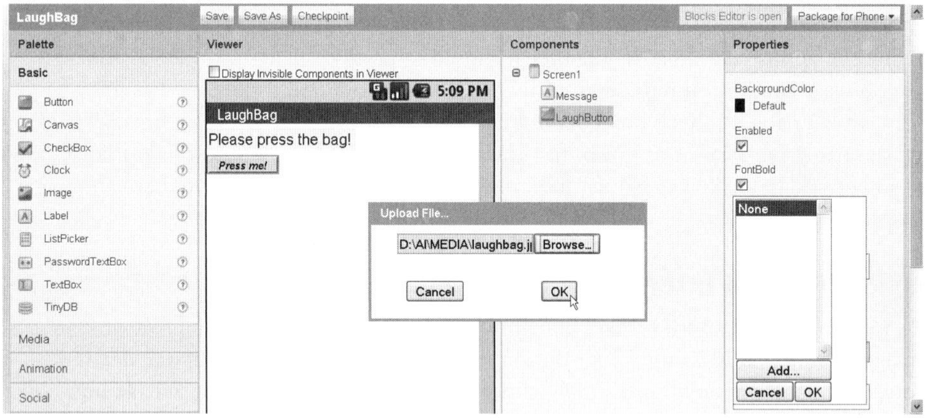

Figure 3.9 Uploading the image file laughbag.jpg to AI IDE

This starts the image file upload, indicated by the AI status message "Uploading laughbag.jpg to the App Inventor server." Once the upload has been completed, our laugh bag in all its beauty appears in the Viewer (and on the connected smartphone), as shown in Figure 3.10. The name of the image file now assigned to the button is displayed in the LaughButton Properties in the "Image" field. The image file `laughbag.jpg` is still available for general use in the current LaughBag project, as indicated by the corresponding list item in the Media panel. If you decide, for example, that you want to assign the same image file to another button, the image file will appear in the selection list of the "Image" field concerned, so you do not need to upload the file again, but instead can reference it within the project to reuse it again and again. If you wanted to delete the image file from the AI IDE or the provider servers, you would have to click on it in the Media panel and select "Delete" in the pop-up menu. The file would be deleted and the LaughButton would be displayed without an image on it.

Figure 3.10 The LaughButton button with the image laughbag.jpg

Optimizing the App Design

This step basically concludes the optic design of our LaughBag app. We say "basically" because we still want to do a bit of fine-tuning. Take a look at the user interface in the Viewer and on the smartphone: The Message is all the way over on the left side of the screen, as is the LaughButton. It would look better and more professional if both elements were centered in the middle of the screen, not only in the static Viewer, but above all on the differently sized screens of the various Android smartphones. You can guess how we can optimize the optic design. Click on the label in AI and go to its Properties to change the setting for the horizontal Width property to "Fill parent." Now the label width automatically matches the width of the parent object "Screen1" and consequently fits the screen width of the relevant smartphone. You can check this immediately in the Viewer and on your smartphone. The text is still in the left corner of the label, however. Center it by changing the Alignment property to "center."

> **Texturing**
>
> In computer graphics, an image that is applied to a 2D or 3D object is sometimes referred to as a *texture* and the process of doing so as *texturing*.

We now want to optimize the button in the same way. Select it and change the Width property to "Fill parent." As the underlying image has a smaller width than the now enlarged screen-wide button in the Viewer and on the smartphone, the image plus label is automatically centered on the screen, thanks to the default setting "center" for Alignment. The optically optimized user interface of our LaughBag app now looks neat and tidy on the smartphone, as you can see in Figure 3.11.

Figure 3.11 Optimized user interface on smartphone LG P500

If You Cannot See the Image

If the bag image should not be visible on your systems, there is no need to panic. Unfortunately, with the many different computer systems and Android smartphones around, it sometimes happens that the image is either displayed in the Viewer only or the smartphone only, or on neither. For example, the image is displayed on the smartphone LG P500 with Android 2.2 or the default emulator of AI with Android 2.1, but does not display on the HTC Tattoo with Android 1.6. The Google developers are aware of this problem and working to fix it; temporary solutions are available on the AI "Troubleshooting" website (see "I set the image property of a button to an image file, but nothing shows on the phone"):

`http://experimental.appinventor.mit.edu/learn/troubleshooting.html`

Even if an image still fails to display on your development systems at this stage, chances are that it will display correctly on your smartphone in the finished app later. Just be patient, and wait until we reach the later section where you learn how to load and run the app on your smartphone. At that point, you should have the pleasure of seeing your image. Until then, you can simply imagine the image in your development environment. As mentioned previously, improvisation and patience are virtues that are most appropriate during app development in general and in the AI beta phase on the highly dynamic Android operating system in particular.

Non-Visible Component "Sound"

Even if the optic design of our LaughBag app already looks rather convincing with just two components and one media file, we are still missing something important. Right—what good is having a laugh bag without laughter? We need to add another media file to our app, an audio file with some nice loud laughter. Once more you will find a sample file `laughter.wav` on the companion website in the directory `/MEDIA`. As with all media files, you have to make sure that the audio file's format is supported by AI or Android.

Audio Formats

For more information on the audio file formats supported by Android, please go to the section "Audio Formats" in Chapter 15, "Tips and Tools."

To insert the audio file into your app, you need to drag another component into the Viewer. The "Sound" component for playing audio files can be found in the "Media" component group. Open it by clicking on the group name in the Palette. Grab the "Sound" component and drag it into the Viewer as before. If you drop the component with the default name "Sound1" in the Viewer, it does not appear within the represented screen area, but rather below it. As a *non-visible component*, the sound object is not displayed in the visible area of the Viewer, but simply listed in the special area "Non-visible components"; see Figure 3.12 (the bottom edge of the Viewer).

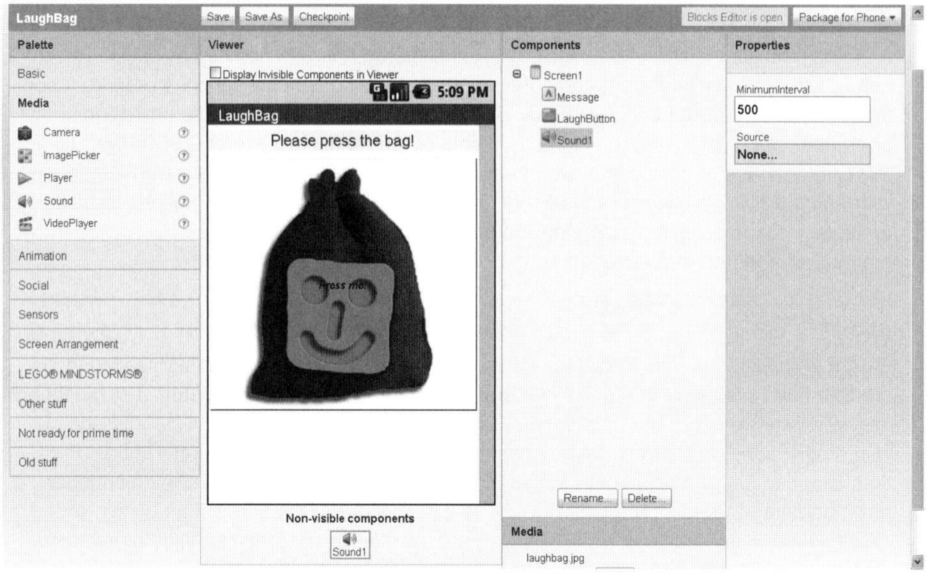

Figure 3.12 Listing the non-visible component "Sound" in the Viewer

Even though the component "Sound1" is naturally not displayed in the visible area of the Viewer (and not on the smartphone either), it does appear in the other panels just like any of the visible components. Under Components, it is subordinate to "Screen1"; under Properties, its specific properties are listed as usual, if the component object "Sound1" was selected and highlighted with a green border (see Figure 3.12). You can change the settings accordingly, just as described earlier in this chapter. Right now, you should change the name from "Sound1" to "Laughter" in Components.

The number of properties of the sound object "Laughter" in Properties is manageably small. You can use the MinimumInterval property to set the playback time of the audio file in milliseconds. If the length of the audio file is shorter than the interval, the file is played repeatedly. As a general rule, the playback time and interval time should match each other as closely as possible, unless you want to achieve a corresponding acoustic effect. We can fine-tune this feature later if necessary.

More interesting for our purpose is the second property of "Laughter" for uploading and integrating the audio file into the app by specifying the audio source in the field "Source," which currently—similar to the case for the image file—contains the value "None." In fact, you use exactly the same process for integrating any media file, whether it is an image or audio file. So, click on "Source" and you will see the list of available media files. This time you can readily see the file `laughbag.jpg`, as the selection list does not distinguish between the media types. Use the Add button to choose a file on your local hard disk and upload it into the AI IDE. Proceed in exactly the same way as when you uploaded the image file, but this time choose the audio file `laughter.wav` in the directory `/MEDIA` of this book's companion website. If all went well and no errors occurred during the upload, you should now see the file `laughter.wav` in the Media panel and the "Source" field in Properties, as shown in Figure 3.13.

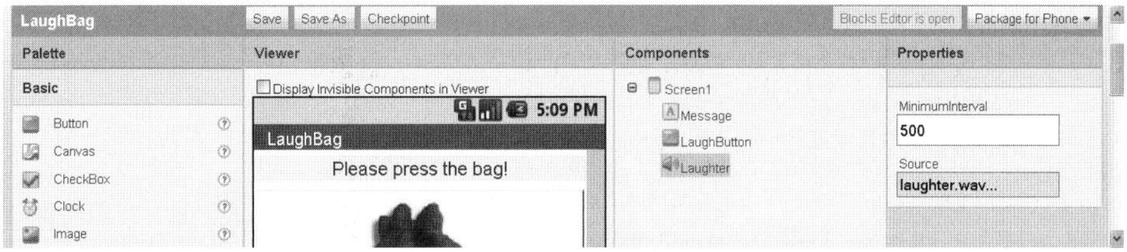

Figure 3.13 Successfully integrated audio file laughter.wav

Now the design of the user interface of our LaughBag app with components is complete. Of course, if you now try to press the LaughButton in the Viewer or even on your smartphone, nothing happens. The reason is that the objects of your app user interface are still unconnected and without functionality. To change this situation, we need to go to the second AI interface, the Blocks Editor.

Developing App Functionality

In this step, we will determine the tasks we want the component objects we placed in the AI Designer to have within our app. To do so, we will connect the active components (button and sound) with each other in the AI Blocks Editor and combine them into an interactive functionality (laughter when the button is pressed). This description of the development work we are about to undertake may sound a little pompous, but is the basic element of each and every app development process with AI, regardless of how complex and complicated, or simple and basic, the resulting app may be. If you fully understand this step, you will have mastered the basic principle of app development with AI and be ready to tackle bigger projects in the future.

This step takes us into a development area that comes close to classic app development with a programming language such as Java. Up to now, you have created the objects of the user interface in AI Designer and optically arranged the visible objects accordingly. Now you will access the functions of these objects (component-specific blocks) in the AI Blocks Editor and use them to design part or all of the app's functionality (block structure). In addition to the object functions, you can use general functions (generic blocks) for completing and developing the application logic and app functionality. Essentially you will start "programming" an app straight away, without using a programming language in the narrower sense. Do not feel put off by this process as a beginner; on the contrary, you should enjoy learning the principles of object-oriented programming as if in passing. Perhaps you would like to be able to develop apps in a programming language such as Java one day—in that case, your experience with AI will prove very useful.

The development process here will not get especially complicated. If you have not yet started the Blocks Editor, please do so now by clicking the button labeled "Open Blocks Editor" in the AI Designer. In the block selection area on the left, select the My Blocks tab. Now you can see the components with their component names that you dragged into the Viewer and renamed with a memorable name in the AI Designer (see Figure 3.14). For example, you can see the label "Message," the sound "Laughter," and the button "LaughButton." You can also see the screen component with its still unchanged default name "Screen1," plus a "My Definitions" area where you can enter your own definitions.

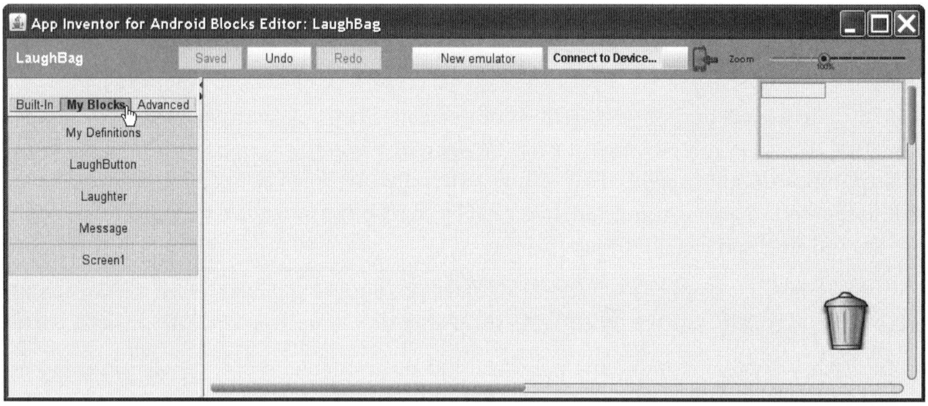

Figure 3.14 The component objects in the AI Blocks Editor under My Blocks

Just as described in Chapter 2 using the example of the "Screen1" component, you can now display the available function blocks for each of the custom component objects you created by clicking on the object name. Remember the "Visible" property in the Message label? In the preceding section on setting the properties of objects in AI Designer, we pointed out that the default settings there for app runtime can be dynamically changed with function blocks of the same name. In Figure 3.15, you can see the corresponding blocks `Message.Visible` for these dynamic changes.

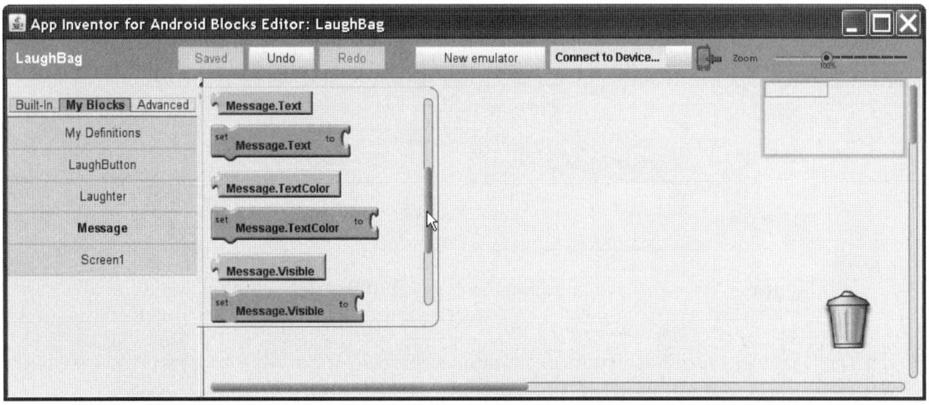

Figure 3.15 Properties of component object label "Message"

Create Interactive App Logic

For now, we want to leave the label text of Message in our LaughBag app unchanged and will not yet use any of these function blocks. Instead, we want to add an interactive function to the button LaughButton. We want to receive user input (i.e., tapping the LaughButton) and respond with a reaction by the app (i.e., playing the sound Laughter). We can express this function of the LaughButton in words as follows:

When user presses LaughButton, play the sound Laughter!

As a beginner without programming knowledge, you may find it hard to believe, but this is already an instruction similar to programming, in the form of an informal *pseudocode*.

We will now implement this function in our LaughBag app to instruct the app to play the Laughter if the user presses the LaughBag. In programming, you generally talk about an event handler—a routine that is carried out only if a certain *event* occurs. In our example, pressing the button is the *event*, the instruction "If click, then [action]" is the *event handler*, and playing the sound is the *action*.

> **Events and Event-Driven Programs**
>
> The term *event* is an important keyword for a basic principle of object-oriented programming, *event control*. In contrast to the classic sequential program flow, an event-driven program waits for input or events of various kinds and reacts with an appropriate function. A program or an app can react to different kinds of events, such as haptic, text, acoustic, or other sensory input, as well as to input from other applications, such as phone calls, SMS messages, e-mails, or news from web services such as Twitter.

To express the function instruction described earlier in the visual developer language AI, we need just two component-specific blocks (see Figure 3.16). The first block forms the frame of the event routine and contains the instruction: When the LaughButton receives a click-event, then do something. The second block forms the action and performs the task: Open the audio player and play back the audio file Laughter.

Figure 3.16 The two components LaughButton.Click and Laughter.Play

To create a continuous instruction sequence, the two individual blocks now have to be connected with each other; that is, the action has to become part of the event routine. That can happen only if the syntactic rules of our visual development language allow it. In our case, you can see this result immediately. The executing component `Laughter.Play` fits like a puzzle piece into the calling component `LaughButton.Click`. This results in the instruction sequence or the block structure shown in Figure 3.17.

Figure 3.17 The block structure for the instruction sequence of the pseudocode

That's it! By connecting these two blocks, you have sufficiently described the functionality of the LaughBag app. That step may seem trivial at first, but only because the visual development language AI hides the complexity behind the block functions. As an app developer using AI, you do not need to worry about the complicated process with which your Android app loads an audio file, plays it, and outputs it via the system loudspeakers. You do not need to write a program routine in which you supervise the touch screen area of the graphically represented button for touches and then combine this event with the audio player. Thanks to the high level of abstraction of the visual description language, you can fully concentrate on describing the functionality of your app and leave the program- and system-technical implementation almost entirely to AI and Android. Even this basic step can become quite challenging, however, as you will notice later during the other projects described in this book.

An Aside: The Power and Abstraction of the Visual Development Language AI

Of course, this convenience comes at a price in terms of the flexibility afforded for function design. The Java programmers among the Android developer population, for example, might argue that they would like to decide themselves which audio player they access and in which way. It is important to recognize that *all* development languages, with their different levels of abstraction, have specific advantages and disadvantages. AI has a very clear advantage: You can very quickly and simply develop appealing apps on your own. Despite their occasional complaints about AI's limitations on design, the Java developers resort to using class libraries that offer prefabricated objects and functions for use in their program code.

App development is also usually subject to a cost–benefit relation. If you can develop the "same" app more quickly and easily with AI, then you should make use of this advantage. Conversely, if you have a specific requirement that cannot be implemented with even a creative use of the AI components, then you will have to accept the need to put in more effort and become familiar with Java programming. Before doing so, however, you should think twice and remember the saying "There are many ways to skin a cat": Perhaps there is a way in AI after all to implement the desired app functionality. AI is much more powerful and more flexible than this first example might suggest, and its functionality is constantly being expanded. Don't forget that AI is only in its infancy (i.e., in the beta phase), yet already offers an impressive range of functions that continues to grow exponentially. You will see for yourself later on what is already possible with AI, even if it is just the "tip of the iceberg."

Implementing Functional Block Structure

Now that we have developed the program logic of our app with the block structure described previously, we can specifically implement it within our LaughBag app. You first need to drag the blocks mentioned earlier, one after the other, into the AI Blocks Editor. Let's start with the interactive component object "LaughButton." Open the available blocks by clicking on the corresponding object name in the block selection on the left. This opens the selection menu shown in Figure 3.18, in which you can see the suitable instruction block `LaughButton.Click` at the top.

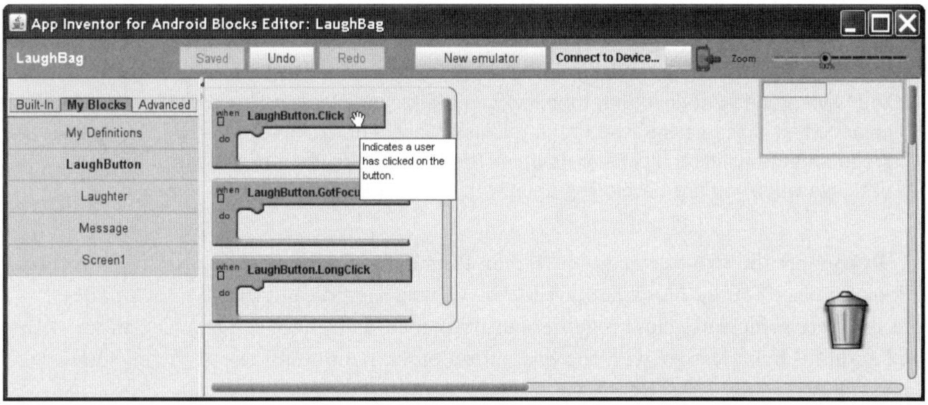

Figure 3.18 Selecting the function block LaughButton.Click in the AI Blocks Editor

If you touch this block with the mouse pointer, a brief description of its functions pops up. As soon as you grab the block with the mouse pointer, the selection menu becomes hidden and you can now drag the selected block into the Editor and drop it in the place you want. Then select the function block `Laughter.Play` in the same way. Open the block selection of "Laughter" and search for the right block—to facilitate the search, you can use the scroll bar on the right-hand side of the selection menu to scroll the selection up and down. In third position, you can see the function block `Laughter.Play` (see Figure 3.19); grab it and drag it into the Editor.

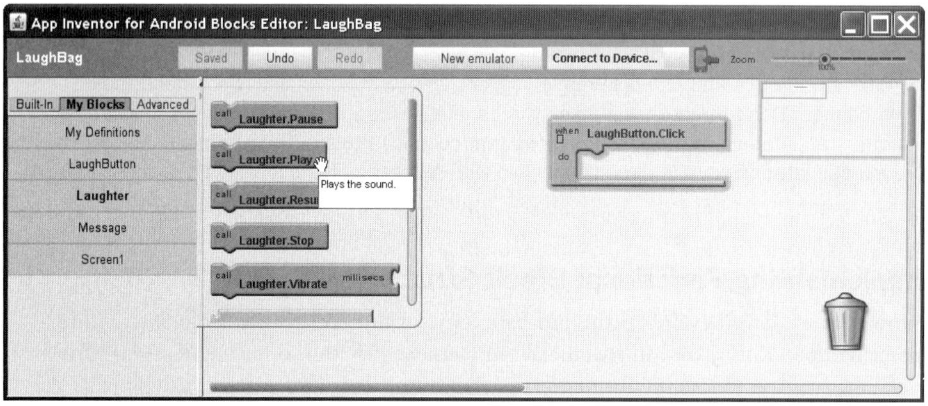

Figure 3.19 Adding the function block Laughter.Play to the LaughBag app

You can "temporarily" drop the function block `Laughter.Play` anywhere in the Editor and then drag it somewhere else later or directly connect it to the instruction block `LaughButton.Click` to form the desired block structure.

Color Coding of the Different Block Types

You have probably noticed that the blocks in the block selections have different colors. The color coding indicates the type of the relevant block. For example, all instruction blocks are green and the function blocks are purple. The different colors make it easier to keep track of things when you are developing apps with complex block structures.

To connect the two selected blocks, drag the block `Laughter.Play` to the correct "docking place" of the block `LaughButton.Click`, then drop it. If the two "puzzle pieces" were sufficiently close together (and provided the syntax is right), `Laughter.Play` will audibly click together with the instruction block `LaughButton.Click`, as shown in Figure 3.20.

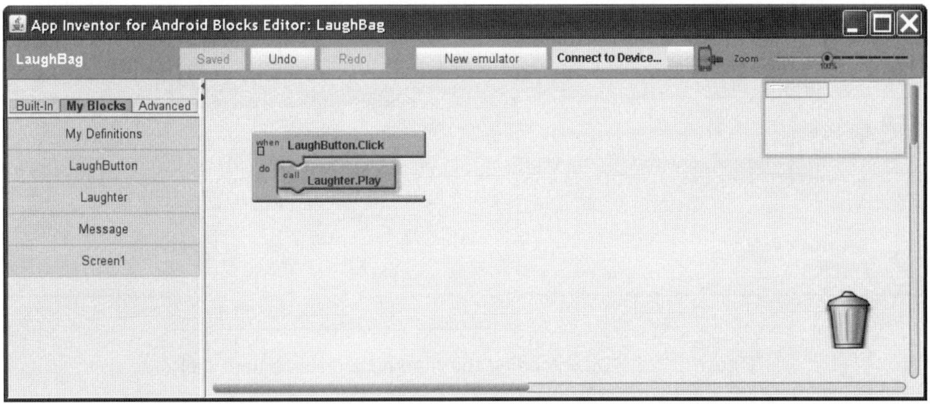

Figure 3.20 Finished implementation of the block structure in Editor

This completes the implementation of the functionality of our LaughBag app. Now you can check that it really does work, provided your smartphone (or even the emulator) is connected. Go to your smartphone and press the laugh bag; you should hear loud laughter every time you press this button.

Save Project Locally

As soon as you have finished developing your AI project, you should immediately save it. As described earlier in the context of the AI IDE, AI saves your project automatically on the provider's servers each time you close the AI IDE. This ensures that you always see the most recent version of your project when opening the AI IDE. You also have the option of saving the current project stage in AI Designer via three buttons—Save, Save As, and Checkpoint—on the provider's servers in the previously described variations. These saved versions of your project are available only online within your personal account in the AI IDE, however, and using them requires that the provider's servers be functioning without errors. If you want to use your AI projects under other accounts or make them available to third parties—for example, as a didactic model, for discussing possible solutions or as a basis for their own projects—then it makes sense to save the project on your local hard disk. You also reduce the risk of losing your projects when you maintain a backup copy in your own sphere of influence.

To save one or more projects together with all components and block structures in the AI Designer and Blocks Editor, you need to go to the project view of AI Designer by clicking the My Projects button. There you can mark the projects to be saved locally with a green check mark. For now, check the LaughBag project, as shown in Figure 3.21, and then click the More Actions button and select the menu item "Download Source" below it.

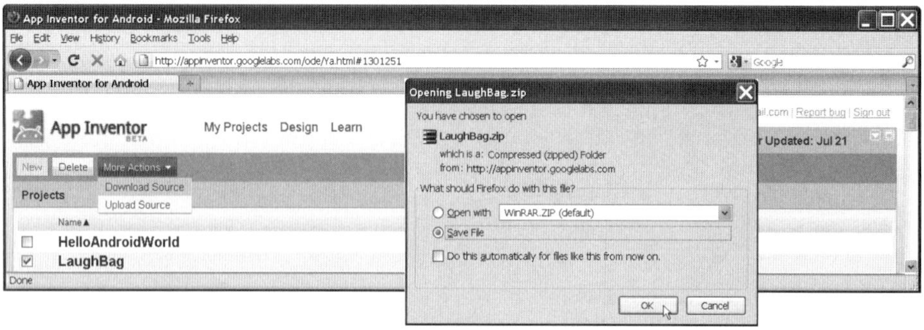

Figure 3.21 Downloading the marked project to hard disk

This series of steps opens the download window shown in Figure 3.21, which asks what you would like to do with the generated project file `LaughBag.zip`. Choose the option "Save File," click OK, and enter the desired location on your hard disk where you want to save the project. Now the project file is safe and sound on your local hard disk.

Downloading All of Your Projects at Once

At the end of 2011, an additional button labeled "Download All Projects" was added to the Google AI's My Projects overview menu. With it, all projects created by a user can be downloaded at once and saved locally as one large ZIP file. The resulting file, `all-projects.zip`, contains all projects in turn as individual ZIP files. After downloading and unzipping the collective file `all-projects.zip` to the local hard disk, you can then upload the individual project ZIP files one by one to the development environment of another AI provider (for example, MIT AI) and process them further as part of your project.

Project Files from This Book on the Companion Website in the /PROJECT Directory

You can find all project files from this book on the companion website in the `/PROJECT` directory (see the link in the Introduction). The website also includes the current file `LaughBag.zip`. You can upload all of the AI projects described in this book directly into the AI IDE after downloading them from the companion website, without having to input the interface components and block structures yourself. Nevertheless, you should not underestimate the benefit of the learning experience you achieve when you recreate the app step by step.

In case the block structures we develop later in this book become so big that they cannot be adequately printed in this book, be aware that you can access the companion website and upload the block structures from the project files into your own AI Blocks Editor. You can then study them in their entirety and develop them further for your own purposes if you wish.

If you should wish to edit the project later under a different account, you can upload it to the corresponding provider's server. Once more, uploading projects in AI happens via the More Options button in AI Designer. Click on the option "Upload Source," and then click on "Choose File" and select the desired local project file with the extension `.zip` in the file manager. Click OK, as shown in Figure 3.22, to upload the project from your hard disk to the provider's servers and open it as the current project.

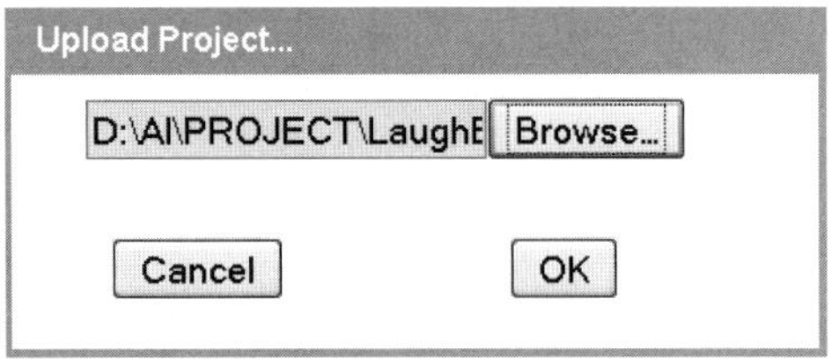

Figure 3.22 Uploading a locally saved project in AI

In this way, you can make your project files available to other AI developers as well, so that they can upload your project to their AI IDE for their own use. It is common practice for AI developers to share their projects and swap opinions on block structures, difficult problems, and common solutions. This cooperative attitude makes it also possible to offer tried and tested block structure functions to other users, which other developers can then use in their own projects as ready-made building blocks.

The file extension `.zip` indicates that the project file is not a single file, but rather a file archive. Surely you have a program installed on your computer that can extract zip files, such as WinRAR (`www.win-rar.com`). Double-click on the project file `LaughBag.zip` in your File Manager and take a look at the contents of the project archive.

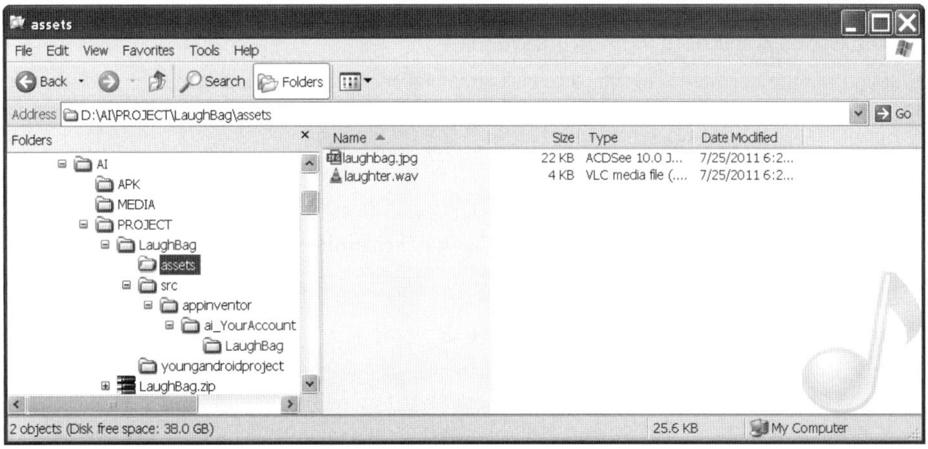

Figure 3.23 Directory and files in project archive LaughBag.zip

In Figure 3.23, you can see the directories and projects of the project archive `LaughBag.zip`. The actual source code with the system-specific description of the interface design and functionality of your app is hidden away in three files in the subdirectory `/src/appinventor/ai_YourAccount/LaughBag`, although on your computer the name of your actual Google account will appear instead of the placeholder `ai_YourAccount`. The directory `/assets` contains all of the media files used in your project and shown in Figure 3.23. You can't really do much with these individual files outside of the AI IDE, but the directory structure gives you an additional impression of how AI internally manages your app projects.

If There Is No Laughter

If the final function test of your app was unsuccessful, first check the obvious sources for the absence of sound. Have you set the volume on your connected smartphone high enough (or the volume of the computer, if you are using the emulator)? If yes, check the setting from the previous section on correctly integrating an audio file into the AI Blocks Editor or the app. Can you see the file name `Laughter.wav` in the button Source property, and is the file still located in the directory specified? Or are you using another sound file that may not fulfill the format requirements of AI or Android and, therefore, cannot be played because it is not supported? Even if you can't see an image yet (see the problem description in the "Optimizing the App Design" section), the sound should be audible if you press the button.

It may be small consolation in this situation, but you are not alone with your problem. We based our first app deliberately on the official beginner's project "HelloPurr" described on the AI online pages. This project uses the same components and blocks for its app in which you can press the image of a cat to hear a meow sound. If you are trying this app, you can assume that you would encounter the same problems as with our LaughBag app.

> **Analogous Beginners App on AI Website**
>
> If you want to compare projects, the analogous beginners project "HelloPurr" can be found at: `http://experimental.appinventor.mit.edu/learn/setup/hellopurr/hellopurrphonepart1.html`

Even if you do not want to test the project "HelloPurr" yourself right now, you can still use the troubleshooting tips if you are having any problems with our LaughBag app. Check the AI Forum or the "Troubleshooting" page if there is no sound.

> **AI Troubleshooting**
>
> This page contains "Working with Sounds and Images," which includes the entry "I set the source property of a Sound or Player component, but there's no sound when I tell the phone to play." This entry, which is found at the following address, provides even more help:
>
> `http://experimental.appinventor.mit.edu/learn/troubleshooting.html#ImagesSounds`

In the document "No Meow for Hello Purr" the Google AI Team also described some steps for problem solving. If you are still having problems, try going through the following steps in order and see if one of them helps:

1. Click the button "Connect to device" in the AI Blocks Editor with your smartphone connected and test the app again.
2. Unplug the USB cable from your smartphone and then plug it back in. Now click the button "Connect to device" and try the app again.
3. Close the AI Blocks Editor, and then start it again from AI Designer. Now click the button "Connect to device" and try the app again.
4. Delete the audio file `laughter.wav` from the AI Blocks Editor, by clicking on the file name in the Media panel and then selecting the "Delete" option. Now load the audio file into the project again as described earlier. Disconnect the smartphone, and then reconnect it to the computer and the AI Blocks Editor.
5. Reboot your smartphone by switching it off completely (not just changing to standby mode) and then restarting it. Now reconnect it to the AI Blocks Editor.
6. Try a different USB connection mode. For information on how to do this, refer to the section on setting up the Android device in Chapter 1. Connect your smartphone to the AI Blocks Editor in the different modes.

Even if none of these steps solves your problem, there is still a chance that you will both see the LaughBag image and hear the laughter sound when you later download the app to your smartphone and run it as an independent app. This advice applies, for example, to the smartphone HTC Tattoo, which we also used for testing the apps in this book. Just be patient and don't give up! The next few sections will show you how to download the LaughBag project as an independent app to your smartphone.

Creating and Installing the App

If you have taken a break at some point during the previous development steps of the LaughBag project and shut down your computer or disconnected your smartphone from the PC and the AI IDE, you may have noticed something. First, there is the reassuring fact that the most recent version of the app project is displayed when you restart AI Designer and Blocks Editor and reconnect your smartphone, even if you did not save it explicitly—you can thank the automatic saving function of AI for that benefit. Second, you may have noticed that the LaughBag app was nowhere to be found among the other apps on your smartphone. That is because our LaughBag app up to now has existed only within the corresponding project on the AI IDE or the provider's servers. Now we need to create it explicitly as an independent app and download it to the smartphone to make it a "proper" app. AI offers three alternative methods for doing this, which we describe in the following sections:

- Direct installation on a smartphone
- Online installation via a barcode
- Downloading of the APK file to the computer

All three approaches can be accessed in AI Designer by clicking the button labeled "Package for Phone" and selecting the relevant option from the pop-up menu.

Direct Installation on a Smartphone

Let's start with the most direct option of creating and downloading the LaughBag app to your smartphone. The key requirement is that your smartphone be correctly connected to the AI IDE via the Blocks Editor. Of course, the app project you want to turn into an app also has to be selected for editing or active in the AI Designer. To create the app and at the same time download it to your smartphone, click the Package for Phone button in AI Designer. In the pop-up menu, choose "Download to Connected Phone" (see Figure 3.24) to start the download process.

Figure 3.24 Selection of an app for direct installation on a connected smartphone

Now AI starts creating the app and downloads it to your connected smartphone. The progress of this process is indicated with the status messages "Packaging" and "Downloading to phone." After a certain processing time and many messages on data transmission in the browser's status line, the extra window shown in Figure 3.25, together with an acoustic signal, announces that the download and installation of the app on your smartphone were successful and are complete.

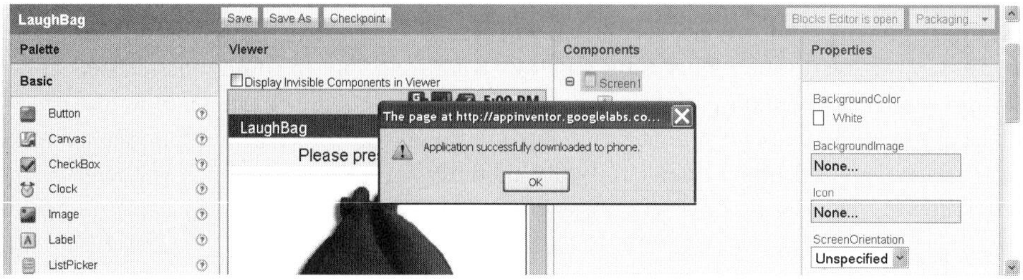

Figure 3.25 Message on successful app installation in AI Designer

Before you can now go looking for the app on your smartphone, you first need to close the still active AI development environment or display of the app project on your smartphone. You can do so with the options described earlier. Press the menu button on your smartphone; select the only menu item that appears, "Stop this application" (see Figure 3.26); and confirm your choice by selecting "Stop and exit" or, alternatively, by just unplugging the USB cable.

Figure 3.26 Closing the connection between the AI development environment and the smartphone

Now you can go to the app overview of your smartphone and search for the app with the title "LaughBag." Figure 3.27 shows an example of the app on the LG P500 smartphone, where we used the manufacturer-specific option of putting our LaughBag app into a separate category "AI Apps" (which will hold our future AI projects), just to make things clearer. If you now select the "LaughBag" app, it will start just like any other app on your smartphone. You can confirm that the app really does run independently of the AI IDE by noting that the USB connection symbol is absent in Figure 3.27 on the left-hand side of the top status line, whereas the connection icon is present in Figure 3.26.

Figure 3.27 The independent LaughBag app on the smartphone

The icon for the LaughBag app shown in Figure 3.27 is the default icon for all apps created with AI. If you would like to replace the small default icon depicting two little androids with your own custom app that matches the theme of your app, we will show you how in the next section.

A Matching Icon for Your App

Normally it would be sufficient to mention this subject in one or two sentences in the context of interface design with AI Designer—from today's point of view. Until the AI update of November 10, 2010, it was not officially possible to replace the default AI app icon with a custom icon. Many heated debates focused on the possibilities of retrospectively unpacking the project files, editing them, and adding another icon in the most adventurous ways. After all, how could people create more or less professional apps, and in some cases market them, if the app could not even have a suitable and appealing icon, just like every other app?

Against this backdrop, one of the early AI beta users had requested the inclusion of this feature by the Google developers. Feature requests are generally submitted via the "Issues List" introduced by the Google developers to enable them to more quickly and clearly structure and edit the numerous requests for improvement and bug reports submitted by AI users in the beta phase. The desire for the option of assigning custom app icons, for example, is listed as Issue 43 under the title "Add the ability to change the icon of apps." The numbers under which the issues are listed (IDs) do not indicate their order of priority, but simply the order in which they are addressed.

> **Bug Reports and Feature Requests in the "Issues List"**
>
> The Google developer team provides the "Issues List" as a collection point for all open technical matters regarding the AI beta software:
>
> `http://code.google.com/p/app-inventor-for-android/wiki/ReportingBugs`
>
> Beta users are encouraged to report any AI bugs in a standardized form and to submit feature requests for AI using this list. Before starting a new issue, the AI beta user should check that the topic has not already been raised by another user and perhaps been discussed and resolved in the Google Group. The topics raised here should be of general interest and not concern individual problems, such as questions on the setup of your own smartphone—that is what the AI Online Documentation and the Google Group are for. The more focused the "Issues List" requests, the more readily the Google developers can concentrate on the important topics and continue developing AI, without getting sidetracked with minor issues. For that reason, each issue is evaluated by the Google developers, processed in various stages, and its status documented as follows:
>
> **Open issues**
>
> | | |
> |---|---|
> | New | Issue has not yet been reviewed or queued |
> | Investigating | Further information is required |
> | Noted | Issue has been noted but not yet been accepted for work queue |
> | Accepted | Issue has been accepted and will be worked on soon |
> | Started | Work on this issue has begun |
> | Testing | Issue is resolved and being tested to be published in the next new AI release |
>
> **Closed issues**
>
> | | |
> |---|---|
> | Fixed | Issue has been resolved |
> | Invalid | This was not a valid issue report |
> | Duplicate | This report duplicates another issue report |
> | Won't fix | The Google team is not working on this issue |
> | Forum | Refer this issue to the Google Group |

Issue 43 now has the status "fixed." If you are curious and want to read up on the suggestions other AI beta users came up with in the past in connection with this feature, however, you could set the filter to "All issues" and search for "43" or "icon" on the "Issues Search" page.

Searching Issues and Checking Status

You can search open issues with various filter options and submit new issues via the "Advanced Search" page:

http://code.google.com/p/app-inventor-for-android/issues/advsearch

You can find Issue 43 directly at this page:

http://code.google.com/p/app-inventor-for-android/issues/detail?id=43

Since November 10, 2010, Issue 43 has had the status "Fixed" (see Figure 3.28). As a general rule, fixed issues are announced as new features in the next official update of App Inventor in the AI Forum. Given this fact, you do not need to search the "Issues List" regularly to find out about new features.

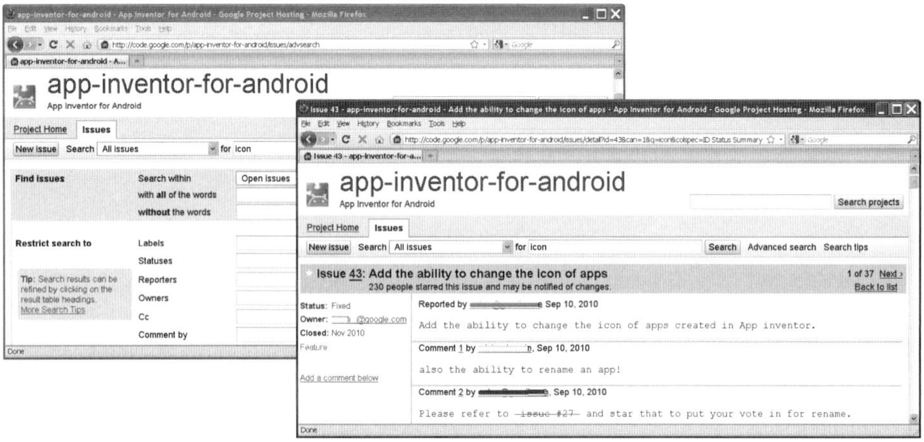

Figure 3.28 Status of Issue 43, "Change the icon of apps"

Now that Issue 43 is fixed, you can add a custom icon to your app really easily. Of course, you still have to keep your masterpiece within the specified format. Apart from guidelines on file formats, a detailed set of instructions in the form of "Icon Design Guidelines" applies to all developers of Android apps.

"Icon Design Guidelines"

A very detailed description of the requirements for format and design of icons for Android apps can be found in the Android Developers Forum:

http://developer.android.com/guide/practices/ui_guidelines/icon_design.html

The "Icon Design Guidelines" contain not only templates and examples, but also recommendations for resolutions (in pixels) for different icon types such as a launcher icon, menu icon, and so on. Try to follow these guidelines when designing your app icons to give them a professional look. You can even use the templates provided in professional graphic programs such as Adobe Photoshop and Adobe Illustrator. Even if you are not a graphic designer, it can make sense to provide your images in the correct format so as to optimize their representation on the smartphone. Almost every graphics program offers the option of cropping your images and reducing them to a specified pixel size. Thus, if you immediately reduce the image you want to use as icon to the recommended size of 48 × 48 pixels, you reduce both the memory requirements and the risk of distorting the icon on the smartphone through automatic display adjustment in Android. For the file formats, the same requirements as specified in Chapter 15, "Tips and Tools," also apply.

Designing a Custom Icon with a Graphics Program

For our LaughBag app, it makes sense to use the existing laugh bag image for the icon as well. We want the icon to stand out a bit from the mass of other icons, however, and the bag should have a greater contrast to the white background.

Using the graphics program Corel Paint Shop Pro, shown in Figure 3.29, we edited the image from left (the original image) to right (the edited result). In the first step, we selected the outline of the bag with the "Magic Wand" and colored the background green using a "Gradient." To the resulting image we then added the optical appearance of a button with the menu sequence Effects > 3D Effects > Button. We then made the button round with Effects > Geometric Effects > Circle, and selected the background again with the "Magic Wand" to color it red.

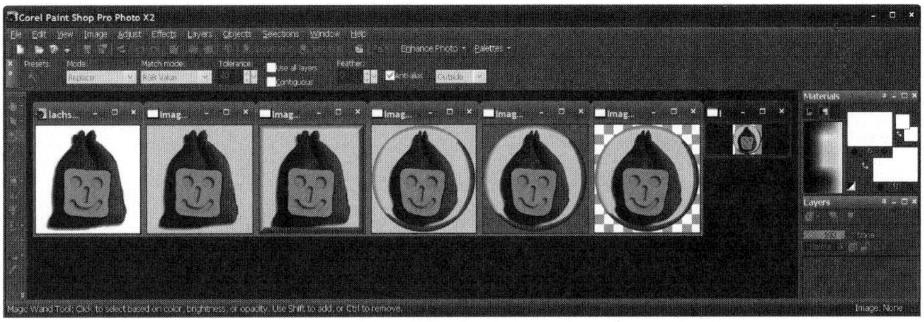

Figure 3.29 Designing the default icon using the laugh bag image

We chose to use the graphics file format PNG (*Portable Network Graphics*), which allows us to define transparent areas, enabling us to achieve smoothly rounded transitions between the originally rectangular or square icon and the screen background. In Corel Paint Shop Pro, we used the menu sequence File > Export > PNG Optimizer to select the Red color values (RGB 255/0/0) as the transparent image area, so that only the round button shown in Figure 3.29 on the right remains visible. We then reduced the image from the original 288 × 288 pixels to the recommended default icon size of 48 × 48 pixels via the menu items Image > Resize, and saved it as `laughbag_icon.png`.

If you do not want to design your own icons in a graphics program, you can use special programs or web services for creating buttons. The website "Glassy Buttons," for example, offers many options for creating and downloading custom buttons or icons in any sizes.

Website "Glassy Buttons" for Creating Custom Icons

The free button generator on the "Glassy Buttons" website (`http://www.netdenizen.com/buttonmill/glassy.php`) lets you create attractive buttons and icons with gloss effects. You can choose from many settings to customize the size, gradients, text labels, and many other characteristics of images, and upload images as textures. The finished button can then be downloaded in the file format PNG and JPG (packaged as a ZIP file) and used directly as icon subject to the conditions of use.

Assigning an icon to your app is just as simple as integrating the LaughBag image into our project and follows the same process. We could have done this in step 2 of designing the user interface described earlier, but then you would not have seen the default icon. With app development, it is quite common to skip back and forth between development steps and to correct, adapt, or expand work done in previous steps. To change the icon, please reconnect your smartphone to your computer and the AI IDE by plugging in the USB cable and clicking the button labeled "Connect to phone." Then go to AI Designer, and select the component object "Screen1." In its properties, you can see the property Icon in last place. As seen earlier with the two media files, its (default) value is "None." Now load a suitable image file for the default icon into your LaughBag project by clicking on "None" and choosing the image file on your computer via the Add button in the pop-up menu. Of course, you can once again find an example file on the companion website for the book in the directory `/MEDIA`—namely, the just-created image `laughbag_icon.png` (shown in Figure 3.29). When you select it, the image name once again appears in the Media and Properties panel, but the image itself is not displayed (see Figure 3.30).

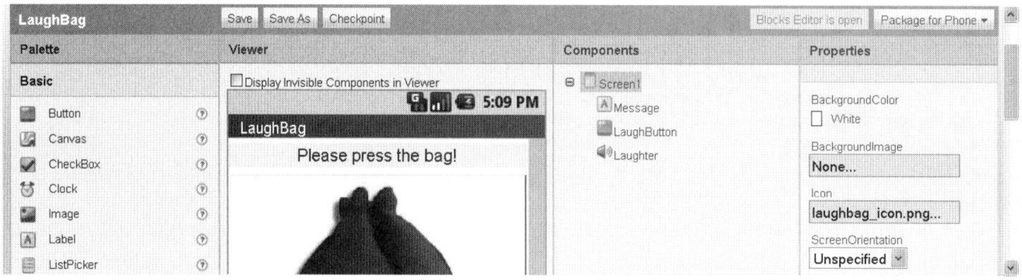

Figure 3.30 Adding an image file for the default icon of the LaughBag app

At this point, you have added your own default icon for the LaughBag project. Now you just have to download the app once again to your smartphone and install it. Remember to delete or deinstall the old LaughBag app from your smartphone before you install the new version with the default icon.

Deleting/Uninstalling AI Apps on Your Smartphone

Proceed in the same way as when deleting or uninstalling other apps. Drag the default icon of the app you created with AI into the waste basket, or select Settings > Applications > Manage > LaughBag > Uninstall, as shown in Figure 3.31.

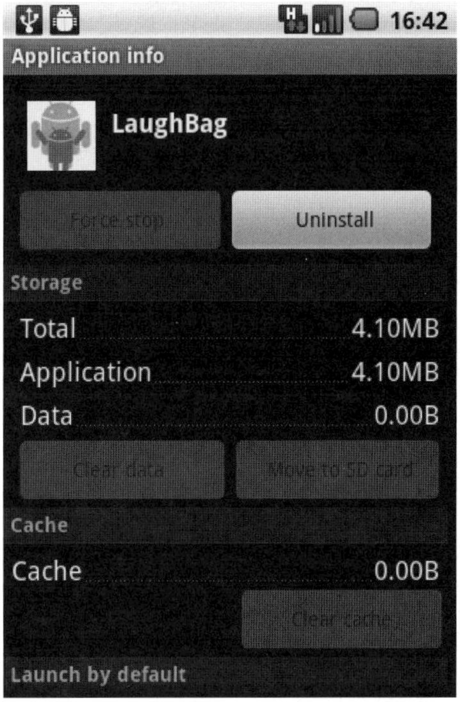

Figure 3.31 Uninstalling the LaughBag app with the default icon

In the uninstall dialog shown in Figure 3.31, the file size shown for our LaughBag app is an impressive 4.10MB. This is the file size of the *installed* app on the smartphone, which is usually much larger than the app installation file you downloaded earlier.

Once the old app with the default icon is deleted, you can install the edited LaughBag app. Proceed as described earlier in the section on direct installation on the smartphone. After you have successfully completed the installation, the LaughBag app appears in your smartphone's app overview with the custom default icon shown in Figure 3.32.

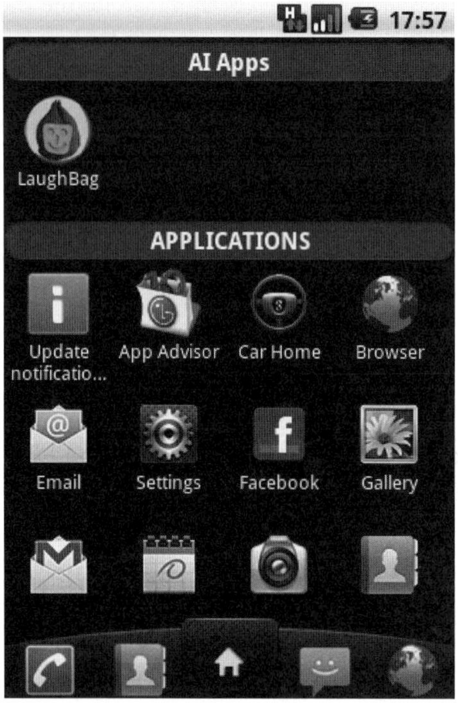

Figure 3.32 The LaughBag app with custom default icon on the smartphone

You can now use your LaughBag app just like any other app on your smartphone. In addition to the app icon in the app overview (Application menu), you can create a widget (link icon) for it directly on the home screen or the other panels.

Correct Reproduction of Image and Sound in the Independent App

If reproducing the laugh bag image or playing back the sound has been causing problems up to now, you may now both see the image and hear the laughter sound in the independent app. This is the case, for example, with the HTC Tattoo with Android 1.6: Whereas neither the image nor the sound works during the app development process, the independent app works perfectly on the smartphone. If you experience the same issue with your development environment and smartphone, then you can assume that in your future development work you will not be able to check and use certain components directly in the AI IDE, but that they will work correctly on the smartphone later as independent apps. This makes developing a bit more awkward, but at least not impossible.

Assigning custom icons for apps developed with AI is, of course, possible at stages other than during the direct installation. Assignment of the default icon occurs independently of the installation process. By assigning an image in the default component "Screen1," the app automatically gets the corresponding default icon.

Online Installation via a Barcode

For the second method for downloading and installing our LaughBag app, you do not need a USB cable connection between your computer or the AI IDE and your smartphone. To demonstrate this the approach, please unplug your smartphone's USB cable from the computer now. If you have already installed the LaughBag app on your smartphone in the step described in the previous section, please delete it so we can be sure that you download the app without the USB cable this time. Keep the AI Blocks Editor and AI Designer open, as you will need the block structures to generate your LaughBag app.

To use the barcode approach, you need an Internet data connection on your smartphone (and on your computer, of course), either via WLAN and your WLAN router or directly via the mobile data net of your cellphone provider in form of GPRS (*General Packet Radio Service,* which offers up to a 172 Kb/s download rate with GSM channel bundling), EDGE (*Enhanced Data Rates for GSM Evolution,* which offers up to a 473 Kb/s download rate with GSM channel bundling), UMTS (*Universal Mobile Telecommunications System,* which offers a 384 Kb/s download rate in the 3G net), or the speedy HSDPA (*High-Speed Downlink Packet Access,* which offers up to a 7.2 Mb/s download rate in the 3.5G net). You also need to have an app for reading barcodes on your smartphone.

Barcodes, QR Codes, and Barcode Scanners

A barcode is generally a method of encoding data using bars (lines) that can be read and processed by optic reading devices. You are certainly familiar with the 1D codes used on almost all product packaging, such as in the supermarket. 2D codes are becoming increasingly more common on the Internet in form of QR codes (quick response codes), which are used to encode web addresses and the like with a *barcode generator*. The encoded information can then be read and decoded by a smartphone, allowing direct access to the website. To use QR codes, you first need to install a *barcode scanner* as an app on your smartphone; such an app can check the filmed or photographed camera image on the smartphone for a QR code and then process the code.

To use the AI option for installing your app online, you need to have a barcode or QR code scanner installed on your smartphone. If you do not yet have one, go to the Android Market and search for "barcode"; then choose one of the many free scanners to install on your device. We used the barcode scanner ixMAT by ZXing, but Google Goggles also works well for QR codes.

(Continues)

Figure 3.33 QR codes for downloading ixMAT (on the left) and Google Goggles (on the right)

Of course, you cannot do anything with the two QR codes shown in Figure 3.33 unless you already have a barcode scanner installed on your smartphone. If you do have one, these two QR codes will give you direct access to the appropriate app from the Android Market. We provide a quick description of how to use the barcode scanner for downloading AI apps using the ixMAT app as an example.

If you have fulfilled the requirements for a mobile Internet connection and a barcode scanner installed on your smartphone, you can start with the online installation of the LaughBag app. Open the menu in AI Designer by clicking the Package for Phone button and this time choose the option "Show Barcode," as shown in Figure 3.34.

Figure 3.34 Selection for online installation of the LaughBag app on the smartphone

After displaying the usual status messages "Saving" and "Packaging," AI opens the window titled "Barcode link for LaughBag" and shows a QR code (see Figure 3.35). This QR code encodes the download link under which AI offers the generated LaughBag app for download. Unlike the case with the direct download described in the previous section, AI has now saved your app on a Google server from which you can download the app.

Figure 3.35 QR code or barcode containing a download link for the LaughBag app

Note that the QR code shown in Figure 3.35 was deliberately distorted before being printed in this book, so that your barcode scanner can no longer read it. Instead, you must scan your *own* barcode generated under your personal account and now displayed by AI. You can also take a "photo" of your QR code (under Windows with the keyboard shortcut Alt + Print) or save it for later downloads. You could also pass the QR code on to third parties, who could use it to download your LaughBag app to their own smartphone and install it; however, the requirement in this case would be that you make the login data for your own Google account (i.e., the account in which you are working with AI) available to others. For security reasons, this practice is not recommended, so this download option is not a suitable choice for making your future apps available to the public. We will discuss possible alternatives in the next few sections.

To get the app onto your smartphone via the QR code shown in AI, you need to scan the barcode with the barcode scanner installed on your smartphone. Start the scanner app and hold your smartphone's camera at an appropriate distance in front of your computer screen (or a printout). If you can see the barcode clearly and in its entirety in the view finder, follow the instructions of the scanner app. In case of Google Goggles, for example, you need to take a photo of the QR code by pressing the appropriate keys before the image analysis is started. In contrast, ixMAT processes the running camera view automatically and quickly indicates the recognition and decoding of the QR code with a signal tone (see Figure 3.36). If your smartphone has a low camera resolution without autofocus, try enlarging the QR code a little to make it scan correctly.

Figure 3.36 Decoding the QR code with the barcode scanner ixMAT

If the QR code was successfully recognized, the decoded download link is displayed in the scanner; Figure 3.36 shows the display in ixMAT. Depending on the feature range of the barcode scanner used, it will offer different options on how to proceed with the link. With ixMAT, you can choose to click "Share via email" or "Share via SMS" to send the link to other e-mail addresses or phone numbers, if appropriate (see the earlier cautionary comments). For our purpose, we want to use the decoded web link to "Open browser" so as to display the download page for the LaughBag app. Your smartphone then opens the web browser and takes you to the HTTPS-secured login page for your Google account, as shown in Figure 3.37 on the left. Enter the same login data as for your login to the AI development environment, and then press the Sign In button.

Figure 3.37 Log in to the Google account and download the LaughBag app

Once you have successfully logged in, the download of the LaughBag app to your smartphone commences. The progress of the download is indicated by the corresponding download icon in the smartphone's status line. If you drag down the status line, you can see a confirmation after successful download telling you that the application file `LaughBag.apk` has finished loading, as shown in Figure 3.37 on the right under "Notifications."

APK Files

An Android file has an extension of `.apk`. The file extension APK stands for *Android Package*. As the term "package" indicates, the app not only comprises a single file, but also forms an archive of several files. This organization explains why the AI status message says "packaging" during the download process: The generated app files are combined together into a "package" before being downloaded. The archive format resembles the Java archive format JAR (Java Archive) and is also used for app development in Java. We will briefly discuss the contents of the APK archive in the following section on downloading the APK file.

Now click on the file `LaughBag.apk` in the "Notifications" section, or follow the other necessary steps for installing the downloaded application file `LaughBag.apk` on your smartphone.

Allow "Unknown Sources"

One requirement for the installation of the downloaded APK file is that you have checked "Unknown sources" in Settings > Applications with a green check mark, to allow app installation of sources from outside of the Android Market. As you have downloaded your LaughBag app from your Google account on a Google server, this setting must be enabled.

Installation takes place via the steps shown in Figure 3.38, just as with other apps. Once you have selected the file `LaughBag.apk`, you are notified of the app's access rights before you start the actual installation by clicking on the Install button. After a brief installation period, you can "Open" the LaughBag app directly from the installation confirmation by clicking on the corresponding button, or go to the application overview of your smartphone to start it.

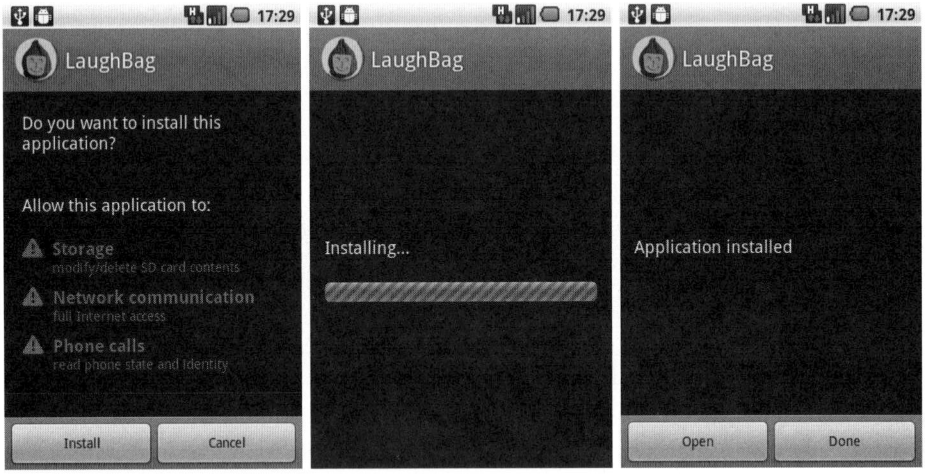

Figure 3.38 Installation of the downloaded LaughBag app on the smartphone

This completes the online installation of the LaughBag app using the second approach (barcode). But wait, there's more: AI offers a third alternative of downloading and installing your app.

Downloading an APK File

As third alternative, you can download your LaughBag app as the file `LaughBag.apk` to your computer and get it to your smartphone via this "detour" to install it. Considering the ease of the other two options, this approach seems rather awkward, but it is the easiest option for passing your app on to third parties without having to go via the Android Market or giving others access to your Google account for the barcode installation. It enables you to offer the file `LaughBag.apk` online on your web server for downloading or to send the file to others via e-mail so that they can also download your LaughBag app to their smartphones.

To try out this method, you again need to uninstall the LaughBag app from your smartphone as described earlier. At first you will not need to connect the smartphone to your computer for downloading the app, but later it will need to be connected when you copy the APK file from the computer to your smartphone. You do not need a mobile

Internet connection for this installation method, as all data required for the app are available locally on your computer and are copied over to your smartphone via USB. Start the download of the file `LaughBag.apk` to your computer by clicking the Package for Phone button in AI Designer, but this time choose the option "Download to this Computer" (see Figure 3.39).

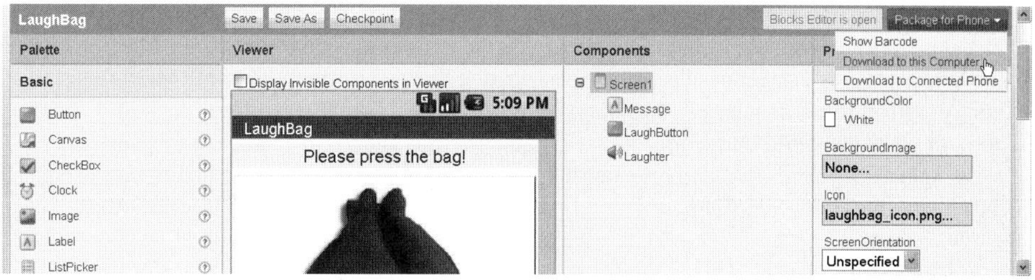

Figure 3.39 Option to download the file LaughBag.apk to the computer

After displaying the usual status messages "Saving" and "Packaging," the system window shown in Figure 3.40 pops up to ask if you want to open or save the file. Choose the option "Save file," click OK, and then select the target directory on your local hard drive to save the file `LaughBag.apk`.

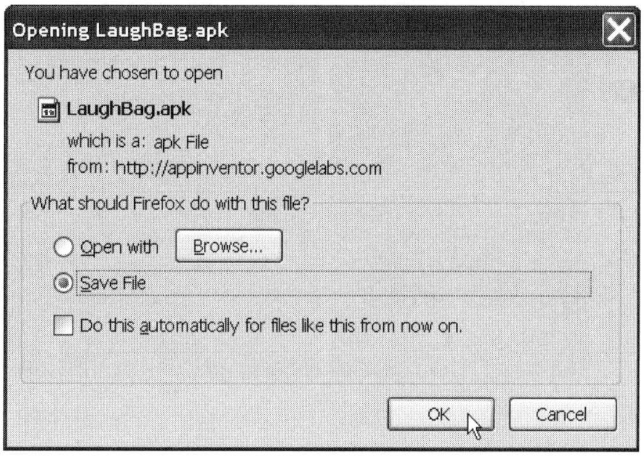

Figure 3.40 Pop-up window for downloading the file LaughBag.apk

After the download is complete, you will find the file `LaughBag.apk` in your specified target directory. The companion website also contains this file, in the directory `/APK`. In contrast to the app's installation size of 4.10MB as shown in Figure 3.31, the downloaded APK file is only about 1.15MB in size.

We now want to copy this APK file from the computer to the smartphone. First you need to ensure the smartphone is connected to the computer via USB. Enable USB debugging and turn on USB storage. To check this status, you can open the file manager on your computer and determine whether your smartphone (or, more specifically, its SD card) is registered or listed as an additional hard drive in addition to the other drives (e.g., `C:/`).

> **An SD Card Is Obligatory**
>
> Having an SD card on your smartphone is a requirement for working with AI—although, of course, it is valuable for many other reasons. The other installation methods also download the apps created with AI to the SD card of your smartphone. The relevant APK files are then usually placed in the SD card's `/downloads` directory. The media files of the installed AI app, referred to as *assets*, can be found in the directory `/AppInventor/assets`. Take a look at your own directories: You may even still see the files `laughter.wav`, `laughbag.jpg`, and `laughbag_icon.png` used in the previous installations. Not all traces vanish after you uninstall a program.

If you cannot see your smartphone in the file manager, you can enable USB storage explicitly on your smartphone by pulling down the status bar, clicking on "USB connection," clicking the button "Turn on USB storage," and confirming your choice by clicking OK (see Figure 3.41 using the example of LG P500 from left to right). Now your smartphone—or, more correctly, its SD card—should appear as a separate drive in the file manager.

Figure 3.41 Enable the USB connection to copy the APK file

Once your smartphone is connected to the computer as a USB storage device, you can easily copy the downloaded file `LaughBag.apk` to the SD card of your smartphone (see Figure 3.42). Go to the download directory in the file manager (for example, `E:/AI/APK`), copy the APK file (Copy in Windows or use the keyboard shortcut Ctrl + C), go to the smartphone's desired target directory in the file manager (such as `F:/downloads`), and paste the copied file there (Paste in Windows or use the keyboard shortcut Ctrl + V). Remember this directory, as you will later need to access it on your smartphone and select the APK file to install it.

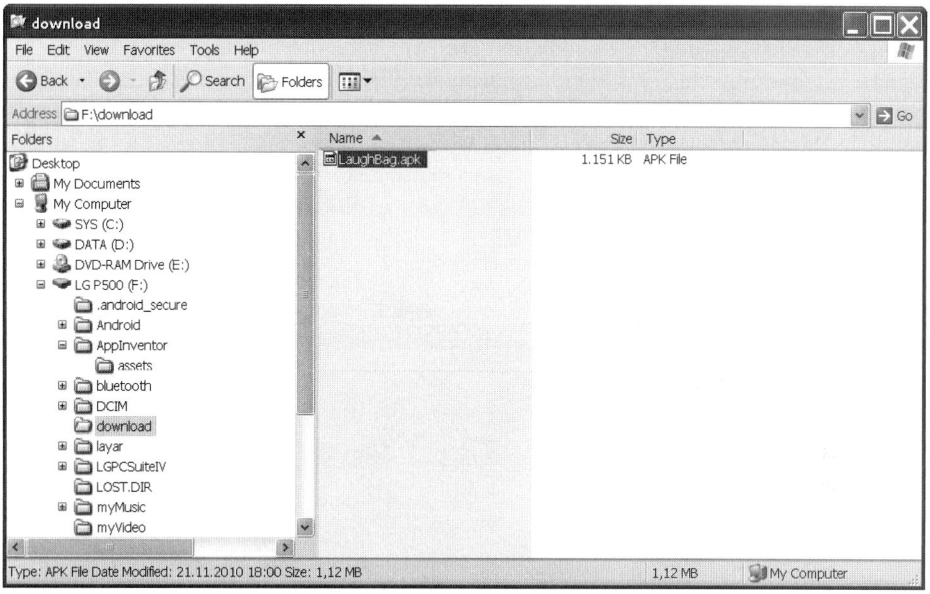

Figure 3.42 Copying the file LaughBag.apk to the SD card of an LG P500 smartphone

Once you have copied the file `LaughBag.apk` onto the SD card of your smartphone, you can disconnect the smartphone from the computer. Close the USB connection by clicking on the button "Turn off USB storage" (see Figure 3.41 on the right), or unmount the drive from your computer just like any other USB device (in Windows, use the icon "Safely remove hardware," which is found in the status bar).

Now you have the APK file on your smartphone, but you can neither start it nor see it in the app overview. Before the app can appear in the application overview, you must first install it. The APK file is merely the installation file. If you tap on an APK file on your smartphone, Android automatically installs the app archived within that file. But how can you find the file `LaughBag.apk`, which you copied into the `/downloads` directory on your smartphone's SD card using the file manager? To do so, you need an app that lets you access the directories and files on your smartphone and its SD card in the same way as the file manager does on your computer.

File Manager for Android Smartphones

To access the files and directories of your smartphone and its SD card, you need an additional app, similar to the file manager on a computer. The current Android smartphones do not usually include a mobile file manager, so you need to obtain one from the Android Market—for example, by searching for "Explorer." The free version AndExplorer, by Lysesoft, is a good choice.

If you have an Android Explorer, such as the AndExplorer program created by Lysesoft, installed on your smartphone, you can start it now to find the copied file `LaughBag.apk` on your SD card. After starting AndExplorer and pressing the SDCard button, you should see the same directories (shown in Figure 3.43 on the left) as were visible in the file manager on the computer (shown in Figure 3.42). Now you can simply press the directory name `/download` to go to that directory; there you will find the copied file `LaughBag.apk`. Click on the file name to start the installation process, as shown in on the right-hand side of Figure 3.43.

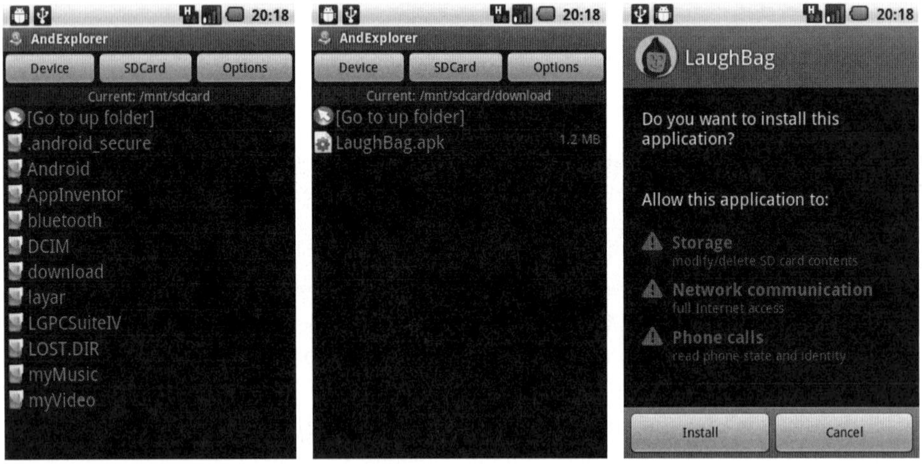

Figure 3.43 Installing the file LaughBag.apk using the AndExplorer file manager

As described in the previous section, an APK file is an archive of several files and directories. With a program for unpacking—for example, 7-Zip (`www.7-zip.org`)—you can take a closer look at the contents of this archive. Figure 3.43 shows the unpacked directory structure of the file `LaughBag.apk`. It is a bit bigger than that of the project file `LaughBag.zip` (shown in Figure 3.23), but still resembles it. In addition, the APK file now includes the Java-type files of an Android app—for example, the Android Manifest in the XML file of the same name, various meta files, and the integrated Java classes in `classes.dex`, plus the three media files as *assets* in the directory `/assets` (see Figure 3.44).

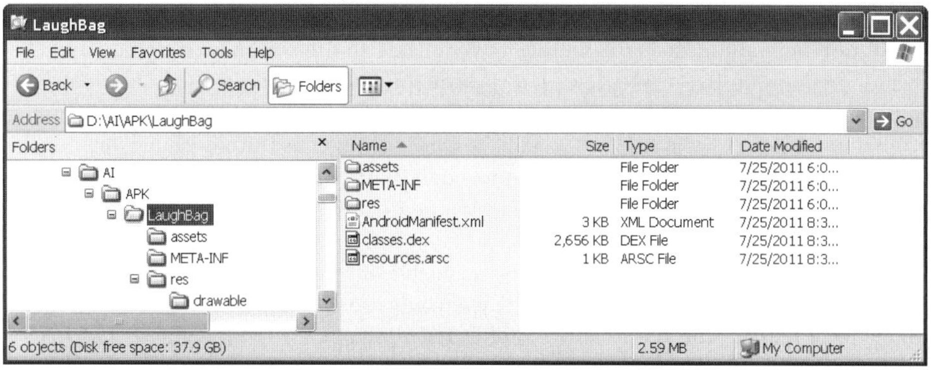

Figure 3.44 Directory structure of the unpacked app archive file LaughBag.apk

Now that you have used all three methods for downloading and installing the LaughBag app on your smartphone, it is entirely up to you which installation method you decide to use and when. If you want to test your independent app quickly during your development work, the direct installation is certainly the fastest option. If you are using several smartphones for testing, the quickest way of getting the app to the various Android devices is probably using the QR codes with online installation. If you want to make your app available to third parties for testing or general use, however, the best option is downloading the APK file.

Google Play and other Android Markets

In the context of exporting your own app as an APK file, you are probably wondering whether you could offer apps created with AI within Google Play (formerly known as Android Market), where apps are also available as APK files. Any developer who wants to distribute an app on Google Play first has to register, regardless of which development language has been used or whether the app is free or sold for a fee.

Registering as a Developer on Google Play

Before you can distribute your apps on Google Play, you first need to register and pay a one-time fee (currently $25). You can register online at this website:

`http://market.android.com/publish/signup`

For further help, refer to the Help page on the registration process:

`http://market.android.com/support/bin/answer.py?hl=en&answer=113468`

Before you think about registering to publish the apps you have developed with AI on Google Play, please read the rest of this section first.

On the Help page mentioned in the note, you can read a statement explaining the motivation behind this financial "hurdle": "We charge this fee to encourage higher-quality products on the market (e.g., less spammy products)." Just like other distributors of competing platforms for marketing apps, Google is trying to keep the quality of apps offered on Google Play as high as possible. Whereas some competitors require each of the apps to undergo a complicated approval procedure with more or less transparent evaluation criteria, the requirements for Google Play are not yet as restrictive. Despite the registration fee, the number of apps available on Google Play continues to grow rapidly, and it is becoming increasingly difficult to find a suitable app among the multitude of available apps. To keep the growing Google Play attractive to consumers as well as developers, Google is trying to limit the excessive proliferation of apps.

Against this backdrop, it should not be surprising to find that for a long time, apps created with AI were not intended or officially allowed to be distributed on Google Play. AI is aimed mainly at beginners and seeks to didactically provide basic methods of developing mobile apps; it is not targeted toward professional Java developers who want to develop commercial apps for Google Play. The prospect of hundreds of additional "HelloWorld" apps inundating Google Play understandably did not seem to be a good idea. Some of the discussions in the AI Forum, therefore, debate the question of whether professional apps can be created at all under the current limitations of AI and whether keeping them off Google Play altogether might be justified. Also, you should not forget that AI is only in the beta stage.

As there was no built-in export-to-market function integrated into AI for a long time, some clever alternative tools have been developed. You can still use the search term "market" in the AI Forum to find tips about publication tools such as Marketizer and AppToMarket, which have been available online and sometimes even free. With these tools, you are still supposedly able to sign the APK files created with AI relatively simply and convert them to compatible APK files, which you can then upload to Google Play with a valid registration.

Tools for Converting AI Apps for Google Play

According to the product information, the following tools enable you to convert, sign, and publish the APK files created with AI under a valid registration on Google Play:

AppToMarket: `http://amerkashi.wordpress.com/`

Marketizer: `http://www.taiic.com/marketizer/`

Since the release of AI Version 125 (see `http://beta.appinventor.mit.edu/ReleaseNotes.html`) from May 6, 2012, apps created with AI can be uploaded to Google Play. There is a complete description about how to download your apps from AI and upload them to Google Play on the documentation sites of the MIT AI.

How to Upload AI Apps to Google Play

You can find a complete description of how to prepare and upload your AI apps to Google Play at the MIT AI documentation website:

`http://beta.appinventor.mit.edu/learn/reference/other/appstoplay.html`

We should also mention that apart from Google Play, a growing number of alternative or additional online platforms are emerging on which you can offer your apps either free or for a charge. Please refer to the terms and conditions on the respective websites for details.

Alternatives to Google Play

In addition to or as an alternative to the official Google Play, you can offer your apps among all the others on these platforms:

Amazon Appstore for Android: `http://www.amazon.com/mobile-apps/b?ie=UTF8&node=2350149011`

AppBrain: `http://www.appbrain.com/`

GetJar: `http://www.getjar.com/`

Yet Another Android Market: `http://yaam.mobi/`

Regardless of where and how you want to offer your AI apps, it is essential to keep your target audience in mind. The success of an app depends not solely on marketing, but primarily on a good idea and its appealing and appropriate implementation—which is what we will concentrate on in the rest of this book.

Part II

Easy Projects as a Warm-Up

In keeping with the title of this part of the book, and continuing on the path we set out on with the LaughBag app, we want to further expand the practical implementation of your theoretical knowledge to lead you quickly toward developing Android apps with AI. At the same time, we do not want to neglect the structured approach of a course book enabling you to gain a quick overview of the scope of functions and relevant topics involved. For these reasons, we will not just list examples and tell you which functions of AI you need to create them. Instead, the second part of this book presents the wealth of features in AI in a structured manner, introducing the individual areas progressively with a focus on practical application. The example apps are adapted to the appropriate topics to illustrate these subjects and inspire your own developments.

The idea behind this structure is to present each individual component of AI as far as possible and demonstrate its functions briefly within examples. Once you have the chance to see a component live in action on your smartphone, you will certainly grasp its function better than if you simply read about the underlying theory. Even if the individual examples do not always correspond to a sensible or useful app, they intuitively impart new knowledge to you as future app developer. The aim is to get you to develop your own ideas for apps that you can build from these components or, conversely, to get you to think about how you can break down your existing app ideas into these functional building blocks. To inspire this creative process, the introductory description of the components is followed by a number of examples demonstrating what useful little apps can be developed using these few blocks. The later chapters on more advanced app development with AI follow the same structure.

This approach also matches the organization of the official AI documentation and has the great advantage of sharing the same mindset as that of the AI developers. As a consequence, it will become easier for you to find your way around the online documentation, search for further information, and have discussions with the other developers. In turn, you will be better prepared for inevitable changes in AI, given its dynamic nature. Any newly developed features of AI will certainly be integrated into the established structure of the AI documentation in the future, and you can use your newfound understanding to quickly navigate to updates and make use of them. The most important part of the AI documentation is the References documentation, which currently contains three types of references—for components, blocks, and concepts. By exploring certain central basic terms and the AI References, this part of the book first presents and demonstrates the basic components for designing the graphical user interface and multimedia apps, and then concludes with a selection of already quite respectable example apps.

Chapter 4

Basic Terms and Central Concepts

To facilitate using the AI documentation in particular and the exchange of information and contents during app development in general, it helps to agree on basic terms and associated concepts. So that we can apply these terms and concepts quickly, we will concentrate here on only a few central aspects specifically required for understanding the topics introduced in this chapter. Of course, these aspects also provide an important foundation for the following chapters. In this chapter, our focus is on elementary terminology and concepts associated with using AI components.

Properties and Property Blocks

As you already know from the LaughBag project, components have specific *properties* that you can set in AI Designer as *initial properties*. You have already assigned several properties to the interactive button component object LaughButton via the Properties panel—for example, the button text "Press me!" via its "Text" property field, and the background image `laughbag.jpg` using the input field "Image," as shown in Figure 4.1.

Figure 4.1 Setting the initial properties in AI Designer

Most of these properties can be changed during the app's runtime—for example, in reaction to an event triggered by the user pressing a button. For this purpose, AI offers the appropriate *property blocks* for the component objects used, in the AI Editor's block selection area under the My Blocks tab. These property blocks can be used to read a current property value (e.g., `LaughButton.Text`) or assign a new value to it (e.g., `set LaughButton.Text to`). Figure 4.2 shows that these two property blocks are found in the selected slide-out panel for the button component object LaughButton.

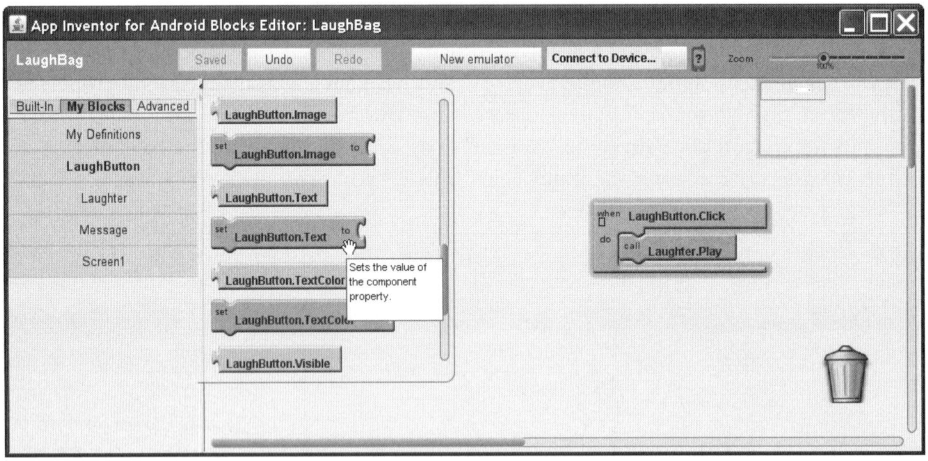

Figure 4.2 Changing properties at runtime via property blocks

The representation of property blocks follows a fixed pattern in the visual development language AI. Blocks for reading property values are light blue puzzle pieces, labeled with the appropriate object and property name separated by a full stop (for example, `LaughButton.Text`). A single *getter* block has a plug on the left and indicates that the property value can be read by another object block. By contrast, the slightly darker blue blocks indicate a *setter* block with a socket on the right, through which the property value of a getter block can be read, overwriting the existing value. The text on the puzzle pieces really says it all: `set LaughButton.Text to`. In Figure 4.3, this assignment principle is demonstrated using the example of "Button1," which gets the text of "Button2," just like "Label1," which has the same text property despite being a different component type and, therefore, can also take on the corresponding value of "Button2."

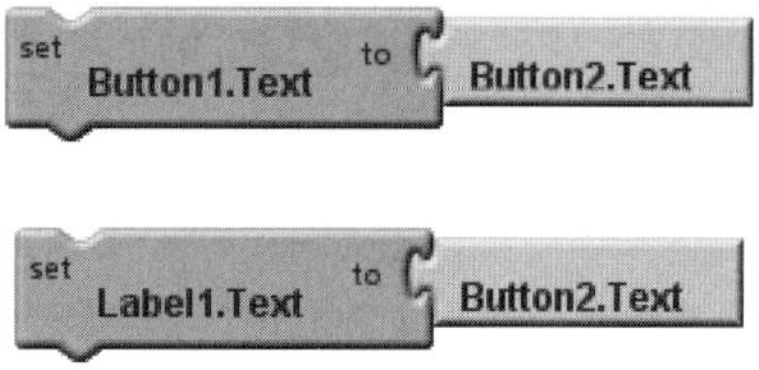

Figure 4.3 Setter and getter property blocks of different objects

Events and Event Handlers

Assigning properties during the app's runtime does not happen just like that, but rather occurs as a consequence of *events*. This makes sense, because otherwise the app would not know when it should assign a property to a particular component object and the app's state would remain undefined. Undefined states must be avoided in app development with AI, as they can lead to errors and even system crashes. That is why you will never see the isolated instructions shown in Figure 4.3 in a functioning app: The app needs to know when it should, for example, assign the text property of "Button2" to the component object "Button1." The events can be of very different nature, such as pressing a button, changing a GPS position, or receiving an SMS message or a reply from a web service. In essence, an app—just like every other event-oriented program, such as in a Windows environment—is in a permanent state of waiting, ready to react in the way determined by the developer as soon as a certain event occurs.

For registering events, most components in AI have specific *event-handling routines,* also referred to simply as *event handlers*. You have already come across a representative of this category in the context of the LaughBag app while designing the interactive app logic in Chapter 3. In accordance with its generic property of being pressed, the button LaughButton has a corresponding event handler "`when LaughButton.Click do`"; expressed in pseudocode, this event handler means "When the user clicks LaughButton, do [the action]." The suitable event handlers are also available in the AI Editor under the My Blocks tab for each corresponding component object. As an example, Figure 4.4 shows the four available event blocks for the button component object LaughButton.

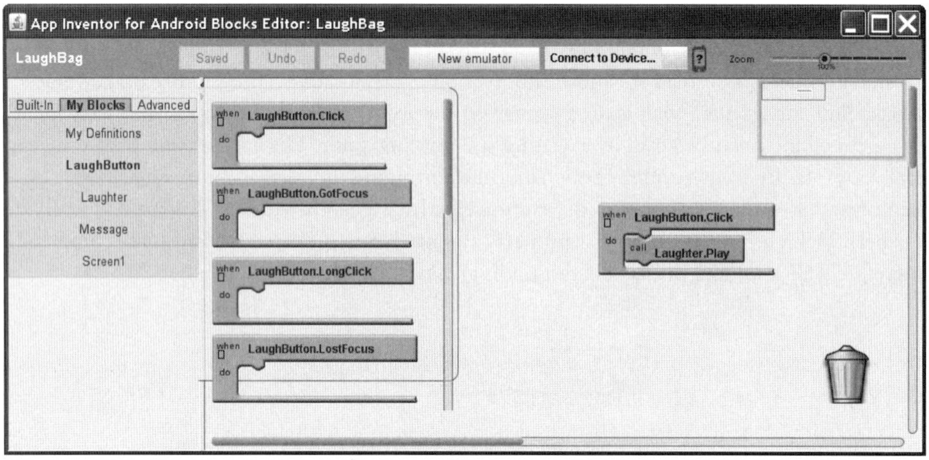

Figure 4.4 The four event blocks of the button component object LaughButton

The puzzle pieces representing an event block in the visual development language AI also follow a consistent pattern. Between the two keywords `when` and `do`, you can see the object and event name in each case, also separated by a full stop (for example, `when LaughButton.Click do`). The event blocks are light green and provide an optical frame around the block structures they can receive and will trigger if a certain event occurs. The individual blocks for event handling can be docked successively on to the event block in the order they are meant to be executed, provided they fit onto the docking point concerned (i.e., they follow the syntax rules of AI). For example, in case of the property blocks mentioned earlier, only the setter property block (`set Button1.Text to`) can be joined directly to the plug in the event block via the socket at its top edge, whereas the getter property block (`Button2.Text`) can be joined only indirectly in combination with the setter (see Figure 4.5).

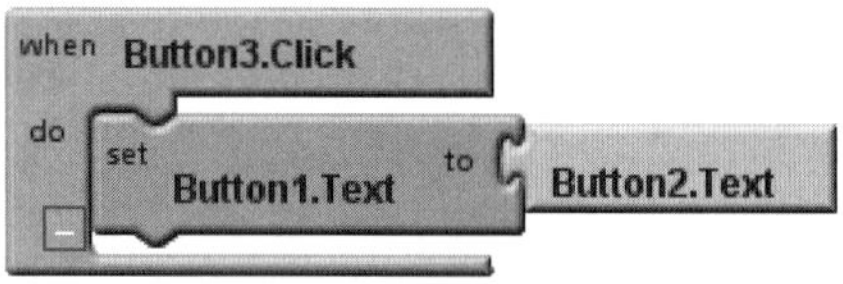

Figure 4.5 Event block with a setter block as the event handler

This syntactic control is quite intuitive to follow if you imagine the pseudocode behind it:

```
When the LaughButton is pressed, do set Button1 to the text of Button2!
```

The smooth edges of the event blocks visually indicate that you cannot dock them onto other blocks; instead, they exist as independent units within an app. The sum of all event handlers contained within the app forms the overall functionality of the app and indicates which interfaces you can use to interact with the app. An event block becomes an event handler only if it is filled with the corresponding functional block structures. These block structures can contain other block types in addition to the property blocks mentioned earlier—namely, methods.

Methods and Method Blocks

Of course, event blocks can fulfill their purpose only if they are filled with at least one functional block structure that can react to the event when it happens. As described in the previous section, these block structures can, for example, change the properties of the component objects contained in the app. In addition to the property blocks, some components include other blocks with which specific tasks can be carried out. These predefined functions are called the *methods* of a component and are available in AI as *method blocks,* also found in the block selection tab (My Blocks) under the relevant component object. You have already come across one of these methods in connection with the LaughBag project. After you assigned the audio file `laughter.wav` as the initial property to the non-visible sound component object "Laughter," you were able to play the audio file by calling the associated component method `call Laughter.Play`. The method was embedded into the event block `when LaughButton.Click do`, so that the method `call Laughter.Play` was called with every click on the LaughButton and the audio file could be played (see Figure 4.6).

Figure 4.6 Embedding the sound method Laughter.Play into an event block

The visual representation of a method also follows a fixed pattern in the development language AI. Each method starts with the keyword `call`, which is followed by the object and method name, once again separated by a full stop (e.g., `call Laughter.Play`). The light purple methods also have a socket at the top edge, so they can be slotted into the same places within event blocks as the previously mentioned setter property blocks. In contrast, very few methods have a socket on the right side; instead, most are closed off as in `call Laughter.Play`. Thus the aforementioned audio file is played once from beginning to end, regardless of how long the playback time is.

A few methods allow or even demand further data before they can be called or to execute their function. For example, in the slide-out panel for the sound component object

"Laughter," you can see four closed methods plus one method that says `call Laughter.Vibrate millisecs`, which has a socket on the right-hand side. As the method's name indicates, you can make your smartphone vibrate by calling this method. Given that the vibration method can be called even if the sound component object does not contain an audio file, the vibration length is not linked to the audio playback time. Instead, you can (actually, have to) specify the length of the vibration explicitly in milliseconds as a *parameter* (argument) by passing it a numeric value via the socket of the method, as shown in Figure 4.7. The block `number` for inputting a numeric value can be found in the AI Editor in the generic block selection in the Built-In tab within the Math group.

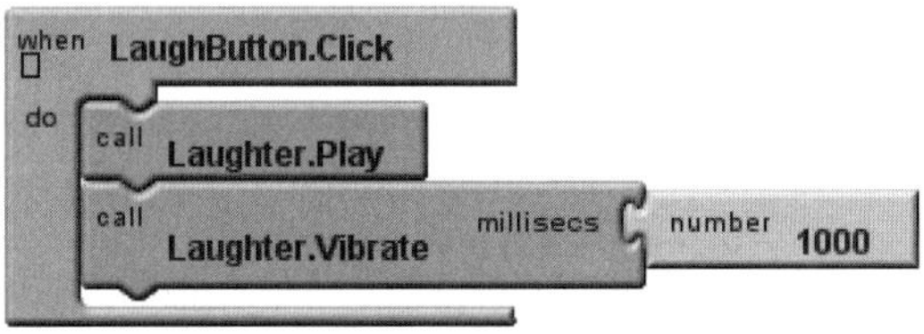

Figure 4.7 Laughter and vibration in reaction to pressing the LaughButton

In Figure 4.7, the length of the vibration is specified as 1 second to provide an example (1 second = 1000 milliseconds). Thus, when you press the LaughButton, you will hear the sound Laughter, while the smartphone also vibrates for 1 second. In the technical terms of the program, this means that the event block `LaughButton.Click` receives an event and then calls the method `Laughter.Play` and the method `Laughter.Vibrate` with the numeric value `1000` as a parameter. In pseudocode, we can express the event handler of Figure 4.7 with the following description.

```
When LaughButton is pressed, do call Laughter.Play and call Laughter.Vibrate
with the value 1000!
```

With this vocabulary, you are already using the developer jargon—and you are ready to work on more components and their property blocks and methods. You can find an overview of all components and blocks in the AI references (see Chapter 5).

Chapter 5

The AI References

Like any programming and development language, AI has a specification; in its case, this specification is found within the *Reference Documentation*. This specification describes all components of the visual development language AI. At the time of writing, it distinguishes between three *reference types*: the Component Reference, the Blocks Reference, and other relevant aspects (Concepts).

> **Online Reference Documentation**
>
> The current online reference documentation can be found at `http://experimental.appinventor.mit.edu/learn/reference/` or at the appropriate website of your AI provider.

Even though the term "specification" or "reference" may seem rather theoretical, this reference work is of highly practical use during your development work with AI—along with this book, of course. You can use the References to quickly check online which properties a component has and which event blocks and methods are available. You can also find out quickly and easily which functions are behind the many component-specific and generic blocks (there are so many that you could never commit them all to memory). It is well worth having a quick look at the References while you are reading the following sections and to practice using them efficiently.

Component Reference

The *Component Reference*, or *Components* for short, contains the specification of all AI components. It reflects the component entries listed in AI Designer within the Palette panel. The Palette entries are linked to the Reference. Thus, if you click on the question mark icon next to each Palette entry, an explanation of the relevant component will pop up that also contains a direct link "More Information" to the appropriate entry in the Component Reference (see Figure 5.1).

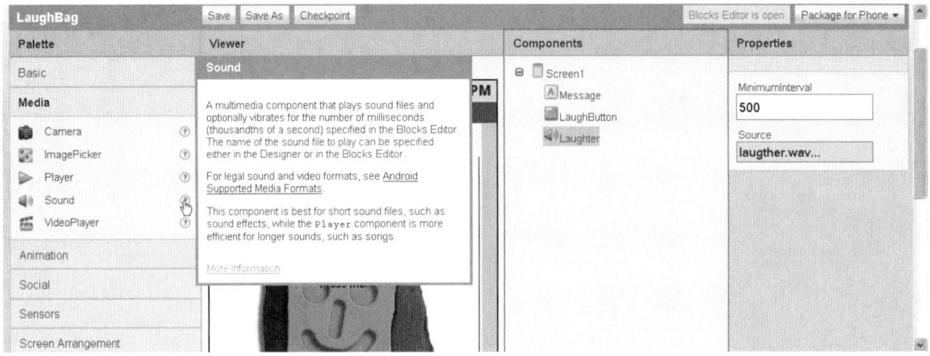

Figure 5.1 Link from the component Palette to the Component Reference

If you click on the link, the Component Reference opens in a new browser tab and skips to the relevant entry. Alternatively, you can go to the Component Reference via the AI Online Documentation.

Online Component Reference

The Component Reference can be found at:

`http://experimental.appinventor.mit.edu/learn/reference/components/`

The start page of the Component Reference (see Figure 5.2) explains that components can have properties, event handlers, and methods, and that the properties can be changed via property blocks that set and get values. (You were introduced to these ideas earlier in this book.) Some exceptions exist, however. For example, the screen size of the smartphone is fixed (evidenced by its properties Height and Width in the "Screen" component). Some properties are read-only (listed in *italics* in the Component Reference) and not writable, and there are no blocks for accessing the initial properties at runtime.

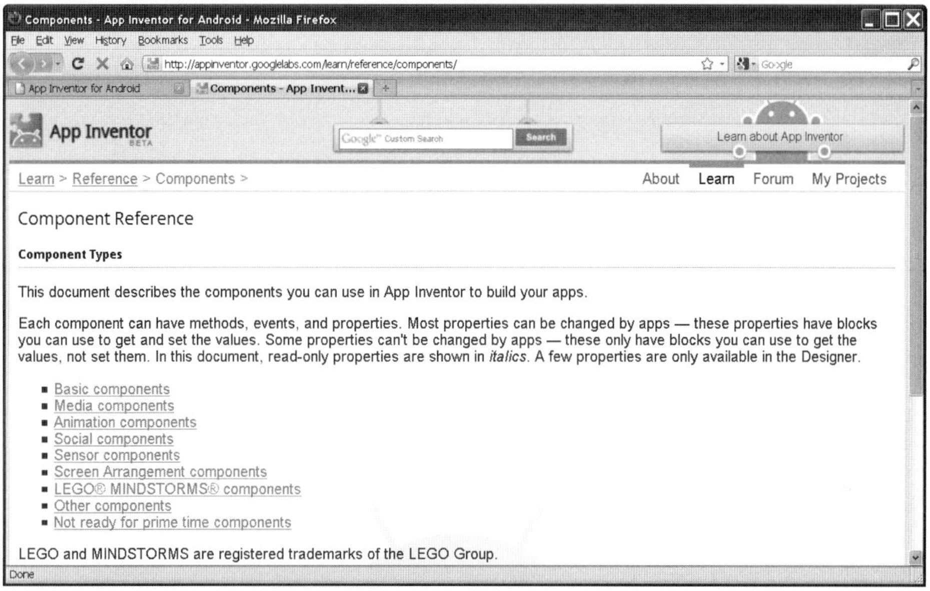

Figure 5.2 Start page and table of contents of the Component Reference

Using the links in the Component Reference shown in Figure 5.2, you can—similar to what happens in the Palette in AI Designer—display the different component groups or their specification. For example, if you click on "Basic components," you can display the Basic group (Basic Components), with the specifications of all components in this group being listed. Its table of contents contains as the first entry the "Button" component with an example button (labeled "Translate"). The explanatory text then tells you at a glance which properties and events are available for the component (see Figure 5.3).

Button

Translate

Buttons are components that users touch to perform some action in your app.

Buttons detect when users tap them. Many aspects of a button's appearance can be changed. You can use the `Enabled` property to choose whether a button can be tapped.

Properties

`Alignment`
  Left, center, or right.
`BackgroundColor`
  Color for button background.
`Enabled`
  If set, user can tap button to cause action.
`FontBold`
  If set, button text is displayed in bold.
`FontItalic`
  If set, button text is displayed in italics.
`FontSize`
  Point size for button text.
`FontTypeface`
  Font family for button text.
`Height`
  Button height (y-size).
`Width`
  Button width (x-size).
`Image`
  Image to display on button.
`Text`
  Text to display on button.
`TextColor`
  Color for button text.

Events

`Click()`
  User tapped and released the button.
`GotFocus()`
  Button became the focused component.
`LostFocus()`
  Button stopped being the focused component.

Figure 5.3 Specification of the "Button" component in the Component Reference

Whereas the "Button" component only has properties and event blocks, the "Sound" component in the Media group also has typical methods needed for playing audio files (see Figure 5.4). The "Sound" component does not have any event blocks because it does not offer direct interaction; rather, it can be triggered only indirectly via the event blocks of other components (such as a button).

Sound

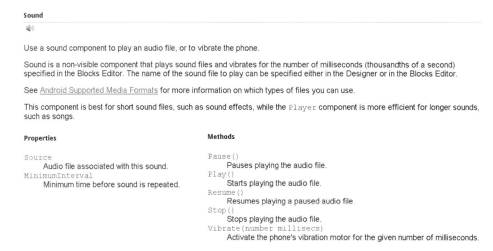

Use a sound component to play an audio file, or to vibrate the phone.

Sound is a non-visible component that plays sound files and vibrates for the number of milliseconds (thousandths of a second) specified in the Blocks Editor. The name of the sound file to play can be specified either in the Designer or in the Blocks Editor.

See Android Supported Media Formats for more information on which types of files you can use.

This component is best for short sound files, such as sound effects, while the `Player` component is more efficient for longer sounds, such as songs.

Properties

`Source`
  Audio file associated with this sound.
`MinimumInterval`
  Minimum time before sound is repeated.

Methods

`Pause()`
  Pauses playing the audio file.
`Play()`
  Starts playing the audio file.
`Resume()`
  Resumes playing a paused audio file.
`Stop()`
  Stops playing the audio file.
`Vibrate(number millisecs)`
  Activate the phone's vibration motor for the given number of milliseconds.

Figure 5.4 Specification of the "Sound" component in the Component Reference

In the general description of the "Sound" component's function in Figure 5.4, you can also see a direct reference to the online overview of Android-supported media formats. This example shows how the Reference serves as a central pool of information, giving you access to all other relevant information and documentation related to each component. It is strongly recommended that you use this source of information for your daily work with AI.

Blocks Reference

The second reference type, the *Blocks Reference*, or just *Blocks*, can be just as useful in your daily developing work with AI. You can not reach this reference from AI Designer or AI Editor, but rather via the online pages of the AI documentation.

Online Blocks Reference

The Blocks Reference can be found at:
`http://experimental.appinventor.mit.edu/learn/reference/blocks/`

The Blocks Reference specifies all generic blocks available in AI Editor in the block selection in the Built-In tab. Although we have addressed this area only in passing up to now, you have already used one of these blocks in the example in Chapter 4, for expanding the event handler `LaughButton.Click` (see Figure 4.7). To the event handler, we added a way to call the method `Laughter.Vibrate` and passed the value `1000` to this method as numeric parameter (argument) to set the duration of the vibration in milliseconds. In the `number` block of the generic block Math group, we edited the default value `123` by clicking on it and replaced it with `1000`. We were then able to pass the number block as the parameter value `1000` to the method `Laughter.Vibrate` through its socket (see Figure 5.5).

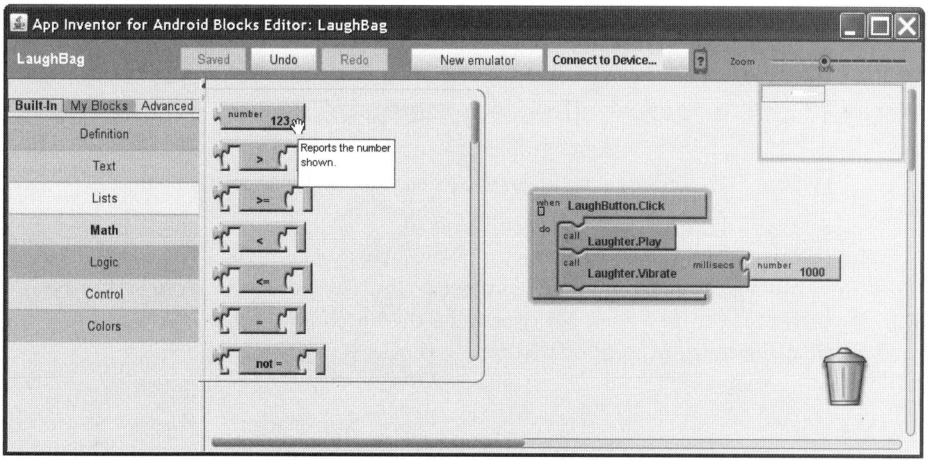

Figure 5.5 Selecting the generic number block as a parameter

The Blocks Reference provides the specification for all generic blocks. Similar to the case for the Component Reference, the table of contents of the Blocks Reference reflects the groups of each block selection in AI Editor. By using the links shown in Figure 5.6, you can access the blocks of each particular group.

Figure 5.6 Start page and table of contents of Blocks Reference

The entries on the individual generic blocks are relatively concise, as you can see from the example of the generic block `number` in Figure 5.7.

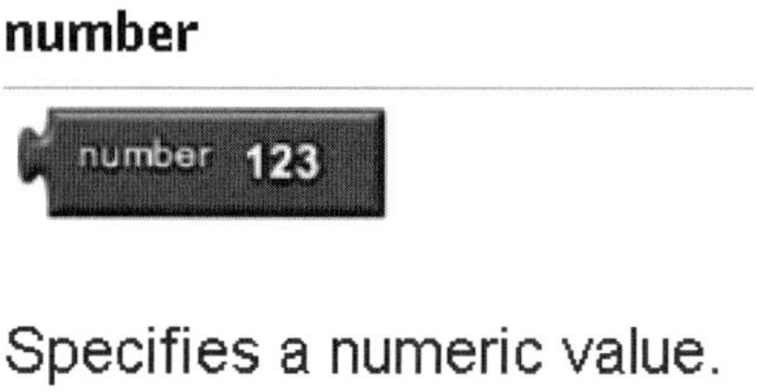

Figure 5.7 Specification of generic block "number" in Blocks Reference

While browsing the Blocks Reference, you are likely to stumble across an interesting block or two whose function you had completely forgotten during your development work or that gives you new ideas for expanding the functions of your own app. Make the most of these additional insights offered by the Blocks Reference.

Concepts Reference

In addition to the central references on AI components and blocks, a selection of other documents on important and basic *Concepts* (previously *Notes and Details*) is included with the AI References as third reference type. You can find these items within the general online documentation on AI.

> **Online Concepts Reference**
>
> Links to other documents providing additional info on AI topics are listed at:
> `http://experimental.appinventor.mit.edu/learn/reference/other/`

This reference type is more of a list of links to many other interesting documents pertaining to AI (see Figure 5.8). In this collection, you can find important notes and information on more complex topics that may prove useful, especially if you are just starting to discover a particular topic.

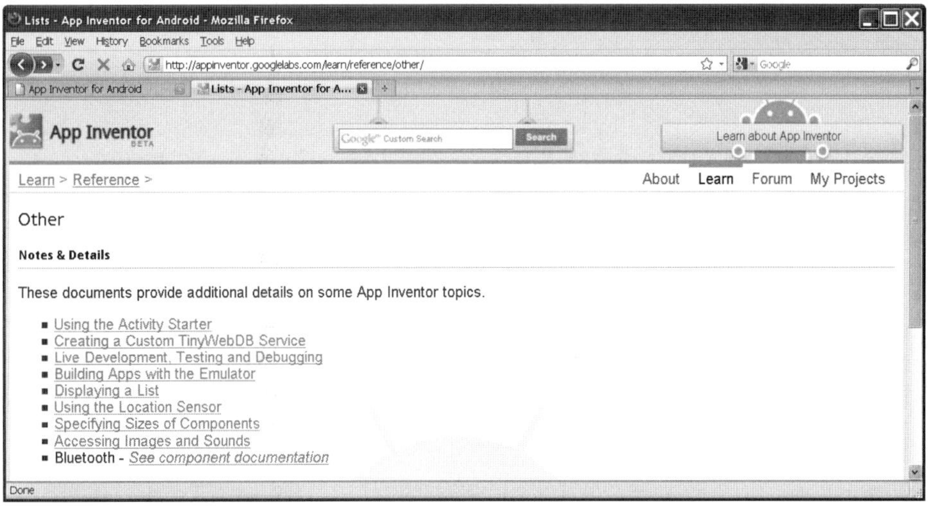

Figure 5.8 Start page and overview of Concepts Reference

Use this source as necessary while you are working with AI. We will also occasionally refer you to additional documentation in the rest of this book's chapters, as these sources may provide expanded and up-to-date information.

Chapter 6

Graphical User Interface

Equipped with the central basic terms and the AI References, we can now turn toward systematically working through the individual AI components and their properties, event handlers, and methods. We will not strictly follow the categories of the Palette in AI Designer or those of the Component Reference, but instead will form our own thematic categories through which we will discover increasingly demanding concepts for developing apps. Using small apps to demonstrate and illustrate a few selected component functions, you will gain a sense of the scope of AI's feature and be able to use them effectively for your own projects. You can easily gather information on any individual functions that we do not address explicitly by accessing the AI References and investigating any new functions that are added in the future to the constantly expanding AI feature range.

This chapter focuses on the graphical user interface, a topic relevant to all development and programming languages used to develop apps for graphical operating systems. AI provides a variety of graphical elements, such as buttons or text fields, that may seem familiar to you from other apps available on the Android Market. To illustrate the functionality of these elements for designing the user interface, we will use one of these components in a relatively pointless app and then gradually add other components to this app, demonstrating and discussing each of them in turn. In addition to their visual properties, the components have event blocks that are triggered in a component-specific way. We will demonstrate these event blocks in the demo app by displaying the name of each activated event block in the app. In other words, the event handler should display the name of the event setter block when an event occurs. Thus, if a button is pressed, we want the app to display the text "Button1.Click". To display text, AI offers the Label component.

Displaying Text with the Label Component

The main function of a label is to display a text. In earlier chapters, you added a label when you placed the message text "Please press the bag!" above the LaughButton in the LaughBag project. You also changed some of the initial properties of the label by editing the color and size of the text and the background color of the text field. With these initial properties and corresponding property blocks, you have already used all of the available features of the Label component; a quick glance at the Component Reference will confirm this. Although there are neither event blocks nor methods associated with a label, this component still provides some appealing text design options with which you can design your text output just as if you were using a text-editing program.

As mentioned earlier, we want to use a label in our demo app to display the name of each event block that reacts to an occurring event. We will take care of the various event blocks and events later in this chapter; for now, we simply want to start a new AI project and place the label as the first component object. Launch the AI Designer in your web browser and then open the AI Blocks Editor by clicking the "Open the Blocks Editor" button. If you like, you can also connect your smartphone via USB and integrate it into the AI IDE; alternatively, you can start the emulator. Go to the My Projects overview in AI Designer and open a new project by clicking on the New button. We will name all our demo apps with the prefix "demo_" so we can spot them more easily in the project overview. Our first demo project will have the name `demo_GUI`, as *GUI* is an acronym for *graphical user interface*.

Once the new demo project opens in AI Designer, you can use the Title property of "Screen1" to give the app the fitting name "Demo App: GUI." Now drag the Label component from the Palette group Basic into the Viewer, and rename the resulting component object "Label1" via the Rename button in the Components panel to "EventLabel." Next, change the default text "Text for Label1" in the Text label property three dots "..." so that the project now appears as shown in Figure 6.1.

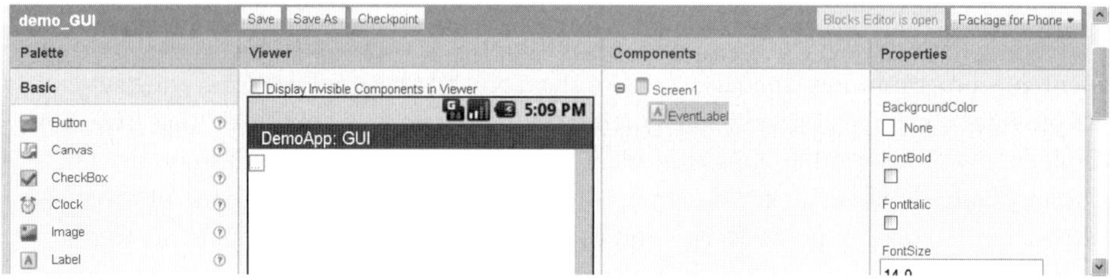

Figure 6.1 The project demo_GUI in its first stage

So far, the app `demo_GUI` does not look very exciting. To jazz it up a bit, we will add a second label showing a short static informative message on the dynamic EventLabel; we will separate this label from the other components we will add later. Drag another Label component into the Viewer, position the created component object above EventLabel, and name it "DivisionLabel1." To emphasize the character of a dividing line, set the initial properties of DivisionLabel1 to those shown in Table 6.1.

Table 6.1 **Edited Initial Properties of the Component Object DivisionLabel1**

Initial Property	New Value
BackgroundColor	Gray
Text	"Last active event block:"
TextColor	White
Width	Fill parent

Assignment in Efficient Table Form

To make things clearer, we will use tables more often in the remainder of this book to present assignments of all kinds in a compressed and efficient form. Please note that although text input as in the property field Text in Table 6.1 is shown enclosed by quotation marks in this book, that you should omit the quotation marks in AI Designer. In the table, we use the quotation marks simply to indicate that you need to enter some text at that point and cannot select an existing preset value, as is the case with the other entries.

After setting the initial properties to those listed in Table 6.1, our demo app should look like Figure 6.2. The setting "Fill parent" within the Width property causes the label to stretch horizontally across the entire screen, so it acts as a separator. This role is emphasized by the negative text color (white on gray) that optically stands out from the components to be added later.

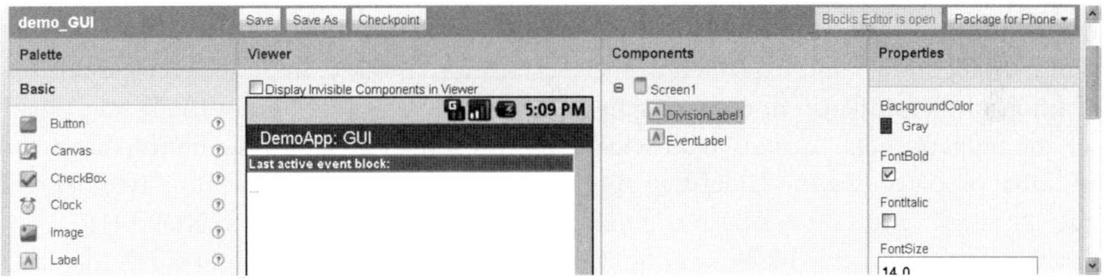

Figure 6.2 The project "demo_GUI" with the two labels

This concludes the first step of our demo project. In AI Editor the event setter block `set EventLabel.Text to` is now available (see Figure 6.3), which we will need later for displaying the currently active event block.

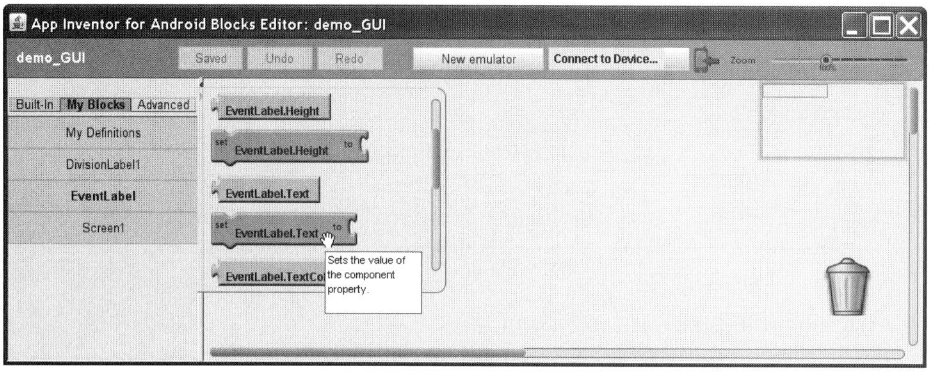

Figure 6.3 Event setter block "set EventLabel.Text to"

Now we can turn to the next component to add to our demo project `demo_GUI`.

Triggering Actions with the Button Component

Now we want to add a Button component to our demo project `demo_GUI`. Of course, we have already dealt with buttons extensively in earlier examples. The button, as one of the most frequently used elements of graphical user interfaces, serves as an intuitive user element in its many forms. The user can start actions with the button or confirm answers to queries. By adding text or even images to a button, you can use this component in a multifaceted way in a great variety of contexts—for example, as the interactive laugh bag in our LaughBag app. The Button component also has a multitude of properties, as shown in Figure 5.3 and explained in the specification in the Component Reference. In addition to the properties for text design (similar to those available for a label), you can see the property field "Image," with which you can add an image to the button, both as an initial property (see the LaughBag app) and during runtime via the property block `set Button1.Image to`. Also intriguing is the option of using the initial property Enabled or the property block `set Button1.Enabled to` for displaying a grayed-out button, signifying that it is disabled. This option is often used when a function is available only after certain conditions have been met—for example, an OK button may become active only after the user has selected an option. This approach is commonly used as an alternative to displaying and hiding options via the Visible property.

In contrast to the label, the button is an interactive element of the graphical user interface and, therefore, has blocks for event handling. We have already used the event block `when Button1.Click do` in the LaughBag app, describing it in the section on events and event handlers. This event block takes on the generic functions of a button—namely, recognizing and reacting to being clicked on. In addition to this event, the button component recognizes two other events: when the button has the focus (`when Button1.GotFocus do`) and when the focus changes to a different object (`when Button1.LostFocus do`). "Focus" in this context means, for example, switching between the selectable elements of a user interface via the arrow keys or a joystick, without selecting and at the same time activating the selected item by pressing it with the mouse button or finger. Such events are relevant if, for example, the button that has the focus is meant to display a short explanatory text before the button is pressed.

In our demo project, we want to explore the button by using its typical event block `when Button1.Click do`. Drag the Button component from the palette group Basic into the Viewer, position the resulting component object above "DivisionLabel1" and leave the name set to the default "Button1." To make the display of different events in the EventLabel clearer in later iterations of the app, drag another button into the viewer, place it beneath Button1, and retain its default name "Button2." Our demo project now looks like in Figure 6.4.

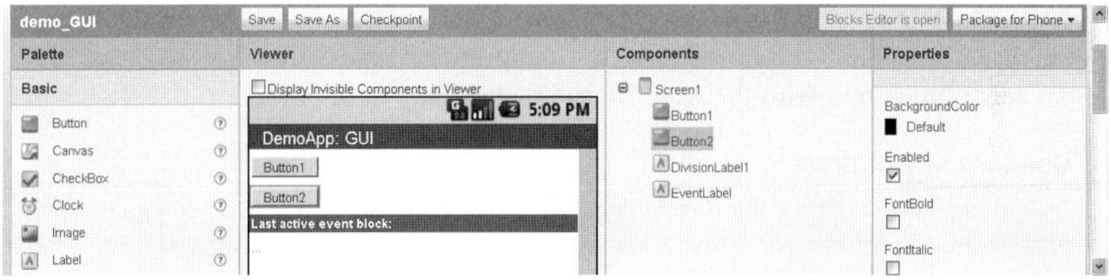

Figure 6.4 The project "demo_GUI" with two additional buttons

Now we want to determine the modest functions of the two buttons within our project `demo_GUI`. You first need to go to the AI Editor. In the block selection under My Blocks, you can now see the two component objects Button1 and Button2. Depending on which button is being pressed later, we want the EventLabel to display the event block name as text, "Button1.Click" or "Button2.Click."

Let's first create the event handler for Button1. Click in the block selection on the block name "Button1" to open the slide-out panel, and then drag the event block `when Button1.Click do` into the Editor. In the next step, this event block is filled with a corresponding block structure as its event handler. As part of this change, we want to assign a new text to the EventLabel. We will use the property setter block `set EventLabel.Text to`, which you can find under the block name "EventLabel." Drag the property block from the slide-out panel into the Editor and position it in the event block so that the former slots into the latter. Now you still need to assign the desired text "Button1.Click" to the property block. You do this by creating a generic text block, which you can find in the block selection under Built-In as first entry in the Text group, similar to the number block we used earlier to specify the duration of the vibration. Drag the text block text into the Editor, position it next to the property block, and slot the plug into the socket. Now you can edit the default text "text" by clicking on it and changing it to "Button1.Click." Your event handler `when Button1.Click do` should now look like Figure 6.5.

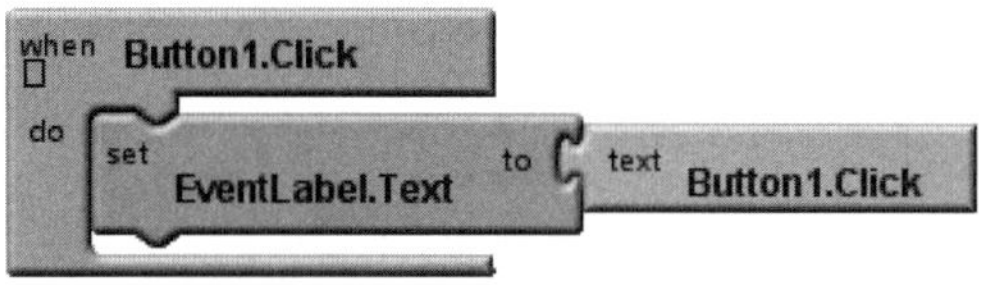

Figure 6.5 The event handler for displaying "Button1.Click" in the EventLabel

To make things clearer, we will express the event handler shown in Figure 6.5 once more in pseudocode:

```
When Button1 is clicked, do set the EventLabel to the text "Button1.Click"!
```

Now you can develop the same event handler for Button2. Drag the event block `Button2.Click` into the Editor, slot it into the property setter `EventLabel.Text`, and assign a text block text with the text "Button2.Click" to the setter.

Condensed Notation

As you may have noticed, our descriptions are becoming more efficient as you gain experience in dealing with components. Some component objects—such as `Button1.Click`—are clearly described as event blocks even without the surrounding keywords `when` and `do`, while others—such as the property block `EventLabel.Text`—are more or less clearly recognizable as setters from their context. Try to get used to this more condensed notation on your way to becoming an app developer, because good development has a lot to do with efficiency. While at first you had to consciously think about how to assign components clearly, you will find it becomes increasingly easier in the course of the projects to come in this book, until eventually it becomes second nature.

Now that we have added the second event handler to the project `demo_GUI`, the exemplary use of the Button component is complete. In the AI Editor, your project should now look like in Figure 6.6.

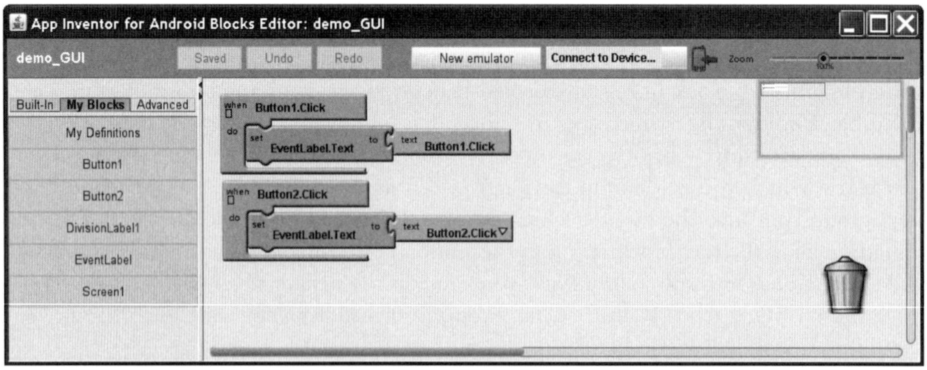

Figure 6.6 Event handlers for both buttons in the project "demo_GUI"

If you have not yet tested the current function range of `demo_GUI`, do so now. Figure 6.7 shows what the app currently looks like in the emulator.

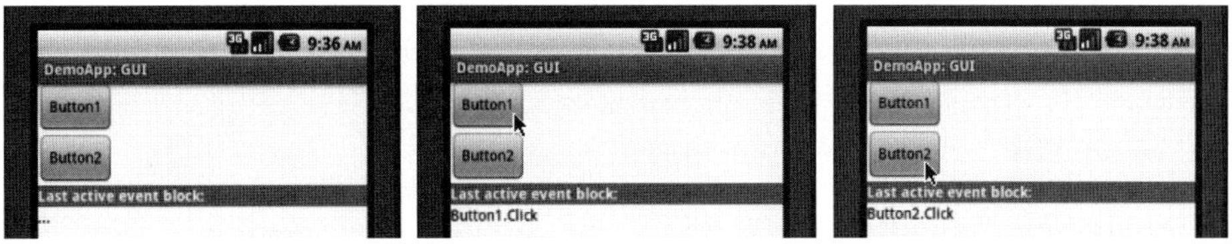

Figure 6.7 Interactive display of current events in the app "demo_GUI"

While the EventLabel still has the three dots as its initial text (on the left) when you start the app in Figure 6.7, pressing Button1 displays the text "Button1.Click" (center) and pressing Button2 displays the text "Button2.Click" (on the right). Thus, at this stage in the app's development, the functionality of the demo app comprises two event handlers, each of which changes the property of a central text field.

Selecting Options with the CheckBox Component

A check box is a commonly used instrument within graphical user interfaces that users can select (or not) to change and check settings in an application. By clicking on the check box, you can enable a setting with a green check mark; to disable it, you click on the check box again. The green check mark is a clear indicator for the user of which settings are currently enabled and which are not. These settings, in turn, determine specific aspects of the app's function. For example, in your Android smartphone you will find numerous check boxes in the Settings menu that you can use to enable or disable button tones, notifications, or, for example, the screen lock. The check box indicates the state of the relevant setting option; that is, it shows whether the option is enabled (*true*) or not (*false*). In programming logic, these two states (true and false) are referred to as *Boolean* values and are often used as the basis for decisions in the program routine. In the course of this book we will encounter other logical structures in Chapter 9, but here we want to concentrate on the two "integral" states of the CheckBox component.

If you look at the initial properties or the specification of the CheckBox component (see Figure 6.8), you can see that the properties available for designing the check box, including the text field positioned on the right side of it, are similar to those available for buttons. A special feature of the check box is the Value property, which represents the Boolean value mentioned previously. If the initial property Value is not set (not checked), its value is `false`; if it is set, its value is `true`. Later you can examine the AI Designer's Viewer as well as the integrated smartphone or emulator to see how the green check mark in the check box displayed is either shown or hidden, depending on the setting of the initial property.

CheckBox

☐ Supersize

Check box components can detect user taps and can change their boolean state in response.

A check box component raises an event when the user taps it. There are many properties affecting its appearance that can be set in the Designer or Blocks Editor.

Properties

`BackgroundColor`
    Color for check box background.
`Enabled`
    If set, user can tap check box to cause action.
`Value`
    True if the box is checked, false otherwise.
`Height`
    Check box height (y-size).
`Width`
    Check box width (x-size).
`Text`
    Text to display on check box.
`TextColor`
    Color for check box text.
`Visible`
    If set, check box is visible.

Events

`Click()`
    User tapped and released check box.
`GotFocus()`
    Check box became the focused component.
`LostFocus()`
    Check box stopped being the focused component.

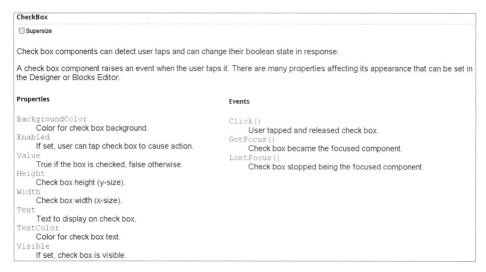

Figure 6.8 Specification of the CheckBox component

In handling events, the event blocks of the check box are mostly identical to those of the button. Again you have three event blocks available, reacting to the check box being clicked (`CheckBox1.Changed`), having the focus (`CheckBox1.GotFocus`), and losing the focus (`CheckBox1.LostFocus`).

Occasional Documentation Delay in Case of Changes

If you look at the block selection in the AI Editor, you will notice that the first event block of the CheckBox component no longer has the keyword `Click` as in Figure 6.8, but instead says "Changed." The specification here seems to lag behind the rapid changes in AI, yet the description of the function is still accurate. Thus you cannot always blindly trust the information in the Component Reference; sometimes the changes are applied directly to the AI IDE and added to the documentation only later.

We now want to see the CheckBox component live in action in our demo project `demo_GUI`. When we click on the check box, we want the app to display both the event in the usual form with the name of the event setter block and its current Boolean value. Drag the CheckBox component from the palette group Basic in AI Designer into the Viewer between Button2 and DivisionLabel1. In the initial properties of the resulting component object CheckBox1, you change just the label in the "Text" field to "CheckBox1." All other properties can remain the same—even the name of the component object. To demonstrate the initial property Value, drag a second CheckBox component into the Viewer below CheckBox1. Use the "Text" field to label this new component as "CheckBox2" and enable the Value property field with a check mark. The second check box now appears preselected and with a green check mark both in the Viewer and on your connected smartphone, as shown in Figure 6.9.

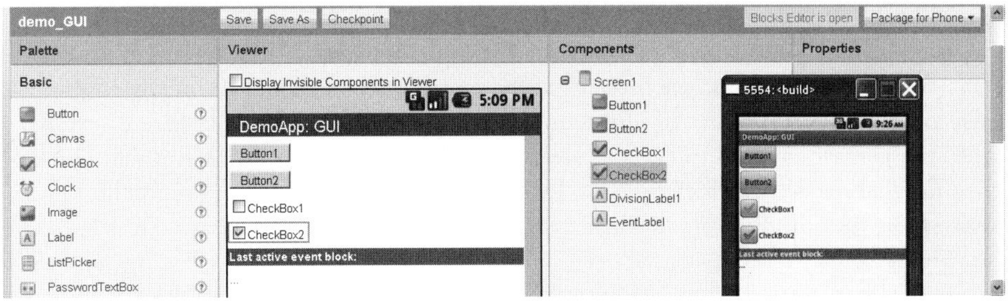

Figure 6.9 Two check boxes with and without preselected property Value

In the next step, we will integrate the two check boxes into the event mechanism of the demo app `demo_GUI`. Similar to the case for the buttons created earlier, we want a corresponding text to be displayed in the EventLabel if we click on one of the check boxes. Let's start with CheckBox1. Go to the AI Editor and the block selection My Blocks. In the block group "CheckBox1," drag the event block `when CheckBox1.Changed do` into the Editor. To display the name of the active event block, take another event setter block `set EventLabel.Text to` from the block group "EventLabel" and slot it into the event block `CheckBox1.Changed` (see Figure 6.10).

Figure 6.10 Preparation for writing the event block name in EventLabel

Note on Incomplete Event Handlers

In Figure 6.10, you can see a yellow exclamation mark icon on the puzzle piece of the event block between the keyword `when` and `CheckBox1.Changed`. This icon is used in AI Editor to indicate that something is not quite right with your block structure. If you move the mouse pointer over the exclamation mark, AI displays additional text to explain what is wrong. In this case, it displays the message, "Warning: This clump contains an empty socket and won't be sent to the phone." This warning tells you that the event handler is incomplete and will not be sent to the smartphone in its current state. This is only one of many support functions that AI offers during your app development.

Now we could just add a generic text block and use it to assign the name of the enabled event block to the `EventLabel.Text` by entering text "CheckBox1.Changed." In this demo, however, we want to add the current Boolean value of CheckBox1 to the name text. We get this value from the property getter block `CheckBox1.Value`, which we also find in the block group "CheckBox1." To add the current Boolean value to the text "CheckBox1.Changed" and form a complete sentence "CheckBox1.Changed with the value [Value]," we expand the text block text to "CheckBox1.Changed with the value " (note the whitespace at the end of the text passage) and join it directly to the value of `CheckBox1.Value`. To join (concatenate) text passages into a coherent text, AI offers the generic method call `make text` in the group Text within the Built-In block selection (see also Blocks Reference > Text Blocks > make text). Drag the method `make text` into the Editor and slot it into the property setter block `EventLabel.Text` (see Figure 6.11).

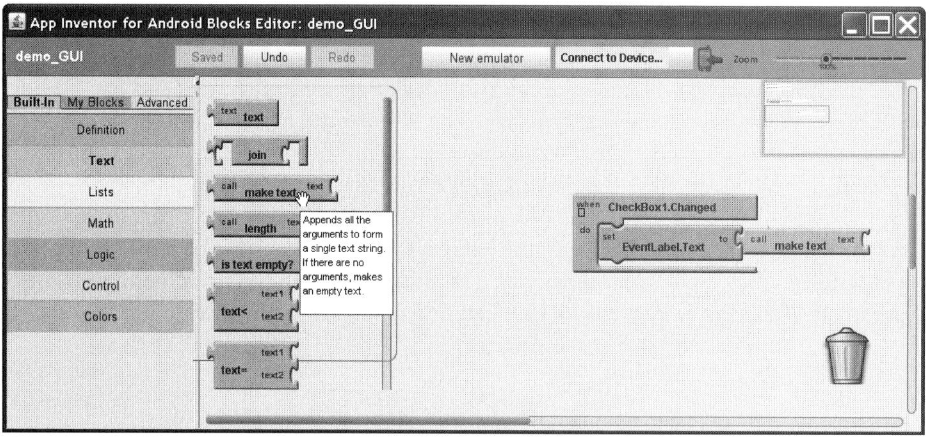

Figure 6.11 Adding the generic method "make text" for joining text

The method `make text` serves as a kind of joining piece into which you can slot the individual text passages. Do not be surprised that the method initially has only a single socket joint. Each time you add a text passage, the puzzle piece will dynamically grow a new socket. First slot the text block with the expanded text "CheckBox1.Changed with value " into the method. Into the now available second socket, you then slot the property getter block `CheckBox1.Checked` (see Figure 6.12).

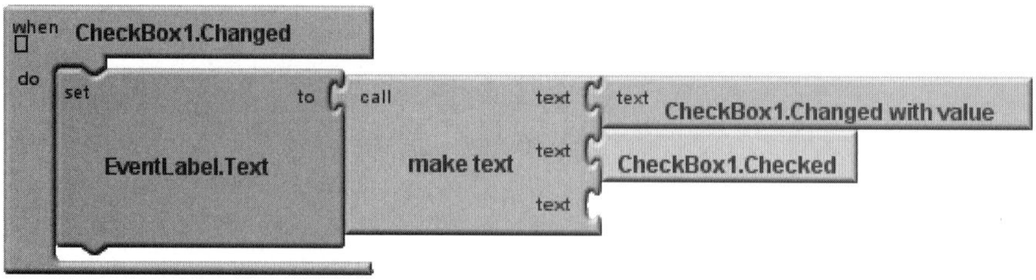

Figure 6.12 Joined text from event block + state value for label display

This completes the description and development of the functionality of CheckBox1. You can now observe the changing text display on your connected smartphone or emulator each time you click on the check box. To clarify, we will express this event handler in pseudocode:

```
When CheckBox1 is clicked, do join the value of text block text to that of
CheckBox1.Value into a coherent text and display it in EventLabel!
```

Now you can add the same functionality or block structure for the second check box with the object name CheckBox2 to our current demo project. The complete block structure of `demo_GUI` is shown in Figure 6.13.

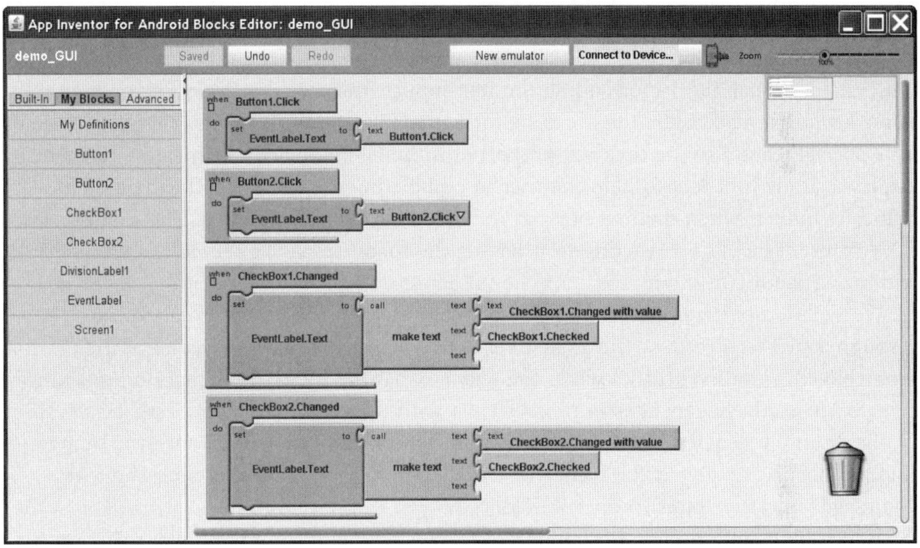

Figure 6.13 The demo project with two interactive buttons and check boxes

This gives you two more interactive elements in the user interface. If you go to the demo app on your smartphone, the text field now tells you not only which check box was last clicked, but also its current Boolean value, as shown in the emulator in Figure 6.14.

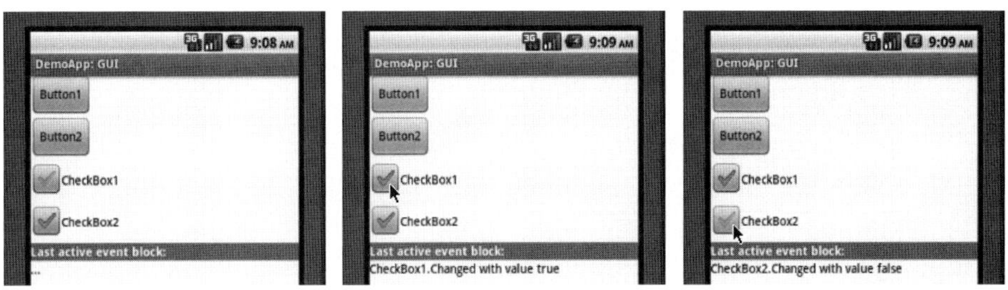

Figure 6.14 The two check boxes in action, displaying their Boolean values

On launching the demo app `demo_GUI` in Figure 6.14, only CheckBox2 is enabled (left). The first click on CheckBox1 enables it and displays the event setter block, including the current Boolean value "true" (center), while the first click on CheckBox2 disables it and displays the event block with the Boolean value "false" (right). With this step you have expanded the functionality of the demo app to four event handlers in total and gotten your first taste of dynamic program states.

Entering Text with the TextBox Component

An important and central function of the graphical user interface is providing a method for receiving text input by the app user. AI offers the TextBox component in the Basic group for that purpose. The user can enter any text into the text box, and then the text can be processed, analyzed, or used in many ways by the app. Often the user is provided with an additional button for ending the text input, similar to the Enter key on a computer keyboard. The entered text can be formatted as usual with various property fields. One special feature in the text box properties is the "Hint" field, which can be used to display a subtle hint text to help the user in completing the text field; this hint is automatically hidden when the text box has the focus for entering the text. The text box also has two event blocks for reacting to it having the focus (`when TextBox.GotFocus do`) and losing the focus (`when TextBox.LostFocus do`).

We will demonstrate the text box functionality within the demo project `demo_GUI` through a two-step process. In the first step, we will again display the name of the event setter block in the EventLabel when the text box has the focus. Implementing this functionality is relatively easy after our experience with the earlier examples. First go to AI Designer and drag a TextBox component from the Palette group Basic into the Viewer under CheckBox2, give it the name "TextBox" (see Figure 6.15), and enter the text "Message" into the "Hint" property field. Now you can develop the event handler in the AI Editor by dragging the event block `TextBox.GotFocus` from the block selection My Blocks into the Editor. Now slot it as usual into the event block `EventLabel.Text`, and pass it a text block `text` with the value "TextBox.GotFocus" (see Figure 6.16). You have now implemented the usual display function in the EventLabel. If you test your demo app on your smartphone or the emulator, you will notice that Android automatically displays the default keyboard for entering text when the text field has the focus. Close it after entering the text (with the usual close key) so that you can check the event display in the EventLabel without it being covered by the keyboard.

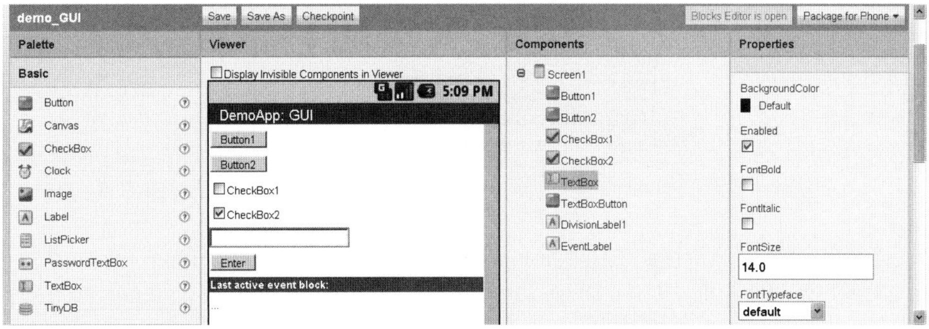

Figure 6.15 Adding components to demonstrate creation of a text box

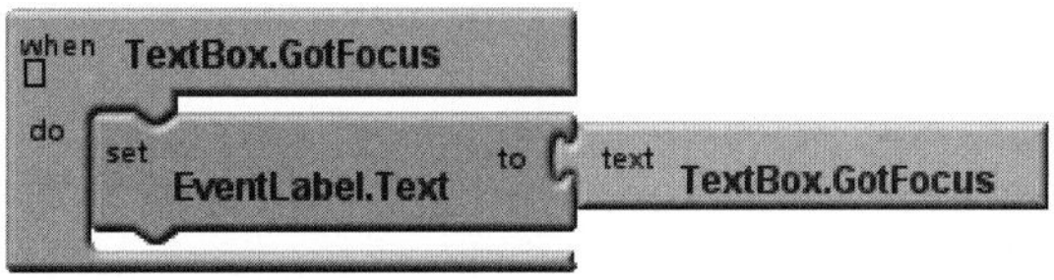

Figure 6.16 Displaying the event setter block in the EventLabel

In the second step of our text box demonstration, we want the text entered by the user to be displayed in the EventLabel. We cannot achieve this display with the event block `TextBox.GotFocus` (it would overwrite the text "TextBox.GotFocus") or `TextBox.LostFocus` (it would be overwritten by the next activated event block); instead, we need another event block. As mentioned earlier, text input is often ended by pressing an Enter button. We now want to add an additional button and use its event block to output the text entered into the text box in the EventLabel. Drag a new button in AI Designer under the TextBox, name it "TextBoxButton," and write the text "Enter" onto it (see Figure 6.15). In the AI Editor, you can now drag the matching event block `TextBlockButton.Click` into the Editor and slot it into the property block `EventLabel.Text`. The latter now does not get a text block as its input value, but rather the value from the property block `TextBox.Text`, which contains the current user input from the text box (see Figure 6.17).

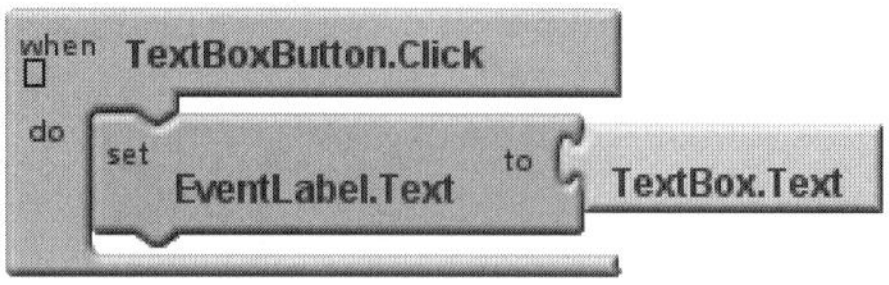

Figure 6.17 Displaying the user input from the text box in the EventLabel

With the block structure shown in Figure 6.17, the instruction to output the entered text from the check box in the label when the Enter button is pressed is complete. Expressed in pseudocode, it would read like this:

```
When the TextBoxButton is pressed, do assign to EventLabel the current input
value from TextBox!
```

Figure 6.18 shows the text box with its Enter key in action in the emulator. While the TextBox still shows the "Message" as its initial property in the "Hint" field when the demo app `demo_GUI` is launched (left), giving the focus to the TextBox causes three actions to occur almost simultaneously: The message text disappears, the activated event block appears in the EventLabel, and the Android keyboard pops up (center). After the user enters a text (for example, "hello"), this text is displayed in the EventLabel once the user presses the TextBox button (right).

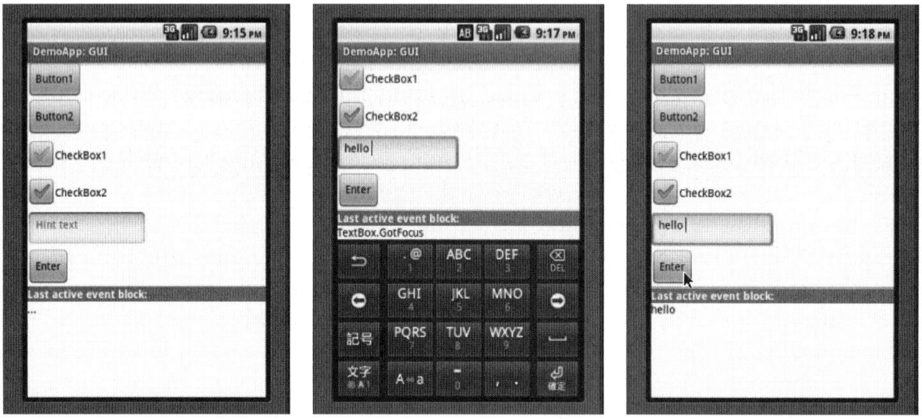

Figure 6.18 Displaying the event block and text input from the text box

By expanding the demo project, you have not only demonstrated the text box but also laid the foundation for your future development work: You now know how to receive and process user text input.

Switch Android Keyboard in the Emulator to Another Language

The default setting for the emulator has the Android keyboard set to the U.S. English keyboard layout. If you want to set the keyboard to another layout or another language, you can do so in the emulator just as you would on your smartphone. Close the demo app in the emulator with the Menu key, and then call up the Application Overview on the home screen. Now click on the app icon "Settings" and scroll to "Language & keyboard." Click on this menu to display the submenu "Select language," and choose the language to be used on the emulator. Disable all check boxes for languages you do not want to select and return to the home screen. If you now restart the app by clicking on the button "Restart app on device" in the AI Blocks Editor, you will see the new keyboard layout when you select the text box. To switch back to a QWERTY keyboard, proceed as above and set "Select language" back to "English (United States)" (see Figure 6.19). By the way, you can also type the text directly via your computer keyboard instead of painstakingly clicking on the virtual emulator keyboard.

Figure 6.19 Setting the emulator back to English QWERTY keyboard

Entering Confidential Text with the PasswordTextBox Component

As you might guess from the title of this section, AI offers an interesting variation on the text box functionality for confidential text information; this component is also found in the Basic group. Whereas the previously described TextBox component shows the text in plain text during and after user input, you can use the component PasswordTextBox to render the text unreadable by displaying a number of dots corresponding to the number of characters entered. As the component name suggests, this choice is especially suitable for entering any kind of password that you do not want others to see. You can imagine numerous specific examples where this capability would be useful.

As the functionality of the password box is largely identical to that of the text box, we will just briefly demonstrate the password box with the same two-step mechanism in the demo project as used in the previous section. The interesting thing is that, once the user completes his or her input by pressing the Enter button, the entered text will be readable only in the EventLabel. Thus we want to create a password box and another Enter button for the user and depict their functionality once again with two event handlers. Drag the component PasswordTextBox from the Basic group in AI Designer into the Viewer under the last button and rename the resulting component object to "PasswordTextBox." Offer the user-friendly hint "Password" in the "Hint" property field. Now add another button ("PasswordButton") under the password box, on which you also write "Enter." The user interface of the project `demo_GUI` now appears as shown in Figure 6.20.

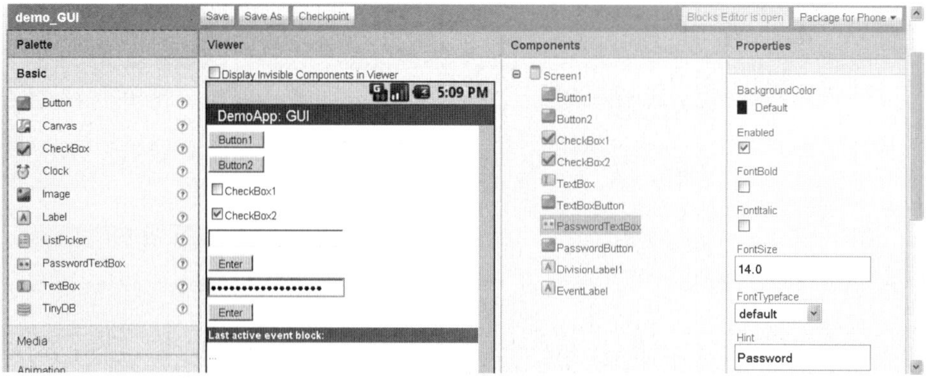

Figure 6.20 Adding a password box and Enter button to the demo project

The two event handlers for displaying the focus event of the password box and displaying the text entered by the user are almost identical to those used for the text box in the preceding section. For the first event handler, drag the event block `PasswordTextBox.GotFocus` (see the block selection under My Blocks in AI Editor) into the Editor, slot a property block `EventLabel.Text` into it, and add a text block "PasswordTextBox.GotFocus" (see Figure 6.21, top).

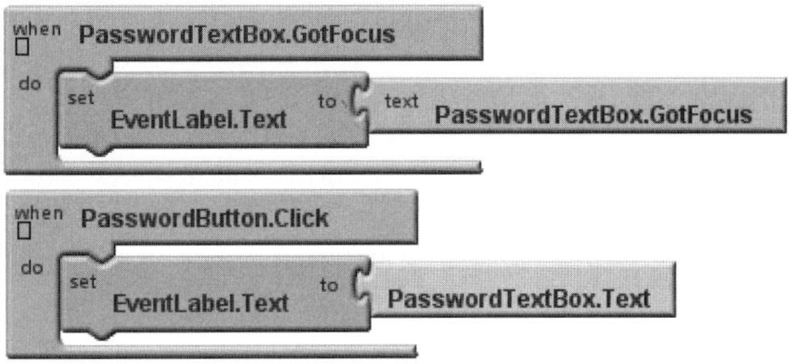

Figure 6.21 Event handlers for displaying an event block and password

The second event handler also follows the same procedure as demonstrated earlier for the text box and reads the hidden input text when the user presses a button. Drag the event block for the second Enter button, `PasswordButton.Click`, into the Editor and slot `EventLabel.Text` into it, to which you assign the content of `PasswordTextBox.Text` (see Figure 6.21, bottom). The functionality of the password box is now analogous to that of the text box described previously. If the user now gives the focus to the password box with its hint text (left) in the demo app shown in Figure 6.22 and enters some text, the event setter block is displayed in the EventLabel and each letter of the entered text in the password box is represented only as a dot (center). Only if the user presses the corresponding Enter button does its event handler become activated and display the password in the EventLabel in plain text (right).

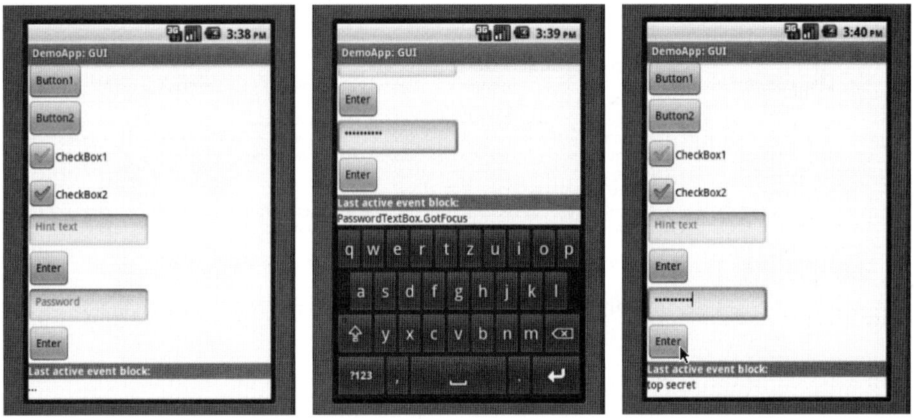

Figure 6.22 Input and displaying the password "top secret" in the demo app

By taking advantage of this additional option of receiving text input from the user without others seeing it, you can use AI to develop suitable user interfaces even for apps dealing with critical data. This level of security, of course, extends only to stopping others from reading the text, but implicitly offers numerous security measures. For example, you can use a password to protect access to a function or even the whole app, or to enter confidential information via hidden input for internal processing. For the user, the password box is the visible expression of a security concept, whichever form it may take. Do not underestimate this effect; many users find security concerns very important.

Displaying Notices and Alerts with the Notifier Component

In certain situations, it can be useful to notify the user of a particular fact. If a simple message text within a label does not seem appropriate or sufficient, AI offers the Notifier component in the group "Other stuff"; you can use this component to display especially important information in a pop-up window. While the pop-up window is open, the app itself can no longer be used, forcing the user to deal with the notifier in a manner depending on the component method used by the developer. The user either has to wait until the notifier disappears automatically (`ShowAlert`), or has to confirm the notifier explicitly by pressing an OK button (`ShowMessageDialog`), choosing between two alternative buttons (`ShowChooseDialog`), or entering some text (`ShowTextDialog`), as described in the Component Reference extract shown in Figure 6.23.

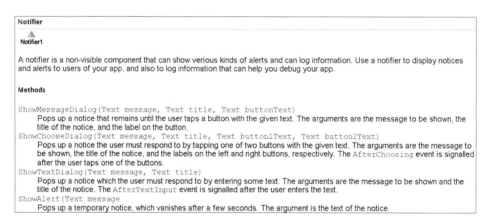

Notifier

Notifier1

A notifier is a non-visible component that can show verious kinds of alerts and can log information. Use a notifier to display notices and alerts to users of your app, and also to log information that can help you debug your app.

Methods

`ShowMessageDialog(Text message, Text title, Text buttonText)`
Pops up a notice that remains until the user taps a button with the given text. The arguments are the message to be shown, the title of the notice, and the label on the button.

`ShowChooseDialog(Text message, Text title, Text button1Text, Text button2Text)`
Pops up a notice the user must respond to by tapping one of two buttons with the given text. The arguments are the message to be shown, the title of the notice, and the labels on the left and right buttons, respectively. The `AfterChoosing` event is signalled after the user taps one of the buttons.

`ShowTextDialog(Text message, Text title)`
Pops up a notice which the user must respond to by entering some text. The arguments are the message to be shown and the title of the notice. The `AfterTextInput` event is signalled after the user enters the text.

`ShowAlert(Text message`
Pops up a temporary notice, which vanishes after a few seconds. The argument is the text of the notice.

Figure 6.23 Extract from the Component Reference: the Notifier component

In addition to these methods, the Notifier component is accompanied by two event blocks with which it can either react to one of two buttons being chosen (`AfterChoosing`) or process the text entered in the dialog (`AfterTextInput`). The Notifier component also has special `LogError` methods that support app development work by providing expanded debugging capabilities (alerts in case of program errors), but not any functionality in the app itself. Interestingly, the Notifier is a non-visible component (like the Sound component we used in the LaughBag app), as it is not visible immediately in the app, but rather is displayed only in reaction to an event.

We want to illustrate the Notifier component and its functionality by using it within our demo project `demo_GUI`. After addressing the importance of security aspects in the previous section, we can now expand on this theme by including a notifier window. After all, it makes sense to alert the user regarding safe use of passwords. Once the user has entered his or her password in the PasswordTextBox as in the preceding example and pressed the PasswordButton, the password is displayed in plain text in the EventLabel. When the user presses the PasswordButton, we now want to alert the carefree user of the fact that his or her password is being displayed visible to anyone (so the user can, for example, press another button to obscure the display again). For that purpose, we want to display a pop-up window with the title "Security advice!" and the message "Your password is displayed below.", which the user then has to confirm explicitly by pressing an OK button to close the window.

To implement this function, drag the Notifier component in AI Designer from the component group "Other stuff" into the Viewer. As a non-visible component, Notifier is displayed below the Viewer area (see Figure 6.24). The Notifier component does not have any initial properties, so your only task in AI Designer is to rename the resulting component object as "Notifier."

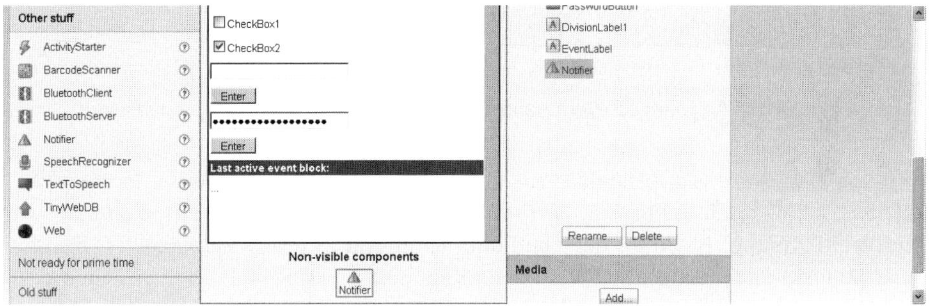

Figure 6.24 The non-visible component Notifier in AI Designer

The development work per se happens in the AI Editor. Because we want the alert to pop up when the user presses the PasswordButton, we do not need an extra event block, but simply add the method `Notifier.ShowMessageDialog` to the existing event handler `PasswordButton.Click` (see Figure 6.21, bottom). We pass it three texts as parameters for the `title`, the `message`, and the button (`buttonText`) of the alert window. Our aim is to develop the functionality expressed in pseudocode as follows:

```
When the PasswordButton is pressed, then do
  assign EventLabel the input value of TextBox and
  call Notifier.ShowMessageDialog with the parameters
    message "Your password is displayed below." and
    title "Security advice!" and
   buttonText "OK"!
```

The indentation in the pseudocode visually indicates the hierarchical relationships between the individual lines of the pseudocode. All entries with the same indent level are on the same hierarchy level and belong as subordinates to the next higher level. This view and notation are already quite close to those used in classic programming languages. In the visual development language AI, the functionality of the event handler appears as shown in Figure 6.25.

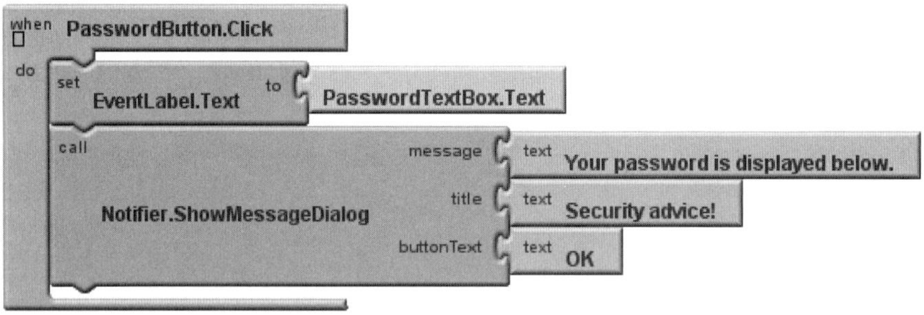

Figure 6.25 Expanded event handler with alert about the displayed password

If you have not already assembled the block structure shown in Figure 6.25 yourself, here is how to do it. Drag the method `Notifier.ShowMessageDialog` in the My Blocks group of AI Editor into the Editor and slot it in below `EventLabel.Text`. Next, you add three text blocks with the corresponding text passages to the method as parameters in the relevant sockets. You have now successfully developed the functionality described previously and can try it in practice within the expanded demo app `demo_GUI` (see Figure 6.26).

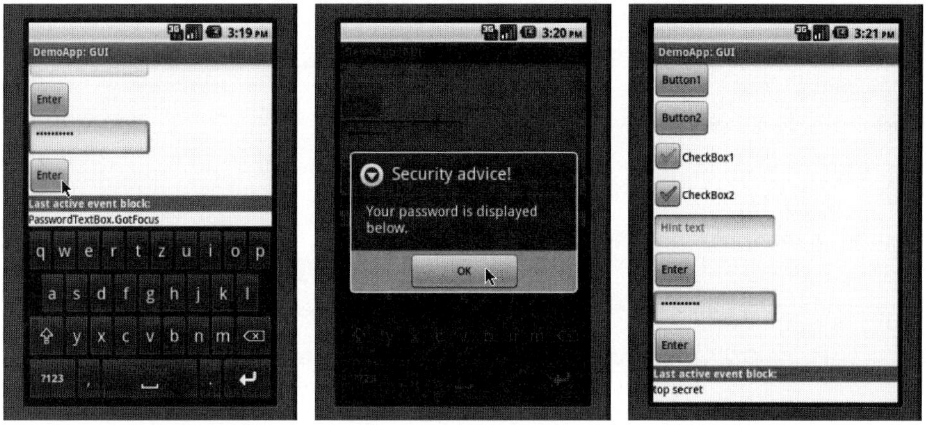

Figure 6.26 Displaying the alert after entering the password

With the pop-up alert shown in Figure 6.26, our demo app has now gained another typical feature of a graphical user interface. In addition, you have seen how simple it is to add other functions to event handlers and to then call them collectively. It really is impressive how easily the graphic elements in AI can be used as building blocks of a professional user interface.

Tidying the Screen with the Screen Arrangement Components

When the number of graphical elements on the app's user interface reaches a certain point, it becomes necessary to arrange them in some kind of order on the screen. Even in our demo app `demo_GUI`, we may already need to scroll to see everything depending on the screen size, and the user elements listed below one another look messy because there is no clear structure. You should not underestimate how this aspect of the app influences its appeal. Often an app that looks clearly structured gives a more professional impression than one in which the user interface was designed following only functional criteria, not ergonomic ones. This is one of the reasons why the AI IDE gives you a Designer, where you can manage this design task. In the Palette of AI Designer, you can see a Screen Arrangement component group with which you can flexibly arrange the graphical elements of the user interface and break up the rather linear appearance of the graphical elements (which are currently listed below one another). In this section, we will demonstrate all three components within this group at once (see Figure 6.27) by tidying up the appearance of the demo app `demo_GUI`.

Figure 6.27 Three components for arranging the graphical user interface

> **Additional Information in the AI "Concepts Reference"**
>
> In addition to the specification of the component group Screen Arrangement in the Component Reference, another document relevant to screen design—"Specifying Sizes of Components"—is available online within the Concepts Reference. Here you can find a description of size setting criteria for the properties Width and Height in general, but also in particular for the components of the Screen Arrangement group. You can find this document at:
>
> `http://experimental.appinventor.mit.edu/learn/reference/other/sizes.html`

Although the description of the three components in the group Screen Arrangement in the AI References might seem a bit overwhelming, they are really easy and intuitive to use. All three components serve to spatially arrange other graphical elements of the user interface on the screen of the Android device. The Screen Arrangement components form the frame into which the other elements can be placed, similar to little tables in a text editing or table calculation program (see Figure 6.27). As the component names indicate, the elements can be arranged next to each other (`HorizontalArrangement`), below one another (`VerticalArrangement`), or in a particular matrix (`TableArrangement`) of x columns and y rows, where you can also set the height and width of the cells. AI also allows almost unlimited *nesting* of these three components in all kinds of combinations, thereby meeting practically all conceivable design wishes.

Designing the screen arrangement is mainly done directly in the AI Designer's Viewer. Using the mouse, you can easily arrange and nest the individual components and place the graphical elements of the user interface into them. The Screen Arrangement components are shown in the Viewer as outlines. These outlines are not visible in the finished app; instead, only the elements they contain appear in the appropriate position. Let's implement these theoretical comments straight away as examples in our demo app. You need only the AI Designer (not the AI Editor) for this task, as the arranging work is purely a design task. We start with the initial version of our demo app `demo_GUI`, as shown in Figure 6.28.

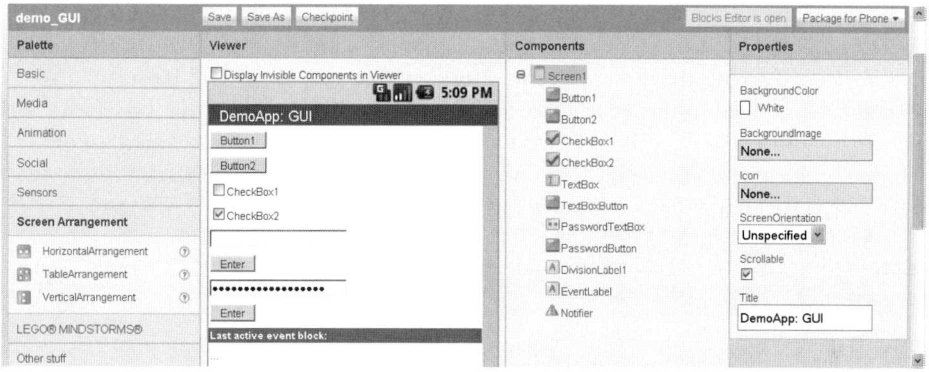

Figure 6.28 Arrangement of screen elements in the initial state of an app

We begin by dragging the table-shaped arrangement component TableArrangement into the Viewer and placing it right at the top above Button1. For the table arrangement, we need just the four default cells; thus we include two columns (Columns, `x`) and two rows (Rows, `y`), as shown in Figure 6.29, in the properties of the resulting component object TableArrangement1. We can then drag the desired elements of the user interface into the TableArrangement1 and place them in the appropriate locations. To do this, click on the relevant component object in the Viewer, hold the mouse button, and drag the object into the TableArrangement1 marked with a green outline. While dragging, the TableArrangement1 uses a blue border to indicate the cell where the dragged component object will be inserted when you drop it. In Figure 6.29, we are dropping Button1 in the top left cell (`x=1` and `y=1`).

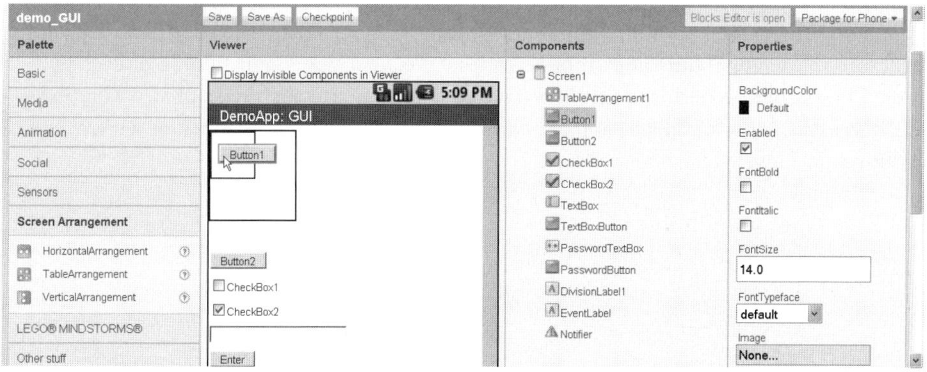

Figure 6.29 Placing Button1 at the top left of TableArrangement1

In the same way, you can now move Button2 into cell 1,2; CheckBox1 into cell 2,1; and CheckBox2 into cell 2,2. If you find that the horizontal distance between the buttons and the check boxes is too small, you can insert an additional column in between them or change the size of the cells in the property field Width from "Automatic" to the desired number of pixels. AI gives you great design freedom. To finish our work, we add two horizontal arrangement components, HorizontalArrangement1 and HorizontalArrangement2, and add to them the TextBox with the TextBoxButton or the PasswordTextBox with the PasswordButton, respectively. The newly designed user interface of the demo app now appears a lot more tidy, structured, and space efficient, as you can see clearly by comparing Figure 6.30 with Figure 6.28.

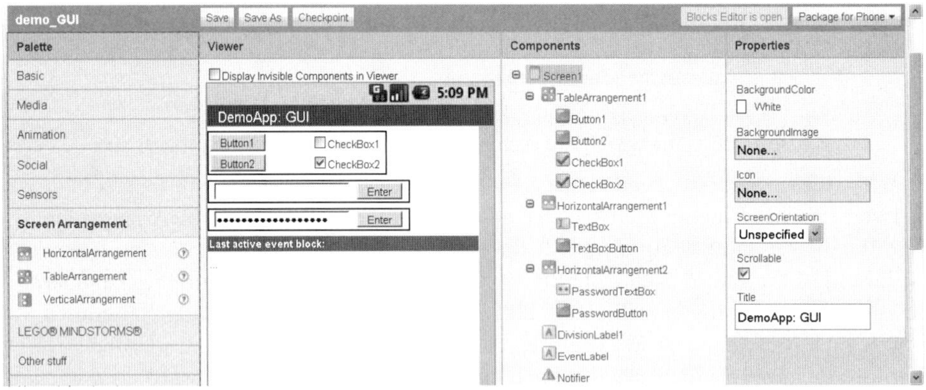

Figure 6.30 Space-efficient and tidy arrangement

As you can see in Figure 6.30, not only has the arrangement of the user elements in the Viewer changed, but also the arrangement of the component objects in the Components panel. In a similar way as the arrangement components visually gather up the user elements into a spatial group, they do the same internally within the program—that is, they insert the corresponding component objects as subordinates into the hierarchical structure of the app. Thus the components for Screen Arrangement fulfill a double purpose: They structure both the user interface for the user and the program structure for the developer. Now the demo app appears nice and tidy on the smartphone or emulator, as shown in Figure 6.31.

Figure 6.31 The finished demo app "demo_GUI" after the facelift

Make good use of the simple, yet powerful, design options provided by AI with the components for Screen Arrangement and the many other elements of the graphical user interface. Thanks to the visual development environment in the AI IDE, it is possible to tackle the visual design of your app at any stage and to carry out design changes before, during, and even after you have developed the block structures. This offers you a very high degree of flexibility—one that you will not find in other code-based programming languages in the same simple and effective way.

Actions at App Start with the Screen Component

Now that we are approaching the end of our overview of the process of designing the user interface, we want to introduce another component separately that you have already been using more or less consciously in the previous examples. When we introduced the AI IDE, we pointed out the special features of the Screen component at the time of printing, which appears just once in every app developed with Google AI. Any app developed with Google AI is currently limited to only one screen and cannot have any additional screens apart from the message windows mentioned previously. You do have the option of simulating several screens by showing or hiding different Screen Arrangements, but at the time of writing this book a specific function for "Multiple Screens" was only available in the experimental version of MIT AI, not in Google AI. As the use of the existing Screen component is still restricted in this way, it is not available for selection in the AI Designer component palette, but instead is present as the highest-level hierarchy component object, "Screen1," when you create a new app project. If you look at the AI References specification shown in Figure 6.32, however, you can see that the Screen component already has some interesting properties.

Screen

The screen does not appear in the palette like other components, but if comes automatically with the project. Each project has exactly one screen, named Screen1. This name cannot be changed.

Properties

`BackgroundColor`
Color for screen background.
`BackgroundImage`
An image that forms the screen's background.
`Height`
Screen height (y-size).
`icon`
An image to be used as the icon for the installed application on the phone. This should be a PNG or a JPG image; 48x48 is a good size. *Warning*: Specifying images other that PNG or JPG, for example .ico files, may prevent App Inventor from being able to package the application.
`Scrollable`
This is set by a checkbox in the designer. When checked, there will be a vertical scrollbar on the screen, and the height of the application can exceed the physical height of the device. When unchecked, the application height is constrained to the height of the device.
`Title`
Title for the screen (text). This will appear at the upper left of the phone when the application runs. A natural choice for the title is the title of the App, but you could make it something else, or even change it while the app is running.
`Width`
Screen width (x-size).

Events

`Initialize()`
Signaled when the application starts. It can be used setting initial values and performing other setup operations.
`ErrorOccurred(component component, text functionName, number errorNumber, text message)`

Figure 6.32 The specification of the special component Screen in the AI References

With the Screen component, you can specify a background color, a background image, and the familiar title. Remarkably, this component has one of the few component properties that is read only, but not writable or changeable at runtime. These two properties, Height and Width, are marked in the Reference in italics (see Figure 6.32). The reason for this regimented approach is that an Android app is automatically adapted to the screen size of the Android device used; thus specifying the app screen size is superfluous.

Although we have used the Screen component in all of our previous examples, we want to demonstrate a new, very useful and basic function in our demo project `demo_GUI` that will play an important role in future app development. Through its event block "Initialize," the Screen component offers the option of executing an action during the app call without requiring an additional event such as a user interaction. You can use this function to carry out important preparations required for the actual running of the app, such as loading data from web sources, determining your own geographic position with GPS, and many more. All of these desired "preparatory tasks" can be slotted into the event handler of the event block `Screen.Initialize` and then triggered and executed by the event of calling the app.

To demonstrate the basic operation, we want to show users a brief greeting when they start the app and then hide the greeting again after a short period of time. As you might guess, we will use the Notifier component and its ShowAlert method for briefly showing and hiding our message. We begin by creating the event handler in the existing demo project `demo_GUI`. As the Screen component is already part of the project as the component object "Screen1," we need only the AI Editor for our additions. Drag the event block `Screen1.Initialize` from the block selection My Blocks under the entry "Screen1" into the Editor area. Then slot the method `Notifier.ShowAlert` into this event block and add a text block `text` with the greeting "Welcome to the DemoApp!" to the method through its setter joint `notice` (see Figure 6.33).

Figure 6.33 Displaying a greeting when the app is called

Each time our demo app is called, the user now receives a friendly greeting, thanks to the event handler shown in Figure 6.33. The Android smartphone or the emulator shows the greeting as message text against a gray background with shading (see Figure 6.34), and hides it again after a few seconds.

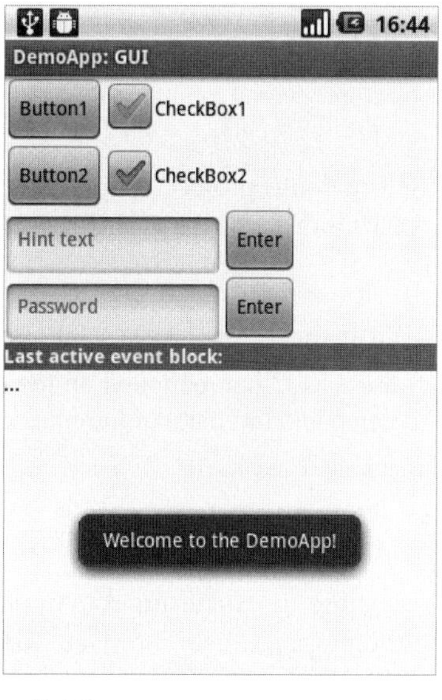

Figure 6.34 Temporary display of a greeting message on an Android device

With the user-friendly gesture and the edited design of our user interface, our development of the demo app `demo_GUI` has come to a close. You can now review what you have accomplished and take another look at the individual components used in creating the graphical user interface of Android apps. Notice how simply and, at the same time, efficiently AI's powerful options enable you to design professional user interfaces for your own apps. Have another look at the block structure as a whole, which serves as the basis for the overall functionality of the demo app (see Figure 6.35).

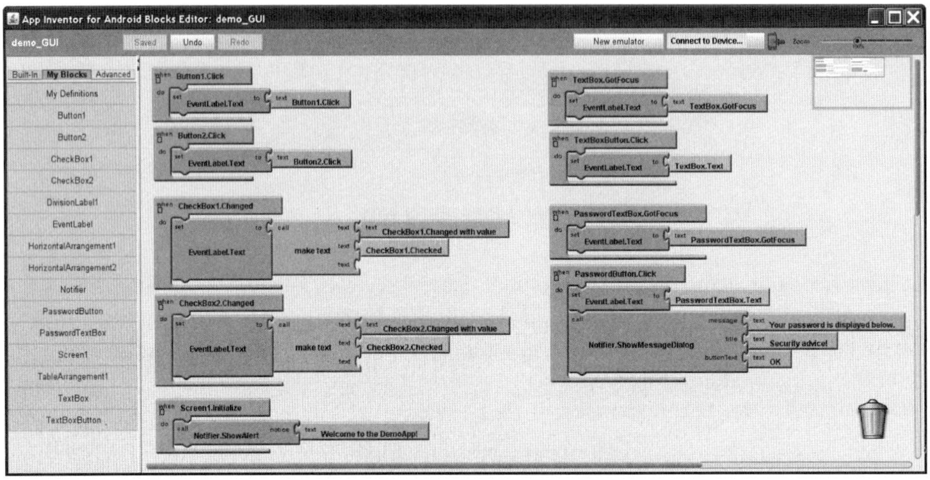

Figure 6.35 Block structure and overall functionality of the demo app "demo_GUI"

If you like, you can now use the demo project `demo_GUI` to create an independent app and download it to your smartphone. You have already learned how to do this in the context of the LaughBag app.

> **Project Files for demo_GUI on the Companion Website**
>
> All files for the demo project `demo_GUI` can be found on the companion website in the following directories (see link to companion website in Introduction):
>
> `/APK`: executable app file `demo_GUI.apk`
>
> `/PROJECT`: packaged project file `demo_GUI.zip`

Of course, we have not come close to exhausting AI's options with our description of the components for designing the graphical user interface. Today it is no longer enough to offer pretty user interfaces both on the computer and on the smartphone. Above and beyond the looks, you need to add pictures, music, and videos.

Chapter 7

Multimedia

Normally it would be unusual to discuss the topic of "multimedia" so soon within a beginning-level project, as multimedia apps are quite challenging and generally better suited for advanced developers. But AI's powerful functions and high degree of abstraction make it possible even for beginners to develop impressive multimedia apps using relatively simple methods. We want to not only present different multimedia files, but also describe how to handle them and even produce them. In this chapter, we again develop a demo app, `demo_Media`, in progressive fashion and use it to demonstrate the different multimedia components and explain how they can be applied. At the end of the chapter, you will have developed a surprisingly powerful multimedia app that will give you great inspiration for your own multimedia projects.

Media Access Options

Nearly all multimedia applications are based on corresponding media files that contain images, sound clips, or videos as different *media types*. The various media types form the central elements for creating multimedia applications, similar to the previously discussed elements of the graphical user interface. Although the number of media types is rather manageable, there is quite a variety in terms of how you access them or save them. For example, local access is limited to media files stored on the Android device either as part of the multimedia app, in the internal smartphone memory, or on the SD memory card. Beyond this local approach, you can also access the practically unlimited amount of multimedia content on the Internet. You can integrate image, music, and video files from the Internet or World Wide Web directly into an app and display or play them there. But that's not all: If the content of these media sources should change over time, you can create dynamic multimedia apps, for example, to display the current image captured by a webcam.

> **Supported Media Formats**
>
> An overview of the media formats supported by Android can be found in the section "Supported Media Formats" in Chapter 15, "Tips and Tools."

In connection with the topic of multimedia, we will need to take a closer look at these options. To proceed in a structured way, we begin our description of the individual components by presenting a brief overview of the different methods for integrating media files, which is applicable to practically all media types. These methods are also documented online in the AI Reference type, "Notes and Details."

Options for Integrating Media Files in Android Apps

The integration of media files can take place in different ways and is also described in the AI Concepts Reference under "Accessing Images and Sounds":

`http://experimental.appinventor.mit.edu/learn/reference/other/media.html`

For integrating media files, AI offers the following options for file storage or file access:

- **As the initial property of a component within the app package.** You have already used this method for integrating a media file in the LaughBag project, when you assigned the image file `laughbag.jpg` as the initial property to the button `LaughButton` via the "Image" field. This approach is also possible for audio and video files; you can make the media file a fixed part of the app project and package it as a file attachment (*application asset*) together with the later APK file. This strategy has the advantage that the media file is always available when the app is executed, but the disadvantage that the size, download time, and memory requirement of the APK file can increase significantly.
- **As a reference to a media file in the internal smartphone memory.** Here you specify the full path to the local directory where you want to save the desired media file. The media file is then not part of the app, but rather a reference to where the file is saved. This approach has the advantage that the APK file remains smaller and the content of the media file can be changed if you keep the same file name, but the disadvantage that the specific reference to a locally stored media file usually applies and works only on your individual smartphone. The specification of the file path follows the conventions of your Android device and takes the format of a *content URL*. As a general rule, the files of the different media types will be stored in the following example directories on your smartphone:
    - Image file: `content://media/external/images/media/image1.jpg`
    - Audio file: `content://media/external/audio/media/music1.mp3`
    - Video file: `content://media/external/video/media/video1.3gp`

- **As a reference to a media file on your smartphone's SD card.** For integrating media files stored on the local SD card, the same statements apply as for accessing the internal memory. Data access also requires specifying a path, but the individual *file URL* is even more dependent on the individual path structure of your smartphone and can vary to a greater degree. For example, the directory path may look very different, but the prefix `file:///sdcard` is always the same (note the three slashes):
  - Media file: `file:///sdcard/downloads/video.3gp`
- **As a reference to a media file on the Internet.** To integrate media files from the Internet or World Wide Web, you need to enter the complete web address, including the connection protocol (`http://`), as the complete *Web URL*. This URL (Uniform Resource Locator) is basically the same as a directory path, except that it is not found locally on your individual smartphone, but rather on a server somewhere in the vast depths of the Internet. The advantages of this method are obvious. Although the external media files do not make the APK file size any bigger, the media files are available to all users of your app, provided they are using an Android smartphone with Internet access. Thus this method offers the best of both worlds—relatively small APK files for fast downloading with access to elaborate multimedia content on all conceivable Android devices. Moreover, the media content can be managed centrally; new images, songs, or videos can be updated and changed on the server and saved under the same file name, without having to change the APK file or download it again. This approach delivers a significant increase in efficiency—a major criterion for professional multimedia apps. As you know from accessing other content on the web, the integration of media files via their web address follows the same pattern:
  - Media file: `http://beta.appinventor.mit.edu/images/logo.png`

Finding the Local Directory Path for Media Files on Your Smartphone

Not many Android devices include a file manager app as a standard feature. To find the directory path for your media files in the internal memory or on the local SD card, you can download a file manager from the Android Market. (We particularly liked AndExplorer by Lysesoft.) Using your chosen file manager, you can search for the desired media files and copy and paste the displayed file path into your AI apps. You can also use the file manager to move or copy the media files into another directory if you do not want to use the default directory. Please refer to the instructions of the file manager to find out how.

Figure 7.1 shows the typical directory paths and some contents of the internal memory for images (left) and the SD card (right) on an Android smartphone, displayed with the file manager AndExplorer.

Figure 7.1 Accessing internal memory and the SD card with AndExplorer

Along with these four options for integrating media files and different types of media, you have countless options for designing your own multimedia apps. In the course of developing the new demo app, you will get to know and practically implement different combinations as examples.

The Basic Principle: Synergy

The smooth transition from local to remote resources on the Web is a central principle in the Android operating system and is also reflected in the AI IDE's cloud approach. Not only are the boundaries between local and online data resources becoming blurred with Android and AI, but those between individual applications on a smartphone are eroding. Instead of constantly having to reinvent the wheel, develop new functions, bloat apps with identical basic functions, and over-stretch the limited mobile resources, Android and AI promote and make use of synergetic "cooperation" between apps. While this has benefits in terms of the limited capacity of the mobile devices, you as AI developer also profit from it, because you can use the functions of other apps for your apps. AI incorporates in many of its components seamless cooperation with system applications and offers the option of adding interfaces to other applications both locally and online.

Especially in the context of the multimedia example apps in this chapter and the demo app we will develop, we will repeatedly come across this central principle of synergy. Synergy allows us to develop impressively powerful apps with remarkably little effort and minimal complexity in our block structures. Admittedly, the shared use of existing system applications and functions can be detrimental to the individual character of your apps. Convinced Java programmers like to point this limitation out, but even they make use of well-known libraries of operating system functions to keep software production viable. Moreover, too much individuality can even be detrimental to the ergonomics of apps. Both on stationary desktop systems and mobile devices, users generally appreciate having a familiar environment that provides for quick orientation and operation, even with new apps. For example, using an individual virtual keyboard for each app that expected text input would certainly be counterproductive and would be accepted only reluctantly by the users.

Against this backdrop, the combined advantages of the myriad synergies far outweigh the disadvantages. Android and AI are very advanced in implementing this concept—and perhaps that is exactly the reason why this mobile operating system is so successful. The rapidly growing number of professional apps on the Android Market is not least due to the fact that the developers can fall back on powerful functions and system applications in the open operating system Android, and can integrate interesting applications from the house of Google. Even professional Android apps for displaying geographical information make use of *Google Maps*, *Google Earth,* or *Google Street View*, without which many applications would not be feasible in the first place. For your own apps, you, too, should make good use of the available options to realize synergy with system apps and other applications. In this chapter, which focuses on multimedia apps, you will get a first taste and an introduction into the impressive options of synergistic app development.

Displaying Local and Online Images with the Image Component

Even if images or photos are a rather simple media element, they are probably the most used media type in multimedia apps. Displaying an image is not just used for the purpose of looking at the image as in a photo album; rather, the image can also be used as background image to give the app a specific character plus a higher degree of perceived complexity and professionalism. For example, the simple display of a textured button can be turned into an interactive laugh bag, or several buttons for selecting audio files can be turned into a stylish jukebox. Moreover, changing the content of image sources can add a dynamic character to the image displayed—for example, by retrieving the current image of a webcam online and displaying it.

For using images with the aforementioned wealth of functions, AI offers the Image component in the component group Basic. This component has only few properties related to loading, displaying, and specifying the height and width of an image, and no event blocks or methods. Thus the flexibility mentioned previously results mainly from the creative use of images in the app context and the exploitation of the various options for accessing images from different sources. To illustrate the basic function and flexible media access, we will demonstrate two options for using the media type "Image" in the next section: We integrate an image as static initial property and an image from a dynamic online source.

> **Supported Image Formats**
>
> Information on the supported image formats can be found in Chapter 15, "Tips and Tools."

As in Chapter 6, we demonstrate the practical application of this and other media components within a successively expanded demo app. Let's start by creating a new app project. Open the AI Designer, go to My Projects, and use the New button to create a new project with the name `demo_Media`. In the Screen properties, give your new app the title "Demo app: multimedia." To visually separate the different media components in the demo app from one another, we precede each one with a corresponding header in form of a label, starting with the Image component. Drag a Label component into the Viewer, rename the resulting component object as "DivisionLabel1," and change its initial properties as shown in Table 7.1.

Table 7.1 **Initial Properties for DivisionLabel1**

Initial Property	New Value
BackgroundColor	Gray
Text	"Webcam image: retrieve online [Image]"
TextColor	White
Width	Fill parent

After these preparations, we can now turn to the Image component itself. Drag it from the Basic palette into the Viewer under the DivisionLabel1 and rename the resulting component object as "WebcamImage." It is now temporarily displayed as graphic placeholder in the Viewer. While the name WebcamImage indicates that there is more to come, for now we want to assign a static image file to this component object as the initial property in our first step, which will consequently be integrated into the APK file as fixed file attachment (asset). The image file we want to integrate is `testpattern.jpg`, a rather small file (around 5KB) that will only marginally increase the file size.

> **Media Files on the Companion Website**
>
> Like all other media files and resources for this book, you can find the image file `testpattern.jpg` on the companion website (see the link in Introduction) in the directory `/MEDIA`.

You learned about the process of integrating an image file in the LaughBag project, where you assigned the image file `laughbag.jpg` to the button LaughButton using its "Image" property field. In the same way, you can now assign the image file `testpattern.jpg` to the component object WebcamImage by loading the image file into the project with the "Picture" property field and assigning it to the WebcamImage (see Figure 7.2). The example integration of an image file as the initial property of the Image component and, therefore, the asset of the APK file is now complete with this step.

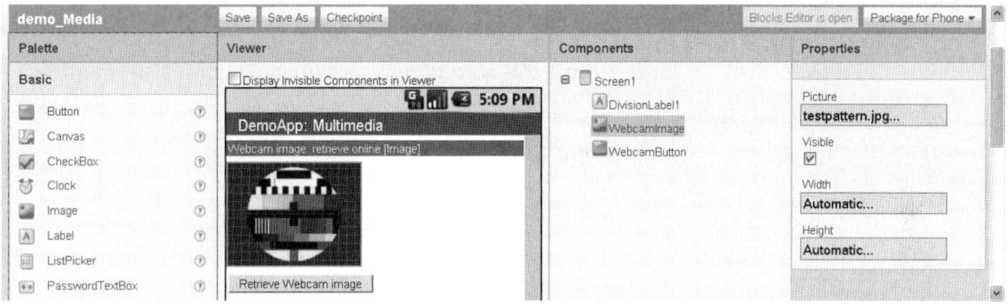

Figure 7.2 Initial design and display of the static test image in "demo_Media"

Of course, we are not satisfied with integrating a static image into our app—we want a dynamic image for our multimedia app. The test image merely represents a temporary initial property, which will be changed during the app's runtime. By clicking on a button, the user should be able to retrieve the current and constantly updated image from an online webcam in the app. Now, however, we have all the essential elements we need to develop the final functionality. Let's first add the button in AI Designer. Place it into the Viewer as the component object WebcamButton below the WebcamImage and write the text "Retrieve Webcam image" onto it. Next, go to the AI Editor to develop the described functionality.

The functionality for retrieving and displaying a current webcam image is remarkably simple to implement with AI. Just as you assigned new text to the EventLabel by pressing a button in the previous section, you can now assign an image to the WebcamImage by pressing a button. Then, with each click on the WebcamButton, the image will be updated by downloading the most recent version from the website you specify. A webcam on the Internet works by saving the current image under the same address and the same file name each time it is updated (overwriting the old image in the process), so you simply need to retrieve and display the same file over and over again with each click on the button. The user then sees the current, updated image and gets the impression of a dynamic mobile online application. The event handler is correspondingly simple to create, as you can see in Figure 7.3.

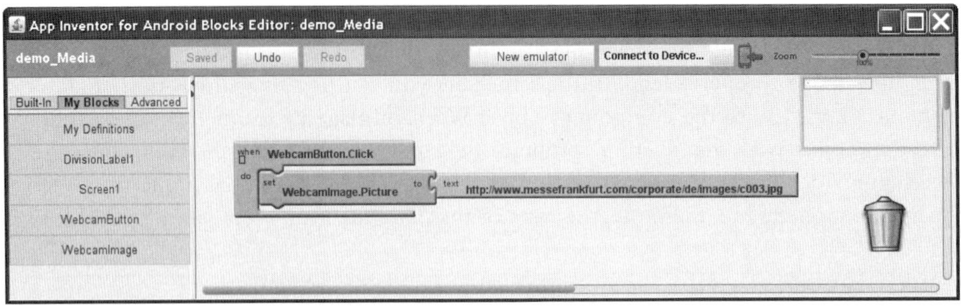

Figure 7.3 Event handler for retrieving the current webcam image by pressing a button

Instead of a particular text, the property block `WebcamImage.Picture` shown in Figure 7.3 is passed a text block `text` via its setter socket, which contains the complete web address of the image file we want to retrieve. This image file is then loaded and displayed in the component object WebcamImage. On first loading the file, the initial property "Picture" of WebcamImage, which was previously set to the test image, is overwritten by the latest version of the image. Loading the specified image file happens again with each event `WebcamButton.Click`, so that the user gets the most recent image from the webcam with each click on the button. The pseudocode is simple to follow:

```
When WebcamButton is clicked, do set WebcamImage to the image retrieved from
the specified web address!
```

The web address and webcam file used in our demo project serve only to demonstrate the AI functionality. For your own apps, you can, of course, use any web address you choose. When using webcam images, however, you should always check the terms and conditions of use first.

On the smartphone, the demo app `demo_Media` appears as shown in Figure 7.4. The figure shows the skyline of Frankfurt, Germany, as it appears at each retrieval moment: when the app is launched (left), after the first click on the retrieve button (center), and after the second click (right).

Figure 7.4 Static launch image and dynamic webcam image in the demo app

This example within the demo app demo_Media has illustrated how easily and quickly you can develop multimedia apps with the AI tools and, at the same time, efficiently integrate web resources. In the course of this and the subsequent chapter, you will come across many other examples of the central synergy concept underlying Android and AI, through which you have access to impressively powerful and capable functions in the simplest possible way. In the next section, you will find out how you can use AI to create a camera as an app, by simply sharing the camera functions of the operating system.

Taking Photos and Displaying Them with the Camera Component

Like the preceding section, this section is devoted to images. This time, however, we will not just load and display existing images from local storage media or from the Web, but rather will produce the images ourselves, save them locally, and then display them together with their directory path. If you are surprised to find such a complex task in an introductory beginners' text, you will be even more astonished how easy it is to implement it with AI. In essence, we will develop our own camera. As you may have guessed after reading the previous section, we will not develop the functionality of the camera completely from scratch, but instead will share what the Android system provides on the hardware it uses. This demo app (demo_Media) assumes that we have integrated the Android smartphone into the AI IDE and not the emulator, so that we can test and see the functionality of our demo app directly on the device and in connection with its system components (for example, the camera). Thus, if you haven't already integrated your smartphone with AI, please do so now.

As promised, you do not need to program the hardware-dependent interface to your smartphone camera yourself, read out the image information from the sensor memory and convert it to a common image format, or program a file manager for saving, choosing, and displaying the image files. All of these functions are already present in one form or another as part of different applications on the Android system or smartphone. When developing apps with AI, you merely need to creatively recombine these elements to develop a new app for a new app context.

To handle the basic functions, AI offers a single component with the obvious name "Camera" in the component group Media. As shown in Figure 7.5, the Camera component is very clear as it abstracts the complexity of the task itself completely and leaves it to other system components. The non-visible component Camera actually has no properties of its own—only a method TakePicture for calling the system camera and an event block AfterPicture for processing the resulting image file.

Camera

Use a camera component to take a picture on the phone.

Camera is a non-visible component that takes a picture using the device's camera. After the picture is taken, the path to the file on the phone containing the picture is available as an argument to the AfterPicture event. The path can be used, for example, as the Picture property of an Image component.

Properties

none

Methods

`TakePicture()`
Opens the phone's camera to allow a picture to be taken.

Events

`AfterPicture(Text image)`
Called after the picture is taken. The text argument `image` is the path that can be used to locate the image on the phone.

Figure 7.5 Specification of the Camera component in the AI References

The individual design options of the camera function are correspondingly small when you are using the Camera component. This trade-off is necessary to realize the greater benefit of simple development of powerful apps.

Compromise Between Simplicity + Powerfulness Versus Flexibility + Individuality

Some sort of compromise is always necessary when you are using a simple, yet powerful development language such as AI. Of course, you could create a camera app with a more individual design by using the programming language Java, but the effort involved in designing it and having to learn the language in the first place is significantly greater.

Just as simple as the specification of the Camera component is its use within AI. We want to integrate it as part of the demo app `demo_Media` into the typical context of a camera. By pressing a button, the user should have the option of calling the camera function and taking a photo, which is then displayed along with the directory path of the saved image file. To develop this overall functionality, we need a total of five components, as shown in Table 7.2. We will implement them in the order in which they are listed in this table and edit the properties as specified.

Table 7.2 **Components and Initial Properties for Camera**

Component	Object Name	Edited Properties
Label	DivisionLabel2	"Text": Photo: take photo + show [Camera] Otherwise, see Table 7.1
Camera	Camera	
Image	CameraImage	
Button	CameraButton	"Text": Take photo
Label	CameraPathLabel	"Text": Local path to photo file

To design the camera user interface in AI Designer, drag the components listed in Table 7.2 into the Viewer below one another in the order specified and edit the properties listed there as shown. The more complex our user interfaces and block structures become, the more we will use tables to represent the individual elements in a clearly structured and compressed form. After you have edited the details as shown in Table 7.2, the demo app should look like Figure 7.6 in your Viewer.

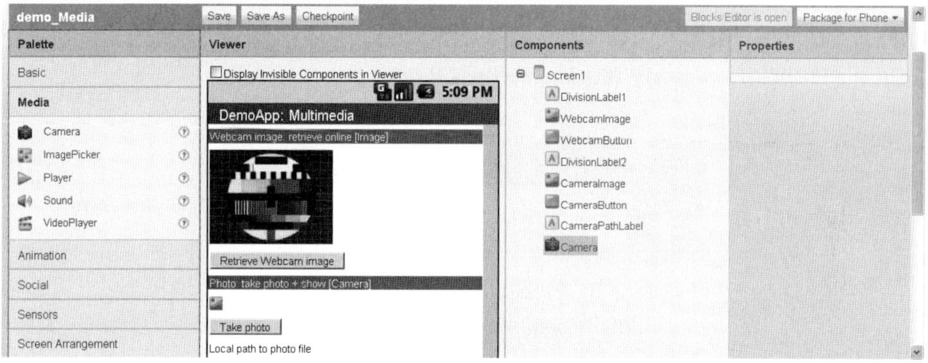

Figure 7.6 User interface of the camera based on the properties in Table 7.2

Once DivisionLabel2 takes care of the optical separation from the previous webcam demo, we want the CameraButton to call the system camera. After the photo is taken, the system app should close again and return the user to the demo app's user interface. There, the photo taken should be displayed in CameraImage, and the complete directory path of the image file, which was automatically saved system-side, should be displayed in CameraPathLabel. We will implement this functionality in two event handlers in AI Editor.

The first event handler for calling the system camera when CameraButton is pressed is quite easy to implement, thanks to the high degree of abstraction. Drag the event block `CameraButton.Click` into the Editor area and slot the Camera method `Camera.TakePicture` into it (see Figure 7.7). This method carries out or encapsulates all tasks required for calling the system camera. With this simple event handler, the system camera is called within our demo app by the user pressing the button, and you can take photos with it (although they are not yet displayed in the demo app).

Figure 7.7 Event handler for calling the system camera when the CameraButton is pressed

For the second event handler, we use the only event block present in the Camera component, `AfterPicture`. As described in the specification of this event block in Figure 7.5, this method is called automatically after the system camera is activated. The trigger event is ending the system application after the user takes the photo. The system application tells the event block `AfterPicture` the relevant directory path where the current photo is saved as an image file on the smartphone. The directory path is written as a text line by the system application into a *variable* with the default name `image`; this variable is then passed to the event handler via a block with the same name (see Figure 7.8). To implement this functionality, drag the event block `Camera.AfterPicture` from the block selection My Blocks into the Editor.

Figure 7.8 Event block "AfterPicture" receives the file path in the variable "image"

The current file path is automatically passed to the event handler `CameraAfter-Picture` so the file path can be used by the block structures contained within the event handler. To make the variable `image` available to other blocks within the event handler, we make it available in the block selection My Blocks in the special category "My Definitions." We will use the file path for two purposes in our demo project—for displaying the photo and for displaying the file path.

As you would expect, displaying the photo is done via the Image component object CameraImage, to which we assign the file path of the variable `image`. This happens in almost the same way as described in the previous section for assigning the static web address of the webcam image. There is one difference of which you should be aware: While the web address mentioned earlier was entered statically in the Editor via a text block `text` and only the image was exchanged when the file was updated under the *same* file name (see Figure 7.3), the event block `CameraImage.Picture` gets a file path with a *new* file name in each case (see Figure 7.9).

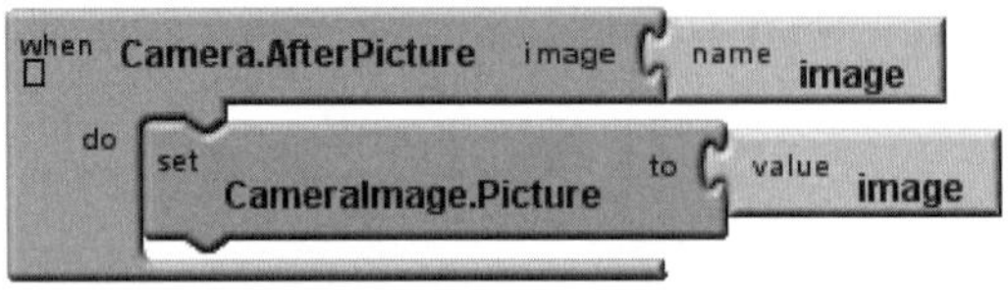

Figure 7.9 Displaying the photo from the file path of the variable "image"

Of course, we also want to display each current file path as text in the CameraPath-Label. This function is easy to add as part of the event handler `Camera.AfterPicture`. Slot an additional event block `CameraPathLabel.Text` into the event handler and assign it the variable `image` (see Figure 7.10). Given that the file path is specified as text line in the variable `image`, the label can simply output it.

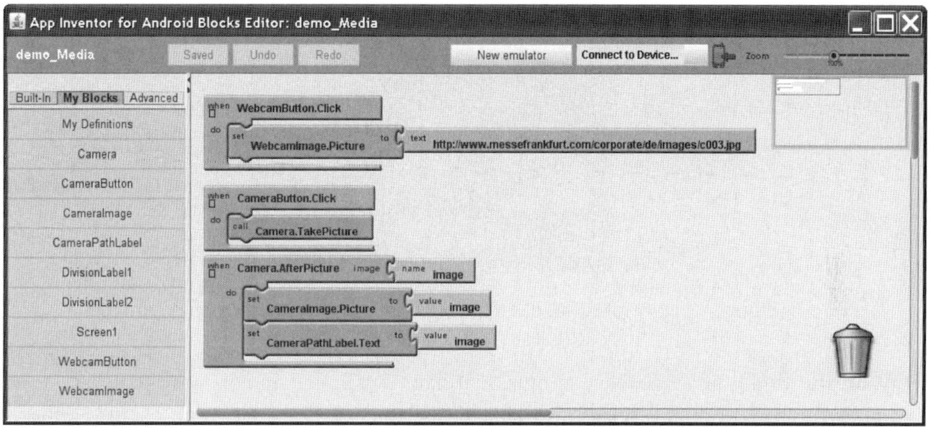

Figure 7.10 Complete event handler for displaying a photo and its file path

The intended functionality of the camera is now completely implemented. You can try it out on your smartphone at this point, if you haven't already done so (see Figure 7.11). Because we did not specify a test image, the image display is empty when we call the demo app `demo_Media` (left). By pressing the button labeled "Take photo," you start the system camera and can take a photo with it as usual. You then need to close the system camera properly to make sure the photo is saved and the file path is passed back to the demo app. This does not usually happen if you just press the Back button or Home button on your smartphone after taking the photo. With the system camera on the LG P500 smartphone, for example, you have to press a button with a paper clip symbol (see the bottom left of the center picture in Figure 7.11) to ensure the photo is saved, the system application is closed, you return to the demo app, and then the photo and file path are displayed (right). Try out several function buttons on your system camera if necessary to find the right way of closing the camera.

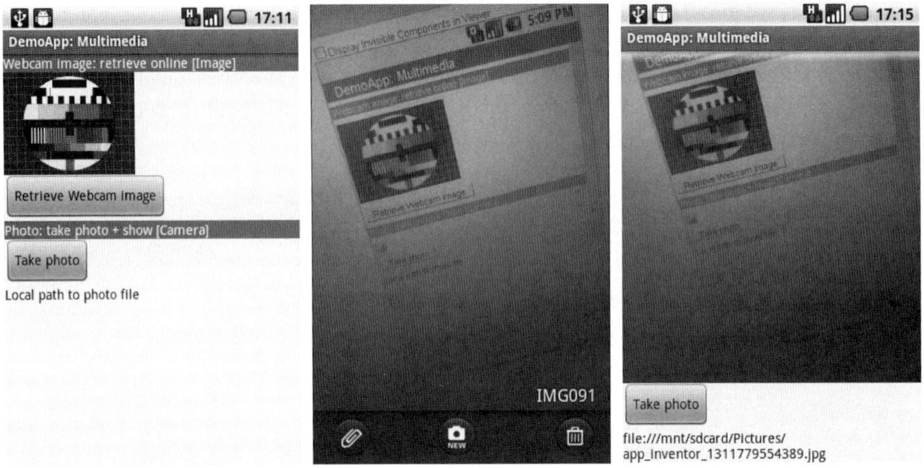

Figure 7.11 Taking and displaying photos with the camera app

With this highly manageable example, you have developed an app with which you can take photos and then display or otherwise use them. You might think of some other ways of expanding this function within your own app projects. For example, you might take photos from within an app and then send them automatically to your friends via e-mail. In the course of this book, you should find many more inspirations for interesting app projects.

Managing Images with the ImagePicker Component

Surely it is no coincidence that the component this section focuses on comes directly after the previously introduced Camera component in the AI References. It makes sense to be able to access photos taken by yourself or others from within the app on the smartphone and to open them like a photo album. With the component ImagePicker, AI provides this function in the Media group in the usual comfortable way. Again, the functionality of another system application is shared—namely, the Picture Gallery, which can be found on almost all Android devices.

> **Picking Files**
>
> The term "Picker" in the component name indicates what the ImagePicker does: It helps you pick images. Later, you will come across other "pickers" for choosing contacts, telephone numbers, and e-mail addresses from system applications.

Much as with the Camera component, you can use the ImagePicker to launch the Picture Gallery with which a user can then select an image from the local storage options in the usual way. The selected image is passed back to the calling app and can be displayed there with the usual procedures, or used in some other way. Using the ImagePicker component is even easier than using the Camera component, however, because you do not need a separate variable when passing the image path, and you don't need an additional button for triggering a calling event, as it is already contained in the component. As you can see from the specification extract in Figure 7.12, the ImagePicker component has the familiar properties of a Button component.

ImagePicker

Tap to pick a picture

Use an image picker component to choose an image from your image gallery.

An image picker is a kind of button. When the user taps an image picker, the device's image gallery appears, and the user can choose an image. After the user picks an image, the property `ImagePath` is set to a text string that represents that image. You can then use that result, for example, to set the image of a button.

Properties

`ImagePath`
The image the user chose, represented as a text string that gives the location of the images.
`Enabled`
If true, image picker can be used.
`Alignment`
Left, center, or right.
`BackgroundColor`
Color for image picker background.
`Enabled`
If set, user can tap image picker to cause action.
`FontBold`
If set, image picker button text is displayed in bold.

Events

`AfterPicking()`
User selected an item from the image picker.
`BeforePicking()`
User has tapped the image picker but hasn't yet selected an item.
`GotFocus()`
Image picker became the focused component.
`LostFocus()`
Image picker is no longer the focused component.

Figure 7.12 Specification of the ImagePicker component

In addition to the usual properties for designing the ImagePicker button's visual appearance, the read-only property "ImagePath" (see Figure 7.12, in italics) is especially important for our demo app. We will later pass the file path to the selected image file to this property field, similar to the use of the variable `image` used in the context of the Camera component. The ImagePicker component also has an event block `AfterPicking`, which is also triggered by the system application Picture Gallery once it is closed after the image was selected.

To implement the component ImagePicker within our demo project `demo_Media` as a photo album, we can follow closely the same instructions given in the previous section for the camera. The creative design of the user interface in AI Designer is specified in Table 7.3.

Table 7.3 **Components and Initial Properties of "Photo Album"**

Component	Object Name	Edited Properties
Label	DivisionLabel3	"Text": Image: pick + display [ImagePicker] Otherwise, see Table 7.1
Image	PickerImage	
ImagePicker	ImagePicker	"Text": Pick image
Label	PickerPathLabel	"Text": Local path to image file

Once you have added and, where necessary, edited the components shown in Table 7.3 in the specified order in AI Designer, the demo project should look like Figure 7.13.

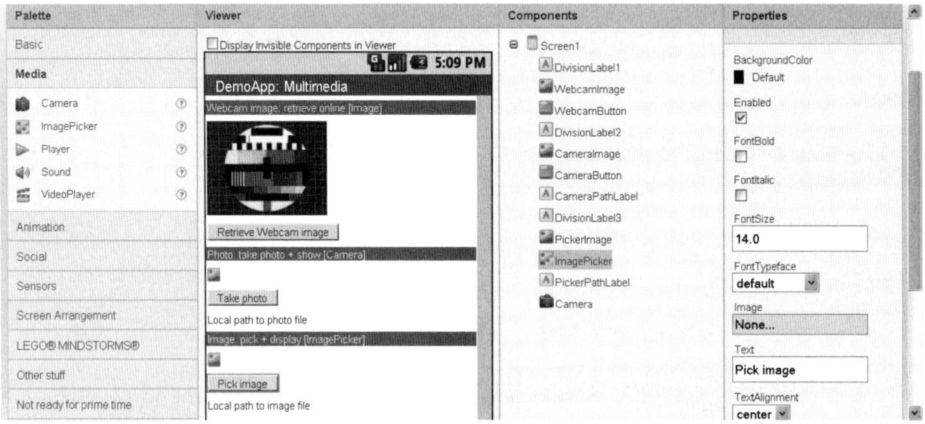

Figure 7.13 Demo project with components for a "photo album"

Now we can go to the AI Editor to develop the event handler for calling the Picture Gallery and selecting and displaying an image. As mentioned previously, the event handler for implementing this functionality is surprisingly short and simple, as the ImagePicker component, with its high degree of abstraction, already contains almost all of the needed functions. The button including the automated event handler for launching the Picture Gallery is effectively integrated into the ImagePicker component, so that we do not need to create it. Instead, we just have to develop the event handler for accepting and displaying the selected image.

Drag the event block `ImagePicker.AfterPicking` into the Editor area and slot the property block `PickerImage.Picture` into it. Just as with the event handler `Camera.AfterPicture`, we want the image received from the system application to be displayed in an Image component. Instead of an additional variable, the file path within the "fully integrated" ImagePicker is already present in its property block `ImagePicker.ImagePath`, so that the latter can be assigned to the property block `PickerImage.Picture` for displaying the image. To display the file path as a line of text, we pass `ImagePicker.ImagePath` to the property block `PickerPathLabel.Text`. In the visual development language AI, the overall functionality of the photo album is present within the event handler shown in Figure 7.14.

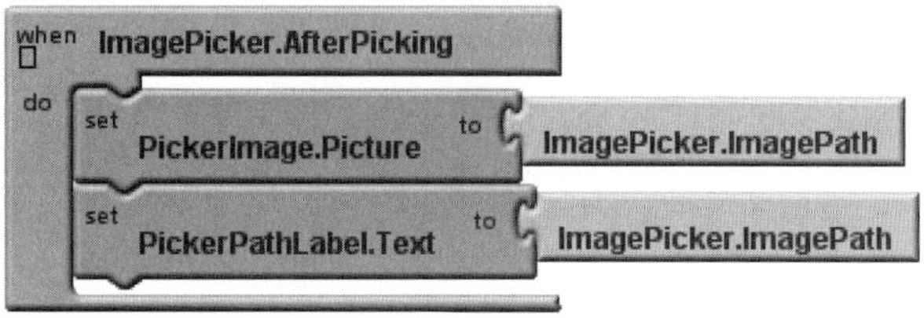

Figure 7.14 The entire photo album functionality in one event handler

Even though it seems hard to believe that the short event handler shown in Figure 7.14 implements the entire photo album functionality, you can easily check whether it works by launching the demo app (see Figure 7.15). When you tap the ImagePicker button (left), the Picture Gallery is launched as a system application (center). Once you select an image from the gallery, the system app closes automatically and you go back to the calling demo app, which then displays the selected image and the corresponding file path (right).

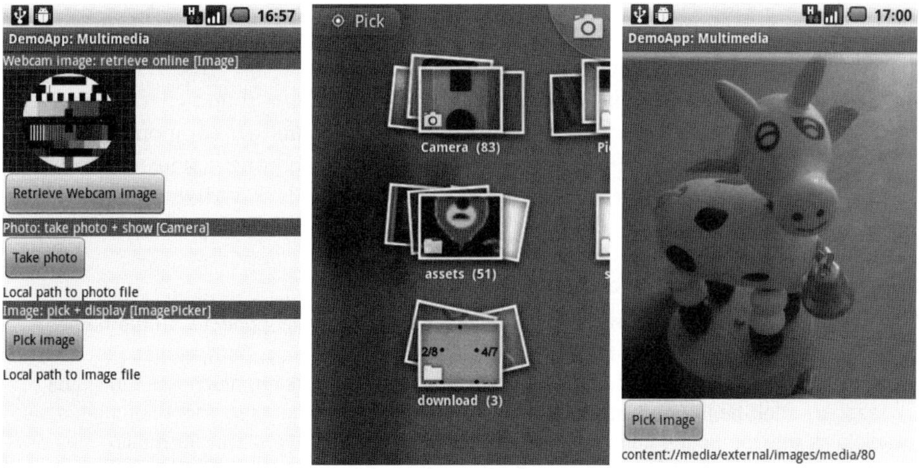

Figure 7.15 Calling, selecting, and displaying images from the Picture Gallery

The demonstration of the ImagePicker component shows once again the impressive ease with which you can use the powerful resources of the Android operating system in your own apps. Now that you have learned much about the myriad ways of handling images, we turn to another media type and see to what extent system apps can be used efficiently in connection with it.

Sound Effects and Vibration with the Sound Component

In this section, we will add another media type to the colorful world of images within multimedia apps, addressing another sensory channel in our app's users. Integrating acoustic signals into an app can make it much more user friendly. Short audio signals, for example, can notify users of newly received messages or a low battery, remind them of imminent appointments, confirm pressing a key, and much more. Even if some of these sound effects can be annoying (but fortunately can be switched off), such acoustic feedback is an indispensable feature, especially for the small mobile all-rounders. We may not even notice sound effects consciously, but if we did not have them, their absence would certainly seem odd—which goes to show how much this media type is (subconsciously) ergonomically useful. While we prefer to leave the design of appealing and appropriate audio signals to the sound designers, we will briefly demonstrate the integration of sound effects in this section.

> **Supported Audio Formats**
>
> Information on the supported audio formats can be found in Chapter 15, "Tips and Tools."

AI offers the non-visible component Sound in the Media group for the integration and playback of short sound effects. As the specification shown in Figure 7.16 indicates, the Sound component is intended only for short sounds such as sound effects, not for playing whole songs or music titles, which can be done via another component (Player). The Sound method `Vibrate` can be used to make the smartphone vibrate, as we saw earlier in the expansion of the LaughBag app in the "Methods and Method Blocks" section in Chapter 4.

> **Acoustic, Haptic, and Visual Feedback**
>
> Combining a sound effect and a vibrate function within one component with the name Sound may seem odd at first, but it makes sense if you consider both acoustic (sound) and haptic (vibration) output as a pure signal or notifying function, much like the visual feedback that the Notifier window provides from the app to the user. This relationship also explains why the Sound component is not intended as an audio player for music titles or similar. Consider the Sound component as another multimedia instrument for designing the user interface.

Similar to the case for the vibration method, you can specify the playback time of the sound effect via the "MinimumInterval" property. The Sound component also has typical methods for playback control of the audio file (`Pause`, `Play`, `Resume`, `Stop`), similar to your DVD player or other devices. For the short sound effects, these methods are used much less frequently than when playing complete songs.

Sound

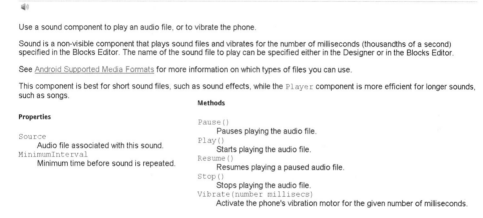

Use a sound component to play an audio file, or to vibrate the phone.

Sound is a non-visible component that plays sound files and vibrates for the number of milliseconds (thousandths of a second) specified in the Blocks Editor. The name of the sound file to play can be specified either in the Designer or in the Blocks Editor.

See Android Supported Media Formats for more information on which types of files you can use.

This component is best for short sound files, such as sound effects, while the `Player` component is more efficient for longer sounds, such as songs.

Properties

`Source`
    Audio file associated with this sound.
`MinimumInterval`
    Minimum time before sound is repeated.

Methods

`Pause()`
    Pauses playing the audio file.
`Play()`
    Starts playing the audio file.
`Resume()`
    Resumes playing a paused audio file.
`Stop()`
    Stops playing the audio file.
`Vibrate(number millisecs)`
    Activate the phone's vibration motor for the given number of milliseconds.

Figure 7.16 Specification of the Sound component

Using the media type audio is, in many respects, similar to using the previously described media type image. Audio files in AI are also integrated into an app via their file paths. Instead of the Image component for displaying images, we now have the Sound component for playing sounds. In addition, an audio file can be integrated into the app as the initial property in AI Designer via the Sound property "Source" as a file attachment (asset) or, alternatively, can be retrieved at runtime from local or online sources via the property block of the same name. In case of the short sound effects typically used in the context of the Sound component, it rarely makes sense to load them online every time they are played. In fact, a delay in the acoustic feedback for a user interaction due to overly long download times has the tendency to unsettle the user. The same applies if the expected acoustic signal fails to occur. For these reasons, it is recommended that the small sound effect audio files be integrated as assets as fixed parts of the APK file.

You already know from the LaughBag project how to load an audio file as the initial property into an app. For the sake of completeness, we will integrate this functionality once again into our current demo project, and once again use the existing audio file `laughter.wav` (see the companion website, under the directory `/MEDIA`). Each time a button is pressed, we want the smartphone to vibrate and play the short laughter sound. To implement this functionality, add the components shown in Table 7.4 to the demo app `demo_Media`.

Table 7.4 **Components and Initial Properties for the Sound Demonstration**

Component	Object Name	Edited Properties
Label	DivisionLabel4	"Text": Sound: play + vibrate [Sound] Otherwise, see Table 7.1
Sound	Sound	"Source": laughter.wav
Button	SoundButton	"Text": Play sound

With the components and properties shown in Table 7.4, the demo project should now look like in Figure 7.17.

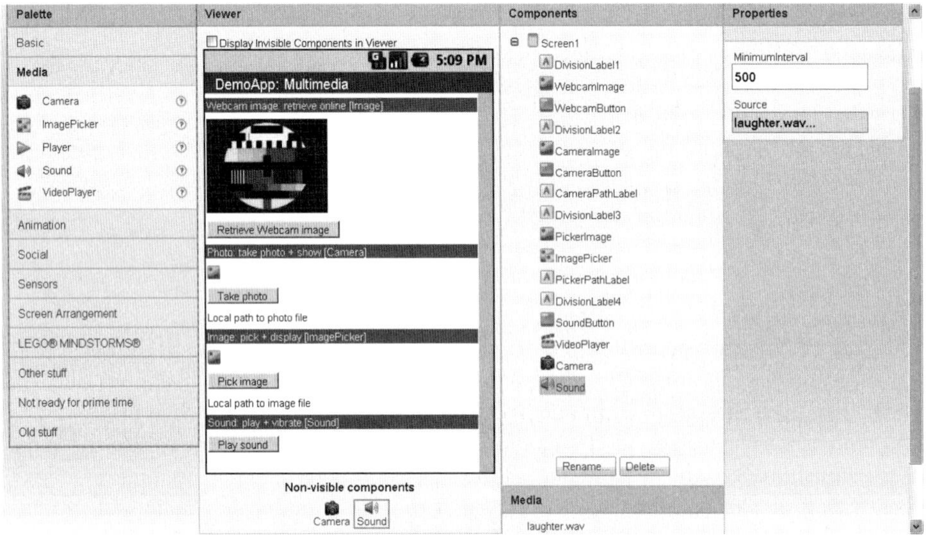

Figure 7.17 Expanding the demo project by adding a Sound component

Regarding the implementation of the functionality in AI Editor, we do not need to explain much more: The event handler used is identical to the one used in the expansion of the LaughBag project in the section "Methods and Method Blocks" in Chapter 4 (see Figure 7.18).

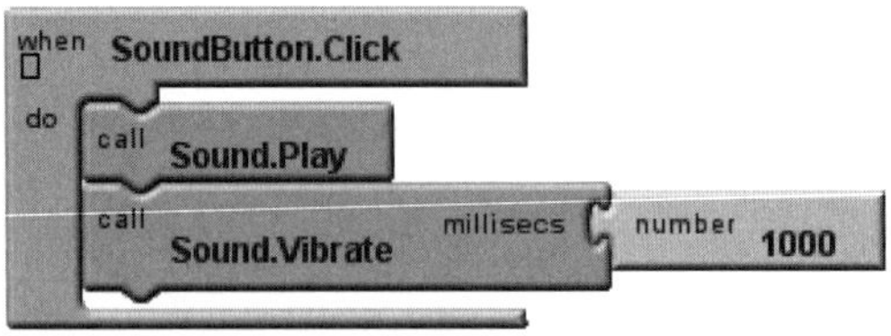

Figure 7.18 Event handler to produce laughter and vibration when a button is pressed

Pressing the SoundButton triggers the associated event handler, which incorporates the Sound methods `Sound.Play` for playing the audio file and `Sound.Vibrate` for simultaneous vibration with a duration of 1 second (1000 milliseconds). Try it out on your smartphone; it should seem very familiar.

Playing Audio Files with the Player Component

For playing back longer audio files, such as whole songs or chapters from audio books, AI offers the component Player in the Media group. According to the specification, it is intended for playing back both audio and video files, but in practice it is mostly used for audio files. This is partly due to the fact that AI also has an extra component for playing back videos, which we will discuss in the next section. In this section, we investigate the Player component mainly in terms of its function as a convenient *audio player*. In many respects, the Player component shown in Figure 7.19 closely resembles the Sound component shown in Figure 7.16, but has one less property and method. The Player component does not need the property "MinimumInterval," among others, because a song or similar piece of music has a fixed length and is usually played back once from beginning to end. In the case of a sound effect, it can make sense to shorten or lengthen it. The fact that the method `Resume` is missing is difficult to understand, however, as this functionality is required for longer audio files to resume playback after a pause.

Player

Use a player component to play an audio or video file, or to vibrate the phone.

Player is a non-visible component that plays audio or video and controls phone vibration. The name of a media file is specified in the `Source` property, which can be set in the Designer or in the Blocks Editor. The length of time for a vibration is specified in the Blocks Editor in milliseconds (thousandths of a second).

See Android Supported Media Formats for more information on which types of files you can use.

Use a player component for playing long sound files, video files, and vibrating the phone. For playing short sound files, such as sound effects, use a `Sound` component instead.

Properties

`Source`
Audio or video file associated with this player.

Methods

`Pause()`
Pauses playing the audio or video file.
`Start()`
Starts playing the audio or video file.
`Stop()`
Stops playing the audio or video file.
`Vibrate(number milliseconds)`
Activate the phone's vibration motor for the given number of milliseconds.

Figure 7.19 Specification of the Player component

The other properties, such as the supported audio formats, are also largely identical to those of the Sound component. Nevertheless, for the Player component, it makes sense to use the options for different media access. As the audio files used for pieces of music or audio book chapters are usually quite large, it is even recommended to save the files externally instead of integrating them as assets of the APK file. You can use either the local storage options or the Web as data pool (but check the terms and conditions!).

Of course, accessing large audio files from the Internet can take quite a long time (and quickly become expensive unless you have a flat rate for mobile Internet access!), so downloading large pieces of music to listen to them only once does not make much sense. Against this backdrop, accessing locally saved audio files is probably the best choice, whether they are stored in the internal memory or on the SD card of your own smartphone.

Use Your Own Audio Files for the Examples

Surely you already have a song or other audio file in MP3 format or one of the other supported audio formats (see Chapter 15, "Tips and Tools"). If not, you can download an MP3 file from the Internet or copy one from your PC to your smartphone via USB. If necessary, use a file manager (such as AndExplorer by Lysesoft) to find the directory path of the saved MP3 file on your smartphone. Please use your own audio files for working through the examples, and replace the directory path in the examples with your own file path on your smartphone. If you have no MP3 files available, you can use the audio files on the companion website in the directory `/MEDIA`, but these are just short sound effects and must be copied onto your smartphone for local access first.

The methods for audio playback control are also present in the Player component and make a lot more sense for use with longer audio files. You can use them to equip the audio player with corresponding user control elements to handle audio playback, just as you would from your personal music-playing devices (for example, a CD player). In our demo app, we want to give you a taste of this functionality by adding an almost complete audio player. You can use the audio player to start, pause, and stop playback of a music file from the local SD card with the touch of a button. Thus, in addition to the Player component, we need three buttons and the other components shown in Table 7.5 to design the user interface of our audio player in AI Designer.

Table 7.5 **Components and Initial Properties of the "Audio Player"**

Components	Object Name	Edited Properties
Label	DivisionLabel5	"Text": Music: play [Player] Otherwise, see Table 7.1
Player	Player	
HorizontalArrangement	HorizontalArrangement1	
Button	PlayerPlayButton	"Text": Play "Width": 100 pixels
Button	PlayerPauseButton	"Text": Pause
Button	PlayerStopButton	"Text": Stop "Width": 80 pixels

We separate the audio player from the other areas by inserting another DivisionLabel5. To arrange the control buttons of the audio player next to each other instead of one on top of the other, we insert a component object HorizontalArrangement1, into which we place the three buttons. The Play and Stop buttons need to be enlarged a little to visually emphasize their importance.

Once you have entered the settings shown in Table 7.5, the demo project should look like Figure 7.20. As you can see, the Viewer is now no longer big enough to display all visible components at once. Just as on your smartphone, you can now scroll the visible area with a scroll bar.

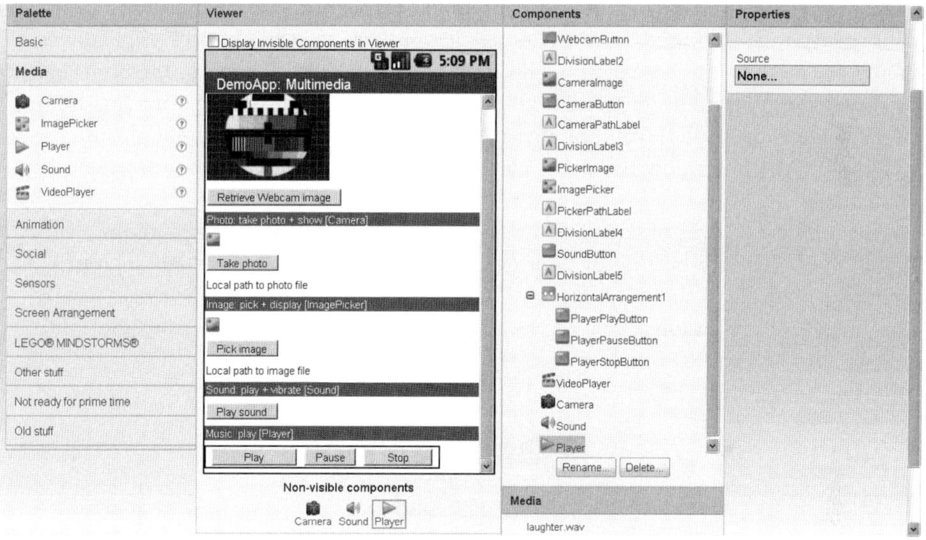

Figure 7.20 Control interface of the audio player in the demo project

Now that we have designed the control interface, we can create the functionality of the audio player in AI Editor. Let's start by implementing the Play button, or the corresponding component object `PlayerPlayButton`. Pressing this button should start playback of the audio file. To provide this function, we need the event block `PlayerPlayButton.Click`, which you can drag into the Editor area. Before an audio file can be played, it first needs to be loaded. Just as with our earlier example of the Image component, you need to tell the Player component the complete file path so it can find the audio file. To do so, assign the property component `Player.Source` a text block `text` with the appropriate file path as text; then slot both into the event handler (see Figure 7.21). You will need to replace the text shown in Figure 7.21 with a valid file path on your own smartphone, so the audio player can play an audio file present on your own smartphone!

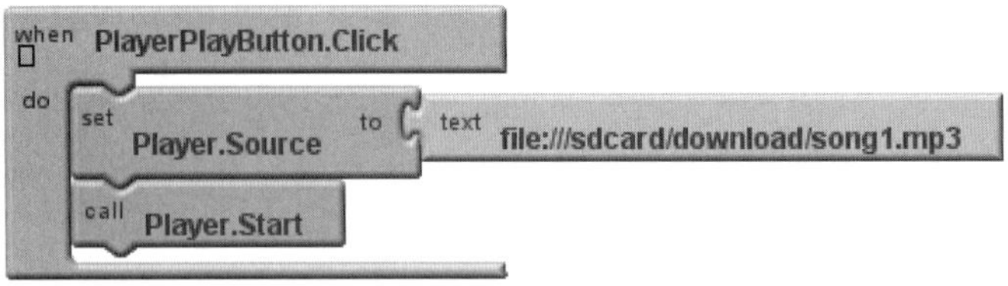

Figure 7.21 Event handler for the audio player's Play button

As you can see in Figure 7.21, the functionality of the Play button is not yet completely implemented. Now the Player component only knows where the audio file on your smartphone is located. In order to play it, you have to start playback explicitly by calling the method `Player.Start`. This method still has to be added in the event handler *below* the file path assignment. If you now test the audio player on your smartphone (and the file path is valid), you can already listen to the audio file. Without a pause or stop button, the file is now inevitably played to the end (unless you close the demo app prematurely).

As promised we will of course add a pause and stop function to our audio player We use the other two buttons or their event blocks and slot them into the appropriate Player methods as shown in Figure 7.22. So we insert the method `Player.Pause` (top) into `PlayerPauseButton.Click` and add the method `Player.Stop` (bottom) to `PlayerStopButton.Click`.

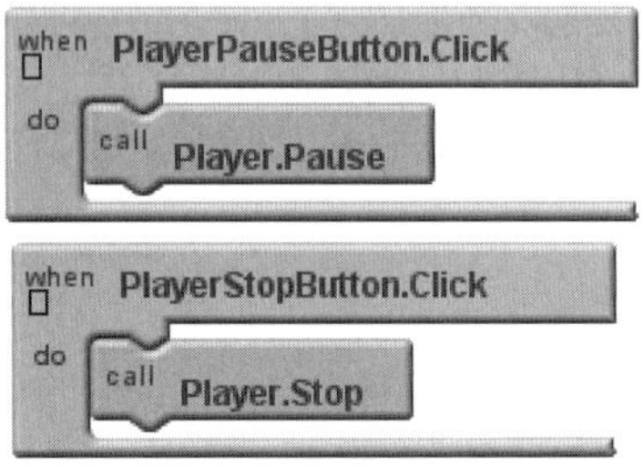

Figure 7.22 Adding event handlers for pause and stop buttons

With these three event handlers, you have fully implemented the audio player with start, pause, and stop buttons and can now try it out on your smartphone. Even if AI also makes use of a system application for playing back the audio file, you have full freedom with the synergistic Player component, at least with regard to the visual design of the user interface. In contrast, the control elements are included in the component for video playback, which we discuss in the next section.

Playing Movies with the VideoPlayer Component

For playing back video files, AI offers the component VideoPlayer in the Media group. Even though this component has a high degree of abstraction and even includes the usual control buttons for playback, it does not simply call the video player of the Android operating system and switch the view accordingly. Instead, the VideoPlayer component—or rather the video display—is fully integrated in the app in which it is implemented, so the call does not produce a visible "break" between the calling app and the external auxiliary application for playing video files. As an alternative or an addition to the user elements provided, you can implement custom control elements for your own *video player*, as you can see from the specification of the VideoPlayer component in Figure 7.23.

VideoPlayer

Use a VideoPlayer component to play a video file.

Video player is a media component that plays videos. A video player appears in your app as a rectangle. If the user taps the rectangle, media controls appear: play/pause, skip ahead, and skip backward. Your app can control playback behavior by calling the `Start`, `Pause`, and `SeekTo` methods.

Video files should be in Windows Media Video (.wmv), 3GPP (.3gp), or MPEG-4 (.mp4) format. For more details about formats, see Android Supported Media Formats.

App Inventor accepts video files up to 1 MB in size and limits the total size of an app to 5 MB, not all of which is available for media files. If your media files are too large, you might get errors when packaging or installing your app, in which case you should reduce the number of media files or their sizes. Video editing software, such as Windows Movie Maker or Apple iMovie, can help you decrease the size of videos by shortening them or re-encoding them into more compact formats.

Properties

`Source`
Video file associated with this player.
`Visible`
If set, VideoPlayer is visible.

Methods

`Pause()`
Pauses playing the video file.
`Start()`
Starts playing the video file.
`SeekTo(number millisecs)`
Seeks to the requested time (specified in milliseconds) in the video.
`GetDuration()`
Returns the duration of the video in milliseconds.

Figure 7.23 Specification of the VideoPlayer component

In addition to the general comments on supported video formats (see also the corresponding section in Chapter 15, "Tips and Tools"), the specification shown in Figure 7.23 provides important information on the maximum size of video files when using AI. As you can see, a video file is supported by AI only up to a file size of 1MB. This limit seems to apply only to video files that are integrated as assets of an APK file, for which the total file size is in turn limited to 5MB. Bear these comments in mind and refer to the tips for reducing video file sizes if necessary. Similar to the case for the large audio files mentioned in the previous section, we can assume that the generally even bigger video files will rarely be integrated into the app as an initial property, but instead will be retrieved from external file sources either on the smartphone or the Web. For accessing video files on the Internet, the same comments and tips as given previously in relation to online audio files apply.

As the component name indicates, the video player functionality is in many respects identical to that of the audio player discussed earlier. Just like an audio file, a video file must be loaded before it can be played back, and the potential use of additional pause and start buttons follows the same principle.

After your experience with the Player component, it is now easy to demonstrate the VideoPlayer component in a similar way within our demo app. We want a video file on the local smartphone to be played back when the user presses a play button. We do not need to implement the other buttons for playback control this time, as they are already included with the VideoPlayer component.

> **Use Your Own Video Files for the Examples**
>
> Just as with the audio files, you should use your own videos on your smartphone for the examples. Adapt the file paths as required. If you do not have video files in the supported video formats (see Chapter 15, "Tips and Tools"), you can record your own video with the smartphone and then use that file, usually saved as 3GP, for the examples. If necessary, check the file path for your video files with a file manager (such as AndExplorer by Lysesoft).

The user interface of our video player is quite easy to implement and can be designed in AI Designer using the settings specified in Table 7.6.

Table 7.6 **Components and Initial Properties of the "Video Player"**

Component	Object Name	Edited Properties
Label	DivisionLabel6	"Text": Video: play [VideoPlayer] Otherwise, see Table 7.1
VideoPlayer	VideoPlayer	
Button	VideoPlayerPlayButton	"Text": Play "Width": 100 pixels

The functionality of the video player is just as easy to implement in AI Editor and follows the pattern of the audio player. As we are creating just a play button this time, we need only one button or its event handler `VideoPlayerPlayButton.Click` for loading and playing back the video file. Again, the video file must be loaded first, by passing the file path as a line of text within the text block `text` to the property block `VideoPlayer.Source` (do not forget to adapt the file path to your own smartphone!). Only then can the previously loaded video file be played via the method `VideoPlayer.Start` (see Figure 7.24).

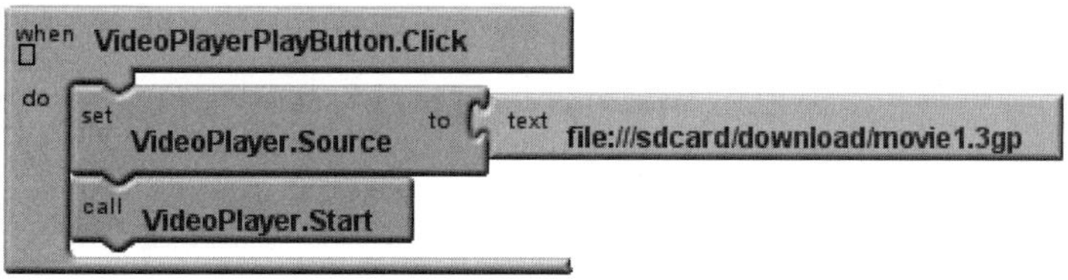

Figure 7.24 Provisional event handler for the video player's play button

The main functionality of the video player is now fully implemented, and you can watch the video on your smartphone with one press of the play button. Unfortunately, before and after playback, the *video area* on your smartphone still appears as an ugly black box that sometimes obscures the play button or other components of the demo app while you are scrolling. To fix this problem, you can hide the video area as long as no video is being played back, and show it again for playing a video. This can be done via the VideoPlayer property "Visible." Disable the initial property "Visible" in AI Designer by removing the check mark from the "Visible" check box. The black video area then disappears from the integrated smartphone.

Of course, playing back the video by pressing the play button is now no longer possible because the video display area is not visible. Thus you need to show it explicitly at runtime when you press the play button. To do so, we need to add the property block `VideoPlayer.Visible` to the event handler `VideoPlayerPlayButton.Click` in AI Editor by slotting it into the first position in the event block. In addition, you need to switch the state of the property block `VideoPlayer.Visible` from the current default state `false` (check box disabled) to `true` (see the comments on Boolean values in the section "Selecting Options with the CheckBox Component" in Chapter 6). You do this by using the generic block `true` in the Logic group in the Built-In block selection, which you slot into the property block `VideoPlayer.Visible`. Now the video area is displayed if you press the play button and the video is played back. After the video ends, the video area remains on the screen as a black box, so you have to hide it again at runtime by using the VideoPlayer event block `VideoPlayer.Completed`, which is activated automatically at the end of the video. Into this event block you slot another property block `VideoPlayer.Visible`, but this time you assign it the Boolean value `false` via the corresponding logic block. The expanded block structure for the video player in the demo app looks like Figure 7.25.

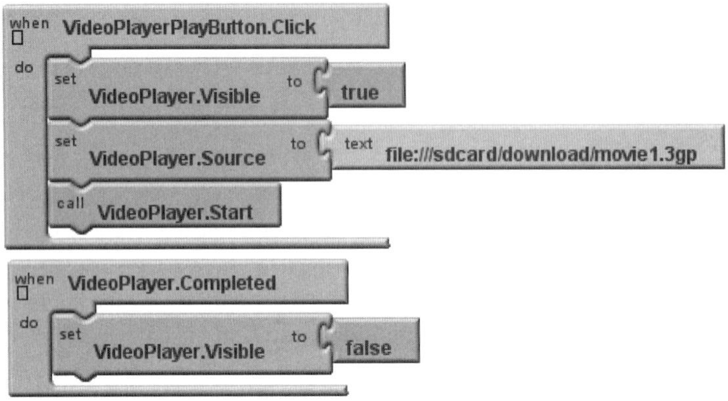

Figure 7.25 Event handlers for dynamically showing and hiding the video player

By implementing the block structure shown in Figure 7.25, you can now enjoy the video playback on your smartphone (see Figure 7.26). While the video player user interface appears without the annoying black box when the app is called (left), pressing the play button displays the video area, loads the video file, and plays it. During playback, you can access the control elements provided with the VideoPlayer component by pressing anywhere on the video area and use them to control playback (center). After the video has finished playing, the video area is automatically hidden again (right) until the user presses the play button again.

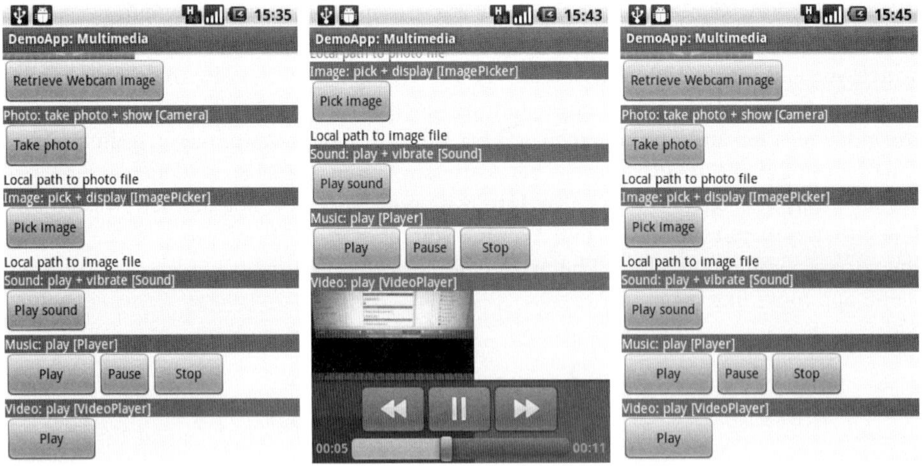

Figure 7.26 The “tidied” video player in action on the smartphone

With this step, we have added a powerful video player to our multimedia demo app `demo_Media`. In addition to dynamic webcam images, a photo album, acoustic and haptic signals, and an audio player, you have now encountered the last media type for developing impressive multimedia apps with AI. Except for the photos we took ourselves with the Camera component, we have mainly concentrated on retrieving ready-made media files. In contrast to the mere *consumption* of multimedia contents, we want to finish our consideration of multimedia by discussing another component for *producing* media files in the next section.

Recording Audio with the SoundRecorder Component

During our multimedia project, we have been mainly accessing and playing ready-made files. To finish off this chapter, however, we are going to get creative and produce our own media files with our demo app. Although we have already created our own image files in the context of the Camera component, this process took place almost entirely outside of our demo app and within the camera app provided by the operating system. Now we want to create files of a different media type—namely, audio—and this process is to occur without noticeable "break," entirely within the demo app. We want to design a user interface similar to that of the audio player described earlier, with the difference that the three buttons will now be used to start, end, and save a sound recording and play it back. In essence, what we are adding to our app is the functionality of a *dictaphone*, which normally has exactly those user elements.

For sound recording, AI offers the non-visible component SoundRecorder in the group "Not ready for prime time" (see Figure 7.27). As you would expect, the SoundRecorder component has two methods to "start" and "stop" recording. Plus there are event blocks for actions at the beginning (`StartedRecording`) and the end (`StoppedRecording`) and for passing and using the file path of the recorded audio file (`AfterSoundRecorded`).

SoundRecorder

●

Multimedia component that records audio.

Properties

none

Events

`AfterSoundRecorded(text sound)`
Provides the location of the newly created sound.
`StartedRecording()`
Indicates that the recorder has started, and can be stopped.
`StoppedRecording()`
Indicates that the recorder has stopped, and can be started again.

Methods

`Start()`
Starts recording.
`Stop()`
Stops recording.

Figure 7.27 Specification of the SoundRecorder component

After our experiences with the other multimedia components, you probably already have a general idea from looking at the event blocks and methods in Figure 7.27 about which ones we will use for our dictaphone. Let's start by creating the user interface, which we will make a bit more elaborate this time. The record button should stand out in color from the horizontally arranged stop and play buttons, and we want the status line to show a text during recording, indicating that the file path will be displayed later. Use the information in Table 7.7 to design the dictaphone and arrange the three buttons within the HorizontalArrangement2.

Table 7.7 **Components and Initial Properties for the "Dictaphone"**

Component	Object name	Edited Properties
Label	DivisionLabel7	"Text": Audio: record + play [SoundRecorder] Otherwise, see Table 7.1
SoundRecorder	SoundRecorder	
HorizontalArrangement	HorizontalArrangement2	
Button	RecorderRecordButton	"FontBold" enabled "TextColor": Red "Text": Record "Width": 100 pixels
Button	RecorderStopButton	"Text": Stop "Width": 80 pixels
Button	RecorderPlayButton	"Text": Play "Width": 80 pixels
Label	RecorderPathLabel	"Text": Local path to audio file

With the settings shown in Table 7.7, the user interface of the dictaphone should appear as shown in Figure 7.28.

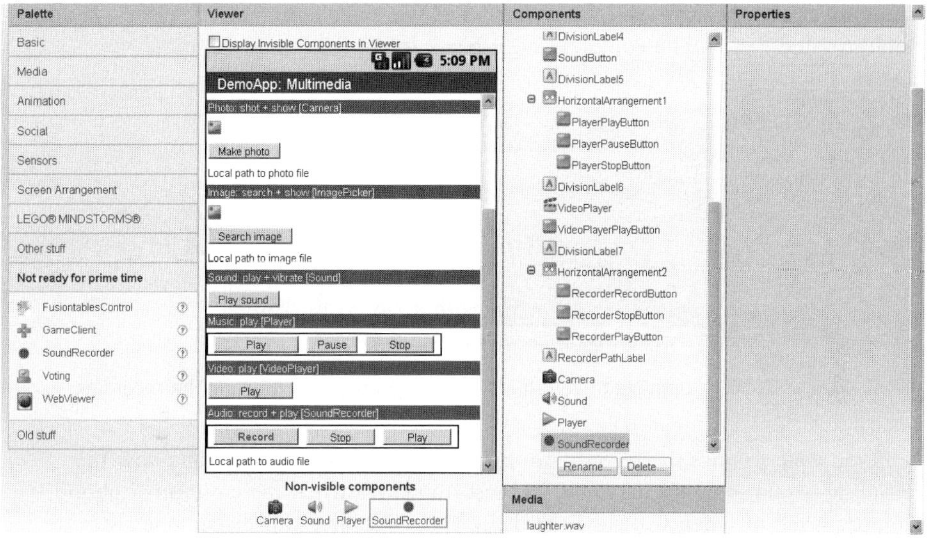

Figure 7.28 The demo project including the user elements of the "dictaphone"

Now we have made all preparations and created the component objects we need in AI Editor for implementing the dictaphone functionality. Next, let's create the record button with which the user can start the sound recording. For this basic function, we need only the event block `RecorderRecordButton.Click`, into which we slot the SoundRecorder method `SoundRecorder.Start` (see Figure 7.29).

Figure 7.29 Preliminary event handler for starting the recording

As mentioned earlier, we want the user interaction for the dictaphone to be somewhat more elaborate and more ergonomic than in the previous examples. For that reason, we want to add two more component objects to the event handler shown in Figure 7.29. During the recording, we want RecorderPathLabel to show the important notice "RECORDING!" as feedback to the user, who would otherwise not know whether the smartphone is recording. Also, we want the record button to be disabled during recording, to avoid it being pressed again and as an additional visual indication that recording is currently in progress. For these additional functions, we add a property block `RecorderPathLabel.Text` to the event handler shown in Figure 7.29, and we assign it a text block `text` with the corresponding notice text. Then we add a property block `RecorderRecordButton.Enabled`, with which we disable the record button via the Boolean value `false`. The complete event block looks like Figure 7.30.

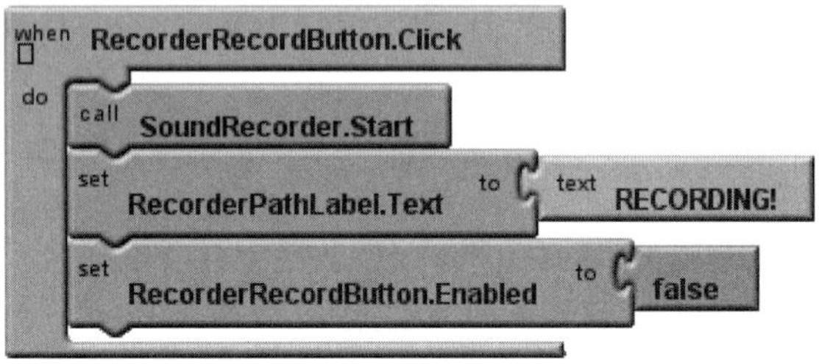

Figure 7.30 Completed event handler for ergonomically starting the recording

If you were to press the record button on your connected smartphone now, the recording would start, but then it would just stop again when the entire smartphone memory is full or when you close the demo app. Of course, our dictaphone also needs an option for explicitly stopping the recording. You implement this functionality in the event handler of the stop button, by slotting the SoundRecorder method `SoundRecorder.Stop` into the event block `RecorderStopButton.Click`. In addition, you must ensure that the disabled record button gets enabled again so that the user can start another recording if necessary. To do so, you again use a property block `RecorderRecordButton.Enabled`, but this time assign it the Boolean value `true`. The overall functionality of the stop button results from the event handler shown in Figure 7.31.

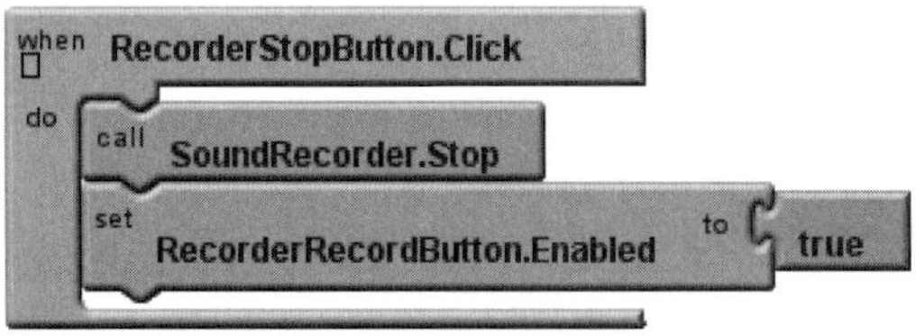

Figure 7.31 Handler for stopping the recording and re-enabling the record button

As we want a high degree of ergonomic appeal for our dictaphone, we want to offer the user the option of automatically listening to the recording he or she has just made. To do so, we use an "After" event, which triggers the system application on which the recording function is based immediately after the sound recording is stopped. Similar to the "After" event we used in the context of the Camera component to automatically display the photo we took (`Camera.AfterPicture` with the variable `image`), we achieve the automatic playback of the recorded audio file with the event block `SoundRecorder.AfterSoundRecorded`. Once again, it returns the complete file path to the current recorded audio file as a line of text within a variable with the (preset, but amendable) name `sound` that is now available in the event handler (see Figure 7.32).

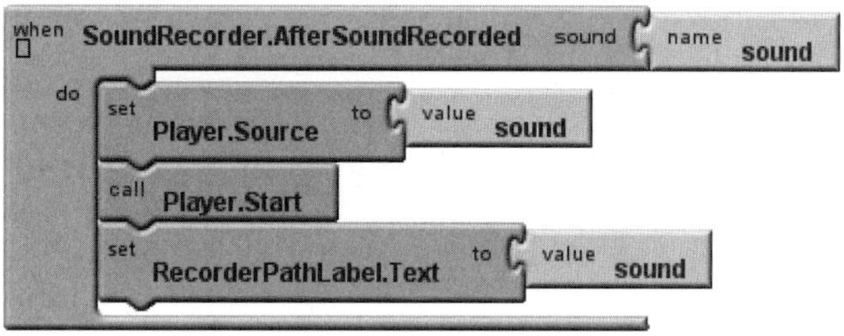

Figure 7.32 Automatic loading and playing back the recorded file, as well as displaying its path

To play the recorded file, we simply use the non-visible object Player, which is already present in the demo project `demo_Media` (we added it to the project in the section "Playing Audio Files with the Player Component"). Instead of passing the audio player a fixed file path as a text block via the property block `Player.Source`, we assign it the variable `sound`, which contains the file path of the current recorded file as a line of text. Then we can start the audio player as usual by calling the method `Player.Start`. For the sake of completeness, we also display the file path as a line of text by assigning the value from the variable `sound` to the property block `RecorderPathLabel.Text`. With this event handler (shown in Figure 7.32), we can now load and play the recorded file after pressing the stop button; in addition, the notice "RECORDING!" is replaced by the current file path.

Of course, the dictaphone functionality makes sense only if the sound recording can also be played back later at any time. This is the task of the play button, or rather its event handler. As we have already passed the file path of the current sound recording to the audio player in the event handler shown in Figure 7.32, we do not need to repeat this step to replay the same sound recording. Instead, we can simply restart the audio player in the event block `RecorderPlayButton.Click` with the method `Player.Start` (see Figure 7.33) and play back the current recording with each press of the play button.

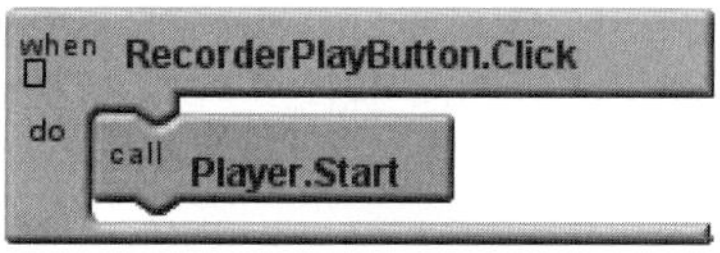

Figure 7.33 Event handler for replaying the sound recording

Now the functionality of the dictaphone is complete. To summarize the interplay of the individual components and event handlers, Figure 7.34 shows an overview of all the underlying block structures.

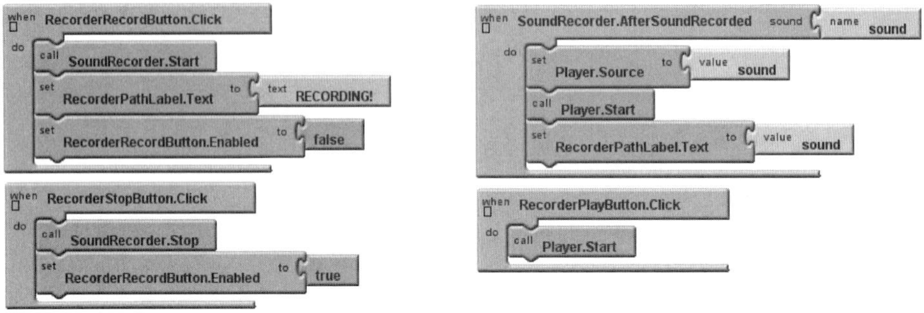

Figure 7.34 Overall functionality of the "dictaphone" with four event handlers

Go ahead and try out this rather elaborate dictaphone functionality on your smartphone (see Figure 7.35). By pressing the record button in the default state (left), you disable it, display the notice "RECORDING!," and can record a spoken text into your smartphone microphone, sing a song, or make any other audio recording you like (center). When you are finished, you can stop the recording by pressing the stop button, which re-enables the record button, replaces the notice with the file path of the audio file you just recorded, and automatically plays this file via the system speakers (right). After this automatic playback, you can listen to your recording over and over again by pressing the play button; alternatively, you can start a new recording by pressing the record button.

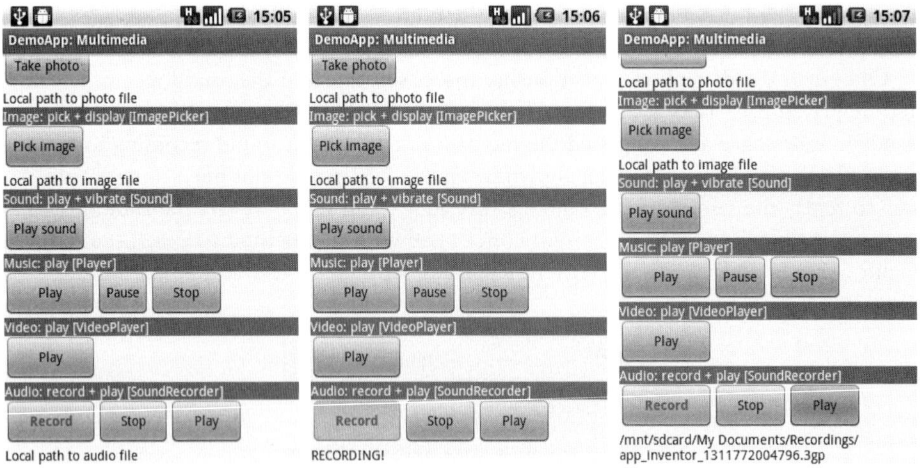

Figure 7.35 The dictaphone in action on the smartphone

In completing the implementation of the dictaphone functionality, we have delved a bit further into programming work and gone beyond the mere demonstration of a basic function of the SoundRecorder component. You have seen how important ergonomic functions (such as displaying the recording notice and disabling or re-enabling the button) can be implemented virtually along the way, how you can synergistically share the use of existing component objects (such as the audio player), and use existing data (for example, the already loaded file path in the audio player) repeatedly and even via different event handlers. In the remainder of this book as well as in your future development work with AI, you will undoubtedly find new ways of increasing the already high efficiency of the visual development language even more with skillful and effective development approaches.

> **Demo Project demo_Media on the Companion Website**
>
> As always, you can find the multimedia project `demo_Media` in the usual directories on the companion website.

In your future work, you may find it helpful to reduce the complexity of large app projects by breaking down the event handlers and components they contain into smaller, more manageable chunks. For example, the complete block structure of the demo project `demo_Media` shown in Figure 7.36 seems rather complicated and difficult to keep track of. But if you look at each area individually, as we did over the course of this chapter, you will discern a manageable structure that can make it easier for you to keep your bearings in most cases. All developers have to face this challenge, whether they are trying to keep track of hundreds of code lines written in a specific programming language or the elements of a visual development language. But do not worry—this is also a matter of practice: The more experience you gain, the easier it will become. In the remaining chapters of this book, we will also introduce some tools that will make working with the AI IDE even easier for you.

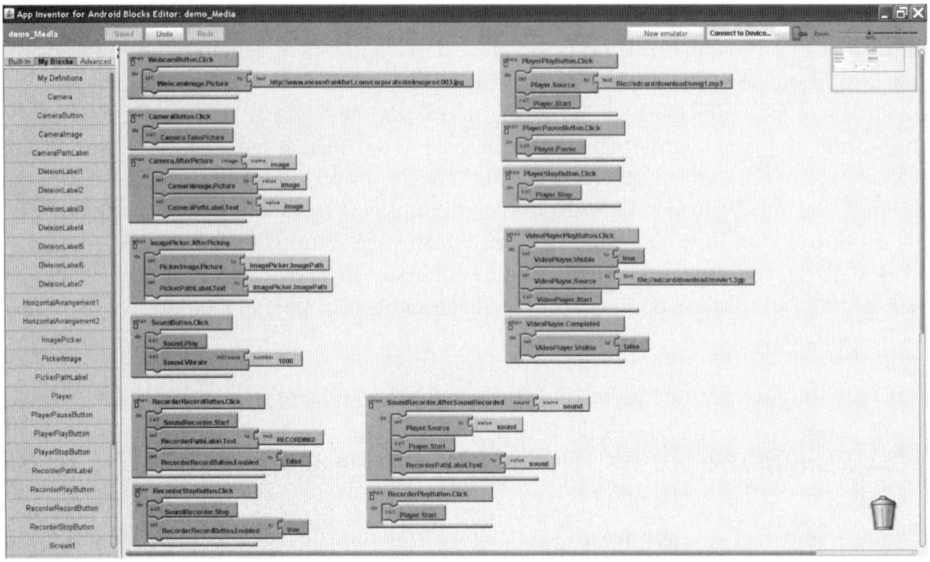

Figure 7.36 Complete block structure of the demo app "demo_Media"

With the experience gained in the previous beginners projects, you should have achieved the right mindset for tackling the next steps on your way to becoming an app developer with AI.

Chapter 8

Example Project: Creating a Media Center

As promised at the beginning of Part II of this book, we want to use specific example projects to illustrate what we have learned, above and beyond the demo projects. An example project usually focuses on one more or less narrowly defined topic, for which the app you are developing provides one solution (out of potentially many) based on the previously demonstrated components. Here the primary function is no longer demonstrating the function of individual components (bottom-up), but practically applying what you have learned within a concrete and realistic task on an appropriate scale (top-down).

From this point of view, we operated very much in demonstration mode in the first demo project `demo_GUI`. In contrast, we used the elements of the graphical user interface with a clear focus on practical application in the second demo project `demo_Media`, with the goal of demonstrating the new multimedia components (i.e., without a button, you cannot start an audio or video player). Thus the transitions between the two approaches and between the demo and example projects are sometimes not clear-cut. This blurring of lines will continue in the next few chapters, as the new projects generally build on the knowledge accumulated during the earlier ones.

Ergonomic Redesign of a Media Center

Against this backdrop, and given the fact that our second demo project `demo_Media` had a practical focus by realizing the functions of a webcam, a camera, a photo album, audio and video players, and a dictaphone, you already have usable examples for working multimedia applications. We close this part of the book with an example project that is not meant to go further into any of these areas of application, but instead give an overview of the two topics addressed previously, by expanding the multimedia functions within an visually and ergonomically more appealing graphical user interface to create an integrated *media center*. We can use the functions created in `demo_Media` as a starting point without having to make many changes, but we will redesign the access to and operation of these functions to make them considerably more fit for practical use.

In the process, you will perceive how you can generally expand the demo projects in this book to create professional-looking apps that will be comparable in quality to some of the apps available on the Android Market. Moreover, the example project will suggest how you can simulate the effect of *multiple screens* in your apps developed with Google AI, despite the current limitation to one single screen. Take a look at Figure 8.1, which shows the media center into which we will expand the demo app `demo_Media` during the course of this chapter.

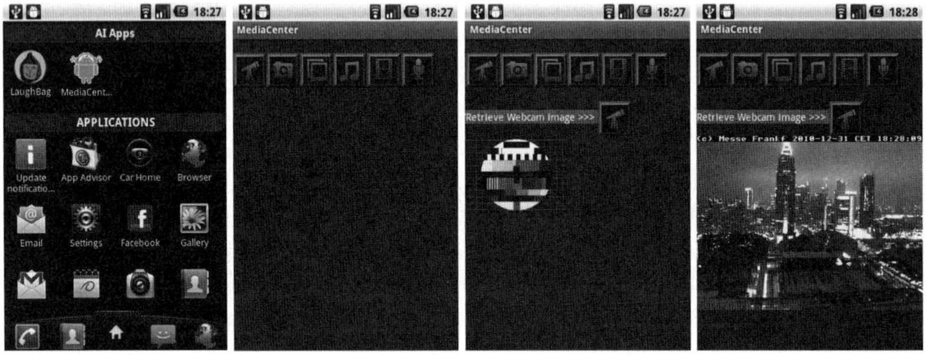

Figure 8.1 The Media Center app on the smartphone

As you can see in Figure 8.1, the appearance and user concepts of our previous multimedia components from the demo app will change considerably in the full-fledged media center. When you launch the media center by pressing the corresponding app icon (Screen > Icon: `media_appIcon.png`) in your smartphone's application menu, the app opens with a tasteful gray background (Screen > BackgroundColor: Dark gray) and nothing more than a subtly stylish menu bar with elegant *menu buttons* (icons by Joseph Wain, `glyphish.com`).

> **Media Center on the Companion Website**
>
> All image files for recreating the media center, plus the entire project and APK file, can be found on this book's companion website in the corresponding directories (see the link in the Introduction).

Once you select a menu key, the relevant media area is displayed in a separate *subscreen*, overlaid by a function notifier and the selected *media key*, with which you can also trigger the media function in most cases (*active* media key). For example, pressing the active media key (telescope icon) in the subscreen shown in Figure 8.1 will retrieve the webcam image as previously described. As you might have guessed, this function notifier and the media key are nothing more than the adapted component objects DivisionLabel1 and WebcamButton created in the section "Displaying Images with the Image Component" in Chapter 7, together with the current image in WebcamImage. In the same way, you can use the other menu keys (from left to right) to activate the camera, the photo album, the audio player, the video player, and the dictaphone. (The audio signal with vibration has not been integrated into the media center, so delete all relevant component objects and blocks in AI Designer and Editor where necessary.) Figure 8.2 shows all six media areas in action after they have been activated in turn.

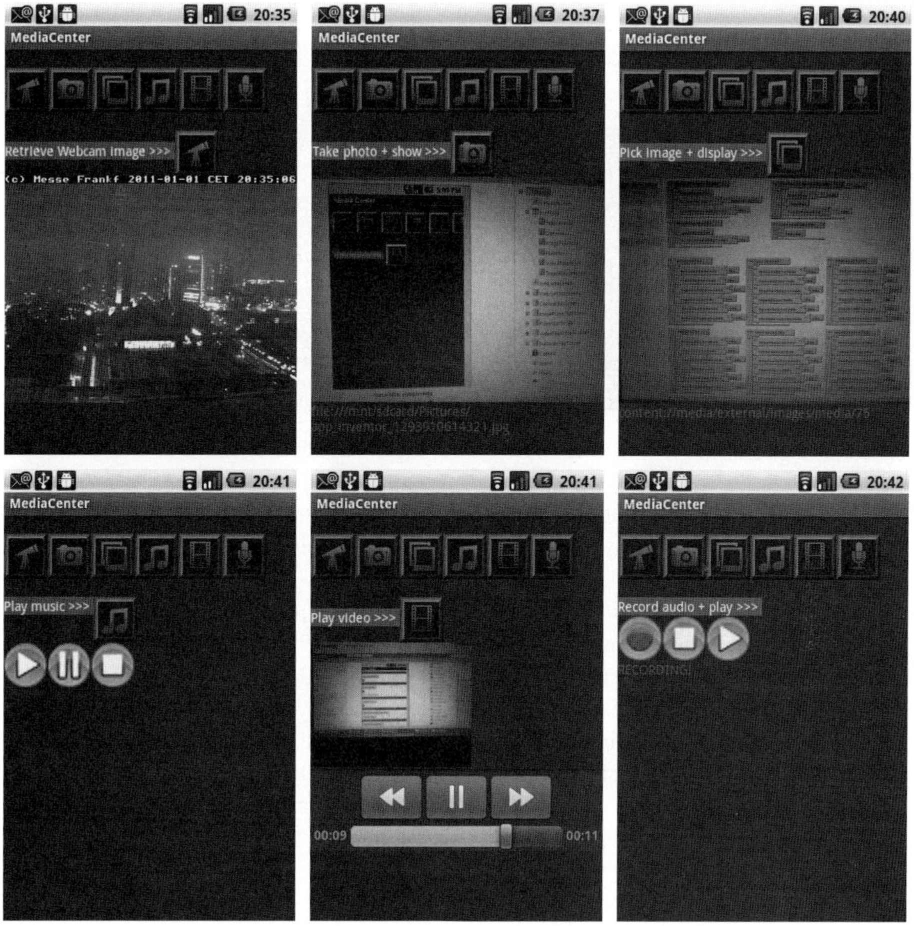

Figure 8.2 The six media areas of the media center in action

Editing the individual media areas from the previous demo project to redesign them structurally and ergonomically as shown in Figure 8.2 is quite easy. In the media areas where a single button triggers the functionality (webcam, camera, photo album, video player), you simply need to texture the button with an image file for the media icon instead of the previous text, and arrange it together with its DivisionLabel in a

HorizontalArrangement to form a *header*. The term "header" is used in an analogy to e-mail in our example, where you have a *header* and a *body* (text content). In Figure 8.3, you can see from the example of the Webcam media area how the component objects DivisionLabel1 and WebcamButton are now combined into a HorizontalArrangement component object with the name WebcamHeader into one structural unit. In the same way, we create the headers for the other media areas with an active media key.

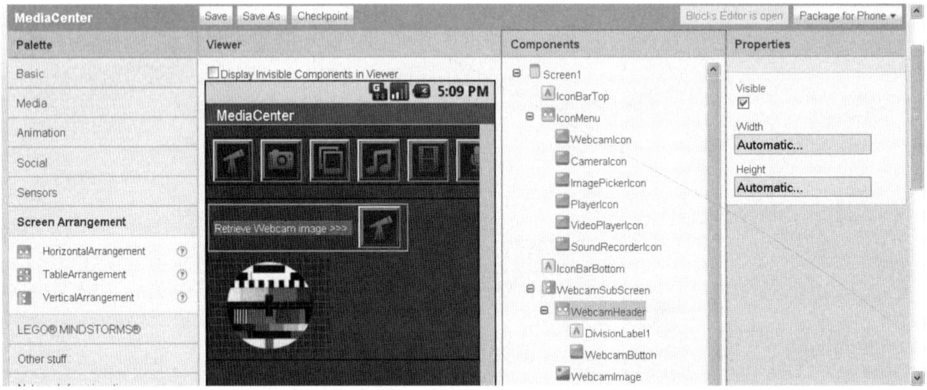

Figure 8.3 Combining a label and an active media key into a header

In the media areas with their own control elements (audio player, dictaphone), the media key is displayed as a symbol for the currently selected media area in form of a textured Image component object (*passive* media key). For example, Figure 8.4 shows the Musicplayer media area, where the PlayerHeader contains only an Image component object PlayerImage in addition to the DivisionLabel5. The functional start button Player-PlayButton of the music player, however, is located within the *body* of the subscreen. The function keys PlayerPlayButton, PlayerPauseButton, and PlayerStopButton have also been textured with corresponding image files instead of the text labels used earlier, and combined within a HorizontalArrangement component object PlayerBody. In the same way, we adapted the header and body of the Dictaphone media area.

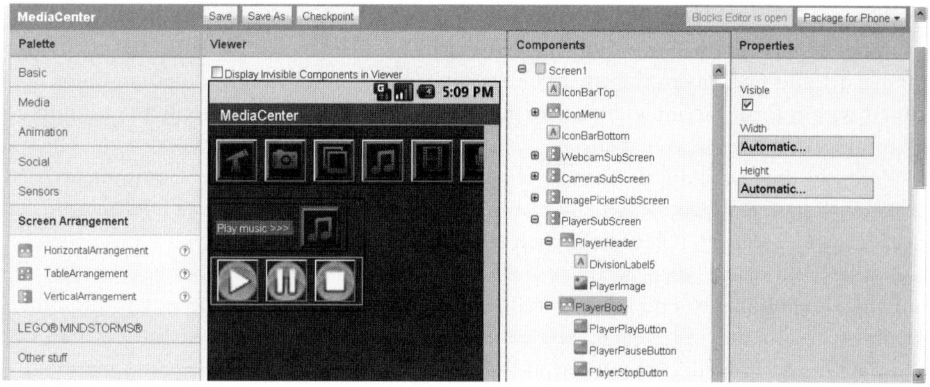

Figure 8.4 Passive media key in the header with function keys in the body

With the knowledge you have acquired in the section "Tidying the Screen with the Screen Arrangement Component" in Chapter 6, you should be able to easily reproduce the structural adaptations described here and carry them out yourself in AI Designer by using `demo_Media` as your starting point. Simply save a copy of this demo project (Save As > "MediaCenter"), and work on the new project in AI Designer. You won't need AI Editor until you start creating the multiple screens.

Multiple Screens for the Media Center

Although Google AI does not officially support multiple screens at the time of writing (see Issue 46), you as app developer do not have to miss out on the effect of having several screens in your app. Even if this function becomes available (such as the way the MIT AI offers it in its experimental version), you may still prefer to use alternative or more flexible design options for this basic effect. Using multiple screens—in whatever form—is an important element of the clear, ergonomic, and structured design of complex apps that comprise multiple functions. Your demo app `demo_Media` also had more than one function, and you saw how quickly both the display for the app user and the structure for you as developer became confusing and cluttered in AI Designer. By introducing a separate screen for each media type, we can significantly improve the structure of our media center in both respects.

We completed the first step of this redesign in the previous section. You as developer have now structured the individual media areas in AI Designer by hierarchically grouping all components of a media area into the structural elements of a header and a body. In the second step, we will combine the header and body of each media area under a single category, the so-called subscreen. The subscreen, which hierarchically gathers all components of a media area under itself, is exactly the structural element we want to display when a media area is selected via the menu keys. From the developer's point of view, the subscreen is nothing more than another component from the group Screen Arrangement, which contains the header/body combination in a hierarchy instead of as individual components. Within this *nested* hierarchical structure, the subscreen is the main category, the header and body form the two subcategories, and the individual components contained within form the individual elements (in the tree analogy commonly used in programming, the leaves and branches).

Precisely, this hierarchical structure is reflected in AI Designer in the Components panel. In Figure 8.5, you can see an example of the hierarchical structure in Components: first the main category RecorderSubScreen, and subordinate to it the two subcategories RecorderHeader and RecorderBody, and then subordinate to these subcategories the individual components. The hierarchical structure is applied in the same way to the other media areas. The only difference between the media areas with active media keys and those with passive media keys is that in the former the executing media components are directly subordinate to the main category subscreen without any intermediary body category; this organization is shown in Figure 8.5 using the example of the subscreen VideoPlayerSubScreen and its media component VideoPlayer.

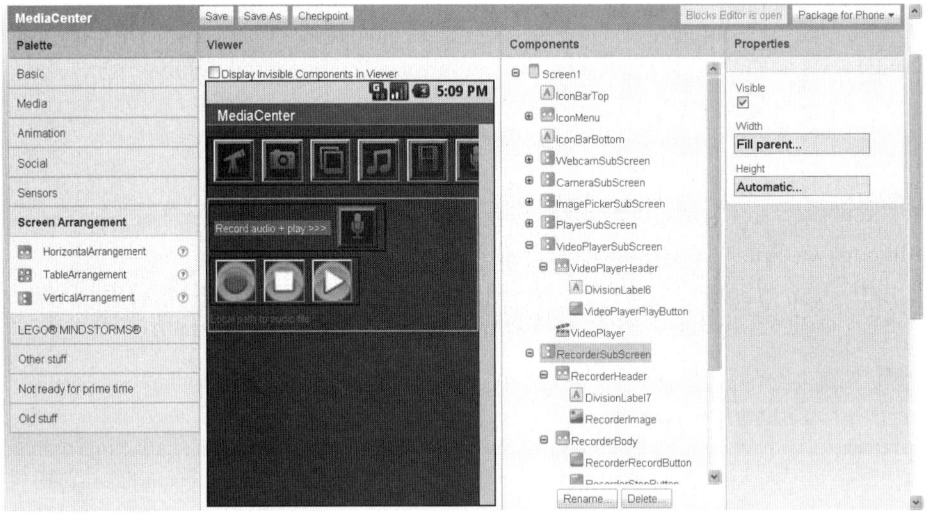

Figure 8.5 Hierarchical structure of subscreens with header, body, and elements

In Figure 8.5, you can see how tidy the program structure now appears in AI Designer. All subscreens are directly subordinate to the *root element* "Screen1" and can be hidden (–) or displayed (+) by clicking on the small square on the left in the AI Designer Components panel. As you can see, all subscreens in Figure 8.5 are collapsed, except for the VideoPlayerSubScreen and RecorderSubScreen, which makes it much easier for you as developer to keep track of the project as a whole.

But this step does not complete all of the preparations in AI Designer for realizing multiple screens. We still need one important default setting in the initial properties of all subscreens. To make sure that the media areas are not displayed one beneath the other all at once, but rather that none of the media areas is visible when the media center is launched, we need to assign to all subscreens the initial property non-visible via the initial property field "Visible" (remove the check mark from the check box). The app then shows only the menu bar when it is launched, as intended. However, the Viewer area also shows only the menu bar. To ensure that all components remain visible in the Viewer during your development work, you can display the normally invisible components by enabling the check box "Display Invisible Components in Viewer," as shown in Figure 8.6.

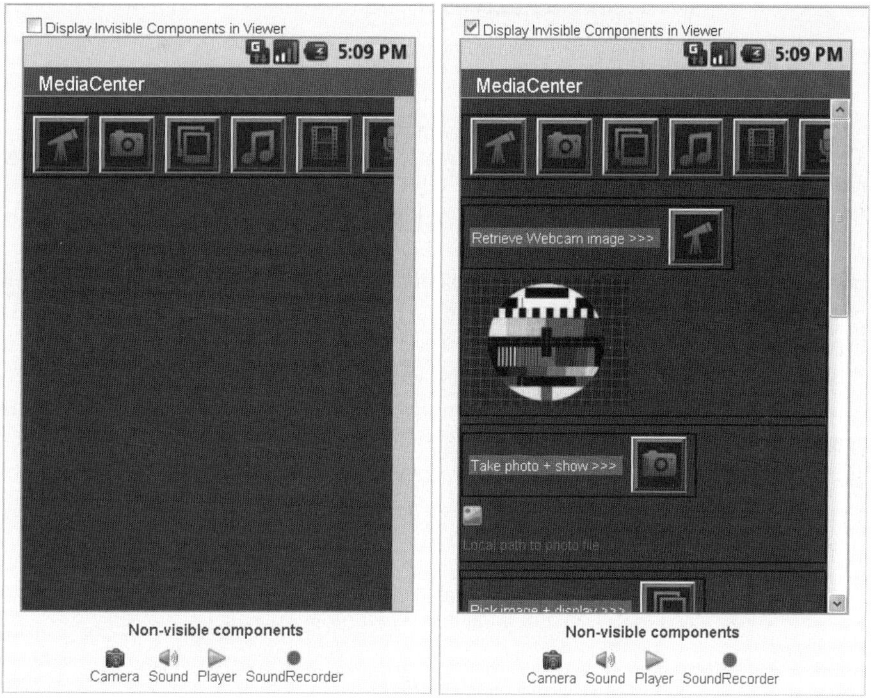

Figure 8.6 Displaying and hiding invisible components in Viewer

The individual menu keys, which are visible in the menu bar, are also combined within a structural component object IconMenu, which groups the various menu keys in the Components panel as shown in Figure 8.7.

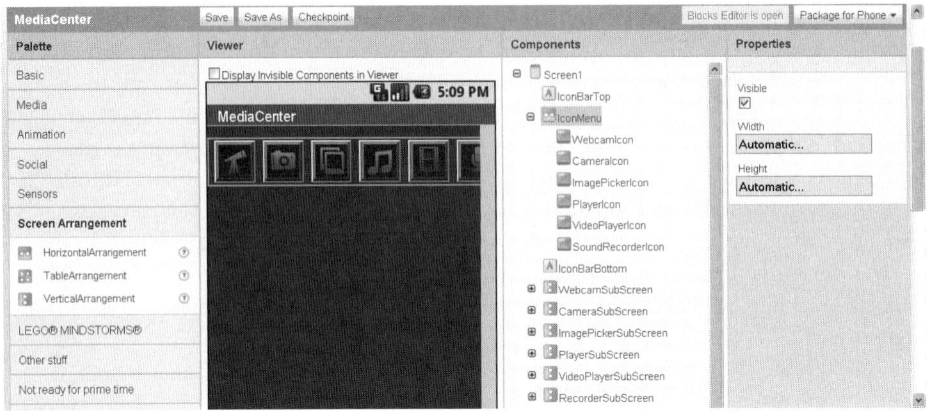

Figure 8.7 Always visible structural component IconMenu with menu keys

Now we need to develop the functionality of the menu bar for displaying the multiple screens in AI Editor. Although that sounds like a major undertaking, the functionality merely consists of displaying the appropriate subscreen when a menu key is pressed and hiding all other subscreens. After our structural preparations, this is no big deal. We simply set the "Visible" property of all menu keys in the event blocks of the menu keys to the desired value of either `true` or `false`. For example, we need to slot the "Visible" property blocks of all six menu keys into the event block `WebcamIcon.Click` shown in Figure 8.8 and to assign a Boolean value to each of them via a logic block. We want to make only the Webcam subscreen visible if the corresponding menu key is pressed—none of the other subscreens should be visible—so only its own property block `WebcamSubScreen.Visible` is assigned the value `true`. We need to slot the same property blocks into the other event handlers of the six menu keys in the same way; in each case, only the relevant event block's "own" property block "Visible" is set to `true`.

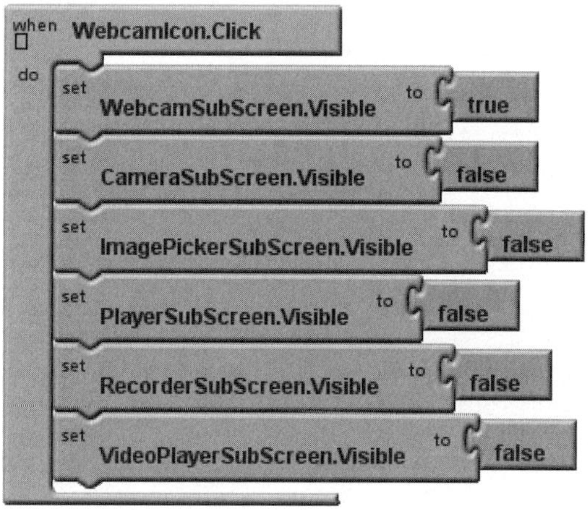

Figure 8.8 Event handler for displaying the Webcam subscreen

Thus a total of six times six property settings is required for switching between the media areas via the menu keys. You now need to add these properties in AI Editor within the six different event handlers, either manually or by using copy and paste.

Copy and Paste in AI Editor

To make your task less tedious, you can take advantage of the handy function *copy and paste* in AI Editor. Once you have manually created the first event handler in AI Editor, you can copy it by clicking on the event block with the mouse and then pressing the keyboard shortcuts **Ctrl+C** and then **Ctrl+V**. Push the resulting copy of the entire event handler to a free space in AI Editor, grab the top property block in it, and drag all property blocks along with it into a free area in the Editor. Now delete the empty event block (put it in the recycle bin) and drag a new event block for the next menu key from the block selection into the Editor. Then grab the copied pile of property blocks again and slot it into the new event block. You can then adapt the settings for the Boolean values in the copied property blocks by clicking on the logic blocks to the right of the value and choosing either `true` or `false`. Repeat this process until you have created event handlers for all six menu keys.

In Figure 8.9, you can see the result: all event handlers of the six menu keys that we need to add to the existing demo project. (Do not forget to delete the previous block structures for the sound effect with vibration where necessary.)

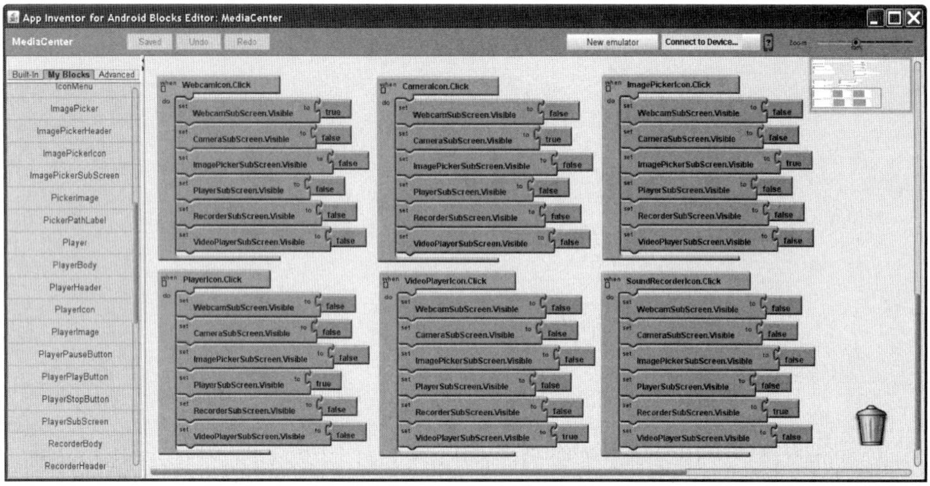

Figure 8.9 All event handlers for switching between the subscreens

By adding these six event handlers, the functionality of the menu bar for switching between the media areas is fully implemented. By working with the redesign in AI Designer, we have turned the former demo-app `demo_Media` into a professional-looking, ergonomic, and structured media center. Of course, you can easily transfer this concept of multiple screens to other areas of application. You have now acquired the fundamental knowledge and tools for developing appealing apps with graphical user interfaces and multimedia content—lessons that will serve you well in developing your own future app projects.

Multiple Screens with the MIT AI system

In the MIT AI Experimental version, a dedicated function was introduced on December 20, 2011, to set up multiple screens. With the two new buttons `Add Screen` and `Remove Screen`, screens can be added and removed to Screen1 in the AI Designer. The different screens and their components communicate with each other by exchanging arguments via new events like `Screen1.OtherScreenClosed` and methods like `open another screen` or `close screen with result`. A good tutorial on how to use the new multiple screen function in the MIT AI Experimental can be found at:

`http://cs.wellesley.edu/~eni/aitutorial/multiplescreen.html`

It is your choice which method you prefer for multiple screens.

Part III

On the Way to Becoming an App Developer

You have already taken the first few steps on your way toward becoming a developer of Android apps with AI. In the introductory beginners' projects, you have learned how to equip the user interface with various graphical control elements, how to use different multimedia components, and how to create an impressive app by adding multiple screens. In the process, you have been using the central concepts of the visual development language AI by setting the initial properties of the components used in AI Designer, changing these properties during runtime via block structures in AI Editor in response to events, and calling system applications via predefined methods to integrate their return values into your app. On this basis, you have managed to create an impressive app in form of the media center—but the capacity of AI is by no means exhausted.

In our previous projects, we have, from a developer's point of view, mostly concentrated on ensuring that the created app reacts to a user action one-dimensionally by executing a fixed functionality. For example, pressing a button always led to the same result, such as displaying the event name or playing a sound effect. While this behavior may be sufficient for some simple apps and their functions, the application context of most apps requires taking additional factors into account. For example, the result of pressing the equals key on a calculator app depends on which calculating function was selected and which numbers were entered previously; moreover, in the case of a color coding for negative numbers you have to take into account whether the result of the calculation is smaller than zero. Any such calculations, interim results, and dependency checks are based on *data* and data structures that vary in form and nature. Without these data structures, most of the apps on your smartphone would be just an empty shell without any proper purpose (like a car without gasoline). Which data varieties AI or Android distinguishes and how you can process and manage them is the subject of Chapter 9, the introductory chapter in this third part of our book. You will have the chance to apply these concepts while developing your own calculator, quiz game, and vocabulary trainer apps.

With this foundation of sound developer know-how, you will get to know even more powerful components of AI. You will find out how to save data persistently on your smartphone, or work with databases locally or online in the cloud. At the end of this third part of our book, you will be able to develop apps that are impressive not just because of their powerful components but also because of their clever use in the block structures that you as developer have implemented. The successful combination of these elements makes for a really good app. Once more, we will conclude with example projects to give you inspiration for your own app projects.

Chapter 9

Program Development Basics

Yes, you read the title of this chapter right. After working your way through this chapter, you will be able to develop *programs*, because apps are nothing more than programs for your smartphone, and AI is nothing more than a visual programming language. Up to now, we have mainly dragged ready-made components into the AI Designer and used the corresponding blocks in AI Editor to liven them up a bit. Now, however, we will give more program structure and individual character to the apps we are designing. To do so, we will make use of the *generic blocks* (from the Built-In block group), which are documented in their own section of the AI References and form the basic building blocks for elaborate apps with complex program flow control and real data processing. But do not worry—as always, we will proceed in well-measured small steps when creating our apps. No knowledge other than what you have gained in the previous chapters is required. We will lead you step by step on your way to becoming a successful app developer.

When introducing the generic blocks, we mainly want to show you how to develop *algorithms* (program flow control), which are what every program and every app is based on. These can be very simple algorithms, some of which you have already encountered, developed, and implemented within the *pseudocode* used in the context of the example app LaughBag in Chapter 3, for example:

```
When user clicks LaughButton, do play the sound Laughter!
```

Each program instruction describing the whole or a self-contained part function of the app corresponds to an algorithm in the wider sense. Nevertheless, we want to apply the term *algorithm* primarily to those program structures in which we divide a complex task into program instructions that, in their entirety, contribute to solving a problem. For example, in a calculator app, each button has its own task to fulfill, but all buttons must work together to create the overall functionality of the app—in other words, the functionality of a calculator. Please be aware of this distinction between individual functions and the overall function of an app, before you start exploring the building blocks for developing algorithms.

Perhaps another analogy for the relationship between the components (component blocks) and the generic blocks will help you better understand this concept. Imagine the previously used components and their component blocks as individual instruments (control elements) in an airplane cockpit. Each component, such as the altimeter and the compass, has its own function, but the details of how this function is implemented are neither transparent nor of much significance to the (auto) pilot. For example, you have been using the Camera component to take photos. Exactly *how* the relevant system application took these photos was not very relevant to you as developer of the media center, only the fact that the photos *were* taken and could then be *used* by your app. Just as important for the (auto) pilot is receiving the correct data from the altimeter, compass, and other cockpit instruments, so as to be able to stay on course and determine the right flight altitude, which in turn fulfills the overall task of the cockpit and the entire airplane, which is taking the passengers safely from point A to point B. The generic blocks work in a similar way: They connect the individual components or the data produced by these components (creating an interaction rather than existing side-by-side), following the motto "The whole is more than the sum of its parts" (Aristotle, 384–322 BC). If you can also manage to fulfill the needs of potential users with this overall system, then you have created a successful app.

Elements of Data Processing

Let's get back to the building blocks that AI offers you for connecting the parts to create a whole. As with the components, we will base our discussion of the generic blocks on the corresponding AI Reference (see the section "Blocks Reference" in Chapter 5) and introduce each of the seven different groups of blocks (Definition, Text, Lists, Math, Logic, Control, Colors) in turn. To ensure that our explanations are not purely theoretical, we will briefly demonstrate the functions of some blocks in a run-capable context when introducing the blocks. This will be just a very brief demonstration, as the individual block groups can unfold their full effect only in combination with one another, as we will show in the example projects. Thus the brief demonstrations are meant purely to illustrate the functions of the blocks. Have a look at the companion website under `demo_Data` if you would like to try out the little demos.

> **Mini-Demos on the Companion Website**
>
> You can find the mini-demos of the generic blocks within a demo project on the companion website, under `demo_Data` in the directories `/APK` and `/PROJECT`.

Apart from the unique aspects of their content, the various block groups differ regarding their role within the program flow structure. For example, some mainly have the task of receiving data and individually processing it. Others combine the data into larger data structures and make these structures available for further processing in a formal way. Yet others direct how the data and data structures are processed, via corresponding control structures. Within the context of developing algorithms, we can divide the generic block groups into three categories: data types, data structures, and control structures.

Data Types

In the category of *data types,* we gather those generic block groups that are connected to an *individual* value of a specific type and its processing. For example, a text corresponds to a different data type than a number. You have already encountered these two data or block types in the examples in previous chapters, where a text block contained a word or line of text and a number block contained a number. In addition to these two data types, there are two others, with which you can record, assign, and process color values and Boolean values. Thus the category of data types comprises, in the narrower sense, four block groups:

- Color
- Math
- Logic
- Text

In contrast to other programming languages, AI is quite tolerant regarding the use of data types. For example, you can add together a number `2` from a number block and a digit "3" from a text block, although the mathematical addition function really requires two numbers. However, if you try adding a number `2` and a letter `b` or the word (*text string*) `two`, AI will generate an error message, as the letter and text string cannot be turned (*converted*) into a number. As you see, you do have to be a little bit careful when using the various data types, but AI still makes life for you as developer as easy as possible.

Data Types in Other Programming Languages

In other programming languages, distinctions may be made between even more data types. For example, many programming languages differentiate the number range further, by making distinctions between integers and floats or doubles, plus variations based on their lengths (short, long). The text area is also frequently subdivided into single characters (char) and character strings (string). Once more, AI reduces the complexity involved in program development to a minimum.

For each data type, you have specific *methods* for processing values of its own data type (similar to the component methods). For example, the method + is used for adding two numeric values and the method `length` is used for determining the length of a text string.

Data Structures

Even though the category of data structures is less homogeneous than the category of data types, common characteristics can still be identified for all data structures. These structures do not form their own data types, but rather receive values regardless of their type. These values are then usually passed on for further processing, mainly within control structures. Thus the category data structures comprises two block groups:

- List
- Definition (procedures and variables)

As a program generally has to deal with many individual pieces of data, it is helpful for purposes of clarity, management, and structured processing to combine the individual data in well-organized data structures. A database can contain many hundreds or even thousands of entries, such as names and telephone numbers. For example, if you want to add the international dialing code for the United States, +1, to all of the phone numbers saved on your smartphone, it is more efficient to read as many phone numbers as possible at once into a *list,* edit the list, and then write the numbers back in a single operation, rather than reading out every single phone number from the database individually and then editing and saving each one. AI offers numerous helpful methods in a separate block group that you can use for creating, processing, and managing lists containing values of all kinds of data types.

In a wider sense, we can also consider the stringing together of text entries in a string as an aggregation of individual entries and, therefore, as data structure. The Text block group, for example, contains specific methods for breaking down a text string and generating a list from the individual entries. If you consider that all values of the various data types can also be represented as text and converted accordingly, the function of the Text block group comes very close to that of the List group, at least as far as storing individual data is concerned. To process the individual data elements, however, you then need to convert the text string into a proper list so that you can edit it with the appropriate list methods.

Data Structures in Other Programming Languages

In many other programming languages, other data structures are available in addition to lists—for example, arrays, stacks, and hash tables. Procedures and variables are not usually counted among the data structures in other programming languages, but rather represent their own category. For the sake of clarity, we will subsume them under the data structures category here, as they can also receive other data and contribute to program structuring.

The Definition block group also contains blocks that can receive data and other elements. Within *procedures,* you can aggregate entire block structures and use them efficiently as a whole within the program structure. Procedures can also receive values; they do not usually merely manage these values passively, but rather pass them on for processing within the procedure. As carriers of values of any data type, you will also find *variables* within the program structure. Although variables do not aggregate any values, but merely receive them individually, they do not form their own data type; instead, they take on the data type of the values they transport between the program structures.

Control Structures

The last category, control structures, contains only a single block group that includes all blocks with which you can check conditions, process data structures, and control program flow.

> **Control Structures in Other Programming Languages**
>
> The term *control structure* originates from the area of imperative programming languages, which distinguish between *branches* and *loops*. We will find and use both of these types of control structures in AI.

We will address the various control structures in the following sections. We start with the basic building blocks of data processing, the data types.

Using Colors with the Color Block Group

We begin by looking at the most exotic of the data types, the color value, for which AI offers its own generic block group. With the blocks in this group, you can color elements of the graphical user interface according to your own wishes.

Predefined Colors

This data type is somewhat exotic in as far as it does not usually appear in other programming languages. Unlike the other data types, its use is very strictly defined and offers little flexibility. The individual blocks in the generic block group known as "Color" have the sole purpose of representing a certain color. AI currently offers 14 *predefined* color blocks, including black and white plus the option of no color, for quick use. With these, you can easily set the color property of a component, such as TextColor or Background-Color (see Figure 9.1), and change the color (see also `demo_Data`).

Figure 9.1 Changing the color property of a component with a color block

Defining Your Own Colors

In programming, colors are usually referred to as *color values.* In reality, a color in itself does not exist as a single entity, but rather is mixed together on the fly from various amounts of the primary colors, red, green, and blue (RGB), within the so-called additive color system. Each amount is defined by a value of 0 (minimum) to 255 (maximum). Thus it is possible to mix the three primary colors to achieve more than 16.7 million (256 × 256 × 256) different colors or shades of colors and represent them on the smartphone, provided the system supports that many colors. In AI, you can mix your own colors in addition to using the predefined colors in the Color block group. Apart from the three proportionate basic colors RGB, you also have a fourth value available for mixing, with which you can set the color's *transparency* or *opacity*. This spectrum goes from fully opaque (255) to fully transparent (0). Mixing the four values in AI is not done simply by specifying four individual values; instead, these first values have to be processed within a formula to produce a total value, which can then be specified as a corresponding color value.

> **Calculating and Using Custom Color Values in AI**
>
> You can find a detailed description of how to calculate and use individual color values when developing with AI in the Blocks Reference, under the entry "Color Blocks." It also offers an algorithm with block structure for calculating any custom color value. You'll find this information at the following site:
>
> `http://experimental.appinventor.mit.edu/learn/reference/blocks/colors.html`

The explanation of the formula and an algorithm for calculating any custom color value can be found at the previously mentioned link in the Blocks Reference. In compact form, this formula can be expressed as follows:

Color value = ((((((opacity amount * 256) + red amount) * 256) + green amount) * 256) + blue amount) – 4294967296

For example, mixing the primary colors R = 139, G = 69, and B = 19 at full opacity O = 255 produces the color value –7650029, which is brown. This calculated color value can then be assigned to the color property of a component, although you have to use a number block with the corresponding (negative) number (instead of a color block; see Figure 9.2 and also `demo_Data`).

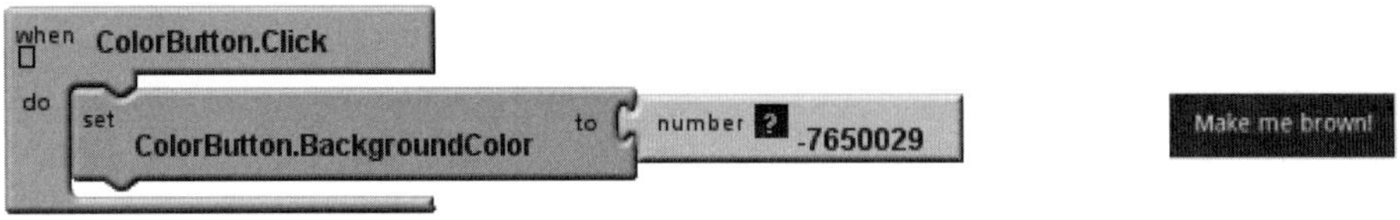

Figure 9.2 Assigning the color value for brown in the color property of a button

By taking advantage of this option for mixing custom colors, you as developer can enjoy full freedom when designing the color of your apps. The modest selection of colors in the Color block group can be vastly expanded in this way. For using color values, it helps to refer to *RGB color tables,* which you can find on the Internet by entering the appropriate search term.

> **RGB Color Tables on the Internet**
>
> For selecting and calculating suitable colors, it helps to make use of RGB color tables available on the Internet. In addition to color samples, they often include the relevant RGB values (instead of or in addition to the frequently listed hexadecimal value), which you will need for calculating the AI color value. An example of such a list can be found on the following website provided by the University of Muenster: `http://gucky.uni-muenster.de/cgi-bin/rgbtab`.

It is a good idea to use the options of individual color mixing so that your app stands out from all the other apps and to create an appropriate setting for your specific area of application.

Processing Numbers with the Math Block Group

Many processes within a program flow are influenced by numeric values or work directly with these values. Even so, programming for you as developer need not have much to do with mathematics, because thankfully the basic calculations of the binary processes are taken care of by the smartphone processor. Nevertheless, you will often fall back on mathematical values and operations, whether in the proper sense (e.g., when developing a calculator app) or indirectly (e.g., as aids for selecting an index from lists or flow control). Appropriate to its multiform and flexible areas of use, the Math block group offers a multitude of blocks that can be roughly divided into groups based on their fields of application. The Blocks Reference provides more detailed information on their functions.

Basic Arithmetic

In addition to the familiar number block `number` for setting an individual numeric value (see Figure 9.3), there is another block for each basic arithmetic operation, as you can see in Figure 9.4. Each block can receive two `number` blocks with which the operation is carried out. The result can then be passed, for example, to a component `Label1.Text` for display on the screen, whereby the numeric value is automatically converted into text.

Figure 9.3 Number block "number" for specifying a numeric value

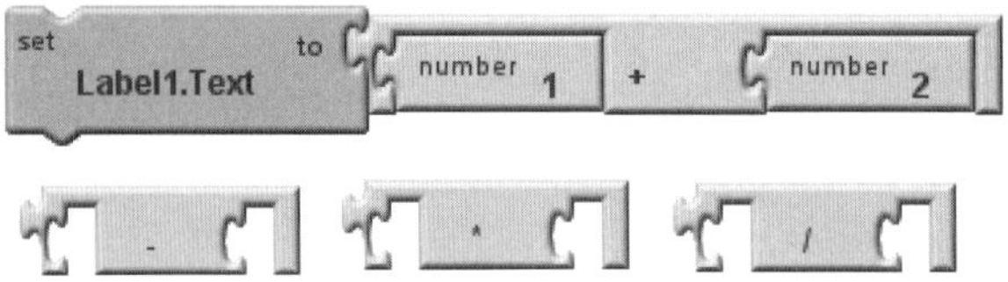

Figure 9.4 Blocks for the four basic arithmetic operations

Scientific Arithmetic

If basic arithmetic is not enough, AI offers additional arithmetic operations (see Figure 9.5) that those of us who are inexperienced in things mathematical will probably only vaguely remember from the scientific calculators we used at school. The "Math" section in the Blocks Reference provides a more detailed explanation of these operations.

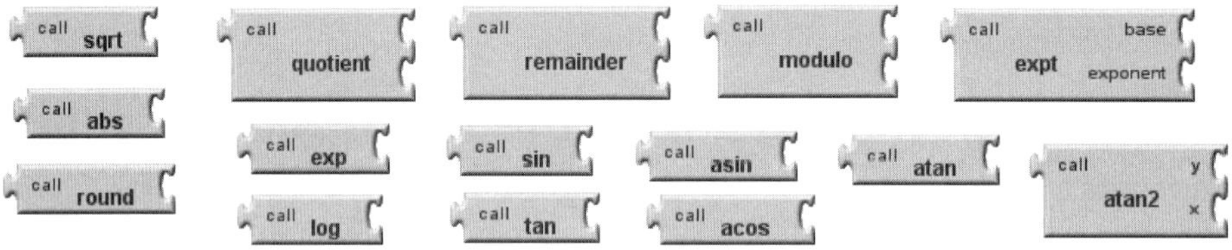

Figure 9.5 Blocks for scientific arithmetic

Generating Random Numbers

Anyone who wants to do calculations, or otherwise work with numbers, requires numbers as a starting point. If no existing numbers are available or if existing numbers should not be used as the seed values, you can use AI to generate random numbers for you. You will need random numbers during app development more frequently than you might think. Most games, for example, are based on random numbers, as otherwise there would be no element of surprise for the user. AI provides two methods for generating random numbers (see Figure 9.6).

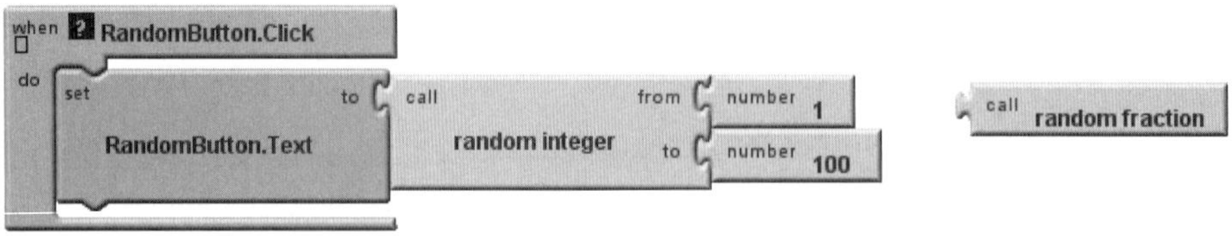

Figure 9.6 Blocks for generating random numbers

With each call of the method `random integer`, you can create an integer from any value range that you can define by specifying the smallest (`from`) and largest (`to`) possible value. In Figure 9.6, a new random number between 1 and 100 is displayed on the RandomButton every time you press the button (see also `demo_Data`). Alternatively, you can create a decimal number between 0.0 and 1.0 by calling the method `random fraction`. This value range is also used more often than you might think. In graphical games or animations, for example, it is used to place a graphical object randomly in a relative position within the screen area (>0.0 and <1.0) but not beyond it (<0.0 and >1.0). We will illustrate the use of this random-number generator later in an example project.

Sorting and Converting

In addition to performing calculations of and with numeric values, the Math block methods provide an ideal basis for creating and maintaining order in various databases. For example, allocating an ascending number sequence when reading in individual data elements from a database makes it possible to write back the number sequence in the same order to the original positions in the database after the program has processed the numbers. A numeric index usually serves as an obligatory access key for values within a list structure. If the order in a database becomes mixed up for some reason, AI has various methods for quickly accessing the first/smallest (`min`) or last/highest (`max`) or next lower (`floor`) or next higher (`ceiling`) position, thereby enabling you to invert the order (`negate`) or sort the database entries in ascending or descending order via a corresponding algorithm (for example, *Bubblesort*) in combination with these methods (see Figure 9.7).

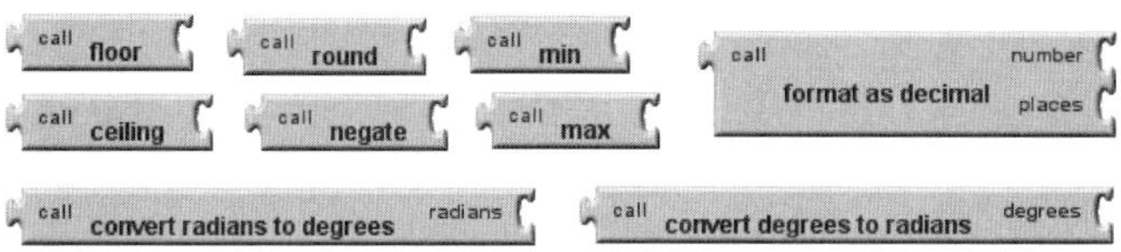

Figure 9.7 Blocks for selecting and converting numeric values

If the granularity of integers proves insufficient for your app, you can use the method `format as decimal` to convert these values into decimal numbers with the desired number of fractional digits. You can also convert angle values from degrees (0 – 360°) to radians (0 – 2*PI) with the method `convert degrees to radians`; the method `convert radians to degrees` reverses this conversion.

Relational Operators

As mentioned earlier and demonstrated in the context of the Math block group, the methods in this group are used for more than simply calculating numeric values; they also have utility in terms of other functions and areas of application. Just as an ascending number sequence reflects the index values for accessing the elements in the data structure of a list, the logical-mathematical *relational operators* are used for checking conditions in the control structures of both loops and branches. For example, a processing loop will be repeated again if the total number of data elements present in the list has not yet been processed (number of loops < number of elements), and this repetition of the loop will continue until all data elements are processed (number of loops = number of elements). Figure 9.8 shows the blocks available for checking these conditions.

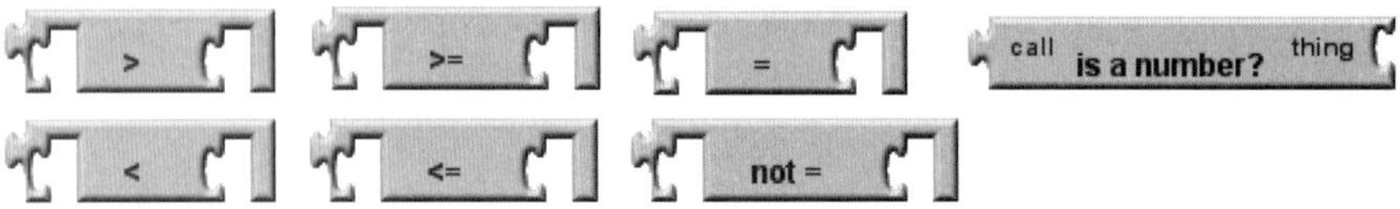

Figure 9.8 Blocks for comparing numbers and checking conditions

Of course, you have to make sure that these checks are really comparing a number with a number, and not a number with a color or anything else; otherwise, the loop will be repeated indefinitely. AI offers a dedicated block `is a number?` to ensure that this initial condition is met. With these blocks, the boundary between the Math block group and the Logic block group becomes quite blurred. It is, therefore, not surprising to find that the relational operator = is present in both groups.

Checking Program States with the Logic Block Group

Most of the decisions in a program flow are based on logical states. Does the list contain elements at all? Have all elements in the list been processed? Is a check box enabled? These and other questions can always be answered with either yes or no (i.e., true or false), following the *Boolean logic*. AI provides several blocks in the Logic block group so you can use the laws of Boolean logic within the algorithms of your apps.

Boolean Values

The two basic states "true" and "false" are represented in the program structure by the Boolean values `true` or `false` (see Figure 9.9), which you have already encountered and used in the context of the CheckBox component. Without these Boolean values, many of the initial checks (conditions) in the control structures that we will address later would not be possible. Together with the mathematical relational operators mentioned previously, the Logic blocks satisfy the basic requirement for using control structures.

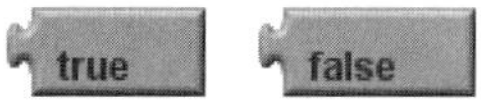

Figure 9.9 The Boolean values "true" and "false"

Boolean Operators

Often it is not enough to check the state of an individual component; sometimes the decision within an algorithm can be reached only based on a condition involving several factors. To take the states of several components into consideration when making a decision and to create higher-order dependencies, AI offers the two logical *operators* AND (conjunction) and OR (disjunction) as methods in the Logic group (see Figure 9.10).

Figure 9.10 The Boolean operators "AND" and "OR"

With the Boolean operators AND and OR, you can create a relation between not just two or more states (*operands*) and then connect them to create an overall state. Each time you add a new component with a Boolean value, the relevant operator puzzle piece shown in Figure 9.10 gets a new setter socket. By connecting individual logical states to combined logical *expressions,* you can create dependencies of any degree of complexity and check conditions.

We want to illustrate the use of the operator AND in an example with two CheckBox components, whose two individual states (enabled = `true`, disabled = `false`) determine a common overall state (both enabled = `true`, neither or just one enabled = `false`). Expressed in pseudocode, this task can be expressed as follows:

```
When CheckBox1 is pressed, test if
 CheckBox1 AND CheckBox2 are checked,
and write the Boolean result in Label1
```

If CheckBox1 is pressed and its logical state thereby changed, the corresponding event handler `CheckBox1.Changed` tests whether CheckBox1 now has the value `true` and whether a second check box CheckBox2 also has the value `true`. The result of this test is `true` only if both check boxes are checked (enabled), and `false` if only one or neither of them is enabled. Figure 9.11 shows the corresponding event handler, where the Boolean result for displaying in the label is written as text "Both check boxes checked: true / false" (see also `demo_Data`).

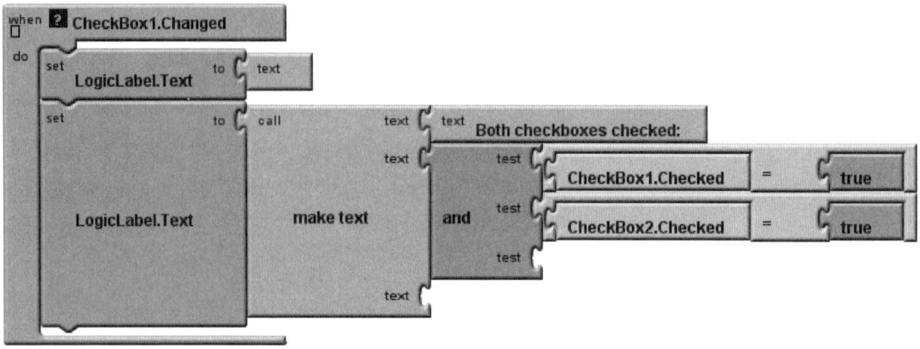

Figure 9.11 Testing whether either or both check boxes are enabled

In addition to the two Boolean operators AND and OR, AI offers the special operator NOT (negation) in the Logic group. You can use it to check whether a condition does *not* apply (see Figure 9.12). This operator is also used more often than you may perhaps think.

Figure 9.12 The "NOT" operator

The relational operators from the Math group mentioned earlier can also be used for corresponding checks with a logical value. The comparisons between two operands (<, <=, >, >=, =) also result in a Boolean value. As mentioned previously, the relational operator = is even present in both block groups.

Editing Text and Strings with the Text Block Group

Another fundamental data type for the most varied range of applications is text in any form from the Text block group. Despite today's options for expressing ourselves through multimedia, a significant part of communication with app users remains based on text input and output. If you consider that numerical, logical, and even color values can also be processed like text, entered via text boxes and output via labels as *alphanumeric characters* (characters, digits, special characters) thanks to automatic conversion, it becomes difficult to conceive of interactive programs that do not the data type "text." Formally, AI does not distinguish in this data type between individual alphanumeric characters, an individual character sequence, or a whole text passage (*string*). All three variations can be set in the familiar text block `text` shown in Figure 9.13.

Figure 9.13 The text block "text"

The many methods in the Text group are just as extensive as those found in the Math group. Also like the Math methods, the Text methods can be grouped roughly by their area of use. For further in-depth details, the Blocks Reference provides additional information about the functions related to editing and processing text.

Comparing and Sorting

For text, there is also a kind of set of relational operators, similar to those found in the Math and Logic block groups. For example, you can check whether two character sequences are equal by comparing the two strings character by character with the method `text=`. Thus, if you press the button TextEqualsButton shown in Figure 9.14, the current input in TextBox1 is compared to that in TextBox2 (see also `demo_Data`). If the input in both text boxes is identical (for example, "hello" and "hello"), the result `true` is shown in the label; otherwise, the result is `false`. Please note that AI does make a distinction between uppercase and lowercase letters (it is *case sensitive*), so "hello" is identical to "hello", but not to "Hello".

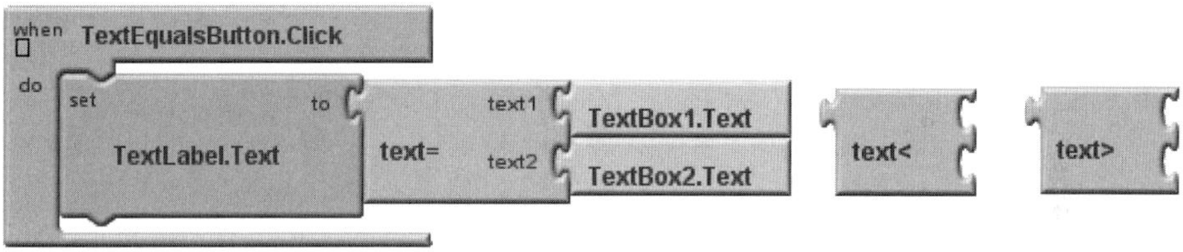

Figure 9.14 Checking two strings for equality with relational operators

In the same way, you can also check whether the character, character sequence, or text passage in TextBox1 is bigger than (`text>`) or smaller than (`text<`) that in TextBox2. The basis for the comparison is the order of the alphanumeric characters of the *ASCII character table,* which specifies both the alphabetical order of letters and the numerical order of numbers (and any other alphanumeric characters) in their relation to one another. The ASCII value of the first different character in a string determines which string is bigger. For example, if you are using the method `text>` in the event handler shown in Figure 9.15, then "James" (TextBox1) is bigger (`true`) than "Emily" (TextBox2), but smaller (`false`) than "Jason" (TextBox2). Think about this for a minute or try out different text input in `demo_Data` until this principle becomes clear (see also `demo_Data`).

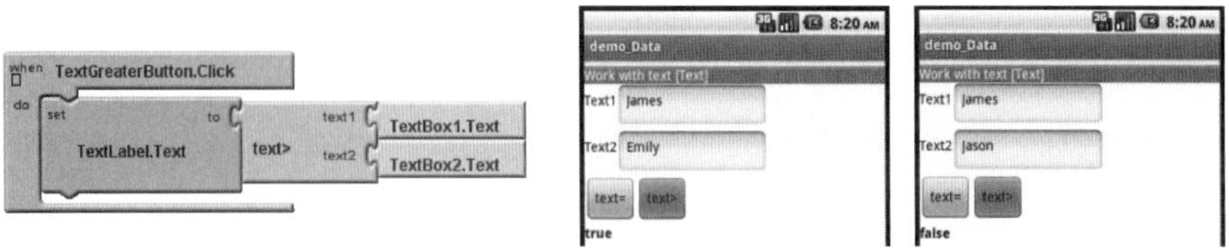

Figure 9.15 Comparing the size of two text strings

These relational methods of the Text block group provide an excellent option for sorting all kinds of alphanumerical data from databases or other sources by using the corresponding algorithms. In addition, you can use the relational operator =, which you already know from the Math and Logic groups and which is present in the Text group as well. When the = operator is used, strings made up of only numerical symbols are interpreted as numbers, whereas the relational operator `text=` treats them as pure character strings. The difference becomes clear if you look at Figure 9.16. In a numerical comparison (=) of the two (automatically converted) text inputs "0123" and "123", the result is `true`, as both numbers correspond to the same numerical value `123`. In contrast, the alphanumeric comparison of both strings returns the result `false`, because the strings are different (see also `demo_Data`).

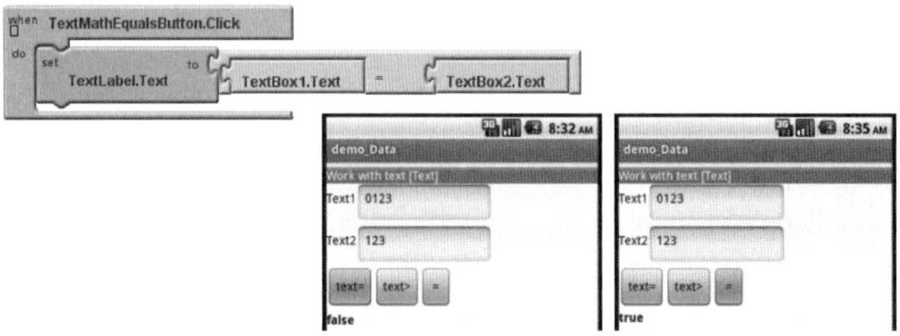

Figure 9.16 Comparing two strings, as text and as numbers

Joining and Changing

As you already know from some of the previous examples, text can be assembled from any number of text sections (*concatenation*). For example, result values can be spontaneously combined with text passages to form coherent sentences at output, as we did in Figure 9.11 with the method `make text`. Alternatively, if you want to create a new string from a series of individual character sequences that should be joined together as a unit, you can use the method `join`, which is shown in Figure 9.17.

Figure 9.17 Methods for joining and changing character sequences

For automatic processing, character sequences often must be adapted and changed. For example, if you want to avoid the problem of the ASCII-based alphabetical order of surnames you entered becoming mixed up because you accidentally input the first two letters in uppercase while typing, all entries can be automatically converted to lowercase (minuscule) or uppercase (majuscule) with the methods `downcase` or `upcase`, respectively. You can also automatically remove any spaces (accidentally) entered at the beginning or end of a text string by using the method `trim`. Have a look at Figure 9.18 to see the nested use of these methods.

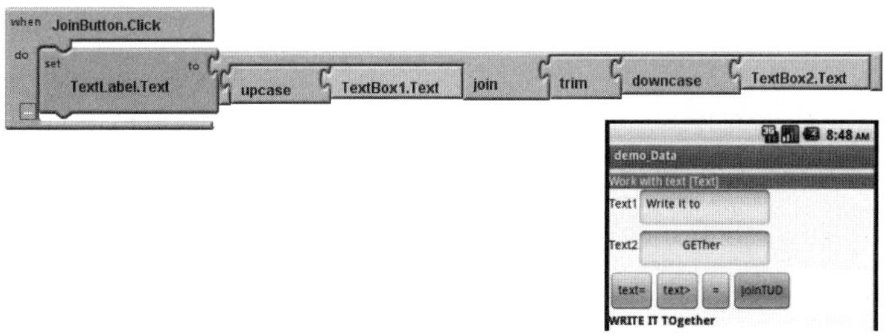

Figure 9.18 Changing two text strings, removing spaces, and joining strings

As the abbreviation "JoinTUD" (for "JoinTrimUpDown") on the button in Figure 9.18 indicates, pressing the button triggers a number of edits of the two text strings in the input fields. The string "GEther" of TextBox2 is converted to lowercase (`downcase`) and its empty spaces are removed (`trim`); it is then joined (`join`) with the string "Write it to" (which is converted to uppercase, `upcase`) to form a new string "WRITE IT TOgether", which is then displayed in `TextLabel.Text` (see also `demo_Data`).

Checking and Searching Content

Another group within the Text block group serves mainly for getting information on a text string or its content. The method `length` returns the absolute length of a string, defined as the number of characters contained in it. With the method `contains`, the resulting Boolean value tells you whether a certain character sequence (`piece`) is contained in a text string (`text`). The method `starts at` returns the character position instead, where the character sequence (`piece`) first occurs in the text string (`text`), or `0` (zero), if it is not found in the string at all (see Figure 9.19).

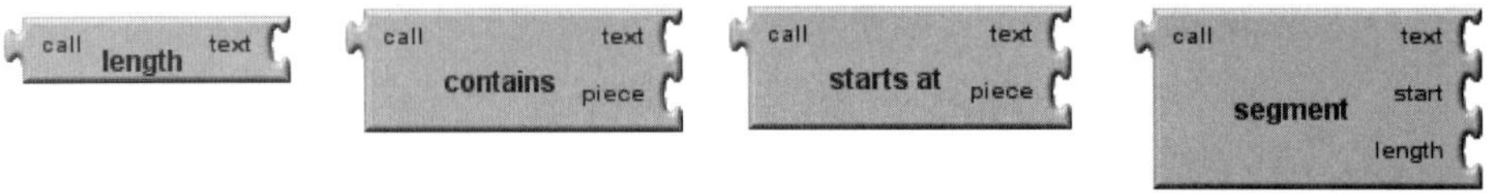

Figure 9.19 Methods for getting information on and from a string

With the method `segment`, you can extract a character sequence of any length (`length`) from a text string (`text`) at any text position (`start`). This function is helpful if, for example, you want to read out a certain information from database entries with a uniform structure. The example shown in Figure 9.20 shows how you can easily specify a certain pattern (YEAR:USD) to search a text string with many items (for example, insurance contributions of recent years) via a search term (search for year `2009`) to find and display the suitable item and corresponding value (`119` USD).

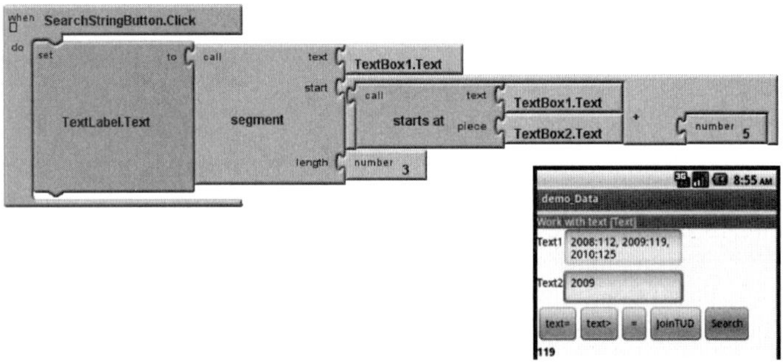

Figure 9.20 Searching and displaying items in a text list

The event handler shown in Figure 9.20 uses the method `starts at` to check whether and in which position (x) the search term entered in TextBox2 is present in the string found in TextBox1. The determined position value is increased by 5 (x + 5), as only the value (USD) stands behind the search term (year) and the colon (a total of five places behind). From this position onward, the next three characters (from x + 5 to x + 8) are displayed in the TextLabel (see also `demo_Data`).

Splitting Strings and Generating Lists

Although the blocks from the previous section can be used to access individual information within a character sequence, the structured access and management of data sets is rarely done via text strings. Instead, a list structure has been specially designed for this purpose, which we will introduce in the next section. Due to the text string's universal character, its great degree of data type independence, and its central interface function for input and output of user data, character sequences within a text string are typically used to handle much of the data within the program flow. To transform string data into a list data structure that is optimized for processing, the Text block group offers a number of methods that are exclusively designed for splitting a text string into list elements or creating a list from these individual pieces. These five methods can be recognized by the fact that they all start with the word `split`; we, in turn, will refer to them as *split methods*. With these methods, the text string is split in the place where a particular alphanumerical character sequence occurs, which is specified in the specific split method. We will refer to this character sequence as a *split element*. The particular split element is removed in the resulting individual pieces when the original string is split into sections.

Three of the split methods work with only a single split element. The method `split at spaces` sets the split element, as the name indicates, to a space—which makes sense because spaces are often used to separate database entries. With this method, the string (`text`) is split wherever a space occurs, and the resulting string pieces are combined in a list. The method `split` is more flexible, allowing you to specify any alphanumeric character as the split element (`at`) and splitting the text string (`text`) at every occurrence of this character. The method `split at first` splits the text string (`text`) only at the first occurrence of the specified split element (`at`) (see Figure 9.21).

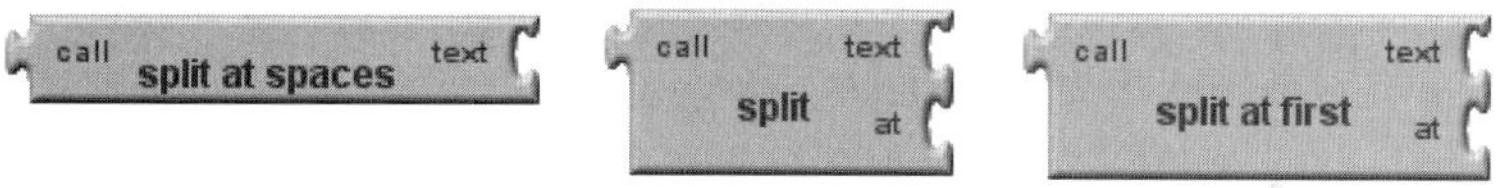

Figure 9.21 Split methods with only one split element

The differences between the three methods become clearer if we use a text string as an example and split it up: "Water, Soda, Beer, Wine, Liqueur", as shown in Figure 9.22. The method `split at spaces` (left) splits the text string at each space and writes the five pieces including commas into a list `(Water, Soda, Beer, Wine, Liqueur)`, whose elements are separated by spaces and represented enclosed in brackets. For the other two methods, a comma (`,`) is specified as the split element. If you apply the method `split` (center) to the same text string, it is split in all positions where a comma occurs, so it results in the list `(Water Soda Beer Wine Liqueur)` with five elements without commas, but with the original spaces. With the method `split at first` (right), the text string is split only once, at the first occurrence of the split element (`,`) between the two entries `Water` and `Soda`; this results in a list with only two elements, one with `Water` and the other one with `Soda, Beer, Wine, Liqueur` in form of the displayed list `(Water  Soda, Beer, Wine, Liqueur)`. Try experimenting using different text strings with the demo app `demo_Data` to get a better feel for how the various split methods work.

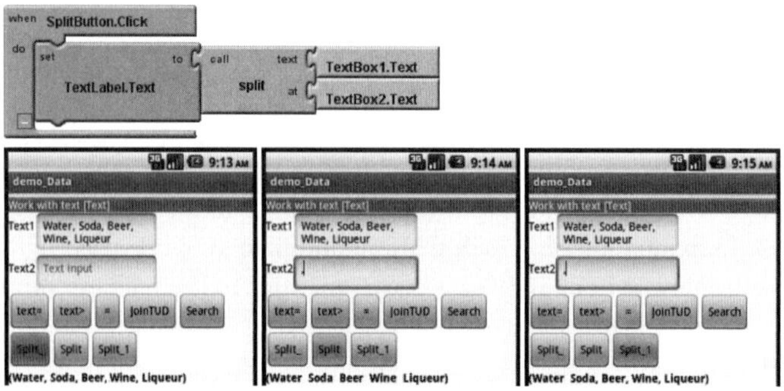

Figure 9.22 Using methods to split a text string into different list elements

In addition to the three split methods described previously, the Text group offers two other methods, `split at any` and `split at first of any`, with which you can specify any number of split elements. This time the split elements are not specified individually, but rather are passed to the split method as elements in a list. We will not examine the list structure in detail until later in this book, so for now we will just concentrate on the basic operation and the results when using these two split methods. If you continue reading and then return to this section, you will be better able to understand the details of the block structure shown in Figure 9.23; it shows a list `demoList` with the two alphanumerical split elements of a comma (`,`) and an equals sign (`=`), which then serves as input (`at`) for the two split methods.

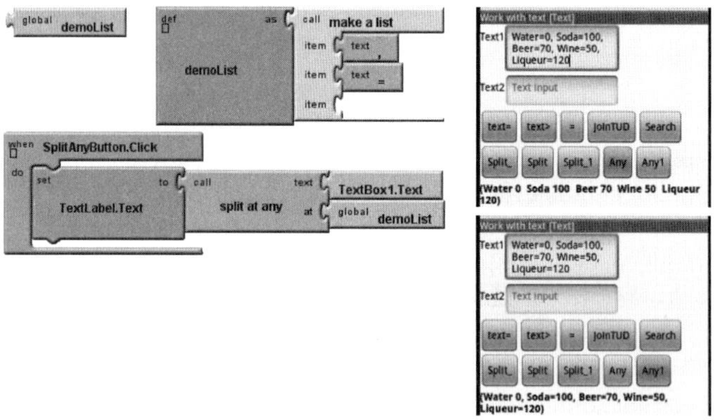

Figure 9.23 Splitting via methods with multiple split elements

In Figure 9.23, the number of calories per drink is entered as a text string (and purely intended as an example without worrying about the values' accuracy): "Water=0, Soda=100, Beer=70, Wine=50, Liqueur=120". This text string is split by the method `split at any` at all places where a comma or equals sign appears. The split results in a list of 10 elements (`Water 0 Soda 100 Beer 70 Wine 50 Liqueur 120`). When the method `split at any at first` is used instead, the same text string is split only at the first occurrence of one of the two split elements—namely, between `Water` and `0, Soda=100, Beer=70, Wine=50, Liqueur=120`, so that it results in a corresponding list of only two elements (see also `demo_Data`).

Take some time to understand the differences between the individual split methods. Next, we explore the structural units in AI projects.

Defining Container Structures with the Definition Block Group

Processing large databases usually requires high efficiency in the processing algorithms. In a database containing hundreds or even thousands of entries of the same data type and the same structure, it would make little sense to process each entry individually and pass it on for dedicated further processing with a separate program structure. If you did, the program code of database programs would increase proportionally to the number of database entries, which, of course, is not the case. Instead, when developing efficient algorithms, it is important to design the program flow generically, so that the flow is identical for each individual element and can be applied to all elements in the same way. Rather than you being forced to engage in laborious manual work, the principle of machine-driven production chain work applies for developing apps and executing program flows, too.

For developing generic algorithms, AI offers a variety of data structures in the Definition block group, which can all receive other elements in some form, just like a *container*. These container structures can be used to generically describe and implement program flows that are then processed at the app's runtime with the specific container contents. Apart from this essentially important function, the container structures make it possible to define custom function blocks (which is probably why the group name is "Definition"), which can be used universally in your developing work as custom "self-built" data types or methods. This capability enables you to define your own blocks and expand the preset repertoire provided by AI. The value of this important expansion option should not be underestimated, as it is an essential part of developing demanding algorithms. In the future, you will likely deal with such container structures more often when developing apps, even if your own apps do not process mass data. Let's have a closer look at the container structures to illustrate the theoretical description.

The Term "Container"

The term "container" normally refers to a data format that can contain various data formats. For example, an AVI container can contain an MPEG-4 video track and an MP3-audio track. In a similar way, the container structures in AI can contain other elements.

Variables

Due to their universal nature, *variables* can be used in many ways for the most varied tasks. For example, they form the basis for creating lists (as an alternative to deriving lists from text strings), as shown in Figure 9.23 and described in the section on list structure yet to come. You can also use variables to expand the spectrum of predefined data types, by assigning to the variable a specific value that you will need repeatedly during the program flow. This capability is useful, for example, if you need the value *PI,* which is not predefined in the Math group for frequent math operations, or if you want to add the color brown to the Color group. To do so, you can drag a new variable `def variable` from the Definition group into the AI Editor, give the variable a suitable name (click on "variable," and edit and overwrite the name), and then assign the desired value to it (see Figure 9.24).

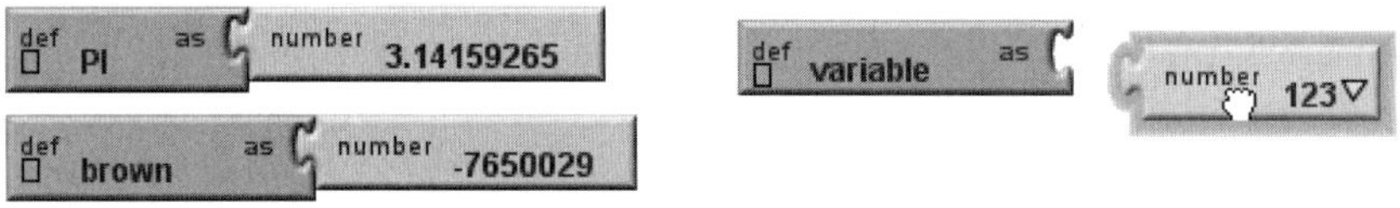

Figure 9.24 Custom-defined variables "PI" and "brown"

Simply select a block of the desired data type from the Built-In panel (e.g., `number` or `text`), slot it into the variable (see the right side of Figure 9.24), and perhaps also enter an initial value for the variable. Depending on the value provided, the variable automatically takes on the corresponding data type and can be used within the app just like a predefined representative of this data type.

> **Variables and Constants**
>
> A variable with a fixed value is referred to as a *constant*.

Because the variables in AI are variables with *global* validity, they are defined outside of the other block structures of an app, and each must have a unique name (one that does not appear repeatedly in the app project). This has the advantage that the global variables or their values can be accessed in all event handlers and block structures of the entire app project, and can be read and overwritten with new values anywhere. For example, an event handler `A` can increase the initial value `0` of the variable `X` by `X+5`, another event handler `B` can increase the current intermediate value `5` of variable `X` again by `X+7` to `X=12`, and so on. Such a variable can then be used in any event handler as a constant, just like any other predefined block. This behavior is shown in Figure 9.25 using the example of the variable/constant "brown" with the corresponding fixed color value.

Figure 9.25 Using the variable "brown" as a constant with a fixed color value

To make sure the custom variables can be used just as other blocks, AI automatically generates two blocks for each created variable for reading (`global`) and writing (`set global`) the variable values. These blocks are then available in AI Editor under "My Blocks" in the My Definitions group (see Figure 9.26).

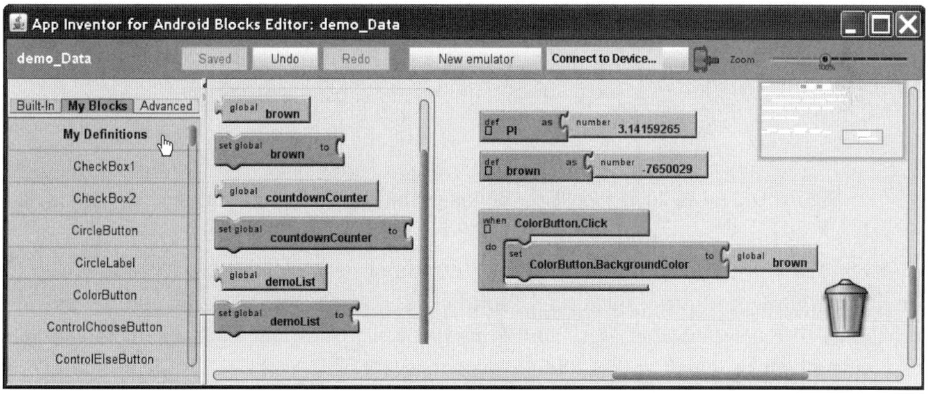

Figure 9.26 Automatically created blocks for reading and writing the variables

Should you wish to change the variable's name retrospectively, you can simply do so in the corresponding `def` block with which you originally created the variable. All variable blocks already in use are then adapted automatically by AI Editor in the other block structures.

Procedures and Arguments

Whereas you can use variables to create your own or additional data types, you can use *procedures* to develop your own methods. Similar to the constants with their fixed values, you can encapsulate generic subtasks or fixed block structures in procedures, thereby creating methods that are processed frequently and run through during the program flow. The equally *global* procedures can then be called by definition simply from other block structures without requiring the latter to implement the subtasks themselves. In this way, the procedures contribute to making the program structure less crowded, more efficient, and clearer, and to organizing it generically. The scope of the block structures encapsulated within a procedure can vary greatly and comprise all kinds of conceivable constructs, ranging from small auxiliary functions to large subtasks that are complete in themselves.

For defining a procedure, AI offers the two blocks shown in Figure 9.27 in the generic block group known as "Definition." The block structures of the procedure are specified within the enclosing block `to procedure do`, similar to an event handler. Once again, you should assign unique names to your custom procedures, which should describe the relevant function as accurately as possible (rename a method by clicking on "procedure1," and then edit and overwrite its current name). As some predefined methods do, you can define values for your custom procedures. These values are received as *arguments* and are then made available within the procedure for further processing. You can define arguments with the block `name`, which you also need to give a unique name.

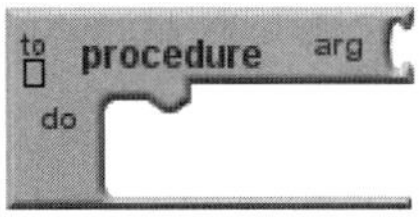

Figure 9.27 Building blocks for defining custom procedures with arguments

Note that you can define more than one argument per procedure. Each time you insert an argument into the socket `arg`, another socket `arg` automatically appears in the procedure to receive another argument. Thus you can pass as many arguments as you like to your procedure, which makes using it a lot more flexible. You can also define procedures entirely without arguments, simply by leaving the socket `arg` empty.

Difference Between Parameter and Argument

In programming, a distinction is sometimes made between the terms "parameter" and "argument." *Parameter* refers to the general placeholder in a procedure that expects a specific value as argument. Thus, in AI, the socket `arg` in the "procedure" block would be a "parameter" and the inserted value would the "argument." We will ignore this semantic nicety and simply use the term "argument" throughout this book.

Let's use an example to make things clearer. In a geometry app, the calculation and display of any circumference (`PI * 2 * r`) could be handled by a separate procedure. As the two values `PI` (see the constant `PI` in Figure 9.24) and `2` are constant, they can be fixed in the procedure. Only the radius `r` is variable; it must be passed individually to the procedure at each call as an *argument* to calculate the circumference for the particular radius of the circle. In Figure 9.28, the example procedure `showCircumference` receives an argument `radius`, inserts it into the calculation `PI * (2 * radius)`, and outputs the result in a label `CircleLabel` (see also `demo_Data`).

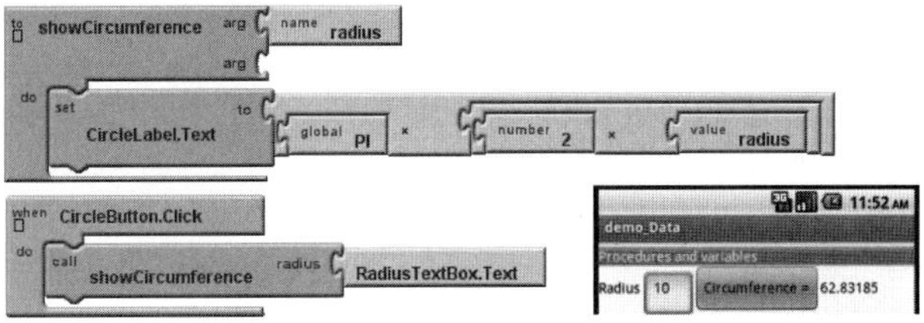

Figure 9.28 Procedure for calculating and displaying a circumference

Now the procedure `showCircumference` in Figure 9.28 (top) can simply be called from any event handler `CircleButton.Click` (bottom) with its name `call showCircumference` and any value as the argument `radius`. As an example, we entered the value `10` into the RadiusTextBox. When we pressed the CircleButton, the value was passed to the procedure `showCircumference`, which calculated the circumference based on the implemented formula and displayed it in CircleLabelText. Please familiarize yourself with this process by looking at the example in Figure 9.28 and perhaps also `demo_Data`, as you will repeatedly come across this efficient development method in this book and almost certainly use it in your own projects.

Just as when you are creating a variable, corresponding blocks are provided automatically for custom procedures, with which you can call the procedure (`call`) and read out and use the value of the argument (`value`) within the procedure. These blocks are also available in AI Editor in "My Blocks" in the My Definitions group (see Figure 9.29).

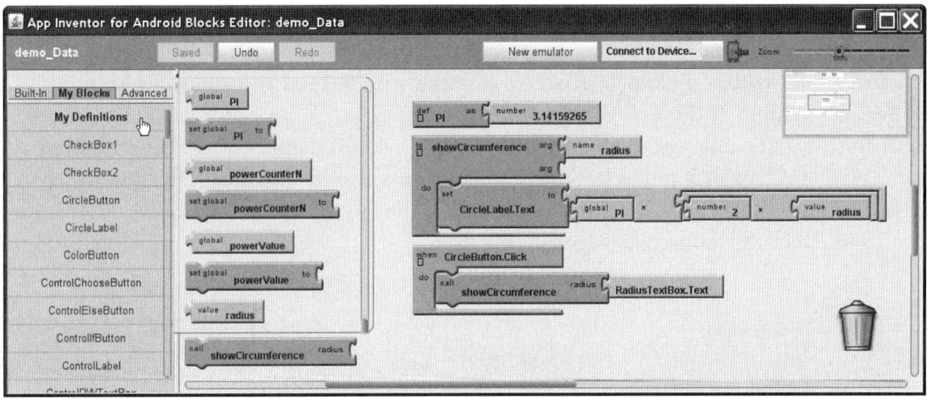

Figure 9.29 Provided blocks for calling procedures and passing arguments

Procedures with Results

In addition to the basic procedure with optional arguments described previously, AI offers a method in the Definition block group that returns a return value after running through the basic procedure. As this value is usually a result of processing within the procedure, it is referred to as result value. It is not necessarily a specific result—for example, in the form of a calculated number—but could also be the simple confirmation of successful completion of a subtask consisting of the Boolean value `true`. More complex return values are also possible, such as the file path to a photo or audio file that was received or processed within a procedure (as we saw with some of the multimedia components described in Chapter 8).

To help you build such methods yourself, AI offers the block `procedureWithResult`. It has an additional `return` socket at the bottom (see Figure 9.30), but otherwise functions in the same way and can receive arguments in the same way as the basic method `procedure`.

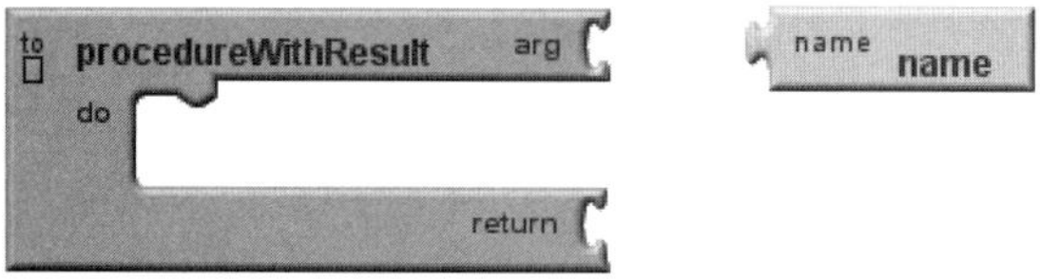

Figure 9.30 Building blocks for defining custom procedures with results

To demonstrate the use of the block `procedureWithResult`, we will address a "real" need that you may have felt yourself while reading the section on mixing your own colors. Instead of having to calculate the suitable color value yourself with a calculator every time you assign an RGB color, you can define a procedure to which you pass four initial values (the proportions of red, green, blue, and opacity in the color) as arguments and which returns the relevant color value. This procedure is particularly efficient because it can be used within the block structure just like a predefined color block. Figure 9.31 shows an example of the use of the `calculateColorValue` procedure, which receives four initial values and returns the calculated color value, for direct display as a number in an rgbColorValueLabel and as background color in an rgbColorLabel. On the right-hand side of Figure 9.31, you can see the input and output in the demo app `demo_Data` using the example of the color value `brown`.

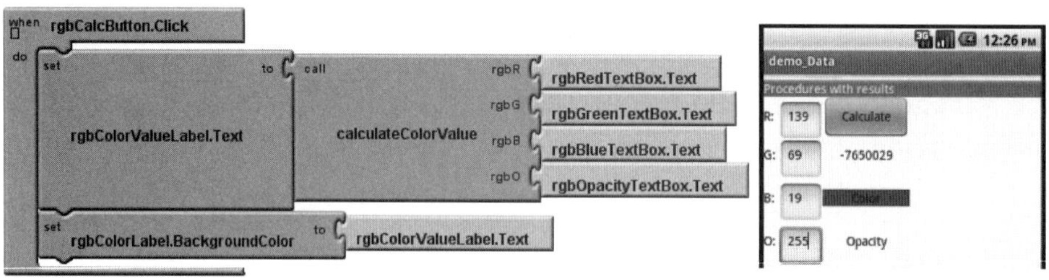

Figure 9.31 Assigning the color value as a direct return value from a procedure call

The section "Defining Your Own Colors" provided the underlying formula for calculating color values in AI. If you implement it as a nested mathematical calculation statement with AI, it should look like Figure 9.32.

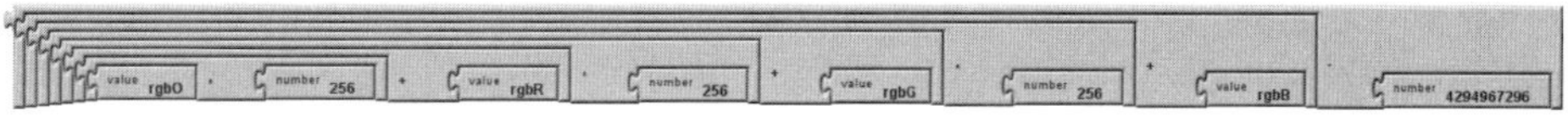

Figure 9.32 Complete calculation of the color value for brown in AI

With the four arguments `rgbR`, `rgbG`, `rgbB`, and `rgbO` (opacity), the corresponding procedure `to calculateColorValue do` shown in Figure 9.33 looks almost as bulky as the procedure call `call calculateColorValue`. It may seem surprising but the entire calculation of the color value takes places directly as input for the return value `return`. This is possible because with the four arguments, the procedure has all of the initial data required for calculating the result; it does not have to determine this data first in any further block structures. The procedure's `do` space is simply filled with a dummy that shows a status text during the calculation. Alternatively, you could slot in the "dummy socket" from the Definition group or leave the `do` space empty. You could also carry out plausibility tests to see whether the four initial values are really within the permitted value range of 0–255.

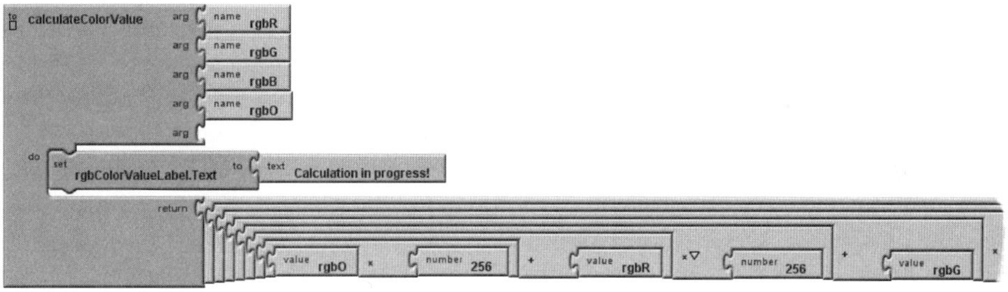

Figure 9.33 Procedure for calculating and returning a color value

Using procedures with results gives you additional options for further optimizing your app's program flow and program structure. The deeper you dive into the world of programming, the more often you will use these structures to make your apps more efficient.

Managing Lists with the List Block Group

Now that you have encountered the various container structures of AI, we are going to turn to the proper representative of the classic *data structures*. As mentioned earlier, *lists* are currently the only dedicated method of combining, arranging, and managing individual data elements in a structured way and passing them on for further processing.

Lists, therefore, form the most important basis for dealing with large amounts of data, as in reading and writing database entries, but also reading out user inputs or other file contents. Although text strings are certainly capable of indirectly managing individual pieces of data as character sequences, dealing directly with the individual elements usually requires converting them explicitly into a list of separate list items, using the split methods described earlier in this chapter. In addition to this indirect approach for generating lists from text strings, AI offers a number of dedicated methods for creating, editing, and managing lists directly, all of which can be found in the List block group.

The method `make a list` has a central role in list management. This method is used to create (*initialize*) a list in the first place. Each list requires a container where the list—or rather the *list items*—can be stored. This task can be handled by any variable, as you saw earlier. By assigning the method `make a list` to a variable to which you then give an appropriate list name, you can initialize any kind of list. Just as with any other variable, the corresponding methods for the list are then available in "My Blocks" in the My Definitions group. After the initialization process, you can replace or remove individual items from the list at any time. Figure 9.34 shows an empty list consisting of the two basic blocks `variable` (renamed to "emptyList") and `make a list` (left), plus the list named `digitList`, to which we assign the first two text blocks with the values `one` and `two` during initialization as list items (right).

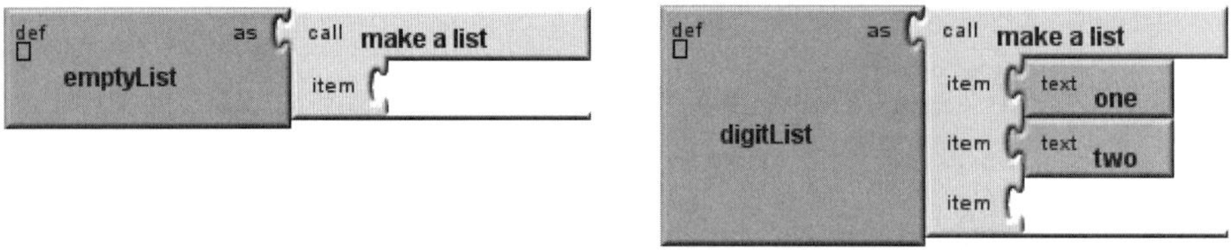

Figure 9.34 Initializing an empty list and a list with two initial items

Lists in AI are displayed according to a fixed *notation*. For example, every list is shown at output (such as in a label) enclosed by opening and closing brackets, and list items are listed separated by blank spaces in the order they were placed. For example, the list `digitList` shown in Figure 9.34 would be displayed at output as follows: `(one two)`.

Checking the Content of and Converting Lists

Before you start working in an algorithm with a list—for example, passing the list to a procedure for processing or starting a process for each list item—it can be useful to check the list for its content first. To do so, AI offers the three methods shown in Figure 9.35 in the List group. The Boolean method `is a list?` allows you to check whether a variable or variable value is a list at all or perhaps another data type. Potentially you may be able to skip one or more editing steps altogether if the Boolean check with the method `is list empty?` should reveal that a list is empty.

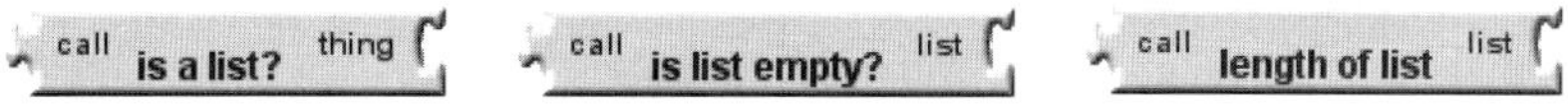

Figure 9.35 Methods for checking list content

The method `length of list` allows you to indirectly determine whether a list is empty, which is the case when this method returns the value `0`. When repeating an editing step for each individual item of a list, determining the number of list items via the method `length of list` is also a basic requirement for using corresponding loop constructs (see "Control Structures").

In Figure 9.36, you can see a demonstration of how the method `length of list` is used within the demo app `demo_Data`. For the list `digitList` shown in Figure 9.34 (by assigning it in the event handler `Screen1.Initialize`, the list can be displayed in Box1), we can determine the correct length `2` by pressing the ListLengthButton; the length of the list is then displayed below the button.

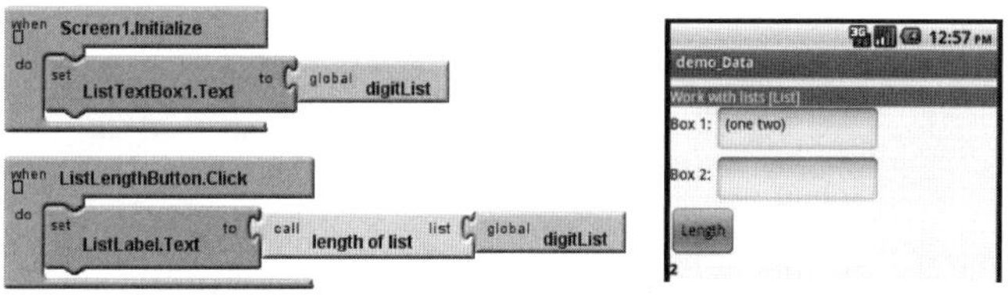

Figure 9.36 Determining the number of items in the list "digitList"

For certain applications, it may also make sense—or even be necessary—to work with other list formats than the AI format. For example, when importing and exporting whole data tables (similar to table calculations) from databases, you would typically use the file format *CSV* (comma-separated values). With this format, each table entry is listed enclosed by quotation marks and separated by commas from the next entry. Each table row is represented as a separate file line that is separated from the next line by a line break or the two nonprinting ASCII characters CR (carriage return) and LF (line feed).

To enable you to work effectively with files in CSV format, AI offers the four methods shown in Figure 9.37 in the List group, which you can use to convert lists to tables, and vice versa. With the method `list to csv row`, you can convert lists to individual table rows; with `list to csv table`, you can convert lists to whole tables. In addition, rows and tables in CSV format can be converted to lists via the methods `list from csv row` and `list from csv table`. To protect the data content in the initial format of AI before converting it, the method `copy list` gives you the option of saving a list prior to its conversion.

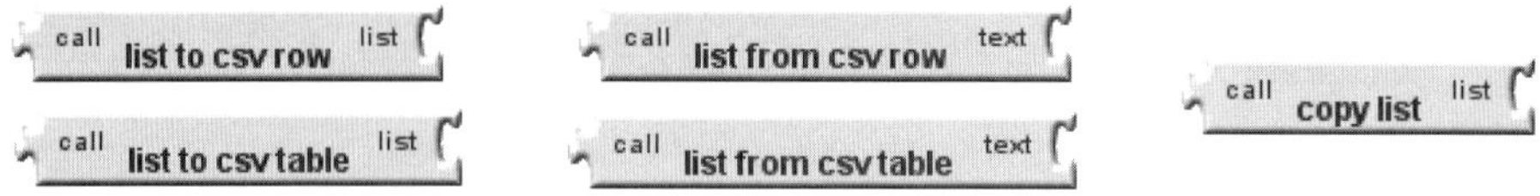

Figure 9.37 Methods for converting between lists and CSV tables

Figure 9.38 demonstrates the conversion between the two formats using a simple and clearly structured example. By pressing ListToCsvButton, you convert the `digitList` of Box1 to the CSV row format `"one","two"`. The reverse option is also possible: By pressing ListFromCsvButton, you can convert the CSV row of Box1 to the familiar list format of AI `(one two three)`.

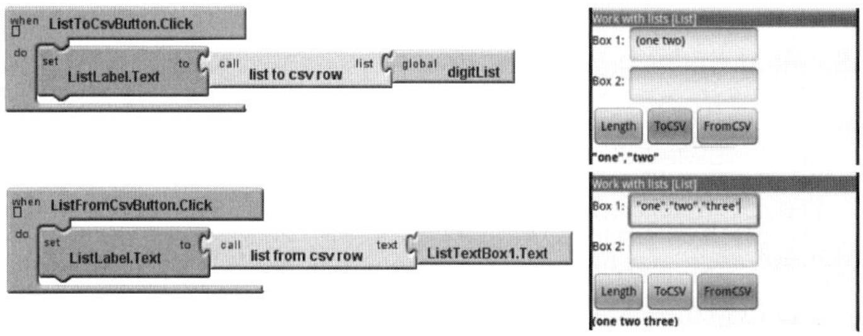

Figure 9.38 Converting a list to a CSV row, and a CSV row to a list

Searching and Reading List Items

One of the essential functions when working with lists is searching the list for certain list items, along with reading list entries to display or otherwise process them. For this purpose, AI offers the four methods shown in Figure 9.39 in the List group. With the Boolean method `is in list?`, for example, you can check whether an item `thing` is contained in the list `list`. The alphanumeric sequence specified in `thing` must match the list item exactly for it to be found (*case sensitive*!).

Figure 9.39 Methods for searching and reading list items

Once again, an indirect check is possible with another method, `position in list`, which will return `0` if no matching list item is found. The main function of this method is actually to determine the position of the desired item `thing` in the list `list` and to return it—for example, to enable the method `select list item` to use the position as an *index* for accessing exactly this item in the position `index` in the list `list`. In Figure 9.40, you can see how the index position of the desired item "two" in the list `digitList` is determined and displayed (see also `demo_Data`).

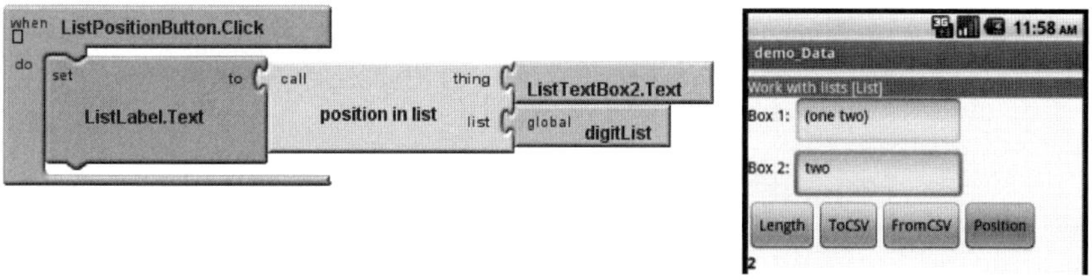

Figure 9.40 Searching for an item in a list and returning its index position

The numbering of the list items in AI starts at 1 (not at 0, as in some other programming languages). The method `pick random item` presents a special case for accessing a list item. In this method, the index selection is based on a random number.

Adding, Replacing, and Deleting List Items

Of course, a list is not a static element, but rather a dynamic structure in which new items can be added at any time, old items can be deleted, or old items can be replaced with new ones. A list behaves like a working memory, which is made available to the app at runtime by the smartphone's operating system to load data, edit it, and record intermediate and final results. For these access methods, AI offers the five methods shown in Figure 9.41 in the List block group.

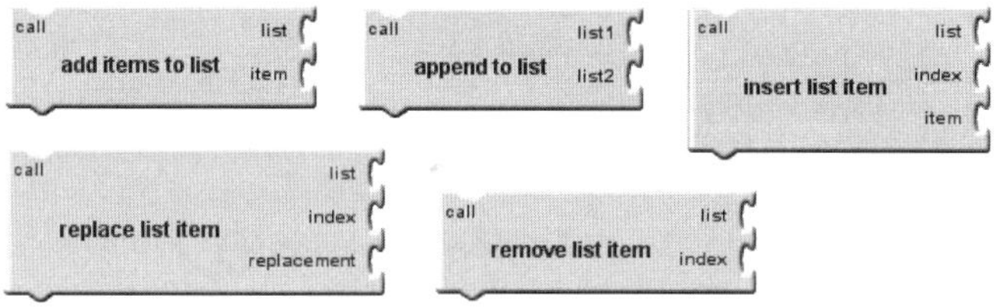

Figure 9.41 Methods for adding, replacing, and removing list elements

Whereas the method `append to list` can be used to expand a list `list1` by appending a whole list `list2` (as a result, `list1` gets longer and `list2` remains unchanged), the method `add items to list` can assign to a list `list` one or more individual entries `item` (after each new item, a new socket automatically appears in the method block). In both cases, the new items are added to the end of the first or existing list. In Figure 9.42 (right), you can see how the user input `three` in Box2 is added as a new item to the existing list `(one two)`, which then grows to the displayed list `(one two three)`. In the block structure, these changes are implemented as follows: When the ListAddButton is pressed, the list `digitList` is assigned the current value of ListTextBox2 and the newly expanded list is then displayed in ListLabel (see also `demo_Data`). Alternatively, you can use the method `insert list item` to add a new item `item` in a list `list` exactly in the position `index`.

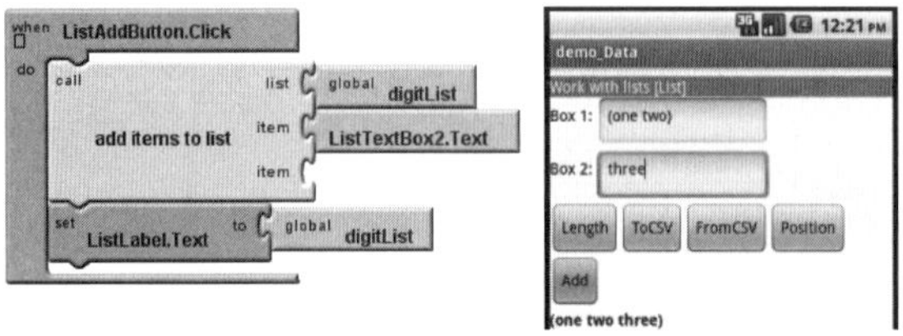

Figure 9.42 Adding a new item to the end of a list

To replace an old list item with a new one, we must pass three arguments to the method `replace list item`: the initial list `list`, the position `index` of the item to be replaced, and the new item `replacement`. In the example shown in Figure 9.43 (right), Box1 contains the initial list, Box2 contains the new item, and the input field next to the Replace button contains the index position. In terms of the underlying block structure (left), pressing the ListReplaceButton in `digitList` causes the item `one` in position `ListIndexTextBox` (1) to be replaced with the value of ListTextBox2 (`three`), resulting in the displayed new list `(three two)` (see also `demo_Data`).

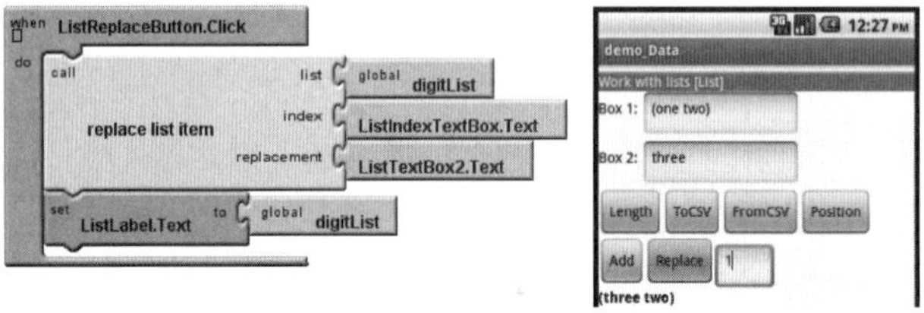

Figure 9.43 Replacing a list item at an index position with a new item

In a similar way, you can then use the method `removeListItem` to remove an item from a list `list` at the index position `index`. In this case, of course, the third argument (replacement) is redundant because you are deleting an item. The next section describes how you can apply these individual access methods in turn to each item of a list.

Controlling Program Flow with the Control Block Group

A fundamental basis for developing structured program flow and dynamic algorithms is provided by the *control structures* of a programming or development language, which AI combines in the Control block group. To ensure that an app does not always react to every possible user interaction in the same way regardless of the current conditions, program state, or data, the program must be able to check conditions and react differently and appropriately depending on the state. The conditions are checked mainly based on logical and sometimes mathematical operators, which you have already encountered in the context of the corresponding data types.

For example, receipt of a new SMS message may be indicated with a sound effect only if the corresponding checkbox is enabled, or confidential information may be displayed only if a valid password has been entered. In structured programming, this concept is referred to as a *conditional statement*, meaning a statement that is executed only if a certain condition is fulfilled. A conditional statement mainly consists of two parts: the condition and the appropriate program statement (*if-then*). Whereas the conditional statement is carried out only if a condition applies, a *branch* determines *which* statement is to be carried out in case of a positive answer versus a negative answer. For example, correctly entering a password can be acknowledged with a greeting tune as a sound effect, whereas an incorrect password generates a dull alert sound. A branch consists of three basic parts: the condition plus the statement sequence for fulfillment and the statement sequence for non-fulfillment, where one of the two statement sequences is carried out in any case (*if-then-else*).

In contrast to the control structures mentioned previously, in which the condition is checked only once and the appropriate program statement run through only a single time, other processes must occur repeatedly in a *loop* or an *iteration*. If the condition is fulfilled, the statement is executed and the condition is checked again. If it is still fulfilled, the statement is executed again, and so on (*while*). Only once the condition is no longer fulfilled does the program flow stop the loop and continue from the next block structure, if appropriate. To avoid *infinite loops,* the program statements in the loop body usually change the value checked in the condition, so that the latter is no longer fulfilled at some point and the loop stops. In the special case of a *for loop,* the number of loop repetitions is predetermined by a maximum value, which, for example, might reflect the number of items in a list that are to be processed consecutively in the loop (*for each*).

Let's take a closer look at the generic control constructs, their differences, and their specific applications.

Conditional Statements and Branches (*if-then-else*)

We will discuss the conditional statements and branches at the same time, as their structures are very similar and, therefore, distinct from the other category of control structures, the loops. If you look at the three methods that AI offers for creating conditional statements and branches (see Figure 9.44), you will notice that they appear almost to be a successive expansion of the basic function (from left to right in the figure). Similar to the structure of a procedure, all three control structures first check the condition `test` in the header and then determine the statement sequence `then-do` in the body of the control construct. Whereas the conditional statement `if` (normally referred to as an *if-then* statement) has only a `then-do` area for inserting an statement sequence, the two branches `ifelse` (*if-then-else*) and `choose` each have two areas: `then-do` for the statement in case of a positive result and `else-do` in case of a negative result.

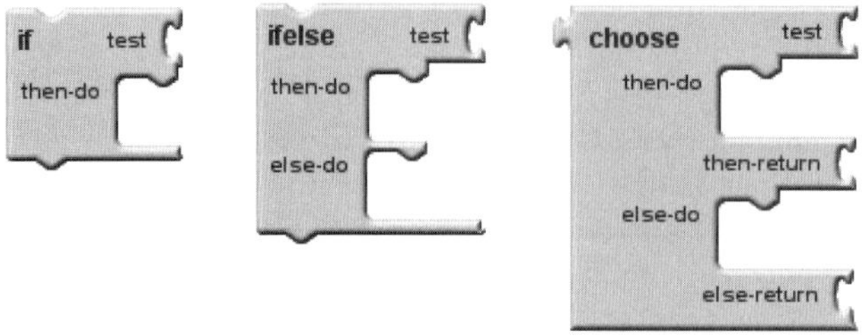

Figure 9.44 Methods for creating conditional statements and branches

The main purpose of a conditional statement is to carry out an individual statement or sequence of statements within an app if a condition is fulfilled or a certain state prevails within the program. Thus a program subsection is not invariably executed if a certain event occurs, but rather is executed only under certain conditions, which allows a certain degree of influence over the program flow as a whole.

Difference Between "when-do" and "if then-do"

Even if the two block types are clearly separated from each other, it can be helpful to make yourself aware of the fundamental difference between an event handler `when-do` and a conditional statement `if then-do`. An input-oriented event handler usually reacts with its block structures directly to an *external* event occurring outside of the app, such as pressing a button or receiving an SMS message. A structurally oriented conditional statement generally evaluates an *internal* state of the app, which can be the consequence of an external event, but this event triggers the condition check indirectly as a consequence of the program structures. The event handler carries out the block structures it contains in any case, whereas the conditional statement carries them out only if the condition check returned a positive result. Usually both constructs work together, and the conditional statement is part of the block structure within the event handler—which is what makes the differentiated reactions of an app to user input and other events possible in the first place.

To illustrate a conditional statement, we will use the example of requesting a password. Figure 9.45 depicts the typical interaction between an event handler and a conditional statement, where the former reacts to user input in any case, but the latter outputs the text "Password correct!" only if the condition of a correct password input is fulfilled. To achieve this outcome, we slot the conditional statement as an `if` method block into the event handler `ControlIfButton.Click`. As a condition `test`, we check with the logical-mathematical relational operator = whether the word entered by the user in the text box ControlPWTextBox is identical to the specified password `confidential` (case sensitive!). If the two are identical, the statement is carried out under `then-do` and the text `Password correct!` is displayed in a ControlLabel. If the passwords do not match, then nothing happens (see also `demo_Data`).

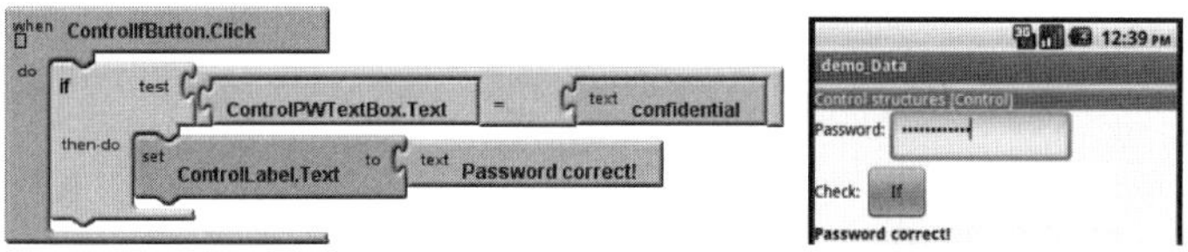

Figure 9.45 Confirmation appears only if the correct password is entered

If you also want to explicitly notify the user of the fact that an incorrect password was entered, you can use a branch or *if-then-else* statement. Depending on the user input, one of two program statements is then carried out, so either a positive or a negative notifier will be displayed. In Figure 9.46, you can see the use of the `ifelse` method block in a similar block structure. Here, the same condition is checked as previously, and the program reacts with the same notifier in case of a positive result. Now however, each time an incorrect password is entered, the statement in the `else-do` area also displays the notifier `Password invalid!` (see also `demo_Data`).

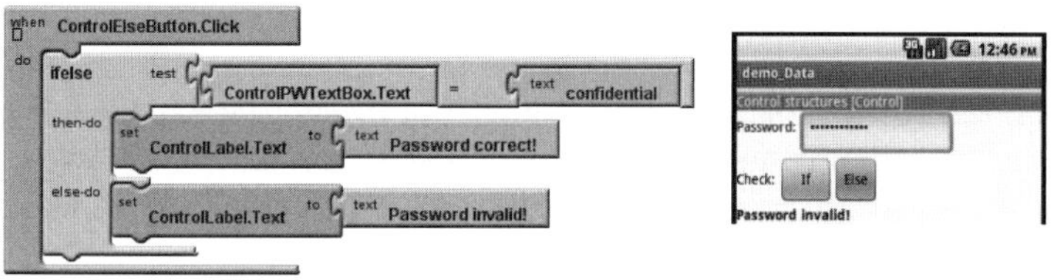

Figure 9.46 Different notifiers in response to correct and incorrect passwords

Expressed in pseudocode, we can describe the event handler shown in Figure 9.46 and the implemented algorithm as follows:

```
When the button is pressed
  check whether the entered character string equals "confidential"
    if yes, display the text "Password correct!"
    if no, display the text "Password invalid!"
```

The branch with the method `choose` offers an alternative to the `ifelse` block. It also comprises the condition check `test` and the two statement areas `then-do` and `else-do`. Additionally, the `choose` method has a return value for each of the two statement areas, `then-return` and `else-return` (similar to the procedure block procedureWithResult and its return value return). With this method, a condition check can be used very efficiently directly in a block structure. For example, in Figure 9.47 the choose block can be used like a static text block, but it can dynamically return the appropriate notifier text for display depending on the result of the test (see also demo_Data). Here, too, the statement blocks themselves can remain empty if no other processing blocks for determining the return value are required.

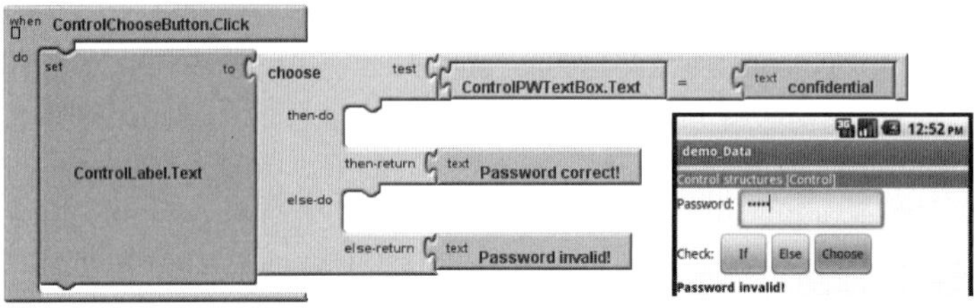

Figure 9.47 Direct display of the appropriate notifier text

List-Specific and Numeric Loops (*for*)

The second significant group of control structures comprises the *loops*, in which a program section is usually repeated several times. If the same data structure is accessed repeatedly—for example, to process all items of a list in order with the same statements—the process is referred to as *iteration*. If the number of iterations is fixed from the start, the program runs take place within a *for loop*. There are different kinds of *for* loops, but as the name indicates, the loop is usually repeated once *for* each item, either from beginning to end, or vice versa. A *for* loop does not necessarily have to be based on the items in a list, but can also be applied to other data types or structures. A numeric value is counted up or down up to a certain end value, and the statement is executed the corresponding number of times.

For each of these two fields of application, AI offers a method in the Control block group (see Figure 9.48). Whereas the loop method foreach is dedicated to list editing, the numeric counting loop for range can be used for general iterative tasks for which you specify the number of repetitions.

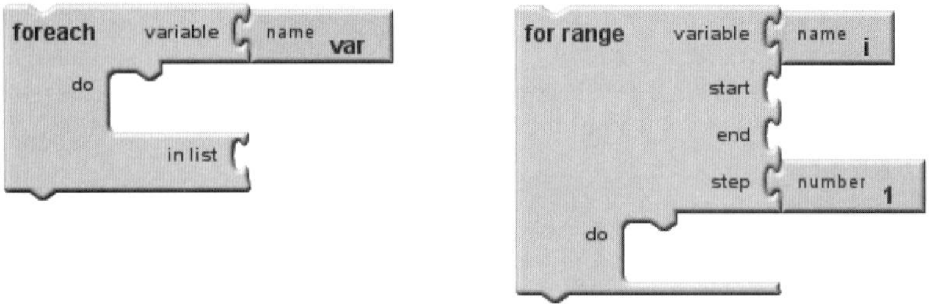

Figure 9.48 The two "for" loops: foreach and for range

With the method `foreach`, you are on the safe side if you want to process all items of a list consecutively. That is, you do not have to worry about either the specific number of list items or a condition check with which the loop can be stopped again. This type of loop also eliminates the risk of infinite loops, as the method `foreach` takes care of all these things automatically. You as developer can then concentrate on implementing the program statements for processing the individual list items in the loop body. The `foreach` loop simply passes over the list items individually for processing.

The structure of the `foreach` loop shown in Figure 9.48 resembles somewhat a procedure with a return value. The `foreach` loop also has two sockets: one that says `variable` at the top and a concluding one that says `in list` below the loop body. If you start dragging the method block `foreach` from the Control block group into the AI Editor, the suitable variable `var` is added automatically; you should then rename it with an appropriate name. In this variable, the current list item is later available in the loop body at each loop iteration and can be used by the inserted block structures for further processing. In the concluding socket `in list`, you can slot the list that you want to process.

To demonstrate the practical application of the `foreach` loop, we will use it to format the output of any list. The formatting consists of listing the items in our list one below the other, with a separate row for each item, instead of listing items consecutively and enclosed by brackets as in the standard output. The user can enter any kind of list as shown in Figure 9.49 (right) and format it by pressing a button (see also `demo_Data`). To keep the list flexible, it is initiated as an empty list in the variable `forList`. Once the button ForEachButton is pressed, the text entered in the ForTextBox is split at all spaces with the list method `split at spaces` and the resulting list is passed to the variable `forList`. The `For Label` that we want to output the formatted list to is first overwritten with the text `List items:`, in a step that occurs before the loop starts. Note the additional character `\n` in the assigned text block; it is a *control character* for a line break (ASCII character 10). This character will not be displayed later but ensures that the next text input or the next list item appears at the beginning of the next line.

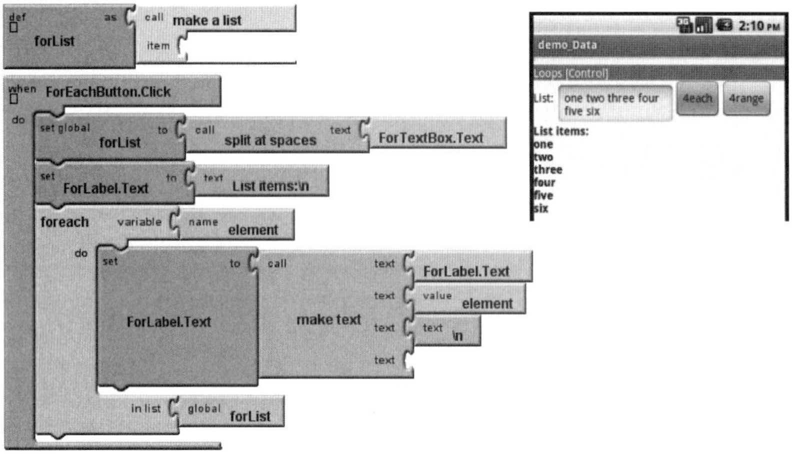

Figure 9.49 Formatted output of a list using a "foreach" loop

The preparations for the loop iteration in Figure 9.49 are now complete, and the `foreach` loop can start its work. As recommended, the default name of the loop variable was changed from `var` to the more accurate term `element`, as the variable contains the current list element at each loop iteration. Now the proper processing of the list can start. It consists of outputting the current list item of `element` in the label ForLabel, followed by the control character `\n`. To ensure that the previous list item is not just overwritten by the new item at each iteration of the list, all items are combined into a coherent text string with the method `make text`, with the current item being appended to the end of the string in each case. In this way, the text string placed in ForLabel grows by another list item with each repetition of the loop. As the control character `\n` is written after each item in the string, the whole text string then appears in its final output in ForLabel with the corresponding number of line breaks, in which is the desired output format (see also `demo_Data`). Expressed in pseudocode, the block structure shown in Figure 9.49 can be described as follows:

```
When the button is pressed
  generate a list from ForTextBox and assign it to forList
  write in ForLabel the text "List items:\n"
  For each element of forList
      take the current text of ForLabel
      and append to it the current element plus \n
     and write this new text again into ForLabel
```

Take your time and have a good look at the block structure and the program flow shown in Figure 9.49. It is important that you thoroughly understand the basic mechanism of how the current list item is read out in a `foreach` loop and then becomes available as a variable for processing in the loop body. For programming newbies, it can be difficult to fully grasp the general operating principle of a loop structure. Once you have taken that step in understanding, however, you are ready to use one of the most important elements for developing efficient and demanding algorithms. Do not let yourself be distracted too much by the specific processing of the individual items in the preceding example or become worried if you cannot grasp the processing steps immediately. The iterative combination of several list items into a new whole is no trivial task. Without the use of the `foreach` loop in our example, however, only the last item would have been displayed in the label ForLabel after the loop was completed and all list items were processed.

Displaying Formatted Lists with the foreach Loop

The AI Reference "Notes and Details" contains a special section "Displaying a List" that provides a detailed description of how to output a formatted list with a `foreach` loop. Please have a look at the following link if you need further help understanding how this loop works:

`http://experimental.appinventor.mit.edu/learn/reference/other/displaylist.html`

To demonstrate the numeric loop `for range`, we do not require a list as the basis for the iteration. As you can see in Figure 9.48, this method instead requires a specified start value `start`, beginning from which the loop counts during the iteration with a specified step value `step` up to the end value `end`. The variable step size makes it possible to have steps larger than +1 or –1. The intermediate value is recorded in the predefined variable `i`. The function can be easily demonstrated in the loop iteration shown in Figure 9.50. Similar to the example for the `foreach` loop, the individual values are again combined into a text string in each iteration with the method `make text` with line breaks (\n), such that the values are listed one below the other.

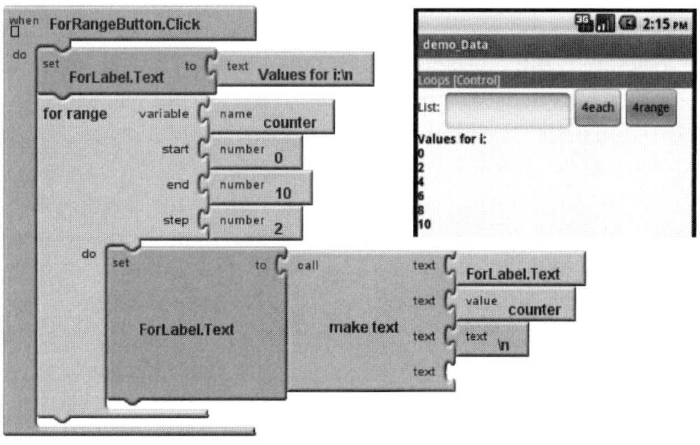

Figure 9.50 Displaying a number sequence with step size 2 with the loop "for range"

The resulting values correspond to the different counters produced during the course of the loop iterations. To create the number sequence `0 2 4 6 8 10` shown in Figure 9.50, we assigned a starting value of `0`, a target value of `10`, and a step size of `2` to the method `for range`. We renamed the default counter variable `i` to `counter`. The statement in the `do` area of the method `for range` simply counts from 0 to 10 in steps of +2, appending the intermediate value to the previous intermediate values as text and displaying the resulting text string in `ForLabel.Text`. In pseudocode, we can describe this process as follows:

```
When the button is pressed
   write in ForLabel the text "Values for:\n"
   and set counter to start value 0
   Until counter is bigger than end value 10
        take the current text of ForLabel
        and append to it the value of counter plus \n
        and write the new text again in ForLabel
      and increase the current value of counter by 2
```

With this approach, you can controllably repeat almost any process, independent of the length of a list, with the number of iterations determined by a value range to be passed through with an incremented counter. But that is not all: This flexibility in executing iterative tasks can be enhanced even further with another loop method available in AI, which means that the potential area of application of the powerful loop structures can be expanded almost universally.

Generic Loops (*while*)

For creating other efficient, iterative (repeatedly applied) program structures and algorithms, AI offers the loop block `while` in the Control block group. Its area of application and range of tasks are far more varied and more flexible than those for the previously introduced `for` loops. It is difficult to clearly assign the `while` loop in AI to a specific loop type, because you can use it to represent the typical constructs and functions of a *while loop*, but also use it as a counting or *for* loop. During the course of this section, we will introduce several ways of using this loop group, which will give you a first impression of the great degree of flexibility and power offered by this method for creating efficient and demanding algorithms. Take your time and explore the iterative processes of the `while` loop, which has a condensed form that includes just a few block structures. If you are a programming beginner, please do not be put off if you do not understand how everything works straight away; as with anything else, practice makes perfect! First let's take a closer look at the seemingly mild-mannered `while` block shown in Figure 9.51.

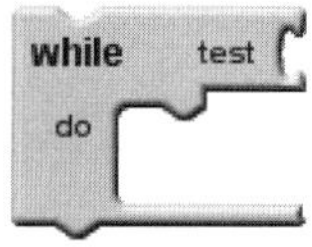

Figure 9.51 The "while" loop for many different iterative tasks

Just as with the conditional statements and branches, the `while` loop shown in Figure 9.51 first checks whether a condition `test` is fulfilled, before executing the program statement(s) in the loop body under `do`. Once the statements have been executed, the condition is tested again. If it remains fulfilled, the statements are executed again, and so on. Only when the condition is no longer fulfilled is the loop exited; the program then continues with the block structure that follows the `while` block in the program structure, if applicable.

Pre-Test Loops and Post-Test Loops

The `while` loop in AI corresponds to a *pre-test* loop (*while-do*), which executes only if the condition is fulfilled at least once. By contrast, a *post-test* loop (*do-while*), which appears in many other programming languages, executes at least once in any case, even if the condition is never fulfilled. Some programming languages support both types of loops.

In accordance with their generic character, `while` loops usually make use of the equally flexible variables required either as counters or for recording intermediate and end results. When the variable is used as a counter, its numeric value is usually increased by 1 with each loop pass (*incremented*) or, conversely, decreased by 1 with each iteration (*decremented*). Thus we can easily implement a countdown timer with a `while` loop and a decrementing variable `countdownCounter` as shown in Figure 9.52. The variable in this example takes on a double function as a counter for the loop pass and an intermediate value of the countdown. Once the user has entered any number in the text box and pressed the Countdown button, the `while` loop counts backward starting from that number to 0, and then displays the text "Countdown over!" (see also `demo_Data`).

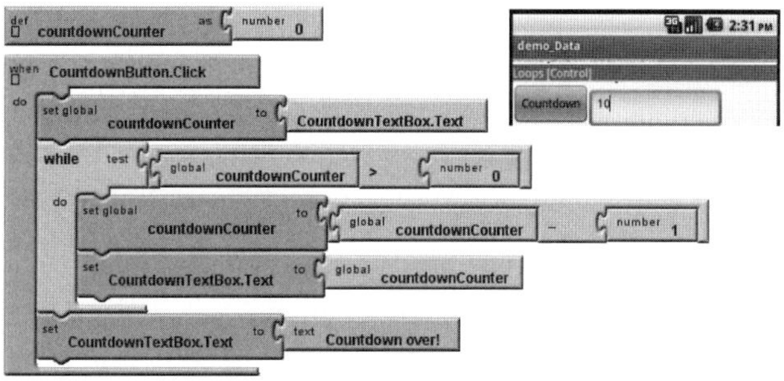

Figure 9.52 Countdown timer implemented in a "while" loop

To implement the countdown counter shown in Figure 9.52, we create it as the variable `countdownCounter` and initialize it with the value `0`. If the user has, for example, entered the number `10` into the CountdownTextBox and then clicks the CountdownButton, the value `10` from the CountdownTextBox is first passed to the variable `countdownCounter` in the button's event handler. Now the `while` loop becomes active and checks whether the current variable value is larger than `0`. As this is the case with the current value `10` and the condition is fulfilled, the loop can be run a first time. With the first statement in the loop body, the current value of `countdownCounter` is reduced by `1`. The new value should now correspond to the old value minus 1, which is expressed in the statement `countdownCounter = countdownCounter - 1`. The current value `9` is displayed with the second statement of the loop body in the text box. Now the loop condition is checked again. As the current variable value `9` is still larger than `0`, the loop is run again, and the value is reduced to `8`, checked again, and so on. Only when the variable value in the loop body is reduced from `1` to `0` does the repeat condition check produce a negative result (the Boolean value `false`). In that case, the loop is exited and the next statement in the event handler is executed, which displays the text `Countdown over!`. Expressed in pseudocode, the block structure shown in Figure 9.52 looks like this:

```
When the button is pressed
  set the countdownCounter to the value of the text box
  While the value of countdownCounter is larger than 0
    reduce the value of countdownCounter by 1
    write the new countdownCounter value into the text box
  Then write "Countdown over!" into the text box
```

Take your time and make yourself aware of the sequence of the block structure shown in Figure 9.52. With the generic `while` loops, you need to be much more careful than with the predefined—and therefore safer—`foreach` loops. With these loops, you are responsible for ensuring that the correct number of loop iterations occurs. You decide when a loop is to be exited, which condition must be fulfilled first, in which way the elements are passed in turn to the processing block structures, and in which steps the counter should count up or down. Try to recreate the individual runs in your mind's eye, because when creating your own loop constructs, you will have to do this in advance during planning and implementation. Pay close attention to every detail during implementation, especially to the statements that influence the value for the condition check. For example, look at the loop body shown in Figure 9.52. If you had merely replaced the operator `-` with `+` (addition instead of subtraction) in the calculation of each new variable value `countdownCounter`, the variable value would increase by 1 with each loop instead of being reduced by 1, so it would always be larger than `0`, the condition would always be true, and the loop would iterate endlessly.

Avoid Infinite Loops!

Try to avoid *infinite loops* by assessing the conditions and parameters for the loop exit carefully and picturing the program flow in your mind's eye before starting the app on the emulator or smartphone. Otherwise, you will have to forcibly terminate the loop. If necessary, make use of the debugging methods to analyze and fix the cause of an infinite loop.

In the later section on debugging, we will provide additional tips on checking the critical loop constructs that work with variables to ensure they run correctly. When troubleshooting, it is often helpful to be able to track the changes in the variable's value that occur during each loop run, which is possible in the AI IDE. With this method, you can also track the countdown counter in the variable `countdownCounter` live. Unfortunately, no intermediate value is displayed in our example in Figure 9.52, even though the loop body contains this instruction, as any other input and output are completely blocked during the repeated loop run. This makes it all the more important that you avoid infinite loops right from the start.

As emphasized previously, `while` loops are characterized mainly by their high degree of flexibility when used in the most varied functional contexts. To illustrate this flexibility, we will show another example of their use: We will use a `while` loop to recreate the mathematical function of exponents. *Exponents* are basically a repeated mathematical operation, where a factor is multiplied repeatedly. In the power a^n (a to the power of n), the base a is multiplied by itself as many times as is specified by the exponent n ($a^n = a * a * a \ldots$). Thus, for example, the value of 2^3 is calculated as $2 * 2 * 2 = 8$. A `while` loop is ideal for this kind of mathematical operation. In Figure 9.53, the user can enter any base a in the PowerATextBox and any exponent n in the PowerNTextBox. When the user presses the equals button, the `while` loop is repeated n times; with each run, the current intermediate value of the power is multiplied again with a. After the loop is exited, the cumulative value of the power is displayed as the result (see also `demo_Data`).

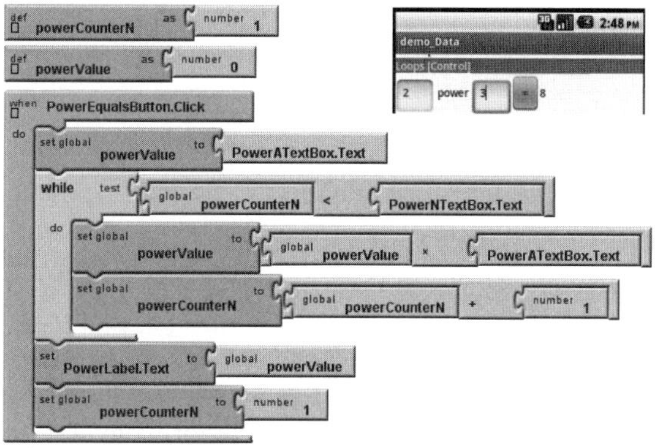

Figure 9.53 Computing exponential powers with a "while" loop

To implement this function within the block structure of Figure 9.53 (left), we need two variables. The variable `powerCounterN` reflects each current exponent n, which determines the number of loop iterations and has the initial value `1`. Later in the loop, the iterative intermediate result or final result (product) of the repeated multiplication is recorded in the variable `powerValue`. If the user has entered the base $a = 2$ and the exponent $n = 3$ as in Figure 9.53 (right), pressing the PowerEqualsButton assigns the base 2 taken from the PowerATextBox to the variable `powerValue` as the initial value of a^1. Next, the initial condition of the `while` loop checks whether the current exponent in `powerCounterN` with the value `1` is still smaller than the exponent 3 entered by the user in the PowerNTextbox. As this is the case, the loop is executed for the first time. In the first *do* statement, the existing `powerValue` 2^1 (= 2) is multiplied for the first time with the base 2 from the PowerATextBox and the result 2^2 (= 4) is recorded as the new `powerValue`. Then the `powerCounter` is increased in accordance with the current exponent by 1, to a value of `2`. As this value is still less than the specified exponent 3, the loop is repeated, the old `powerValue` of `4` is again multiplied by the base and the result 2^3 (= 8) recorded as the new value in `powerValue`. After the `powerCounter` is incremented to the value `3`, the condition of the loop is no longer fulfilled, and the program flow continues after the loop body. There, the current value `8` of the variable `powerValue` is displayed as the result of the calculation of 2^3 in the `PowerLabel`. To be ready for the next calculation when the PowerEqualsButton is pressed the next time, the `powerCounterN` is then set back to its initial value of `1`.

Phew, take a deep breath and let this already rather complex process within the condensed block structure shown in Figure 9.53 sink in for a while. As mentioned earlier, loops can be used to develop very efficient and rather demanding algorithms. Their operation is not really all that complicated, as you can see in this pseudocode, which is provided to help you understand the explanations of the previous paragraph:

```
Assign powerCounterN the initial value 1
When the button is pressed
  assign powerValue the base of PowerATextBox
  While powerCounterN < exponent of PowerNTextBox
    multiply powerValue by the base and
      write this result back to powerValue
    increment powerCounterN by 1
  display the value of powerValue in PowerLabel
  set powerCounterN back to the initial value 1
```

We are not going to leave it at that, however. No, we want to demonstrate the flexibility of the `while` loop using another example: We will use a `while` loop to recreate the `foreach` loop that we used earlier to hold the formatted list output. This is no problem at all and easily done, but this time you must take care of managing the number of repetitions and reading the individual list items yourself. Despite this extra effort, the required block structure shown in Figure 9.54 is not considerably longer or more elaborate than the original one shown in Figure 9.49. Both the base data and the result are identical—that is, in both cases the individual items are output line by line from any list from the same text box (see also `demo_Data`).

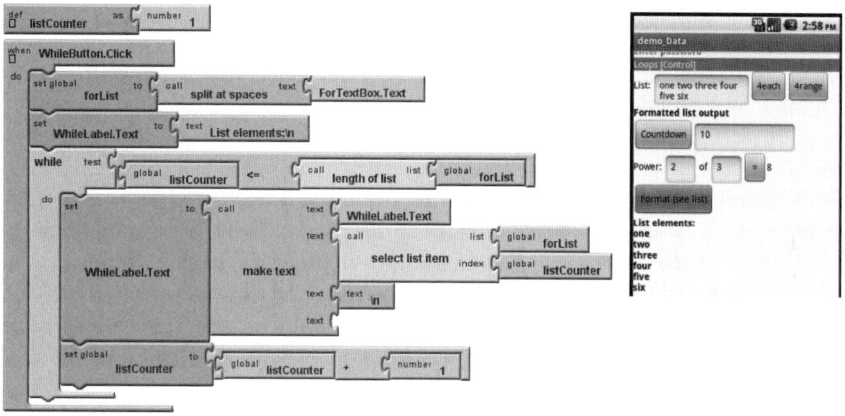

Figure 9.54 List output with a "while" loop, same format as in Figure 9.49

The first difference from using the `foreach` loop is that in the `while` loop shown in Figure 9.54 we need an additional variable `listCounter` to serve as a counter for the loop iterations; we will initialize this variable to have the value `1`. In the event handler `WhileButton.Click`, we use the original text box `ForTextBox` and even the list variable `forList` from the `foreach` example; our only new item is the label `WhileLabel` for recording the text string to be lengthened. Before entering into the `while` loop, the program checks whether the `listCounter` with the current value `1` is smaller than or equal (<=) to the length of the list `forList` (using the list method `length of list`), which is the case. The appending of each current list item to the growing text string in each iteration takes place in the loop body as before, but with the second difference that now each current list element has to be explicitly read at the current index position `listCounter` with the list method `select list item`. So that we call the next list item during the next loop iteration and at the same time increase the loop counter, the value of the variable `listCounter` is also incremented at each loop run, which constitutes a third difference. As soon as the value of `listCounter` is equal to the list length, the initial condition of the `while` loop is no longer fulfilled and the process is terminated.

To make things clearer, we can describe the block structure shown in Figure 9.54 in pseudocode as follows:

```
Assign listCounter the initial value 1
When the button is pressed
  generate a list from ForTextBox and assign it to forList
  write in WhileLabel the text "List elements:\n"
  While listCounter <= the length of forList
      take the current text from WhileLabel
      and append to it the list element
        of the index position listCounter
      plus \n,
    and write this new text back into WhileLabel
   increment listCounter by 1
```

The fundamental significance of this highly flexible and powerful method for programming in AI should have become clearer in the course of this last example while we were using the `while` block. By condensing complex program flows in generic program structures for iterative processing of homogeneous databases, we have already dived deeply into the typical subject area of developers and, ultimately, programmers. The existence and great potential of these control structures, as well as the previously discussed and underlying data types and structures, illustrate once again that the ostensibly simple and easy-to-use visual development language AI is actually a serious and powerful development tool. In the connection and interaction of component-specific and generic block groups, you can use AI to implement any conceivable algorithms, functions, and apps, provided you have the necessary knowledge of their existence, function, and use, along with the required creativity during development. But that is, after all, why you are reading this book.

Closing an App Properly

The Control block group contains four other methods that do not influence the program flow of an app directly but merely affect its start and end. The method `close screen` can be used to close the running app. Thus, for an app developed with AI, it represents an alternative to the standard stop method via the menu item "Stop this application." Of course, the final quitting of the app is then still up to the memory management of the Android operating system, just as with any other Android app. In Figure 9.55, you can press the EndButton to close a running app such as `demo_Data`. To quit the app completely and remove it from the working memory, you can use the alternative method `close application`. Calling this method also quits any sounds or timers that may have continued running in the background if the app was simply closed.

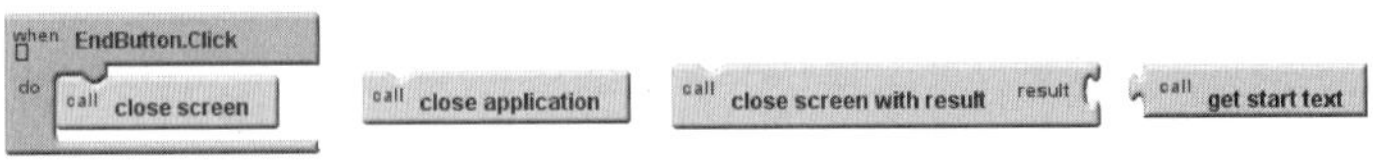

Figure 9.55 Methods for starting and ending an app

For the sake of completeness, we also want to briefly address the other two methods shown in Figure 9.55, even though their full potential will not be revealed until Chapter 13, "Communication." On the one hand, if the app that you want to close should previously have been called by another application, the closing app can return a result to that application via the method `close-screen-with-result` (in the preset variable `APP_INVENTOR_RESULT`). On the other hand, an app can receive a passed value via the method `get start text` if such a value was passed by a calling application. The reciprocal calling of apps and passing values between apps is an advanced topic that will be discussed in more detail in Chapter 13, in the context of the Activity Starter component.

In the other projects in this book and as you continue on your way toward becoming an app developer, you will frequently fall back on the generic blocks, regardless of the context and the component involved. If you are familiar with the generic blocks, you will be able to deal more flexibly with the functions of the various components and get a lot more out of them than you did in the beginner's projects presented in earlier chapters. Even if you have not yet grasped the workings of all generic blocks fully and feel that you have not completely mastered their use, you will do just that and deepen your knowledge further in the course of the projects yet to come. If you want, you reread certain sections of this chapter on program development basics. Nevertheless, once you have reached the end of this chapter, you will certainly have gained some important knowledge on your way toward becoming a full-fledged app developer.

Tips for Program Development

To conclude this chapter on program development basics appropriately, we introduce a few tools and resources that can make life easier for you as app developer. In the same way that the development language AI has the performance characteristics of a proper programming language, so the development environment AI IDE offers the typical tools and properties of a programming environment, which can be valuable resources for you when developing more advanced apps. In the following sections, we will describe these tools and properties briefly to round off the topics on program development in general and with AI in particular.

> **Additional Tips in the AI References**
>
> The AI "Concepts Reference" offers additional tips and information, as well as the documentation "Live Development, Testing, and Debugging" on tools available in the AI IDE:
>
> `http://experimental.appinventor.mit.edu/learn/reference/other/testing.html`

Let's start with a feature that you probably thought would be useful or even necessary while you were trying to enter all examples of the chapter within the demo project `demo_Data` into the AI Editor yourself or to recreate them. Although you will probably come across even more extensive projects when you are developing your own apps, the space available in AI Editor while we were developing the project `demo_Data` became so small that the individual event handlers with their block structures could hardly be displayed without overlapping (see Figure 9.56).

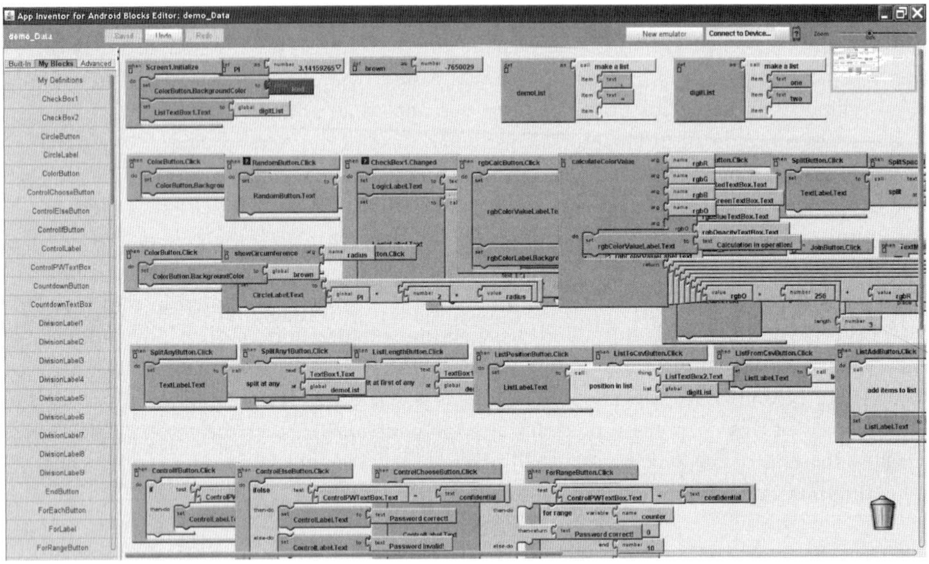

Figure 9.56 Lack of space and clarity with large projects in AI Editor

Compared to the code lines of a classic programming language, the program structures of the visual development language require much more display space. Even if the displayed workspace can be enlarged through its virtual extension, you quickly reach the limits of the maximum workspace when developing large app projects. Further enlarging the virtual workspace would help to only a certain extent, because the bigger the virtual program structures become, the more unclear and difficult to navigate they will be for you as developer. Against this backdrop, the AI IDE offers an alternative strategy for handling large projects and keeping track of the visual structures: The individual event handlers and procedures can be collapsed selectively to display only a header. For example, the event handler `WhileButton.Click` shown in Figure 9.57 can be reduced from a full view (right) to a minimized view (left).

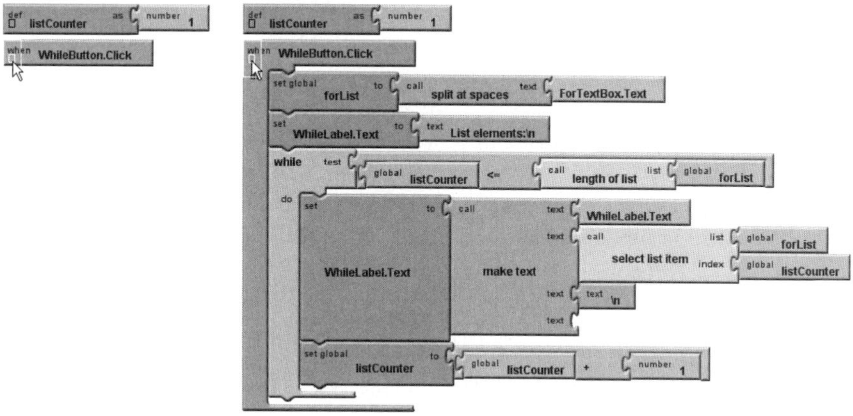

Figure 9.57 Collapsing and expanding an event handler in AI Editor

The *block collapsing* of an event handler or procedure in AI Editor can be activated or deactivated by clicking on the little square in the left side of the block (see Figure 9.57). Using this technique, you can expand only those block structures you are currently working on, while the others remain collapsed to save space. With this option, you can make much better use of the workspace in AI Editor, and keep track of things more easily in large projects. As an alternative to the expanded view shown in Figure 9.56, you can display the demo project `demo_Data` in collapsed view as shown in Figure 9.58.

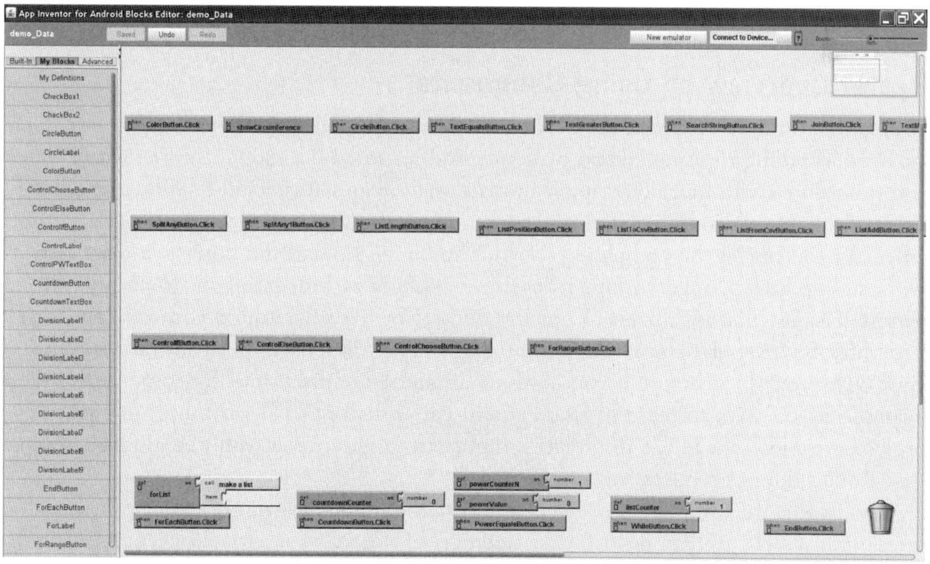

Figure 9.58 The same project as in Figure 9.56, now with blocks collapsed

In Figure 9.58, the individual collapsed block structures are arranged next to each other, with a certain distance separating them from the block structures in the next row. With this arrangement, you can extend the currently required structures as far as possible so that they generally do not overlap with the other structures. This is just one of many options for arranging the block structures—you can find your own preferred way.

The AI IDE can also help you tidy up your workspace. Simply click in AI Editor in a free space and select "Organize all blocks" from the context menu (see Figure 9.59). The individual block structures are then automatically arranged in table form.

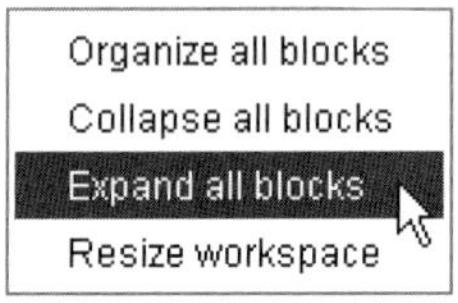

Figure 9.59 Context menu in AI Editor for organizing the workspace

With the context menu shown in Figure 9.59, you can also hide all of the block structures at once (Collapse all blocks) or show them all (Expand all blocks). With the menu item "Resize workspace," you can adapt the workspace in the Blocks Editor to the size you really need—for example, after deleting previously used large block groups. Different *context menus* will appear in AI Editor depending on which area or block you right-click and what seems appropriate to the relevant function and the current development stage. In the following section, you will also encounter a few more context menus.

Better Overview by Using Comments

Even after you have collapsed the block structures, arranged them in relation to one another according to some certain principle, and renamed the individual event handlers and procedures with more descriptive and accurate names, it can still be difficult to keep track of the connections between, and functions of, the various block structures. That is especially the case as the complexity of your app increases and the time since your last work session grows longer. Another developer looking at your program structures will almost certainly find it difficult to quickly find his or her way around your program structures, but even for you it will potentially become difficult to get your bearings in your own program structure if you have not immersed yourself in it for some time. For example, if you want to reuse or adapt an old part structure or algorithm from a past project at some point in the future, it is important to ensure that you can still find your way around the old program structure.

Against this backdrop, it can be very important to add *comments* to your block structures, with which you can describe the function of the relevant variable, event handler, or procedure. In AI Editor, you can also visually emphasize the structural separation between the individual thematic areas, similar to what we did in the Viewer of AI Designer or in the app itself with the DivisionLabel for the particular topic. In Figure 9.60, you can see some of the headings we have previously used as the DivisionLabel in the form of comments.

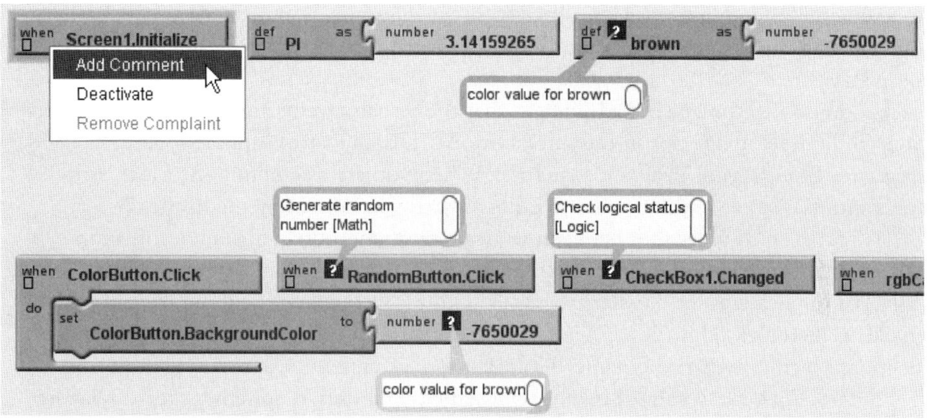

Figure 9.60 Blocks and block structures in AI Editor with added comments

You can add comments to an event handler, a procedure, or any other kind of block individually by right-clicking on that item with the mouse and selecting "Add Comment" from the context menu (see Figure 9.60). Then you can write your comment in the input field, resize it, and drag it anywhere you wish. Once a comment has been created, you can expand and collapse it by clicking on the little question mark icon on the block.

Complaints and Error Messages During Live Development

A major source of help for developing Android apps is a feature in the AI IDE that we have not yet mentioned explicitly, but have already used intensively. In classic compiler languages (such as C and C++), the program code has to be first entered as run-capable source code into an editor, then translated into executable machine code (compiled), and finally tested as an independent application. In contrast, you can use the interpreter language AI to simply drag one new component after the other in the AI IDE to the Viewer and test its functionality directly in the emulator or even on the connected smartphone. This *incremental* development is mainly what makes *live development* with AI so easy, as individual program blocks can be tested without any great effort, and the developer can get direct and selective feedback on everything that is working correctly (or incorrectly).

In addition to saving a considerable amount of time that would otherwise be devoted to the editing–compiling–testing cycle with traditional programming languages, the AI developer has to deal with far less complexity in terms of the initial considerations required when designing the algorithm to be implemented. It is precisely this intuitive, spontaneous, and sometimes even playful approach to tackling the tasks that makes the interactive development process with the AI IDE generally simpler, especially for programming novices, and leads more quickly to a feeling of success (which should not be underestimated in terms of impact on personal motivation). Once you have grasped the fundamental underlying principles that both programming approaches are equally based on, you will find it much easier to switch to a classic programming language later on if necessary.

In addition to the general advantages that the visual development language AI offers you while developing apps in the interactive AI IDE, the latter supports you directly by *preventing errors* in your program structures. When you are assembling the block structures into the larger program, the AI Editor warns you about any inconsistencies or errors and even distinguishes between critical errors and potential sources of errors. For example, in Figure 9.61, the AI IDE displays a warning (complaint) "Warning: This is a duplicate event handler" together with a yellow square with an exclamation mark on the block. This message indicates that two event handlers exist for one event, or more specifically that the name "ColorButton" is present twice, so that the event `ColorButton.Click` cannot be clearly assigned. The only requirement for displaying the error messages is that the AI IDE is connected to an Android device or the emulator.

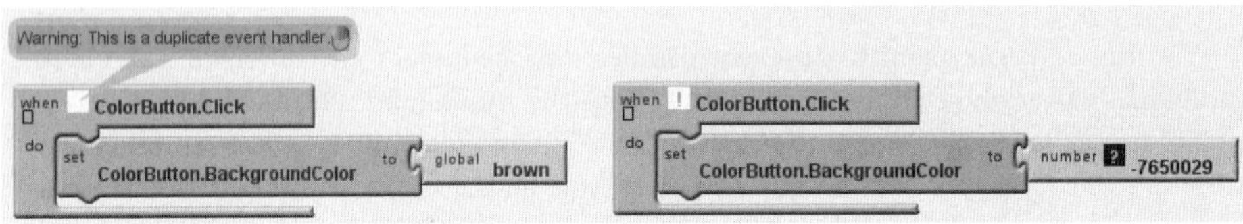

Figure 9.61 Warning about two event handlers with the same name

If the duplicate event handler in Figure 9.61 is not a mistake and you want to leave both of them in the AI Editor for now as alternatives during project development, you can use the context menu to temporarily deactivate (Deactivate) one of the event handlers and remove the other complaint explicitly in the other one (Remove Complaint), as shown in Figure 9.62. The deactivated block then stays marked in white in the AI Editor, but will not become part of the APK file when the app is downloaded (Package for Phone). Generally, AI is rather *error tolerant*, so that the app can be started even with the duplicate event handler and will behave normally otherwise.

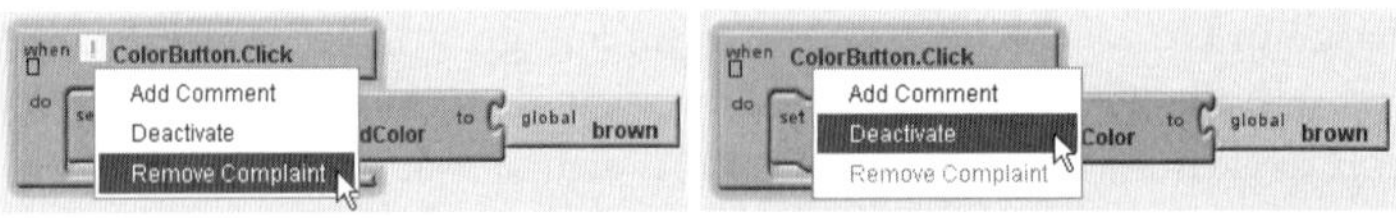

Figure 9.62 Ignore the complaint or deactivate the duplicate event handler

A program structure that generates complaints in AI Editor is still run capable, whereas a critical error would cause the program to be aborted. For that reason, AI Editor will prevent you from attempting to join blocks that do not fit together, by displaying an error message that you must acknowledge explicitly. For example, the property setter block `ColorButton.BackgroundColor` shown in Figure 9.63 can receive only a number block or a corresponding variable, not a text block.

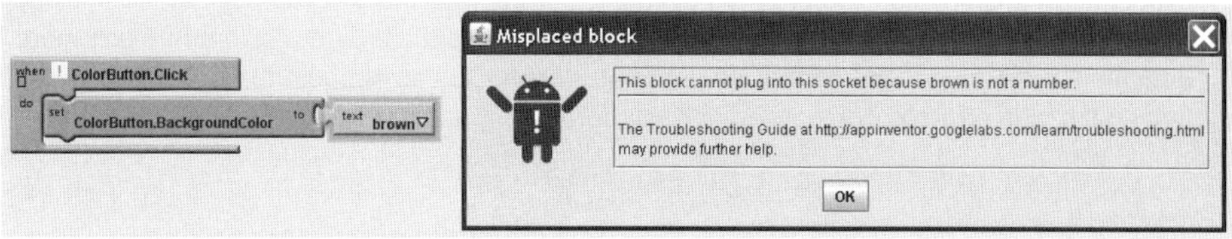

Figure 9.63 Error message in case of incompatible block combinations in AI Editor

Despite its utility, you cannot place all of your trust in the AI Editor. It will not spot all errors during input, for one thing. For example, the AI Editor does display a warning in Figure 9.64 if an input value `from` is missing for the method `random integer` (top left), and prevents you from connecting a block with an incompatible data type (`text` instead of `number`) by displaying an error message. If a number block already connected to the `from` field is accidentally transformed into a text block (bottom left) later, however, this error will become apparent only during program execution and results in the program aborting (right).

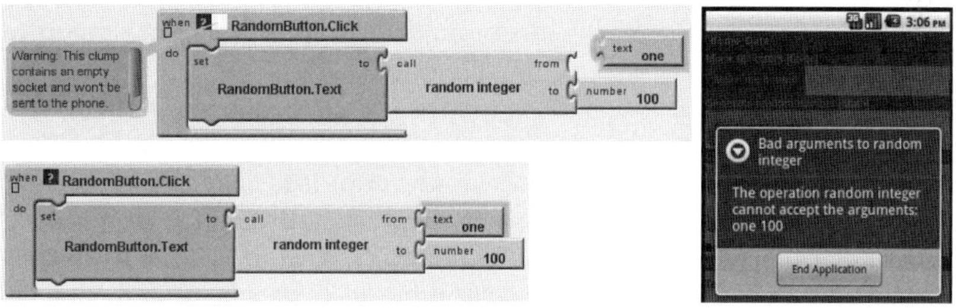

Figure 9.64 Some problems may not be discovered in time and lead to the program aborting

But even if the program aborts as shown in Figure 9.64, the cause of the error will be analyzed and listed very clearly, so that it should be relatively easy for you to fix the problem. While AI Editor provides a very high degree of support in the face of the *syntactic* program errors described previously, fixing any *semantic* errors in the program logic is mainly up to you.

Syntactic Versus Semantic Program Errors

The errors that AI Editor can spot on your behalf are *syntactic* program errors. The connection of individual blocks to block structures and event handlers follows the rules set out in the grammar/syntax of the visual development language AI. The AI Editor can check whether these syntax rules have been followed, and point out syntax errors with the appropriate complaints and error messages. By contrast, *semantic* errors are characterized by the fact that the program is running but produces results with the wrong content or does not behave as expected. In such a case the program syntax is correct, but the program logic does not work as intended by the programmer. Analyzing and fixing semantic program errors is much more difficult in most cases and cannot be automated. The IDE can support the developer in analyzing semantic errors only by providing tools for testing and debugging.

Testing and Debugging

If you can start and use your app on the emulator or the smartphone without an error message, then you can assume that your program has no—or at least no serious—syntax errors. If the app does not behave as you intended, however, a semantic error may be lurking in your program. For example, the countdown counter may get stuck in an infinite loop or the block structure for calculating the exponential value may produce the wrong results. Often such semantic errors occur within control structures such as *for* and especially *while* loops, as the iterative program flow represented by them can quickly become very complex and the developer is then less able to predict or mentally follow the program behavior. Semantic errors and their causes cannot be automatically analyzed and tracked down by AI Editor, because they do not have a formal underlying grammar whose correctness could be checked. Thus the developer must deal with troubleshooting and fixing errors—but thankfully once again the AI IDE offers some support for this quite challenging task.

In complex block structures, nested branches, and even highly efficient loop constructs, it can be difficult for you as developer to check the entire functionality as a whole for correctness. Sometimes the origin of a semantic error is hidden away in a single faulty statement, omission, or incorrect order. Against this backdrop, the AI Editor enables you to execute and test each individual statement in a block structure separately. In case of a visible action, you can also follow the result of this single statement on the integrated emulator or smartphone, or simulate the corresponding user input. Even more important and helpful is that you can observe the program's internal state during each execution directly in AI Editor and assess it as part of your analysis. Simply right-click on the statement block in which you are interested and select "Do it" from the context menu. The statement is then executed and the program-internal result is displayed in a notifier (see Figure 9.65).

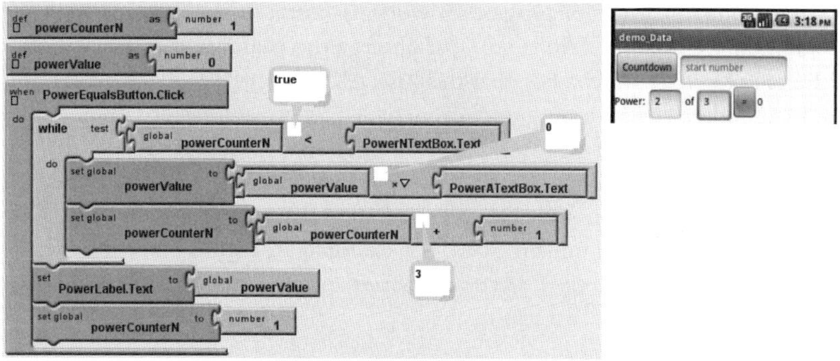

Figure 9.65 Error analysis by testing individual statements with "Do it"

In Figure 9.65, you can see how we can proceed in troubleshooting the event handler for calculating any exponential value, shown in Figure 9.53. This program still calculates the result correctly as `2 to the power of 3 = 8`, but this time an error has crept in that causes the same input values to produce the incorrect result `0`. To find the cause of the error, you can check the individual statements in the event handler for their result values. For example, selecting "Do it" from the context menu for the `while` condition check that utilizes the relational operator < produces the answer `true`. This means that the condition for entering the loop with the current input values 2 (base) and 3 (exponent) is fulfilled correctly. Calculating the exponential value with `powerCounterN` up to the correct loop repeat value `3` also works correctly, as we see displayed when selecting "Do it" at that point. But something seems to go wrong when we multiply the `powerValue` by the value from the PowerATextBox, as the value of "Do it" stays at `0` even after the multiplication is complete. To further pinpoint the problem area, we use "Do it" to display the value of PowerATextBox, which is also correct (`2`). Thus the error must be due to the first factor of the multiplication. Indeed, performing a "Do it" check on `powerValue` reveals the result `0`. Now we have found the cause of the problem and know why the event handler kept producing the incorrect overall result of `0`—namely, repeated multiplication by `0`—despite the loop running correctly. As the developer of the algorithm, you recognize immediately that this value should actually be the intermediate value in each case, starting with the initial value for a^1—in our example, the factor 2. A review of the block structure in Figure 9.65 reveals that the statement `set global powerValue to PowerATextBox.Text` was omitted, which should be the first statement in the event handler, appearing before the loop, and assign the initial value accordingly. If you now add this statement, the error is fixed and the program will calculate the correct results.

To further confirm that your program is working correctly or, alternatively, to explore additional sources of errors, you can observe the changes in critical values during the entire program flow. For that purpose, AI Editor offers another function found in many other programming environments—namely, a *debugger* (a type of diagnostics tool). For each variable, as well as for other block types, you can use the context menu item "Watch" to open a little pop-up window that displays the current live value while the program is running. This feature allows you to follow live what happens "behind the scenes" of your program. For example, in Figure 9.66 (left), you can track the two variables `powerCounterN` and `powerValue` while the event handler `PowerEqualsButton.Click` is running.

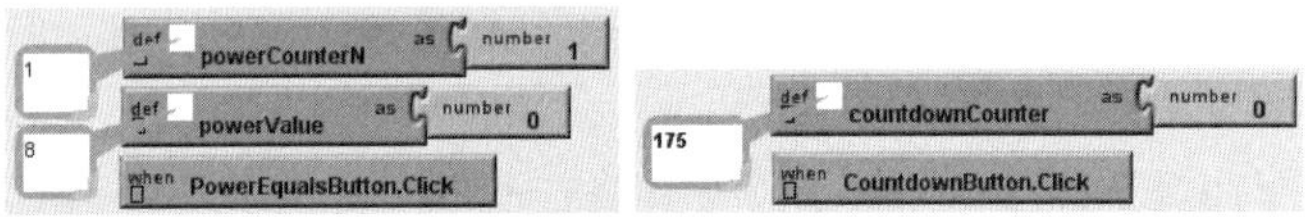

Figure 9.66 Tracking the current variable values live with "Watch"

In the Watch window shown in Figure 9.66 (right), you can watch the countdown counter from Figure 9.52 while it is counting down and check that your program is really working correctly. The individual Watch windows can be closed again at any time by selecting "Stop Watching" from the context menu.

Through its testing and debugging functions, the AI IDE offers important and helpful tools that will support you during the process of finding, analyzing, and fixing semantic program errors. Make liberal use of these tools, because especially in complex branch and loop structures they are often the only way of approaching the problem systematically and illuminating what is happening in these condensed processes. You can also construct your own debugging functions from the AI components—for example, by displaying the values of variables in the emulator or on the smartphone in a label, or by setting *break points* with the Notifier component, with which the program flow can be interrupted and intermediate values displayed for analysis. By using a certain amount of creativity, you can conceive of other aids that might also support you during program development and error analysis.

Apart from program-internal errors, problems with an app can be caused by system errors, although these are less likely to occur in case of programming novices. Such errors can occur both within the Android environment in which your app is running and within the Java environment in which you are developing your app with the AI IDE. Both environments document their processes and any errors in *log files*. Access to and analysis of these log files is an advanced method used primarily by professional Java programmers. You can find more detailed information on the *Android Logs* and the *Android Debug Bridge* in the general Android documentations.

Android Logs, Android Debug Bridge (ADB), and Java System Logs

For professional developers, other general tools for error analysis are available. These programs assume the developer has an in-depth understanding of the processes on the operating system level and, generally, Java programming knowledge. Further general information can be found at:

`http://experimental.appinventor.mit.edu/learn/reference/other/testing.html`

For information on Android Debug Bridge (adb), see:

`http://developer.android.com/guide/developing/tools/adb.html`

For further information on the *Java System Logs,* see the section "Control with the Java Console" in Chapter 15, "Tips and Tools."

Developing More Quickly and Comfortably

Although the active support in avoiding and fixing sources of errors can be a great help in completing your app project more quickly and successfully, the AI IDE offers a few other ways of increasing your work efficiency. For example, you can click the left mouse button on an empty space in AI Editor to access all generic block groups under the "Built-In" heading as *shortcuts*. Click on one of the groups to select an individual method (see Figure 9.67, left).

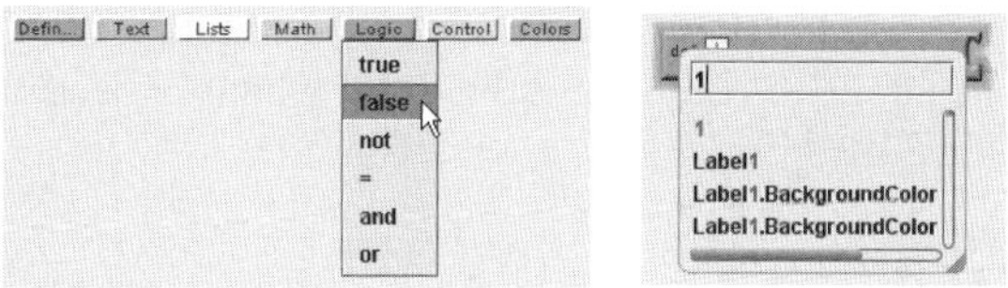

Figure 9.67 Speed up your work with shortcuts and typeblocking in AI Editor

With the technique known as *typeblocking,* you can simply insert a block in AI Editor by typing an alphanumeric character on your keyboard. The AI Editor then opens a menu with all kinds of data types, methods, and other items that contain this character or character string. You just need to choose one of these options, and the suitable block is inserted. If a setter block is active, the block selected via typeblocking is even inserted automatically into the setter. In Figure 9.67, for example, you can initialize a variable with the value `1` by simply typing a 1 on the keyboard and pressing **Enter**. You could hardly develop more quickly, conveniently, and intuitively than that.

Also, do not forget the effective options of *copy and paste*, which are also available in AI Editor. Simply highlight the desired block, block structure, or even an entire event handler by clicking on it, press **Ctrl+C** to copy it, and then press **Ctrl+V** to paste the copy in the desired location. The copied block structure is then immediately available for further use in AI Editor. Especially with copied event handlers, you must ensure that you just reuse the block structures contained within them and replace the event handler with another one; otherwise, you will have two different event handlers for a single event, which will cause inconsistencies in the program structure (see also Figure 9.61).

To delete a block, you can use the recycle bin or, alternatively, press the **Del** key on your keyboard and then confirm that you really want to delete the block. In the course of your work as app developer, you will probably increasingly make use of these kinds of little aids to help you optimize your development work and make it more efficient.

Example Projects

A theoretical chapter like this one on program development basics should be capped off with some practical example projects. Even if the companion demo project `demo_Data` has already helped you gain a first impression of how the Built-In block group can be used in practice, the potential of these generic blocks in particular will only become clear if you can see concrete examples of how they are used and, of course, try them out yourself. Their potential fields of application are far broader than those for the multimedia components, for example; the latter are more geared toward a particular area. With the Built-In blocks, you are hardly tied to a certain field of application—on the contrary, you can use them efficiently in connection with all of the other topic-specific components, thereby adding important and fundamental functions. To demonstrate how this works, we will apply the knowledge gained in the course of this chapter very often in the following sections, and you can also do so in your future work as developer. The following projects are intended to give you a little taste of this process and demonstrate the use of some of the Built-In components, without which projects with a challenging program logic would be inconceivable.

Classic Calculator

At first glance, implementing a calculator app does not seem to hold many challenges. For what else is a smartphone nowadays except a small computer—and, therefore, a calculating machine. That statement is basically correct, but even at a second glance you will probably look in vain (at least in the private sector) for apps in which any kind of visible calculation is carried out. It is probably no coincidence if even a progressive operating system such as Microsoft Windows, despite its mighty table calculation programs, still includes a simple calculator among its tools, and some users probably still have classic calculators on their desk right next to the PC. When on the move (e.g., when shopping), however, it can be useful and helpful to have a calculator with you on your smartphone. This app should behave and be operated in the same way as the familiar classic calculator to the greatest degree possible. In other words, it should have separate keys for entering numbers and arithmetic operators, a single screen or text field for displaying the input values and the result of the calculation, and so on. Requiring several screens for the individual operands of an arithmetic operation and using the smartphone keyboard would not be very practical or ergonomic and probably even get in the way.

Terminology: Operands, Operators, and Expressions

In mathematics, an *operand* is the number on which a mathematical operation is performed. A mathematical operation is represented by an *operator*. In the mathematical *expression* `2 + 3`, the two numbers `2` and `3` are the operands, which are linked by the operator `+`.

This is the point where things become challenging for our calculator app shown in Figure 9.68, which has to do a lot more than just calculate a coherent mathematical expression entered via the Android keyboard using the blocks of the Math group. The multiple-digit operands have to be entered character by character in the app via the keyboard, then combined with the operators to form an expression, whose value is then calculated when the user presses the equals key, and the result displayed on the same screen. Negative results are displayed in red. In addition to the number and operator keys and the equal key, two more function keys should be available: the C key (Clear) for deleting and resetting the current input and the Off key for switching off the calculator (i.e., ending the app).

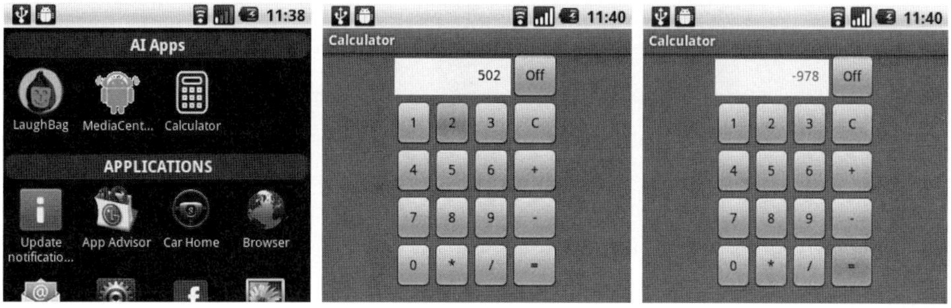

Figure 9.68 Starting and operating the calculator app with an ergonomic design

To develop the Calculator app project (Figure 9.68), we first create a new project in AI Designer in "My Projects" with the New button and name it "Calculator." Assign the corresponding title to "Screen1," set its background color to "Gray," and load the image file `calculator.png` (see the files on the companion website, in the directory `\MEDIA`) as the app icon.

Project Files on the Companion Website

As usual, you can find all files for the Calculator project on the companion website in the corresponding directories (see the Introduction for the link).

Now we need to take up the chore of creating the buttons that will serve as the keys of our calculator. To achieve the symmetrical arrangement of the keys shown in

Figure 9.68, we need to arrange them within the components of the Screen Arrangement group. Create a HorizontalArrangement with the name "DisplayHArr," for displaying the result in the box at the top and the Off button; a TableArrangement (3 × 4) with the name "NumbersTArr" for the number block below the display; and a Vertical-Arrangement with the name "FunctionVArr" for the C function key and the keys below it ("+", "–", and "=") (see Figure 9.69).

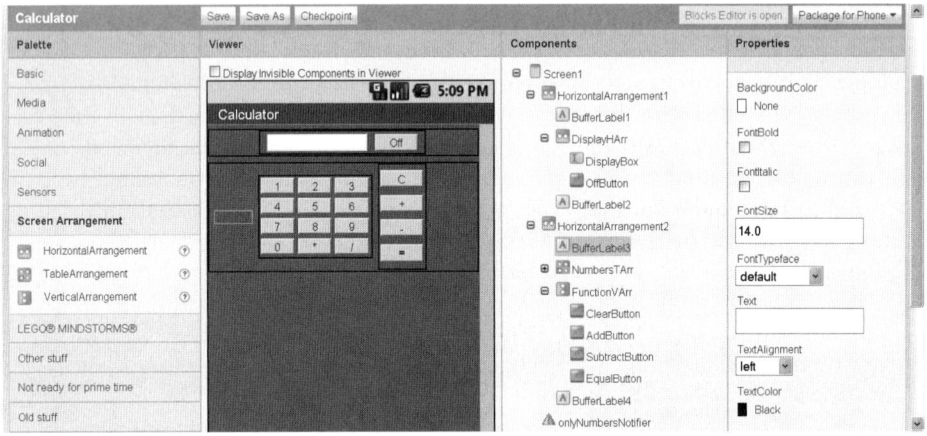

Figure 9.69 Designing the calculator's user interface in AI Designer

Next, drag the keys shown in Table 9.1 into the Viewer one after the other, and then to their appropriate positions within the Arrangement components as shown in Figure 9.69.

Table 9.1 **Components and Initial Properties for the Calculator**

Component	Object Name	Edited Properties
TextBox	DisplayBox	"Alignment": right "Enabled": disable "BackgroundColor": White "Width": 120 pixels
Button	OffButton	"Text": Off "Width": 50 pixels
Button (12x)	Button0-9, MultiplyButton, DivideButton	"Text": 0–9, *, / "Width": 40 pixels
Button (4x)	ClearButton, AddButton, SubtractButton, EqualButton	"Text": C, +, –, = "Width": 50 pixels
Notifier	onlyNumbersNotifier	

Once you have positioned the components of Table 9.1 in the Arrangement components accordingly, the elements of the calculator should appear in the upper-left corner of the screen both in the Viewer and on the emulator or smartphone. To align the calculator so it is displayed horizontally centered in the app, irrespective of the smartphone's screen size, we can use a simple trick. We place the elements we want to *center* horizontally into another HorizontalArrangement and insert an empty label (not visible without text) on its far left and right edges, setting the Width property of each empty label to "Fill parent." This causes the two invisible labels to expand dynamically so that they push the visible fixed-size components in between them together, thereby positioning them in the center of the screen.

Trick: Dynamically Centering Components in the Middle of the Screen

At the time of this book's writing, AI did not offer a preset function for centering components on the screen. For this reason, you need to use a HorizontalArrangement and two empty labels on either side where you set the Width property to "Fill parent." Now when you insert any components in between the two empty labels, they will be squashed into the center of the screen, irrespective of the different screen sizes of the various smartphones.

In our example of Figure 9.69, DisplayHArr is arranged together with its components and the two flanking labels BufferLabel1 and BufferLabel2 in the HorizontalArrangement1. The two arrangements NumbersTArr and FunctionVArr with the labels BufferLabel3 (highlighted in Figure 9.69) and BufferLabel4 are arranged in the HorizontalArrangement2, and thereby centered horizontally on the screen. Like the BufferLabel objects, these two HorizontalArrangement component objects must have their Width properties set to "Fill parent" so that the calculator app appears as shown in Figure 9.68.

Now we have created the user interface of the calculator and all required components are present. At this point, you can switch to AI Editor to implement the calculator functions. Let's start with the easiest part, the event handlers for the number keys. Like its traditional counterpart, our calculator shows the input operands right-justified in the display (see the Alignment property of the DisplayBox component object). Because an operand can have more than one digit, each character shown on the calculator display after the user presses a number key must be added to the end of the existing character string. This ensures that if the user presses the keys "5", "0", and "1", the three-digit number "501" appears in the calculator display, not "105". To join the individual numbers together to form multiple-digit numbers, we treat them as alphanumeric characters to which we can apply the methods of the Text generic block group. That is, we use the method `join` to add the number of the key we just pressed to the end of the existing string in the text box DisplayBox and then display the expanded string again in the DisplayBox. This process and the corresponding event handler are the same for all of the number keys; Figure 9.70 shows these steps for the keys "1" and "2".

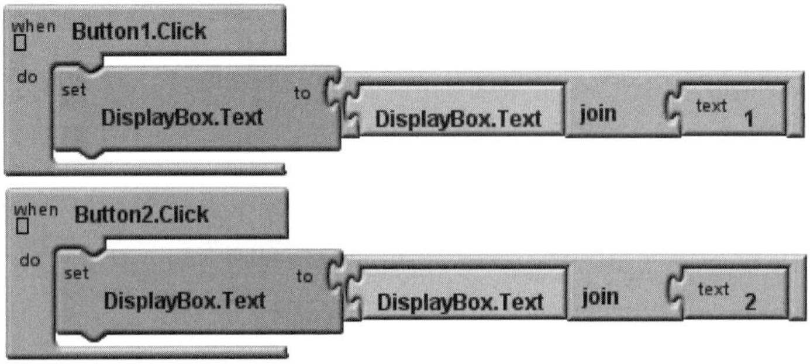

Figure 9.70 Event handlers for the number keys "1" and "2"

The next challenge is that we want to have only one display in our calculator, through which we join two operands with an operator key to form a mathematical expression and calculate its result with the equals key. For the two operands we need two auxiliary variables, where the variable `lastValue` is to receive the first Operand1 and the variable currentValue the second Operand2. Later, we can select the appropriate mathematical operation with the variable `calculationType`. Thus all variables are initialized with the numeric value `0` (see Figure 9.71).

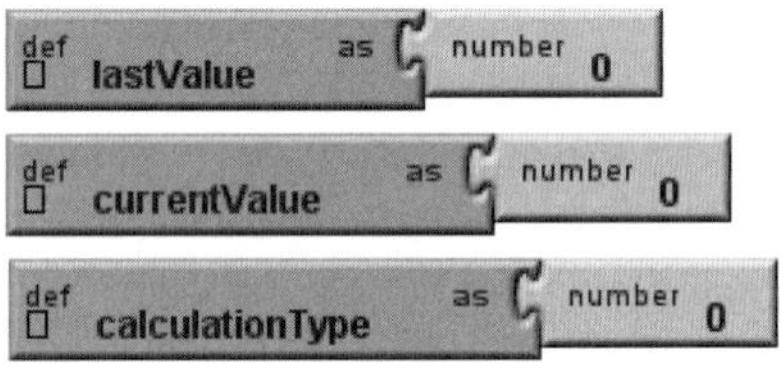

Figure 9.71 Two variables for the operands and one for the operator

Pressing an operator key should trigger various tasks in the relevant event handler—tasks that arise in all mathematical operations in the same way. It makes sense to create a central procedure to take care of these tasks. We can then invoke this procedure in the event handler for each operator key. In Figure 9.72, you can see how this procedure `buttonClicked` is called using the examples of the two operator keys "+" and "–". You can also see how an operator-specific index value is assigned to the variable `calculationType` in each case.

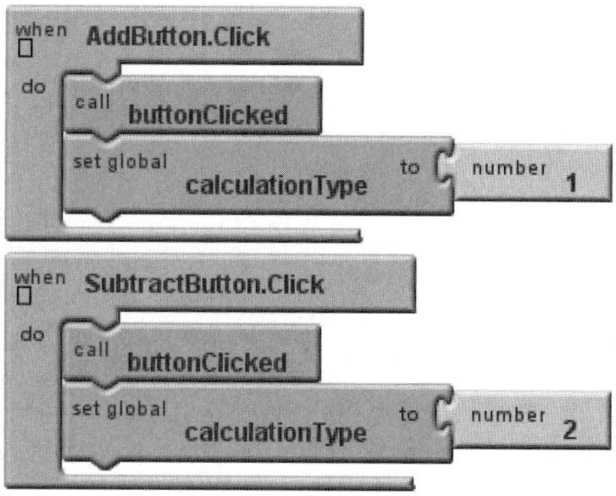

Figure 9.72 Calling the same auxiliary function for each operator key

Before you can use the method `call buttonClicked` shown in Figure 9.72, you must first create the corresponding procedure `buttonClicked` (see Figure 9.73). The main task of the procedure `buttonClicked` is to write the current number sequence in the calculator display as operand1 to the global variable `lastValue`. This temporarily saves this value and makes it available later for the mathematical operation. The display screen DisplayBox can then be deleted again with an empty text block `text`, so that the user can enter the operand2. It is important to recognize this generic task of the procedure `buttonClicked`: No matter which operator key the user presses, the current value shown at that time in the display will be temporarily saved as operand1 in `lastValue`.

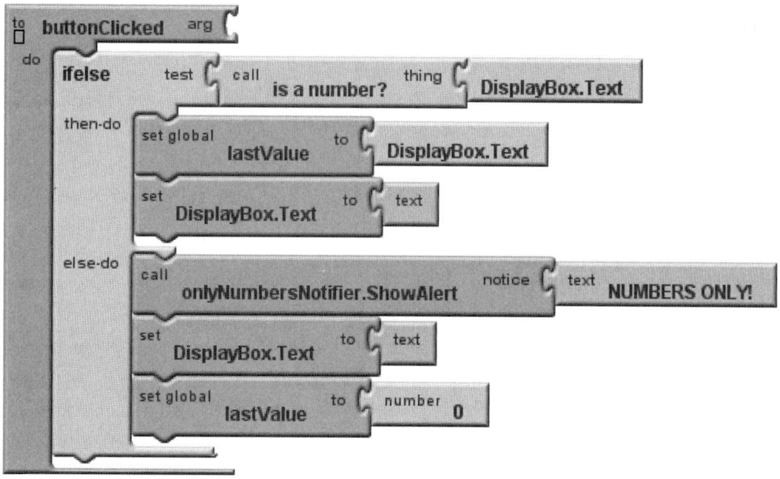

Figure 9.73 Procedure for checking operand1 and overwriting it with operand2

In addition to this main function, the procedure shown in Figure 9.73 takes on other functions. For example, the `ifelse` branch checks in its initial condition whether the current input in the display really is a number and not a letter. Here, we make use of the automatic conversion in AI, by simply applying the Math method `is a number?` to the alphanumeric string in the DisplayBox. This ensures that the mathematical operation later is carried out only with numeric values and not text strings; the latter input would cause a serious runtime error and program crash. If anything other than a number was entered, a corresponding notifier "NUMBERS ONLY!" is displayed via the `onlyNumbersNotifier`, the calculator display is deleted for new input, and the variable `lastValue` is set back to `0`.

The appropriate mathematical operation starts only when the user presses the equals button. The event handler `EqualButton.Click` (shown in Figure 9.74) encapsulates all of the mathematical operations and, therefore, appears rather cumbersome. In contrast, an individual calculation is rather simple. In the first statement in the event handler, the current input value from the DisplayBox is written to the variable `currentValue` and thereby saved as operand2. Now we have all data for carrying out the calculation, the two operands in the variables `lastValue` and `currentValue`, and the index value in the variable `calculationType` for selecting the specific mathematical operation. The index value of `calculationType` now determines which conditional statement is selected, and whose test value matches the index value, and the mathematical operation contained within it is applied to the two operands and displayed in the DisplayBox.

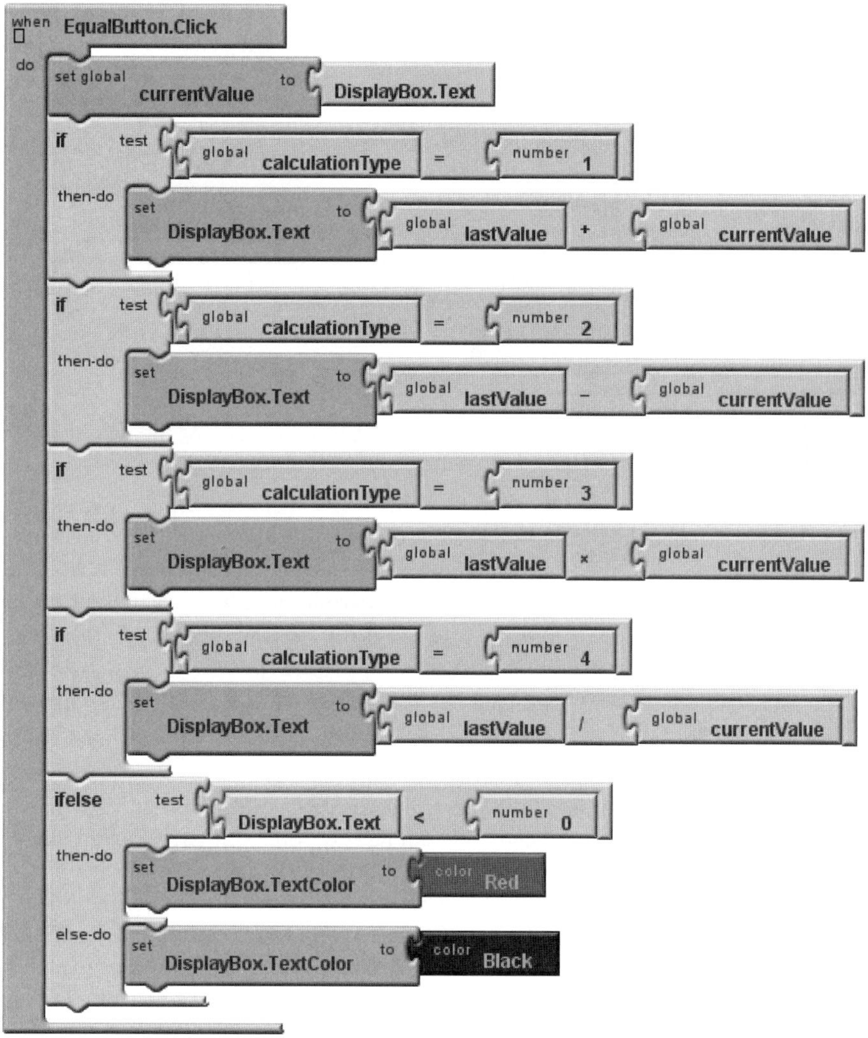

Figure 9.74 Executing a mathematical operation when the user presses the equals button

After one of the four mathematical operations in the event handler shown in Figure 9.74 is executed, a final `ifelse` branch is followed. It switches the font color in the DisplayBox to red if the result is a negative value (<0), and to black if it is a positive value (>0). As the result of the calculation also appears in the display, it can be used straight away for the next mathematical operation.

Now we must deal with the two remaining buttons on our calculator, or more specifically their event handlers. When the user presses the C (clear) button, the entire calculation is reset within the event handler `ClearButton.Click`, so both saved operands are set to the value `0` and the display in the DisplayBox is deleted (see Figure 9.75, left).

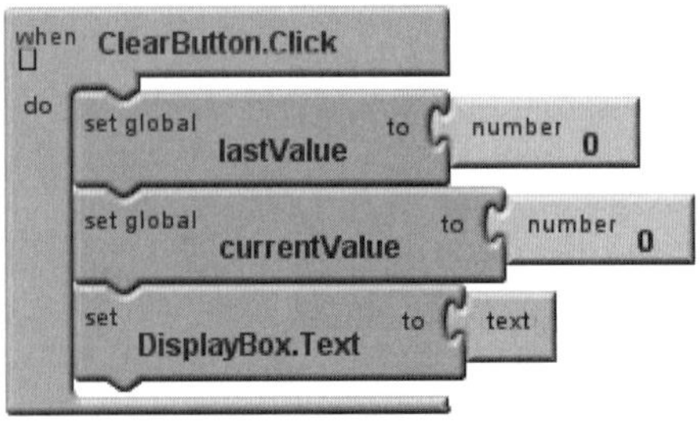

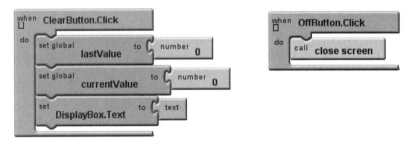

Figure 9.75 Event handlers for resetting input and closing the app

Pressing the Off key calls the Control method `close screen` within the event handler `OffButton.Click`. It switches off the calculator—or rather closes the calculator app.

Now you have fulfilled the program requirements and implemented the look and feel of a classic calculator as an Android app for your smartphone. Go ahead and put the app through its paces and see where you can improve it if necessary. Perhaps you want to expand the functions and add more mathematical functions to the four basic arithmetic operations of the calculator.

Quiz Game with Numbers

As the heading of this section indicates, we will again deal with numbers in our next example, but this time in a playful and entertaining way. After you have worked your way through the chapter on program development basics—which was probably not very easy and in part somewhat dry, especially for programming novices—it won't hurt to have some fun. You have now left the hard fundamentals of programming behind you and should have grasped them fully, and the next few chapters will introduce many more components with a certain "wow" factor. It's getting interesting, and this example project is just the start.

In our quiz game with numbers, we want to skip the elaborate design and concentrate mainly on the functionality. For you as developer, this project focuses mostly on efficiently determining the state of the app, which is influenced by several factors, and giving the user independent feedback interactively. To make games entertaining, it is important to react dynamically, quickly, and appropriately to as many different conditions as possible. The underlying decision structures and dependencies can become as complex as you want. Our version of the number guessing game will not become quite so elaborate, although it is intended to give you ideas for developing your own games. With games on the technologically less advanced smartphones, elaborate 3D graphics effects are not yet so important, as a good and simple game idea is still sufficient to fascinate the user, just as with card or board games. Let's have a closer look at the simple game shown in Figure 9.76.

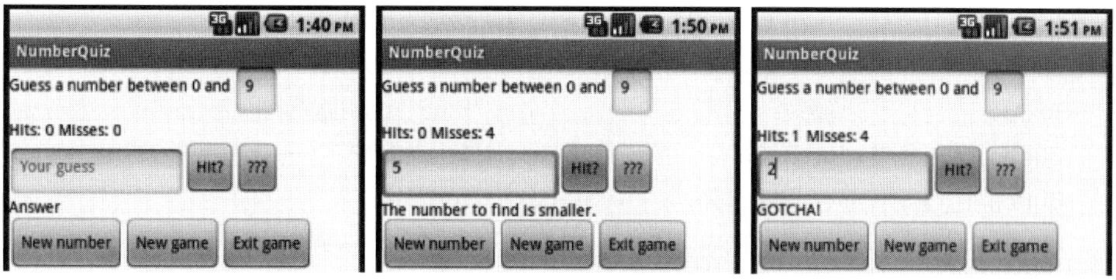

Figure 9.76 Interactive number guessing game

In our interactive number game, the user has to guess a number between 0 and 9 that is generated randomly by the program. The user enters the guess in the input field "Your guess" and presses the button labeled "Hit?" to check whether the answer is right. If the desired number is larger or smaller than the guess, an appropriate hint is displayed in the hint window and the wrong guess is counted as a miss. If the user manages to guess the right number after several program hints, it is also displayed and counted as a hit. The user can then generate a new random number by pressing the button labeled "New number" and keep on guessing. The hits and misses counter keeps track of the user's records, so the user can see and record his or her overall score over several games. If, for example, a user manages to get five hits and wants to know if he or she managed to beat the hits and misses ratio of the previous player, the counters can be reset by pressing the button labeled "New game." If the number range from 0 to 9 is getting too boring as the player's experience increases, the range can be increased as desired via the input field with the preset number 9. If the user then finds the game too difficult and cannot manage to find the desired number, he or she can press the button labeled "???" to display the correct number. To close the app, the user presses the button labeled "Exit game."

Project Files on the Companion Website

You can find all of the files for the NumberQuiz project on the companion website (see the link in the Introduction).

Regardless of whether you personally would find the idea of a number guessing game fascinating for long, if at all, let's consider how the interactive, dynamic, and expandable behavior of the app presents itself from the developer's point of view. The app interface is easy to design, with the components and settings shown in Table 9.2.

Table 9.2 **Components and Initial Properties for the NumberQuiz**

Component	Object Name	Edited Properties
Label	IntroLabel	"Text": Guess a number between 0 and
TextBox	MaxTextBox	"Text":
Label (2x)	Label3, Label4	"Text": Hits: , Misses:
Label (2x)	HitsLabel, MissesLabel	"Text": 0, 0
TextBox	Guess	"Hint": Your guess
Button	HitsButton	"Text": Hit?
Button	ToFindButton	"Text": ???
Label	AnswerLabel	"Text": Answer
Button	NewNumberButton	"Text": New number
Button	NewGameButton	"Text": New game
Button	ExitButton	"Text": Exit game

The components shown in Table 9.2 are arranged within four HorizontalArrangement components, as shown in Figure 9.77. This determines the appearance of the number quiz app, and we can now turn to developing the program logic.

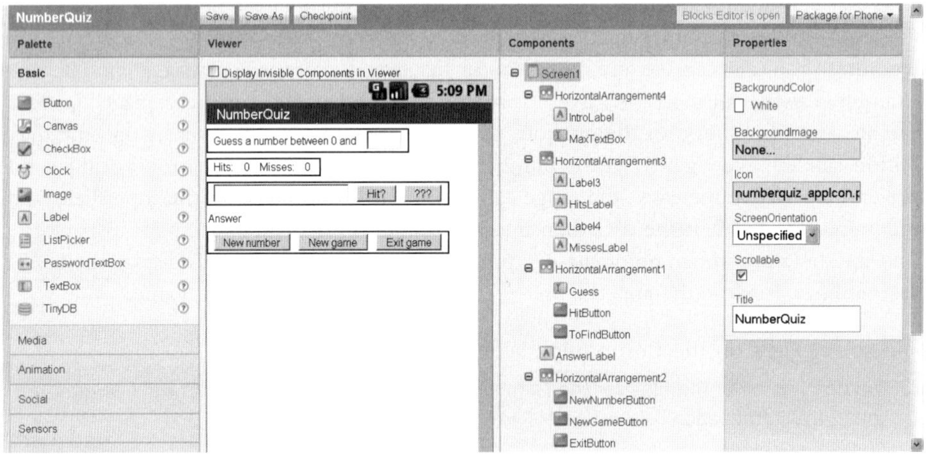

Figure 9.77 Components in the NumberQuiz project

In the AI Editor, we first create the three variables shown in Figure 9.78. In the variable `number`, we will later record the current random number. By initializing the two variables `min` and `max`, we determine the number range from which the random number is chosen.

Figure 9.78 Variables for recording the current random number and the number range

As we want to generate a new random number when different events occur, we combine the required block structures in a procedure with the name new. For creating a random integer in the number range determined by the two variables min and max (initially 0–9), we call the Math method random integer and assign the random number to the global variable number. Creating a new random number in the app is also meant to reset the Guess input box and the AnswerLabel, so we also include these instructions in the procedure shown in Figure 9.79.

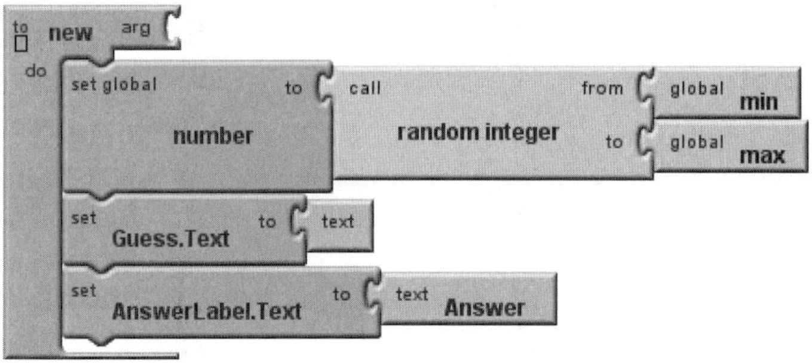

Figure 9.79 Procedure "new" for creating a new random number

Now the event handlers in Figure 9.80 can be used to generate a new random number and the display can be reset by calling the procedure new again. Whereas calling the app in the event handler Screen1.Initialize also reads out the value of the variable max for displaying the editable maximum number range, pressing the "New game" button calls the event handler NewGameButton.Click and causes the hits and misses counters to be reset to 0.

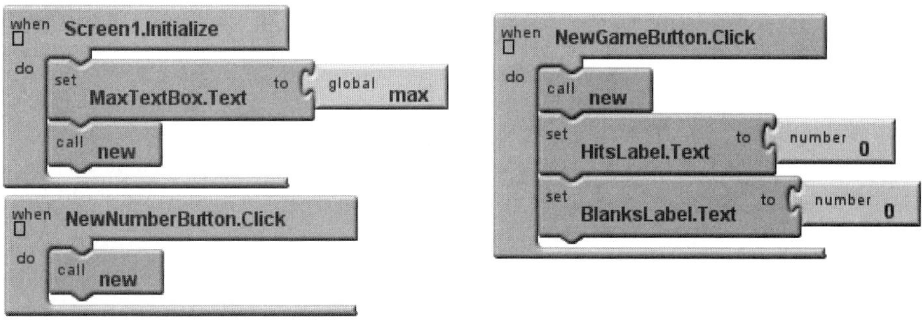

Figure 9.80 Generate a new random number for different events

The actual analysis of user input and the appropriate response occurs when the "Hit?" button is pressed, which calls the event handler `HitButton.Click`. Even at first glance you can see the multitude of dependencies in the factors to be checked within the rather complex construct of three *nested* `ifelse` branches, as shown in Figure 9.81.

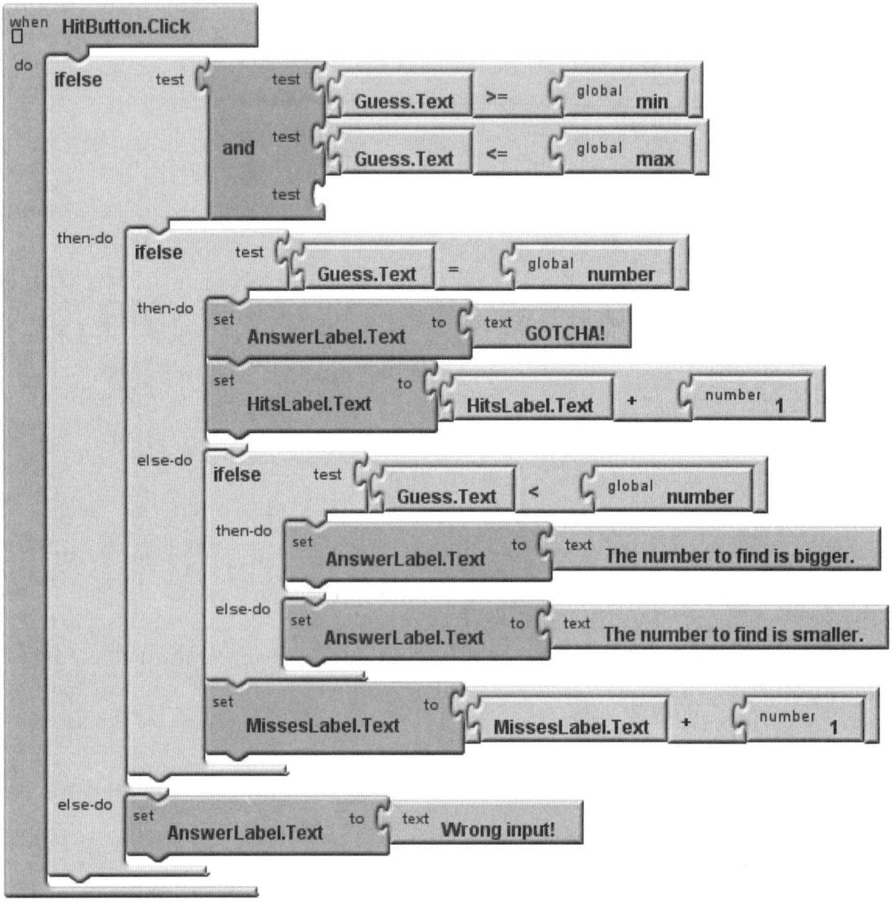

Figure 9.81 Evaluating user input and responding appropriately

By nesting the condition checks, multiple dependencies can be represented more efficiently than if they had to be retrieved and executed in full for each individual program action. For example, a hit can be achieved only if the entered guess was within the specified number range. If the guess is outside the range, the program does not even need to check whether the guess matches the target number, as such an outcome is not possible. Similarly, you need to check only whether the guess is larger or smaller than the target number if the guess is within the specified range and is not a hit. These logical dependencies are used in the nested `ifelse` branches shown in Figure 9.81 to keep the laborious checks for each new guess to a minimum. Although the advantage of this efficient approach with this straightforward task has hardly any measurable effect on the app performance, it can make a big difference when there are thousands of inputs or conditions to check.

Checking a guess entered by the user takes place within the event handler `HitsButton.Clicks` as follows. The first `ifelse` branch checks whether the guessed number is within the number range—that is, whether the guess is larger than or equal to the value in the variable `min` *and* smaller than or equal to the variable `max`. If this is not the case, the entered guess is outside of the number range or possibly not even a number. Thus the notifier "Wrong input!" can be displayed in the `else-do` area. If the guessed number is within the number range, the second `ifelse` branch is triggered; it checks whether the guess is identical to the random number in the variable `number`. If it is, it is a hit, which is displayed and counted in the hit counter. If not, it is a miss, which is also counted in the misses counter. Now the third `ifelse` branch checks whether the guessed number is smaller or larger than the random number, and the appropriate hint is displayed. This sufficiently describes the algorithm for evaluating user guesses.

Now only three functions are left within the number quiz app, or more precisely the three event handlers shown in Figure 9.82. As the user should have the option of making the number range larger or smaller as desired, he or she can change the default value `9` in the corresponding text box to another numeric value. We are using the event block `MaxTextBox.LostFocus` for this purpose, so the change will take effect only with the next guess entered in the Guess text box, because the event `LostFocus` for the MaxTextBox is triggered only then and the new number range is set at that point.

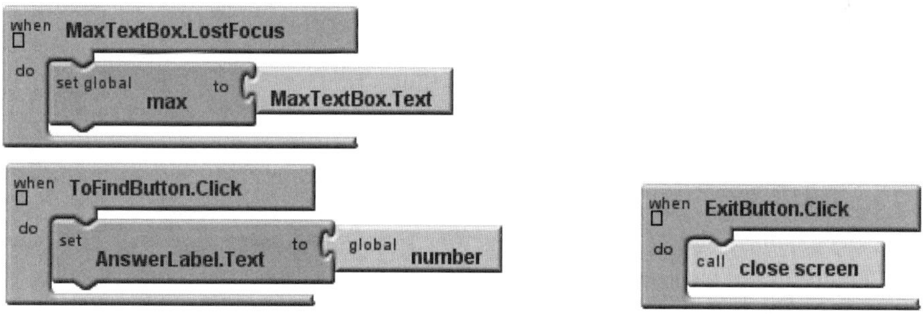

Figure 9.82 Remaining event handlers in the NumberQuiz app

The other two remaining event handlers shown in Figure 9.82 are pretty much self-explanatory. Pressing the "???" button causes the event handler `ToFindButton.Click` to display the random number. Pressing the "Exit" button in the event handler `ExitButton.Click` closes the app. This little quiz game may well be fun and entertainment for a user who is a numbers fan.

Vocabulary Trainer: English–German

In our last example project in this chapter, we will once more deal with processing lists. Our intensive examination of lists here will emphasize the enormous potential of this data structure. We frequently used databases and lists in the demo project `demo_Data`, as a way of saving, editing, and retrieving many data elements in a structured manner. As one of countless other potential uses, we will now use some of the many list components of AI within a fully equipped vocabulary trainer and combine them to create a really useful app. The app we will develop, which we will call "Vocab," will not just allow linear checking of words in one language, but also provide many other sensible features that can really help the user learn words in a foreign language. This *vocabulary trainer* hides a whole range of functions under its user interface (as shown in Figure 9.83), which are necessary for learning new words in a foreign language.

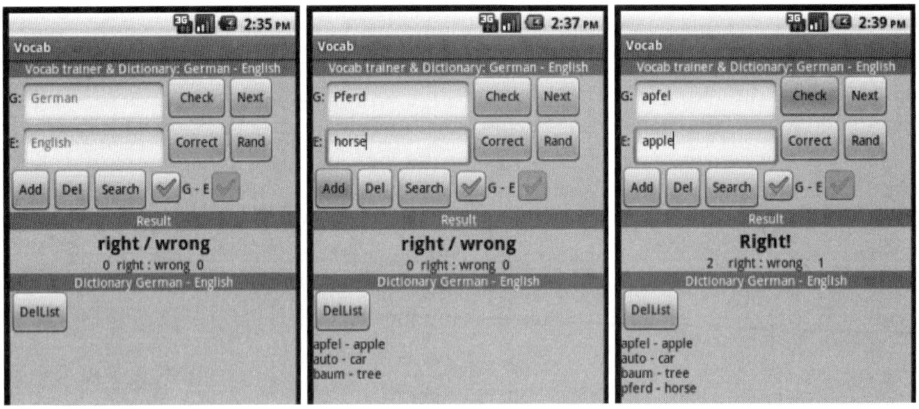

Figure 9.83 Vocabulary trainer app for learning and checking new foreign words

When the user starts the vocabulary trainer shown in Figure 9.83 (left), the database is still empty, so there are no foreign words displayed yet. The user generally starts by entering words via the two input fields "G" and "E" and then adds them to the dictionary via the Add button or deletes them individually via the Del button. Once the dictionary has words in it (center), the user can start checking the vocabulary he or she wants to learn (right). For checking the words, several methods are available. With the Next button, the user can go through the words from the dictionary one by one; with use the Rand (Random) button, he or she can go through the words in random order. The language used can also be switched via the check boxes—for example, training with the German words or the English translations. The entered answer is checked by pressing the Check button, and the result is displayed in the appropriate section as "Right!" or "Wrong!" and counted in the score of "right : wrong". If the user simply cannot remember what the translation of a word is, he or she can use the Correct button to show the solution. To look up a word in the dictionary, the user can press the Search button to find the translation for a word entered in German or English, and if it is in the dictionary it will be displayed. The last button, DelList, can be used to delete the entire entered dictionary all at once, after confirming that you really want to delete it.

Project Files on the Companion Website

You can find all files for the Vocab project on the companion website (see the Introduction for the link).

Before implementing these functions, you first need to design the user interface as shown in Figure 9.83. Open a new project in AI Designer with the name "Vocab" and place the components shown in Table 9.3 with the edited initial properties in the order listed. You can add the DivisionLabels, BufferLabels, and Arrangements yourself.

Table 9.3 **Components and Initial Properties in the Vocab Project**

Component	Object Name	Edited Properties
Screen	Screen1	"BackgroundColor": Light gray "Icon": vocab_appIcon.png (see the companion website, `/MEDIA`)
Label (2x)	Label1-2	"Text": G:, E:
TextBox (2x)	GerTextBox, EngTextBox	"Hint": German, English
Button (4x)	CheckButton, CorrectButton, NextButton, RandButton	"Text": Check, Correct, Next, Rand
Button (3x)	AddButton, DelButton, SearchButton	"Text": Add, Del, Search
CheckBox	GerEngCheckBox	"Text": G - E "Checked" enable
CheckBox	EngGerCheckBox	"Text": "Enabled" disable
Label	ResultLabel	"Text": right/wrong
Label (2x)	HitsLabel, MissesLabel	"Text": 0, 0
Label	Label9	"Text": right : wrong
Button	DelListButton	"Text": DelList
Label	DictLabel	"Text":
Notifier	Notifier	

Together with the DivisionLabels, BufferLabels, and Arrangements, the user interface should appear in AI Designer as shown in Figure 9.84.

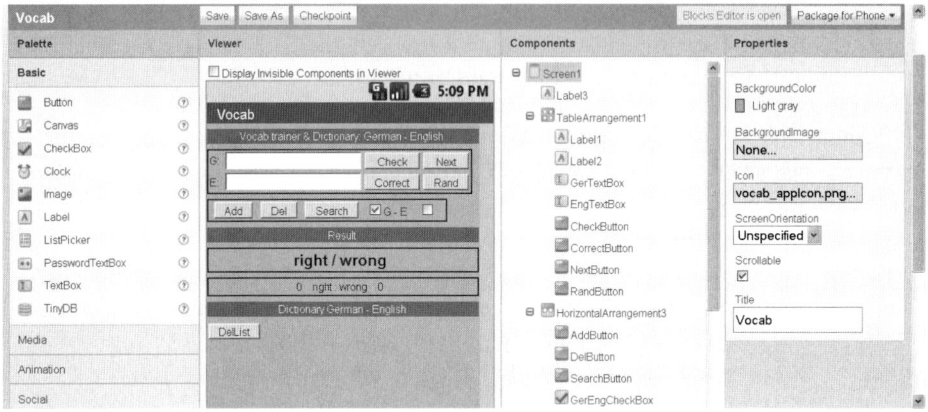

Figure 9.84 Vocab Project in AI Designer

The design preparations are now complete, so we can start implementing the functions in AI Editor. We begin by creating and initializing the universally required variables shown in Figure 9.85. The two empty lists `gerList` and `engList` will receive the words later, separated into German and English, but matched together within the same index. Accessing the current pair of words is done via the global index value of the variable `listIndex`, which is required in several event handlers. Meanwhile, the auxiliary variable `i` helps with counting and controlling the local loop runs in various handlers.

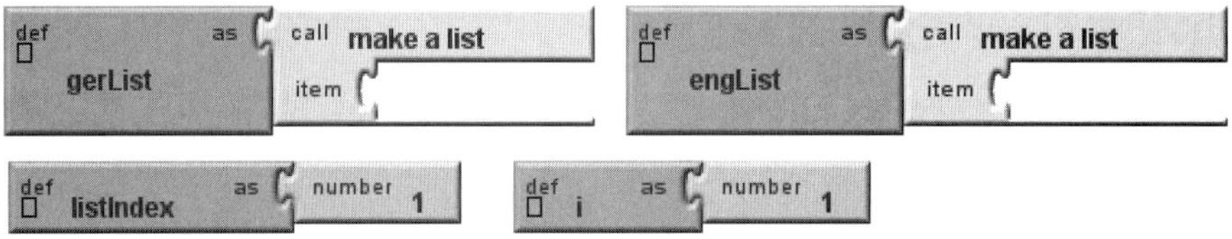

Figure 9.85 List variables for vocabulary and index variables for access

We will introduce the event handlers based on the use of the function keys when starting or operating the vocabulary trainer. Let's start with the event handler `AddButton.Click` (shown in Figure 9.86), which is called by pressing the Add button to insert a new word pair in the lists. Through the two list methods `add items to list`, the two words entered in the text boxes GerTextBox and EngTextBox are received and appended to the end of the lists `gerList` and `engList`. To make matters easier later and to enable us to check the vocabulary words no matter they are entered as uppercase or lowercase (*not* case sensitive), the entered words are immediately converted to the more neutral format lowercase with the method `downcase`.

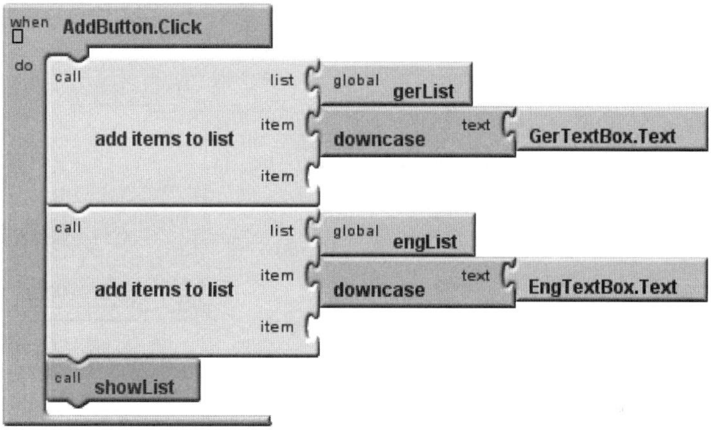

Figure 9.86 Adding a new word pair to the lists with the Add button

Every time the user adds a new word pair, the expanded vocabulary lists are displayed fully in the dictionary area. The formatted display of the two lists is handled by the procedure `showList`. Similar to the technique used in `demo_Data` in Figure 9.54, `showList` (Figure 9.87) a `while` loop in which all elements are read out of the two lists `gerList` and `engList` one by one via the auxiliary counter `i`, appended as separate text lines to the continuously expanded text of DictLabel, and finally output as a whole in DictLabel. To allow the next word pair to be entered as soon as one pair has been saved, the first word pair is deleted from the two input fields GerTextBox and EngTextBox via another auxiliary procedure, `emptyBoxes`.

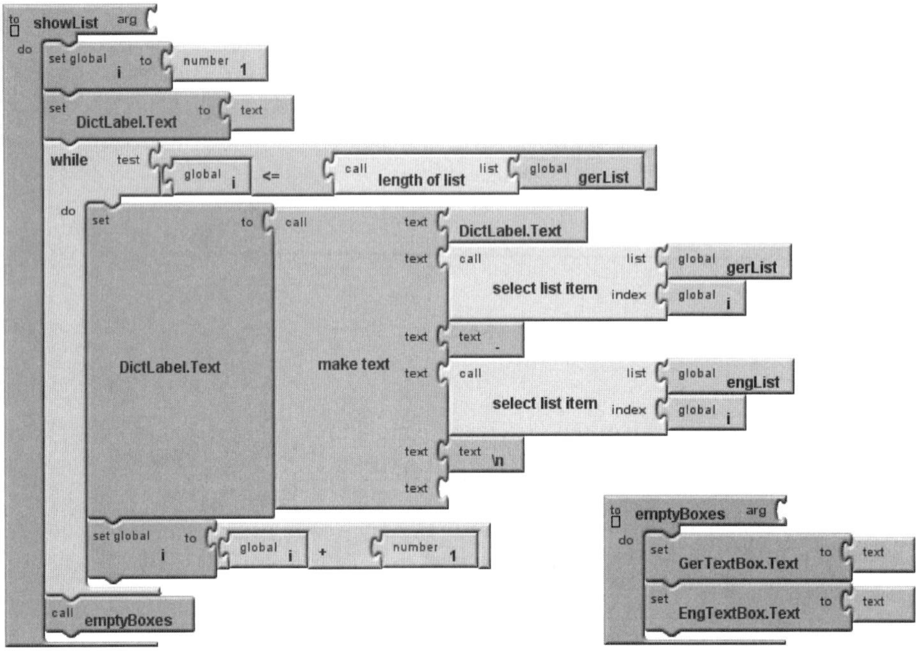

Figure 9.87 Formatted display of the word lists and clear input fields

If you want to delete a word pair from the lists that were just displayed previously, you can do so with the event handler `DelButton.Click` shown in Figure 9.88. Based on the current index position `listIndex`, the corresponding element is simply removed from both lists with the method `remove list item`. Calling the procedure `showList` then updates the formatted view of the dictionary.

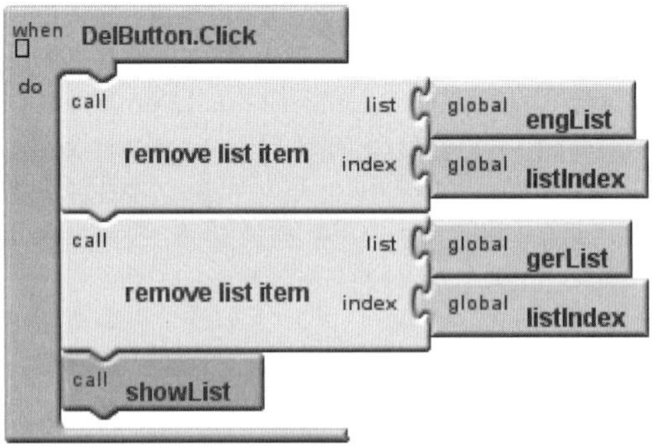

Figure 9.88 Deleting a word pair from the dictionary with the Del button

Once the dictionary has been filled with several word pairs, the vocabulary training can begin. You can set which direction you want to check in, either German–English or English–German, with the checkboxes GerEngCheckBox and EngGerCheckBox, using the rather efficient algorithm shown in Figure 9.89 for switching from one to the other. To implement it, we need the event handler `GerEngCheckBox.Changed` and a Boolean variable `gerEng` set to the initial value `true`, corresponding to the initial property `Checked=true` of Table 9.3. If the user now clicks on the checkbox GerEngCheckBox for the first time, its new value `false` is recorded in the variable `gerEng` and the other checkbox EngGerCheckBox is set to the opposite value (`not false = true`). The next time the GerEngCheckBox is pressed, the values of the two check boxes are switched again. In this way, both check boxes can be set to oppose each other via the GerEngCheckBox alone, which is why the manual operation of the EngGerCheckBox was disabled in the initial properties (`Enabled=false`). The current value of the variable `gerEng` later determines the direction of word checking.

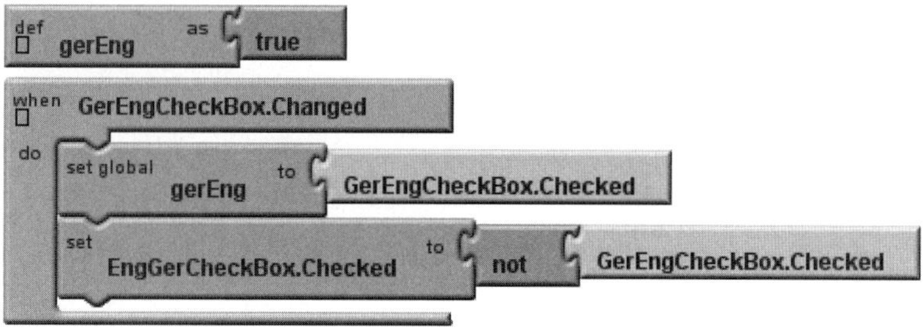

Figure 9.89 Setting the direction of word checking with just one check box "G–E"

As described earlier, the user can choose between two ways of checking. When the user presses the Next button and the event handler `NextButton.Click` (Figure 9.90) is called, the words are checked *serially*, in the order they were entered into the dictionary. After both text boxes GerTextBox and EngTextBox are deleted with the procedure `emptyBoxes`, the first `ifelse` branch uses the list `gerList` to check whether the last list item or dictionary entry has been reached. If this is not the case, the `then-do` section of the branch increments the global index counter `listIndex` by 1. But if the last item has been reached, the `listIndex` is reset to `1`, so that the serial word check can start over in an endless repetition. Based on the now reset global index counter `listIndex`, the procedure `showVocab` is then called. In another `ifelse` branch, it selects the next word by applying the method `select list item` to one of the two lists and displays the word. The selection of the list and the appropriate text box depends on the direction of the word check, which was set previously in the variable `gerEng` (see Figure 9.89) with `true` (G–E) or `false` (E–G).

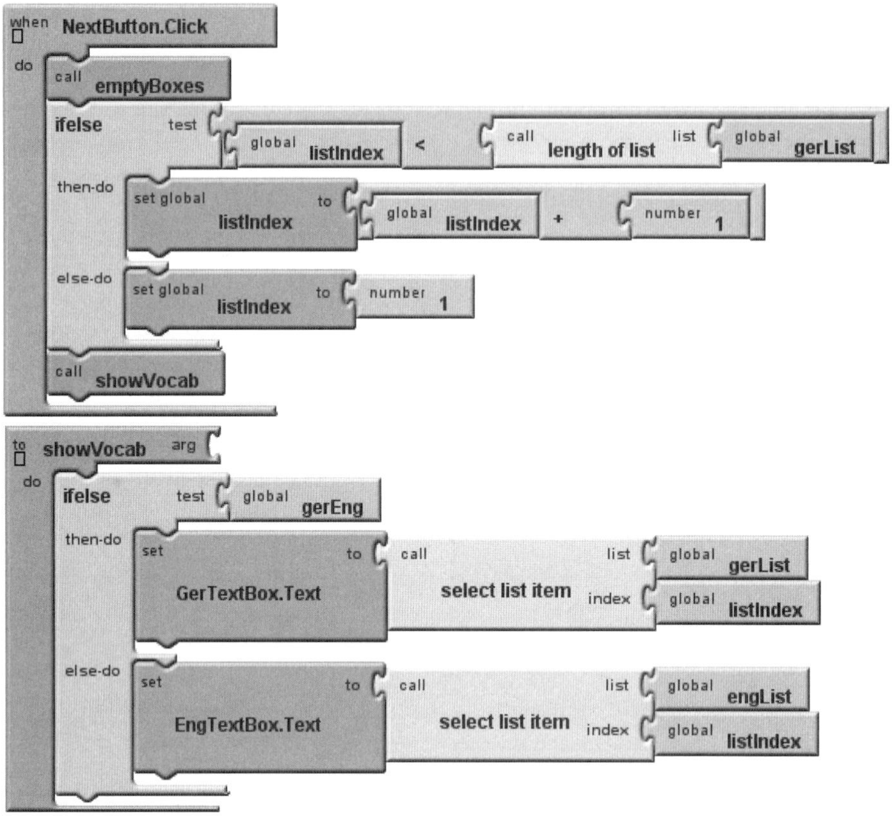

Figure 9.90 Serial word training with the Next button

The alternative approach of checking the user's knowledge of words in *random* order via the Rand button works in a similar way. With each press of the button, the event handler `RandButton.Click` (Figure 9.91) is called, and the method `random integer` generates a random number between `1` and the current list item number (`length of list gerList`) and assigns it to the global index counter `listIndex`. Based on the now reset index counter, the suitable word is selected via the procedure `showVocab` and displayed in the appropriate text box.

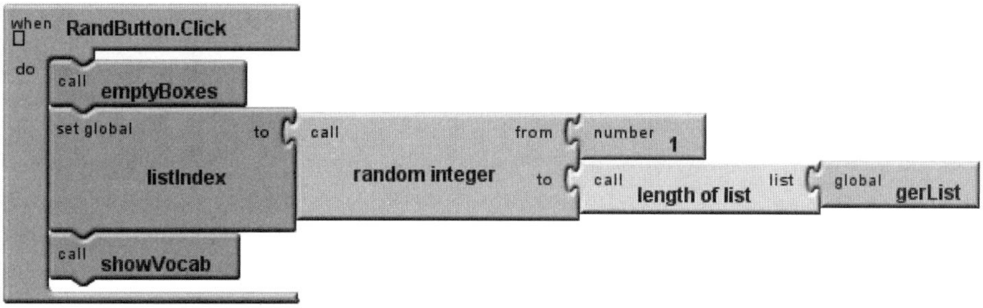

Figure 9.91 Word training in random order with the Rand button

Using the "Check" button, the user can get the vocabulary trainer to check the translation he or she entered to see if the word was right—that is, if the input word matches its saved counterpart. The corresponding event handler `CheckButton.Click` (Figure 9.92) takes care of this check in the initial condition of an `ifelse` branch. Ignoring the direction of the word check, it determines whether the two current inputs in the GerTextBox and EngTextBox match the word pair in the current index position of the global counter `listIndex` in the lists `gerList` and `engList`. To ensure the check accounts for words that are entered in either uppercase or lowercase (*not* case sensitive), the words to be checked are converted to lowercase via the method `downcase` and only then compared to the word pair (which was also saved in lowercase). If both (`and`) words match, the user input was correct, and the `then-do` section of the branch displays "Right!" in the ResultLabel and increments the number of correctly translated words in the `HitsLabel` by 1. If the translation is wrong, the `else-do` area displays the text "Wrong!" and increments the number of misses.

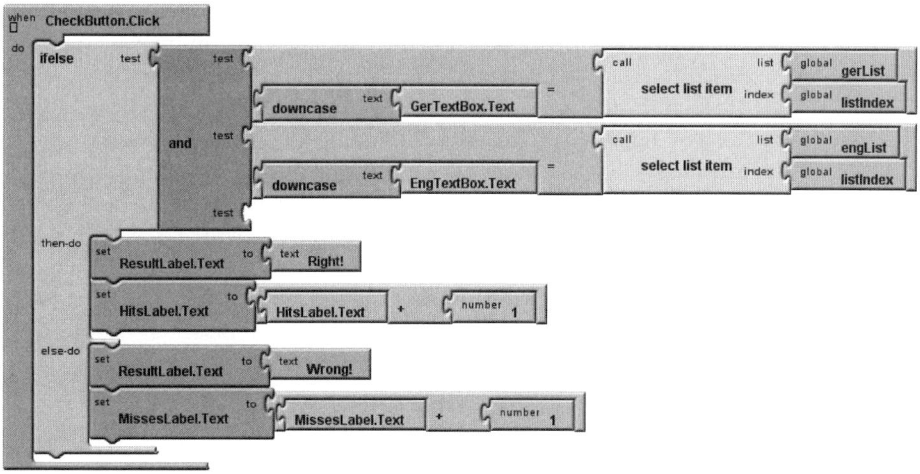

Figure 9.92 Checking whether the entered translation is correct with the Check button

If the user simply cannot remember the translation of a word or is reading the word for the first time while learning vocabulary, he or she can press the Correct button to display the appropriate translation. The corresponding event handler `CorrectButton.Click` (Figure 9.93) then retrieves the word pair from the current index position `listIndex` regardless of the word check direction and displays it in the two text boxes.

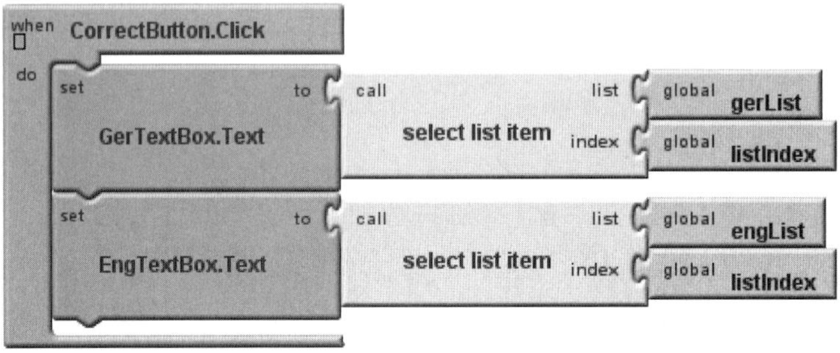

Figure 9.93 Displaying the correct translation with the Correct button

Matters become more complex with the translation of a particular word that the user enters in the appropriate text box depending on the translation direction. This operation is triggered by pressing the Search button. Such a query is comparable to a typical *database query* in which a database is searched for the occurrence of a particular entry, the content of which is displayed as a result if it is found. In our vocabulary trainer, the dictionary represents the database and the entered word represents the search term. In the corresponding event handler `SearchButton.Click` (Figure 9.94), the auxiliary variable `i` plays an important role. In the first `if-else` branch, the entered search term is searched in the appropriate list (`gerList` or `engList`) depending on the language direction set previously (`gerEng` = `true` or `false`). The list method used in this case, `position in list`, returns the appropriate index value if the item is found and assigns the value to the auxiliary function `i`. If the word is not present in the dictionary, the variable `i` is assigned the value `0`. The new value of `i` is then used for the initial check of the second `ifelse` branch. If it is larger than `0` (i.e., if a suitable word was found in the dictionary), the statements in the `then-do` area are executed and the word pair is retrieved at the index position `i` and displayed in the text boxes. If no translation was found, the `then-do` area deletes the two text boxes and the text "Search term unknown!" is displayed.

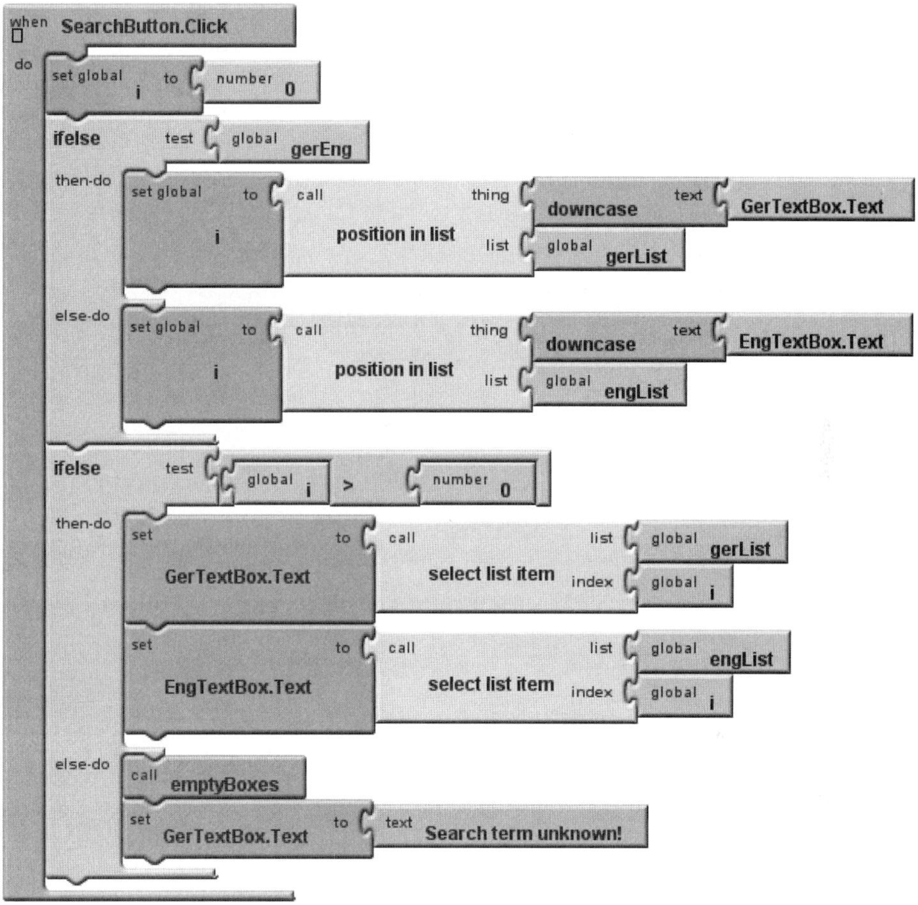

Figure 9.94 Retrieving the translation of any word with the Search button

Now all the core functions of the vocabulary trainer are implemented. We still need to implement the feature in which we delete the entire dictionary at once after the user responds to a corresponding confirmation prompt, however. To combine the deletion operation with a confirmation prompt, we need the two short event handlers shown in Figure 9.95. Pressing the DelList button and activating its event handler `DelListButton.Click` displays a notifier via the method `Notifier.ShowChooseDialog` with the corresponding prompt text and the two alternative buttons for confirming ("Yes") or canceling ("No") the deletion. Once the user has made a choice by pressing one of the two buttons, the event handler `Notifier.AfterChoosing` is called automatically and is passed the chosen answer in the local variable `choice` as the text `Yes` or `No` (this text appears on the two buttons the user can choose). To ensure that the dictionary is deleted only if the user explicitly confirms this choice with "Yes," the statements for deleting it are embedded in a conditional `if` statement, whose `then-do` area is executed only if the value of `choice` corresponds to the text `Yes`. If this is the case, the two lists `gerList` and `engList` are deleted by simply overwriting them with an empty text. In addition, the cleared dictionary is displayed as empty in the DictLabel.

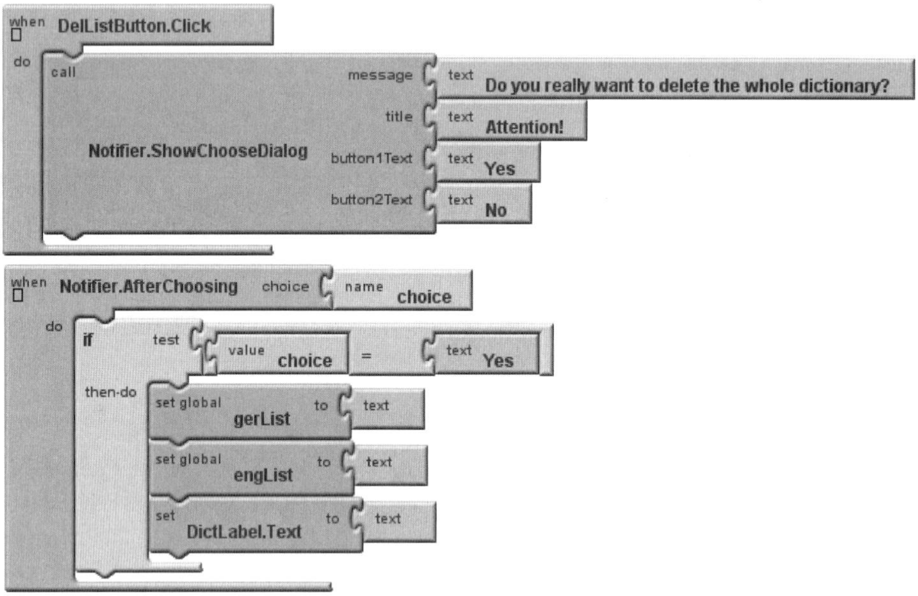

Figure 9.95 Deleting the entire dictionary with the DelList button

Now that all functions of the vocabulary trainer are implemented, you can see that they go far beyond merely checking words in a foreign language. Perhaps you might even want to use the vocabulary trainer for yourself, or expand it further and make it available to third parties. In any case, our development of this rather large app should have given you an impression of how more complex tasks can be divided among several event handlers that utilize the same data pool and interact indirectly via global variables. Given the greater function range of this project, the amount of space it requires in AI Editor is likewise increased. As you can see in Figure 9.96, we had to resort to "block collapsing" to fit all of the block structures onto the workspace. If you have been developing this project along with the book and tried out individual functions in advance, you may well have been making use of the debugging methods—for example, the helpful "Watch" function in AI Editor—to track down undesirable results in the program logic and understand the complex interaction of the individual event handlers based on the common data.

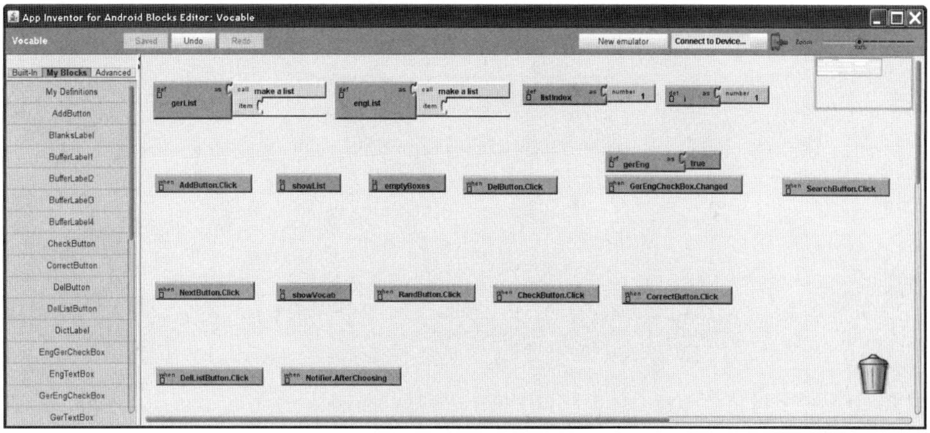

Figure 9.96 Overview of the Vocab project

Congratulations: You are now right in the middle of developing Android apps that are becoming increasingly elaborate and can be of proper use to their users. In particular, the generic blocks described in this chapter on program development basics hold an enormous potential and are part of the basic tools of every programmer and app developer. Both in the remaining chapters of this book and in your own future projects, you will hardly manage to do without them, because only with these generic blocks can you fully exploit the potential of the many other functions and components of AI and develop really impressive Android apps.

Chapter 10

Storage and Databases

Storing data is one of the most elementary tasks performed by a computer—and today, by a smartphone as well. You take it for granted that your smartphone still has all of your apps, icons, and phone book entries after you restart it from standby mode or after it was switched off. But if you have been trying the previous demo and sample apps in this book, you will have noticed that the data entered by the user disappeared after you stopped and restarted the example apps. This is particularly annoying if the user has entered data that he or she would like to reuse, expand, or change when next using the app, without having to enter all the data again—be it names, addresses, phone numbers, or words in a vocabulary list. Perhaps you felt during the Vocab example project that this app was potentially useful but almost pointless without the option of saving the entered vocabulary permanently. The same concept applies to almost any app in which the user gathers data—that is, the majority of apps. Thus data storage is an indispensable and essential feature with which you as developer can and generally probably need to equip your apps.

AI offers three variations of data storage. During the app's runtime (i.e., while it is being used in the foreground, but also in the background for a period of time dependent on the operating system), all data required by the app and entered by the user is saved in the smartphone's *working memory*. The working memory is a *volatile* memory that is reserved for the app only during runtime but not afterward. The long-term storage of data beyond the app's runtime requires *nonvolatile* storage methods. This includes saving the data *locally* on the internal memory or SD card of the smartphone. Alternatively, the data can be saved in the *cloud*—that is, on a server on the Internet that can be accessed worldwide not only by your own smartphone, but also by other authorized smartphones and computers as if from a database. This kind of permanently saved data is referred to as *persistent* data. The web-based storage method in particular offers incredible and countless options for globally distributed applications based on common data, such as traditional groupware, collaborative and shared applications, and social networks, mobile communities, multiuser games, and geotracking or life logging.

In this chapter, we will deal with the two nonvolatile storage methods. You will be surprised at how simply local and even web-based storage in the cloud can be achieved with AI. We will use the vocabulary trainer from Chapter 9 as our example app, but expand it to become a really useful app with a persistent dictionary as its database. After we make the dictionary available in the cloud, other users can use a corresponding client app to learn vocabulary based on the common data of your dictionary, translate words, or look them up. This modest example merely hints at the incredible potential for apps that use this concept and should inspire you when you are developing your own mobile and distributed applications.

Saving Data Locally with the TinyDB Component

Persistent data is data that is created or changed during the runtime of an app by the app and/or the user, and that is available after closing and restarting an app without having to recreate or reenter the data. Generally, this process is referred to simply as saving data, and it corresponds to what you do with the text processing or spreadsheet programs on your PC on a daily basis. Exactly this process takes place just as naturally on your smartphone when, for example, you enter a new contact address, phone number, or appointment in the corresponding apps. The apps then usually ensure automatically that the new data is saved in the local memory of the smartphone or on the SD card and is made available persistently.

To enable you to store data persistently with the same ease in your apps, AI offers the non-visible component known as TinyDB in the Basic group. Although the abbreviation "DB" (database) suggests something big, the prefix "Tiny" reduces your expectations to a sensible degree. The TinyDB is a storage area that the operating system Android makes available to each app created with AI permanently in the smartphone's internal memory, but in dynamic relation to the actually required amount of space. The dynamic reservation of memory space ensures that data-intensive apps can have more memory space than other apps, so that the system resources are always used optimally by the operating system. Despite (or perhaps because of) its essentially important function for most apps, the TinyDB component has a very simple range of functions. It is also simple to use in developing applications, as you can see from the specification in Figure 10.1.

TinyDB

Use a TinyDB component to store data that will be available each time the app runs.

TinyDB is a non-visible component.

Apps created with App Inventor are initialized each time they run. If an app sets the value of a variable and the user then quits the app, the value of that variable will not be remembered the next time the app is run. TinyDB is a *persistent* data store for the app, that is, the data stored there will be available each time the app is run. An example might be a game that saved the high score, and retrieved it each time the game is played.

Data items are stored under *tags*. To store a data item, you specify the tag it should be stored under. Subsequently, you can retrieve the data item that was stored under a given tag. If there is no value stored under a tag, then the value returned is the empty text. Consequently, to see if a tag has a value stored under it, test whether the return value is equal to the empty text (i.e., a text box with no text filled in).

There is only one data store per app. If you have multiple TinyDB components, they will use the same data store. To get the effect of separate stores, use different keys. Also each app has its own data store. You cannot use TinyDB to pass data between two different apps on the phone.

Properties

none

Events

none

Methods

`StoreValue(text tag, valueToStore)`
Store the value under the given tag. The `tag` must be a text string; the value can be a string or a list.

`GetValue(text tag)`
Gets the value that was stored under the given tag. If no value was stored, returns the empty text.

Figure 10.1 Specification of the TinyDB component

Without any property or event components, the component TinyDB offers just two methods with which saving and loading data can be achieved with the highest possible efficiency. Each has a single *data store* available, in which any amount of data can be stored and retrieved, identified by a unique identifier (*tag*). The data to be stored corresponds to the values present in the corresponding variables during the program runtime.

Storing and Loading Values of Variables as Data

To store data from an app, the data must be present as values within a variable and be passed to the method `StoreValue`. During loading, a variable of the same or compatible data type is also required into which the value from the memory can be written by the method `GetValue`.

Just as the global variables in AI can contain values of different data types, so the TinyDB component can be used to save text, numbers, or even whole lists and later load them back into the variables. In our vocabulary trainer, for example, the entire dictionary, the hits and misses counter, and the last direction of the word check could be stored and reloaded. Saving takes place via the TinyDB method `StoreValue`, to which a unique `text tag` and the variable with the data to be stored (`valueToStore`) are passed. For loading the data, the method `GetValue` requires the `text tag`, so that it can read the value from the memory and assign it to a variable at runtime.

Saving Values of Variables as Persistent Data

To make the explanations of saving and loading data easier to understand, we will implement them in practice by expanding the vocabulary trainer (`Vocab.apk`) created in Chapter 9. Right now, the user has to first laboriously fill the dictionary by entering new word pairs manually in the text boxes GerTextBox and EngTextBox and pressing the Add button; these words then become available for vocabulary training in the two lists `gerList` and `engList` while the app is active. Each time the app is restarted, the lists and the dictionary are empty—the values from the previous session(s) are not saved. We will now change this unsatisfactory behavior by locally storing the two lists with each new entry. If the user or another app (for example, if a phone call is received) then quits the vocabulary trainer app, we can ensure that the latest dictionary content is permanently saved. The next time the app is launched, the dictionary will be automatically loaded from memory at the program start and be available for checking words within the app. This new example will also demonstrate how to deal with more complex list structures as saved values of variables—a concept on which most database-oriented applications are based, but is not really any different from dealing with variables having just a single value in terms of saving and loading data.

> **Persistent Data Only for Apps, Not Within the Development Environment!**
>
> Permanent storage is possible only from within an independent app that has been installed as an APK file on your smartphone. Only then will the operating system reserve a data store for the app, which can then be used for saving and loading. If the app is running within the AI development environment on an integrated smartphone, however, every restart of the application is equivalent to reinstalling the app, so the reserved data store is deleted and recreated from scratch (see also the AI "Component Reference" under the entry "TinyDB"). Thus you need to download the expanded vocabulary trainer as an independent app to your smartphone to try out its storage function.

As the expansion of the vocabulary trainer takes place almost exclusively in the non-visible area, we need the AI Designer to add and adapt a few things. To get start with the revision of this app, load the previous example project Vocab into the AI Designer via My Projects > Vocab, and then save a copy with the Save As option under the new name "Vocab1." In the new project, change the title from "Screen1" to "Vocab1 (auto save)," to visually distinguish the new version *Release 1.1* of our original vocabulary trainer with the new auto-save function of the dictionary from the old version. Now you just have to add the two additional components shown in Table 10.1.

Table 10.1 **Additional Components in the Follow-up Project Vocab1**

Component	Object Name	Adapted Properties
Screen1	Screen1	"Icon": vocab1_appIcon.png (companion website `/MEDIA`)
TinyDB	TinyDB	
Button	OffButton	"Text": OFF

Project Vocab1 on the Companion Website

The files for this project are available on the companion website in the usual directories (see the link in the Introduction).

We add the Off button so that the user can now lightheartedly switch off the app without having to worry about losing the data. After you make the changes shown in Table 10.1, the Vocab1 project should look in AI Designer like the screen shown on Figure 10.2. As you can see in the Properties section, the component TinyDB really does not have any properties at all.

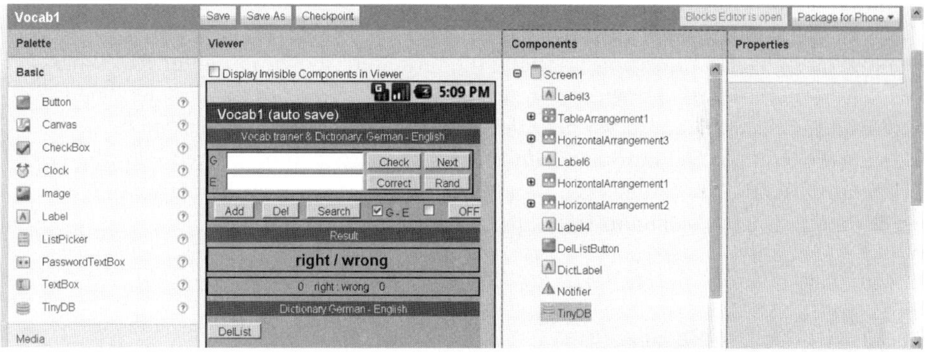

Figure 10.2 Expanded Vocab1 project in AI Designer

The event handler for closing the vocabulary trainer with the Off button is easy to implement. You are already familiar with the method `close screen` from previous projects (see Figure 10.3).

Figure 10.3 Closing the Vocab1 app

Now we can directly implement the statements for saving the two lists `gerList` and `engList`. As this process is required by various event handlers, we simply put it in a separate procedure, `saveLists`. As you can see in Figure 10.4, saving in AI is done in a really simple and comfortable way. You just pass the appropriate variable `gerList` or `engList` for each list as a `valueToStore` to the TinyDB method `TinyDB.StoreValue`, together with a unique `tag` such as `gerListTinyDB` or `engListTinyDB`. When this procedure is called, the two lists with their current values are saved locally under the corresponding tags.

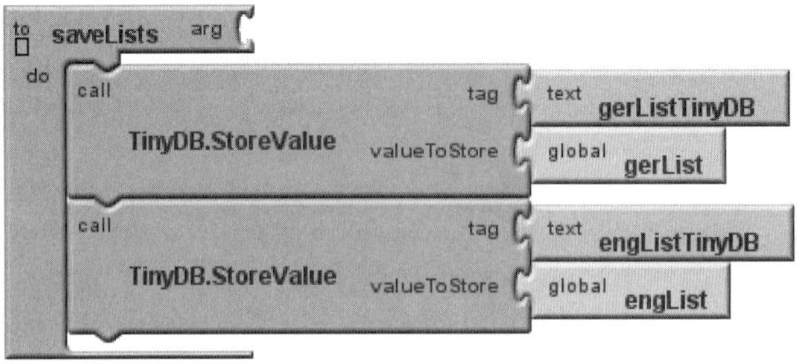

Figure 10.4 Saving both lists locally under separate tags

Now saving is just a question of calling the procedure shown in Figure 10.4 whenever saving at runtime seems appropriate. In our vocabulary trainer, this is the case when a new word pair is to be added via the Add button, an existing word pair is to be deleted individually with the Del button, or the entire dictionary is to be deleted with the Del-List button. We just need to add the procedure call `saveLists` to the corresponding event handlers shown in Figure 10.5.

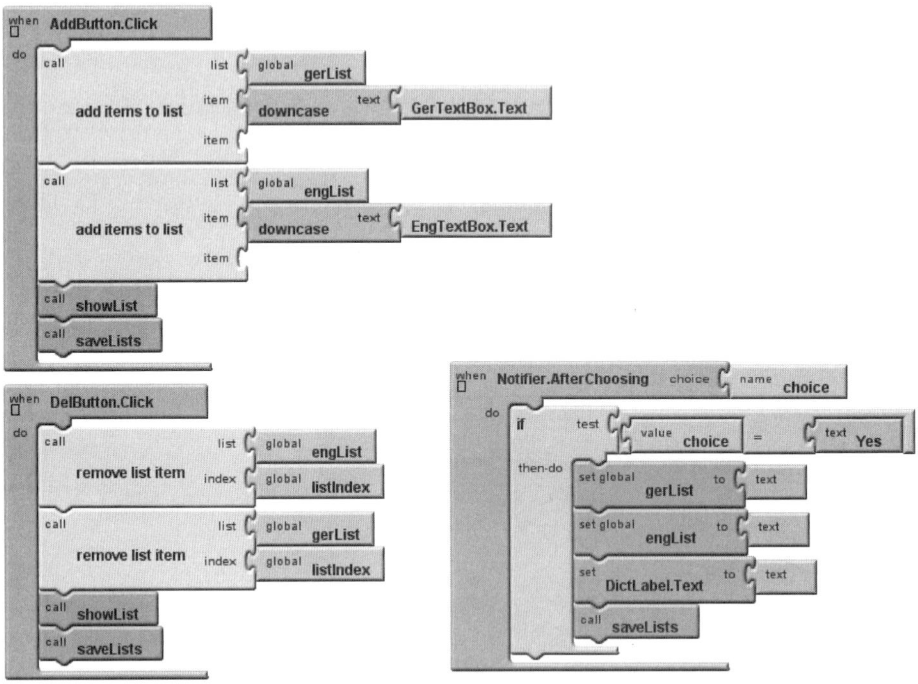

Figure 10.5 Saving from within various event handlers

Now the lists are saved automatically with every change and are always available permanently with their current data content.

Loading Local Data from a Dictionary

Now that we have saved the two vocabulary lists automatically as described in the previous section, we want to load them automatically into the dictionary when the vocabulary app is relaunched, so that the user can carry on working with the most recent version of the dictionary. To make sure the two vocabulary lists are immediately available without requiring any further action on the user's part, the loading instructions are embedded in the event handler `Screen1.Initialize`. The loading process is just as easy and comfortable with the TinyDB component as the saving process, but there is one thing to watch out for.

> **Be Careful When Loading Empty Lists!**
>
> Loading empty lists usually causes problems because the returned text string is empty. To avoid this problem, you should check lists on loading them or before assigning them to a variable. Otherwise, applying list operators to an empty text string typically leads to a system crash.

If the dictionary was empty the last time it was saved, retrieving the saved values of variables does not return an empty list, but rather an empty text string (`text`). This return value does not usually cause any problems when retrieving individual values of variables of the data type `text` or `number`, but it needs to be *intercepted* explicitly when the method expects to receive a value of the data type `list`. The statements, which should work with the loaded values of the variables (discussed later), are geared toward a list and try to access, for example, the list item 1. Of course, this item does not exist in an empty text string, so this attempt causes a program crash. To check a saved value to see whether it corresponds to a list or an empty text string, we use the auxiliary construct shown in Figure 10.6. Here, we first provisionally load one of the saved lists via the TinyDB method `TinyDB.GetValue` and the suitable tag `gerListTinyDB` into the auxiliary variable `i`. We can then check the value of `i` in the initial condition of a conditional `if` statement to see if its text length `length i` is larger than 0—in other words, to see if it is not an empty string.

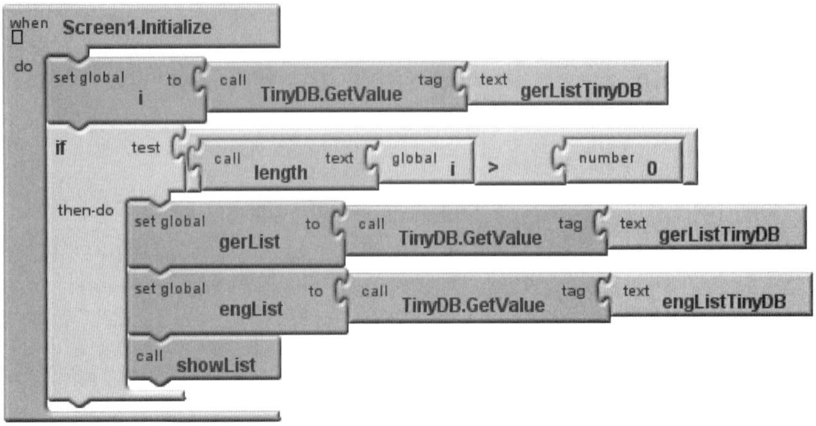

Figure 10.6 Loading the two lists and checking for empty strings

If this initial condition is met and the loaded value is not an empty string, we can then retrieve the saved lists via their tags `gerListTinyDB` and `engListTinyDB` with the method `TinyDB.GetValue` and pass them to the list variables `gerList` and `engList`, respectively. After these loading processes have been executed within the event handler `Screen1.Initialize`, the two lists are available immediately after the program launch and are also displayed in the dictionary via the final call of the procedure `showList`. Apart from the additional check regarding empty strings, which you can use in the same way in your own projects, the loading of saved data into an app is very simple with AI. With these few statements, you have expanded the limited functions in the version of Vocab and turned it into the really useful Vocab1 app, as shown in Figure 10.7.

Figure 10.7 Persistent dictionary in the Vocab1 app

Notice that Release 1.1 of the vocabulary trainer has an Off button now with which you can close the app and its dictionary (left). When restarting the app (center), the last state is restored (right). Now you can use the persistent dictionary straight away to check your knowledge of words, add new words, or delete existing ones.

Deleting App Data from the Android System

Not every app has such a comfortable function as our vocabulary trainer, in which you can use the Del button to delete an individual item or the DelList button to delete the entire persistent dictionary. If you need to delete persistent data manually one day, you can do so on a system-wide level via the Settings menu of the operating system. Go to Settings > Applications > Manage Applications on your smartphone. Once you have selected the desired app as shown in Figure 10.8, the "Application info" can be viewed by choosing Storage > Data, which brings up the current amount of storage space used by the persistent data of this app. If you want to delete this data, you can press the button labeled "Clear data." After you confirm your decision, the persistent data no longer takes up any storage space; that is, it has been deleted.

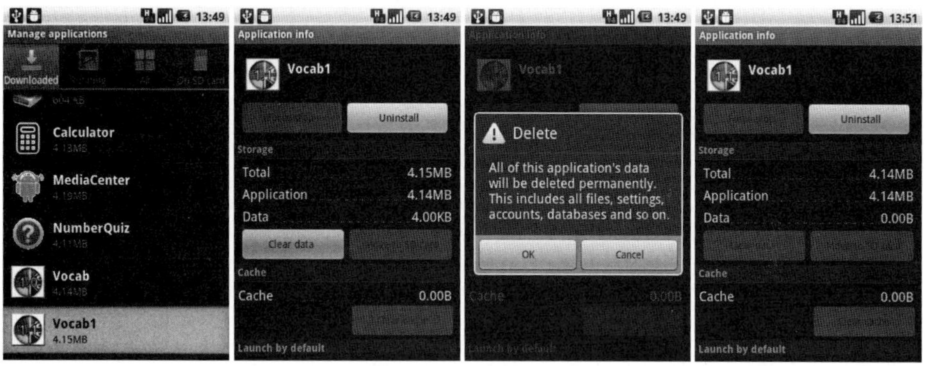

Figure 10.8 Deleting app memory through the system menu

In Figure 10.8, you can see that the data in the vocabulary trainer—that is, the three word pairs shown in Figure 10.7—takes up 4KB. Compared to the more than 4000KB (4.14MB) of storage space required by the app program code, the dictionary is rather modest in terms of memory usage.

Saving Data on the Web with the TinyWebDB Component

As mentioned earlier, the data in apps developed with AI can be stored not only in the more traditional way by saving them locally, but also on a server on the Internet as part of the *cloud*. Although storing and retrieving data externally (i.e., on the Web) is just as easy with AI as storing data on and retrieving it from local storage media, the potential inherent in flexible and distributed online access is far greater. For example, you can store data in almost unlimited amounts centrally on powerful servers, which can then be accessed, edited, and amended worldwide by various users and devices. Generally the requirements for developing professional applications with a distributed common database (shared databases) are relatively high, as critical data obviously requires advanced methods for ensuring its consistency and safeguarding access to it. Nevertheless, the basic mechanisms are easy to use, especially with AI, and you can take advantage of the options provided by Google (whose services were among the forerunners of so-called cloud computing), in which smartphone apps are integrated with other web services.

For saving data online, you do not need to have your own web server. Google makes storage resources available online through its web services, which you can use, for example, to store data for your apps. In an environment especially designed for quick and experimental use of online data storage, developers can access a dedicated shared data server that can hold up to 1000 entries. This service is explicitly declared as a *test platform* and should be used only for demo purposes for two reasons: (1) all data on the server can be viewed by all users of the server and (2) if the capacity limit is exceeded, the data is overwritten without warning. Go ahead and have a look at the example data provided by your fellow developers, by typing the address of the test server into your web browser.

Shared Data Server for Test Purposes for AI Developers

For testing online data storage with AI apps, Google offers an AI web service at:

`http://appinvtinywebdb.appspot.com/`

This server address also corresponds to the default setting for online storage in the corresponding AI components, so that accessing it is done automatically from within AI. The server can store up to 1000 entries. Be careful, though: Any visitor of this site can view, load, and manipulate the data. When the capacity limit is reached, the data is successively overwritten without prior warning. As you can readily see, this public web service is definitely *not* suitable for permanently storing confidential and important data!

For storing confidential and important data online persistently, you need to create your own web service with the corresponding features. This can be done via Google and is described online as a "Custom TinyWebDB Service" in the AI "Concepts Reference" and at:

`http://experimental.appinventor.mit.edu/learn/reference/other/tinywebdb.html`

For further alternatives and similar services, please check your AI provider's website.

Don't let these limitations stop you from using this great service and the impressive options of online storage, or at least trying them out for yourself. Even if responsible and secure saving of data in the cloud is not to be taken lightly, it is becoming more important, especially for mobile devices, which have only very limited storage and computing resources of their own. In general, the ability to access a central repository of data from more and more different devices of a user and from anywhere is becoming increasingly important. It is worth having a closer look at this exciting topic, and as usual the effort required to become part of this movement is incredibly small thanks to AI. Despite its promise, however, you should be aware, and make the users of your apps that utilize online storage aware, that each access to the data via the smartphone is subject to additional charges unless you have a data flat rate or are surfing via a free WLAN access.

For comfortably storing data in the cloud—in other words, for saving and loading app data on the Web—AI offers the non-visible component TinyWebDB in the group "Not ready for prime time." As its name indicates, this component is similar to the local variation TinyDB; its functions are also just as easy to use as the familiar ones for working with local storage media. The complex and involved processes for network communication are made almost completely abstract, such that for you as AI developer, web-based data storage hardly differs from local data storage. The specification of the TinyWebDB component shown in Figure 10.9 again lists the two methods `StoreValue` and `GetValue` for writing and reading the online data; the methods have similar functions to the corresponding TinyDB methods.

TinyWebDB

TinyWebDB1

Non-visible component that communicates with a Web service to store and retrieve information.

See Creating a Custom TinyWebDB Service.

Properties

`ServiceURL`

Events

`GotValue(text tagFromWebDB, any valueFromWebDB)`
Indicates that a GetValue server request has succeeded.

`ValueStored()`
Event indicating that a StoreValue server request has succeeded.

`WebServiceError(text message)`
Indicates that the communication with the Web service signaled an error

Methods

`GetValue(text tag)`
GetValue asks the Web service to get the value stored under the given tag. It is up to the Web service what to return if there is no value stored under the tag. This component just accepts whatever is returned.

`StoreValue(text tag, any valueToStore)`
Asks the Web service to store the given value under the given tag

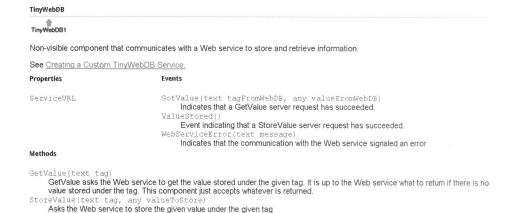

Figure 10.9 Specification of the TinyWebDB component

Saving and loading the online data take place in a two-step process, as the online communication generally happens *asynchronously*; in other words, the answers from the Internet do not arrive immediately, but may be delayed for some period of time after the request is submitted, depending on the available bandwidth, traffic, and data volume to be transferred. By contrast, retrieving data from local storage happens almost instantaneously. The successful storage of data on the web service via the method `StoreValue` is confirmed with a time-delayed event `ValueStored` and the retrieval via the method `GetValue` with the event `GotValue`, which also returns the retrieved value together with the corresponding tag as identification. If an error occurs in the online communication, a message to that effect is returned as text and described in the event `WebServiceError`. In the only property ServiceURL, the address of the web service mentioned previously is preset to the default `http://appinvtinywebdb.appspot.com`, but you can replace it with your own "Custom TinyWebDB Web-Service"—for example, one running on Google AppEngine.

Storing the Dictionary in the Cloud

Next, we will demonstrate the practical use of the component TinyWebDB in the context of the vocabulary trainer. We will expand the existing project Vocab1 even further by adding the option of storing the dictionary on the preset test platform of the Google web service with one press of a button, in addition to the automatic local storage. This makes the app interesting as a *master*—for example, for a teacher or language coach who wants to manage new vocabulary for his or her students locally and then make the dictionary available online in incremental steps, depending on the learning stage reached, with the students using a corresponding *client* app to access the words. The teacher can manage his or her data pool locally, expand or reduce it as needed, and then upload the amended dictionary to the server. We will implement both variations, the master and the client app, to demonstrate the distributed access to a common database in practice. In this section, we begin by developing the master app, which implicitly includes the client function.

As the expansion of the vocabulary trainer once more takes place mainly in the non-visible area, we need the AI Designer for only a few minimal edits and additions. Load the Vocab1 project into the AI Designer via My Projects > Vocab, and save a copy (Save As) under the name "Vocab2." In the new project, change the Title property from "Screen1" to "Vocab2 (web master)," to indicate the new role and function of this *Release 1.2* of the original vocabulary trainer. Now you just need to add the four additional components shown in Table 10.2. As we want to use the Google test platform for saving the dictionary, we leave the value in the TinyWebDB property ServiceURL unchanged from the default path `http://appinvtinywebdb.appspot.com` (you should adapt this value accordingly if you are using another service address).

Table 10.2 **Additional Components in Follow-on Project Vocab2**

Component	Object Name	Adapted Properties
Screen1	Screen1	"Icon": vocab2_applcon.png (see companion website `/MEDIA`)
TinyWebDB	TinyWebDB	
Button (2x)	UploadButton, DownloadButton	"Text": Upload, Download
Label	StatusLabel	"Text": not loaded

Project Vocab2 on the Companion Website

You can find the project on the companion website in the usual directories.

By using the two additional buttons UploadButton and DownloadButton, the user will later be able to start the *upload* (saving) to or *download* (loading) from the web server explicitly. The additional label StatusLabel will indicate the current upload or download status, so that the user is informed of the otherwise non-visible, time-delayed online loading processes and does not, for example, abort a download process prematurely or restart it again. On starting the app, the StatusLabel shows the text "not loaded," as the online dictionary is not loaded automatically but only when the user presses the Download button. With minimal edits and arrangements, the Vocab2 project appears as shown in Figure 10.10.

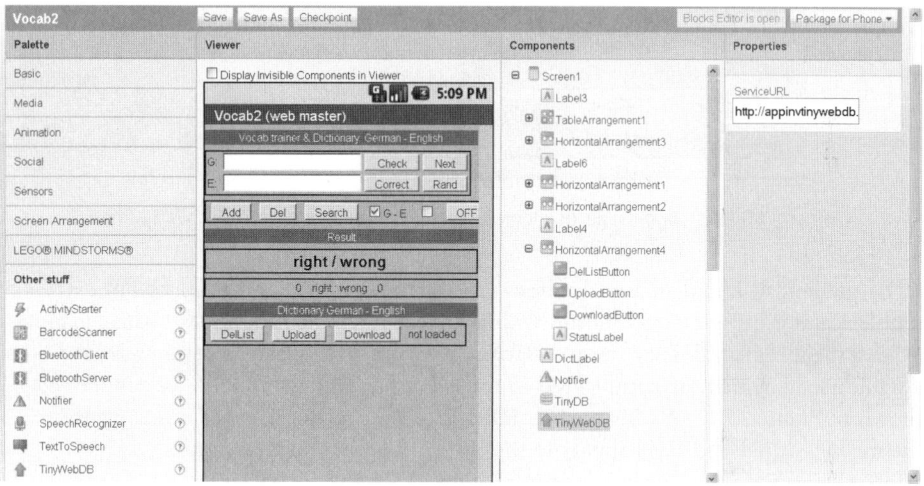

Figure 10.10 Project Vocab2 with a TinyWebDB component

After these design preparations, we can turn to implementing the online access in AI Editor. The existing block structures remain entirely unchanged. Thus, on launching the new vocabulary trainer app, any dictionary already present locally on the smartphone will be loaded automatically and displayed in the dictionary area. The user can amend this initial list as desired by using the Add, Del, and DelList buttons and then upload the edited dictionary to the web server by pressing the Upload button. On the emulator or a smartphone integrated into the development environment, only web access is possible, as described earlier. Uploading the dictionary happens mainly in the corresponding event handler `UploadButton.Click` (shown in Figure 10.11). In the TinyWebDB method `TinyWebDB.StoreValue`, the two lists `gerList` and `engList` are saved online as `valueToStore` under a unique identifier `gerListTinyWebDB` and `engListTinyWebDB` as `tag` at the default web address, similar to the local saving with `TinyDB.StoreValue`. During the upload process, the StatusLabel keeps the user informed of this process by displaying the text "uploading."

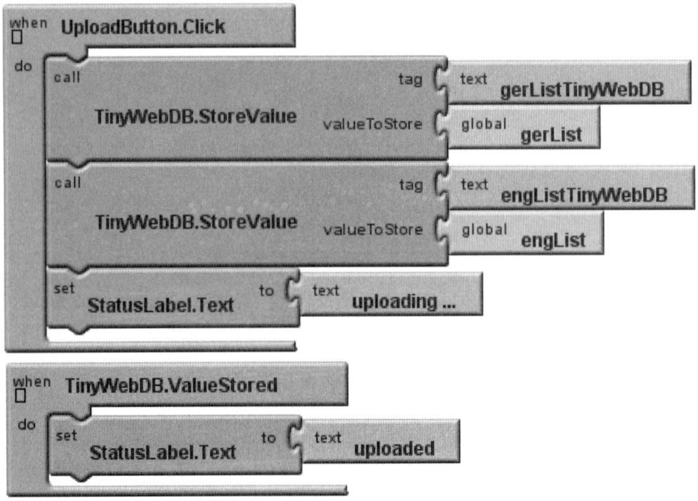

Figure 10.11 Two-stage asynchronous upload process onto the web server

As the upload is also an asynchronous process, the confirmation of successful data transfer cannot happen directly from within the event handler `UploadButton.Click`. With a slight temporal delay, the web service returns a `ValueStored` event after successful upload, which the app receives in the event handler `TinyWebDB.ValueStored` shown in Figure 10.11. As this event handler is called only in case of a positive answer, the message "uploaded" will appear in the StatusLabel only in that case.

If an error should occur in the transfer, however, the web service sends a `WebServiceError` event back to the app, which is received via the event handler `TinyWebDB.WebServiceError` shown in Figure 10.12 and displayed in the StatusLabel. In some cases, the cause may be a temporary network failure, which perhaps might not occur again if the user presses the Upload button a second time. In case of permanent errors, you should first check the Internet address of the web service and make sure that your data connection is really enabled. Once you have checked these fundamental sources of errors, you will know that the cause lies elsewhere and will have to start analyzing the problem more closely.

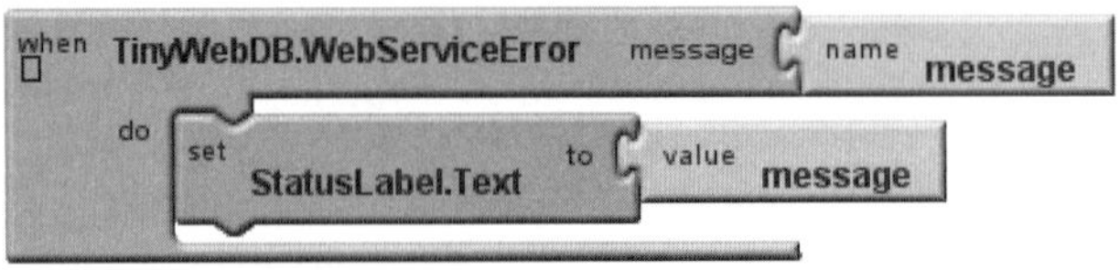

Figure 10.12 Error message in case of failed data transfer via the Internet

Whereas the confirmation of successful data transfer does not necessarily have to be implemented for the upload process, the download of the data stored online only makes sense and is only possible if both stages of the process are implemented. In the first step, pressing the Download button triggers the event handler `DownloadButton.Click`, which requests and begins the download from the web service with the method `TinyWebDB.GetValue`. This method does not receive the data that is downloaded, however.

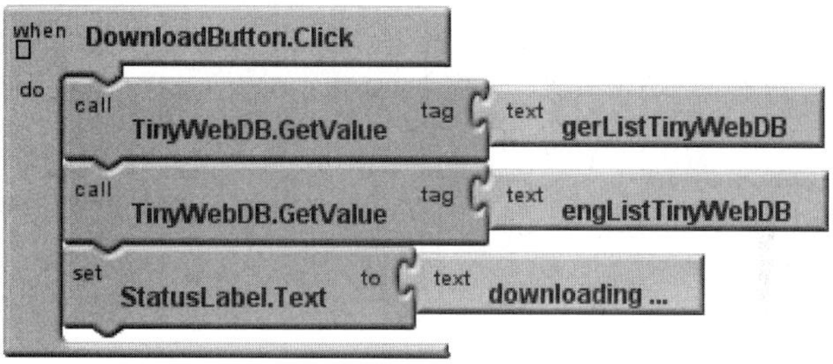

Figure 10.13 Requesting and triggering the download from the web service

This decisive difference between the two otherwise analogous methods `TinyDB.GetValue` and `TinyWebDB.GetValue` is expressed in their visual puzzle shapes: The latter does not have a getter joint for passing on a received data value (see Figure 10.13). Requesting and receiving data from the Internet are strictly separate processes. This basic principle of asynchronous data transfer is more than sensible, because it ensures that the app will not be completely blocked during the sometimes lengthy downloading periods, but rather can continue to execute other event handlers in the meantime. Only when the online data has been fully downloaded does it make sense to deal with the data and start processing it. The same principle applies in our example of the vocabulary trainer. Only after the data set requested online has been fully received on the smartphone is the corresponding `GotValue` event triggered in the app, with the data set then being passed in the local variable `valueFromWebDB` together with its identifier in the variable `tagFromWebDB` to the event handler `TinyWebDB.GotValue` shown in Figure 10.14. At that point, processing of the retrieved data can begin.

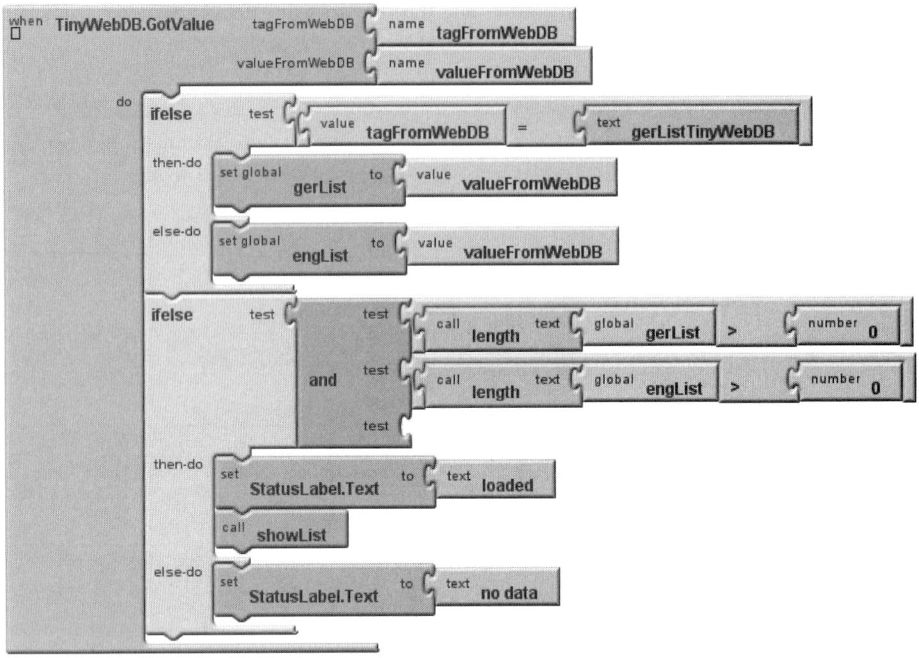

Figure 10.14 Receiving and testing the requested data from the web service

The event handler `GotValue` plays a central role: It appears only once per app and receives every incoming data set. Thus, if several requested data sets arrive in a time-delayed fashion, the incoming data first must be allocated to the corresponding requests within the handler. In our vocabulary trainer, we have requested two different data sets in the event handler `DownloadButton.Click` (see Figure 10.13)—namely, the two vocabulary lists `gerList` and `engList`, via their identifiers. As these data sets will not necessarily arrive in the app in the same order that they were requested (blame the often unfathomable ways of the Internet), the first `ifelse` branch in the `GotValue` handler shown in Figure 10.14 deals with allocating the data set passed in the variable `valueFromWebDB`. If the associated identifier corresponds to the previously specified tag text `gerListTinyWebDB`, the data set that has just been received is the complete list `gerList`, and the corresponding value of `valueFromWebDB` can be passed to the global variable `gerList` in the app. If this is not the case, the data set must be the other list `engList` as there are only two requested data sets. After the data set is passed to its corresponding variable, the corresponding list is available in the app as usual.

When downloading lists from the Internet, we also face the challenge of checking the returned data set to see whether it is really a list, before we apply list methods to it. If, for example, there is not yet any data set stored under the specified identifier on the web service when the user presses the Download button for the first time, an empty text string could be returned. If we want to apply a function that requires both lists—for example, if we want to display the dictionary via the method `showList`—we must ensure that both data sets have been received in full. All of these requirements are checked to the fullest extent by the event handler `TinyWebDB.GotValue` (Figure 10.14), within the second `ifelse` branch. If a value has been assigned to each of the two global variables `gerList` *and* (`AND`) `engList` after the download *and* if both values correspond to a *not empty* text string, the successfully completed download process can be indicated with the message "download" and the dictionary (consisting of both loaded lists) output via the method `showList`. In all other cases, we can assume that no data was available on the web server and display the message "no data." Of course, the analysis of the downloaded data could be refined further, but for our purposes it is sufficient that we can deal with empty or nonexistent online lists, without having the app crash with an error message.

Now we have expanded the vocabulary trainer to be a "web master," with which you can continue to edit the dictionary locally, but also save it on the Internet. Go ahead and try out the revised app. In contrast to saving the data locally, you can fully access the data stored on the web server on the emulator and the smartphone within the development environment. In your independent app, you are working with both storage sources—local and online. Of course, the local dictionary is still empty when you first start the app, because the vocabulary lists created for the Vocab1 app are available only for that app. When you launch the Vocab2 app, it will look as shown in Figure 10.15 (left). Once you have entered a few word pairs, you can upload them to the web server by pressing the Upload button, with the success of this operation being confirmed with the status message "uploaded" (center). At that point, you can delete the dictionary locally via the DelList button (right) if you like, as you can download it again any time you want from the online data store by pressing the Download button.

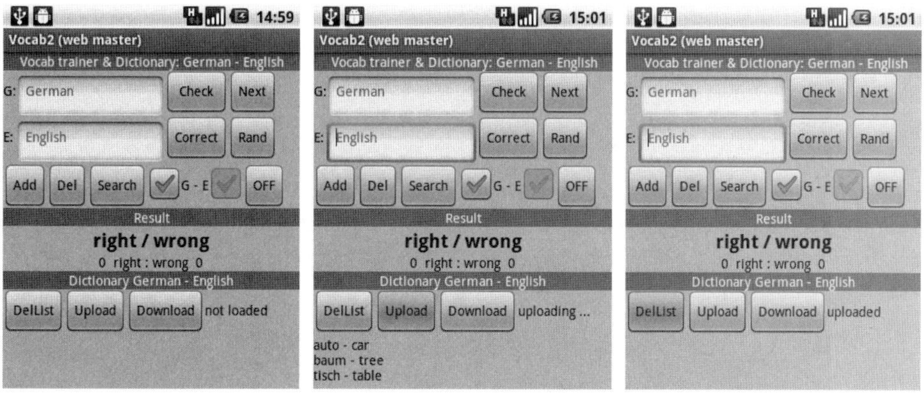

Figure 10.15 Entering, uploading, and local deletion of the vocabulary lists

If you have a look at the Google test server, you will notice that you can also use your web browser (at the address `http://appinvtinywebdb.appspot.com`) to check that the two lists have been saved online as data sets under their respective identifiers. Search for the list identifiers `gerListTinyWebDB` and `engListTinyWebDB`, and you will find the vocabulary entries from Figure 10.15 in your browser as well, as illustrated in Figure 10.16 (provided the identifiers are unique and have not yet been overwritten by another AI developer).

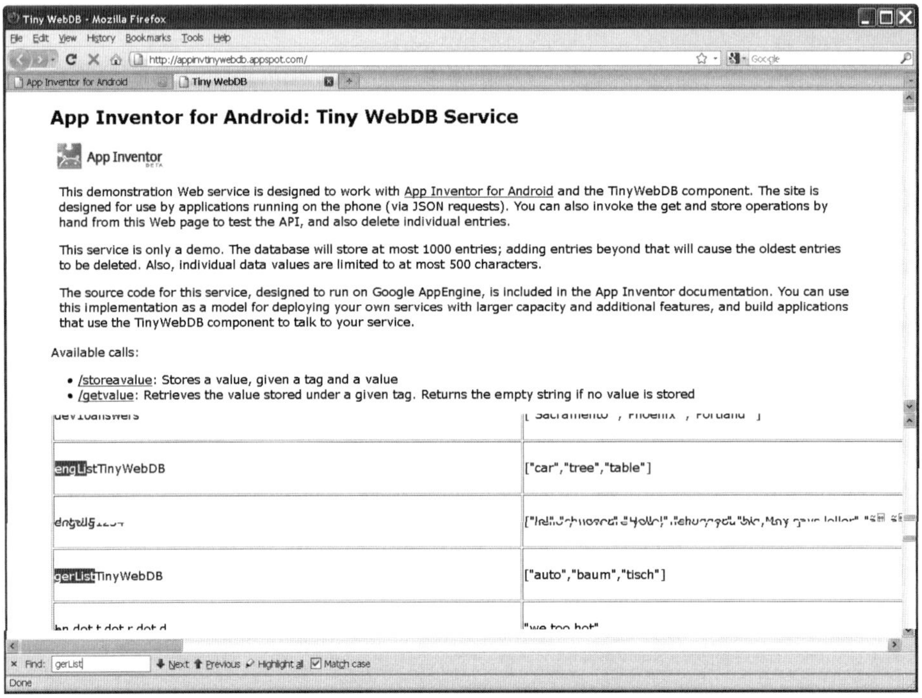

Figure 10.16 The two vocabulary lists on the AI test server

Given that the two vocabulary lists are correctly stored on the AI test server, you can now download them via the vocabulary trainer "web master" to your smartphone. Just press the Download button, watch the status messages, and after a short time observe that the dictionary is again available on the smartphone, as shown in Figure 10.17.

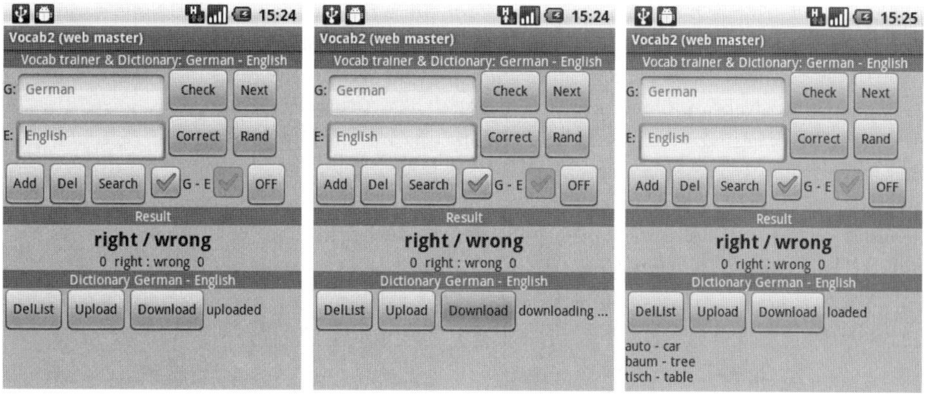

Figure 10.17 Downloading the vocabulary lists from the AI test server

With your master vocabulary trainer, you can now manage the local and online lists rather flexibly. The online lists can also be deleted again, by first deleting the dictionary locally in the app with the DelList button and then uploading the now-empty lists to the test server with the Upload button, which overwrites the previously filled lists with the empty ones.

Shared Database for Master and Client Apps

Thanks to the preparatory work we have already done, it is now really easy to create a *client* app for the vocabulary trainer to complement the *master* app. With the client app, the words can only be retrieved from the Internet; they cannot be altered. Thus a teacher can make new vocabulary lists available online that students are required to learn for the next lesson. To do so, the teacher makes the client app available to the students, so that all students have access to the same shared database online as the teacher. This teaching concept is attractive and useful, and you as developer need only "slim down" the existing master to the limited function of the additional client app. In this revision, you remove those user elements and functionalities from the master that deal with saving data locally, adding and deleting words, and displaying the dictionary.

> **Project VocabC on the Companion Website**
>
> You can find the project on the companion website in the appropriate directories (see the link in the Introduction).

First create a copy of the Vocab2 project for the new client app in AI Designer (using Save As), give it the new name "VocabC," rename its "Screen1" to the new title "VocabC (web client)," and replace the app icon with the image file `vocabc_appIcon.png` on the companion website. Next, delete all event handlers that are no longer required for the client by dragging them to the recycle bin one by one in the AI Editor. Also delete the corresponding interface elements in AI Designer by selecting them in the Viewer one by one, pressing the Delete button below the Components section, and confirming the deletion with OK. Start by deleting the event handlers and then delete the component objects, as listed in Table 10.3.

Table 10.3 **Elements to Be Deleted in AI Editor and AI Designer for the Client App**

Handler/Method	Object	Removed Function
AddButton.Click	AddButton	Add button for adding individual words
saveList		Saving new vocabulary locally
DelButton.Click	DelButton	Del button for deleting individual words
DelListButton.Click	DelListButton	DelList button for deleting the entire vocabulary list
Notifier.AfterChoosing	Notifier	Confirmation prompt for DelList button
showList		Displaying the dictionary
	LexLabel	Display area for dictionary
UploadButton.Click	UploadButton	Upload button for saving data online
TinyWebDB.ValueStored		Confirming successful uploading of data

As the students have no local database available, we want the client to automatically load the online dictionary instead of the local one when the app is launched. For that reason, we also delete the old content (local loading) of the event handler `Screen1.Initialize` and insert in its place the content of the event handler `DownloadButton.Click` (online loading). The now-superfluous event handler `DownloadButton.Click` can also be deleted, together with the corresponding component object `DownloadButton`. In addition, we delete the non-visible component object TinyDB in AI Designer, as we no longer need local data access. All other components and event handlers remain unchanged, so that the now slimmed-down client appears in AI Designer as shown in Figure 10.18.

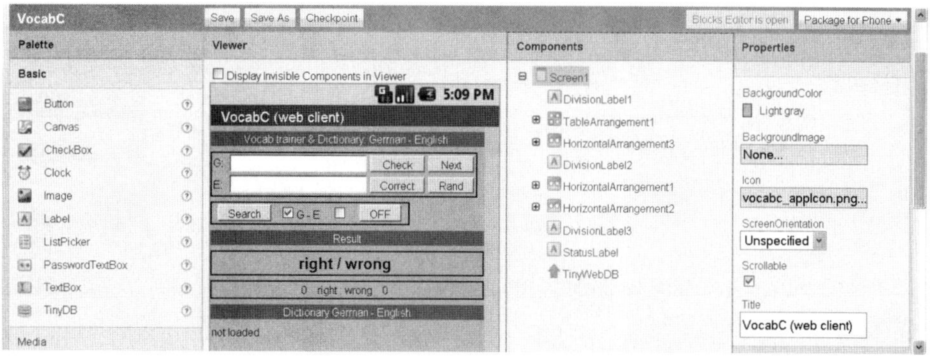

Figure 10.18 Client app VocabC with reduced range of functions

The number of block structures in AI Editor is considerably reduced as well, so that only some of the previous event handlers, methods, and variables remain. In addition to these items, Figure 10.19 shows the newly designed event handler `Screen1.Initialize`, with which the online dictionary is downloaded at app launch.

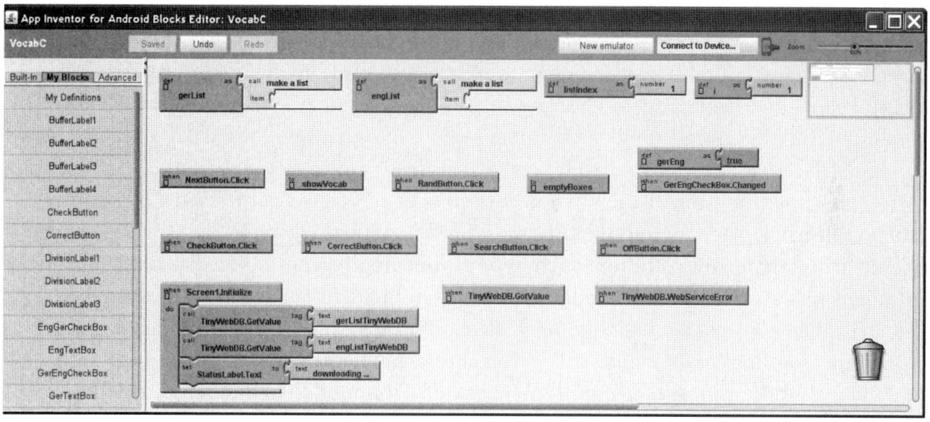

Figure 10.19 Reduced block structures in app client VocabC

Now different users can use the different vocabulary trainer apps—the teachers with the master and the students with the clients—to access the dictionary from anywhere and work in parallel based on shared data, as shown in Figure 10.20.

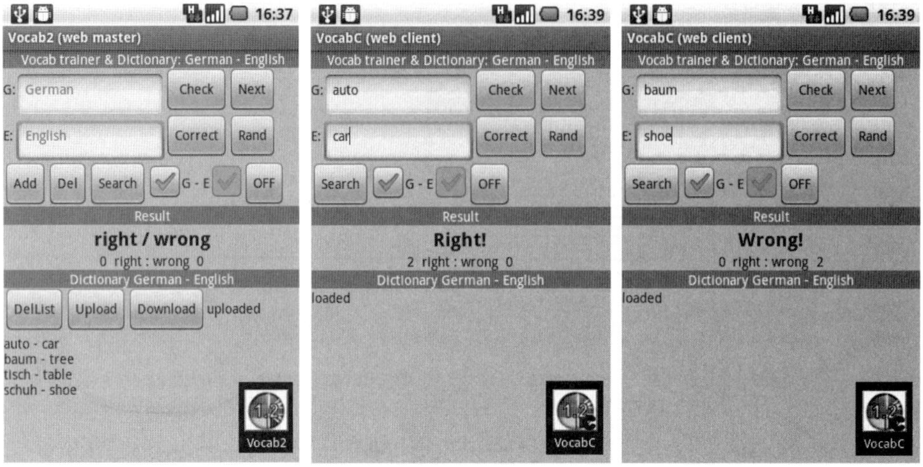

Figure 10.20 Working in parallel with different apps based on the same data

This type of application, in which data are stored in the cloud and different apps are used to access a common database online with different authorizations, has an enormous potential. Think beyond a classic database application (a description that largely fits our vocabulary trainer), and consider new contexts of use for your own app projects. For example, imagine managing and controlling a fleet of vehicles, where each truck driver is equipped with a smartphone containing a client app that saves the truck's geoposition in regular intervals on a central web server. The fleet manager could use the master app to retrieve, track, and direct the current locations of the trucks at any time. In a slightly amended version, such an app would be useful for spontaneously getting together with friends who are nearby. Although such applications might seem rather demanding right now, you will acquire the knowledge needed to implement them in the next chapters. With AI, such projects are easier to realize than you may think at the moment.

By learning how to save and load persistent data, whether locally or online, you have conquered another important requirement for developing demanding apps. Because your new knowledge is combined with your understanding of the program development basics, you have now constructed a broad and generic foundation on which you can build an almost unlimited multitude of apps. The following chapters introduce a variety of special features and unique areas in connection with developing apps for mobile Android devices, which are all based more or less on the basics acquired up to now. Data appears in almost every context, and in most cases you will have to or want to store it permanently. To do so, you will probably fall back frequently on the components for storing and loading data.

Part IV

Developing Attractive Apps

Of course, "beauty is in the eye of the beholder"—and the same is true when determining whether an app is attractive. The title of this part of the book is intended to indicate that we have progressed quite a bit in the path toward becoming app developers. Next, we will continue to encounter new components and impressive functions of AI, which we can quickly implement as part of appealing apps. The topics and examples in this part of the book correspond to fairly advanced development areas and put your already acquired knowledge of AI consistently and almost naturally into practice. With the three chapters in this book part, we venture into advanced topics that can help make your apps more attractive to the users. As on the PC, many users succumb to the fascination of computer graphics and animation on the smartphone. Beyond the intrinsic appeal of these visual elements, an entirely new area of use opens up in connection with mobile and increasingly sensor-equipped smartphones, the potential of which has not yet been fully addressed and where location-based services seem to represent just the spearhead of an entirely new generation of apps. By comparison, the many forms of electronic communication via telephone, SMS, and e-mail seem almost traditional, but even here the combination of mobility with previously stationary web services offers a whole new perspective. In regard to all of these fascinating new trends, you can not only participate in them, but also help actively create them by developing your own corresponding apps with AI. This part of our book will show you how.

Chapter 11

Graphics and Animation

The topic of graphics and animation on computers is a fascinating, broad, and demanding area that we could fill whole books in describing. Even on computers in the private domestic sector, we are now spoiled by incredibly sharp pictures, graphics, and animations of HD quality, free of blurs, and photo realistic. In addition, mass-market-ready, stereoscopic 3D capabilities have become available recently. Of course, on the considerably less powerful mobile smartphones currently available, we remain relatively far from this level of achievement. The processors are too weak, the memory too small, and the battery capacity too limited to realize such sophisticated graphics and animations, even though great strides are being made in this area. On mobile devices, graphics and animation continue to play a more modest role—a disclaimer that also applies to Android smartphones and, accordingly, to AI.

By "animation," we do not mean the colorful animated movies, which can be played back as ready-made video files just like any other movie on a smartphone with impressive quality (see the section "Playing Movies with VideoPlayer" in Chapter 7, "Multimedia"). In this chapter, we are talking about creating such graphics and animations ourselves and having the smartphone calculate and represent them in real time. As you would expect, you as AI developer do not need to deal with the very challenging basics of computer graphics and animation or work at the machine level with graphics functions based on OpenGL ES. With AI, you can use graphics and animations in your apps as usual (and, unfortunately, only) on a very high level of abstraction. But do not expect too much: At the moment, interactive 3D real-time graphics are not yet available in AI (only with Java), although interactive 2D real-time graphics can be used to a limited extent. Especially in the context of mobile devices, however, it is often the good idea behind, and appealing implementation of, a graphics app that determines whether the users will accept it and whether it becomes successful, even without extensive use of the latest and sometimes proprietary features. How else could one explain the success of games like *Moorhuhn* by Witan (*Crazy Chicken* in English) and *Angry Birds* by Rovio?

After being spoiled by elaborate 3D games, we tend to forget the fascination of the earlier painting and graphics programs and simple 2D computer games. These programs have enjoyed a renaissance on the less powerful mobile devices, and this chapter will give you a chance to look into the exciting development of such graphics and animation programs. The effort involved is relatively small, and the number of components provided in AI is quite manageable. While you are getting to know and implementing the basic principles of graphics and animation, you will also glance behind the scenes of current graphics games and animation programs, which are based on similar principles. Thus you will benefit from this chapter in several respects.

Painting as if on a Canvas with the Canvas Component

In an Android app, you cannot simply draw a line somewhere and start painting a piece of art. Before you can even make the first dot within a graphic, you first need to have something to draw or paint on. You would not just paint on your desk in real life, but rather get a notepad, a canvas, a drawing board, or some other suitable surface first. The same applies to painting with AI. In the Basic component group, AI offers the Canvas component, which provides both a surface to paint on and the basis for all pixel-oriented functions in the context of graphics and animation. Unlike with the usual app background of "Screen1," you can specify and navigate to any pixel point within a Canvas component object—a capability that is necessary for placing a point, drawing a line, or positioning or moving a graphic. Before exploring these functions, let's have a look at the specification of the Canvas component, shown in Figure 11.1.

Canvas

A canvas is a two-dimensional touch-sensitive rectangular panel on which users can draw and sprites can move.

Canvas components provide a rectangular space for drawings and sprites. Each location on a canvas can be specified by integral X and Y pixels with (0,0) in the upper-left corner.

The `BackgroundColor`, `PaintColor`, `BackgroundImage`, `Width`, and `Height` of the canvas can be set in either the Designer or the Blocks Editor. The `Width` and `Height` are measured in pixels and must be positive.

Any location on the canvas can be specified as a pair of (X, Y) values, where

- X is the number of pixels away from the left edge of the canvas.
- Y is the number of pixels away from the top edge of the canvas.

There are events to tell when and where a canvas has been touched or a sprite (`ImageSprite` or `Ball`) has been dragged. There are also methods for drawing points, lines, and circles.

Events

`Dragged(number startX, number startY, number prevX, number prevY, number currentX, number currentY, boolean draggedSprite)`
User dragged from `prevX, prevY` to `x, y`. The `draggedSprite` argument indicates whether a sprite is being dragged.

`Touched(number x, number y, boolean touchedSprite)`
Provides the x, y position of the user's touch on the canvas. `touchedSprite` is true if a sprite was in this position.

Methods

`Clear()`
Clears the canvas without removing the background image, if any.

`DrawCircle(number x, number y, number r)`
Draws a circle using the given coordinates and radius.

`DrawLine(number x1, number y1, number x2, number y2)`
Draws a line between the given coordinates.

`DrawPoint(number x, number y)`
Draws a point at the given coordinates.

`Save()`
Saves a picture of this Canvas to the device's external storage and returns the full path name of the saved file. If an error occurs the Screen's `ErrorOccurred` event will be called.

`SaveAs(text filename)`
Saves a picture of this Canvas to the device's external storage in the file named fileName. fileName must end with one of ".jpg", ".jpeg", or ".png" (which determines the file type: JPEG, or PNG). Returns the full path name of the saved file.

Properties

`BackgroundColor`
Color for canvas background.

`PaintColor`
Color used for drawing objects on canvas.

`Visible`
If set, canvas is visible.

`Height`
Canvas height (y-size).

`Width`
Canvas width (x-size).

Figure 11.1 Specification of the Canvas component in the AI References

In the specification of the Canvas component, the focus is on specifying pixel positions on the two-dimensional canvas with the two coordinate values *X* (horizontal position) and *Y* (vertical position), with the upper-left corner always fixed to the coordinates X = 0 and Y = 0. The coordinate position of the lower-right corner depends on the absolute size of the canvas in pixels. Thus, if the canvas had a size of 250 × 200 pixels, the lower-right corner would correspond to the coordinate values X = 250 and Y = 200 (for short: 250, 200). With the two coordinate values X and Y, any pixel on the canvas can be clearly determined, as shown in Figure 11.2 in general (left) and as an example with three specific points (right).

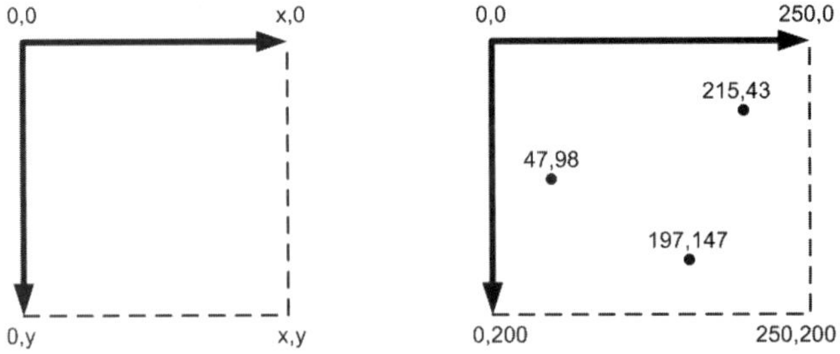

Figure 11.2 2D coordinates within the drawing surface of a Canvas component

The properties of the Canvas component shown in Figure 11.1 are unspectacular. You can set the size, visibility, and background color as usual. Matters get more interesting with the property PaintColor, with which you can specify and change the color you paint with. As in other graphics applications, the methods of the Canvas component offer options for cleaning all drawings off the drawing surface at once (Clear), drawing a point (DrawPoint) in a particular position (*x, y*), drawing a line (DrawLine) from one point (*x1, y1*) to another point (*x2, y2*), or drawing a circle (DrawCircle) in a particular position (*x, y*) with a specified radius (*r*).

Your finished masterpiece can be saved permanently by saving the content of a canvas object on the smartphone's SD card. You have two options for saving your pictures. If you choose the `Save` method, AI automatically assigns a file name and returns it with the complete file path. With the `SaveAs` method, you can choose your own file name to save the picture in JPEG or PNG format. You also need to enter the appropriate file extension: ".jpg" or ".jpeg" for JPEG, or ".png" for PNG.

The two event handlers shown in Figure 11.1 deserve special mention. They make it possible for the user to interact directly with the canvas—in other words, to draw on the smartphone's touch screen with the finger to create dots, lines, and any shapes on the canvas or move graphic objects. The `Touched` event handler returns the coordinates of the contact point for processing a single touch, informing the user whether a graphic object was touched, if applicable. By contrast, dragging the finger over the canvas produces a whole stream of coordinate data continuously in the `Dragged` event handler, with this data then being made available for further processing in the event handler.

Colored Dots with Different Brush Sizes

Even if the analogy to the Impressionist painting style of pointillism certainly does not do this style any justice, we want to start our demonstration of the Canvas component by placing multicolored dots of different sizes on the virtual canvas. As this is already one of the characteristics of a simple painting program, we want our app to have the character of a painting program right from the start. Our demo app should look like the mini painting program shown in Figure 11.3.

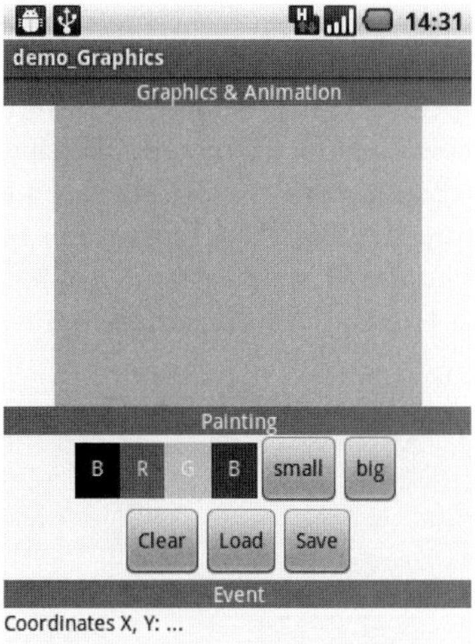

Figure 11.3 Mini painting program in the demo_Graphics project

> **Demo app demo_Graphics on the Companion Website**
>
> You can find the demo app `demo_Graphics` on the companion website in the corresponding directories (see the link in the Introduction).

Create a new project with the name `demo_Graphics`, and rename "Screen1" with the same title. Now you can place all components shown in Table 11.1 in the specified order in AI Designer.

Table 11.1 **Components and Initial Properties for the Painting Program**

Component	Object Name	Adapted Properties
Label (3x)	DivisionLabel1, DivisionLabel2, DivisionLabel3	"Text": see Figure 11.4 Otherwise, see the DivisionLabel discussed previously
Canvas	Canvas	"Width": 250 pixels "Height": 200 pixels
Button (4x)	blackButton, redButton, greenButton, blueButton	"BackgroundColor": as names "Text": B, R, G, B "TextColor": White
Button (2x)	smallButton, bigButton	"Text": small, big
Button (3x)	clearButton, loadButton, saveButton	"Text": Clear, Load, Save
Label	Label1	"Text": Coordinates X,Y:
Label	EventLabel	"Text": ...

To make the demo project look like Figure 11.4 in AI Editor, you need to make a few arrangements. As you would expect, all horizontally arranged components are positioned within a HorizontalArrangement. To get the canvas to be in the center of the screen, we use the same trick as we used in the Calculator app in Chapter 9, and place the Canvas component object into a HorizontalArrangement2 between two BufferLabels with the Width property set to "Fill parent." The gray Canvas then appears centered in the smartphone, framed by two white borders. Using the same method, we center the two button areas below the canvas with a HorizontalArrangement and two BufferLabels each.

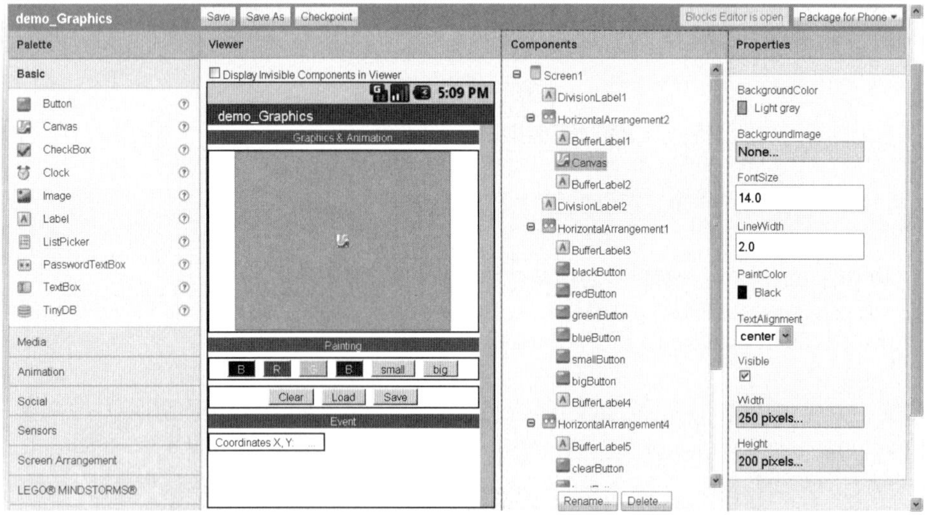

Figure 11.4 Components for the painting program in AI Designer

Now we can implement the functionality in AI Editor. We want users to be able to add dots to the canvas by pressing with a finger, so our program has to be able to register the user's touch on the canvas, determine its position, and paint a dot just in that place. For registering the touch and determining the position, we use the Canvas event block `Touched` shown in Figure 11.5 (left). If the user touches the canvas `Canvas`, its event block `Touched` is called and is passed the X,Y coordinates of the touch position in two *local* variables, `name x` and `name y`. If the touched position should contain a graphic object, this is also displayed via the Boolean value `true` in the third local variable `touchedSprite` (we will discuss sprites later, so let's ignore them for now). Now the X,Y coordinates are available in the two local variables `value x` and `value y` within the event handler `Canvas.Touched`, which are automatically generated and made available after we insert the `Touched` block in AI Editor in its block area (My Blocks > My Definitions). If we were now to slot the Canvas method `DrawPoint`, which is really intended for that purpose, into the `do` area of the event handler and call it with these two variables as arguments (see Figure 11.5, right), a dot of the default size would be painted onto the canvas exactly in the touched position.

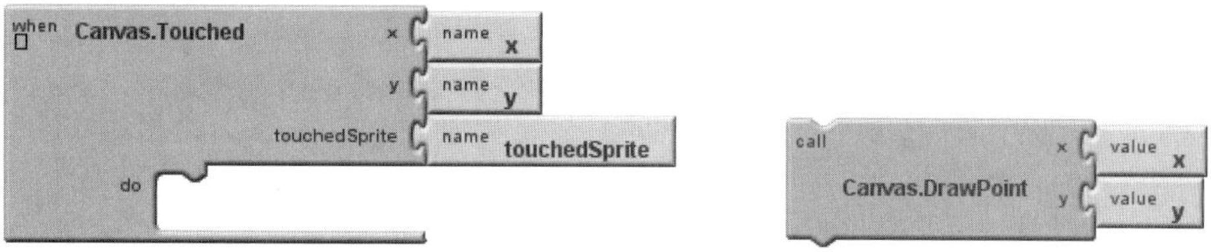

Figure 11.5 Painting a default-sized dot at the touched point

In reality, we do not want to always use the default size for the points we are painting, but rather vary the brush size we use. For that reason, we do not choose the Canvas method `DrawPoint`, but instead the method `DrawCircle` (Figure 11.6). To it, we assign not only the coordinates `x` and `y` but also the value of the global variable `brushSize` as radius `r`. We take advantage of the fact that AI does not represent a circle drawn with `DrawCircle` as an outline, but instead as filled circle; thus we can use this behavior to simulate a dot of any size.

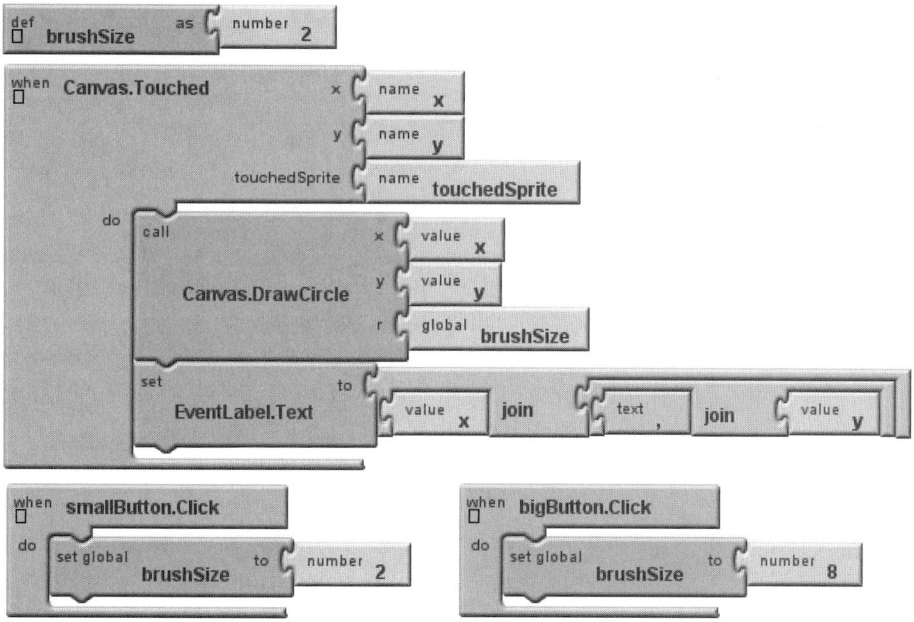

Figure 11.6 Painting a dot with different brush sizes

The user determines the size of the dots by pressing the buttons "small" or "big," thereby triggering the corresponding event handler `smallButton.Click` or `bigButton.Click` (Figure 11.6) to switch between a radius or `brushSize` of 2 and 8 pixels. At this stage of the program's development, you can use the painting program to create reasonably attractive dot pictures on your smartphone, as shown in Figure 11.7 (left). For the purposes of our demo project, we will also display the corresponding X,Y coordinates for each touch of the screen in the EventLabel, joined together as text string via the method `join` and a comma, which also happens in the `do` area of the event handler `Canvas.Touched` via the appropriate statement. To get a better feel for the canvas dimensions, you can place dots in the corners to illustrate the coordinates (compare Figure 11.7, right, to Figure 11.2, right).

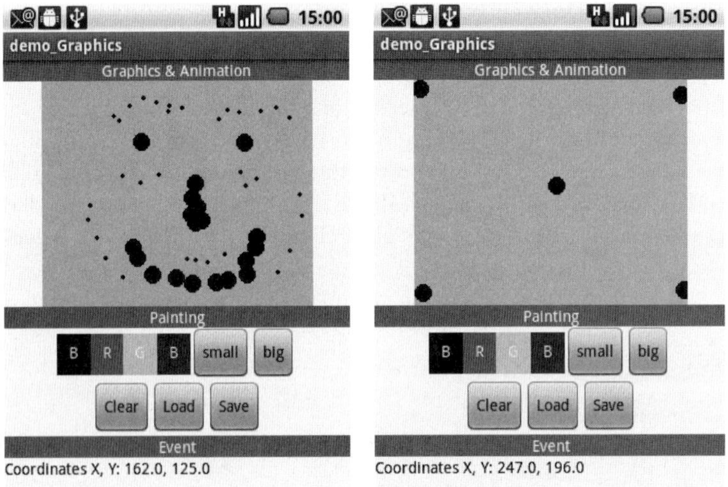

Figure 11.7 Pictures with differently sized dots and displaying coordinates

Now it's easy to give the whole thing a bit of color and paint dots in black, red, green, or blue with the four color buttons "B", "R", "G", and "B". We first assign one of the four available colors to the Canvas property via the corresponding button—or more specifically, via the event handler it triggers—as shown in Figure 11.8.

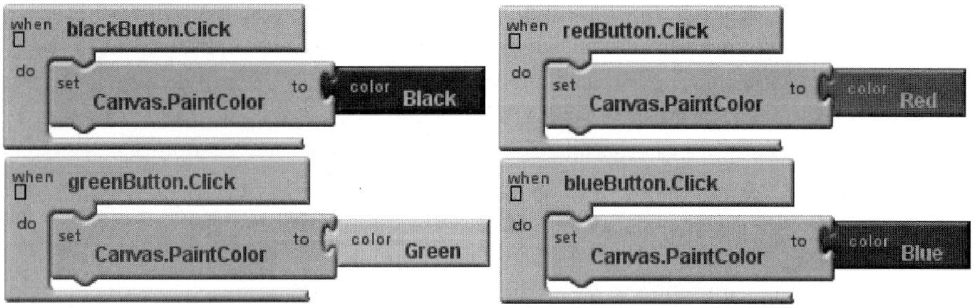

Figure 11.8 Selecting and switching between different colors

You would be surprised to see how much more realistic the dotted face looks in color (shown in Figure 11.9) in comparison to the gray face of Figure 11.7, if you could see this book in color.

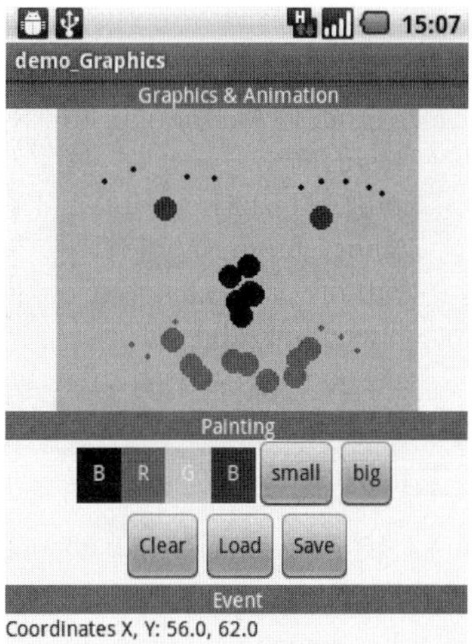

Figure 11.9 A face drawn with colored dots

We now have implemented the first six buttons of our painting program. At this point, we can add other functions; after all, there are other painting styles aside from pointillism.

Drawing Lines by Dragging on the Screen

An essential addition to our painting program is to enable the user not only to place individual dots onto the canvas via *touch*, but also to *drag* a finger over the canvas to draw lines. For registering the finger movement, AI offers the Canvas event block `Dragged`, which writes the coordinates of a continuous dragging movement into various local variables. Whereas the `Touched` event block registers the touched X,Y position only once, a total of six local variables (plus `draggedSprite`) receive the dynamic movement information continuously in the `Dragged` event block and make it available for further processing within the `do` area (variable blocks in My Blocks > My Definitions). In detail, the local variables record the start position (`startX`, `startY`), the previous coordinates (`prevX`, `prevY`), and each current finger position (`currentX`, `currentY`) and make this data available as shown in Figure 11.10. Whereas the start position remains unchanged during a dragging movement, the two other coordinate positions are constantly changing.

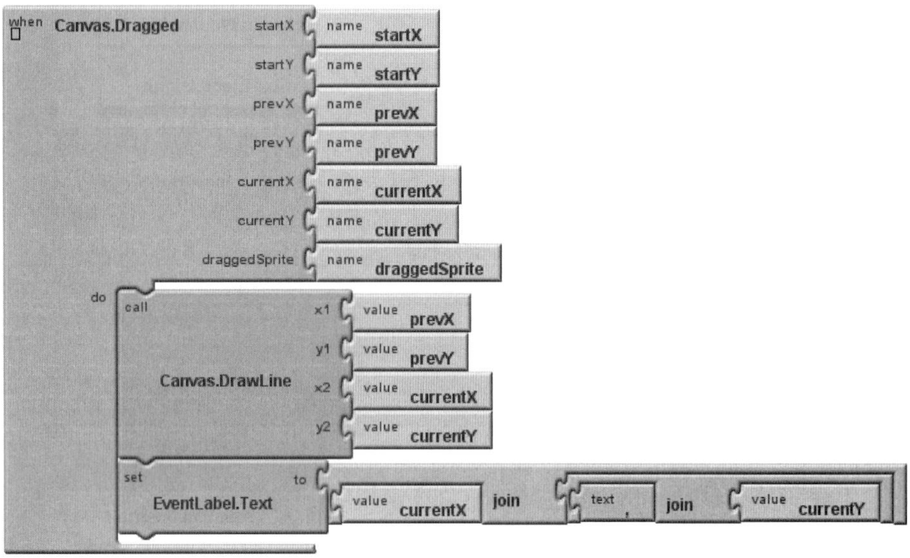

Figure 11.10 Event handler for drawing lines

Just as with drawing a single dot, drawing a continuous line is possible only through the interaction of two components. In Figure 11.10, we slot the Canvas method `DrawLine`, which can use a total of four of the six available coordinates for its purpose, into the `do` area of the event block `Canvas.Dragged`. The task of the `DrawLine` method is to draw a line between the two passed coordinates `x1,y1` and `x2,y2`. In this way, we can achieve different painting effects, depending on which values we pass to the method `Canvas.DrawLine`. If we pass `startX,startY` for `x1,y1` and `currentX,currentY` for `x2,y2`, a straight line is drawn for each individual dragging motion from the start point to the current coordinates. This effect can result, for example, in interesting star pictures, as shown in Figure 11.11 (left). If we instead pass `prevX,prevY` for `x1,y2` values, as shown in Figure 11.10, an extremely short line with a length of approximately one pixel is drawn between the previous and current finger positions. This creates the overall impression of a continuous curve, which follows the finger movement exactly, as shown in Figure 11.11 (center). We will use this setting in our app, as such a drawing function should not be absent from any painting program.

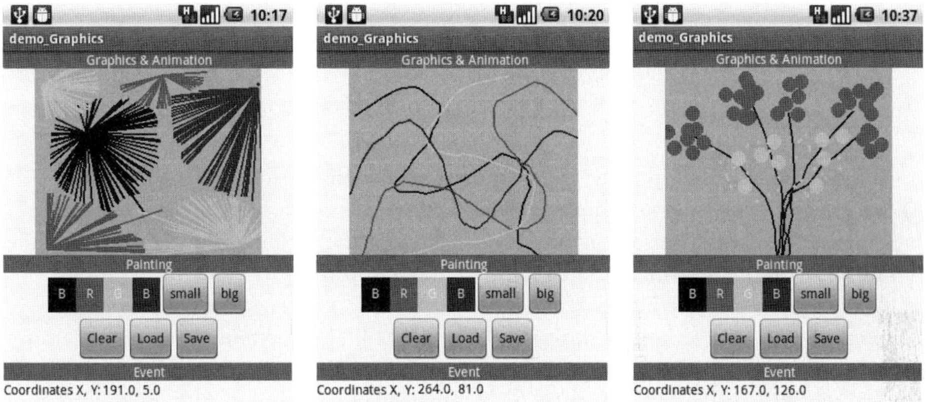

Figure 11.11 Painting with different X, Y variables in the DrawLine method

This concludes the implementation of the proper drawing functions of the demo app `demo_Graphics`. You can now paint pretty and expressive pictures, as shown in Figure 11.11 (right). You can choose dots of different colors and sizes, as well as lines. Of course, you do not want to have to restart the app every time you decide to paint a new picture, so deleting the canvas via a Clear button would be useful. This task is easy to implement thanks to the Canvas method `Clear`, as you can see in Figure 11.12.

Figure 11.12 Deleting the canvas with the "Clear" method

Do you know the drawing game "Haus vom Nikolaus" ("House of Santa Claus"), which is popular with German school children? The object is to draw the house shown in Figure 11.13 in just one go, without lifting the pencil off the paper; that is, you try to draw a sequence of eight connected lines in which you go over each section only once. It's not widely known in English-speaking countries, but you may well have heard of the mathematical principle behind it—the Eulerian path, in which every edge of the graph is visited exactly once. Children say the eight-syllable rhyme "This is the house of San-ta Claus" while drawing the house. See if you can draw this house in our painting program.

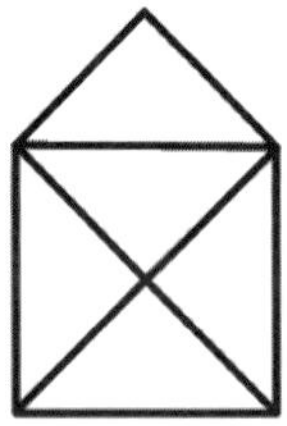

Figure 11.13 "This is the house of Santa Claus"

To help the user with finding one of the possible solutions for drawing the "House of Santa Claus," we want to equip our demo app with another feature. In our example, pressing the Load button is meant to show a guide on the screen as in "painting with numbers," with the user then following the numbered pattern to draw the "House of Santa Claus" correctly. For displaying the background image, we use the property `Canvas.BackgroundImage`, as shown in Figure 11.14. The key requirement is that you must be able to access the corresponding image file on your smartphone. In our example, we are using the image file `painting.png`, which we have saved on the smartphone's SD card (see also the companion website in the directory `/MEDIA`). Of course, you can use an alternative image of your choice if you like.

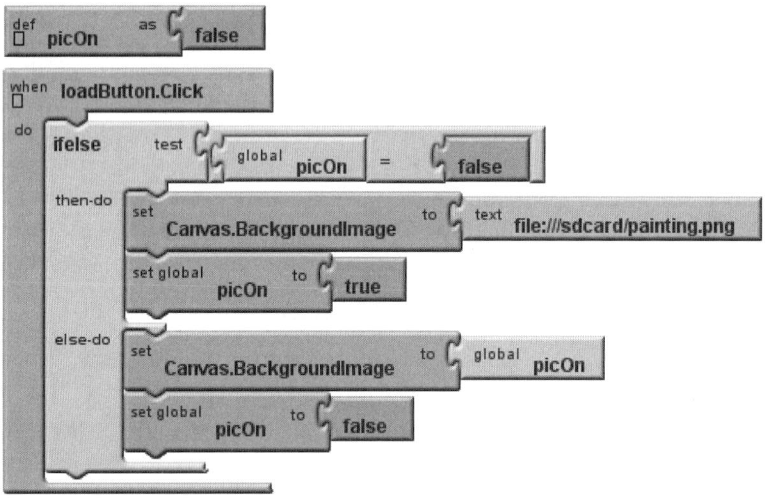

Figure 11.14 Showing and hiding a background image on the canvas

To show and hide the background image in turn, we create a global variable `picOn`, which records the current state as a Boolean value (`false` = off, `true` = on). When the app is launched, the canvas should be empty, without a background image, so the variable `picOn` is initialized with the value `false`. If the Load button is then pressed for the first time and the event handler shown in Figure 11.14 is called, the `ifelse` branch executes the statements in the `then-do` area due to the now fulfilled condition `picOn=false`. The background image is then loaded and the variable is set to the value `true`, because the image is now being shown. The next time the Load button is pressed or the event handler `loadButton.Click` is called, the `ifelse` condition is no longer fulfilled (`picOn=true`), so the statements in the `else-do` area are executed and both showing that the background image and the variable `picOn` are set back to `false`. This alternating process is repeated each time the Load button is pressed. The desperate user can now draw directly on the background image and practice how to do it freehand next time (see Figure 11.15).

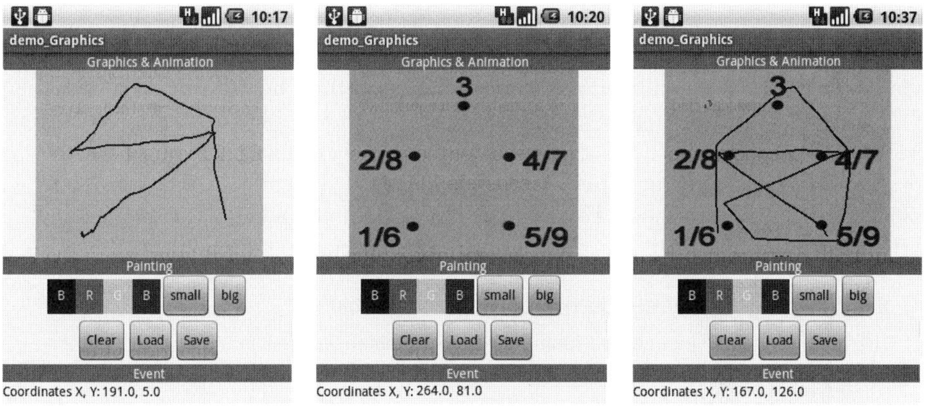

Figure 11.15 Painting with a displayed number guide as the background image

To enable the user to save his or her artwork permanently or to finish it at a later time, we want to make it possible to save the picture on the smartphone's SD card by pressing the Save button, and then load the picture again by pressing the Load button. To make matters simpler, we use the same file name (`painting.png`) for saving the canvas content with the `SaveAs` method as we used previously for loading or showing the background image of the "House of Santa Claus." As a consequence, the first time you press the Save button, the original image of the "House of Santa Claus" is overwritten with the current image in the canvas object; the same thing happens each time the button is pressed. The required event handler is quite clear, as shown in Figure 11.16.

Figure 11.16 Saving the drawing on the smartphone's SD card

To perform this task, pass the file name where the current picture should be saved to the method `Canvas.SaveAs` (Figure 11.16). If you do not specify the appropriate path, the file is saved in the SD card's main directory and the corresponding file path (`/sdcard/painting.png`) is displayed in the EventLabel. The next time the Load button is pressed, calling the event handler `loadButton.Click` (Figure 11.14) loads the previously saved image from the same file path and displays it in the canvas object. By that we have fully implemented the saving and loading function in our little painting program.

A Painting Program with an Undo Function

Now you have become familiar with the painting functions of the Canvas component and used them in conjunction within an appealing painting program. With the knowledge you gained in Chapter 9 on programming basics, you can now add even more functions to the painting program and expand it to become a truly powerful app. Imagine, for example, how useful an Undo function could be, so that you could undo dots put in the wrong place step by step instead of having to clear the whole canvas and restart your painting from scratch. Such a feature is not just a special graphics function unique to the Canvas component, but rather an example of how dedicated basic functions, generic blocks, and a good idea can be combined to develop a useful functionality; we will briefly discuss how to implement this feature while considering this context.

> **Example Project Painter on the Companion Website**
>
> The files for this project can be found on the companion website in the usual directories (see the link in the Introduction).

In a corresponding expansion of the `demo_Graphics` demo project to the Painter example app, it would then be possible to change the dotted sad smiley face shown in Figure 11.17 (left) to a laughing smiley face (right) by undoing the last few dots for the mouth (center).

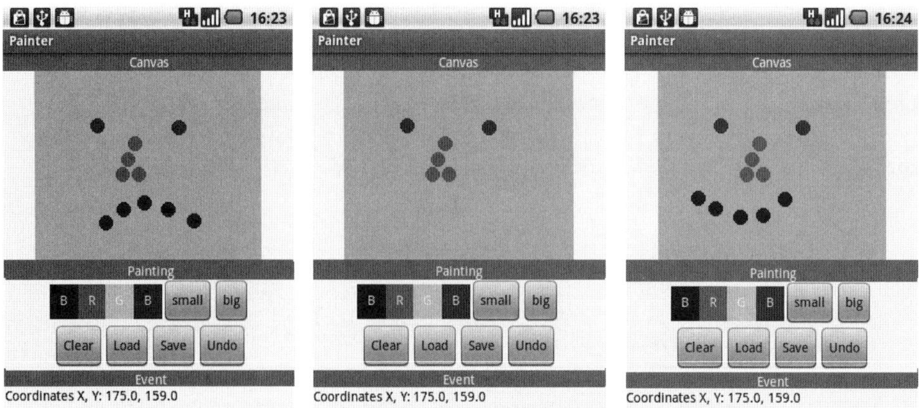

Figure 11.17 The Undo function of the painting program in action

To implement the Undo function, we use two lists `xList` and `yList` in the expanded block structures shown in Figure 11.18. In the event handler `Canvas.Touched`, we add the corresponding X,Y coordinates with each new paint dot to the lists. Additionally, we count each dot by incrementing a central index value in the global variable `xyIndex` by 1 with each touch. This saves the position of each dot in our lists, in the order in which the user draws them onto the canvas.

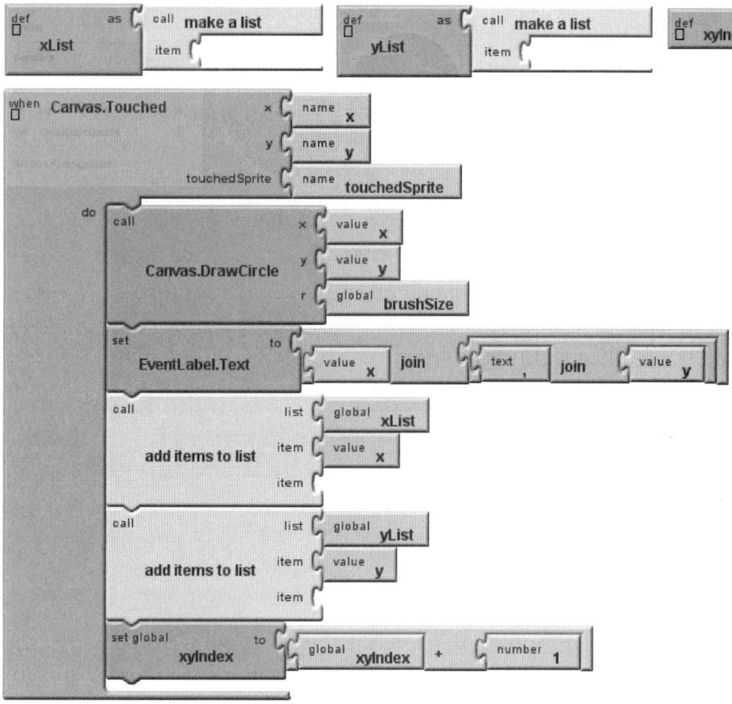

Figure 11.18 Saving the position of the dots in the order they are painted

To delete the dots step by step, we paint over each individual dot with a dot in the background color, but this time in reverse order. This happens in the event handler `UndoButton.Click` shown in Figure 11.19, where the following statements are carried out with each new press of the Undo button. Initially, the paint color `Canvas.PaintColor` is set to the background color "Light Gray," and the method `Canvas.DrawCircle` uses this color to draw a dot onto the coordinates saved in the lists at the current index position `xyIndex`. Once this is done, the last coordinate value is deleted from the lists via the method `remove list item`, the index `xyIndex` is reduced by 1, and the paint color `Canvas.PaintColor` is reset to the default color black.

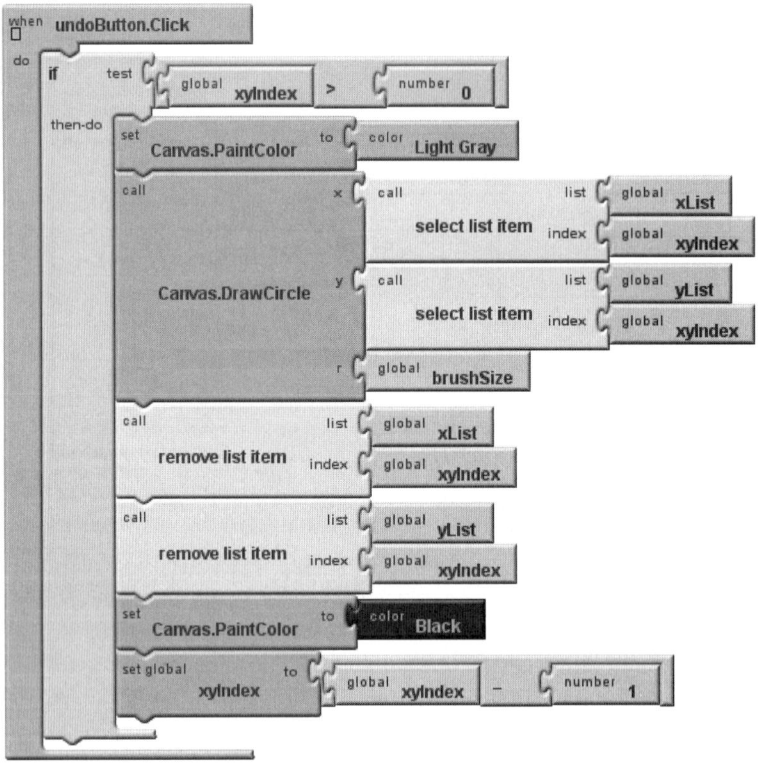

Figure 11.19 Painting over and deleting the dots in reverse order

This process is repeated with every press of the Undo button until the `xyIndex` is 0, the lists are empty, and the canvas is cleared of all dots. The user can switch between adding and undoing dots at will. All new dots are added to the lists dynamically and seamlessly taken into consideration during all Undo actions. Have a go and try it yourself in the app Painter.

In a similar way, we could dynamically save and undo the line drawings in the event handler `Dragged`. In this case, the coordinate pairs for each individual dot of a line would have to be saved, so the amount of data would be much larger. Once such curves are saved in lists, however, you can use them for other purposes. For example, you could use them as *animation paths*, on which a graphic object could move across the canvas—a procedure commonly used in modern animation programs. Thus you could use AI to develop an app in which a user draws an animation path with his or her finger and a graphic object then moves along that same path—a fascinating idea. Before we explore this app, let's first see how animations are possible at all with AI.

Animations with the Ball and ImageSprite Components

Often directly based on the methods of computer graphics, the animation of graphic objects has a special attraction for many computer users and, of course, for smartphone users. Like the graphics functions, the animation functions found within AI are mostly appropriate for the current performance of reasonably priced average smartphones and cannot compete in any way with the extremely compute-intensive 3D real-time graphics of modern PC games. The animation in AI currently uses only two dimensions, but once more the principle applies that what counts is mostly the good idea behind it and the appropriate implementation of an app with 2D animation. As part of a "retro" movement, simple 2D computer games are currently enjoying a renaissance, particularly on the less powerful smartphones. For example, in the forefather of all computer games, the game *Pong,* published in 1972 by Atari, a ball is played back and forth between two vertically movable bars (Ping Pong) just as in a tennis game.

For developing 2D animations, AI offers a dedicated component group, Animation, which consists of only two components. These components have a multitude of powerful blocks whose functionality goes beyond the pure animation function. The two components and their properties are largely identical, except that the Ball component is primarily a geometric 2D object (round disk), whereas the ImageSprite component is any 2D image. Both can be animated, among other things.

> **The Term "Sprite" in Computer Graphics**
>
> The term "sprite" in computer graphics refers to a flat 2D image or 2D graphic object that is moved against a graphic background, similar to the mouse pointer in a Windows system. To be able to calculate sprites quickly even on weak processors, these objects usually correspond to a simple rectangular shape, which can be made to appear with any outline thanks to transparent areas, similar to app icons on the smartphone. Apart from the low processor load they impose, sprites are characterized by automatic collision detection and overlaying with other sprites or graphic objects. Sprites were used mainly in the early days of graphic computer games and are still used today in combination with 3D games. You can find a good overview of the history of sprites in computer graphics here:
>
> `http://en.wikipedia.org/wiki/Sprite_%28computer_graphics%29`

The two Animation components differ only in their specific properties, which reflect the type of the graphic objects to be animated. For example, in the Ball component, you can set the radius (Radius) and color (PaintColor) of the disc, whereas in the ImageSprite component, you can load any image file (Picture) and determine its center (X, Y) and size (Width, Height). If you consider that you can also load the image of a disk of any color into an ImageSprite component and change its size using the Width and Height properties, the differences almost completely disappear, especially given that the specification of the ball component incorporate the notion of a round sprite. Thus, if you happen to want to animate a round disc, use the Ball component; in all other cases, use the ImageSprite component. Figure 11.20 shows the specification of the Ball component. If you would like to read the complete text and the almost identical specification of the ImageSprite component, please go to the AI References.

Ball

A ball component is a particular kind of sprite (animated object) that looks like a ball.

A ball is a round sprite that is contained by a canvas, can react to touches and drags, interact with other sprites (image sprites and other balls) and the edge of the canvas, and move according to its properties. For example, to have a ball move 4 pixels toward the top of a canvas every 500 milliseconds (half second), you can set the `Speed` property to 4, the `Interval` property to 500, the `Heading` property to 90 (degrees), and the `Enabled` property to True. You can change these and other properties to modify the ball's behavior.

The difference between a ball and an image sprite is that the latter can get its appearance from an image, while a ball's appearance can only be changed by varying its `PaintColor` and `Radius` properties.

Properties

`Radius`
: Radius of the ball.

`PaintColor`
: Color used for drawing the ball.

`Enabled`
: If true, ball is active.

`Interval`
: Frequency of ball's movement in milliseconds.

`Visible`
: If set, ball is visible.

`Heading`
: Direction of the ball's travel.

`X`
: Ball's x-coordinate.

`Y`
: Ball's y-coordinate.

`Speed`
: Number of pixels ball moves each period.

Events

`CollidedWith(component other)`
: Called when two animated components (image sprites or balls) hav component in the collision.

`Dragged(number startX, number startY, number prevX, n currentY)`
: The ball was dragged. See the canvas `Dragged` event for a descri

`EdgeReached(number edge)`
: Called when ball reaches the edge of the screen. The `edge` argume follows:
- north = 1
- northeast = 2
- east = 3
- southeast = 4
- south = -1
- southwest = -2
- west = -3
- northwest = -4

Note that opposite directions are negations of each other.

`NoLongerCollidingWith(component other)`
: Called when two animated components have stopped colliding.

`Touched(number x, number y)`
: Called when user touches the ball.

Methods

`Bounce(number edge)`
: Makes the ball bounce, as if off a wall (or corner). The meaning of the argument is the same as in `EdgeReached`. You can set up the `EdgeReached` event to make the ball bounce off whichever edge was reached, causing the ball to appear to bounce elastically from all edges and corners.

`boolean CollidingWith(component other)`
: Reports whether this ball is colliding with the given component.

`MoveIntoBounds()`
: If the ball is out of bounds, this method moves it back in bounds.

`MoveTo(number x,number y)`
: Moves the ball directly to the given point.

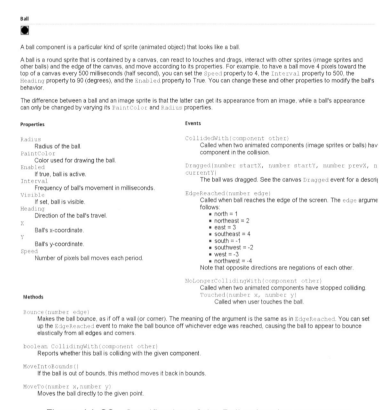

Figure 11.20 Specification of the Ball animation component

If you have prior experience with designing animations outside of AI, you take note of the special approach to animation in AI. The animation mechanisms in many 3D animation tools are present as independent and neutral tools; in AI, however, they are directly and solely linked to the two graphic objects Ball and ImageSprite (an exception will be mentioned in the section on the Clock component). The animation functions of AI are directly integrated into the graphic objects and not applied to them from the outside. Even if the result is similar, the approach is different.

General Basic Principles of Computer Animation

In computer animation, the properties of a graphic object change over time. In addition to the position, these changed properties may include the size, shape, or color of a graphic object. The speed of the animation depends on the size of the change per time unit, such as the number of pixels moved per second in an animation of the X, Y position of a moving graphic object. The bigger the change (Speed) and the smaller the time unit (Interval), the higher the overall speed.

The general basic principles of computer animation also apply to the two animation components of AI, but we can animate the X,Y position only using their Speed and Interval properties. To demonstrate these and the other functions of the animation components shown in Figure 11.20, we will introduce these components in a step-by-step fashion within an example project, the two-dimensional graphics game Squash shown in Figure 11.21. This example game resembles the original arcade game *Pong* in terms of its optical appearance, controls, and underlying idea. In the 2D squash field, the user can play the round ball against the wall and over the lines with the rectangular racquet and score points for every hit. The game speed adapts dynamically to the player's skill.

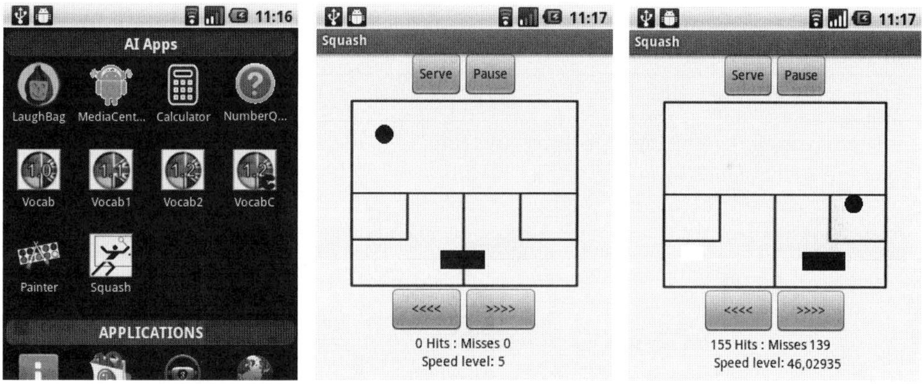

Figure 11.21 Interactive 2D game Squash as target project

Project Squash on the Companion Website

The files for the Squash project can be found on the companion website in the usual directories.

Create a new project with the name "Squash" and place the components shown in Table 11.2 with the specified basic settings into the AI Designer's Viewer. Drag the two animation components Ball and RacquetSprite directly to the desired starting position on the FieldCanvas, as shown in Figure 11.21 (center).

Table 11.2 **Components and Initial Properties for the Squash Game**

Component	**Object Name**	**Adapted Properties**
Screen	Screen1	"Icon": squash_applcon.png (companion website see `/MEDIA`)
Button (2x)	ServeButton, PauseButton	"Text": Serve, Pause
Canvas	FieldCanvas	"Width", "Height": 250 × 200 pixels "BackgroundImage": squash.png (companion website see `/MEDIA`)
Ball	Ball	"X","Y": any position on the canvas "Radius": 10
ImageSprite	RacquetSprite	"Picture": bar.png (companion website see`/MEDIA`) "X", "Y": 100, 160
Button (2x)	LeftButton, RightButton	"Text": <<<<, >>>>
Label	Label1	"Text": hits : misses
Label (2x)	HitsLabel, MissesLabel	"Text": 0, 0
Label	Label2	"Text": Speed level
Label	SpeedLabel	"Text": 5

After creating the components listed in Table 11.2, the user interface of the Squash project in AI Designer should look like Figure 11.22.

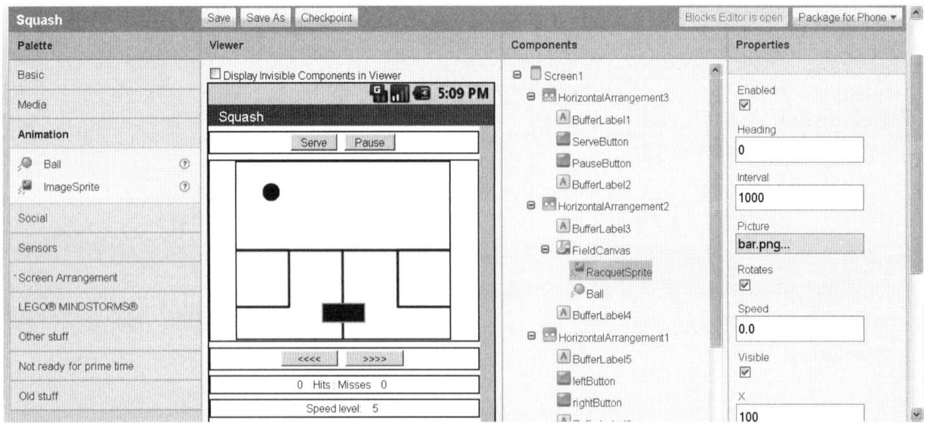

Figure 11.22 User interface and initial properties in the Squash project

Of course, achieving the centered alignment of the individual components requires using appropriate HorizontalArrangement components and BufferLabels, as you should recognize from earlier projects. Add these items on your own to create the appearance shown in Figure 11.22. Once all of these static design preparations are complete, we can begin creating the animation.

Moving Graphic Objects

To move a graphic object (Ball or ImageSprite) across the screen and thereby animate it, we do not even require the AI Blocks Editor for the first step. We can make the two animation components move by setting the initial properties in AI Designer. We just need a Canvas component, in whose boundaries the graphic object can be moved with pixel accuracy in relation to its X,Y position. Similar to the process of drawing with dots and lines on a canvas, the movement range of a graphic object is determined by the area of the Canvas component used, the dimensions of which can be specified at will. In our Squash project, we carry out the animation itself wholly on the basis of the two component objects Ball and FieldCanvas. The movement of the animation object Ball is determined by the following properties:

- Initial position (X,Y)
- Direction (Heading)
- Speed
    - Step size (Speed)
    - Step interval (Interval)

You have already determined the *initial position* of the component object Ball by dragging it into the Viewer and placing it onto the area of the FieldCanvas. In the two Ball properties X and Y, the corresponding 2D position was automatically recorded in the coordinate system of FieldCanvas. For example, if you placed the Ball at the exact center of the FieldCanvas, it would have the initial position 125, 100, as you can see in the schematic representation in Figure 11.23 (left). If you move the ball in the Viewer, the coordinates are automatically adapted accordingly.

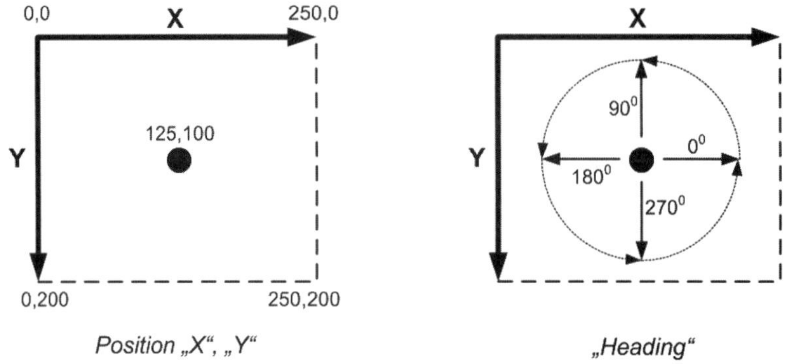

Figure 11.23 Initial position and heading of the animated component Ball

For the Ball to be able to move away from its initial position, you must specify a *direction* in the Heading property field. The direction is specified in the familiar degrees, within the range of 0° to 360°. A movement to the right corresponds to 0°, directly upward is 90°, to the left is 180°, and directly downward is 270°; all other headings can be specified with the appropriate number of degrees in between these values, as shown in the schematic representation in Figure 11.23 (right). The initial value of the component object Ball is a heading value of 0, so it would be moving to the right.

Before our ball can move to the right from its initial position, however, we must specify a *speed* for its movement. The speed of an animation movement results from two factors, comparable to the speed of a walking person. The bigger the *step size* and the shorter the temporal *step interval*, the more quickly the walking person moves in terms of miles per hour (mph) or kilometers per hour (km/h). The same relationship applies to the movement of the animation object on the pixel background: The bigger the step size in the Speed property and the shorter the step interval in the Interval property, the more quickly the animated graphic object moves in the comparable measurement of pixels per millisecond (p/ms).

The animation speed results from the product of the two factors (Speed × Interval). Thus, if one of the two factors has the value 0, the overall speed is also zero ($0 \times x = 0$). This is the reason why our component object Ball is not yet moving after we created it. Because although the step frequency in the Interval property is set to one step per second (1 second = 1000 milliseconds), the step size in the Speed property is still set to the value 0, so the total speed is zero pixels per second, which is equivalent to not moving. If you set the step size in the Speed property to a value of, for example, 5, the Ball starts moving to the right with a speed of 5 pixels per second, as you see on the integrated emulator or smartphone (see also the schematic representation in Figure 11.24). You can then vary the animation movement as you wish through the combined setting of the two factors. For instance, you might make the movement more fluid and slower by decreasing the step size or more bouncy and faster by increasing the step size.

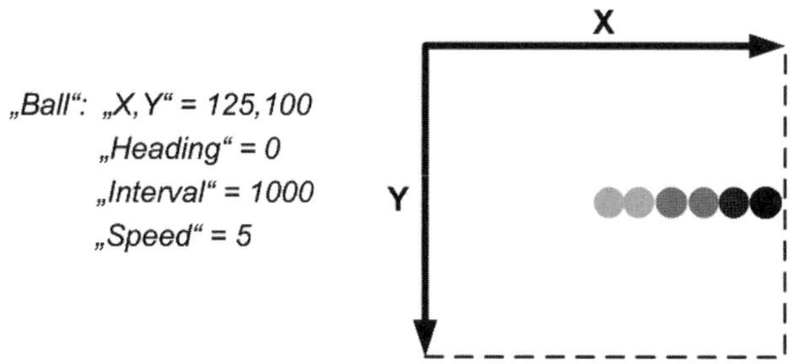

Figure 11.24 Animation of Ball from XY position 125,100 to the right with 5 p/s

Try out several settings for the animation parameters in Figure 11.24, to get a better feel for the fine-tuning of the animation movements. You can also try dropping the Ball from the center downward (Heading = 270) or letting it move diagonally across the FieldCanvas (Heading = 225), combined with different speeds and step sizes.

Collision Detection

Once the Ball reaches one of the edges of FieldCanvas, it stops and stays in that spot. To make the animation continue—in other words, to make the ball bounce off the wall like a squash ball—we must implement this behavior in AI Editor. Before the desired behavior can be achieved, the ball reaching the wall or colliding with one of the edges of the FieldCanvas first has to trigger a corresponding event. For detecting collisions between an animation object and the edges of the underlying canvas object or other animation objects, AI offers corresponding event blocks for both animation object types. Thus, if we want the ball in our squash game to bounce off any of the walls, we can use the event block `EdgeReached` in the Ball component blocks, as shown in Figure 11.25.

Figure 11.25 The animated ball bounces off the side walls

If the animation object `Ball` reaches an edge, the event handler `Ball.EdgeReached` shown in Figure 11.25 is called and passed the hit wall or corner as an encoded numeric value in the local variable with the default name `edge`. The edges or corners of the surrounding canvas object are encoded as shown in Table 11.3.

Table 11.3 **Number Code for Touched Edge or Corner**

Code	Touched Edge	Code	Touched Corner
1	top (north)	2	top right (northeast)
3	right (east)	4	bottom right (southeast)
-1	bottom (south)	-2	bottom left (southwest)
-3	left (west)	-4	top left (northwest)

Once the touched edge is recorded in the event handler `Ball.EdgeReached` via the local variable `edge`, the program can react with the corresponding statements. In Figure 11.25, we use the Ball method `Bounce`, which ensures that the animation object `Ball` bounces back in an angle appropriate to the collision angle and the animation continues appropriately or indefinitely within the canvas limits. Try out this function by implementing the short event handler shown in Figure 11.25 in the Squash project. If you have kept the animation settings shown in Figure 11.24, the ball should now move endlessly between the right and left edges of the canvas object, as shown in Figure 11.26 (left), and as you can see on the integrated emulator or smartphone.

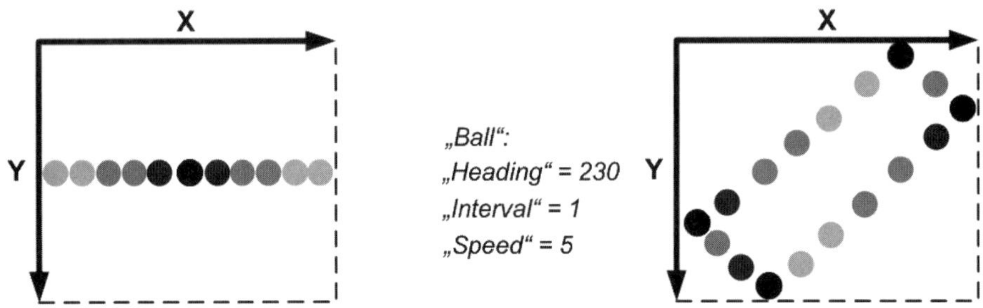

Figure 11.26 Horizontal and diagonal bouncing off the side edges

To make the movement of the `Ball` object more closely resemble that of a squash ball, you can alter the settings for the animation accordingly. For example, if you change the initial settings in AI Designer to those shown in Figure 11.26 (right), the ball will move quite realistically between the edges of the playing field.

Now that we have animated the basic movement of the squash ball, we want to turn to the squash racquet, which you have previously placed into the playing field as the black bar RacquetSprite. The purpose of a racquet is to send the ball upward, without letting the ball touch the bottom edge of the playing field. Up to now the ball has simply passed right through the racquet, ignoring it if the racquet happened to be in its way. We now want to change this behavior to make the ball bounce off the racquet upward and to allow the user to move the racquet across the playing field, just as in a real squash game.

For the racquet movement, we have two alternatives, both of which we will implement. For the first variation, we use an approach that you have encountered earlier in the painting program. Just as we dragged our finger to paint lines onto the canvas, so we can now use the ImageSprite event block `Dragged` to drag a graphic object across the canvas field, thereby moving the object. The event block `RacquetSprite.Dragged` provides the familiar coordinates during dragging, which we can then use as local variables in the statements of the event handler. For our squash game, we use the current X,Y finger position (`currentX`, `currentY`), to place the RacquetSprite at that position by setting its X and Y properties (see Figure 11.27). Try it out by implementing the event handler `RacquetSprite.Dragged`; tap the black bar on your integrated emulator or smartphone and then drag it over the playing field.

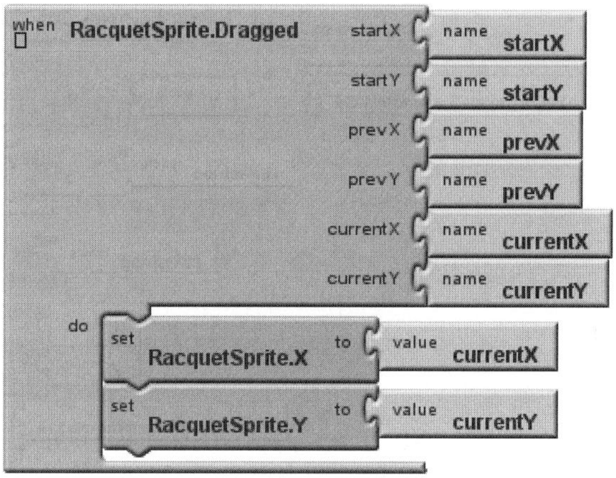

Figure 11.27 Dragging the squash racquet over the playing field with your finger

For the second variant, we use two control buttons, LeftButton and RightButton, that move the racquet horizontally over the playing field. Starting from the X,Y position 125,160 (the initial values of the global variables `goX`, `goY`), the value for the X position (`goX`) is decreased or increased by 30 pixels each time the button is pressed in the event handler `LeftButton.Click` or `RightButton.Click`, as long as the left (`goX > 10`) or right (`goX < 240`) canvas edge has not yet been reached. In the ImageSprite method `MoveTo`, the RacquetSprite is repositioned on the playing field with each press of the button. Try out these two event handlers of Figure 11.28 as well, and move the racquet via the two control buttons.

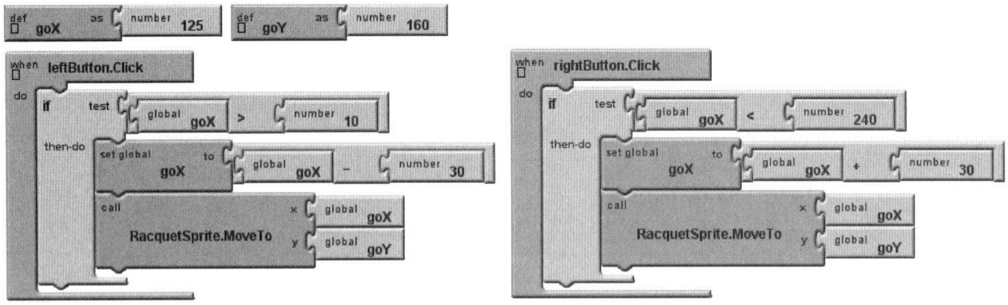

Figure 11.28 Moving the squash racquet via the two control buttons

Now that we have two options for moving the squash racquet on the playing field, we want to be able to play the ball back with it. Up to now, the ball has behaved as if the racquet did not have strings; that is, the ball moved right through it. Just as with the edge collision detection when the ball touches the canvas edges, we now need to detect the collision between the two animation objects `Ball` and `RacquetSprite`. Instead of the `EdgeReached` event block, we now use a `CollidedWith` event block. In its local variable with the default name `other`, the name of the colliding component is passed. The event handler `RacquetSprite.CollidedWith` shown in Figure 11.29 is then called when the ball hits the racquet, and the name of the component object `Ball` is passed as well.

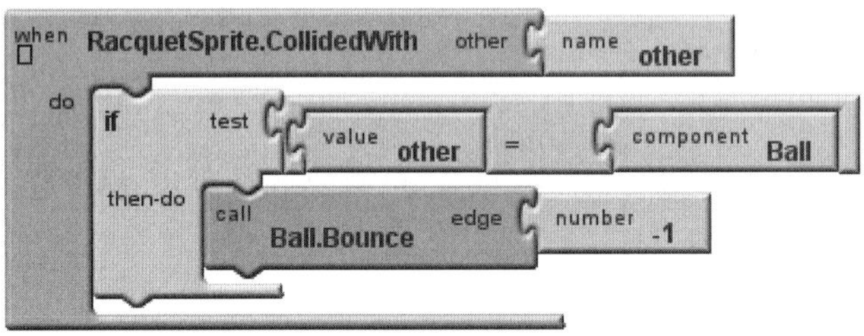

Figure 11.29 Playing the ball back with the squash racquet

Although our squash game includes only two graphic objects that can collide with each other, we want to embed the reaction to the collision with the `Ball` object (My Blocks > Ball > component Ball) into the conditional `if` statement shown in Figure 11.29. This would make it possible to distinguish between collisions with different animation objects. For example, if the `RacquetSprite` object collides with a graphic object and this object is the `Ball`, we want it to bounce back as if from the bottom canvas wall (code `-1`; see Table 11.3) via the method `Ball.Bounce`.

With this event handler, the basic functionality of our squash game is now almost complete. Have a go: You should be able to play the ball off the edges with the racquet.

The only things still missing are typical game elements such as a score counter and difficulty level, plus the functions of the remaining buttons in the squash game.

A 2D Squash Game with Dynamic Animation

To make a game interesting and entertaining even over a longer period of time, random events and a dynamically adapted difficulty level can help surprise the player anew and keep posing a challenge even if the user has gained gaming experience. To a modest extent, we want to achieve this effect in our squash game as well, by providing a random ball serve at the start and dynamically adapting the animation speed and, therefore, the game to the player's skill level. The skill level is measured using the relation of hits (the ball bounces off the racquet) to misses (the ball bounces off the back wall; code `-1`). If the player mostly hits the ball and misses only rarely, we can assume that he or she has mastered the game at this speed. To make the game less boring, pose a challenge, and keep the player interested in the game, we want the ball speed to increase. If the player then misses more often than he or she hits the ball, we want to reduce the speed again to prevent the player from becoming frustrated and quitting the game. With this approach, we adapt the game's difficulty level dynamically to the training level of the player, thereby providing a constant incentive to keep playing. Although the implementation in our squash game is rather simple, this basic principle is present in many games that fascinate their players sufficiently to spend days and nights in front of the PC and provide a stimulus to keep on playing.

To expand our Squash project and add this dynamic behavior—that is, recording the score and linking it to the animation speed—we first need to add the variable shown in Figure 11.30 to the existing project and initialize it. The variable `speed` manages the current speed, `minSpeed` determines the minimum speed (2 p/ms), `Hits` records the number of hits, and `misses` records the number of misses. We initialize the two score counters with the value 1, to prevent errors caused by dividing by 0 in calculating the speed later. As the `Ball` object should stay still both when the app is launched and each time the Pause button is pressed, we create a separate procedure `reset` for resetting the two speed parameters `Ball.Speed` and `Ball.Interval`; this reset procedure can then be called both by the event handler `Screen1.Initialize` and by `PauseButton.Click`. The movement interval is set to the value 1 (once per millisecond), to make the movement as fluid as possible.

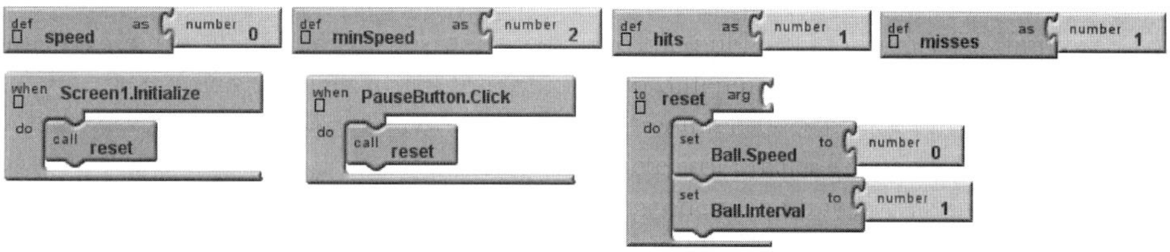

Figure 11.30 Initial values for the squash game

Next we implement the surprise factor: The first serve of the squash ball should come in from a random position at the top edge of the canvas, and at a random angle that can have an effect on the success of the whole match. By pressing the Serve button and calling the event handler `ServeButton.Click` shown in Figure 11.31, the `Ball` object is first assigned the initial speed `Ball.Speed` from the variable `minSpeed` (2 p/ms), which is also displayed as the current speed level in the SpeedLabel. Then a random pixel position `Ball.X` at the top canvas edge is created via the method `random integer` and the `Ball` is placed at that point. Finally, a heading angle `Ball.Heading` between 200° and 340° is generated as a random number, so that the `Ball` now moves at a speed of 2 p/ms from a random position at the top canvas edge downward toward the racquet at a random angle.

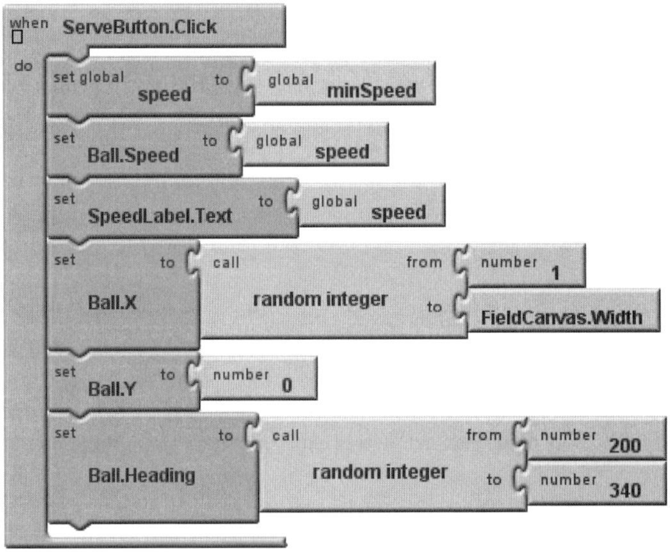

Figure 11.31 First serve of the ball with a random position and a random angle

After the random first serve is implemented, we want to implement the score counter (hits versus misses) for the game, which is then used to calculate the game speed level. We need to expand two existing event handlers. Let's start with the handler `RacquetSprite.CollidedWith` (Figure 11.29), with which we have already implemented playing the `Ball` object back with the `RacquetSprite` object. In the expanded version of Figure 11.32, the counter value in `hits` is now also increased by 1 and displayed in the HitsLabel when the two graphic objects collide. Based on this new number, the speed value is recalculated in the variable `speed`, resulting from a simple calculation of the old speed `speed` plus the value of the quotient from `hits` divided by `misses` [new `speed` = old `speed` + (`hits` / `misses`)]. The higher the number of hits in relation to the misses, the higher the resulting speed. The new and *increased* speed value `speed` is then assigned to `Ball.Speed` and displayed in the SpeedLabel.

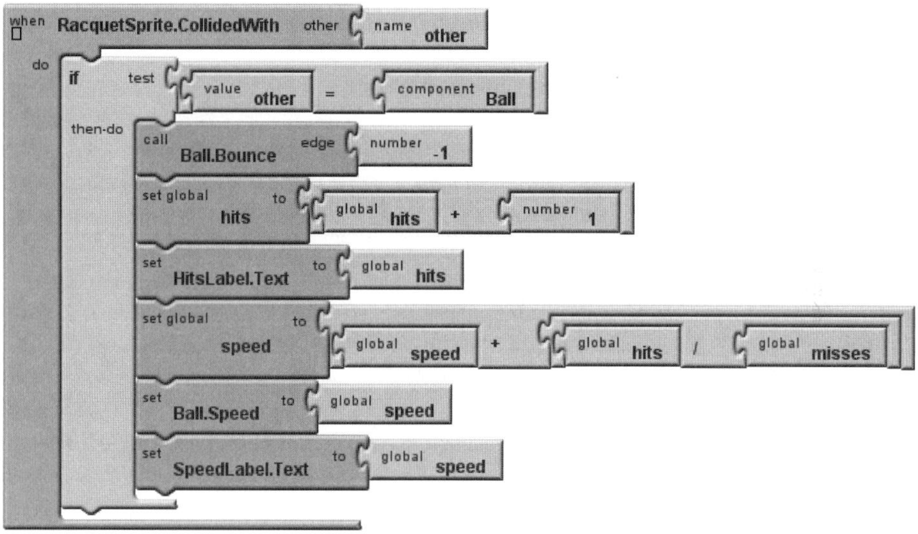

Figure 11.32 Playing the ball back and increasing the number of hits and speed

In a similar way, we can expand the originally very short event handler `Ball.EdgeReached` (Figure 11.25), with which we had implemented the bouncing back of the `Ball` object from the side walls of the canvas. In the expanded version shown in Figure 11.33, we add a nested construct to this event handler, consisting of two conditional `if` statements. Right now the event handler `Ball.EdgeReached` is called with each collision of `Ball` with *any* side wall or corner of the canvas object, but we want to respond only to a collision with the *bottom* back wall (code `-1`). Thus this starting condition (`edge = -1`) is checked with the first `if` statement. If the back wall was hit, the misses counter `misses` is incremented by 1 and displayed in the MissesLabel. To avoid reducing the game speed too much (down to no movement), the second `if` statement checks whether the current speed is larger than or equal to the minimum speed `minSpeed` (2 p/ms). If this is the case, the current value of the quotient of the `hits` is again divided by the `misses`, but this time we subtract it from the old speed value `speed`, to calculate the new speed. The new and *reduced* speed value `speed` is then assigned to `Ball.Speed` and displayed in the SpeedLabel.

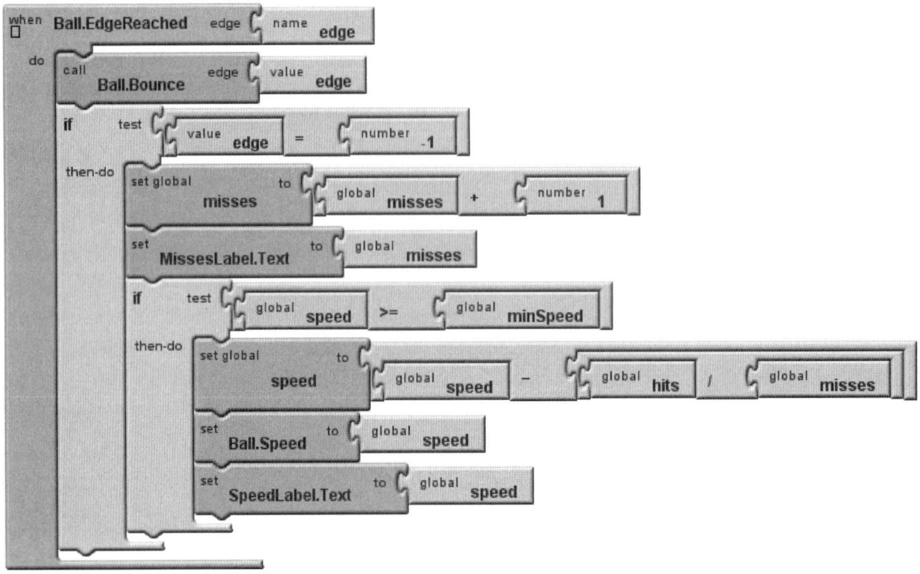

Figure 11.33 Increasing the number of misses in case of a miss and reducing the speed

Now we have fully implemented the dynamic and interactive gameplay of our 2D action game, Squash. The specific and individual course of the game then results only from the interaction with specific user and offers a remarkably high degree of flexibility and variety. It is really impressive how quickly and easily an animated 2D action game with dynamic gameplay can be implemented in AI.

Controlling Automatic Processes with the Clock Component

As mentioned earlier, the animation approach of AI is different from that taken by other animation tools, in that it integrates the animation mechanisms directly into the two graphics components, Ball and ImageSprite. As also mentioned, however, there is an exception to this rule, which makes it possible to animate graphic objects "from the outside" in AI, similar to the approach used in 3D animation programs. For this purpose, among others, AI offers the non-visible component Clock in the Basic group. Its timer function, TimerInterval, forms the central control element for animation and is essentially the external equivalent to the integrated property Interval of the two graphics components described previously. Like a real timer, the Timer property of the Clock component generates events itself in regular intervals; these events can be used universally, not just for fixed step intervals in connection with a step size.

The regular intervals of the events created result from the system clock of your computer or smartphone, whose smallest measurable time unit in AI is 1 millisecond. Thus you can use the timer in AI to generate an event per millisecond (interval `1`), or per second (interval `1000`), per minute (interval `60000`), or per hour, day, month, year, or any other time interval. To what extent a graphic object is moved, enlarged, or otherwise changed per time unit is entirely up to you as developer; the same is true when an e-mail account is checked, an hourly sound effect played, or a geoposition is recorded. Moreover, you use the Clock component to display the current time and date. As you can see, it's a very flexible component, whose basic, generic function supports the development of many kinds of *automated* processes where the factor of time plays a role. Let's have a look at the specification of the component Clock in Figure 11.34.

Clock

Clock1

Use a clock component to create a timer that signals events at regular intervals. The clock component also does various conversions and manipulations with time units.

One use of the clock component is a a *timer*: set the timer interval, and the timer will fire repeatedly at the interval, signalling a timer event.

A second use of the clock component is to manipulate time, and express time in various units. The internal time format used by the clock is called an *instant*. The clock's `Now` method returns the current time as an instant. The clock provides methods to manipulate instants, for example, return an instant that is several seconds, or months, or years from the given instant. It also provides methods to show the second, minute, hour, day, ..., corresponding to a given instant.

Properties

`TimerInterval`
timer interval in milliseconds
`TimerEnabled`
If true, then the timer will fire
`TimerAlwaysFires`
if true, the timer will fire even if the application is not showing on the screen

Events

`Timer()`
This event is signaled when the timer fires

Methods

`SystemTime()`
The phone's internal time in milliseconds
`Now()`
The instant in time read from phone's clock
`MakeInstant(Text from)`
Make an instant specified by MM/DD/YYYY hh:mm:ss or MM/DD/Y
`MakeInstantFromMillis(Number millis)`
Make an instant specified by time in milliseconds
`GetMillis(instant)`
The instant in time measured as milliseconds since 1970
`AddSeconds(instant, Number seconds)`
An instant in time some number of seconds after the given instant
`AddMinutes(instant, Number minutes)`
An instant in time some number of minutes after the given instant
`AddHours(instant, Number hours)`
An instant in time some number of hours after the given instant
`AddDays(instant, Number days)`
An instant in time some number of days after the given instant
`AddWeeks(instant, Number weeks)`
An instant in time some number of weeks after the given instant
`AddMonths(instant, Number months)`
An instant in time some number of months after the given instant
`AddYears(instant, Number years)`
An instant in time some number of years after the given instant
`Duration(Calendar start, Calendar end)`
Milliseconds between instants

`Second(Calendar instant)`
The second of the minute
`Minute(Calendar instant)`
The minute of the hour
`Hour(Calendar instant)`
The hour of the day
`DayOfMonth(Calendar instant)`
The day of the month,a number from 1 to 31
`Weekday(Calendar instant)`
The day of the week. a number from 1 (Sunday) to 7 (Sa
`WeekdayName(Calendar instant)`
The name of the day of the week
`Month(Calendar instant)`
The month of the year, a number from 1 to 12)
`MonthName(Calendar instant)`
The name of the month
`Year(Calendar instant)`
The year
`FormatDateTime(Calendar instant)`
Text describing the date and time of an instant
`FormatDate(Calendar instant)`
Text describing the date of an instant
`FormatTime(Calendar instant)`
Text describing time time of an instant

Figure 11.34 Specification of the Clock component in the AI References

As you can see in Figure 11.34, the Clock component has a multitude of methods. The number of event and property blocks, by comparison, is rather manageable. For example, there is only one single event block `Timer`, in which you embed the statements that are to be triggered in a regular sequence. The timer interval is specified in the TimerInterval property, as usual in milliseconds, and you can use the Boolean property TimerEnabled to switch the timer on and off. Interestingly, you have the option of keeping the timer running via the Boolean property TimerAlwaysFires, even when the app is not actively displayed in the foreground. As a consequence, you can trigger time-controlled events even in the background, which can be useful for an alarm clock, for example, or for checking your e-mails regularly. Thus the user can work with other apps or keep the smartphone in standby mode, yet still be woken up at the specified time.

Almost all of the numerous Clock options relate to the topic of time, and two of the methods can be used to retrieve the current system time. The method `SystemTime` outputs the time passed since January 1, 1970, in milliseconds. This decimal representation of time values makes it possible and easy to perform calculations involving time intervals—for example, setting a timer to ring in 5 minutes or jumping back 1 month in the calendar. For calculating time intervals, the Clock component offers methods such as `Duration` (calculate the interval between two points in time), `AddYears`, `AddMonths`, `AddWeeks`, `AddDays`, `AddHours`, `AddMinutes`, and `AddSeconds`.

System Time in Milliseconds Since 1970

For historical reasons, the system time on digital systems such as the computer or the smartphone is measured and managed internally in milliseconds passed since January 1, 1970, 00:00 o'clock in the coordinated world time UTC (Universal Time Code). Adoption of this standard ensures that systems connected in a worldwide network always have the same time, which makes synchronous communication processes possible in the first place. For converting the system time into a format that humans can read, each programming language generally provides appropriate functions, and AI does so in the form of instants.

With the method `Now`, the system time is returned as an *instant*—that is, in a time and date format that humans can readily understand. An instant cannot be directly displayed in a label, but must be formatted first with appropriate methods such as `FormatDateTime` as a time–date combination (`Feb 3, 2011, 11:45:00 AM`), separated via `FormatDate` or `FormatTime`, or split into its time elements via `Year`, `Month`, `Weekday`, `Hour`, `Minute`, or `Second` before it can be displayed. Additionally, it is possible to convert between the two time formats with the method `MakeInstantFromMillis` or `GetMillis` or to convert readable text specifications (for example, `16:10` or `03/01/2011, 16:45:00`) to instants with `MakeInstant`.

External Control of Animations

If you have read the previous explanations of animation with AI, you can imagine the great potential implied by the heading of this section. With the Clock component, you can animate *any* properties of visible component objects—not just their position, size, and orientation, but also their color, labeling, texture, and so on—as long as the properties are either numeric values or other data elements in a list structure; you can change these properties based on the intervals of the timer or retrieve them one by one. This makes it possible, for example, to simulate moving pictures or sprites by showing them in order from a list of individual pictures on an Image or ImageSprite component, just as with a movie, which is also made up of numerous individual pictures. As we have mainly been concentrating on animating graphic objects by changing their positions (the only option with internally controlled animations), we now want to illustrate the differences between internal and external animation control by demonstrating the manipulation of the position values *from the outside* with the Clock component.

> **Files for Project Animation on the Companion Website**
>
> You can find the files for the Animation project on the companion website in the usual directories.

We want to build on the user interface and functionality of an existing app project, the painting project described earlier in this chapter. Go to AI Designer; in My Projects, load the Painter project and save a copy (Save As) under the new project name "Animation." The aim is to demonstrate three different animations with the Clock component on the existing canvas object. The first animation is reminiscent of the squash example game, not least because of the always constant shape of the animation object `Ball`. Now, however, the movement and speed of the ball will no longer remain constant, but rather the ball will move in a curve with an almost exponential increase in speed. Perhaps this description seems rather theoretical, but it simply describes the falling of a ball from a wall to the floor and, therefore, resembles a movement simulation involving approximately the real laws of physics. In Figure 11.35 (left), the progress of the falling movement is schematically represented to make things clearer: At the beginning, the ball slips slowly over the edge of the wall, drops faster and faster until it hits the floor, slowly rolls into a hole, and then falls off the wall once more.

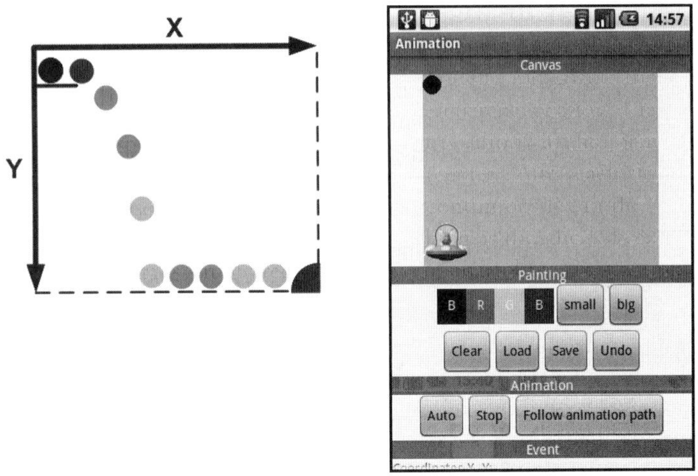

Figure 11.35 Movement simulation represented schematically and in the Animation app

In Figure 11.35 (right), you can see the expanded interface of the Animation project. To create it based on the existing interface of the painting program, simply expand the components of the painting program (see Table 11.1) with the additional components shown in Table 11.4.

Table 11.4 **Additional Components and Properties in the Animation Project**

Component	Object Name	Adapted Properties
Screen	Screen1	"Icon": anim_applcon.png (companion website, see /MEDIA)
Clock	Clock	"TimerEnabled": disable "TimerInterval": 10
Clock	UfoClock	"TimerEnabled": disable "TimerInterval": 100
Ball	Ball	"Interval": 0 "Radius": 10
ImageSprite	UfoSprite	"Picture": ufo.png (companion website, see /MEDIA)
Label	DivisionLabel4	"Text": Animation
Button (3x)	AnimAutoButton, AnimStopButton, AnimPathButton	"Text": Auto, Stop, Follow animation path

With the additional component objects of Table 11.4, the Animation project should now look in AI Designer as shown in Figure 11.36. Place the two animation objects `Ball` and `UfoSprite` into the two suggested positions on the canvas object. (We will get to the `UfoSprite` later.) To make sure the animations are standing still when the app is launched, both component objects `Clock` and `UfoClock` should have the property TimerEnabled disabled in AI Designer. To achieve smoother movements, the timer interval should also be changed from the initial value of one event per second (`TimerInterval=1000`) to one event per tenth of a second (`TimerInterval=100`) for the `UfoSprite` and to one event per one-hundredth of a second (`TimerInterval=10`) for the `Ball`.

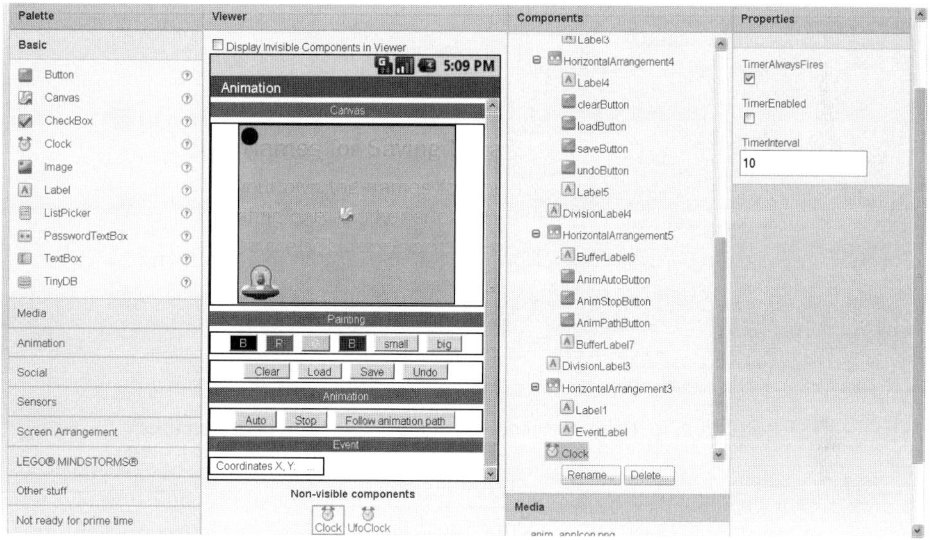

Figure 11.36 Additional components for the Animation project in AI Designer

After sorting out the settings in AI Designer, we are ready to implement the animations in AI Editor. Before we do so, we first determine the behavior of the two buttons, Auto and Stop, in their event handlers `AnimAutoButton` and `AnimStopButton`, with which the animation can be started and stopped. The starting and stopping of time-event generation with the timer `Clock` are carried out by assigning the Boolean values `true` and `false` to its property block `Clock.TimerEnabled`, as shown in Figure 11.37. The `Ball` object is placed into its starting position in the upper-left corner of the canvas object, as determined by the two global variables `posX` (=1) and `posY` (=1).

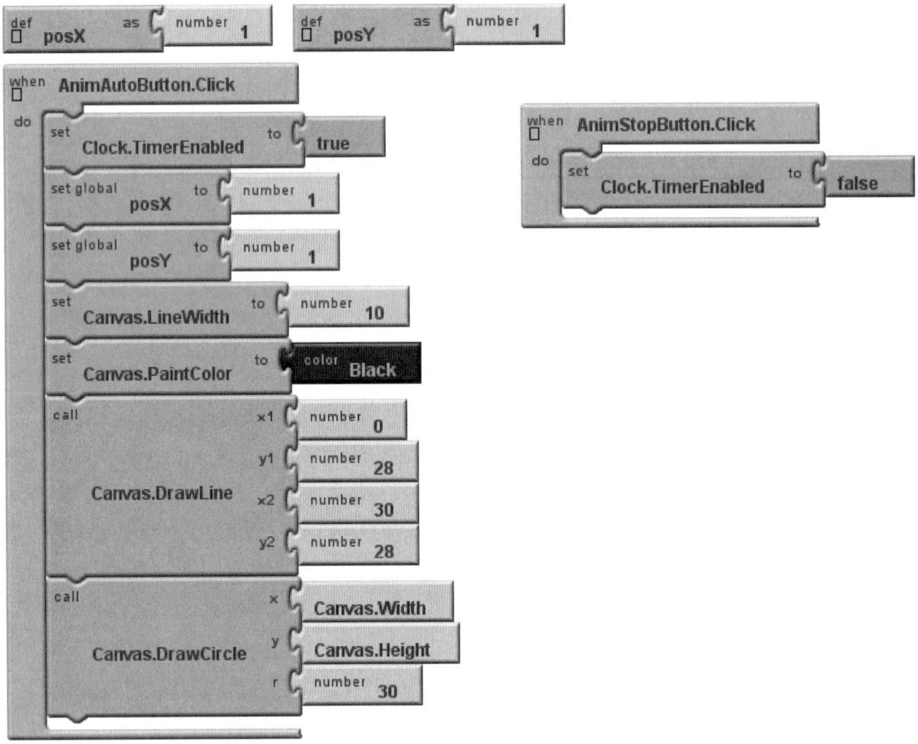

Figure 11.37 Painting scenery and starting or stopping animation

As we want the animation to happen against a "scenery" backdrop consisting of a wall and hole, we must draw these items on the canvas using appropriate instructions in the event handler `AnimAutoButton.Click` (Figure 11.37). We keep the scenery as simple as possible and use only `Canvas.DrawLine` to draw a little ledge at the upper-left corner and a hole in the lower-right corner with `Canvas.DrawCircle` (see also Figure 11.35, right). We can get rid of the scenery at any time by pressing the Clear button, but we want it to be redrawn every time the animation is started.

Now we can implement the animation of the graphic object `Ball` itself. We use the only event block available for the Clock component, `Clock.Timer` (Figure 11.38). This event handler is called with each interval of the timer of `Clock`—that is, every one-hundredth of a second (`TimerInterval=10`)—and all statements are run through each time. You should thoroughly understand this general principle: Depending on the interval to which you set the timer, the contained block structures can be run through and executed in either extremely short cycles or large intervals.

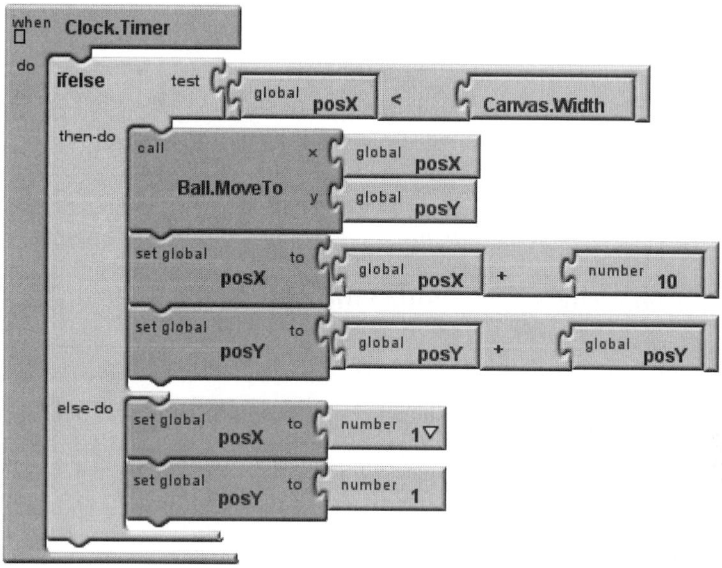

Figure 11.38 Infinite animation of a ball controlled via an external timer

The block structures in the event handler `Clock.Timer` shown in Figure 11.38 are all embedded within an `ifelse` branch. This achieves the infinite repetition of the animation, as long as the timer is running and not stopped by pressing the Stop button. As the initial condition, the `ifelse` branch checks whether the current X position `posX` is still smaller than the width of `Canvas`—in other words, whether the `Ball` object is still within the `Canvas` boundaries. If this is the case, the ball is placed onto the current X, Y position based on the coordinates `posX` and `posY`. Then, a new X,Y position is generated, shifted 10 pixels to the right (`posX + 10`) and twice as many pixels downward (`posY + posY`) in comparison to the previous animation cycle. In the next animation cycle, the `Ball` is placed onto that new position via the method `Ball.MoveTo` and another new position is generated. This cycle continues until the `Ball` has reached the right side of the `Canvas` (`Canvas.Width`), rendering the initial condition of the `ifelse` branch `false` and causing the statements in the `else-do` area to be executed. At that point, the X,Y position of `Ball` is set back to `1,1`, returning the ball to the ledge on the wall, and the animation can start all over again.

Make sure you understand the statements required for external animation of the ball, including the statements of the event handler `Clock.Timer`, and in particular the `then-do` area of the `ifelse` branch. As if with a remote control, this generates new coordinate pairs by which the `Ball` is then positioned. The movement of the `Ball` depends on the results of just the two calculation statements for recalculating the values of `posX` and `posY`. If `posY` were to increase by a constant value of 10 as well, the movement would look very different and would follow a linear diagonal. Because we are adding two increasing numbers, however, the distances from the preceding Y position become increasingly larger, which creates the impression of an increasing falling speed. As the `Canvas` object prevents graphic objects from being positioned outside of the `Canvas` boundaries, the ball continues to glide along the bottom `Canvas` edge despite the mathematically higher Y values, until the X position also reaches the `Canvas` edge; at that point, the X and Y positions are reset and the animation starts all over again.

Keyframe Animations with Your Finger

Perhaps you recall the fascinating idea we mentioned earlier of simply drawing an animation path onto the screen with your finger and getting a graphic object to follow that path. This is exactly the task that we will implement in this section, based on the list of paint dots created in the context of the Undo function implemented in the painting program. The X,Y positions dynamically generated by the user then provide the database with which to move a graphic object along this same coordinate path. This app also demonstrates an alternative to calculating animation data—namely, taking the data from an existing data list. If you consider that this method can be used in areas other than animation, such as for retrieval of data elements from a data structure in regular intervals, then the Clock component we use here really constitutes an incredibly powerful and flexible tool.

For demonstrating the animation from data lists, we will use the painting program as starting project, to which we have already added the necessary components for the Animation project shown in Table 11.4. As the graphic object to be animated, we will use the existing ImageSprite component object called `UfoSprite`, which we want to fly along the animation path marked by the paint dots. To design this animation independently of the quicker animation of the ball, we use a dedicated Clock component `UfoClock`, whose TimerInterval we have already set to `100` (one event per tenth of a second) in AI Editor.

After launching the Animation app, the user can place paint dots with his or her finger along the desired animation path, starting from the initial position of the UFO. Of course, the user can also make corrections via the already implemented Undo button and hide the dotted animation path with the Clear button. The longer the distances between the individual paint dots, the faster the movement will appear, as the UFO then covers a greater distance over the same time interval. The user can place the animation points to create any kind of movement and varying speeds. In this respect, the placement of the animation points resembles the creation of the intermediate points (*keyframes*) that are used in the professional animation method known as *keyframe animation*. In our variation, the definition of the animation path is even more comfortable and spectacularly easy.

Keyframe Animation

Professional animation programs often use an animation method called *keyframe animation*. For the animation of a graphic object, a time interval plus starting and ending points are specified, between which there can be any number of intermediate points (keyframes). The animated graphic object moves in regular time intervals from one keyframe to the next. The larger the distance between the keyframes, the faster the graphic object moves on that section of the path; the smaller the distance, the slower it moves. This way, you can realize animations with varying speeds on the animation paths.

In addition, the animation repeats itself when the user presses the button labeled "Follow animation path," until the button is pressed again. After reaching the last animation point, the graphic object jumps back seamlessly to the first animation point to continue the animation. The user can place the animation points cleverly to create a smooth infinite movement. In Figure 11.39, you can see a few examples of animation paths with varying speeds, closed loops of movement, and even a loop-the-loop.

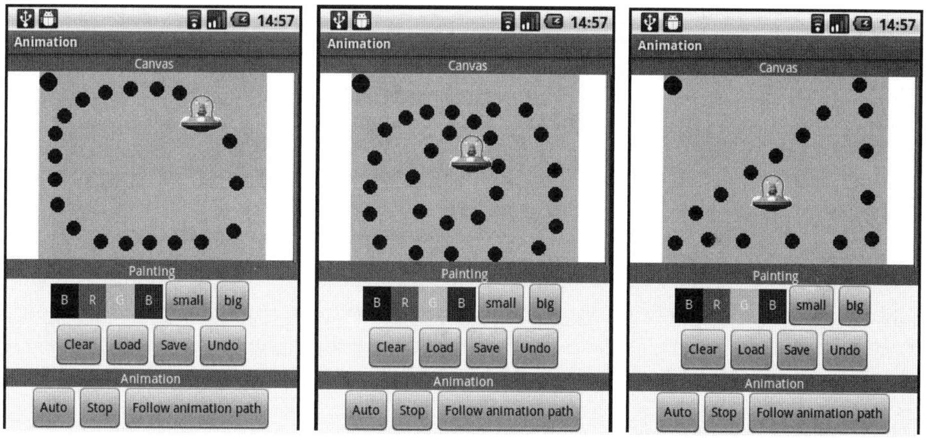

Figure 11.39 Different animation paths with varying speeds and loops

As we have already done some of the preparatory work in the painting program for placing and recording the list of dots, our changes in AI Editor remain comparatively modest despite the powerful new functionality we are adding (which again speaks to the enormous level of efficiency of the visual development language AI). Similar to the changes we made for the animation of the ball, we switch the timer for the UFO on and off via the Clock property `UfoClock.TimerEnabled`, but this time we use a single button, "Follow animation path." To achieve this two-way switching, we use an `ifelse` branch in the event handler `AnimPathButton.Click` shown in Figure 11.40, with which we always switch to the opposite of the Boolean value in the TimerEnabled property field. Thus, if TimerEnabled is set to the initial property `false` when the app is launched (see Table 11.4), the initial check of the `ifelse` branch triggers the execution of the statements in the `else-do` area—namely, assigning the value `true` and starting the timer or the animation. As TimerEnabled is now set to `true`, the next press of the button leads to the execution of the statements in the `then-do` area, which switch the timer off again. This cycle continues with each press of the button. Additionally, each press of the button sets the graphic object back to the first X,Y position (`animIndex=1`) of the animation lists.

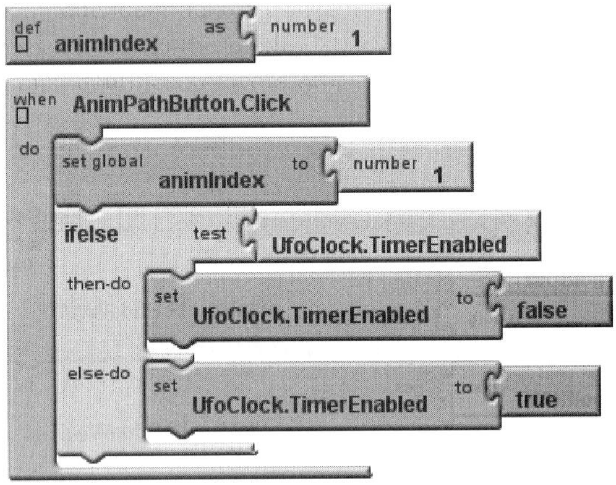

Figure 11.40 Switching keyframe animation on and off

This brings us to the actual animation of the graphic object `UfoSprite` via "remote control" from within the event handler `UfoClock.Timer`. Similar to the ball animation, we again embed the control of the UFO within the event handler shown in Figure 11.41 into an `ifelse` branch. Again, we check whether a limiting value has been reached each time the timer event is triggered; in this case, however, the limiting value is the last index position `xyIndex` in the current lists `xList` and `yList` (see the lists given earlier for saving the X and Y positions for the Undo function). If these two lists are filled with coordinates (i.e., if the index counter `xyList` is larger than 1), the initial condition of the `ifelse` branch is fulfilled and the first animation position can be retrieved via the `animIndex`, with X and Y coordinates from the lists `xList` and `yList`, and assigned to the `UfoSprite` via its method `UfoSprite.MoveTo`. Then the index counter `animIndex` is incremented by 1, so as to collect the X,Y coordinates of the next paint dot from the lists at the next timer event. This process continues until all items of the current lists have been read and the value of `animIndex` exceeds the value of `xyIndex`. Then, the `else-do` area of the `ifelse` branch is executed, in which the index counter `animIndex` is reset to the first list position 1 and the animation cycle begins all over again.

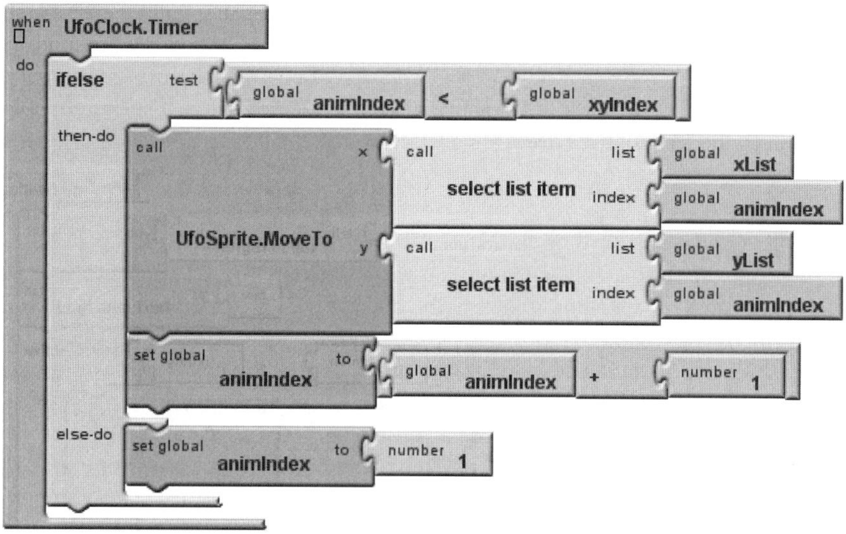

Figure 11.41 Executing, controlling, and repeating keyframe animation

For this example project, we also recommend that you try to consciously understand the rather complex processes underlying the keyframe animation based on the dynamic list elements. Even though the block structures in the Animation project are still rather manageable, the condensed statements contain a high density of processes that become comprehensible only through their interplay with other components, timer events, dynamic data structures, and a controlled process sequence. As mentioned earlier, the topic of computer graphics and animation is both fascinating and demanding, and we are able to give you only a quick glimpse of it in this book.

An Alarm Clock with Timer Events

As discussed earlier, the Clock component can be used not only to animate graphic objects but also to automatically execute other regularly occurring tasks. The connection between these two functions may not be immediately obvious, but displaying the time is also such a regularly occurring task. Although the Clock component might inherently seem to be associated with displaying the time due to its name and its multitude of time-related methods, this is not the case, as we saw in our explanations of the system time and instants. Rather, the system time is completely independent of the Clock component. To allow us to display the current time within an app with second accuracy, we first need to retrieve the time via a Clock component at least once per second (`TimerInterval=1000`). To make this connection and the general principle of time-controlled tasks clearer, we want to demonstrate the generic use of the Clock component by creating a clock with an alarm function. This example is also meant to give you an incentive for using this component in different contexts and conclude the topic of computer graphics and animation, providing a gentle transition to the topics following in the next chapter.

Files for Project Alarm Clock on the Companion Website

You can find the files for the project Alarm clock on the companion website in the usual directories.

With these noble objectives in mind, we want to display the current time and date in an example app, Alarm Clock. Depending on the system used, the time is displayed on an American emulator on a 12-hour clock with a.m. and p.m. (Figure 11.42, left) or on a European smartphone on a 24-hour clock (Figure 11.42, right). Once the alarm time is set, the alarm has to be switched on with the check box "alarm ON" to make sure it displays the text "ALARM!" at the set time and plays the sound effect. As an added bonus, the alarm app runs in the background. As a consequence, the user can work with other apps in the meantime or switch the cellphone to standby mode, yet still be notified by the alarm when the set time has come. The alarm signal sounds for exactly 1 minute or can be manually switched off by pressing the check box. In that sense, it works just the same as a real alarm clock.

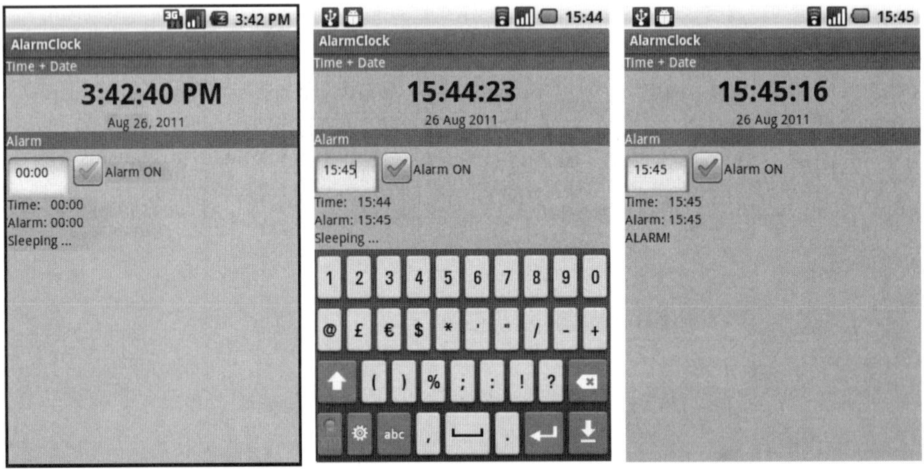

Figure 11.42 Clock with alarm setting shown on an American emulator (left) and a European smartphone (right)

Create a new project with the name "Alarm" in AI Designer and design the user interface with the components shown in Table 11.5. The important thing is that you leave the initial property TimerAlwaysFires of the component object Clock unchanged and still set to *enabled*, so that the alarm can run in the background.

Table 11.5 **Components and Initial Properties in the Alarm Clock Project**

Component	Object Name	Adapted Properties
Screen	Screen1	"Icon": alarm_applcon.png (companion website, see `/MEDIA`) "Background": Light gray
Clock	Clock	
Label	TimeLabel	"Fontsize": 30, "Text": Time
Label	DateLabel	"Text": Date
TextBox	AlarmTimeTextBox	"Hint": 00:00, "Text": 00:00, "Width": 70 pixels
CheckBox	AlarmOnCheckBox	
Label	Label1, Label2, Label3, Label4	"Text": Time:, : , Alarm time:, :
Label	AlarmLabel	"Text": Sleeping ...
Sound	Sound	"Source": beep.wav (companion website, see `/MEDIA`)

Now add the DivisionLabels, Arrangements, and BufferLabels to create a centered display for the alarm clock. Your project should look like Figure 11.43 in AI Designer.

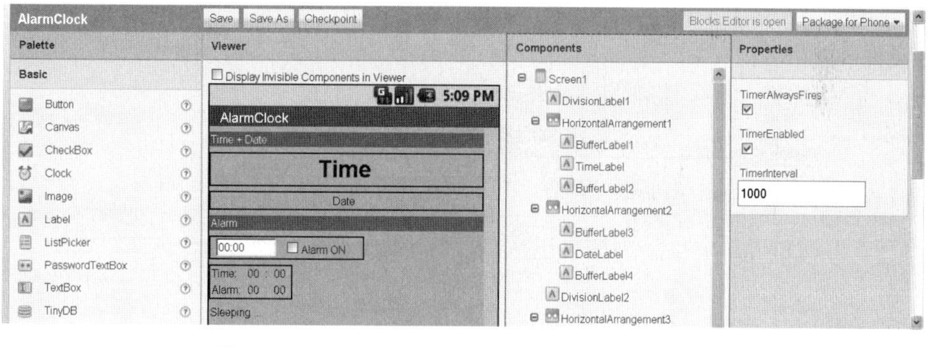

Figure 11.43 Alarm Clock Project in AI Designer

Now we can implement the time display and alarm function in AI Editor. We need just two event handlers to create the full functionality. With the first event handler `AlarmOnCheckBox.Changed` (Figure 11.44), we switch the alarm clock on via the check box, by reading the entered alarm time from the AlarmTimeTextBox, generating the alarm time as an instant from it via the method `Clock.MakeInstant`, and then assigning it to the global variable `alarmTime`. When entering the alarm time, you need to enter the hours and minutes separated by a colon (for example, `15:50`), which would also make it possible to enter and process a time for a particular day (for example, `02/04/2011, 15:50:00`), maybe for a calendar app. The sleep mode of the alarm clock is displayed in the text "Sleeping ..." in the AlarmLabel.

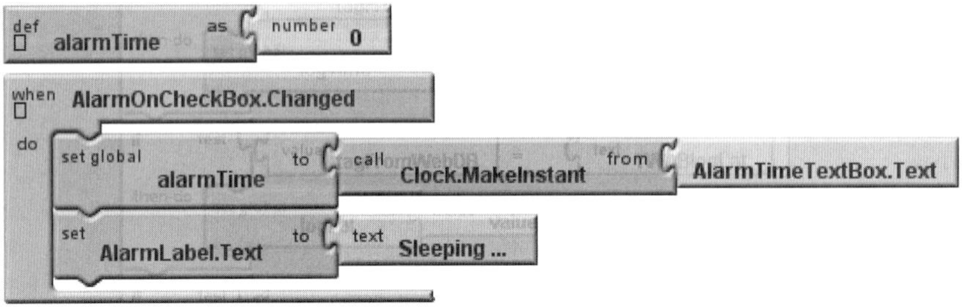

Figure 11.44 Setting the alarm time and switching the alarm function on or off

To get the current system time in intervals of 1 second (`TimerInterval=1000`), we retrieve it in the event handler `Clock.Timer` (Figure 11.45) via the Clock method `Clock.Now`. The returned instant is formatted to a readable time by the method `Clock.Format` and displayed in the TimeLabel. In the same way, we determine the date and display it in the DateLabel. Now we have completely implemented the time and date display of our alarm clock.

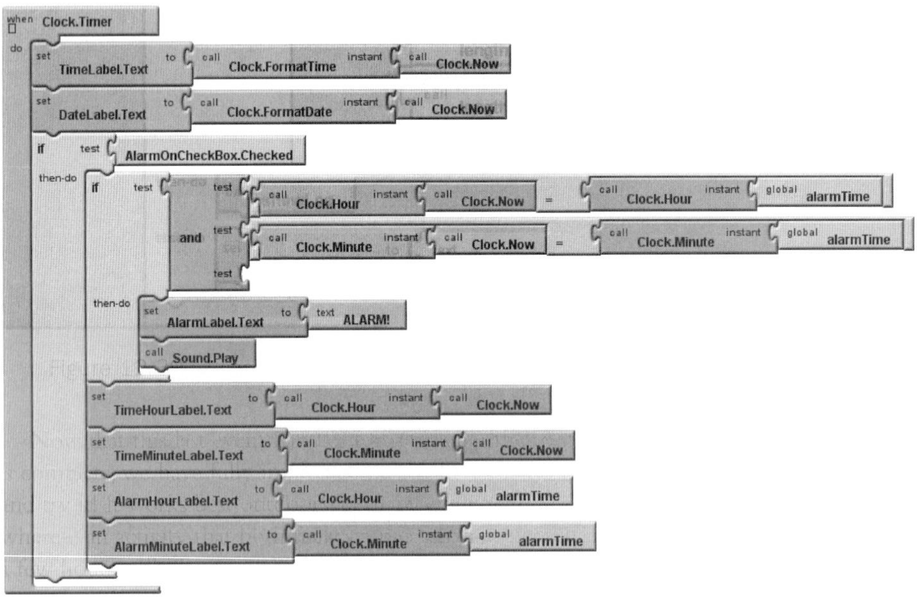

Figure 11.45 Time and date function plus display controls

We embed the functionality of the alarm clock completely in the first `if` condition in the event handler shown in Figure 11.45. The statements in it are carried out (also in intervals of 1 second) only if the alarm clock is switched on, so the check box AlarmOnCheckBox is enabled (set to `true`). A nested `if` condition then checks whether the current hour `Clock.Hour` and minute `Clock.Minute` match the set hour and minute of the alarm time. The two instants are directly compared to each other. If the values match, the statements in the `then-do` area are executed; that is, the text "ALARM!" is displayed in the AlarmLabel and the alarm sound is played with the method `Sound.Play`. As this condition remains fulfilled for exactly 1 minute, the alarm sound also plays for 1 minute. At the end of 1 minute, the current time and the alarm time no longer match, so the sound automatically stops or is manually switched off by deactivating the check box. The functionality of the alarm clock is now fully implemented, but just to make sure, we display the alarm time and current time on our alarm clock—exactly the two values that are constantly being compared.

The alarm clock project shows, in an impressively condensed way, how the Clock component in AI can be used for tasks other than animation—tasks that also require a regular event impulse. If you think about it, you can probably come up with other contexts of use where tasks have to be processed in large, small, or alternating time intervals. The regular checking of e-mail accounts, an hourly sound signal, or recording geopositions to track your own route are just some of the many apps that can be implemented in AI by following the same principles. The description of the Clock component here may have whetted your appetite; you'll find more topic-specific implementations in the examples of Chapter 12.

Chapter 12

Sensors

The integration of sensors is often new territory even for experienced programmers, as reading and processing sensor data on the computer has mostly been a task for special applications and system programmers up to now. Unlike with graphics and animation, where small mobile devices are still clearly inferior to modern computers, the opposite is true for sensors. Hardly any PC has default sensors for registering its own geoposition, current orientation, or direction of movement. Why would it need to? Most computers are intended and usable for stationary (not mobile) use, both now and in the foreseeable future. Only with the growing popularity and availability of powerful smartphones, and in particular those with the mobile operating system Android, has it become almost customary that the small technical miracles contain a whole range of sensors for recording these environment parameters as standard features. Practically all Android smartphones now include sensors for registering the geoposition (e.g., GPS, triangulation), the directional position (location sensor), the orientation (digital compass), and movement (accelerometer). With progressing miniaturization and growing capacity, this trend is poised to continue; accordingly, the prevalence of smartphones, tablets, and other mobile devices with these sensors will increase.

By registering the environment parameters in mobile devices and processing them in the programs and apps running on these devices, new types of applications can be created, beyond the previous horizon of experience of the average PC user. It may be questionable as to how useful it is to have a virtual snow globe that reacts to shaking the smartphone or a virtual glass of beer that you can drink from your smartphone, but these little demonstrations of individual sensors are entirely new and, perhaps because of that fact, real eye-catchers (at least for now). Apart from these fun apps, there are serious applications, such as GPS tracking for geocaching, in social networks, in lifelogging, and in various forms of navigation or other location-based services. Furthermore, new digital paradigms such as *mobile augmented reality* are emerging. Unlike *virtual reality*, in which a user immerses himself or herself in a virtual 3D environment with as many of the human senses as possible, mobile augmented reality is all about enhancing the real surroundings with virtual information; for example, the user may get additional information from the Web on what he or she perceives in the current surroundings, adapted to the individual situation. Such applications and new ways of using digital media are only conceivable with the wide availability of powerful and programmable mobile devices with appropriate sensors. Based on these capabilities, a whole new market of environment- and context-sensitive applications could be created, the potential extent of which we can hardly conceive of today.

Although many of these features might seem to lie in the distant future or to require hardware programming, you can actually participate in this trend today by using AI to develop your own sensor-based apps. With the visual programming language, you can take advantage of the various sensors inherent in Android devices and use the resulting location, position, orientation, and acceleration data in your apps to create real wow effects. In this chapter, you will get to know the components of AI with which you can address the various sensors of your smartphone and read their environment data. Of course, within the scope of this book we can demonstrate only a tiny fraction of the endless possible ways of using these sensors and the data they provide; we will do so with a few example applications that are intended to inspire you in creating your own projects.

Measuring Orientation with the OrientationSensor Component

Knowledge of the smartphone's orientation can be exploited in a multitude of new sensory applications and used for myriad purposes. For example, a navigation app will require information about the direction in which the user is holding the smartphone so as to point the way—for example, with a compass. If the user wishes to use the smartphone as a spirit level when doing a do-it-yourself (DIY) project, for example, the app needs accurate data on the horizontal and vertical position of the smartphone when placed on the surface that is to be measured. In both of these examples, two different physical sensors of the smartphone are involved: the *position sensor* for determining the position on a spatial plane (*x*- and *y*-axis) and the *electronic compass* for determining the direction in which the smartphone is pointing (*z*-axis). Which physical sensor ultimately determines these three values (*x, y, z*) on your smartphone is not really relevant for you as AI developer, as the corresponding AI component abstracts from these details and enables you to use the sensor values independently.

Basics of Sensory Orientation Measurement

The smartphone's orientation in physical three-dimensional space is clearly determined via three values: the rotation via the *x*-axis (*roll*), *y*-axis (*pitch*), and *z*-axis (*yaw*). Borrowed from aviation, the orientation of a smartphone at any particular time can be determined in the same way as the *roll–pitch–yaw (RPY) angle* of an airplane, as the plane's movements are also described in terms of roll, pitch, and yaw. Figure 12.1 shows a schematic representation of these three movement angles around the three axes *x, y,* and *z*. With these values, any conceivable orientation of the smartphone in a three-dimensional physical space can be accurately described.

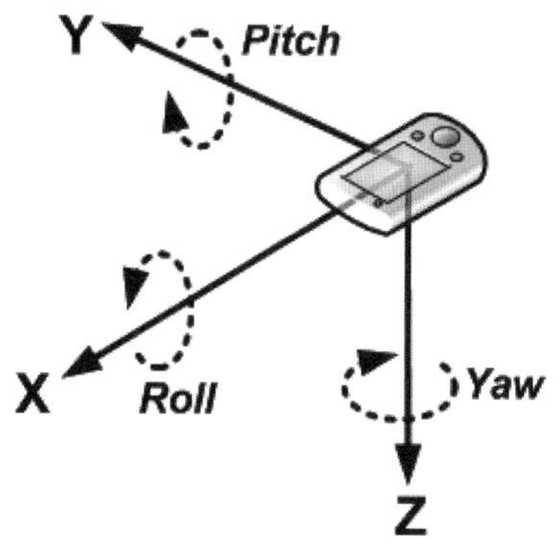

Figure 12.1 Measuring the physical orientation of the smartphone in terms of roll, pitch, and yaw

Exactly these three RPY values are returned in degree values by the OrientationSensor component, which AI makes available in the group Sensor Components. In viewing the direction along the positive *x*-axis, rolling the smartphone goes to the left up to an angle of 90° to the corresponding positive degree numbers; then, if you continue to rotate until the smartphone is on its belly, the degree values go back down to 0°. If you roll to the right, the angle values are returned as negative numbers. If the smartphone pitches around the *y*-axis forward and down, the degree numbers climb up until the smartphone is on its belly at 180°, whereas if you pull it up forward, the degree numbers sink down to –180°. Yawing around the *z*-axis results in continuously positive degree values of 0° if the orientation is toward the *north*, 90° in direction *east*, 180° in direction *south,* and 270° in direction *west.* Figure 12.2 illustrates the connections between the smartphone movements around the spatial axis and the measurement values returned by the OrientationSensor.

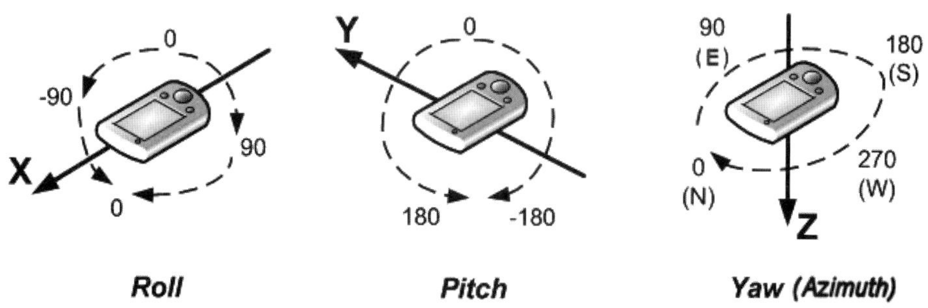

Figure 12.2 AI degree values for rolling, pitching, and yawing around the spatial planes

The specification of the non-visible component OrientationSensor shown in Figure 12.3 describes these connections in the context of the three central values Roll, Pitch, and Yaw.

"Yaw" and "Azimuth"

The aviation-based property term "yaw" for the yaw angle has been changed in the specification (retrospectively) to the more general term "azimuth," which a horizontal angle specifies as a point on a compass—for example, in navigation with a compass. In this book we will use the terms "yaw" and "azimuth" synonymously, such as in the context of the RPY values used to describe spatial position in all three dimensions.

Typical of the sensor component is the Available property, with which you can check whether the corresponding sensor is available on the device used, and the Enabled property, with which the sensor can be explicitly enabled if required. As you would expect, you also have the three RPY values available as the properties Roll, Pitch, and Azimuth, in addition to values for registering how much the device is tilted (Magnitude) and in which direction the tilt is occurring (Angle). These values describe the magnitude and angle that would be felt by an object on the device, depending on how the smartphone is being held.

OrientationSensor

OrientationSensor1

Use an orientation sensor component to determine the phone's spatial orientation.

An orientation sensor is a non-visible component that reports the following three values, in degrees:

- **Roll**: 0 degrees when the device is level, increasing to 90 degrees as the device is tilted up onto its left side, and decreasing to −90 degrees when the device is tilted up onto its right side.
- **Pitch**: 0 degrees when the device is level, increasing to 90 degrees as the device is tilted so its top is pointing down, further increasing to 180 degrees as it gets turned over. Similarly, as the device is tilted so its bottom points down, pitch decreases to −90 degrees, then down to −180 degrees as it gets turned all the way over.
- **Azimuth**: 0 degrees when the top of the device is pointing north, 90 degrees when it is pointing east, 180 degrees when it is pointing south, 270 degrees when it is pointing west, etc.

These measurements assume that the device itself is not moving.

Properties

Available
Indicates whether the orientation sensor is present on the Android device.

Enabled
If set, the orientation sensor is enabled.

Azimuth
Returns the azimuth angle of the device.

Pitch
Returns the pitch angle of the device.

Roll
Returns the roll angle of the device.

Magnitude
Returns a number between 0 and 1 that indicates how much the device is tilted. It gives the magnitude of the force that would be felt by a ball rolling on the surface of the device.

Angle
Returns an angle that tells the direction in which the device is tiled. That is, it tells the direction of the force that would be felt by a ball rolling on the surface of the device.

Events

`OrientationChanged(number azimuth, number pitch, number roll)`
Called when the orientation has changed.

Figure 12.3 Specification of the OrientationSensor component in the AI References

Apart from these properties, the OrientationSensor component also has a single event block `OrientationChanged`, which is called with every change in orientation. The number and frequency of the results produced in this way depend on the sensitivity of the underlying sensors; that is, sometimes very many events and sometimes very few events are triggered, which makes a continuous measuring or using of the measurement results difficult. To get continuous values and use them in an app, the regular events of a Clock component can be used. In its event handlers, the desired measurement values can be retrieved in regular intervals. We will also use this method when we take advantage of the OrientationSensor components in our example projects.

A Compass with a Graphical Direction Indicator

Perhaps while reading the introductory section, you suddenly thought that the roll value of the OrientationSensor component could be used for developing a compass app based on your smartphone's electronic compass. It seems obvious to use the returned value, in degrees between 0° and 360°, for displaying the direction as points of the compass. Of course, users of such an app who are trying to get their bearings would not find it very helpful if you just displayed the track angle via a block statement. Instead, we want to develop an app that offers the user a graphically implemented, analogous compass in which the needle always points north so that the user can see which way he or she is heading. In addition, we want to indicate the direction not just in degrees, but also by the corresponding points of the compass (N, NE, E, SE, S, SW, W, NW). That functionality will make the compass a valuable asset to the user whether he or she is hiking or just wandering around town. With its appealing visual appearance, the compass shown in Figure 12.4 is already quite attractive; in this figure, the app shows both the correct cardinal points and the user's current direction when the user is facing 3° north (left), 60° northeast (center), and 285° west (right).

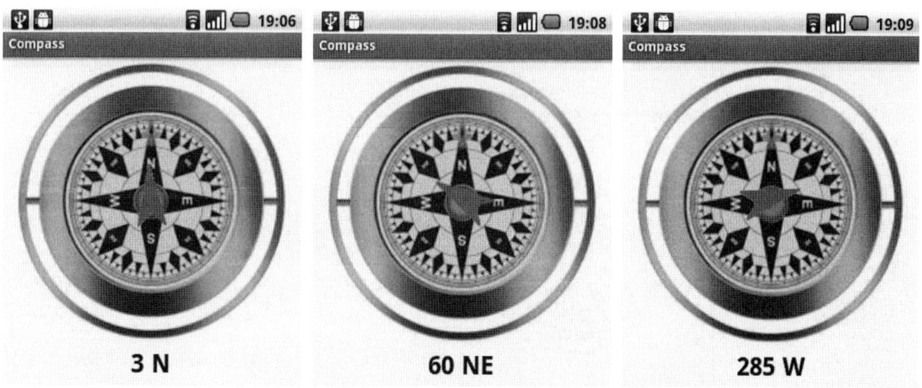

Figure 12.4 Displaying the cardinal points and user heading in the Compass app

The visual appearance might suggest otherwise, but the implementation of this appealing and really useful compass app requires incredibly little effort thanks to the powerful tools provided by AI. The visual design in AI Designer is created remarkably quickly, as long as the required image files are present. First, create a new project in AI Designer with the title "Compass," rename the title of "Screen1" accordingly, and insert the few components shown in Table 12.1 into the new project.

Table 12.1 **Components and Initial Properties in the Compass Project**

Component	Object Name	Adapted Properties
OrientationSensor	OrientationSensor	
Clock	Clock	"TimerInterval": 100
Canvas	Canvas	"BackgroundImage": compass.jpg (see companion website, `/MEDIA`) "Width"/"Height": 300 × 300 pixels
ImageSprite	NeedleSprite	"Picture": needle.png (see companion website, `/MEDIA`) "Interval": 100
Label (2x)	YawLabel, DirectionLabel	"Text": 0, N "FontBold": enable "FontSize": 26

With the appropriate Arrangements and BufferLabels, the interface of our compass app is indeed complete once you have added the few components specified in Table 12.1. Drag the ImageSprite with the image of the compass needle into the proper starting position, oriented to the north-pointing arrow of the Canvas background image, as shown in Figure 12.5.

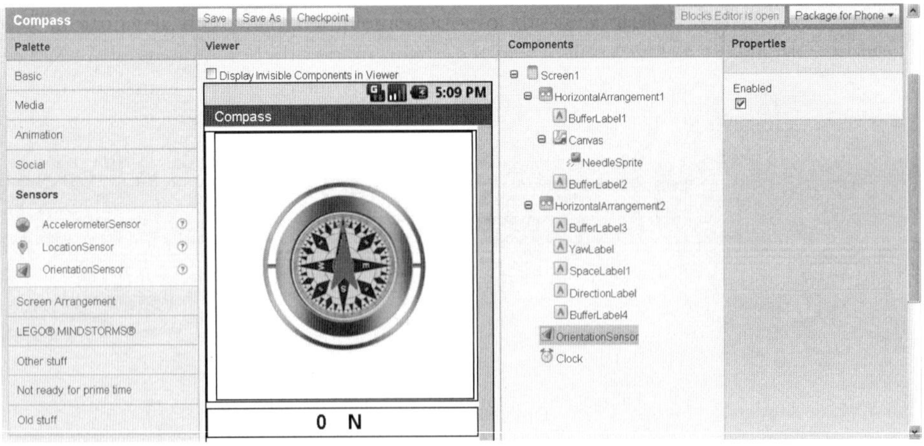

Figure 12.5 The Compass project in AI Editor

It might seem incredible, but it's true: Now you can easily implement in AI Editor the function for turning the compass needle and its permanent orientation toward north, analogous to the movement of the smartphone (or rather the user who is holding it). The block structures for the graphic animation hardly do anything other than display the degree value. As shown in Figure 12.6, you can repeatedly retrieve the current yaw value via the method `OrientationSensor.Azimuth` in intervals of a tenth of a second via the component object `Clock`, and then use this value directly for displaying the degrees in the YawLabel and implementing the rotation of the NeedleSprite in the corresponding angle via its ImageSprite property `NeedleSprite.Heading`.

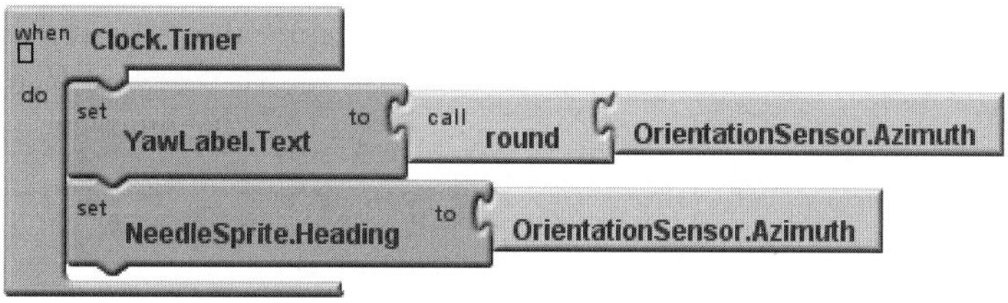

Figure 12.6 Displaying the degrees and animating the needle to point in the direction of the compass

With the minimal block structures shown in Figure 12.6, the compass, including the graphic animation of the compass needle for the corresponding yaw angle, is completely implemented. Now you have encountered yet another way of using the graphic and animation components Canvas, ImageSprite, and Clock described in Chapter 11. As an alternative to retrieving the sensor values via the regular timer events, we could have used the OrientationSensor property block `OrientationChanged`, but you will notice that the resulting needle animation is less even and somewhat jumpy.

Project Compass on the Companion Website

As usual, you can find all files for the Compass project on the companion website in the usual directories (see the link in the Introduction).

To complete the compass app and create a "proper" field compass, we need to display the current direction of travel. Even if this function is not very complicated, its implementation inflates the previously modest block structures many times over. Figure 12.7 shows the previously slim event handler `Clock.Timer` now inflated with an additional nested `ifelse` branch structure with eight hierarchies. The eight nested statements select the eight possible points of the compass depending on the current value in the YawLabel and display them in the DirectionLabel as N, NE, E, SE, S, SW, W, or NW. Even if the complex block structure may not seem particularly efficient at first glance, this hierarchical checking of the current measurement value every tenth of a second occurs quite quickly, as the hierarchical `ifelse` condition checks have to be executed only up to the suitable value each time.

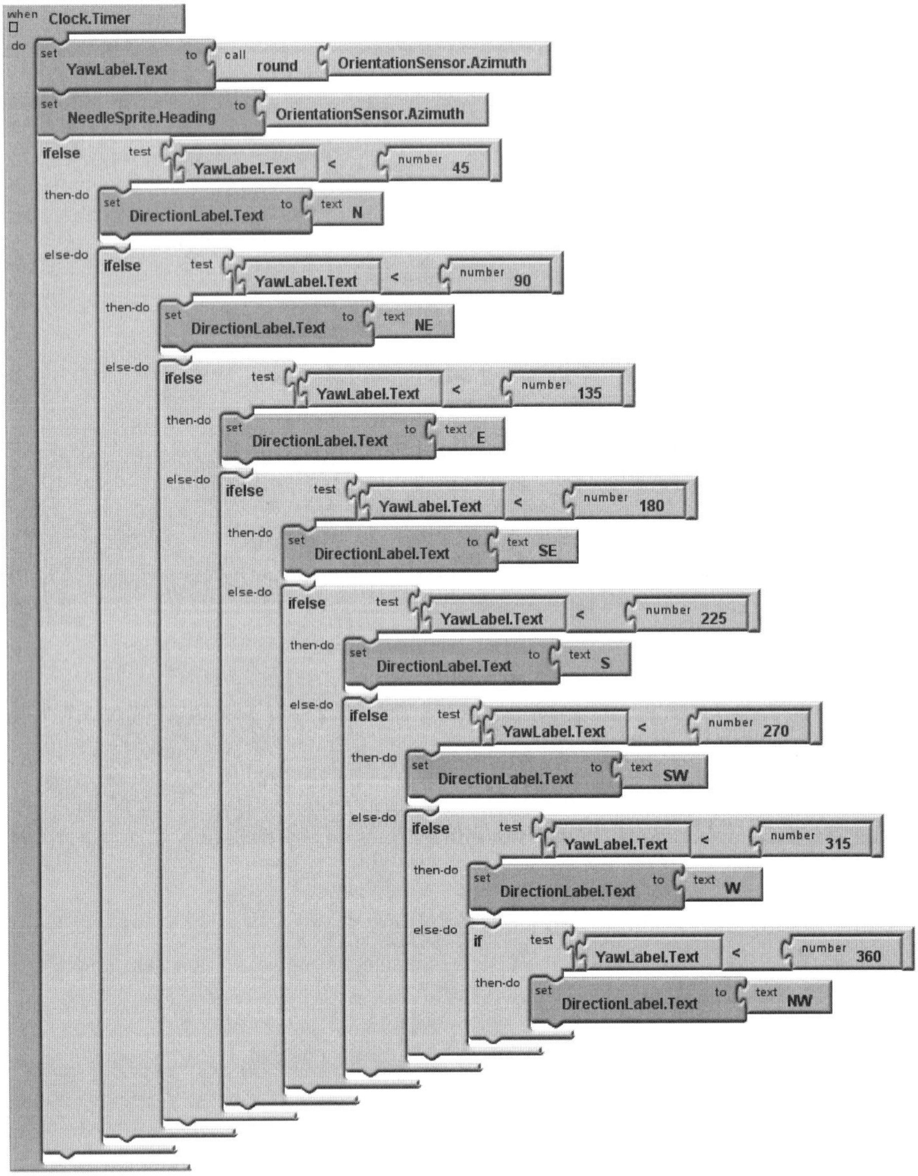

Figure 12.7 Adding the display of the direction of travel to the compass

Assigning the direction of travel to the currently measured yaw value takes place in the nested `ifelse` branches shown in Figure 12.7 based on a rather simple scale: N (0–44°), NE (45–89°), E (90–134°), SE (135–179°), S (180–224°), SW (225–269°), W

(270–314°), and NW (315–359°). Now the hiking compass shown in Figure 12.27 is fully implemented, and you should try it out while you are out and about. If you feel that the displayed direction is not quite correct compared to a real analog compass, then perhaps you need to *calibrate* the electronic compass on your smartphone. While the compass app is active, turn the smartphone several times around all its axes. The correct points of the compass should then be displayed. The best values will be measured outside, at some distance away from reinforced concrete walls (which may block the sensor) and other electromagnetic interference fields created by computers and other electronic devices. Of course, in a truly critical situation, you should never blindly trust the electronic measurement results and displays of your smartphone.

A Spirit Level with a Graphical Level Indicator

Because dealing with sensors is so much fun and leads to surprisingly quick and impressive results in the form of attractive apps, we will illustrate the other two central values of the OrientationSensor component using another example project. This time we will recreate an analog spirit level, like the one you would use in DIY projects or construction work, in digital form on the smartphone. With the spirit level app, we want to be able to identify a level horizontal or vertical plane by placing the smartphone down flat or upright, so as to check whether something is level or which degree of inclination it has, just as with an analog spirit level. Once again, we do not want to display the measured values just as numbers; rather—as with an analog spirit level—we want to use a virtual liquid with a yellow tint and an air bubble inside to represent the inclination of the surface within markings via a graphical animation in an attractive way and in real time, as shown in Figure 12.8.

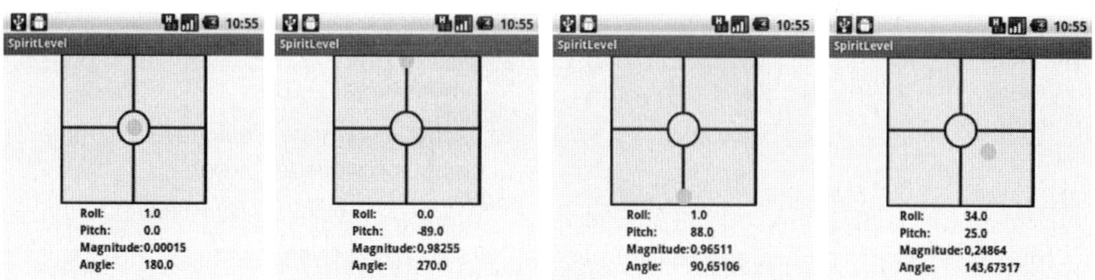

Figure 12.8 Spirit level display when the device is level and at different inclinations

In our spirit level app shown in Figure 12.8, the square area corresponds to the water inside the gauge, the dot over the square represents the bubble, and the lines represent the markings for indicating the degree of inclination. The example readings displayed are from a smartphone that, from left to right, (a) is resting flat on its back on a level surface, (b) is standing upright with its back against a practically right-angled wall, (c) is standing upside down against a practically right-angled wall, and (d) is resting on a surface that inclined downward and to the left. Certainly, you will find it easier to follow these descriptions of the function and readings of a spirit level if you are familiar with its analog counterpart or if you have tried out this app yourself. The values displayed below the spirit level show the unfiltered measurement data that the OrientationSensor returns in the corresponding properties. Here you can see how much more intuitive the graphical display of the measured values is—for example, for a worker who is doing a DIY project—as the values themselves have little significance.

Project SpiritLevel on the Companion Website

You can find the files for the SpiritLevel project in the usual directories on the companion website (see the link in the Introduction).

The development of the SpiritLevel app is also very easy. The major part of the development work takes place in AI Designer. We make use of the fact that the measured roll angle (Roll) returns values between 90° and –90°, and the pitch angle (Pitch) returns values between 180° and –180°, of which we also need only the range between 90° and –90° to represent each degree of inclination adequately on the spirit level. Corresponding to the numeric range of 90° to –90°, we define the size of the spirit level display to exactly match the canvas dimension of 180 by 180 pixels. Now the two measured values (Roll and Pitch) can be placed as X,Y coordinates directly on the canvas field, starting from its center at the coordinates X = 90 and Y = 90 (more on this later). To begin, we create a new project in AI Designer with the name "SpiritLevel," rename the title of "Screen1" accordingly, and add the few components listed in Table 12.2.

Table 12.2 **Components and Initial Properties in the SpiritLevel Project**

Component	Object Name	Adapted Properties
OrientationSensor	OrientationSensor	
Clock	Clock	"TimerInterval": 100
Canvas	Canvas	"BackgroundImage": spiritlevel.png (see companion website, `/MEDIA`) "Width" / "Height": 180 × 180 pixels
Ball	BubbleBall	"PaintColor": Cyan "Radius": 10
Label (4x)	RollLabel, PitchLabel, MagnitudeLabel, AngleLabel	"FontBold": enable "Text": 0, 0, 0, 0

Now add the other text Labels, Arrangements, and BufferLabels so that the new project SpiritLevel appears in AI Designer as shown in Figure 12.9. Make sure that you set the sizes correctly for the component objects `Canvas` (Width, Height) and `BubbleBall` (Radius), as they are important to ensure the correct graphical representation.

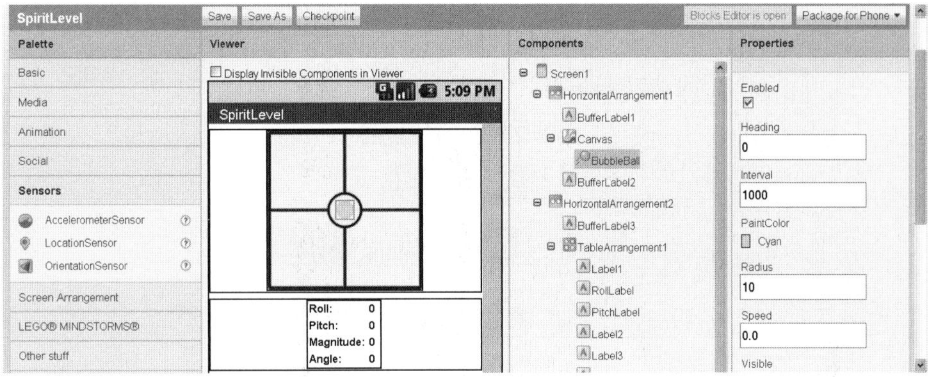

Figure 12.9 The SpiritLevel Project in AI Designer

Now we have completed the most important preparations in AI Designer, which enable us to carry out the implementation in AI Editor once again with remarkable efficiency. In the event handler `Clock.Timer` of Figure 12.10, you can see the entire implementation of the spirit level's functionality. The bulk of the statements serve to display the measured values Pitch, Roll, Magnitude, and Angle directly in the corresponding labels. The graphic animation takes place in the first statement, in which the `BubbleBall` object is placed after each tenth of a second (Timer interval) in that X, Y position onto the `Canvas` object, which corresponds to the current measured value `OrientationSensor.Roll` on the *x*-axis and `OrientationSensor.Pitch` on the *y*-axis. Both values are added to 80 prior to their X,Y positioning, so as to place the new position always relative to the canvas center (90, 90) minus the radius of `BubbleBall` (10 pixels). Each new retrieved roll and pitch value pair is then directly converted to X,Y coordinates and the bubble is placed in that position.

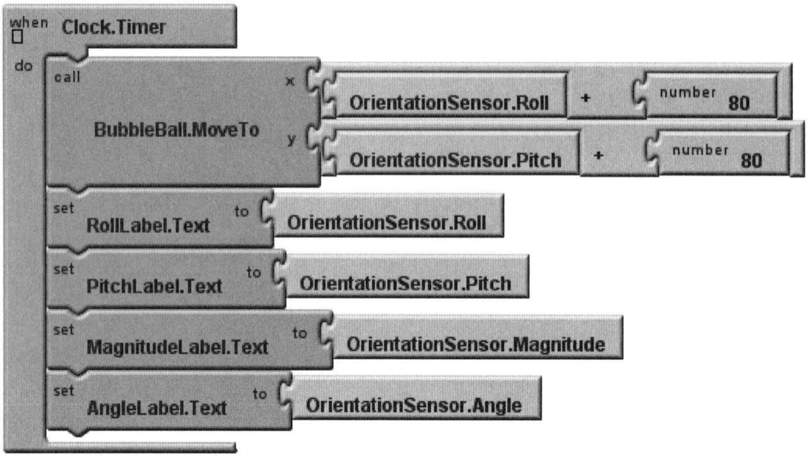

Figure 12.10 Fully implemented functionality of the SpiritLevel app

So that the event handler shown in Figure 12.10 is not looking quite so lost and lonely, we add an initial check to the block structures. When the app is started, it determines whether the smartphone has a corresponding position sensor or orientation sensor in the first place, and whether this sensor is enabled. If this is *not* the case, an appropriate warning is displayed to the user, as shown in Figure 12.11. Adding such an initial check is recommended for any app that relies on the values of one or several sensors to inform the user and, if necessary, prompt him or her to explicitly enable the sensor.

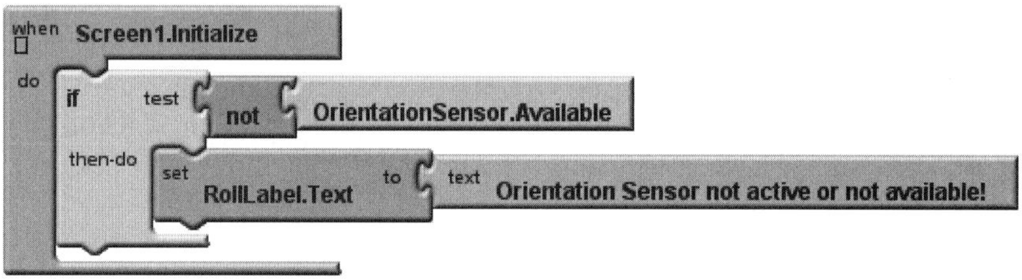

Figure 12.11 Initial check to verify that the sensor is present and enabled

Would you have imagined that sensory apps would be so quickly and easily implemented? The ease with which AI makes it possible for developers to implement innovative concepts and keep up with even rather demanding topics in terms of app development is really impressive. Purely on the basis of regular value measurements, you can realize incredible applications, provided you have the required amount of creativity in developing ideas and apps.

Measuring *g*-Force with the AccelerometerSensor Component

This section's title is an apt description of the physical property we will describe and measure next. The term "*g*-force" describes the force acting on a body (of a human being or any object, such as a smartphone) through acceleration. It is often measured in conjunction with airplanes, but also plays a key role in roller coasters. The unit 1 *g* is based on the average gravitational acceleration that we are normally exposed to on Earth and that corresponds to an acceleration of 9.81 meters per square second (1 $g = 9.81\ m/s^2$) within the International System of Units (*SI*: Système International d'unités). Higher accelerations are divided by the value of the gravitational acceleration (acceleration *a* / gravitational acceleration *g*) and specified as the *g*-force or *g*-factor. In sources on the Internet, you can find examples of *g*-forces acting on humans, such as when driving a racecar from a stopped position (up to 1.5 *g*) and going around corners (up to about 4 *g*), or on a roller coaster (4–6 *g*); the corresponding impact on the human body is also identified, such as a nose bleed from a force of 6 *g*, unconsciousness from a force of 10 *g*, or even death in case of a car crash at a force of 20 *g* (see `http://en.wikipedia.org/wiki/G-force` for more examples). When your smartphone is dropped onto a concrete floor, this event can also produce a destructive force of up to 1000 *g* from the sudden stop at the moment of impact.

Basics of Sensory Acceleration Measurement

With an acceleration sensor, also referred to as accelerometer or *g*-sensor, you can continuously measure the *g*-force that acts on the smartphone. For example, the integrated sensor uses piezoelectric or microelectromechanical sensor parts to determine the inertial force acting on a test mass at acceleration; in this way, it can register any increase or decrease in speed. The real speed is of little relevance; that is, the *g*-force occurs only when a car is accelerating from 0 to 125 mph, but once the target speed of 125 mph is reached and maintained, the *g*-force approaches its initial value again. For a more extensive explanation of this concept, you might want to take a quick look at one of those physics books from your school days to help you better understand the properties and values of the corresponding sensor components in AI. But don't let the theoretical underpinnings of this topic discourage you from using this sensor type to develop interesting apps—the OrientationSensor component handles most of the sticky details for you. In particular, games offer unfathomable possibilities for using multisensor controls, which are becoming increasingly popular at the moment, mainly for registering movements in games consoles. Serious uses are also possible, such as registering when a person in need of care falls and automatically sending an emergency message via SMS, or perhaps issuing a warning when sudden movements or the unauthorized removal of a smartphone is perceived.

For measuring acceleration, AI offers the AccelerometerSensor component, which is found in the group Sensor Components. Similar to the OrientationSensor, the AccelerometerSensor measures the *g*-forces in three sensor values—XAccel, YAccel, and

ZAccel—which act on the smartphone along the *x*-, *y*-, and *z*-axes. At rest, the maximum acceleration through the force of gravity of 1 $g = 9.81\ m/s^2$ is set as the default. Depending on the spatial position, this force is distributed on the *x, y, z* spatial axes such that ZAccel approaches the value 9.81 when the smartphone is on its back; XAccel approaches 9.81 when the phone is rolled over to the left up to 90° and –9.81 when it is rolled to the right; and YAccel approaches –9.81 if the smartphone is pitched forward 90° and 9.81 if it is pitched backward. In Figure 12.12, the corresponding 90° positions for the spatial axes are represented with their values; on the right, you can see the distribution of *g*-forces on two axes when the smartphone is resting at an angle. All values are based on the rest position—for example, when the smartphone is lying in the appropriate position on a table and not moving. If it was falling down in the appropriate position, the acceleration value would increase in the relevant axis direction and would shoot up to its highest value at the moment of impact.

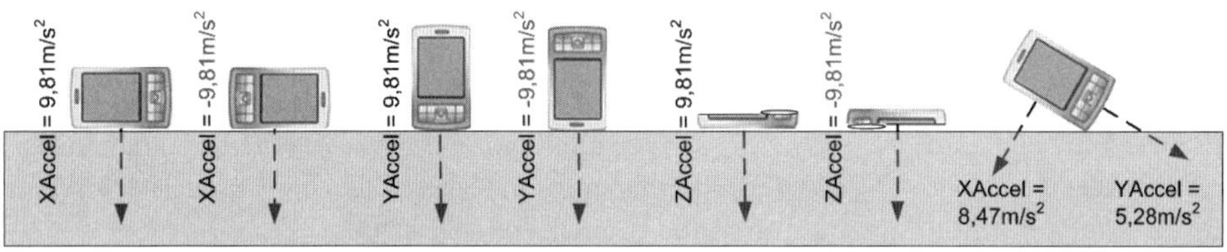

Figure 12.12 Acceleration values of the *g*-sensor in various rest positions

After all this theoretical preparation, the specification of the AccelerometerSensor component shown in Figure 12.13 probably seems anticlimactic—almost self-explanatory. Similar to the OrientationSensor, the AccelerometerSensor has three central values—XAccel, YAccel, and ZAccel—as properties and the typical options of checking whether the physical sensor is Available and Enabled. There is also an event block `AccelerationChanged`, which is called automatically when the acceleration has changed. Additionally, there is a special event block `Shaking`, which is activated when the smartphone is shaken in any way.

AccelerometerSensor

This component senses the Android device's accelerometer, which detects shaking and measures acceleration in three dimensions. Acceleration is measured in SI units (m/s^2). If the device is a rest lying flat on its back, the Z acceleration will be about 9.8.

The component produces three values.

- `XAccel`: Positive when the device is tilted to the right (that is, its left side is raised), and negative when the device is tilted to the left (its right size is raised).
- `YAccel`: Positive when its bottom is raised, and negative when its top is raised.
- `ZAccel`: Positive when the display is facing up, and negative when the display is facing down.

Properties

`Available`
Indicates whether the accelerometer is present on the Android device.
`Enabled`
If set, accelerometer is enabled.
`XAccel`
Acceleration in the X-dimension.
`YAccel`
Acceleration in the Y-dimension.
`ZAccel`
Acceleration in the Z-dimension.

Events

`AccelerationChanged(number xAccel, number yAccel, number zAccel)`
Called when the acceleration has changed.
`Shaking()`
Called repeatedly when the Android device is being shaken.

Figure 12.13 Specification of the AccelerometerSensor component in AI References

Let's move away from theoretical descriptions now and instead demonstrate the functions of the AccelerometerSensor using a practical example. As mentioned earlier, the typical ways of using it exist at two extremes—either for emergency situations or for entertaining applications in games or music.

Use Your Phone as a Shaker Musical Instrument

The non-musicians among you may shake your heads. Indeed, the connection between an accelerometer and a musical instrument such as a shaker might seem tenuous at first. But if you think about it for a moment or two, the connection becomes clear very quickly. The shaker is part of the relatively large group of percussion instruments or rattles that are used in various music styles—for example, as a tube shaker, rattle, or maracas in samba, tango, or jazz. All shakers have a hollow space with a grainy filling in common, which makes a rattling sound when the instrument is moved and shaken. Depending on the type and amount of filling and the speed of the movement, the shaker can produce an amazing range of sounds. Moving it slowly with hardly any acceleration will produce gentle rattling tones, but shaking it quickly with high acceleration will result in short, sharp sounds.

Now you can see the connection between a shaker and our accelerometer. Even though we definitely do not want to reproduce the entire sound repertoire of a shaker on our smartphone, simulating a rudimentary shaker will give us a good insight into, and intuitive illustration of, the measured *g*-forces that would otherwise be difficult to perceive. After all, we cannot just throw the smartphone through the air and simultaneously read the *g*-force on the screen. By shaking the smartphone and getting acoustic feedback based on the degree of acceleration, we can experience the measured force in a special multisensory way.

Instead of representing the range of sounds of the shaker through movements at different speeds, we want to create three different sounds depending on the axis direction, triggered by a certain speed threshold in the relevant direction and played in the same rhythm as the movements. The threshold value for triggering the sound can be set between 10 and 25 m/s^2 (1.1 *g* to 2.4 *g*), so that the musically minded user can regulate the sensitivity of his or her "instrument" to the user's own individual requirements. As a consequence, the smartphone can do much more than, for example, a synthesizer. A synthesizer can play typical shaker sounds but only by having the user press a button; in contrast, you can shake the smartphone rhythmically just like the real shaker instrument, so it offers a very different sensory experience.

Project ShakeIT on the Companion Website

You can find all files for the ShakeIT project in the usual directories on the companion website.

As you can see from the description of how our shaker works, we will not be able to content ourselves with the standard function of the AccelerometerSensor event block `Shaking`, as it reacts to any kind of acceleration in all three axis directions in the same way. Instead, we will process the *g*-values of all three spatial axes individually. Also, instead of relying on the self-calling event block `AccelerationChanged`, we will activate the values in regular intervals ourselves, just as we did with the OrientationSensor. Create a new project in AI Designer with the name "ShakeIT," give the corresponding title to "Screen1," and add the components shown in Table 12.3.

Table 12.3 **Components and Initial Properties in the ShakeIT Project**

Component	Object Name	Adapted Properties
Screen	Screen1	"BackgroundImage": rattles.jpg "Icon": shakeit_appIcon.png (companion website, `/MEDIA`)
AccelerometerSensor	AccelerometerSensor	
Clock	Clock	"TimerInterval": 10
Sound (3x)	Sound1, 2, 3	"Source": rattle1s.wav, rattle2s.wav, rattle3s.wav (comp website, `/MEDIA`)
TextBox	gTextBox	"Text": 15
Button	GoButton	"Text": GO!

To the components shown in Table 12.3, you then just need to add the text labels and arrangements, so that the project ShakeIT appears in AI Designer as shown in

Figure 12.14. The optical appearance of the app is of secondary importance in this case, because we mainly want to stimulate the user's kinesthetic and acoustic perception.

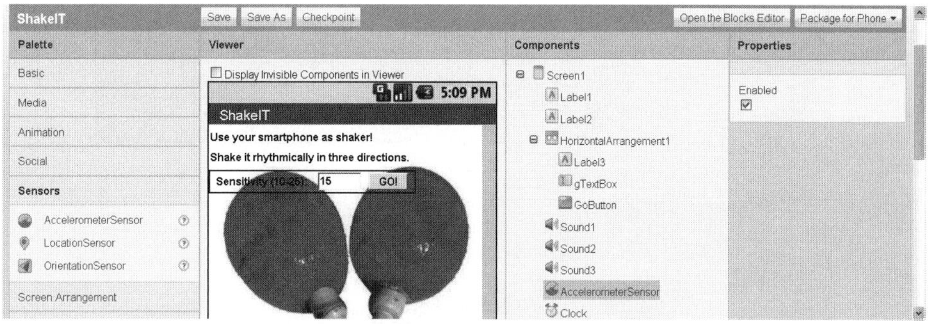

Figure 12.14 Project ShakeIT in AI Designer

Now we can quickly move on to the functional implementation of our shaker. In the first step, we will enable the user to set the sensitivity of the shaker. It is initialized and recorded in the global variable `sensitive` shown in Figure 12.15 with the initial value `15`. This value represents the acceleration in m/s^2 and is set to the default value 15 m/s^2, which corresponds to approximately 1.53 *g*. At this acceleration threshold value, triggering the corresponding tone should be possible without any great effort. The user can actually set the ideal sensitivity on his or her own, by entering the desired threshold value in the gTextBox. To make sure that the smartphone does not constantly produce sounds when it is not moving, we set the minimum threshold value to 10 m/s^2—in other words, just above the gravitational force of 9.81 m/s^2. Also, as the human muscles cannot produce more than 2.5 *g* without suffering damage, we set the maximum value to 25 m/s^2. If desired, you can, of course, adapt these values to your own preference. We check the value range on pressing the GoButton within the event handler `GoButton.Click` via the condition check of the `ifelse` branch. If the value entered in the gTextBox is greater than or equal to `10` and (`AND`) less than or equal to `25`, the set value is accepted and inserted into the global variable `sensitive`; otherwise, it is set back to the initial value `15`.

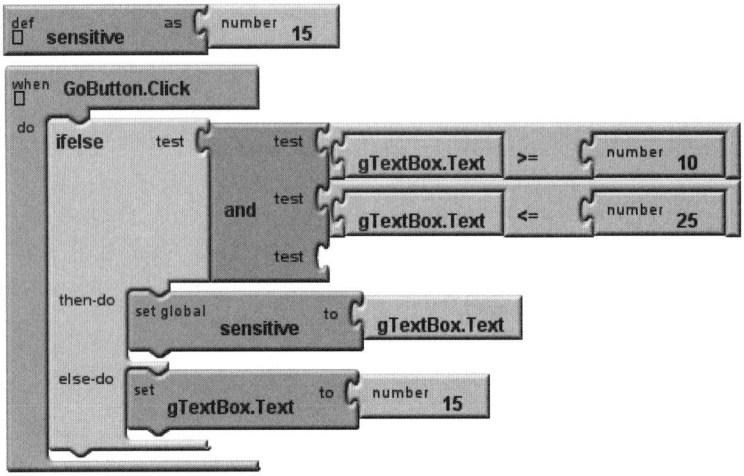

Figure 12.15 Setting the shaker sensitivity and limiting its value range

These steps cover the process of setting the options for our app. The sensor and shaker are immediately ready to make music when the app is started. The music itself is implemented by the few simple statements shown in Figure 12.16. Instead of waiting for the acceleration events of the AccelerometerSensor block `AccelerationChanged`, we check at intervals of one-hundredth of a second (`Clock.TimerInterval = 10`) within the event handler `Clock.Timer` to see whether any of the current values of `XAccel`, `YAccel`, and `ZAccel` are above the threshold value of the variable `sensitive`. For each value that fulfills this condition, the corresponding tone is played via the appropriate method `Sound.Play`.

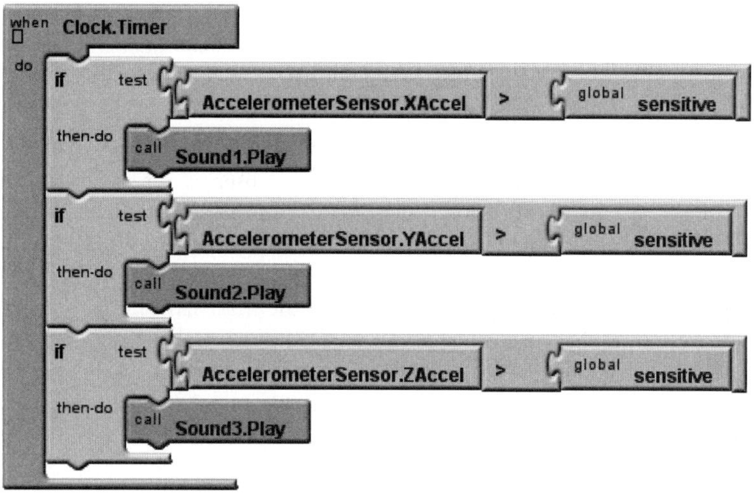

Figure 12.16 Three different sounds depending on direction and acceleration

Now our shaker is already fully implemented. Try it out, find your favorite threshold setting, and test your feeling for rhythm—and acceleration! This app can certainly be refined and expanded musically. Perhaps you might want to turn it into a virtual set of drums, with which you select the relevant percussion instrument by turning and twisting one or even two smartphones in your hands (crash cymbal, floor tom, tom tom, big and small drum, hi-hat) and play the instruments at specific volumes depending on how hard you move your hands through the air.

Setting the Measurement Sensitivity via Slider Control

Of course, a sensitive musician will not want to set the sensitivity of his or her instrument by just specifying cold numeric values. In other contexts of use, the implementation of a slider control for continuously adjusting measurements and other values upward or downward would make sense as an input method, but unfortunately AI does not yet offer the feature by default as a GUI component. We decide to implement the slider on our own, recognizing that it will make the shaker from the previous section a bit more user friendly and intuitive. You can then use the same concept and the slider control in other apps where integrating such a control element seems appropriate.

Project ShakeIT2 on the Companion Website

You can find all files for the ShakeIT2 project on the companion website in the usual directories.

Instead of entering an acceleration value between 10 and 25 m/s^2 in a text box via the system keyboard as in the original app, we want the user of our shaker app to now be able to use a finger to adjust a slider horizontally and thereby regulate the threshold value. That is, the user should be able to adjust the shaker sensitivity continuously between 0 and 25 m/s^2, as shown in Figure 12.17. The figure includes three example settings. With the default setting of 15.0 m/s2 (left), the musician can stay relaxed and make music without tiring out his or her muscles. With the high setting of 21.0 m/s^2 (right), the user has to shake the smartphone quite vigorously to produce sounds. In the center image, the setting of 7.0 m/s^2 is below the average gravitational force of 9.81 m/s^2, which means that the smartphone will constantly produce at least one of the three sounds depending on its position. As such as setting below 1 *g* makes little sense for playing a shaker, we have marked this area of the scale in red. Of course, you can experiment with this setting if you want to test it. The smartphone will respond acoustically to any changes in its position.

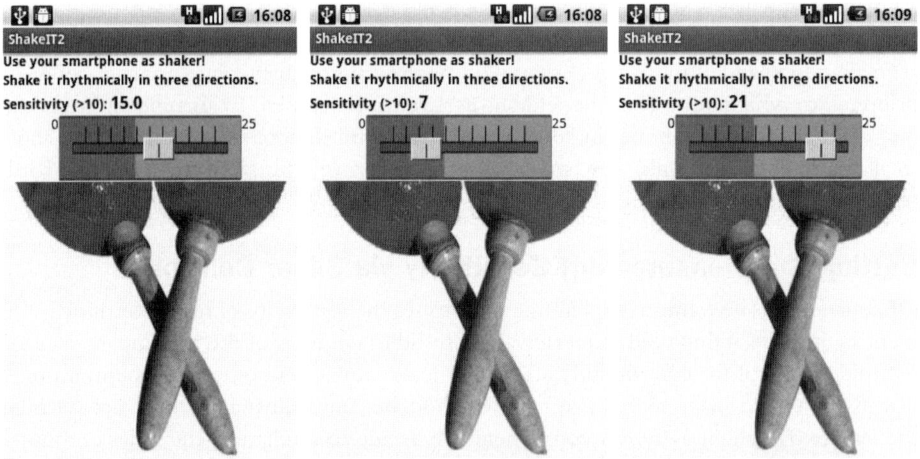

Figure 12.17 Setting the shaker sensitivity via a slider control

As our changes are based directly on the previous project ShakeIT, we can use this project as a starting point. Save the project under the new name "ShakeIT2," delete the gTextBox and GoButton in this new project, and then adapt the remaining components and add the new components as shown in Table 12.4.

Table 12.4 **Adapted and New Components in the ShakeIT2 Project**

Component	Object Name	Adapted Properties
Screen	Screen1	"Icon": shakeit2_applcon.png (companion website, `/MEDIA`)
Canvas	SliderCanvas	"BackgroundImage": sliderField.png (companion website, `/MEDIA`)
		"Width / Height": 200 × 70 pixels
ImageSprite	SliderSprite	"Picture": sliderbutton.png (companion website, `/MEDIA`)
		"Interval": 100
Label	gLabel	"Text": 15.0
		"FontSize": 18
		"FontBold" enabled
Label (2x)	BufferLabeLon1, 2	"Text": 0, 25

Next, arrange the slider control with a corresponding Arrangement and the two BufferLabels (this time labeled with the minimum and maximum values of `0` and `25`) as shown in Figure 12.18. The SliderSprite should be placed in a suitable initial position on the scale of the SliderCanvas. The Width size setting for the canvas object is particularly important, as the value that is later adjusted with the slider control and displayed in the gLabel will be calculated based on this setting and used as the threshold value of the sensor.

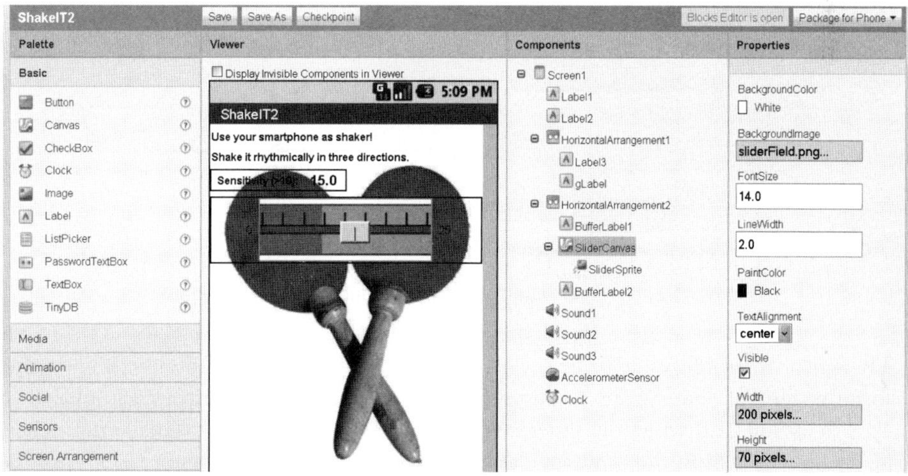

Figure 12.18 The adapted project ShakeIT2 in AI Designer

Once the SliderSprite is placed properly and the Width property of SliderCanvas is set to "200 pixels" as the default, we can implement the functionality of the slider control in AI Editor. We leave the existing event handler `Clock.Timer` and the global variable `sensitive` untouched (the event handler `GoButton.Click` has been removed by deleting the associated "GO!" button). The implementation of the animation and the complete functionality of the slider control now takes place in just a single event handler, as shown in Figure 12.19. To drag the SliderSprite with the finger over the screen, we use its event block `SliderSprite.Dragged`, which records the finger movement. As our slider will move only horizontally, we use only the value passed in the local variable `currentX`, to place the SliderSprite via the method `SliderSprite.MoveTo` onto the current X position of the finger on the SliderCanvas. The vertical Y position remains set statically to the value `25`, so that only a horizontal animation takes place. The sideways limitation of the movement results automatically from the canvas width (Width), which we have preset in AI Designer to 200 pixels.

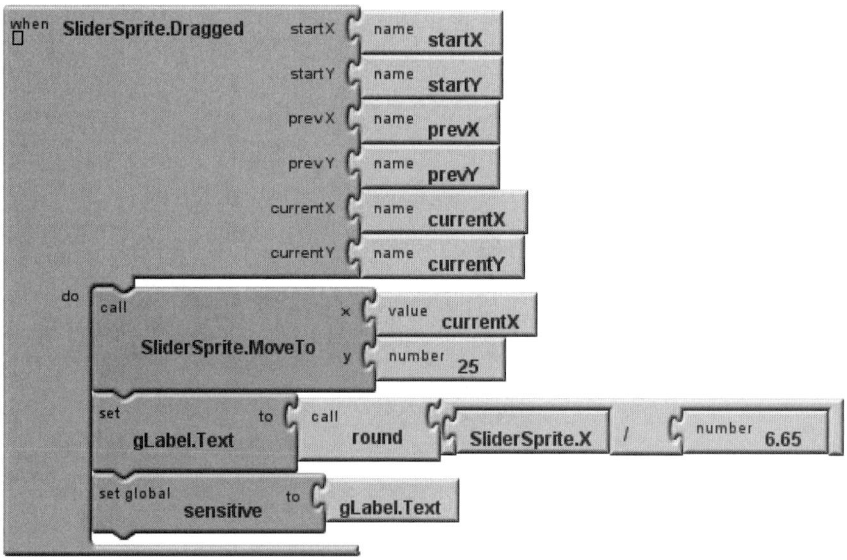

Figure 12.19 Animation and functionality of the slider bar

The sensor threshold value to be set via the slider control is gathered directly from the X position value of SliderSprite. To ensure that the maximum value displayed in gLabel really is the value 25.0 when the slider is moved all the way to the right, we subtract the sprite width (33.7) from the canvas width (200 pixels) and divide the result (166.3 pixels) by 25 m/s^2. We then round this result with the method `round` up to the next whole-integer value and display it as `gLabel.Text`. The displayed value is then passed to the global variable `sensitive`, which is used in the event handler `Clock.Timer` (shown in Figure 12.16) to set the threshold value.

We have now fully implemented the slider control and the app ShakeIT2. We invite you to test it and play around with it, proving that its operation is much simpler now.

A Balance Game for the Whole Body

As mentioned earlier, the accelerometer is well suited not only for use in serious situations such as emergencies, but also for (re)inventing new forms of games. The phrase "(re) inventing new forms of games" is meant to indicate that the user control concepts of the new kinesthetic and otherwise sensor-guided electronic games are often transferred to or simulated in digital games from concepts that have previously been exploited in their analog counterparts and predecessors. For example, you would have used the whole arm holding a tennis racket to swing and hit a real tennis ball, long before it became possible to control a virtual tennis racket through the abstract movement of one finger on a keyboard, a joystick, or a control unit in computer games. With the new sensory games on the various types of game consoles, game producers are now attempting to make the control resemble the original movement sequence again, including creating a perfect simulation in terms of both the visual 3D representation and the body-related input and output for the player. Given the rich set of basic sensory equipment that most Android smartphones and tablets include as standard, they are particularly well suited to these new/old game forms. Instead, this realm is one where they can make full use of their advantages over the otherwise much more powerful consoles and PCs.

We will use the acceleration sensor in an example project for simulating a board game that is reminiscent of the traditional wooden labyrinth. In the analog wooden version of the labyrinth game, you have to roll a marble through a labyrinth to reach the target without the marble falling into the holes on the way. The marble is controlled only by balancing the mobile surface, either by the player holding the board in his or her hands or by controlling its movements via two rotation buttons for tilting the board on the *x*- and *y*-axes. We want to recreate the game control as realistically as possible on the smartphone, albeit with some slight changes to the gameplay. Instead of balancing the ball toward a target, we want the ball that we call "MyBall" to chase another ball, called "GameBall," that pops up in appropriate intervals in different areas of the game board; we want to try to hit the other ball with MyBall. For each hit, the player scores points, but he or she can also lose points for each collision-free appearance of GameBall. As we are using the acceleration sensor, we can make MyBall roll around the game board at different speeds in accordance with the physical laws. Also, depending on how much the user tilts the board, he or she can accelerate the ball even more by moving the smartphone in the desired direction. In Figure 12.20, MyBall is always rolling toward the lowest point of the game board depending on the smartphone's position, and if possible it should hit the current position of GameBall on the way.

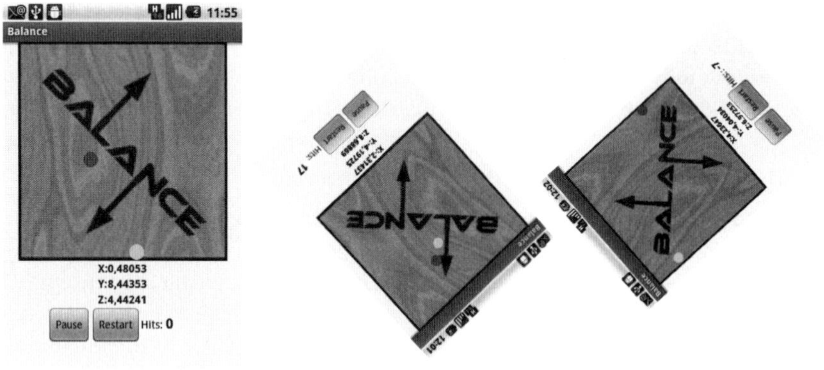

Figure 12.20 Balancing, rolling, and chasing the ball in the Balance game

This sounds a bit more complicated than the previous simulations we have developed with the sensors. Indeed, we will use a few more block structures this time, especially to simulate the almost realistic movement of the rolling ball on the game board. To start designing our game Balance in AI Designer, create a new project with the name "Balance," rename the title of "Screen1" accordingly, and add the components listed in Table 12.5.

Table 12.5 **Components and Initial Properties in the Balance Project**

Component	Object Name	Adapted Properties
Screen	Screen1	"Icon": balance_appIcon.png (companion website, `/MEDIA`)
Canvas	WoodCanvas	"BackgroundImage": balance.jpg (companion website, `/MEDIA`) "Width / Height": 280 × 280 pixels
Ball (2x)	MyBall, GameBall	"Color": Cyan, Red "Radius": 10, 10
AccelerometerSensor	AccelerometerSensor	
Clock	Clock1	"TimerInterval": 10
Clock	Clock2	"TimerInterval": 0 "TimerEnabled": disabled
Sound	Sound	
Label (3x)	XLabel, YLabel, ZLabel	"Text": X, Y, Z "FontBold" enabled
Button (2x)	PauseButton, NewButton	"Text": Pause, Restart
Label	HitsLabel	"Text": 0 "FontSize": 18 "FontBold" enabled

With the appropriate text labels, BufferLabels, and Arrangements (which you can add yourself), the project Balance should appear as shown in Figure 12.21. Make sure you set the dimensions of the component object `WoodCanvas` correctly, to 280 × 280 pixels.

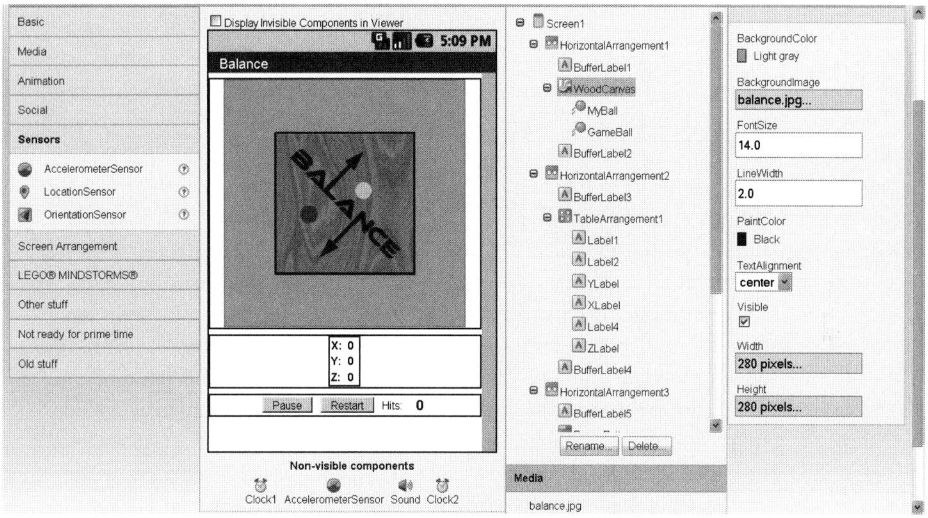

Figure 12.21 Components in the Balance project in AI Designer

After making these preparations in AI Designer, we are ready to move on to the functional implementation in AI Editor. Let's start with the simulation of the rolling movement of the `MyBall` object over the game board `WoodCanvas` (the object that the user balances), and try to make this rolling movement as realistic as possible. The animated graphical object `MyBall` should follow two laws of physics: (1) It should always move toward the "lowest" point of the game board and (2) it should do so with a variable speed, with the increase in speed depending on the degree of the smartphone's inclination. To be able to enter basic settings such as the base speed of the movement centrally and not in all sorts of possible points, we fix it in the form of the variable shown in Figure 12.22. The variables `X` und `Y` determine the initial position of `MyBall` when the app is started, whereas the two buffer values `borderMin` and `borderMax` will later prevent `MyBall` from traveling beyond the game board boundaries of `WoodCanvas` (a distance of 2 pixels on each side f the canvas edges, which are set at 280 × 280 pixels). In the variable `speed`, we set a factor by which the animation speed will dynamically increase in relation to the measured acceleration value.

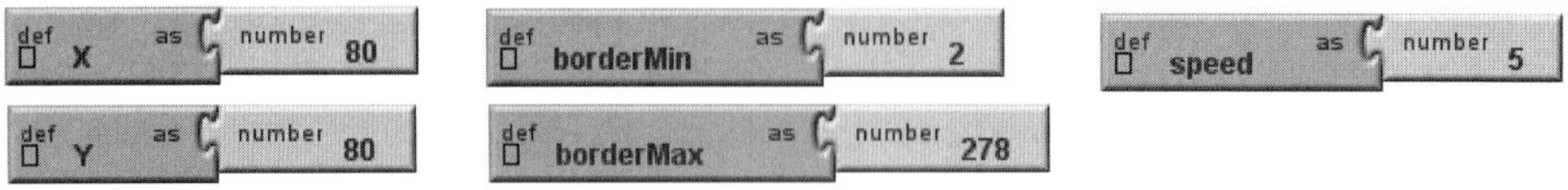

Figure 12.22 Specifying central settings as global variables

As with our other sensor-driven animations, we entrust the timer with controlling the retrieval of the measured values in intervals of one-hundredth of a second within the event handler `Clock1.Timer` (Figure 12.23) and use these values to simulate the falling and rolling movements of `MyBall`. In each cycle, the first nested `ifelse` branch checks two conditions—that is, whether `MyBall` is within the horizontal boundaries of `borderMin` and `WoodCanvas.Width`. If this is the case, then the positive or negative measured value of the current acceleration (see Figure 12.12) is multiplied by the speed factor `speed`, and the positive or negative result of this calculation is subtracted from the current position `X` (of `MyBall`), resulting in either a lower (movement to the left) or higher (movement to the right) new position value for `X`. The higher the value of the product that depends on the *g*-force, the higher the resulting animation speed. If `MyBall` has already reached the right edge of `WoodCanvas` (`X <= WoodCanvas.Width`), however, the value `X` is not reduced any further but remains set to the position value of `borderMax`; that is, `MyBall` stays on the corresponding "floor" of the canvas object. If it has reached the left canvas edge (`X >= borderMin`), the value `X` remains set to the position value of `borderMin` and `MyBall` stays on the opposite floor. Similarly, each timer event causes the second nested `ifelse` branch to recalculate the new value of the variable `Y`.

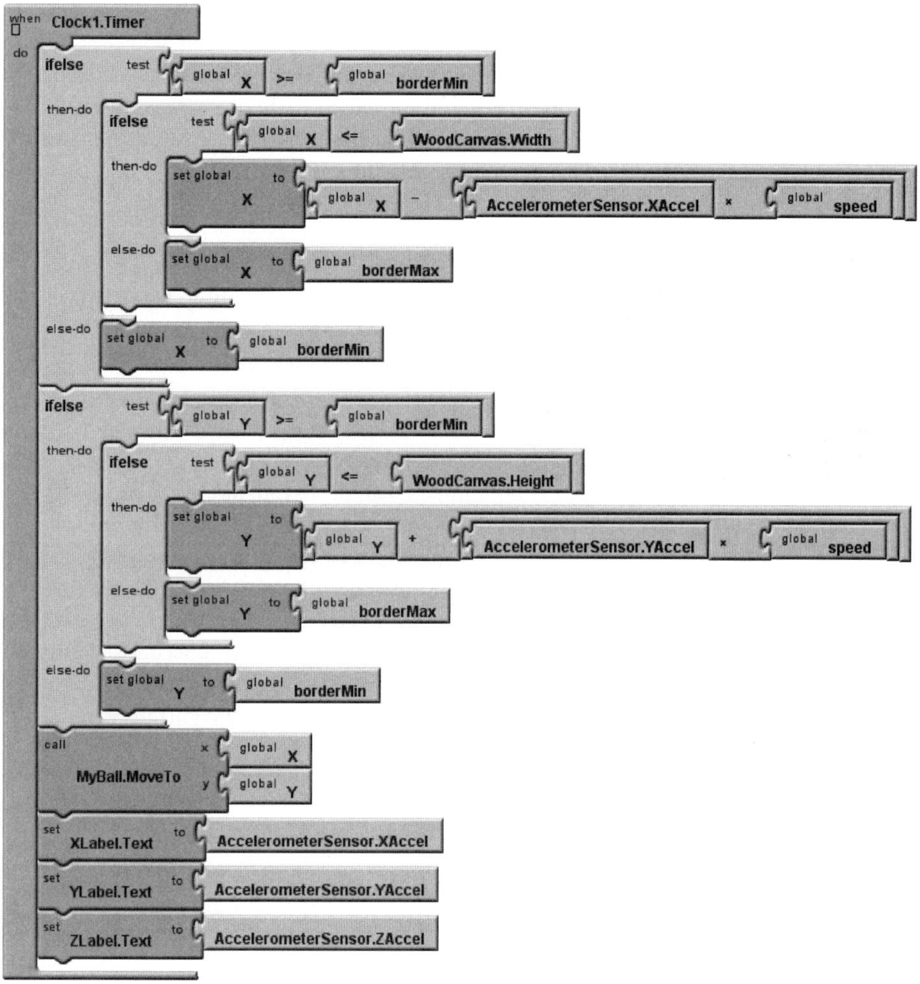

Figure 12.23 Movement simulation analogous to the measured player movement

Although (or perhaps because) the statements for calculating the new X,Y position in relation to the measured inclination angle are so short and condensed, you may need to take some time to fully comprehend them. If you want to track the measured values and calculated intermediate values to understand the processes better, you can use the AI Editor's Watch function to observe what happens when you move the smartphone once this device is integrated into the development environment. After the new values for `X` and `Y` have been calculated in the nested `ifelse` branches, they can easily be assigned as new position values to the animation object `MyBall` in each timer cycle via the method `MyBall.MoveTo` (Figure 12.23). For checking purposes, we also display the underlying measured values `XAccel`, `YAccel`, and `ZAccel` in the corresponding labels. Try the simulation yourself: Balance the blue-green ball and move it around the game board with your smartphone; let it roll around the edges or drop from one corner to another. Vary the tilt angles and move the smartphone in the desired direction you want the ball to go in, so as to test the different rolling speeds. Even though this is not a real physical simulation, the whole thing still feels quite realistic.

As the movement simulation is now fully implemented, we can add the other block structures shown in Figure 12.24 to create the proper game function. Several event handlers are involved, but the connections are quickly explained and easy to follow. Through the Restart button and the associated event handler `RestartButton.Click`, the hit counter is set to the initial value `0`, the second timer `Clock2` is enabled, and its `TimerInterval` is set to the initial value `2000`, to generate a time-controlled event every 2 seconds. Pressing the Pause button, which launches its event handler `PauseButton.Click`, causes the timer of `Clock2` to be switched off and on again, thereby switching from the current state of `Clock2.TimerEnabled` to the opposite Boolean state each time.

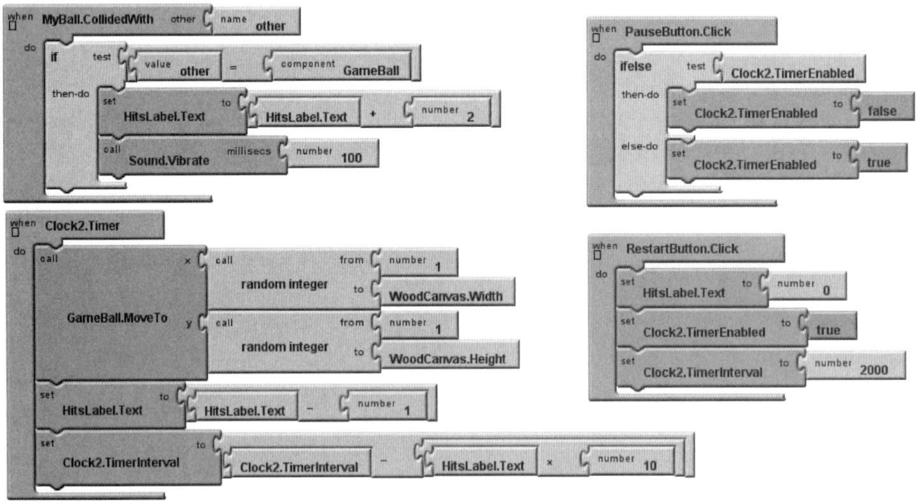

Figure 12.24 Game function for chasing the randomly appearing second ball

The animation of the second ball `GameBall`, which the player chases round the board, takes place in the event handler `Clock2.Timer` (Figure 12.24). As with all other animations, `GameBall` is set to its new X,Y position with each timer cycle via the method `MoveTo`. In contrast to the relatively fluid movements of the other animations, `GameBall` jumps every 2 seconds from one random position on the canvas object to the next; thus its functionality represents less an animated movement and more a regular change of location. The `GameBall` object appears on the game board for 2 seconds somewhere between `WoodCanvas.Width` and `WoodCanvas.Height`, then it disappears again and reappears in another place. For the sake of simplicity, we always reduce the hit score in `HitsLabel` by 1 in each timer cycle and then, to compensate for this change, we increase it again by 2 in case of a hit. To ensure that we do not constantly demand too little or too much of the player, we add a dynamic component to the game by adapting `Clock2.TimerInterval` to the current hit score and, therefore, to the player's performance level.

In these dynamic intervals, the player now has to try to navigate his or her `MyBall` to the `GameBall` and hit the latter to score points. The collision of the two animated objects `MyBall` and `GameBall` is registered via the event handler `MyBall.CollidedWith` (Figure 12.24) and causes the number of hits in the HitsLabel to be incremented by 2; in addition, a brief vibration created via the method `Sound.Vibrate` provides haptic feedback to the player.

Now you have developed a multisensory game that is definitely worth looking at and above all experiencing, and that can provide the basis for many other exciting and impressive game ideas.

Determining Geoposition with the LocationSensor Component

Until a few years ago, the ability to determine your own geoposition was considered very rare and exotic in the private sector, in addition to being rather expensive. Originally developed by the U.S. Department of Defense and intended exclusively for military use, the satellite-based position finding and navigation systems known as *GPS* (Global Positioning System) and *NAVSTAR GPS* (NAVigational Satellite Timing And Ranging GPS) eventually became accessible, useful, and cost-effective for civilian purposes when the intentional signal degradation by the U.S. military was turned off in May 2000. With this move, it became possible to pinpoint locations within approximately 30 feet (10 meters) for the first time. Over the years since GPS was opened up to the public, this accuracy has improved to just a few centimeters thanks to the use of modern differentiation methods such as differential GPS. At the beginning of the millennium, the required GPS parts were still rather fragile, big, expensive, and electricity intensive—characteristics that relegated GPS use to mainly professional aviation and seafaring, in the areas of geodesy and transportation. In recent years, however, GPS-based positioning has experienced a general breakthrough in the private sector with the triumphant success of navigation devices for cars. When a growing group of leisure-oriented users discovered the potential of mobile GPS systems for private outdoor activities such as hiking or geocaching, smartphones with GPS receivers became the norm; that is, smartphones *without* GPS receivers became the exception.

Background of GPS and Location-Based Services

Today, several previously separate systems and applications have been blended together in one single central device, the smartphone, which is increasingly displacing the dedicated navigation systems and mobile GPS systems of the past and opens up entirely new possibilities through the convergence of applications and technologies. Technical advancements such as *A-GPS* (Assisted GPS), in which the satellite-based position finding is supported by additional information from the cellphone network, are helping users achieve more and more precise positioning results faster and faster, even in urban environments and inside buildings. One weakness of mobile position finding via purely satellite-based GPS is that it requires a direct and largely unobstructed line of sight to at least four GPS satellites (three for calculating the position from the signal relay times, and one for synchronizing the time signal), which is often possible only to a limited extent or only with more or less significant interference, especially in urban environments and within buildings. Thus it helps if, for example, the signal relay times between at least three cellular network base stations can be factored into the position finding calculation. The developments in the area of location finding are by no means over, but the present results and technologies are already very impressive.

> **Background Information on GPS**
>
> If you would like to know more about the technology, history, and uses of GPS, you can search under the relevant terms on the Internet. For example, *Wikipedia* contains interesting articles on GPS, A-GPS, and more:
>
> `http://en.wikipedia.org/wiki/Gps`
>
> `http://en.wikipedia.org/wiki/Assisted_GPS`

With the rapid-fire spread and ready availability of GPS-capable devices, a basis for new digital services, applications, and social changes has evolved, whose vast potential, opportunities, and risks we can hardly grasp today. For example, *location-based services* (*LBS*), which were considered visionary not so long ago, have now become part of everyday life: Any navigation system can now show you the way to the next gas station or fast-food outlet when you are in your car and, thanks to the smartphone, on foot. In terms of technology, a GPS receiver and mobile data connection make it easy to tell your friends in a social network your own position data for buddy tracking or lifelogging. Of course, this greater openness in terms of personal data also creates some risks, which are currently the subject of controversy. Whereas the information on a user's current geoposition might be used positively to arrange a meeting point, for navigation, or for recording a hiking route, it could also be exploited for negative purposes such as unwanted advertising, supervision, or profiling someone's movements.

Please be aware of this fact: Your smartphone, which is equipped with GPS, compass, position and acceleration sensors, and possibly other sensors plus a mobile data access and corresponding apps, now "knows" exactly where it is and, above all, where *you* currently are, what you are pointing the smartphone camera at, what you can see and what is around you, where you have just been, who you are in contact with, what you are doing online, where you want to go, and much more. Clearly, location-based applications can and will be expanded to even more context-based applications in future. We cannot enter into the debate of the pros and cons of this trend within this book, nor do we want to. Nevertheless, our examples, in addition to demonstrating the power of AI, are meant to not only hint at the fascinating possibilities of location-based apps and their enormous potential for the future, but also make you aware that the ease of accessing such very personal location data makes it necessary to treat this information responsibly. In the first example project, you will develop an app with the usual ease in AI with which you can, on the one hand, record a harmless hiking route and make it consciously available to others who would like to hike there, but, on the other hand, create a profile of your movements that can be retrieved in real time online and that potentially enables others to track your (or your app's users') every step without your knowledge. Thankfully, you are developing the app yourself, which at least has the added advantage that you know what your own app is doing in the background.

Geocoordinates and Decimal Separators

Before entering into the specific development of location-based apps with AI, let's briefly introduce some basic terms that will make the later explanations easier to follow. A thorough introduction of the technical, geographical, nautical, and mathematical basics and terminology of determining location and the various methods for doing so is beyond the scope of this book. Even so, you should at least know what to do with the "measured values" that AI returns with the LocationSensor component so that you can process and use these values later in your apps. In our explanations, we will keep matters at the basic level and occasionally simplify the discussion. For further details, please refer to the relevant Internet sources under the appropriate search terms.

Find Further Information on Geographical-Related Content

If you would like to know more about the underlying geographical concepts, mathematical models, and navigation approaches, please search under the corresponding terms on the Internet. For example, *Wikipedia* offers interesting articles on longitude and latitude, the calculation of geographical distance and track angles, and much more:

`http://en.wikipedia.org/wiki/Longitude`

`http://en.wikipedia.org/wiki/Latitude`

`http://en.wikipedia.org/wiki/Great-circle_distance`

`http://en.wikipedia.org/wiki/Geographical_distance`

A position on the surface of the planet Earth can be clearly defined by two coordinates, similar to the X,Y positions on the canvas object. As the Earth's surface is not a flat surface, but an almost spherical curved surface, other measurements and units apply. The location of a particular point on Earth is described via *geographical coordinates*, the 360° of *longitude* and 180° of *latitude* shown in Figure 12.25. The lines of longitude (long.) run between the North and South Poles, with the *Prime Meridian* passing through the Royal Observatory in Greenwich, England, having the longitude 0°. From this point, the other degrees of longitude are measured up to 180° east and west. The distance between the lines of longitude is greatest at the equator, where they are separated approximately 111 km (40.000 km Earth circumference /360°), whereas they meet at one point in the poles. The calculation of the degrees of latitude (lat.) starts at the equator with 0° and goes up to 90° at the North Pole (+North, N) and South Pole (–South, S), where the distances between the lines of latitude are always approximately 111 km.

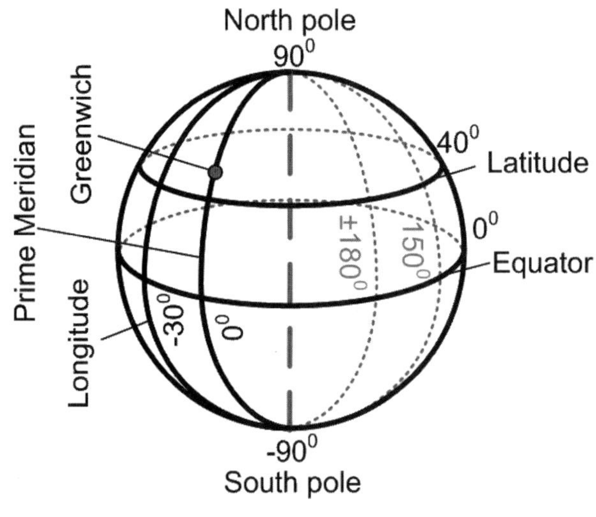

Figure 12.25 Latitude and longitude

Specifying a position on Earth via a geocoordinate is done with the corresponding degrees of latitude and longitude, in that order. Frequently, the degree numbers are still specified in the traditional *sexagesimal format*, as *degrees° minutes' seconds" cardinal point* (e.g., 50° 11' 42" N), where 60 seconds corresponds to 1 minute, and 60 minutes or nautical miles corresponds to 1 degree. In modern GPS systems, the geocoordinates are usually represented in decimals, and this is also the case in AI. The conversion from the traditional to the decimal notation follows the simple formula *degree + minute/60 + second/3600* (e.g., 50° 11' 42" N, 8° 35' 14" E = 50.1951 N, 8.5872 E), but the cardinal point is often omitted, with a negative sign instead being used to denote south and west coordinates (e.g., 50.1951, 8.5872). This notation is then also directly suitable for use as the initial values for any further calculations for navigation or measuring the distance.

When processing geocoordinates, you should also be aware that some European countries (for example, Germany) use a *comma* as the *decimal separator* instead of the *point* (period) commonly used in the United States to indicate the position of the decimal. U.S. systems such as the AI development environment expect a decimal point in their calculations (see *Wikipedia* for a list of countries indicating which use the decimal point which use the decimal comma: `http://en.wikipedia.org/wiki/Decimal_mark`). Thus, if a smartphone (or its GPS or other sensor) built or set up for the European market returns the geocoordinates with a decimal comma (e.g., 50,1951, 8,5872) to an application that expects a decimal point (e.g., 50.1951, 8.5872), this behavior may lead to wrong results (in the best-case scenario) or to a program crash (in the worst-case scenario). That is exactly what would happen if a smartphone is by default set to "comma" countries (for example, in Germany) and its GPS sensor returns values with decimal commas to an AI app that expects decimal points. To ensure that the users of AI apps do not have to change their country settings for the app to work properly and to be able to use the geocoordinate values returned by the AI component LocationSensor no matter which country the app is being used in, you may have to convert the values from decimal comma numbers to decimal point numbers before you can use them in AI for further calculations. We will demonstrate this conversion in the context of our second example project GeoCacher, in which we want to calculate the distance between two measured geocoordinates. For our first example project GeoTracker, we do not require this conversion, as we do not make any calculations with the measured geocoordinates.

Before we get to the location-based example projects, let's take a quick look at the specification of the required non-visible component LocationSensor, which AI also offers in the group Sensor Components (see Figure 12.26). At the beginning of the specification, it emphasizes that the geodata provided via the sensor component does not have to come from a GPS sensor but instead can come from an alternative source (*provider*) such as the cellular network or WLAN, provided the smartphone can receive these values and the system can access them. To check the smartphone equipment, various properties are available. Apart from the general check to determine whether the geo-receiver is set to "enabled," the available geodata sources can be identified via AvailableProviders and the currently active provider can be identified via ProviderName and set permanently with ProviderLocked. With the Has properties, you can also check the general availability of data sources in terms of the accuracy of reception (`HasAccuracy`), the altitude (`HasAltitude`), and the geoposition (`HasLongitudeLatitude`).

LocationSensor

This component provides the Android device's location, using GPS if available and an alternative method otherwise, such as cellular towers or known wireless networks.

`LocationSensor` is a non-visible component providing location information, including longitude, latitude, altitude (if supported by the device), and address. This component can also provide geocoding, converting a given address (not necessarily the current one) to a latitude (with the `LatitudeFromAddress` method) and a longitude (with the `LongitudeFromAddress` method).

In order to function, the component must have its `Enabled` property set to true, and the device must have location sensing enabled through either GPS satellites (if the device is outdoors) or an alternative method.

Properties

Accuracy
Indicates Android device accuracy level, in meters.
Altitude
Altitude of the Android device, if available.
AvailableProviders
List of available service providers, such as *gps* or *network*
CurrentAddress
Physical street address of the Android device.
Enabled
If set, location information is available.
HasAccuracy
If true, Android device can report its accuracy level.
HasAltitude
If true, Android device can report its altitude.
HasLongitudeLatitude
If true, Android device can report longitude and latitude.
Latitude
Android device latitude.
Longitude
Android device longitude.
ProviderLocked
The device will not change the service provider.
ProviderName
The current service provider.

Events

`LocationChanged(number latitude, number longitude, number altitude)`
Called when the Android device reports a new location.
`StatusChanged(text provider, text status)`
Called when the status of the service provider changes.

Methods

`LatitudeFromAddress(text locationName)`
Determines the latitude of the given address.
`LongitudeFromAddress(text locationName)`
Determines the longitude of the given address.

Figure 12.26 Specification of the LocationSensor component in AI References

In addition to the properties for checking the equipment beforehand, you also find the properties for receiving the geodata. The Altitude, Latitude, and Longitude properties correspond to the values for the currently measured geoposition, and the Accuracy property specifies the accuracy of these values in meters. By accessing online data and comparing it to the geocoordinates, the street address of the current location is determined and recorded in CurrentAddress. If the geoposition changes or if new geodata is received, the event block `LocationChanged` is activated and is passed the new geoposition as a series of latitude, longitude, and altitude values. Also, any changes in the geo-provider status are displayed via the event block `StatusChanged` and the new provider is displayed in the form of a status message. Using the two methods `LatitudeFromAddress` and `LongitudeFromAddress`, the geocoordinates of the street address can be determined, which basically reverses the function of the CurrentAddress property.

In addition to describing the many functions of the LocationSensor component, the AI References specification states that the position sensor works properly only in independent apps (installed APK files), although this does not seem to apply for every smartphone. Try it with your own smartphone—perhaps the position sensor will also work within the development environment. The emulator is no help at all in this situation, as the emulator (or, more specifically, your computer) does not typically have a GPS sensor and would need to perform an elaborate simulation to provide the necessary GPS data. It's best if you use your smartphone as the attached device during development, because that is where the geo app is supposed to run later.

Surely you are now eager to see the component LocationSensor in action. Let's get to work.

A Geotracker for Tracking Your Route Profile

In light of the previous discussion of the opportunities and risks associated with location-based apps, the description of our first example project with which we want to demonstrate the component LocationSensor proves somewhat of a double-edged sword. The basic description of the function can be found by searching for terms such as "GPS tracking" and "digital footprint" on sites such as *Wikipedia*. But we want to deal as neutrally as possible with the options offered by AI for developing a geotracker. In geotracking, the route you have traveled is recorded by determining and saving the current geocoordinates of your location (latitude and longitude) in regular intervals (time, but also per kilometer or some other unit), similar to the breadcrumbs used by Hansel and Gretel as trail markers in the forest. On modern GPS systems and smartphones, other geodata (e.g., altitude, address), along with the geocoordinates and the recording time and date, can be automatically recorded and logged in a *track log*. This data can then be used, for example, to create a route and altitude profile after or during a hiking trip, and also graphically represented within a canvas object. Apart from the address data, which must be determined online using the geocoordinates, all of this information is available even if your smartphone no longer has a signal out in the middle of nowhere, provided you have a clear line of sight to the sky and at least four GPS satellites (and the battery is not empty). With the app developed in this example project, you can turn your smartphone into a real geotracker.

> **Example Project GeoTracker on the Companion Website**
>
> All files for the project can be found in the corresponding directories on the companion website (see the link in the Introduction).

> **Enable the GPS Receiver on Your Smartphone!**
>
> To ensure that the geodata can be received in the first place, you need to have enabled the GPS receiver on your smartphone. Just like the other reception options, you usually enable it via the top status bar or another shortcut. If you have questions, refer to the user guide for your smartphone.

In case you are not familiar with how a GPS tracker or geotracker works, Figure 12.27 shows the functions of the geotracker that we will implement later. After starting the app, you can set the time interval for recording the position (left) and enable the tracking via the check box "enabled". During your hiking trip, the current location data is then constantly recorded and displayed in the section "Current position" in the form of geocoordinates, altitude, address (if available), and time stamp (center). After each time interval, the current location is also logged and displayed in a continuous list in the "Track log," with the last entry appearing in first place (right). As long as the check box "online" is not enabled, your position data is simply recorded on your smartphone by the app and then deleted when you quit the app.

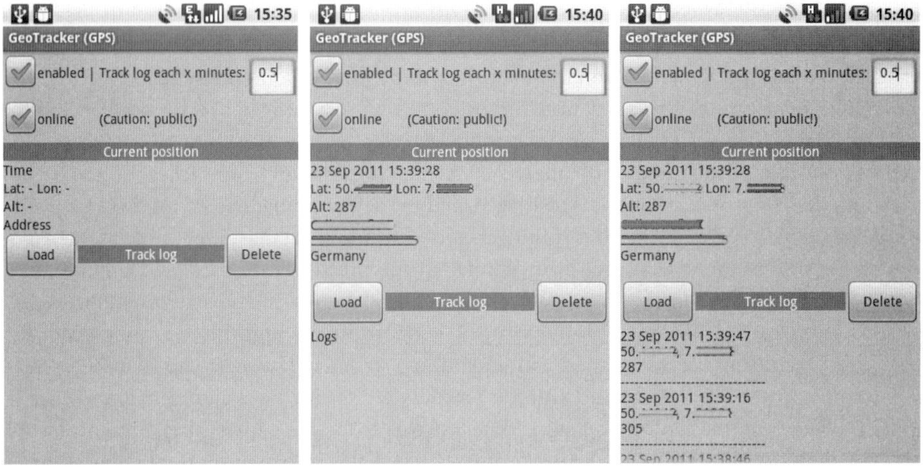

Figure 12.27 The geotracker in the GeoTracker project in action

If the check box "online" is enabled, the position data is also saved online with each new entry in the log. Of course, it would be possible to save this data locally via the TinyDB component, but we want to go one step further and save the position data online in the cloud via the TinyWebDB component. You can later change your preferences at any time and add a local saving function, which can be useful if there is no signal while you are out in the middle of nowhere. With our geotracker, however, we want to demonstrate that it really is very easy to record a movement profile on a smartphone, with this profile later being loaded at the same time or almost simultaneously to another smartphone through the same app by simply pressing the Load button. The profile can then be used for a variety of purposes. In our example of Figure 12.28, the geodata saved online is available as usual on the AI test server online in plain text and can be retrieved from there.

Figure 12.28 Geodata of the route profile online in the cloud

Use Your Own Tag Names for Saving Data Online!

Do not forget to use your *own* tag names for your own app. Otherwise, the readers of this book will keep overwriting one another's log entries on the shared online database at `http://appinvtinywebdb.appspot.com/`!

To make sure you can delete this data again, our geotracker offers the Delete button. With it, you can not only delete the track log locally on the smartphone, but also overwrite the online lists with empty lists, as shown in Figure 12.29.

Figure 12.29 Deleting the log on the smartphone and in the cloud

As you can tell from the figures, the optical design of our geotracker is not very complicated, so we can implement it quickly in our example project GeoTracker. Create a new project in AI Designer and name it "GeoTracker," give the corresponding title to "Screen1," and add the components shown in Table 12.6 for the new project. Make sure you set the Clock property TimerInterval to the correct value (`60000`) so it matches the default value `1` of the MinutesTextBox for recording the position every minute. Both check boxes should initially be disabled to ensure that the position is recorded only when the user consciously turns this function on.

Table 12.6 **Components and Initial Properties in the GeoTracker Project**

Component	Object Name	Adapted properties
Screen	Screen1	"Icon": gpstrack_applcon.png (companion website, `/MEDIA`)
LocationSensor	LocationSensor	"Enabled": disable
Clock	Clock	"TimerInterval": 60000
TinyWebDB	TinyWebDB	
CheckBox (2x)	EnabledCheckBox, OnlineCheckBox	"Checked": disable
TextBox	MinutesTextBox	"Text": 1
Label (3x)	TimeLabel, AddressLabel, LogLabel	"Text": Time, Address, Logs
Label (3x)	LatLabel, LonLabel, AltLabel	"Text": -, -, -
Button (2x)	LoadButton, DelButton	"Text": Load, Delete

With the addition of the appropriate DivisionLabels, text labels, and arrangements, the project GeoTracker should appear as shown in Figure 12.30.

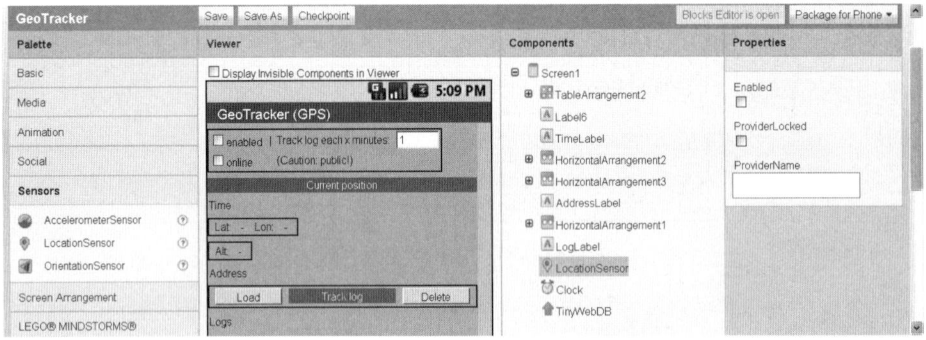

Figure 12.30 Project GeoTracker in AI Designer

Now we can move on to the functional implementation of the app in AI Editor. We want to record the individual log entries for the different geodata in lists, so we need to create these lists at start-up and initialize them as empty lists, as shown in Figure 12.31. We also initialize a global auxiliary variable `i`, which will we will use later as a counter variable—for example, when reading the list values.

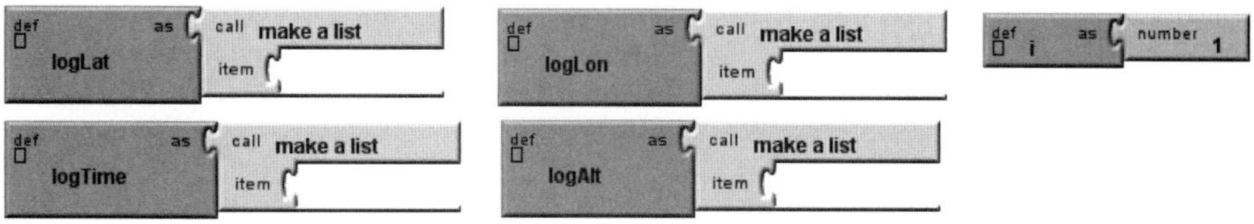

Figure 12.31 Lists for recording the geodata and the auxiliary variable i

By selecting the check box "enabled," the user starts recording the position via the sensor available on the smartphone or, more specifically, from the currently active provider (e.g., GPS, A-GPS). In the corresponding event handler `EnabledCheckBox.Changed` (Figure 12.32), the current Boolean property of the check box determines whether the sensor is turned on (`true`) or off (`false`) via the property `LocationSensor.Enabled`. If the user turns it on, an animated GPS icon typically appears in the top status bar of the smartphone. For the second check box "online," we do not even require an event handler, as its Boolean property will be checked directly later (see Figure 12.34).

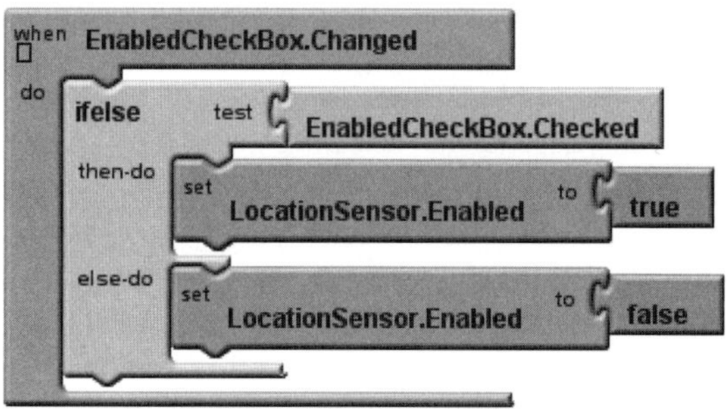

Figure 12.32 Start logging the position

This takes us to the actual retrieval of geodata from the receiving sensor. Instead of retrieving the data controlled by a timer in fixed intervals as we did with the other sensors (though this would also be possible here), we use the corresponding event block `LocationChanged` in the LocationSensor, which is called automatically when the geosensor has received new data. This is usually the case if the location has changed, but it can also happen after signal interference if the sky is cloudy and then clears again or if additional GPS satellites come into range. With each sensor-driven call of the event handler `LocationSensor.LocationChanged` (Figure 12.33), it is passed the currently measured geodata in the three local variables `latitude`, `longitude`, and `altitude`. Within the event handler, we use this geodata for displaying the "Current position" in the corresponding label and add the current time stamp of `Clock.Now` in the format `Clock.FormatDateTime`. Finally, we use the sensor method `LocationSensor.CurrentAddress` to determine the matching street address of the current geocoordinates and display it, if available. Each time a new geoposition is received, the event handler is called again so that the user is always informed of his or her current location in the app section "Current position."

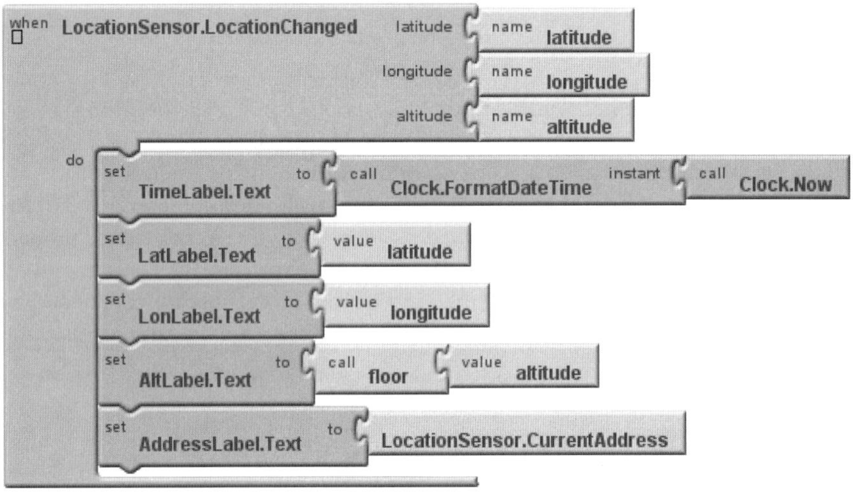

Figure 12.33 Receiving geodata and displaying it with the address and time stamp

After the current geoposition is recorded via the event handler shown in Figure 12.33 and is displayed in the TimeLabel, LatLabel, LonLabel, AltLabel, and AddressLabel, we can also log this data in the data log at the default interval (1 minute) or the interval specified by the user. To that purpose, in the event handler `Clock.Timer` (Figure 12.34) we read in the last-received geodata from the labels and append it to the corresponding lists `logLat`, `logLon`, and `logAlt`. If the user does not move during a period of time that is longer than the specified interval, this fact is also recorded in the log by marking the same constant and unchanging geoposition with each new entry with the current (and therefore different) time stamp. Entries are made in the log only if the check box "enabled" is enabled; its status is checked via the conditional `if` statement at the beginning of the event handler. Once the entries have been added to the lists, the lists are displayed in the appropriate format in the app's Track Log area through statements in the `showLog` procedure (see Figure 12.36 later in this chapter) so that the user can track the log entries live online.

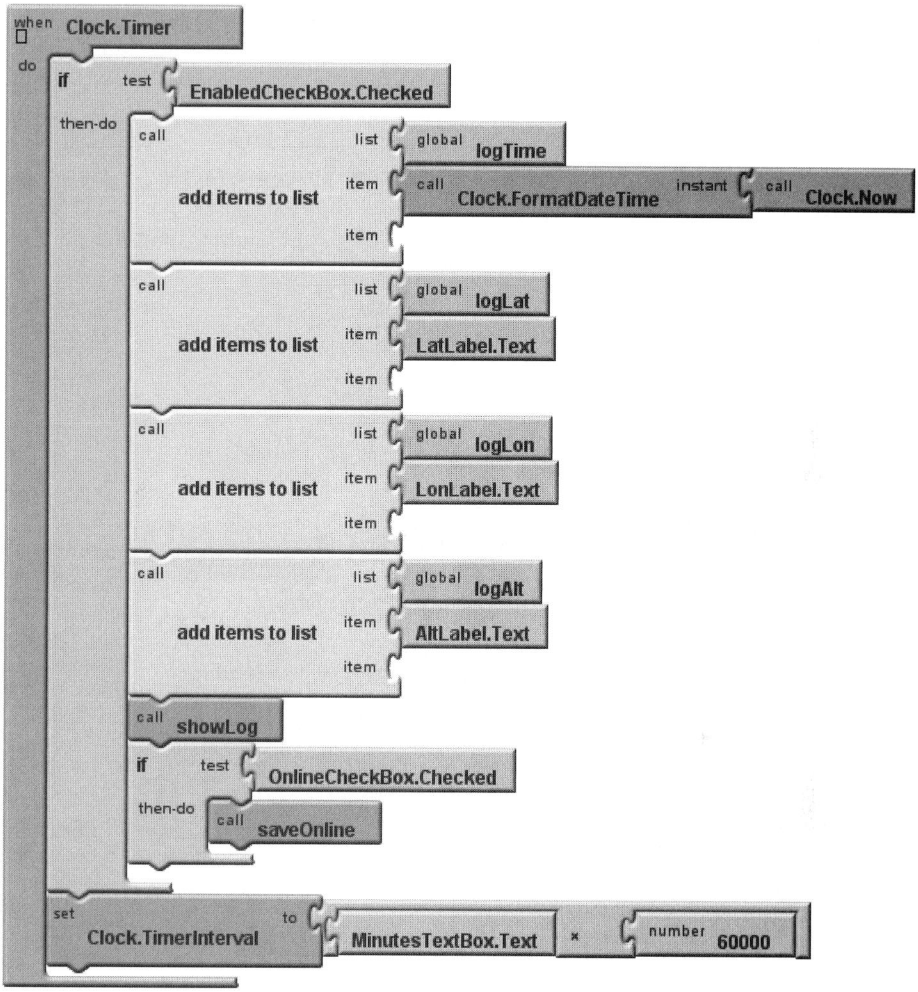

Figure 12.34 Recording the current geoposition with a time stamp in the data log

The first conditional `if` statement in the event handler `Clock.Timer` (Figure 12.34) encompasses a second conditional `if` statement, which has an important function despite its inconspicuous appearance. At this point, the check of the Boolean property `OnlineCheckBox.Checked` determines whether the log should just be displayed on the smartphone (`false`) or whether it should also be saved online on the AI test server (`true`). Only if the check box "online" is selected (i.e., marked with a green check mark) will the condition be fulfilled (`true`), with the log then being saved online in the cloud after each time interval via the statements in the `saveOnline` procedure (see

Figure 12.35). Independent of the settings of the two check boxes (in other words, outside of the two conditional `if` statements), at the end of each cycle of the event handler `Clock.Timer` its own time interval `Clock.TimerInterval` is reset to the new current value (which potentially may have been changed by the user in the meantime) of minutes (* `60000`) taken from the MinutesTextBox.

For the sake of clarity, we took the statements for saving the log on the AI test server and combined them in the separate procedure `saveOnline` shown in Figure 12.35. In the usual way, the current lists `logTime`, `logLat`, `logLon`, and `logAlt` are stored on the AI test server under unique identifiers (tags) `TWDBlogTime`, `TWDBlogLat`, `TWDBlogLon`, and `TWDBlogAlt`, respectively, via the method `TinyWebDB.StoreValue`. Remember to assign your own unique identifiers to avoid other developers and readers of this book overwriting your log!

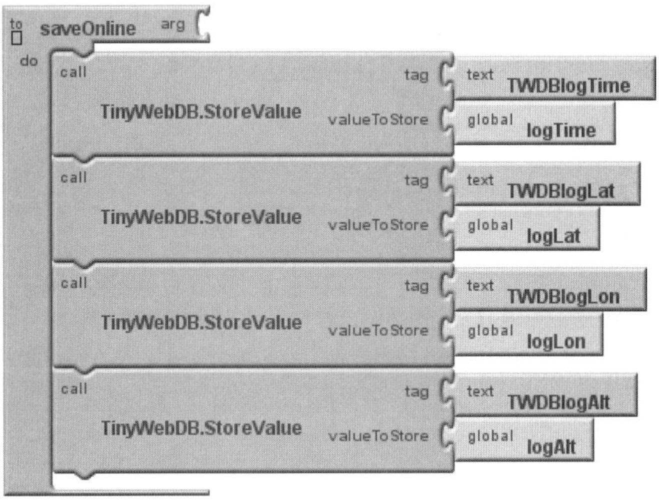

Figure 12.35 Storing the log lists online on the AI test server

Just as easy is the formatted display of the log, which is updated with each timer interval, on the user's smartphone. Again, we combine these statements in a separate procedure `showLog` as in Figure 12.36, to make things clearer. Similar to an example earlier in this book that provided for formatted output of lists with loop constructs, we read all elements of the four lists consecutively in a `while` loop in the event handler `showLog` with each call (at each newly added item), then join the elements together successively to form a coherent text string via the method `make text`, which we then display in

LogLabel.Text. The counter for the while loop is the auxiliary variable i, to which we assign the item number (length of list) of the equally long lists as the initial value, and then use to output the lists in reverse order (i = i - 1) from the most recent to the oldest entry (last in, first out—the *LIFO* principle).

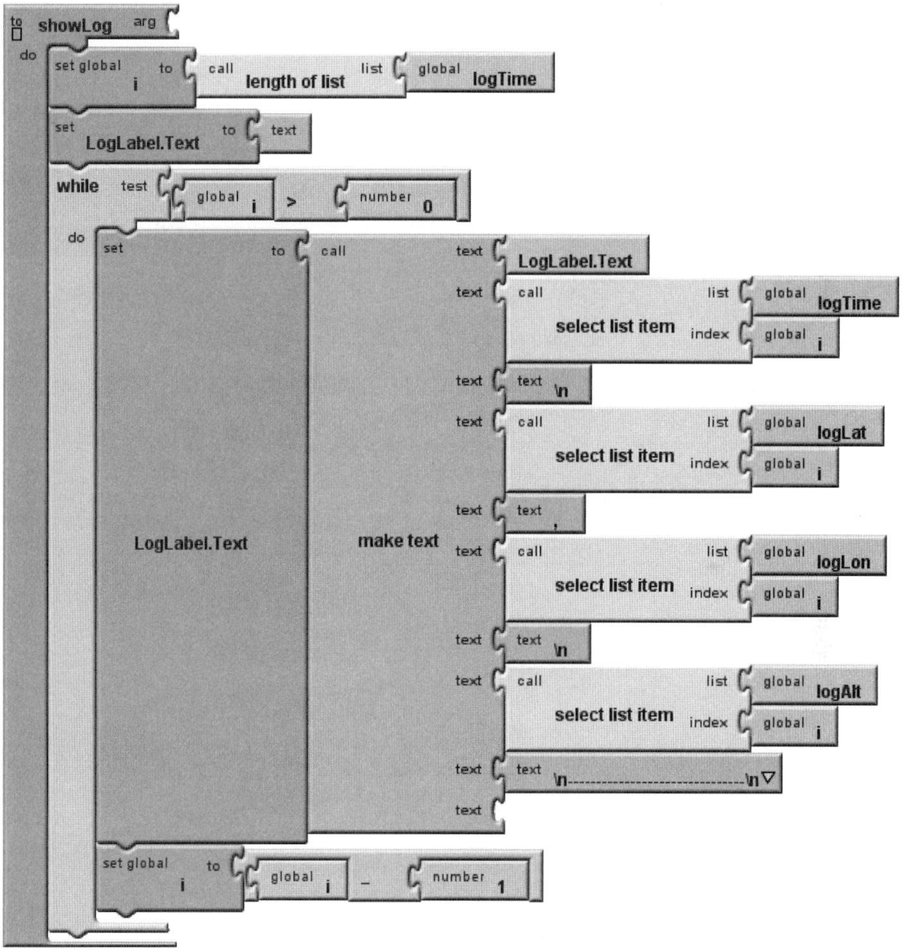

Figure 12.36 Formatted output of the log on the smartphone

The deletion of the log when the user presses the Delete button is carried out by the event handler `DelButton.Click` (Figure 12.37) and follows a similar principle. Like the display formatting procedure, it starts with the last list item. This time, however, all list items are deleted from the lists one after the other in a `while` loop via the method `remove list item` (i.e., the items are removed permanently, not just overwritten), until the lists are empty. With the next call of the procedure `saveOnline`, the filled lists previously stored online are overwritten with the empty lists, so that the log is deleted from the AI test server as well. The local display of the log can be deleted by assigning an empty text string to the LogLabel.

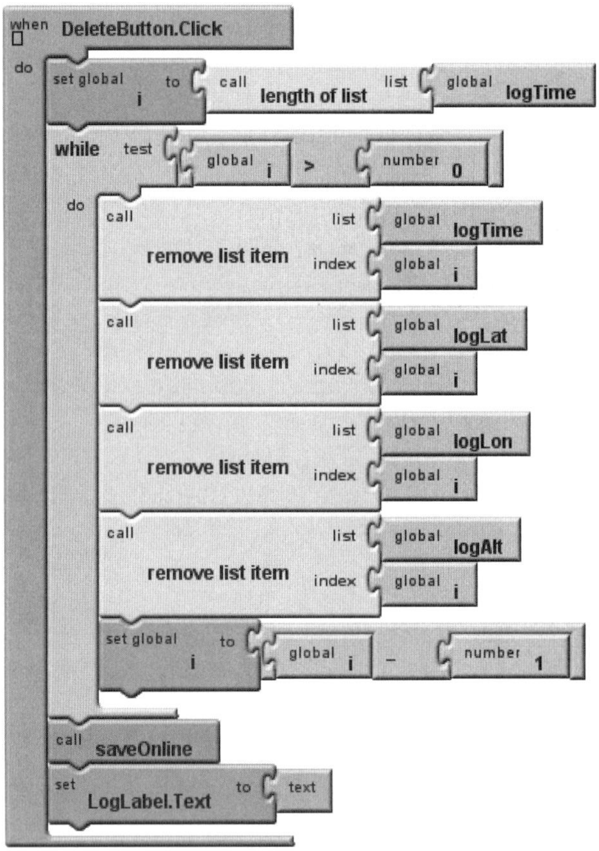

Figure 12.37 Deleting the log both locally and online

If you have not yet deleted your online log but have already closed the GeoTracker app and want to view the log at a later time, you can download it from the AI test server to your smartphone by pressing the Load button and displaying it on your smartphone in the Track Log. Of course, any other user of the GeoTracker app can do this, too, provided he or she is using the same tags for the saved lists. This possibility makes it all the more important that you use custom tags and ensure that your confidential data is stored safely and securely on a separate, protected server. Retrieving the lists stored online follows the familiar two-step process of request and asynchronous reception. In the event handler `LoadButton.Click` shown in Figure 12.38, the saved lists are requested from the web server in the first step with the method `TinyWebDB.GetValue` and the lists' unique identifiers.

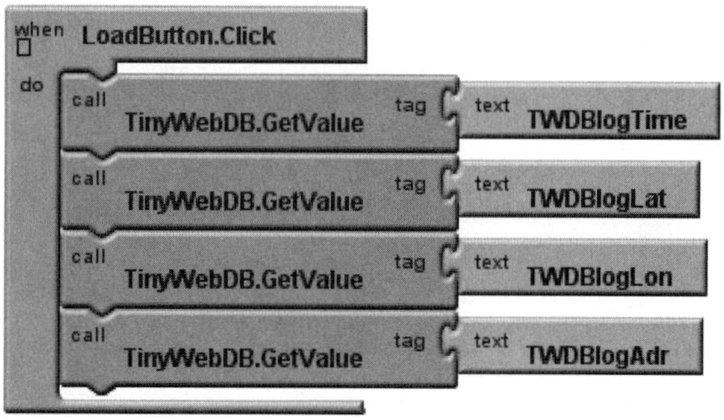

Figure 12.38 Requesting the saved lists on the AI test server

Each arrival of an individual list on the smartphone then results in calling the event handler `TinyWebDB.GotValue` shown in Figure 12.39. In individual conditional `if` statements, the received list is identified from the tag supplied in `tagFromWebDB` and assigned to the matching local list variable (either `logTime`, `logLat`, `logLon`, or `logAlt`). As soon as all requested lists have arrived and the conjunctional `AND` condition in the `ifelse` branch is fulfilled, the loaded lists can be displayed in the usual way with the procedure `showLog` in the app's Track Log area. If no entries were found, the message `no logs` is displayed instead.

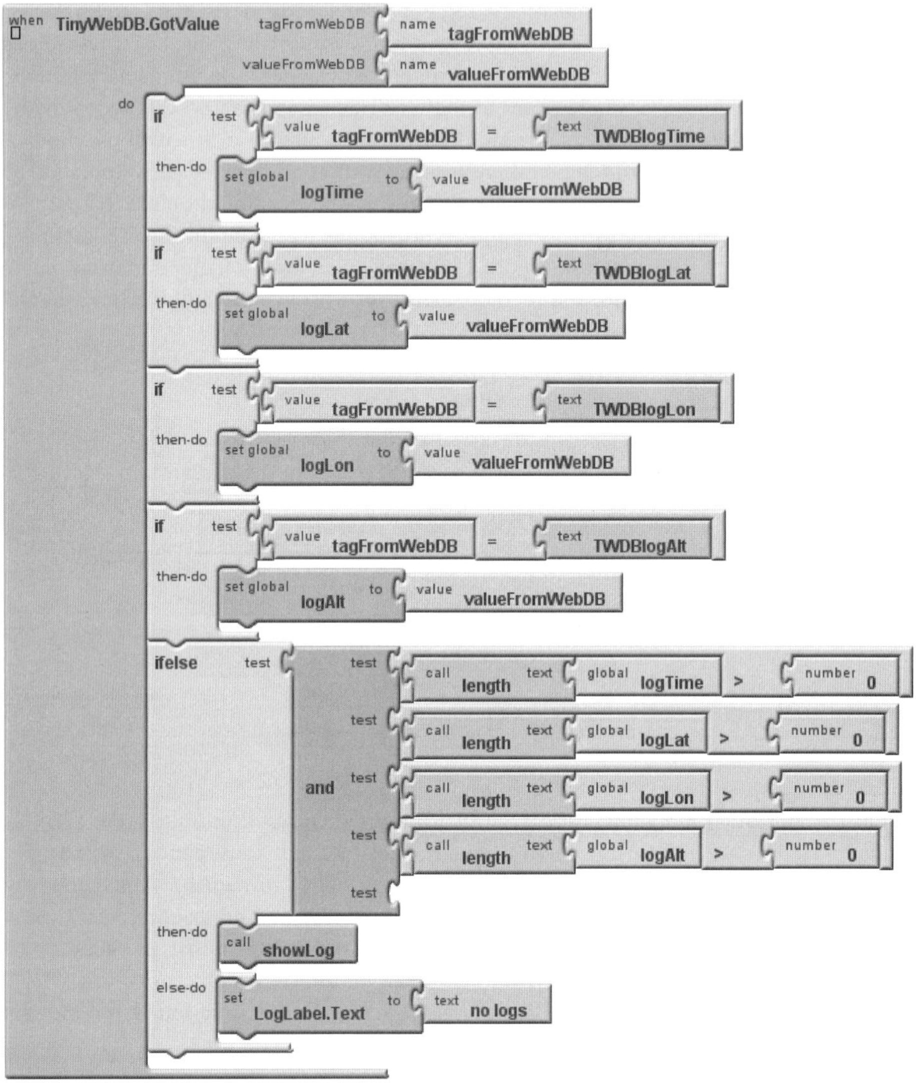

Figure 12.39 Receiving lists from a web server, and assigning and displaying lists

Now that this last event handler for retrieving the route and altitude profile saved online is complete, we have fully implemented the functionality of our GeoTracker app. Have a go and try it! It works best outdoors, perhaps while you go for a nice long walk or hike somewhere—an activity that both makes a nice change after sitting in front of the computer for a few hours and gives you the chance to do a proper field test. Amidst the general controversy regarding opportunities and risks in connection with location-based applications, you should not overlook the impressive special options that AI gives you once again with amazing ease in the form of the LocationSensor component. Would you have guessed that you could turn your smartphone into a geographical measurement device just like that?

Geocaching with Your Smartphone

If you have not yet been carried away by new wave of enthusiasm for *geocaching*, this book and the next example project may bring you closer to this fascinating outdoor activity. Geocaching is something like a modern GPS-based variation on the traditional treasure hunting game. With the growing popularity of GPS use for civilian purposes since the beginning of the millennium, *geocachers* have made it their task (or sport) to hide small waterproof containers (*caches*) with more or less useful contents and little paper log books in all sorts of places around the world. The positions of the hiding places are then published on the Internet with their geocoordinates, and other geocachers try to find the "treasures" by using their GPS devices. The finders usually write something in the log book, exchange one of the found articles in the cache with an article of their own, and hide the cache again in the same place, always wary of the "muggles" who neither know nor suspect anything of this mysterious parallel world. In addition to the *traditional caches* with centrally published geocoordinates, other variations exist—for example, *multi-caches*, where the path to the cache itself first has to be discovered via several stations. In this case, the geocoordinates of the next station are either given directly or are encoded in the form of a riddle. If you are interested in this topic, have a look on the Internet under the relevant search terms to find out more. You should also visit `www.geocaching.com`, one of the biggest international platforms on this topic. You will be surprised to see how many caches are located right near you—and to realize that you did not have the faintest idea they even existed!

To take part in geocaching, you will at least need a mobile GPS system into which you can enter the target coordinates of a cache and that can then lead you to the stash. As many of the caches are located outside of cities in the open countryside, you cannot always rely on a cellphone signal and online navigation (for example, with Google Navigation); instead, you often have only the sensory data of your GPS system and its digital compass to go by for finding your way around. Operating these navigation aids and determining your position with them does take some practice, so you should not venture too far and seek out very remote caches unless you really know what you are doing and have gained some experience. If you should get lost one day, you can fall back on the geocoordinates of your starting position, which ideally you will have written down or saved in the GPS system, so that you can find your way back to the start of your hike.

In our example project, we want to develop a simple geocaching app with AI, which offers some of the described functions to a certain extent. Calculating navigation data is no trivial matter, however, and the development of a truly professional and reliable geocaching app would go beyond the scope of this book, as it is primarily intended to offer an introduction and general overview of AI. Given those limitations, the following example app is intended mainly as inspiration for your own geo-based projects with AI. You can further explore this topic and develop corresponding functions on your own to your taste. In our example project GeoCacher, we will combine the functions of the

GeoTracker project with those of the Compass project to create a GPS system. In addition to displaying all available information on your current location, the geocacher is meant to enable you to enter a target coordinate and show you the distance to and direction toward this target, so that you can use the constantly updated navigational data to find your way to the specified target.

> **Example Project GeoCacher on the Companion Website**
>
> All files for this project are available in the corresponding directories on the companion website.

In Figure 12.40, you can see the geocacher in action. Below the adapted compass, the section "Current location" displays the geocoordinates received via the geosensor, including the altimeter reading, the accuracy of reception, and a time stamp (left). If you scroll down, even more areas become visible (center). In the "Target location" area, you can enter the desired geocoordinates as target data in the two fields "Lat" and "Lon"; you can also use the Current button to enter your current position as a target—for example, as the starting or returning point of a hike. "System status" displays additional information on the equipment and current reception status and provider for your smartphone. Once the target coordinates have been entered and the targeting has been enabled via the checkbox "enabled," the current position is used to display the distance ("Target distance") in kilometers and the direction ("Track angle") in degrees below the compass (right). The second arrow behind the compass needle (green color) indicates the track angle as well. If you point the smartphone north, the green directional arrow rotates toward the direction where the specified target is located the next time new geodata is received. Using the target distance and the direction indicator, you can then plan your journey to the target point and start walking in that direction.

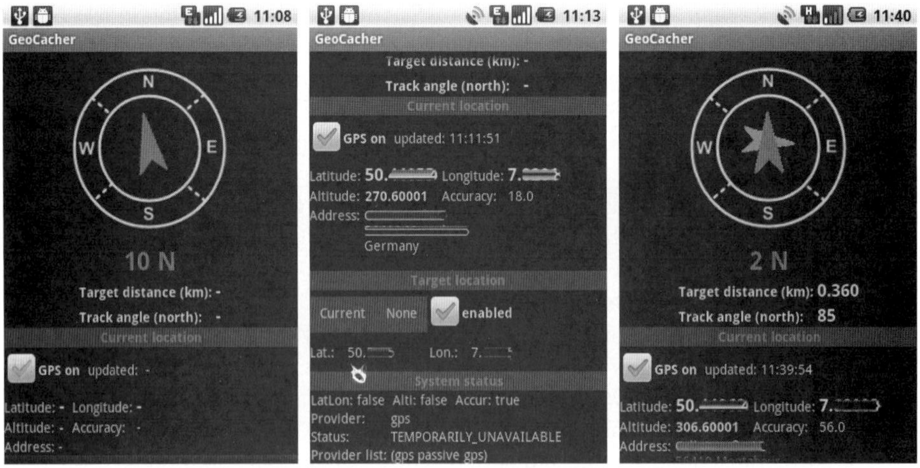

Figure 12.40 Distance and direction indicator in the GeoCacher app

As you can probably guess from the multitude of data displayed in the geocacher in Figure 12.40, the design of the user interface requires a number of display components. As we want to reuse the previously developed compass function from the Compass project, you can simply load that project in AI Designer and save it under the new project name "GeoCacher" via the Save As function. Keep all components of the compass, including the OrientationSensor and the Clock, but replace the BackgroundImage of the canvas object with the image file `compassgreen.png` and then reduce it to 200 × 200 pixels. Now add the components shown in Table 12.7, which we limit to the most important functional components for implementing the desired functionality. You can add the numerous text labels, DivisionLabels, Arrangements, and BufferLabels on your own, as well as the color design of the app for displaying data in a green font on a black background (TextColor: Green) and labels in light gray (TextColor: Light gray).

Table 12.7 **Added Components and Initial Properties in the GeoCacher Project**

Component	Object Name	Adapted Properties
Screen	Screen1	"Icon": geocache_appIcon.png (companion website, `/MEDIA`)
LocationSensor	LocationSensor	"Enabled" disable
ImageSprite	DirectionSprite	"Picture": needlegreen.png (companion website, `/MEDIA`) "Visible" disable
Label (2x)	DistanceLabel, TrackAngleLabel	"Text": Target distance (km), Track angle (north) "FontSize": 18
CheckBox (2x)	GPSCheckBox, EnabledCheckBox	"Text": GPS on, Enabled "FontBold" enable
Label (6x)	TimeLabel, LatLabel, LonLabel, AltiLabel, AccurLabel, AddressLabel	"Text": updated, Latitude, Longitude, Altitude, Accuracy, Address
Button (2x)	CurrentButton, NoneButton	"Text": Current, None
TextBox (2x)	LatTextBox, LonTextBox	"Text": -, -
Label (6x)	LatLonOkLabel, AltiOkLabel, AccurOkLabel, ProvActualLabel, ProvStatusLabel, ProvListLabel	"Text": -, -, -, -, -, -

To place the green directional indicator arrow that you just added (DirectionSprite) *behind* the existing red compass needle, you may have to remove the latter temporarily to a second canvas object and then drag it back to the original `Canvas` object so that the order of the two ImageSprites is reversed in the representation. As the directional arrow should be displayed only if a target has been specified and the navigation is activated, we hide the DirectionSprite in the default setting ("Visible" disabled). During the interface design, you can temporarily show the directional arrow in AI Designer by enabling the check box "Display Invisible Components in Viewer" above the Viewer area. After adding the new components, the project GeoCacher should look in AI Designer as shown in Figure 12.41.

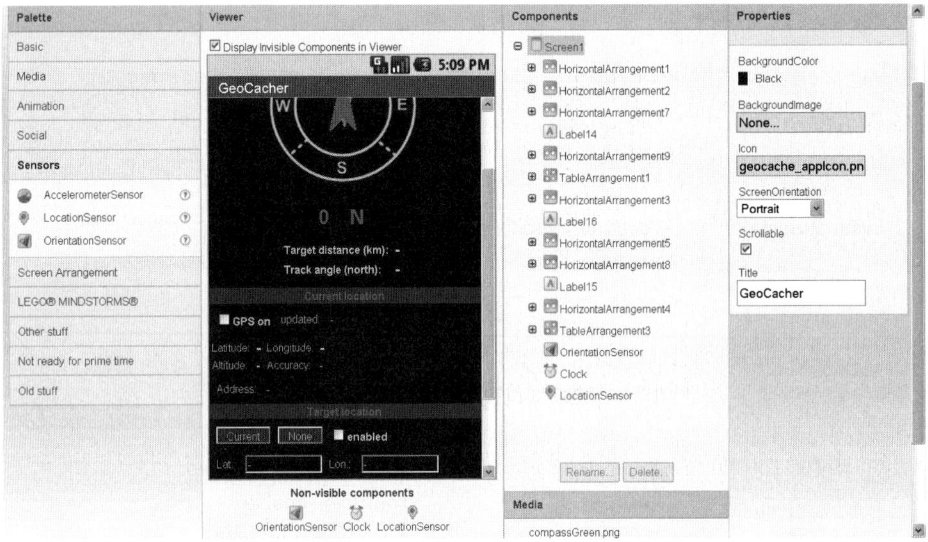

Figure 12.41 Project GeoCacher in AI Designer

Now we can start implementing the functionality of our GeoCacher in AI Editor and filling the numerous display labels with measured and calculated values. We also reuse the entire existing compass functionality from the event handler `Clock.Timer` (see also Figure 12.7) without making any changes, although we collapse the block structure as shown in Figure 12.42.

Figure 12.42 Reusing the event handler of the Compass project

Before we can work with geodata, we first need to enable the geosensor. This is done by the user selecting the check box "GPS on," which calls the event handler GPSCheckBox.Changed (Figure 12.43). In the usual way, it switches the sensor on (true) and off (false) via its Boolean property LocationSensor.Enabled. With each new selection, the capability characteristics of the sensor are checked regarding position (HasLongitudeLatitude), altitude (HasAltitude), and accuracy measurement (HasAccuracy) and the results are displayed in the corresponding labels as Boolean values.

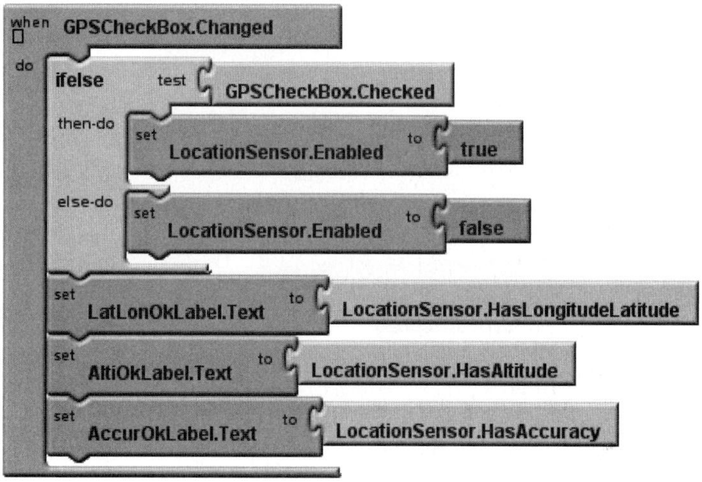

Figure 12.43 Enabling the geosensor and displaying the sensor capability characteristics

If the LocationSensor is enabled, the geodata and other information on the current location (similar to the data collected by the geotracker) are now retrieved with each change in location in the event handler LocationSensor.LocationChanged (Figure 12.44). Here we display not just the geocoordinates latitude and longitude themselves, but also the altitude via altitude, the current accuracy of the received signal via Accuracy, the street address via CurrentAddress (if available), and the time stamp of the last received signal via Clock.Now. In a conditional if statement, we then determine whether the check box "enabled" was checked by the user; if so, the route guidance is enabled. In this case, we trigger the new calculation of distance and direction to the target point based on the currently received geocoordinates by calling the procedure calculateTrack, which we will look at in more detail later.

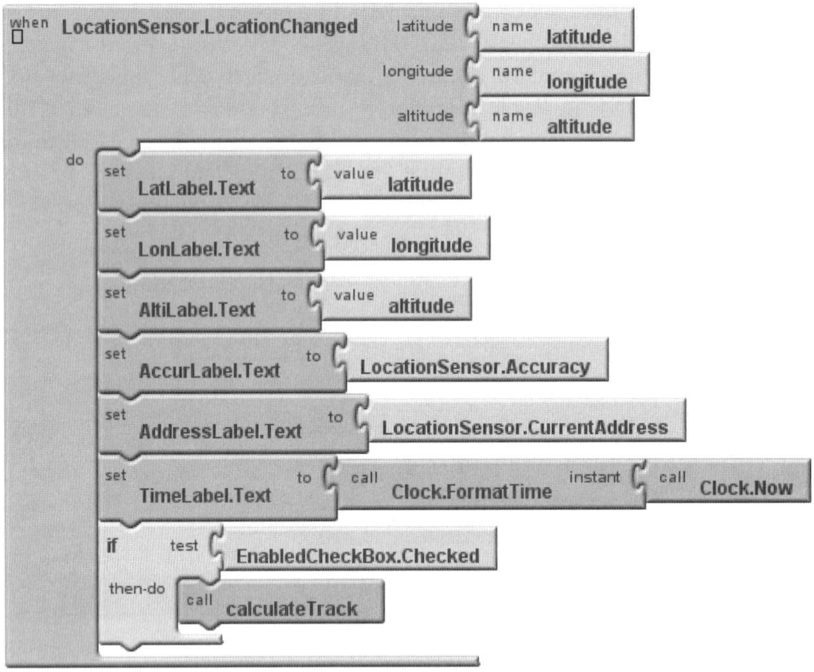

Figure 12.44 Displaying the received geodata and calling the course calculations

From the active `LocationSensor`, we can also request other status information in addition to the geodata itself. For example, we can use the event block `StatusChanged` (Figure 12.45) and its local variables to determine with each status change which *provider* (data source) is being used for receiving the geodata (`provider`) and which *status* (`status`) it has (e.g., `AVAILABLE`, `CURRENTLY_UNAVAILABLE`). In this context, we also want to display the list of available providers via the method `AvailableProviders` (e.g., `gps`, `passive gps`).

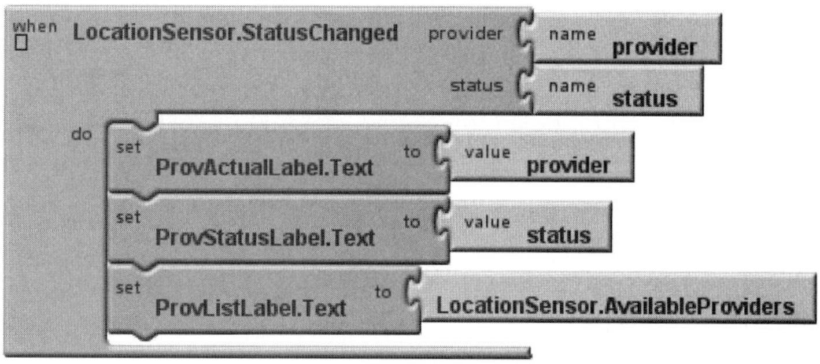

Figure 12.45 Requesting and displaying changes in provider status

After we have requested and displayed all information that the `LocationSensor` offers by itself, we want to process the received geocoordinates further. Thus we turn to the implementation of the route guidance functionality itself, which forms the core of our geocacher. For entering the target coordinates, the user has several options available. For example, the user can insert his or her current geocoordinates into the two text boxes LatTextBox and LonTextBox by pressing the Current button and calling the event handler `CurrentButton.Click` (Figure 12.46) if he or she wants to return to the starting point of a hike. Alternatively, if the user wants to delete the last station of a multicache, he or she can quickly get rid of the relevant target coordinates by pressing the None button, which triggers the event handler `NoneButton.Click`; the user can then enter new target coordinates manually in the two text boxes. By checking the check box "enabled," the user can also activate the route guidance that makes the previously hidden green directional arrow below the compass needle visible (`DirectionSprite.Visible = true`).

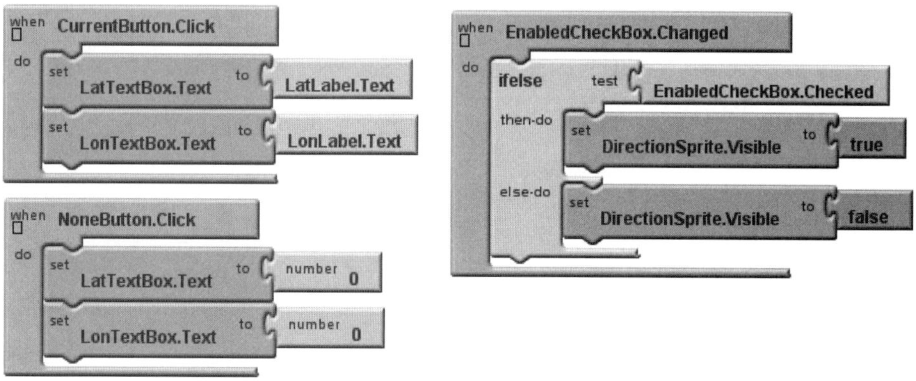

Figure 12.46 Entering target coordinates and enabling route guidance with a directional arrow

When the check box "enabled" is selected, the condition of the previously mentioned `if` statement in the event handler `LocationSensor.LocationChanged` (Figure 12.44) is fulfilled, so that the procedure `calculateTrack` is called in it with each new batch of geodata received via the sensor. In this procedure, a number of calculations are performed to determine the distance (central angle) between the current location and the target location, along with the direction to the target location (track angle). Here we will make use of some general formulas. If you would like to find out more, you can look up the geographical basis, navigation background, and mathematic derivation of these formulas under the relevant search terms on the Internet.

> **Calculate the Distance and Track Angle Between Two Geopositions**
>
> Further background information on calculating the *distance* between two geographical locations and the *track angle* can be found online under the corresponding search terms. A summary of the formula used in our calculations for determining the shortest connection between two points on the surface of a sphere (great-circle distance or *orthodromic distance*) can be found in *Wikipedia*:
>
> `http://en.wikipedia.org/wiki/Great_circle_distance`

In the calculation of the two target values of distance and track angle, we follow the approach of the so-called great-circle distance or *orthodromic distance.* Defined as the shortest distance between two points on the surface of a sphere, it is used mainly in aviation for determining the ideal flight path ("as the crow flies"). In the first step we calculate the *route* between the current location 1 and the target location 2, where the locations 1 and 2 result from the latitude and longitude in each case (Lat1, Lon1 and Lat2, Lon2). The route is specified as the central angle in degrees (not radians) and calculated using the following formula, in which we also use the method names from the AI Math component group:

```
central angle = acos(sin(Lat1)*sin(Lat2)+cos(Lat1)*cos(Lat2)*cos(Lon2-Lon1))
```

Unfortunately, the concrete implementation of this formula is hardly visible in Figure 12.47 due to its length. If you are interested in seeing the full details, the best thing to do is look directly in your development environment using the project file on the companion website (see the link in the Introduction).

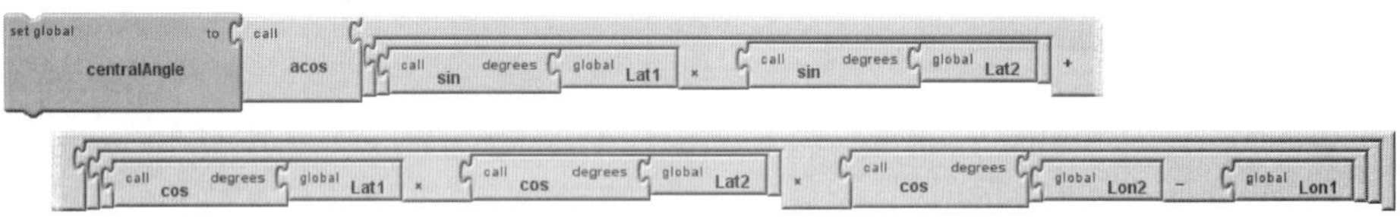

Figure 12.47 Formula for calculating the route as an angle in AI

From the central angle in degrees, we can then calculate the *distance* in kilometers in the second step. Here the following simple formula applies, where we assume a simplified Earth radius of 6.370 km:

```
distance = central angle*6370*6,283/360
```

Its concrete implementation in AI can be seen clearly in Figure 12.48.

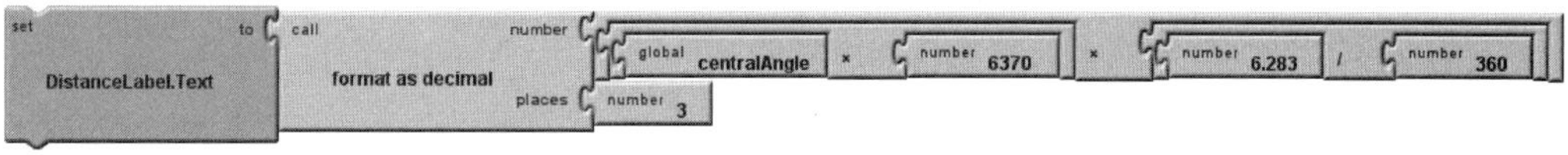

Figure 12.48 Calculating the distance from the central angle

The central angle can also be used to calculate the *track angle* as the true course from the starting location 1 to the target location 2 with the following formula, whose implementation in AI (shown in Figure 12.49) you should also look up directly within your development environment:

```
track angle = acos (sin(Lat2)-sin(Lat1)*cos(central angle))/(cos(Lat1)
-sin(central angle))
```

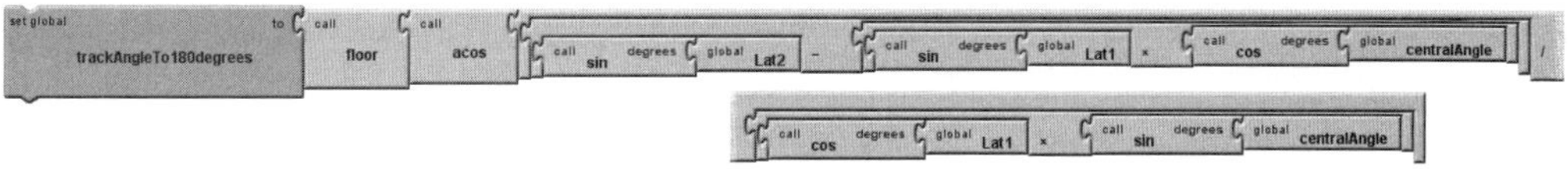

Figure 12.49 Calculating the track angle from the central angle

Now that we have introduced the formulas for calculating the desired distance and track angle, let's take a closer look at the procedure `calculateTrack` shown in Figure 12.50, where the formulas are put into practice. To keep the implementation of the formulas as short as possible, we use the shortest possible names to record the required geocoordinate values in the calculation—that is, `Lat1` and `Lon1` as well as `Lat2` and `Lon2`—and we initialize these variables with a value of `0` in each case. The calculated central and track angles are recorded in the variables `centralangle` and `trackangleTo180degrees`, respectively, and are initialized with a value of `0` as well. In the procedure, we first read the geocoordinates received most recently by the geosensor from the display labels and write them into the corresponding variables. When reading the geocoordinates into the variables, we may need to convert the values with the custom procedure `decimal` from a decimal number with a comma to one with a decimal point, to ensure that our app can run on smartphones with different country settings (including those that use a comma as decimal separator) without producing errors. As described earlier, we require the geocoordinates to be formatted as decimal point numbers for further processing with the Math methods in AI (see the section "Geocoordinates and Decimal Separators"). We will have a closer look at the procedure `decimal` later.

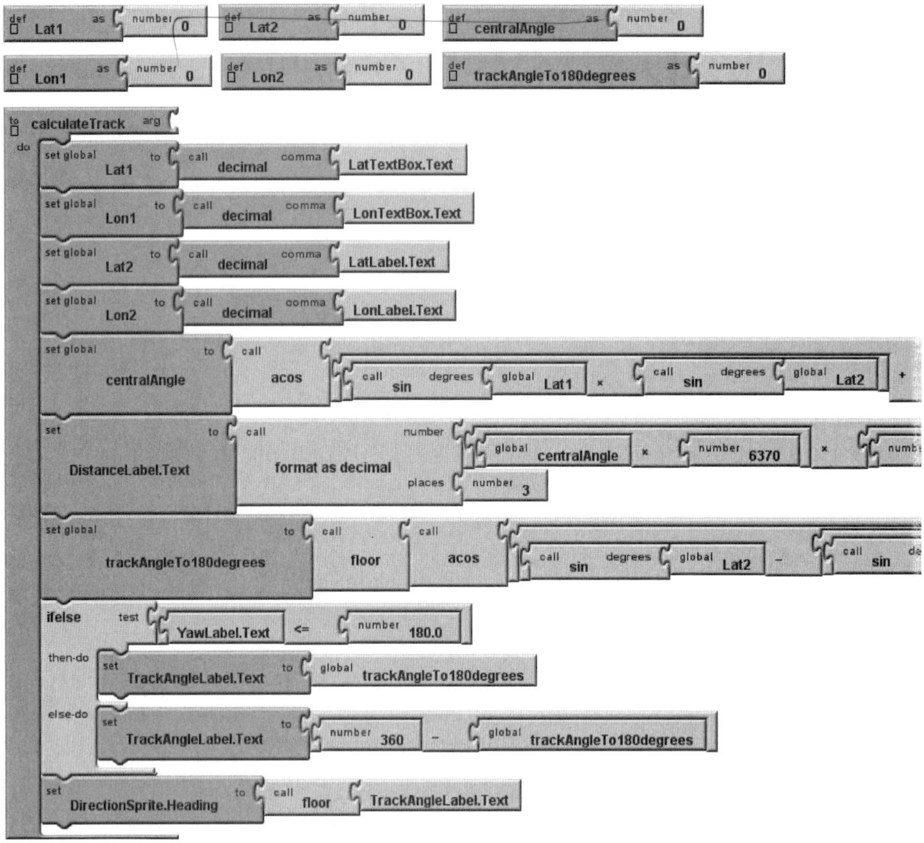

Figure 12.50 Calculating the current distance and track angle to the target point

Once the geocoordinates of the starting location (`Lat1`, `Lon1`) and the target location (`Lat2`, `Lon2`) are present in the correct decimal format, we can use them to calculate the central angle, the distance, and the track angle and display the results in the variables `centralangle` and `trackAngleTo180degrees` directly in the DistanceLabel. In Figure 12.50, the block structures with the calculation statements are cut off so that the picture will remain readable. You may be wondering why the variable has the name `trackAngleTo180degrees`. The geosensor always returns a positive number between 0° and 180° for hikes on the northern hemisphere for western and eastern targets, and we require a value between 0° and 360° for displaying the cardinal direction and the directional arrow pointing toward the target location. Thus we simplify matters by using the check in the `ifelse` branch to make the displayed track angle dependent on whether the compass needle tends to point east or west

(360 - trackAngleTo180degrees). With this rounded-up result (floor), we then turn the directional arrow by the corresponding angle into the suitable course heading via its property DirectionSprite.Heading.

To finish this app, we want to have a closer look at the procedure decimal (Figure 12.51), with which we convert any coordinates returned with decimal commas and received by the geosensor to values with a decimal point, so that we can use those values in further calculations. To make sure we can efficiently use this procedure directly like a component method in statements, we use a procedure with a return value; thus that decimal receives an input value comma and returns a return value dot. Within the procedure, we use the text method replace all to replace every comma with a dot in the numeric value passed as the local variable comma. This ensures that the decimal separator is replaced only if it really is a comma; the numbers that already have decimal points remain unchanged. By using this method, we can make sure that our procedure, and therefore the whole app, works in both countries that use decimal commas and countries that use decimal points.

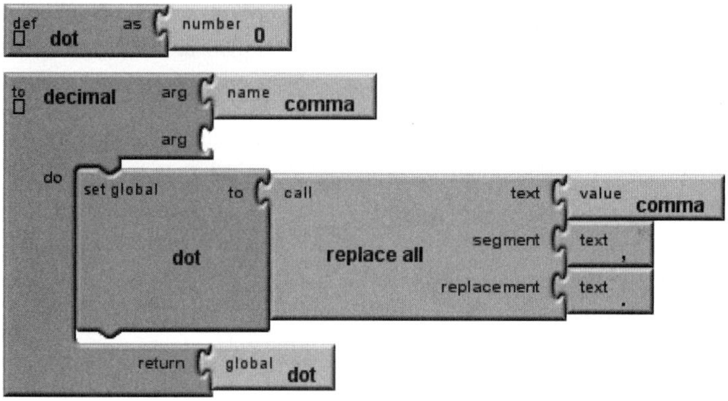

Figure 12.51 Converting the decimal separator from a comma to a point

Now we have completely implemented the already complex geocacher. Of course, you should never blindly trust the displayed navigation values, but rather take them with pinch of salt, especially now that you recognize the highly simplified basis by which the display of the directional arrow is achieved. Feel free to experiment and play around with the GeoCacher app; get to know its strengths as well as its weaknesses. Perhaps you will come up with your own good ideas or already have profound knowledge that you can use to improve the accuracy of the displayed values. If you feel that testing the GeoCacher app during a long hiking trip is too much effort, you can try it out from the comfort of your desk. Go to Google Maps, enter the desired target in the input field "Search Maps," and click in the map on the desired target with the right mouse button. In the context menu that then opens, click on "What's here?" At that point, you can see the geocoordinates in the input field as shown in Figure 12.52. You can enter these values as target coordinates in the GeoCacher app, point the compass north, and test the target course indicated by the directional arrow with the next GPS data update plus the distance "as the crow flies" to see if they are approximately correct.

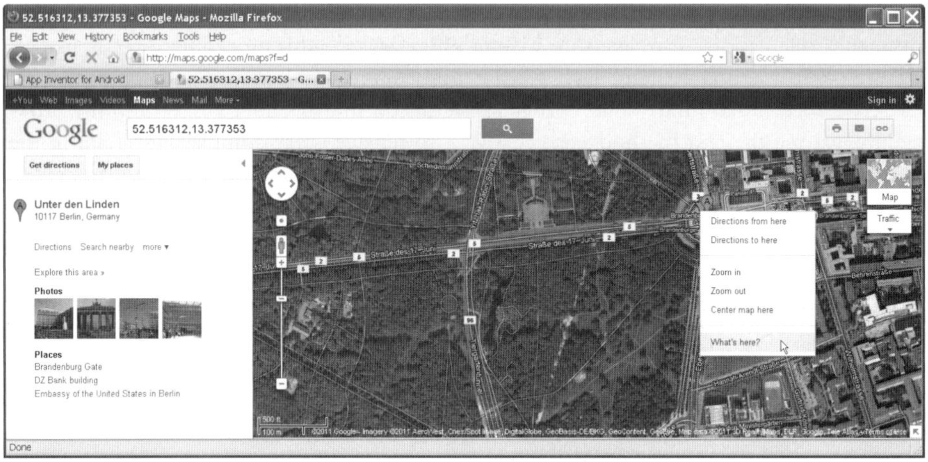

Figure 12.52 Determining target coordinates with Google Maps for testing the GeoCacher app

Use this app as a source of inspiration for your own useful and appealing applications, which you can now develop yourself using AI. You have acquired the required programming knowledge necessary to develop sensor-based graphical applications. From now on, the necessary expertise will be increasingly more important in the apps you develop on your own, and using AI you can turn your know-how into really useful and increasingly demanding apps.

Chapter 13

Communication

Let's not forget that you can also make phone calls with your Android smartphone. Indeed, it was not so long ago that we initiated the mobile revolution by becoming able to make phone calls anywhere via the cellphone. Today, this central technical achievement of the cellphone network appears increasingly less relevant and has become almost routine, at least in comparison to the many other functions that have become part of the smartphone in its role as universal companion and convergent service platform. Even if mobile data service is not yet as widespread as mobile telephony and text messaging (SMS), this has begun to change with the broad introduction of flat rates for mobile voice *and* data services. At the same time, the market for hardware and software that makes use of all of the new options in mobile data communication is virtually exploding, be it on smartphones, tablet computers, or other mobile devices. In addition, it is becoming more socially accepted and even expected, from a sociocultural standpoint, to be connected anywhere and anytime to your social network, your community, and the corresponding web platforms. From this perspective, smartphones represent an ideal breeding ground for an immense new market in which you can participate soon (if you want to) with the apps you develop yourself.

We devoted Chapter 12 to the use of the sensory smartphone components for creating a new type of application for the former cellphone. We now want to return to the classical phone functions on the smartphone. In this chapter, we will cover a wide range of functions—from the traditional phone and SMS functions on the one hand, to the new convergent data services with sensory measurement values on the other hand. These functions can be combined to create useful and powerful apps the offer significant added value. Consider, for example, the many possibilities related to remote servicing devices (*telemetry*) equipped with SIM cards that can be controlled and read with instructions via SMS—manually or automatically (*machine-to-machine*, or M2M)—even in areas and countries where there are not yet any large mobile data networks apart from the GSM cellphone network. But even in electronically based communication between people, the phone call or short text message via SMS continues to play an important role, despite the emergence of the Twitter social network. We want to use the term "communication" in the wider sense in this chapter, with our definition encompassing the data exchange between different apps (*app-to-app*) locally on the smartphone as well as online between apps and the Web (*app-to-Web*), always viewed from the perspective of offering the user of your apps more information, service, and entertainment. As you see, communication in the age of digital *convergence* is no longer merely a one-dimensional exchange of information.

Because you are already used to working with AI, we do not have to start from scratch with using the various communication components in this chapter. Instead, just as we did with previous projects (e.g., the media center), we can make use of system functions that are already available in particularly advanced forms on the smartphone and within the Android operating system, especially in case of the traditional phone and SMS functions. If we look back on previous projects such as the media center, we can see that our general focus in developing apps has been increasingly moving away from the individual components (*bottom-up*) and instead going more toward the specific tasks (*top-down*) performed by the apps. This change in perspective corresponds to the desired learning effect of internalizing the programming tools of AI more and more, which enables us to concentrate more intensely on the proper task of developing useful apps. We want to continue this trend and introduce the communication components using only selected functions within a comprehensive and useful example project. We will no longer seek to demonstrate each and every property method or event block individually, as you now know where to find the component specification and how you can learn more about new functions yourself by using this resource. After all, encouraging you as reader to take advantage of the numerous tools available in the AI development environment independently is one of the aims of this book, so as to prepare you for future expansions in the performance scope of AI within the highly dynamic context of mobile application development.

By now, you should no longer find large and complex block structures daunting—a good thing, given that such structures are becoming more common in our increasingly powerful and demanding apps. In our last example project for this book, we combine several tasks and forms of communication within a single app, but keep them separate in terms of structure, both in the block structures for the developer and on the user interface for the user. We apply the principle of *modularization,* on which the event blocks are inherently based, to the entire program structure as well, which makes dealing with the app easier and reduces the complexity of large apps to manageable subsections. This modular approach becomes all the more important as apps evolve from small auxiliary programs to serious, full-fledged mobile applications. Based on the principles of *software engineering,* your work as developer often starts with analyzing the demands, functions, and requirements for the app, as well appropriately segmenting the program into sensible and definable subtasks.

Task: Developing a Driver Assistance System

As noted earlier, electronic communication is becoming more important today, with myriad applications and extensive service becoming the norm. Thanks to mobile communication devices, we are not cut off or sent offline when out of the house or office, but can still get a connection even while driving in the car at 55 mph. Unfortunately, our human ability to concentrate does not seem able to keep pace with this impressive technical capacity, because all too often you will find when overtaking a dangerously swerving car that the driver is busily searching for phone numbers, reading, or even writing a text message on a cellphone. As the laws and regulations have not always caught up with this phenomenon, and appealing to common sense does not seem to be enough to stop this sometimes-dangerous behavior, there is a real need for an electronic driver assistant that, on the one hand, can satisfy the driver's communication urges and, on the other hand, requires only minimal attention to reduce the danger to the general public.

Demand, Functions, and Requirements

As communication nowadays takes place via many channels, these venues must be managed appropriately—if possible, from just one central app that requires only a single press of the button or is fully automatic. Thus we want the assistance system for the communicative car driver to enable the driver to make phone calls via speed dial buttons, because usually there are only a few numbers that a private traveler calls regularly. As reading and (especially) writing text messages divert a lot of the driver's attention over a dangerously long period of time, these tasks should also be automated to the greatest possible extent. To satisfy etiquette, we want the sender of the text message to get an immediate reply via SMS message informing the sender that the recipient is currently driving a car and will get back to the sender later. To edit the reply, the user can enter a new text or dictate it. Optionally, the sender should also be able to see the current location of the recipient—for example, to be able to tell when he or she is likely to arrive. If the recipient in the car is curious, he or she can also have the received text message read aloud automatically while the recipient continues driving.

> **Project CarAssistant on the Companion Website**
>
> All files for the project can be found in the corresponding directories on the companion website (see the link in the Introduction).

In addition to the reactive services on receiving a text message, the car driver should have the option of actively informing one or several persons via e-mail of his or her current whereabouts. If the driver drives back and forth between home and work on a daily basis or wants to be led to an address quickly from the current location via the navigation system, this should be possible with just one touch of the button. Moreover, if the driver has found a place to park in an unknown area, the assistant should remember the location and later be able to lead the driver back to that location if required. All of these functions should be integrated into the driving assistance system under a clearly structured, easily operated, and attractive user interface. Although you might disagree with the finer points of the design, let's assume that the driver assistance system should look similar to that shown in Figure 13.1 and that the user should be able to operate and control it via the few large buttons, thereby accessing all of its functions in a comfortable and safe way.

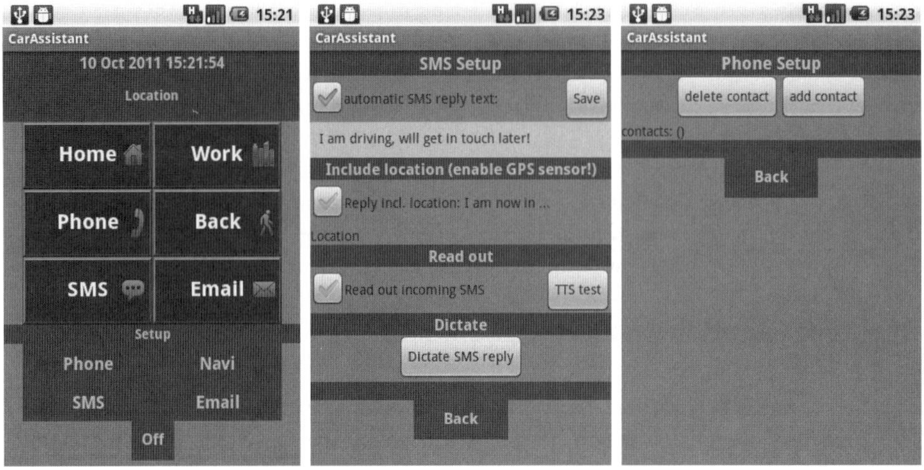

Figure 13.1 Designing the user interface and modular functional areas

While driving, the user should be able to control all of the functions via the *switchboard* shown on the left in Figure 13.1. The colors are quiet grays, blacks, and whites, and the main user elements should be clear and easy to read and use even while driving. The six large *function buttons* make it possible to operate the specific functions with just one press of a button. Any important basic settings and configurations of the function buttons should be carried out via additional *configuration keys* (see the Setup section) in separate screen areas before the user starts driving. Depending on the task, the setup modules can be more or less extensive, as shown in Figure 13.1 for the SMS (center) and phone (right) setup area. To make things clearer, the buttons should have additional function icons to make operating them more intuitive. The car driver should also be able to see important information such as the time, date, and current location displayed on the screen.

Modular Design of the App Structure

Now that we have identified individual subtasks from the needs and requirements for the driver assistance system, and divided them into a central control area and a separate setup section, we have essentially identified the modular structure of the CarAssistant app. Into this basic framework, we can insert the individual functions, which can then be subdivided further without negatively affecting the core requirement of a clear user interface. Do not underestimate the significance of the initial requirements analysis and preparatory structuring effort, which often accounts for more than half of the total project development time in case of large software projects. The earlier an error is discovered, the less expensive it is to fix or even prevent. Even if the outcome of the preparatory structuring process described previously appears obvious, it is still true that most software products are based on just this modular principle. For example, in word processing and spreadsheet programs, the individual functions are activated, configured, and applied to a text or balance sheet via a series of menus and submenus. A smartphone app is also a software product, albeit a rather small one in the case of most apps, and should be developed in the same way as its larger brethren.

> **Software Engineering**
>
> If you are planning larger and perhaps even commercial app projects and would like to find out more about the structured creation and development of software products, have a look on the Internet by searching for the term "software engineering." Even if the sometimes academically oriented principles of software engineering are aimed primarily at very large software projects that are subject to interdisciplinary development processes, these thoughts can serve as an inspiration for your own app projects, which you can also base on the well-defined core processes of planning, analysis, design, programming, and validation or verification. You can find a good summary of this topic at *Wikipedia*:
>
> `http://en.wikipedia.org/wiki/Software_engineering`

Apart from fulfilling the user requirement of providing a clearly laid-out driver assistance system, the modularization of the subtasks supports a structured and, therefore, generally more efficient approach to app development, which might otherwise grow exponentially in complexity with a growing range of functions, thereby becoming much more confusing. In our driver assistance system, the modular structure becomes visible in the central placement of the function buttons in the switchboard. With these buttons, the user activates and/or executes the underlying functions in a structured manner. The settings for the individual subtasks appear on separate screens for each task, such that they are practically independent of the other areas.

Switchboard with Multiple Screens

To achieve this separation both visually and in content, we will use the concept of *multiple* screens, introduced previously in the context of the media center. We will encapsulate the components of the screen areas we want to separate within an overall VerticalArrangement component, which we can then show and hide in turn depending on the menu setting via its Visible property. Within these separate app areas (in terms of separate content), we can then concentrate fully on each task concerned, including both its design and its implementation, largely independent of the other areas.

To begin, let's create a new project in AI Designer with the name "CarAssistant." Give the corresponding title to "Screen1," and create the switchboard of the driver assistance system with the components shown in Table 13.1.

Table 13.1 **Components and Initial Properties of the Switchboard Module**

Component	Object Name	Adapted Properties
Screen	Screen1	"Icon": car_appIcon.png (companion website, `/MEDIA`)
VerticalArrangement	SWITCHBvArr	"Visible" enable "Width": Fill parent
Label	TimeLabel	"Text": Time "FontSize": 16
Clock	Clock	
Button	LocationButton	"Text": Location "FontSize": 14
LocationSensor	LocationSensor	
Button (5x)	HomeButton, WorkButton, BackNavButton, SMSButton, EmailButton	"Image": home.png, work.png, parking.png, sms.png, email.png (companion website, `/MEDIA`) "Text": Home, Work, Back, SMS, Email "FontSize": 22 "Width × Height": 140 × 70 pixels
ListPicker	PhoneListPicker	"Image": phone.png (companion website, `/MEDIA`) "Text": Phone "FontSize" + "Width × Height" (see WorkButton)
Button (4x)	PhoneSetupButton, NaviSetupButton, SMSsetupButton, EmailSetupButton	"Text": Phone, Navi, SMS, Email "FontSize": 18 "Width x Height": 140 × 40 pixels
Button	OffButton	"Text": Off "FontSize": 16

You can add the remaining optical design items on your own by setting and placing the text labels, DivisionLabels and BufferLabels, and Arrangements, and specifying the colors and font sizes based on the figures in this chapter. Set the background color to "Dark gray" for all functional labels and buttons, the font color to "Light gray" and "FontBold," and the font color for the six function buttons to "White." To make sure you do not forget to add the VerticalArrangement component object `SWITCHBvArr` (which is essential for realizing the multiple screens), we have listed it explicitly in Table 13.1. The ListPicker component and the visually identical buttons can be found in the Basic group. With the components and the elements you add yourself, the switchboard for the project CarAssistant should look like that shown in Figure 13.2.

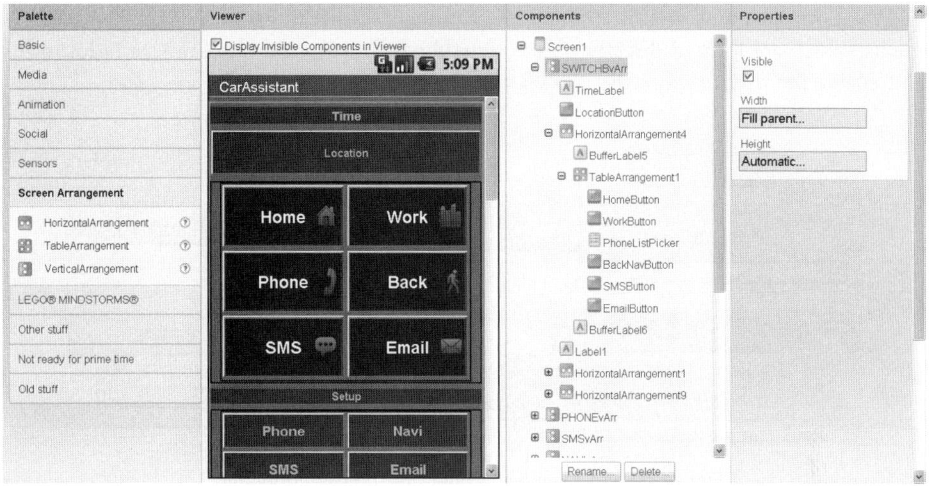

Figure 13.2 The Switchboard module in the CarAssistant project, as seen in AI Designer

In designing the switchboard, we have created the start-up screen as the central module for our CarAssistant app. Now we can add the various functional areas, both as additional screens where the user can specify any desired setting options and in the form of block structures for implementing the functionality behind the function buttons. For switching between the multiple screens, we create the auxiliary procedure `screenBlank` shown in Figure 13.3 in AI Editor, with which we hide all other screens first before showing each new screen. In this procedure, we will later switch off the Visible properties of other subscreens, such as the SMS screen (`SMSvArr`) and the Phone Setup screen (`PHONEvArr`), to hide them along with the central screen `SWITCHBvArr`.

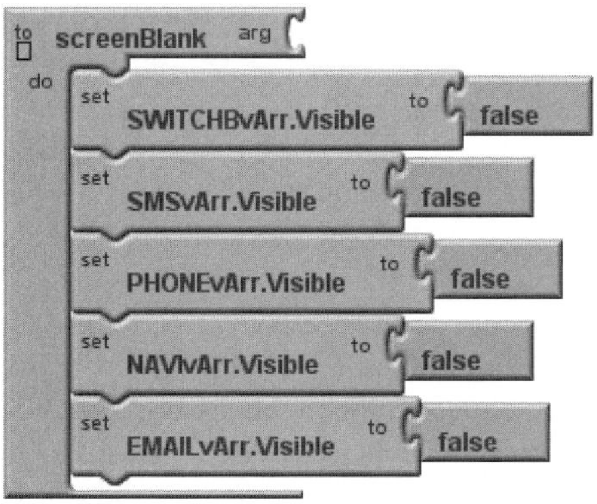

Figure 13.3 Hiding all screens before showing a new screen

We also implement the three functional elements shown in Figure 13.4. These elements, which are located directly on the switchboard, display the date, time, and location and enable the user to close the app via the Off button.

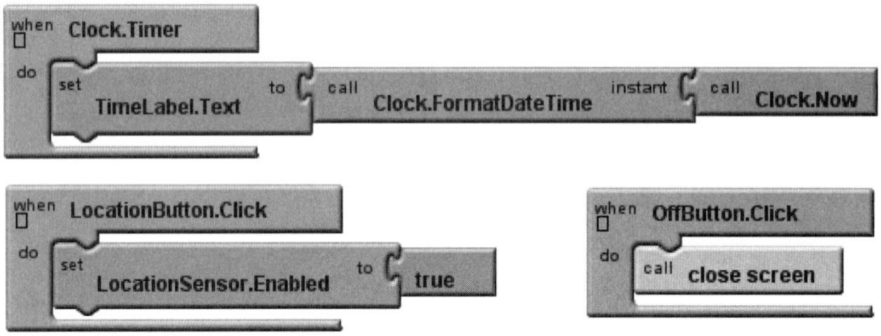

Figure 13.4 Displaying the date, time, and location and closing the driver assistance system

The three event handlers shown in Figure 13.4 hold no significant surprises. The handler `Clock.Timer` calls the current system time every second. From the instant returned by the method `Clock.Now`, the current date and current time are formatted via the method `Clock.FormatDateTime` and displayed in the TimeLabel right at the top of the switchboard. The current location is implemented as label text on a button; thus the user can press this button, trigger the event handler `LocationButton.Click`, and "wake up" the GPS sensor (if it goes into standby mode) via its property `LocationSensor.Enabled`. This step may be necessary in some smartphones to really display the last location (if no Clock Timer is used for active GPS retrieval). By pressing the Off button, which calls the method `close screen` in the event handler `OffButton.Click`, the user can close the driver assistance system.

Making Telephone Calls via Speed Dial List

It is not hard to guess that the Phone function button holds the module for making phone calls in our driver assistance system. That is just as we intended, as its operation should be easy and intuitive. As we outlined in the preliminary analysis of our app, pressing the Phone button should display a clearly structured speed dial list with the names of the most important contacts, which can then be dialed directly. To implement this functionality and integrate it into our CarAssistant app, we need several new components of AI that we will introduce and use in this section directly in the context of the driver assistance system. Significantly, these components are combined in AI in the Social group, as their primary function is making contact with other people. To design these functions as comfortably as possible, the user should not need to laboriously enter the contact data manually. Instead, the data should be conveniently selected and transferred from the general smartphone phone book when creating the speed dial list. The display of the speed dial list should have an attractive design that resembles the operating system, and deleting any item from the list should be just as simple as dialing the number of a selected contact.

The settings for the Phone functionality are entered in the subscreen shown in Figure 13.1 (on the right), which the user displays by pressing the Phone Setup button. To create this module, add the components shown in Table 13.2 in AI Designer, arranging them below the components of the switchboard. The new Phone components can be found in the Social group and the ListPicker component within the Basic group of AI.

Table 13.2 **Adding the Components of the Phone Module**

Component	Object Name	Adapted Properties
VerticalArrangement	PHONEvArr	"Visible" disable "Width": Fill parent
ListPicker	PhoneDelListPicker	"Text": Delete contact
PhoneNumberPicker	PhoneNumberPicker	"Text": Add contact
PhoneCall	PhoneCall	
TinyDB	TinyDB	
Label	PhoneLabel	"Text": -
Button	PhoneSetupBackButton	"Text": Back

Again, you can add the other few arrangements and labels yourself in the Phone module, making sure that you encapsulate all components in the VerticalArrangement component object `PHONEvArr`. Appearing below the components of the switchboard, the Phone module should then look as shown in Figure 13.5.

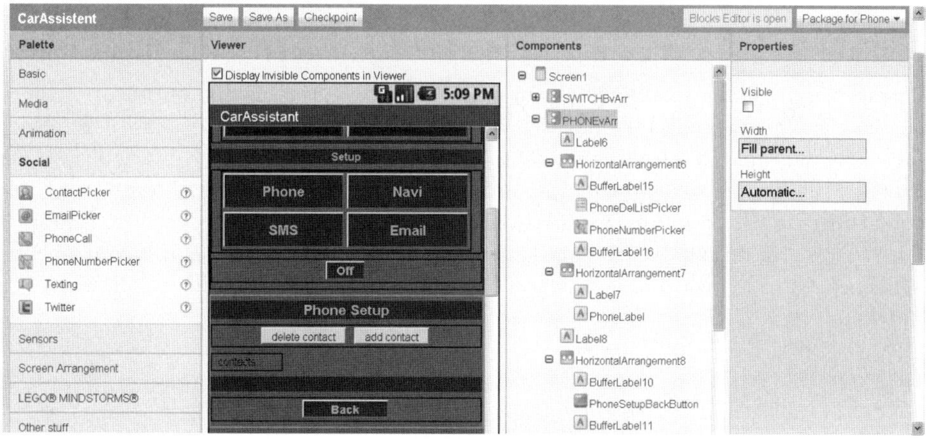

Figure 13.5 Adding the additional components in the Phone Setup module

During the development work, you must leave the Visible property of the subscreen `PHONEvArr` enabled so that the components it contains will be displayed in AI Designer; alternatively, check the check box labeled "Display Invisible Components in Viewer." Just before the final step of saving or installing the app on your smartphone, you should hide all other subscreens (except the switchboard `SWITCHBvArr`) by disabling the Visible setting as the default, so that these subscreens will appear in the app only if the corresponding setup button is pressed. Now we can implement the first switching process from the switchboard to the Phone Setup, which happens when the Phone Setup button is pressed, by calling the event handler `PhoneSetupButton.Click` as shown in Figure 13.6.

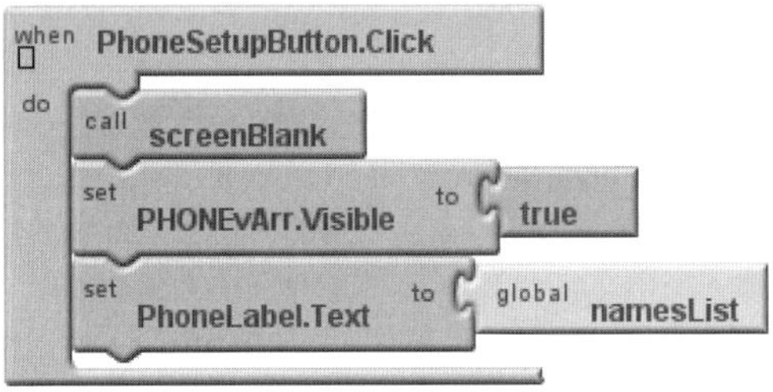

Figure 13.6 Hiding all screens and showing the Phone Setup subscreen

In the event handler shown in Figure 13.6, we first hide all screens via the previously implemented procedure `screenBlank` and then show the subscreen `PHONEvArr` by setting its Visible property to `true`. The same basic principle also applies to all of the other subscreens, as we will see later. Once the subscreen of the Phone module is set up and activated, we are ready to implement its functionality.

Picking Phone Numbers with the PhoneNumberPicker Component

Perhaps you recall the ImagePicker component, which we used within our media center for selecting image files on the smartphone. We did so by using the picture management feature of the Android operating system to pick an image, which we then included in our app. In a similar way, we can access the smartphone's contacts list and pick out individual contact data for our purposes. AI offers the PhoneNumberPicker component in the Social group for this purpose. In addition to its special picker properties, this component behaves just like a normal button, as you can see in the extract from the specification shown in Figure 13.7.

PhoneNumberPicker

Choose phone number

Use this component to allow users to choose a phone number from a list of Android contacts' phone numbers.

When the user taps a phone number picker button, it displays a list of the phone numbers of contacts to choose from. After the user has made a selection, the following properties will be set to information about the chosen contact:

- `ContactName`: contact's name.
- `PhoneNumber`: contact's selected phone number.
- `EmailAddress`: contact's primary email address.
- `Picture`: name of the file containing the contact's image, which can be used as a `Picture` property value for the `Image` or `ImageSprite` component.

Other properties affect the appearance of the button (including `TextAlignment` and `BackgroundColor`) and whether it can be tapped (`Enabled`).

Properties

`Enabled`
    If set, user can tap phone number picker to use it.
`Image`
    Image to display on phone number picker.
`BackgroundColor`
    Color for phone number picker background.
`ContactName`
    Name of selected contact.
`EmailAddress`
    Primary email address of selected contact.
`PhoneNumber`
    Selected phone number of selected contact.
`Picture`
    Picture of selected contact.
`FontBold`
    If set, phone number picker text is displayed in bold.

Events

`AfterPicking()`
    Called after user picks a phone number.
`BeforePicking()`
    Called after user taps phone number picker but before phone number
`GotFocus()`
    Phone number picker became the focused component.
`LostFocus()`
    Phone number picker stopped being the focused component.

Figure 13.7 Extract from the specification of the PhoneNumberPicker component in AI References

If the PhoneNumberPicker button is pressed and a contact is selected, the event handler `AfterPicking` then makes available the phone number (`PhoneNumber`) and contact name (`ContactName`), e-mail address (`EmailAddress`) and associated contact photo (`Picture`) via the corresponding property fields, provided they were present under the original entry on the smartphone.

Differences in Accessing Contact Data

Depending on the smartphone and authorization, the display of the contacts produced by pressing the PhoneNumberPicker button may vary. Some smartphones allow access to only the contacts in the Google address book, whereas others allow unlimited access to contacts on the phone memory and the SIM card.

In our driver assistance system, the PhoneNumberPicker shown in Table 13.2 enables us to compile the speed dial list conveniently from the smartphone's contact list. After going to the Phone Setup screen shown in Figure 13.8, the user can open the contact list (center) by pressing the button "add contact" and choosing an entry, which is then copied into the Phone Setup (right).

Figure 13.8 Selecting contacts from the contact list

From the selected contact data, we record each name and associated phone number in the two lists `namesList` and `numbersList` shown in Figure 13.9. Each selection of a new entry via the PhoneNumberPicker automatically calls the event handler `PhoneNumberPicker.AfterPicking`, in which we append the selected `ContactName` and the `PhoneNumber` to the end of the relevant list. After each new entry is added, we display the complete name list in the PhoneLabel.

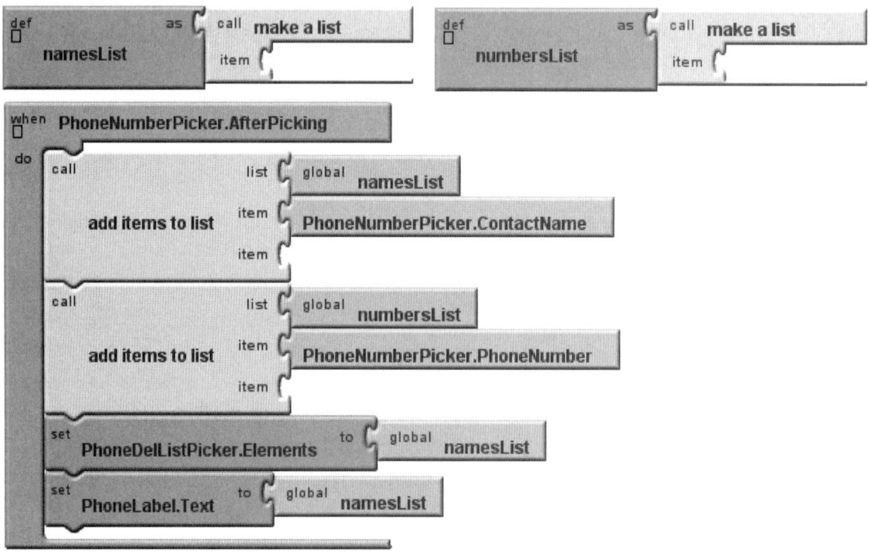

Figure 13.9 Reading, saving, providing, and displaying names and phone numbers

We also assign the name list to another component, with which we can present the elements of our speed dial list just as easily as before when making the selection from the system's contact list.

Selecting Speed Dial Numbers with the ListPicker Component

The user has now created his or her own speed dial list which is displayed as simple list of items in the PhoneLabel so that we can check whether everything is correct. We now want to present this list in an appealing format to facilitate comfortable selection of a contact while the user is driving. This list presentation should match the user's system, and we require it to fulfill two criteria in our driving assistance system: It should provide for conveniently deleting items in the Phone Setup by pressing the "Delete contact" button, and it should support the efficient selection and dialing of a contact by pressing the Phone function button in the switchboard. For creating such a list presentation and selecting from it, AI offers the ListPicker component in the Basic group. This component is essentially the generic counterpart of the other specific "picker" components and can be applied universally to any list. Thus the ListPicker component also has the familiar properties and event blocks, as you can see from the specification extract shown in Figure 13.10.

ListPicker

Pick a number

Users tap a list picker component to select one item from a list of text strings.

When a user taps a list picker, it displays a list of text items for the user to choose from. The text items can be specified through the Designer or Blocks Editor by setting the `ElementsFromString` property to their comma-separated concatenation (for example, `choice 1, choice 2, choice 3`) or by setting the `Elements` property to a `List` in the Blocks Editor.

Other properties, including `TextAlignment` and `BackgroundColor`, affect the appearance of the button and whether it can be tapped (`Enabled`).

Properties

`Selection`
Selected list element.
`Items`
Comma-separated list of items to display in component.
`ElementsFromString`
(Description to come.)
`BackgroundColor`
Color for list picker background.
`FontBold`
If set, list picker text is displayed in bold.

Events

`AfterPicking()`
User selected an item from the list picker.
`BeforePicking()`
User has tapped the list picker but hasn't yet selected an item.
`GotFocus()`
List picker became the focused component.
`LostFocus()`
List picker is no longer the focused component.

Figure 13.10 Specification of the ListPicker component in AI References

The ListPicker component can be passed two types of lists: (1) a finished list of the corresponding data type via the Elements property and (2) a comma-separated text string that is then automatically split at the commas via the ElementsFromString property, so that a list is generated from the remaining elements (similar to the Text method "split at any" with a comma as the "at" parameter). We used the first variation in Figure 13.9 when we assigned the speed dial list (with one additional item added each time) namesList to the corresponding property PhoneDelListPicker.Elements. By assigning it, we ensured that pressing the ListPicker button "Delete contact" (shown in Table 13.2) presents the current speed dial list namesList in the desired format. Now we can implement the corresponding event handler PhoneDelListPicker.AfterPicking (shown in Figure 13.11), to ensure that the entry the user has selected from the speed dial list is returned in the property PhoneDelListPicker.Selection.

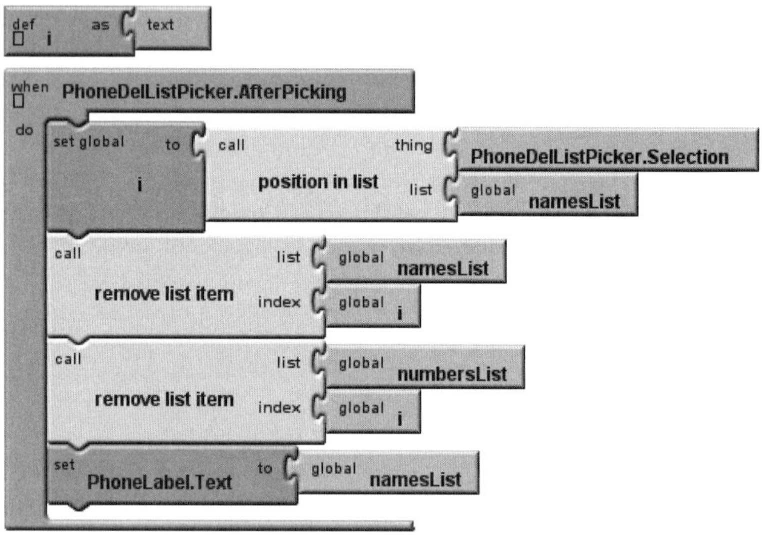

Figure 13.11 Deleting the selected item from the speed dial list

We use the returned selection PhoneDelListPicker.Selection in the event handler to determine the index position of this item in the list namesList via the list method position in list. We record this index position in the auxiliary variable i. Using the index position i, we can delete the corresponding contact name from the namesList and the matching phone number from the numbersList via the list method remove list item. The now-shortened list is then displayed in the PhoneLabel for the purpose of checking it. The next time the speed dial list is called up, this item is no longer present. As an example, Figure 13.12 shows the deletion of the entry "Greta Testar."

Figure 13.12 Deleting an item from the speed dial list

With the two functions "add contact" and "delete contact" now working, the setup options for the Phone function area are exhausted, and the user can return to the switchboard by pressing the Back button. In the corresponding event handler `PhoneSetupBackButton.Click` (Figure 13.13), the Phone Setup is hidden via the procedure `screenBlank` and the switchboard `SWITCHBvArr` is displayed instead. To ensure that the Phone function button (also a ListPicker component) receives the previously updated speed dial list, the current `namesList` is passed to its property field `PhoneListPicker.Elements`. Finally, the two lists `namesList` and `numbersList` are saved locally under the corresponding identifiers (tags) in the app memory via the method `TinyDB.StoreValue`, thereby ensuring that they will still be available the next time the user starts the driver assistance system.

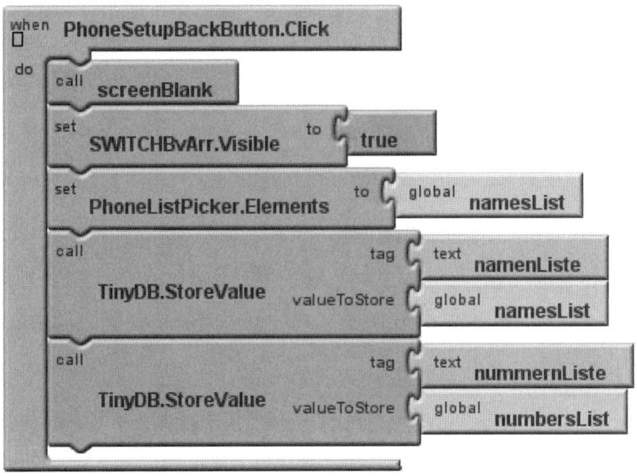

Figure 13.13 Saving the current speed dial list and returning to the switchboard

The speed dial list is now available in the driver assistance system's switchboard and can be used there by pressing the Phone function button to directly call a contact.

Making a Call with the PhoneCall Component

With the speed dial list, we can now access the phone numbers that are to be selected and dialed directly via the Phone function button. For making the phone call, AI offers the non-visible component PhoneCall in the Social group (Figure 13.14). It comprises only one single property and method and, as you would expect, makes use of the system's phone functions with a high degree of abstraction. Basically you can just pass a phone number to the PhoneCall component via the property PhoneNumber, and the number is then called via the method `MakePhoneCall`. The PhoneCall component is rather flexible with regard to the format of the phone number being passed; that is, it accepts numbers with dashes, full stops, and brackets by simply ignoring all of these special characters. Only spaces should be avoided in the phone numbers, and should be eliminated before dialing via text methods such as `split at spaces`.

PhoneCall

PhoneCall1

Use this component to dial the phone and make a call.

`PhoneCall` is a non-visible component that makes a phone call to the number specified in the `PhoneNumber` property, which can be set either in the Designer or Blocks Editor. You can use the `MakePhoneCall` method to make a phone call programatically from your app.

This component is often used with the `ContactPicker` component, which lets the user select from the contacts stored on the phone and sets the `PhoneNumber` property to the contact's phone number.

To directly specify the phone number, set the `PhoneNumber` property to a `Text` with the specified digits (for example, "6505551212"). The number can be formatted with hyphens, periods, and parentheses; they are ignored. You can't include spaces in the number.

Properties	**Methods**
`PhoneNumber` Phone number to dial.	`MakePhoneCall()` Dials the number specified by the component's `PhoneNumber` property.

Figure 13.14 Specification of the PhoneCall component in AI References

The use of the PhoneCall component in our driver assistance system is quite simple. After the user has pressed the Phone function button (a ListPicker component) in the switchboard and selected the desired contact from the speed dial list, the corresponding event handler `PhoneListPicker.AfterPicking` (Figure 13.15) is called automatically. In it, the index `i` for the selected name is determined via the method `position in list`, similar to what happens with the "Delete contact" button (or the event handler shown in Figure 13.11). Armed with the index `i`, we can then use the method `select list item` to find the correct phone number in the `numbersList` and pass it as target number to the PhoneCall component via its `PhoneCall.PhoneNumber` property. Through the method `PhoneCall.MakePhoneCall`, the phone number is passed to the system phone and dialed, and the phone call is carried out in the usual way.

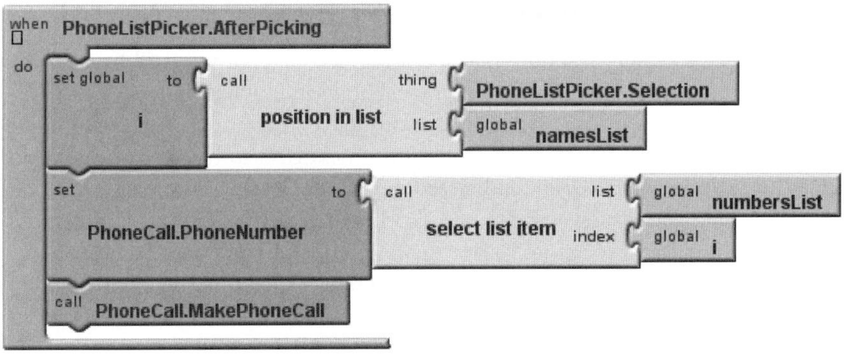

Figure 13.15 Selecting and dialing a phone number

After the phone call is complete, the system phone closes and the program returns to the invoking app. In Figure 13.16, you can see an example of the entire process from invoking the speed dial list via the Phone function button (left) to selecting the contact from the speed dial list (center) to making the phone call (right).

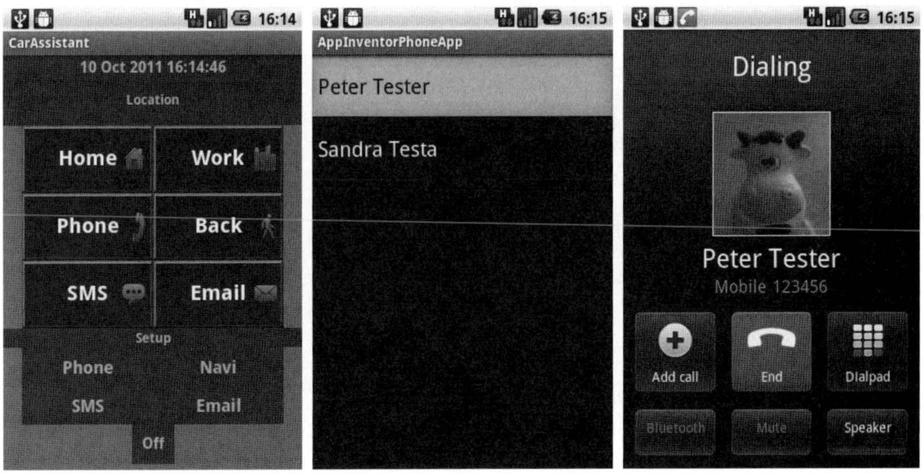

Figure 13.16 Speed dialing via the switchboard of the driver assistance system

The Phone module and its functionality are now almost fully implemented. Only the loading process for the two lists `namesList` and `numbersList` from the TinyDB component when the app starts will be briefly introduced later, together with all other functions needed for starting the app in the event handler `Screen1.Initialize`. For now, however, we will move on to the next module, which we can develop almost completely independently of the phone module.

Managing SMS Messages Fully Automatically

Admittedly, this is a rather presumptuous-sounding heading, but you will be surprised which tricks are possible with AI when receiving and sending text messages via SMS (Short Message Service). The SMS module of our driver assistance system will provide a really powerful tool for the user, with which SMS messages can be processed fully automatically. Incoming text messages can be read out to the driver, and the user can generate replies as outgoing text messages; he or she also has the option of informing the recipient of the driver's current location. To slot the SMS functionality with its many setting options into our driver assistance system, we need to add a new module with the components shown in Table 13.3 below the previous components of the switchboard and the phone module.

Table 13.3 **Adding Components for the SMS Module**

Component	Object Name	Adapted Properties
VerticalArrangement	SMSvArr	"Visible" disable "Width": Fill parent
Texting	Texting	
CheckBox	SMSreplyCheckBox	"Text": auto-reply via SMS
Button	SMSreplySaveButton	"Text": Save
TextBox	SMSreplyTextBox	"Text": I am driving, will get in touch later!
LocationSensor	LocationSensor	
CheckBox	LocationCheckBox	"Text": Reply incl. location: I am now in ...
Label	LocationLabel	"Text": Location
TextToSpeech	TextToSpeech	
CheckBox	TTSCheckBox	"Text": Read out incoming SMS
Button	TTSTestButton	"Text": TTS test
Button	SpeechButton	"Text": Dictate reply
Button	SMSsetupBackButton	"Text": Back

For the SMS module, the same comments apply as for the Phone module. Add the text labels, DivisionLabels, and Arrangements, and set the color design and font sizes yourself, referring to Figure 13.1 as a template. The project—or rather the SMS module `SMSvArr`—should then look in AI Designer as shown in Figure 13.17.

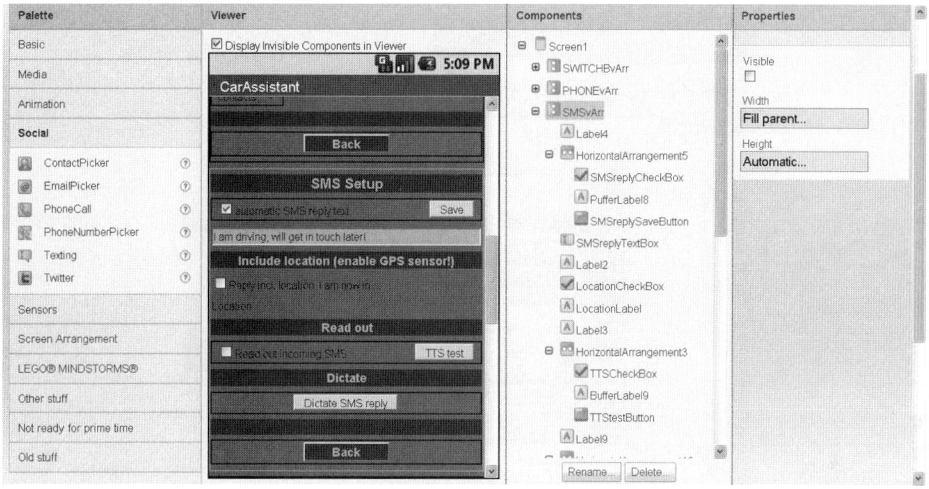

Figure 13.17 Adding the SMS module in AI Designer

All functions of the SMS module are meant to be optional, so that the user can decide whether he or she wants the incoming SMS messages to be read aloud, or whether and how the app should reply to them automatically. The user should be able to enable or disable this individual configuration in the SMS Setup with one touch of the SMS function button in the switchboard. As switching between enabled and disabled does not produce a reaction that is visible to the user, we need to explicitly implement this visual feedback. We want the text on the SMS function button to glow in light-green letters as soon as the SMS management is enabled, and to indicate its disabled state with the normal white font color. Switching between enabled and disabled with one touch of the button is implemented in the corresponding event handler `SMSButton.Click` (Figure 13.18), in which we record the state in the global variable `smsReply` as a Boolean value and switch the corresponding font color via an `ifelse` branch.

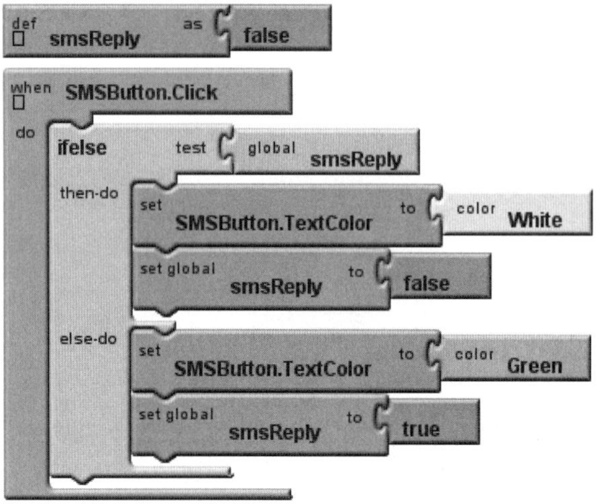

Figure 13.18 Enabling and disabling SMS settings and indicating the state of the SMS function

As with the phone label, the settings and options of the SMS module are displayed and adjusted in a separate screen, encapsulated within the VerticalArrangement component object `SMSvArr`. Invoking the SMS Setup via the SMS Setup button in the switchboard hides the switchboard and shows `SMSvArr`. This happens within the event handler `SMSsetupButton.Click` (Figure 13.19, left) as usual by calling the globally available procedure `screenBlank`. In the same way, pressing the Back button in the SMS Setup implements the return to the switchboard within the event handler `SMSsetupBackButton.Click` (Figure 13.19, right).

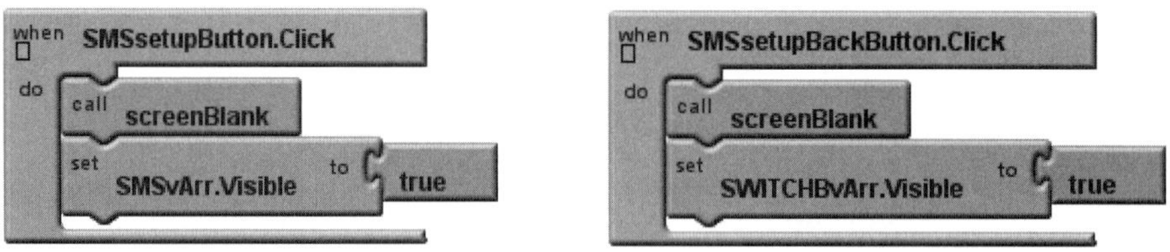

Figure 13.19 Starting and closing (showing and hiding) the SMS Setup

Now that we have added displaying the subscreen for the SMS Setup, we can implement the functions and set the options for the SMS module.

Generate a Reply with an Optional Geoposition

In the SMS Setup, the user can choose from three available settings, some of which have a cumulative effect. In addition to the initial configuration shown in Figure 13.20 (left), where the sender of the incoming SMS automatically receives a simple reply with the suggested text "I am driving ...," the received SMS can be read aloud (center) or the outgoing SMS text can be amended and expanded by adding more text or the current location "I am now in ..." (right).

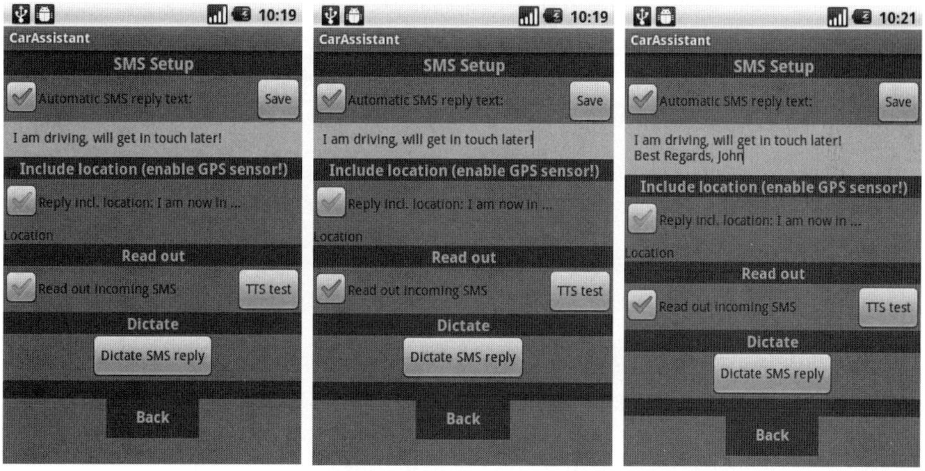

Figure 13.20 Setting options in the SMS Setup

Implementing these options is relatively easy. For two of the three check boxes (`SMSreplyCheckBox` and `TTSCheckBox`), we do not even need to implement a separate event handler, as the relevant Boolean states are checked only when an incoming SMS is received. At that point, the Boolean results lead to the execution of the corresponding statements. Thus, for the first option of "auto-reply via SMS," we implement the Save button in the form of the mostly self-explanatory event handler `SMSreplySaveButton.Click` (Figure 13.21). If the user changes the SMS text in the `SMSreplyTextBox`, he or she can then save this reply permanently in the app's TinyDB component by pressing the Save button.

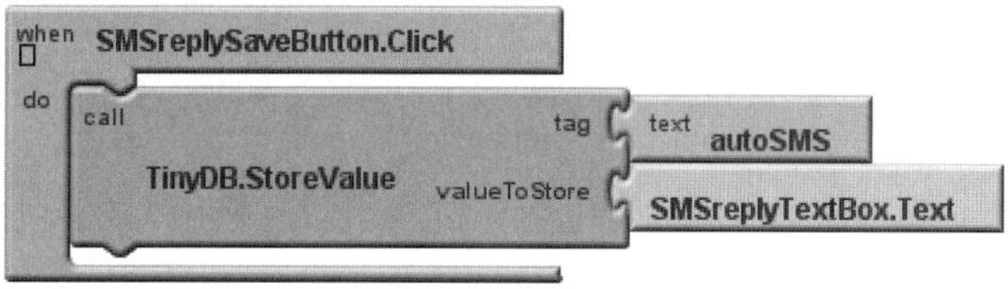

Figure 13.21 Saving the text of the automatic reply SMS

Implementing the option for adding the current location to the SMS reply is almost trivial, thanks to the knowledge you have gained in the previous chapters. To wake up the geosensor from standby mode if required, we use the event handler `LocationCheckBox.Changed` (Figure 13.22, left) and explicitly trigger the `LocationSensor` to retrieve the current location when the check box is enabled. Of course, the user needs to have enabled the GPS receiver on the smartphone for this aspect of our driver assistance system to work, so that the geofunctions can come into effect. The geodata is then received as usual in the event handler `LocationSensor.LocationChanged` (right) and displayed both in the LocationLabel and in the switchboard on the LocationButton.

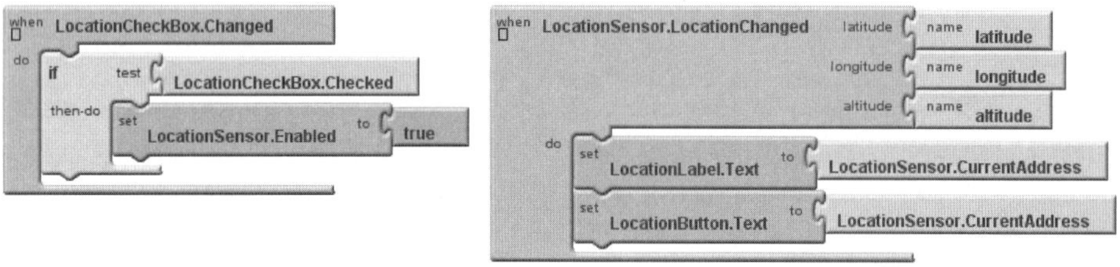

Figure 13.22 Triggering the GPS sensor and retrieving and entering geodata

The actual statements for composing the SMS reply text will be implemented later in the context of the event handler for receiving SMS messages.

Letting Android Read Your SMS Aloud with the TextToSpeech Component

As a third option in the SMS Setup, the user can decide whether he or she wants the incoming SMS message to be read aloud automatically, independent of the other settings. For *speech synthesis*—the speech output based on a text (for example, the text message)—AI offers the non-visible component TextToSpeech in the group "Other stuff." Before you can use it, however, you need to enter some preliminary settings on the smartphone and test them; in addition, you may need to install a separate *text-to-speech* module for outputting speech with AI.

Setting Up the Speech Module

As a general rule, before the TextToSpeech component can be used successfully, you will need to install and/or enable a speech module on your smartphone that is supported by AI and can be used for the speech synthesis. Chapter 15, "Tips and Tools," explains how to check your current setup, determine which settings you need to enter, and identify which app you may have to download, install, and configure. If you have already installed the app "TTS Extended Service" from Eyes-Free Project, chances are that you can use speech output in our driver assistance system straight away. You can check this by pressing the "TTS test" button. If you hear the sentence "Hello, this is a test!", the speech output on your smartphone is configured correctly.

Once the speech module is properly set up, the TextToSpeech component can be used for outputting any text as speech. As this component works on a very high level of abstraction and the speech output itself is left almost entirely to the speech module mentioned previously, its functions remain readily manageable, as you can see in the specification extract shown in Figure 13.23. Using the Language and Country properties, you can set the language (for example, `eng` for English) and the appropriate pronunciation (for example, `GBR` for British English or `USA` for American English); with the two event handlers `BeforeSpeaking` and `AfterSpeaking`, you can add other statements immediately before or after the speech output.

TextToSpeech

TextToSpeech2

Use a text-to-speech component to have the device speak text audibly.

In order for this component to work, the device must have the *TTS Extended Service* app by Eyes-Free Project installed. You can download this from http://code.google.com/p/eyes-free/downloads/list

The text-to-speech component has properties you can set to guide the pronunciation of the text to be spoken. These properties use three-letter codes to specify the language and the country in which the language is spoken. For example, you can specify British English or US English. For British English, the language code is `eng` and the country code is `GBR`, while for US English, the language code is `eng` and the country code is `USA`. The complete list is below.

Events

`AfterSpeaking(Text result)`
Signaled after the text is spoken. The argument is the text result that was produced.
`BeforeSpeaking()`
Signaled just before the text is spoken.

Here are the language and country codes you can use. The codes are organized first by language; then, in each language section are a list of possible country codes:

- ces (Czech)
  - CZE
- spa (Spanish)
  - ESP
  - USA
- deu (German)
  - AUT
  - BEL
  - CHE
  - DEU
  - LIE
  - LUX

Properties

`Country`
The country code for speech production.
`Language`
The language code for speech production.
`Result`
Details to come.

Methods

`Speak(Text message)`
Speaks the given text.

Figure 13.23 Specification of the TextToSpeech component in AI References

For the speech output in our driver assistance system, we will use the TextToSpeech method `Speak`, with which we can get the app to read out any kind of text, such as the content of an SMS message. As the reading out of the incoming SMS message will also be implemented later in the event handler for receiving SMS, we implement just the event handler `TTStestButton.Click` (Figure 13.24) in the context of the SMS Setup now.

Figure 13.24 Testing the speech output via the button "TTS test"

Through the event handler `TTStestButton.Click`, pressing the button "TTS test" in the SMS Setup results in the speech output of the sentence "Hello, this is a test!" If you can hear this sentence, reading out the incoming SMS message will also work when we create this functionality later in the chapter. If you cannot hear anything, please check the speaker volume on your smartphone and then read the appropriate section in Chapter 15, "Tips and Tools."

Dictation and Voice Recognition with the SpeechRecognizer Component

In addition to providing speech output through our app, we want to include input via spoken language in the app. To do so, we more or less reverse the principle underlying the speech synthesis described earlier (text-to-speech) and generate a text string from a *speech input* (*speech-to-text*). For *speech recognition*, AI offers the SpeechRecognizer component, which is also found in the group "Other stuff." Thanks to the speech guidance contained in the Android operating system, this component can be used without any further preliminary settings. The SpeechRecognizer component also has a high degree of abstraction and only a few settings options, as you can see from its specification in Figure 13.25.

SpeechRecognizer

SpeechRecognizer1

Use a speech recognizer component to listen to the user speaking and convert the spoken sound into text using Android's speech recognition feature.

Properties

`Result`
The last text produced by the recognizer.

Methods

`GetText()`
Asks the user to speak, and converts the speech to text. Signals the `AfterGettingText` event when the result is available.

Events

`AfterGetting(Text result)`
Signaled after the recognizer has produced text. The argument is the text result that was produced.
`BeforeGettingText()`
Signaled just before the recognizer is called.

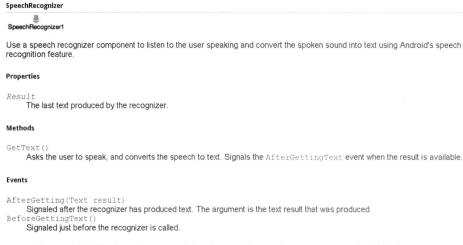

Figure 13.25 Specification of the SpeechRecognizer component in AI References

The method `GetText` invokes the system's speech recognition capabilities, prompts the user to enter speech input, and analyzes the recorded speech. The result of the analysis is then returned to the event handler `AfterGetting` as a text string and made available there in the SpeechRecognizer component's Result property for retrieval and further processing. You might think that it would make sense to use the speech control capability for our switchboard in the driver assistance system, but in fact we would not significantly improve the already implemented one-touch-of-a-button control via the function keys, as the speech analysis functionality must also be triggered explicitly via an event (in other words, by pressing a button). Instead, we can use the speech recognition much more effectively for inputting a new SMS reply. Suppose the user should need to change the default text of the SMS reply after he or she has already started driving—for example, if congestion or traffic jams cause the driver to be late for an appointment and the user wants to reply adequately to impatient SMS queries. He or she can do so in the SMS Setup via speech input by pressing the button "Dictate SMS reply," as an alternative to entering text manually. Figure 13.26 shows an example of the process of speech input (left), the speech analysis (center), and the subsequent transfer of the analysis result to the SMS reply text field (right).

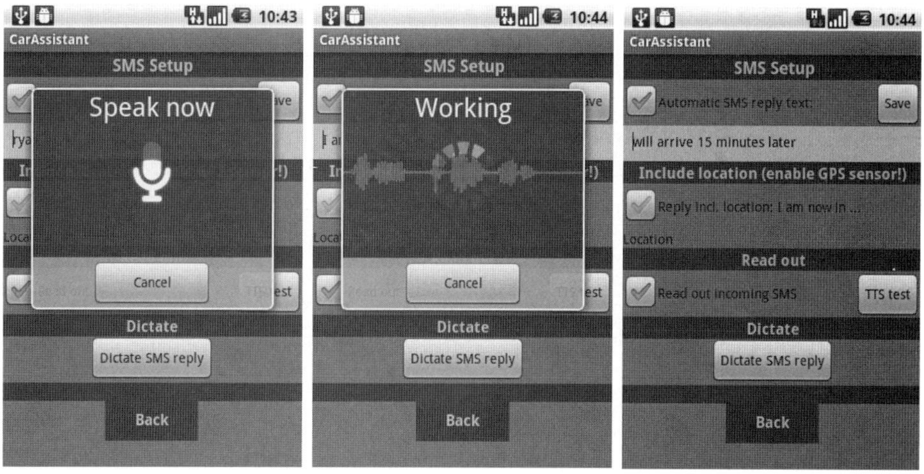

Figure 13.26 Speech input of a new SMS reply text

The implementation of this dictation function within our SMS Setup is extremely simply and brief, as you can see in Figure 13.27. In the first step, pressing the button "Dictate SMS reply" invokes the speech recognition system and carries out the analysis in the event handler `SpeechButton.Click` via the method `SpeechRecognizer.GetText`. After the analysis is completed, the event handler `SpeechRecognizer.AfterGettingText` is called automatically in a second step and is passed a text string in the variable `result` as the analysis result. This string is retrieved from the property field `SpeechRecognizer.Result` and displayed in the SMSreply-TextBox. The new SMS reply text is then available for the next SMS, just as a manually entered text would be.

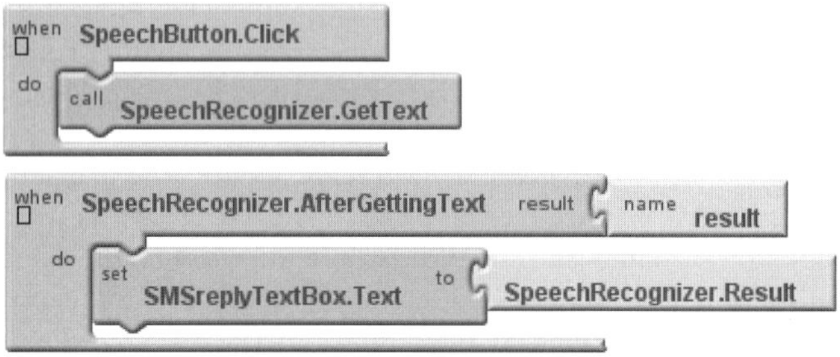

Figure 13.27 Triggering voice recognition and displaying the analysis result

Now that we have implemented all setting options of the SMS Setup, we can move on to implementing the SMS reception and sending process itself, taking into consideration the options we have chosen so far.

Receiving, Evaluating, and Sending SMS Messages with the Texting Component

For receiving and sending SMS messages, AI offers the Texting component in the Social group. As it is implemented on a similarly high level of abstraction as the PhoneCall component, the Texting component consistently uses the SMS system functions of the Android operating system to receive incoming text messages *and* send them. Unlike with phone calls, both *incoming* and *outgoing* SMS messages can be managed with the Texting component, so the entire process of dealing with SMS can be represented fully within an app and automated fully. Between receiving an SMS message and sending a message to the original sender, or to one or any number of other recipients, the content of the incoming SMS message can be processed in any way and the outgoing message can be expanded with desired text information and any data you want. As mentioned at the beginning of the chapter, you can automate not only the SMS communication between human beings, but also that between humans and machines, or even between machines and machines (*M2M*). Consider the incredible possibilities for potential apps exploiting this functionality! All this is possible with AI thanks to the rather inconspicuous but very powerful Texting component, whose specification appears in Figure 13.28.

Texting

Texting1

Use this non-visible component to allow users to send and receive text messages.

When the `SendMessage` method is called, the texting component sends the text message specified in the `Message` property to the phone number specified in the `PhoneNumber` property. Texting components can receive text messages unless the `ReceivingEnabled` property is False. When a message arrives, the `MessageReceived` event is raised and provides the sending number and message.

This component is often used with the `ContactPicker` component, which lets the user select one of the contacts stored on the phone and sets the `PhoneNumber` property to the contact's phone number.

To directly specify the phone number, set the `PhoneNumber` property to a `Text` with the specified digits (for example, "6505551212"). The number can be formatted with hyphens, periods, and parentheses; they are ignored. You can't include spaces in the number.

Properties

`PhoneNumber`
Phone number that text will be sent to.
`Message`
Text of message that will be sent.
`ReceivingEnabled`
If set, this component can receive text messages.

Events

`MessageReceived(text number, text messageText)`
Text message was received, with given text and from given number.

Methods

`SendMessage()`
Sends the text specified by `Message` to the number given in `PhoneNumber`.

Figure 13.28 Specification of the Texting component in AI References

Because it incorporates the complete functional chain from receiving to sending an SMS message, the specification of the Texting component shown in Figure 13.28 has a few more elements than the PhoneCall component, which it otherwise resembles strongly in terms of function. Sending an SMS message requires the recipient's phone number, which is recorded in the PhoneNumber property. There is also a single method `SendMessage` with which the text message is sent from the property field "Message" to the target phone number. The two remaining elements are solely devoted to receiving SMS messages: The basic readiness to receive can be turned on and off via the Boolean property field `ReceivingEnabled` and the incoming SMS message is received as an event in the event handler `MessageReceived`, including the received text message and the sender's phone number.

In our driver assistance system, we use the Texting component both for receiving and for sending SMS messages. If the SMS management is enabled, we want to react to every received SMS message in the way configured in the SMS Setup, have the received text message be read aloud if applicable, and send any reply SMS back to the sender, perhaps with added information about the driver's current location. All of these processes, including requesting and considering the configuration settings from the SMS Setup, are executed in the event handler `Texting.MessageReceived` (Figure 13.29). The event handler is called automatically with each received SMS message, and to it we pass both the sender's phone number (`number`) and the message text itself (`messageText`) as local variables, which are then available for further processing within the handler. To take any new input of an SMS reply text into account in the SMS Setup, we delete the last-sent reply text `Texting.Message` straight away and take the received phone number of the sender as the new target phone number `Texting.PhoneNumber` for our reply back to the sender. In the first conditional `if` statement, we check whether the automatic SMS management was enabled by the user (in other words, if the SMS function button is illuminated in green; see Figure 13.18). Only if this is the case (`smsReply` = `true`) will the program react to the incoming SMS message and the other statements be executed.

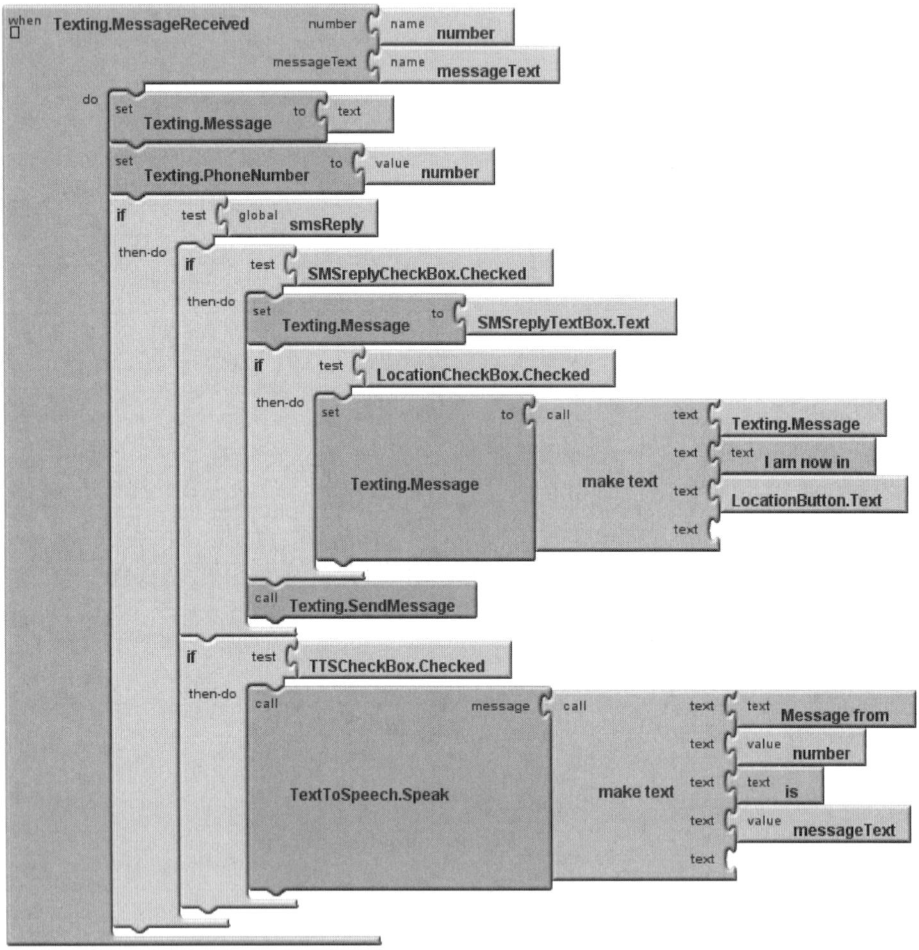

Figure 13.29 Receiving and sending SMS messages with the options of the SMS Setup

If SMS management is enabled, the event handler shown in Figure 13.29 carries out the next check in the form of a second, subordinate `if` statement to verify that the automatic SMS reply was selected previously in the SMS Setup. If this is the case (`SMSreplyCheckBox .Checked` = `true`), we take the text currently entered in the `SMSreplyTextBox` (be it preset, entered manually, or dictated) as the new SMS reply text `Texting.Message`. In another, also subordinate `if` statement, we then determine whether the location information should be included in the reply text. If this option was enabled in the SMS Setup (`LocationCheckBox.Checked` = `true`), we append the text string "I am now in", together with the current location text found in `LocationButton.Text`, to the existing reply text `Texting.Message` via the method `make text`. The hierarchical nesting has the cumulative effect that the location information will never be sent as a reply without the reply text, whereas the reply text *can* be sent without the location. Finally, we send the reply of `Texting.Message`, however it may be filled, to the phone number identified by `Texting.PhoneNumber`, by calling the method `Texting.SendMessage`. Now the functionality of the automatic reply SMS is fully implemented.

After sending—or optionally not sending—the reply SMS, we add the statements for speech output of the received SMS message via text-to-speech conversion in the event handler shown in Figure 13.29. Again we first check in an `if` statement whether this option has been turned on by the user in the SMS Setup. If the answer is positive (`TTSCheckBox.Checked` = `true`), we use the method `make text` to create a coherent text from the text string "Message from", the phone number `number` of the sender, the text string "is", and the received text message `messageText`; the installed speech module reads it aloud when we call the method `TextToSpeech.Speak`. Depending on the speech module, the phone number may not be read number by number, but rather as one big number ("one million five hundred thousand ..."). You can change this behavior by editing the phone number first with the corresponding text methods.

Now the SMS module of our driver assistance system is fully implemented (see also `Screen1.Initialize`). By itself, it has an impressive range of functions. Think about the enormous potential offered by the complete representation of the communication process via SMS message using the powerful AI components, which you can use for your own future projects. Thanks to the modular app structure, we were able to simply slot these new functions into the basic framework of our driver assistance program, without changing the overall structure of the app or impairing the program's clarity in any noticeable way. In the same way, we can now add other modules and successively expand the overall functionality of our driver assistance system.

Data Exchange via an Interface

In this section, we do nothing less than implement all four remaining function keys, whose functionality basically relies on just one central component of AI. Correspondingly, this section does not merely introduce just another component, but rather a basic concept and a more or less universal *interface*, through which the apps developed in AI can communicate with the outside world and exchange data. As a developer, you can use such an interface to remove the boundaries surrounding your own app, and then integrate other apps you have programmed (whether in AI or in another programming language such as Java), any apps from the Android Market, or even apps intrinsic to the Android operating system into the functionality of your own app, thereby letting the new app take advantage of these sources' capabilities. Similar to the system-side components of AI through which we have already made use of individual Android system functions and applications (for example, Image, Camera, Player, PhoneCall, Texting), this integrative spectrum can be expanded to include almost any apps and their functions. We can invoke these functions from our own app, in as far as they allow it and are designed for this type of data communication. Moreover, we are not limited to just other apps that can be used from within our own app via this interface component; instead, any kind of *web services*—whether developed by you or offered by third parties—can be accessed online, integrated, and their functions combined with those of your own app. As you might imagine, the component we introduce in this section provides critical support for the trend-setting approach of *cloud computing,* whereby we can use web services for saving as well as processing data.

Sharing Use of Apps and Web Services via the ActivityStarter Component

The importance of this central component for your work as an app developer cannot be over-emphasized, as it offers you amazing possibilities even beyond the range of functions inherent in the AI inventory. This component shapes both the AI developer language and the apps developed with it into open, expandable, and flexible systems with which you are well prepared to address any future developments in the highly dynamic field of mobile applications.

After all these lofty announcements, we will now reveal the secret and tell you which central interface component we have been talking about. In the group "Other stuff," AI offers this conceptional element as the non-visible component ActivityStarter. Its functionality is described well by its name: With this component, apps, web services, system functions, and other external functions can be started or invoked as *activities*. As is appropriate given its generic function range, the specification of this component is a bit more extensive than usual. The first part of the specification, shown in Figure 13.30, consists of a detailed, general description of the functions and introduces a few example *parameters* for invoking other apps and web services.

ActivityStarter

A component that can launch another activity from your application.

You communicate with the activity starter by setting properties of the component to pass information related to the activity, including the action and activity class. See Using the Activity Starter Component for details and examples.

Activities that can be launched include:

- Starting another App Inventor for Android app. To do so, first determine *class* of the other application by downloading the source code and using a file explorer or unzip utility to find a file named "youngandroidproject/project.properties". The first line of the file will start with "main=" and be followed by the class name; for example,

  `main=com.gmail.Bitdiddle.Ben.HelloPurr.Screen1`

  To make your `ActivityStarter` launch this application, set the following properties:

  - `ActivityPackage` to the class name, dropping the last component (for example, `com.gmail.Bitdiddle.Ben.HelloPurr`)
  - `ActivityClass` to the entire class name (for example, `com.gmail.Bitdiddle.Ben.HelloPurr.Screen1`)
- Starting an activity that is built in to the Android OS, such as using the camera, or performing a web search. You can start camera by setting the following properties:
  - `Action: android.intent.action.MAIN`
  - `ActivityPackage: com.android.camera`
  - `ActivityClass: com.android.camera.Camera`
- Performing web search: Assuming the term you want to search for is "vampire" (feel free to substitute your own choice), set the properties to:
  - `Action: android.intent.action.WEB_SEARCH`
  - `ExtraKey: query`
  - `ExtraValue: vampire`
  - `ActivityPackage: com.google.android.providers.enhancedgooglesearch`
  - `ActivityClass: com.google.android.providers.enhancedgooglesearch.Launcher`
- Opening a browser to a specified web page. Assuming the page you want to go to is "www.facebook.com" (feel free to substitute your own choice), set the properties to:
  - `Action: android.intent.action.VIEW`
  - `DataUri: http://www.facebook.com`

You can also launch third-party applications installed on the phone, provided you know the appropriate *intents* to invoke them, and you can also launch activities that produce text results and get them back to use in your application. The way this data is extracted depends on how the application has been implemented.

Figure 13.30 Part 1 of the specification of the ActivityStarter component in AI References

As examples for the various activities that can be launched with the ActivityStarter, the specification shown in Figure 13.30 lists the parameters for starting another AI app ("HelloPurr"), a system app ("Camera"), a search query for the term "vampire" via the web service "Enhanced Google Search," and going to the website `www.facebook.com`. For better understanding the ActivityStarter, the documentation in the AI Concepts Reference is also very important and useful.

Documentation and Other Examples for the ActivityStarter

As a guide to help you use and better understand the ActivityStarter component, the AI Concepts Reference contains the document "Using the Activity Starter Component," which lists many additional examples, references to additional sources of information, and instructions for determining the interface parameters of other apps and web services. It is a good idea to use this online document as the starting point for your own work with the ActivityStarter, in particular to stay up-to-date with its ongoing evolution:

`http://experimental.appinventor.mit.edu/learn/reference/other/activitystarter.html`

In addition to the general descriptions of the functions and exemplary parameters for starting the activities mentioned previously, the specification of the component ActivityStarter identifies its properties, events, and methods, as shown in Figure 13.31. The property fields specify the parameters that are required for launching the relevant activity and exchanging data with it. For example, in the Action property, the desired *action* (for example, `android.intent.action.VIEW` for viewing a video on YouTube) is started as the *intent* of the corresponding Android system function (similar to retrieving the system time in the Clock component). Launching an activity with AI is already very similar to launching it with Java, so under the ActivityClass and ActivityPackage properties of the ActivityStarter component, you also need to specify the corresponding package name (for example, `com.google.android.youtube`) and class name (for example, `com.google.android.youtube.PlayerActivity`).

Properties

`Action`: text
  Action of the activity to be launched.
`ActivityClass`: text
  Class name of the activity to be launched.
`ActivityPackage`: text
  Package name of the activity to be launched.
`DataUri`: text
  URI passed to activity to be launched.
`ExtraKey`: text
  Key name of text passed to the activity.
`ExtraValue`: text
  Value of text passed to the activity.
`Result`: text
  Value returned by the activity being started.
`ResultName`: text
  The name used to extract the result returned from the activity being started.
`ResultType`: text
  Type information returned from the activity being started.
`ResultUri`: text
  URI (or Data) information returned from the activity being started.

Events

`ActivityError(text message)`>
  Indicates that an error occurred while using this ActivityStarter.
`AfterActivity(text result)`
  Called after activity ends.

Methods

text `ResolveActivity()`
  Returns the name of the activity that corresponds to this ActivityStarter, or an empty string if no corresponding activity can be found. You can use this before starting an external application to ensure that the application is installed on the phone.
`StartActivity()`
  Start the activity associated with this component.

Figure 13.31 Part 2 of the specification of the ActivityStarter component in AI References

Background Information: Intents

If you would like to know more about using intents for launching system functions or want to look up individual intents, you will find information for advanced programmers and an overview of the Java classes and packages under "Android Developers" at the following site:

`http://developer.android.com/reference/android/content/Intent.html`

But do not let these descriptions awe you too much. Although the AI Concepts Reference talks of ActivityStarter as a component intended mostly for "advanced developers," you can simply copy the data for the intents from the templates, enter them as properties, and then use the activity starter just like any other component. For this simplified form of use, you can also find collections of intents on the Internet that are very easy to understand.

Collections of Useful Intents

To help you quickly and easily use known intents, overviews of these elements are available on the Internet. Here is one we recommend:

`http://www.openintents.org/en/node/35`

Simply regard the three pieces of data in the property fields Action, ActivityClass, and ActivityPackage as identifiers for the activity or external application that you want to launch. Of course, once you have started the activity, you need to tell the application what it should do or which data you would like to get from it. That is what the property field DataUri, shown in Figure 13.31, is for. In it, you can pass a specific request to the invoked web service for carrying out a function or providing data. This request may consist of a simple web address as an instruction for going to the address (for example, `http://news.google.com`) or, as in our earlier YouTube example, an extended web address with the request (*query*) for a particular video that you want the activity to play (for example, `http://www.youtube.com/watch?v=8ADwPLSFeY8`). The specific identifier for requesting the desired YouTube video can be obtained by going to the video with your web browser, pressing the Embed button, and copying the complete http address in the shown HTML tag "src" of the embedding code.

Both simple and extended web addresses belong to the *URI* (Uniform Resource Identifier) group, with which you can clearly identify and retrieve any resource on the World Wide Web, be it a website, a video file, or a specific service of a web service. In addition to retrieving websites via an `http` identifier, you can use this method for retrieving maps via geocoordinates through the *scheme* `geo` of the web service Google Maps (for example, `geo:50.19,8.58?z=23`) or use the scheme `mailto` for sending e-mails with a specified recipient, subject line, and text (for example, `mailto:peter.tester@gmail.com?subject=Hello`). When the query is introduced by a question mark (`?`), you can use specific query parameters in the query to formulate your request or instruction even more precisely. Please refer to the documentation of the web service in question to find out which parameters are appropriate in each particular case.

Launching, Invoking, and Sending Search Queries to Web Services via a URI

You can find further information on the general use and structure of a Uniform Resource Identifier (URI) by searching on the Internet under the appropriate search term. *Wikipedia* offers an overview of the common schemes and the two subcategories, URL (Uniform Resource Locator) and URN (Uniform Resource Name), at these links:

> `http://en.wikipedia.org/wiki/Uniform_Resource_Identifier`
>
> `http://en.wikipedia.org/wiki/URI_scheme`
>
> A general overview and further information on web services can be found here:
>
> `http://en.wikipedia.org/wiki/Web_service`
>
> An impressive example of the multitude of potential queries and instructions via query parameters is provided by the page "Google Map Parameters," with which you can direct all sorts of queries to the web service `maps.google.com`:
>
> `http://mapki.com/wiki/Google_Map_Parameters`

In addition or as an alternative to the URI, to some activities the query parameters can be passed via the other property fields of the ActivityStarter component. For example, in a web search via the activity `enhancedgooglesearch`, you can pass the parameter `query` to the action `android.intent.action.WEB_SEARCH` in the ActivityStarter property field ExtraKey and also assign it the exemplary search term `vampire` in the property field ExtraValue. Whereas some activities or external apps display the result directly by themselves when they are launched and the desired action is performed, other activities return an additional or alternative return value (result) to the invoking app. For this case of reciprocal communication and reciprocal exchange of data between the invoking app and the invoked app, the ActivityStarter component offers additional property fields in which the result can be received as text string (Result), together with its identifier (ResultName), its type (ResultType), and, if appropriate, a returned URI.

In addition to the properties described in detail earlier, the ActivityStarter component has the methods and property blocks shown in Figure 13.31. Through the method `ResolveActivity`, you can check whether the desired activity or external application is available on the smartphone and, if so, under which name. This query applies to any kind of activity, be it launching another AI app, another app by a third party, a web service, or a system function, as all variations make use of the Android operating system to a greater or lesser extent. If the smartphone does not have the appropriate facility, it is not possible to use that special kind of service; for example, accessing a website is not possible without the network and browser functions of the Android operating system. If this functionality is available, the method `StartActivity` launches the activity, based on the settings that you established in the properties. Any actions after the external service is used can be implemented in the event handler `AfterActivity`, such as processing of results that are made available in the corresponding Result property fields by the external service. There is also an event handler `ActivityError`, which seems to be intended for receiving any error messages passed by the external app.

If you have not yet gained any personal experience with using web services—for example, in the context of designing your own home page—these topics may have seemed a little unfamiliar. In that case, please make use of the sources identified elsewhere in this chapter for finding out more about this extremely diverse and powerful topic if you are interested. Otherwise, just continue reading, because we will use some of the many possible activities in connection with our CarAssistant project, at the same time demonstrating the really not quite so complicated use of the ActivityStarter component.

Pedestrian Navigation with Integrated Google Maps

For our driver assistance system, we want to use an activity starter to implement the functionality behind the Back function key (actually a button). With the Back button, the user should have the option of saving a location spontaneously and having the app guide him or her back to that location upon pressing a button—for example, when parking a car in a parking space the driver has never used before and might otherwise not find back again in an unfamiliar environment. Saving the geoposition of the parking space does not hold any great surprises, but the seamless integration of the web service Google Maps is a functionality that is not contained in AI itself as an independent component (unlike accessing the system Camera or the VideoPlayer, for example), but that has to be implemented via the generic interface component ActivityStarter. Figure 13.32 shows an example of how this function can be used (from left to right). Once the driver has reached the place where he or she wants to park the car, the user invokes the Navi Setup via the setup menu in the switchboard, and records the current location as the parking location (including its longitude, latitude, and address) under "Back to Car" by pressing the Current button. To find the way back to that location later, the user simply presses the Back function key in the switchboard, which starts Google Maps as an activity, displays the directions to the desired location, allows the user to select the type of navigation ("By car," "By public transit," "Walking," "Bicycling"), and starts the navigation when the user presses the blue navigation arrow on the upper-right edge of the screen in the desired view mode. Once he or she has reached the parking space again, the user can use the Back button of the smartphone to go back to the driver assistance system and immediately select the next desired function by pressing another function key.

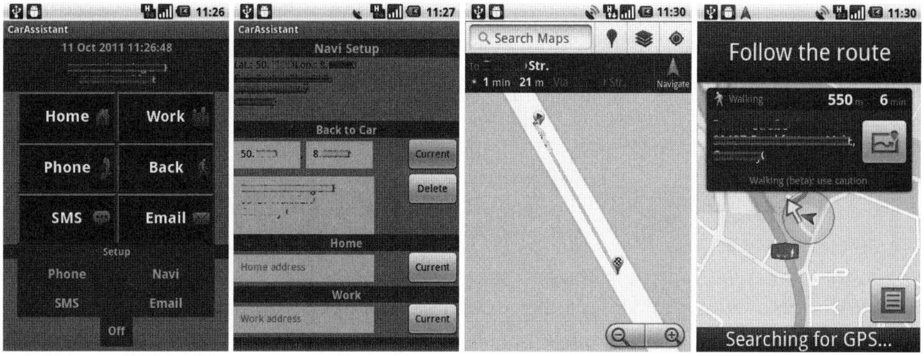

Figure 13.32 Pedestrian navigation via the driver assistance system and Google Maps

The implementation of this integrative functionality starts with the design of the user interface or, rather, by presetting the component properties in AI Designer. After all, this is where the action or the intent, the package, and the class of the desired activity for navigating to a destination of your choice via the web service of Google Maps are preset. Let's add the next module to our driver assistance system by designing the interface of the Navi Setup, in which the settings for both the Back function key and the Home and Work function keys (i.e., buttons; implemented later) are applied. Open the CarAssistant project in AI Designer, and add the components listed in Table 13.4. As with the other modules described earlier, you should add the required text labels, color and font size settings, BufferLabels, SpacerLabels, DivisionLabels, and Arrangements yourself. The entire module is encapsulated for the multiple screens in a VerticalArrangement object component, `NAVIvArr`.

Table 13.4 **Adding the Components for the Navi Module**

Component	Object Name	Adapted Properties
VerticalArrangement	NAVIvArr	"Visible" disable "Width": Fill parent
ActivityStarter	ActivityStarterMaps	"Activity," "ActivityClass," "ActivityPackage": see Table 13.5
Label (3x)	LatLabel, LonLabel, NaviAddressLabel	"Text": -, -, Location
TextBox (3x)	BackLatTextBox, BackLonTextBox, BackAddressTextBox	"Hint": Latitude, Longitude, Address
Button (2x)	BackCurrentButton, BackDelButton	"Text": Current, Delete
TextBox	HomeTextBox	"Hint": Home address
Button	HomeCurrentButton	"Text": Current
TextBox	WorkTextBox	"Hint": Work address
Button	WorkCurrentButton	"Text": Current
Button	NaviBackButton	"Text": Back

With the components of Table 13.4, we have already set most of the items needed for the two other navigation function keys, Home and Work, in the Navi Setup, except for the additional activity starter that we require for these two function items and will add later. With these settings and your other design additions, the Navi module should appear in AI Designer as shown in Figure 13.33.

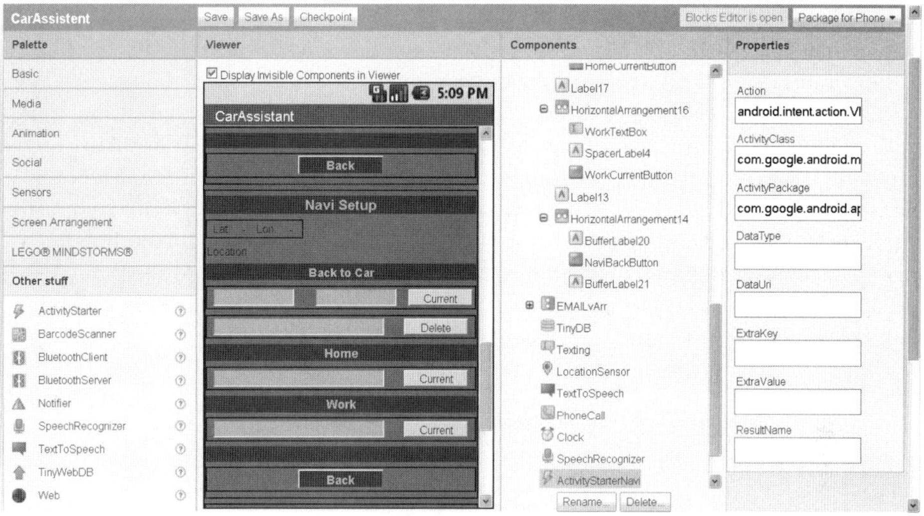

Figure 13.33 Adding the Navi module in the CarAssistant project

In the Properties section of Figure 13.33, you can see the default settings for the activity starter `ActivityStarterMaps`, which we require for launching the Google Maps web service and starting the pedestrian navigation. In Table 13.5, you can see the complete data for the property fields, which you should add to the initial settings of the Navi module.

Table 13.5 **Default Settings of the ActivityStarterMaps Activity Starter**

Property	Default Setting for Object ActivityStarterMaps
"Action"	android.intent.action.VIEW
"ActivityClass"	com.google.android.maps.MapsActivity
"ActivityPackage"	com.google.android.apps.maps

In addition to the Navi Setup user interface, we have now named the activity (i.e., external web service) of Google Maps, which we will invoke later, integrate in our app, and want to use for navigating between two geopositions (which we will need to pass to the web service). Now we can start implementing the functionality of the Back function key as well as the Navi Setup in AI Editor. To give us the option of conveniently inserting the current location of the user with one press of the button as the destination address for navigating to the parking space (Back)—or to the user's home (Home) or workplace (Work)—we insert the geodata determined by the GPS sensor as the topmost position in our Navi Setup. To that end, we expand the event handler `LocationSensor.LocationChanged` (which you encountered earlier, in Figure 13.22) as shown in Figure 13.34, so as to have the current address displayed in the NaviAddress-Label as well (the additional elements for the Email Setup are included here, too). Along with the address, we display in the geocoordinates of the current address, as the user may sometimes park his or her car in a rural location, and because we require these coordinates as parameters for querying the activity Google Maps. The Google Maps web service also expects the geocoordinates to be decimal point numbers, so we convert the values that the geosensor may potentially return as decimal comma numbers to the desired decimal point format first by using the text method `replace all` before we use the numbers in the LatLabel and LonLabel of Table 13.4.

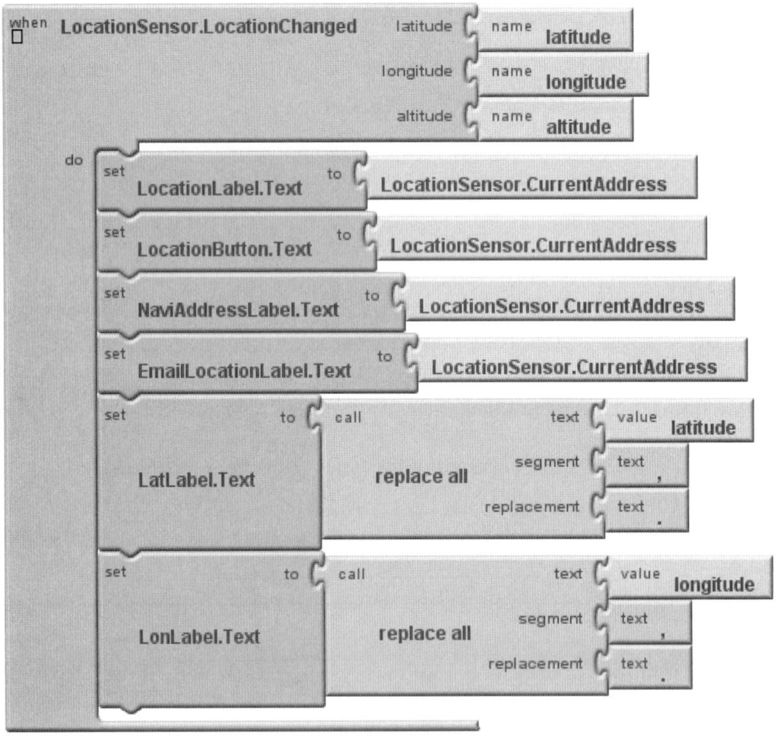

Figure 13.34 Inserting the current geodata in Navi (and Email) Setup

When we press the Navi function key and launch the Navi Setup—or, more precisely, the associated event handler `NaviSetupButton.Click`—the Setup area is immediately overwritten with the correct current geodata. Figure 13.35 also shows the event handler `NaviBackButton.Click` for closing the Navi Setup, which is called when the user presses the Back key in the Navi Setup. This event handler contains not just the usual statements for switching between the multiple screens, but also three calls of the method `TinyDB.StoreValue`, with which the destination addresses for the parking space, the home, and the workplace from the corresponding text boxes are saved locally under a unique identifier, thereby making them persistently available when the driver assistance system is started the next time.

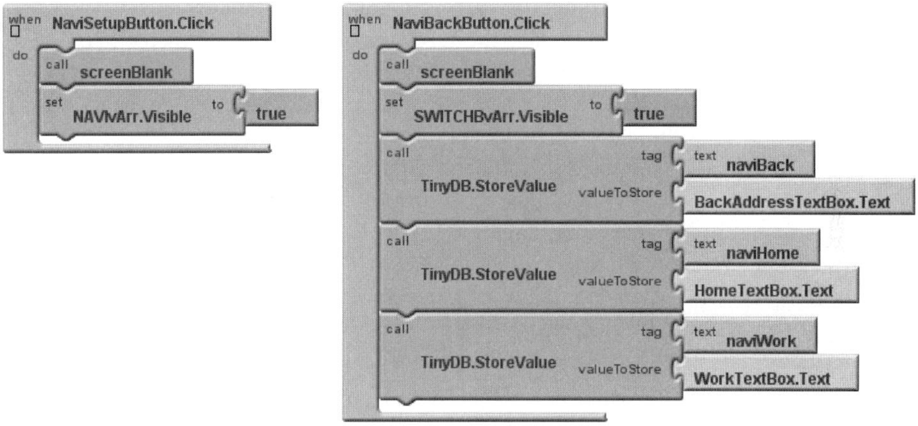

Figure 13.35 Starting and closing the Navi Setup

The two buttons for setting up the "Back to Car" functionality are also easy to implement. Through the Current button, or rather the corresponding event handler `BackCurrentButton.Click` (Figure 13.36), the current address, as determined in Figure 13.34, and its corresponding geodata are simply copied as the destination address into the appropriate text boxes for finding the way back to the parked car and are recorded there for the later navigation. Of course, the user can also enter the address and geodata manually into the text boxes and use the Delete key (or rather the event handler `BackDelButton.Click`) to quickly clear them as necessary.

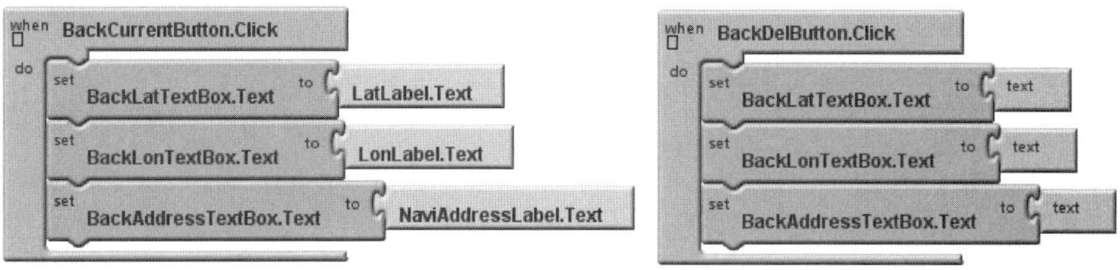

Figure 13.36 Deleting and inserting the current geoposition as the destination address

Now that we are able to record the location of the parked car in the Navi Setup, we can move on to implementing the navigation functionality itself, using the activity starter `ActivityStarterMaps` for launching Google Maps, which we have already selected and preset in AI Designer as an activity. As described earlier, we need to formulate our query or instruction to navigate from the current location address (*start address*) to the saved location of the parked car (*destination address*) as a URI and pass it to the Google Maps web service. This happens when the user presses the Back function key, which calls the event handler `BackNavButton.Click` (Figure 13.37). We use the text method `make text` to assemble the URI as a text string from the components required for the navigation query. The URI begins with the Internet and service address of the web service (`http://maps.google.com/maps`) followed by the query (`?`) for navigating from the start address `saddr=` (source address)—put together from the latitude (`LatLabel.Text`) and longitude (`LonLabel.Text`) of the current location—to the destination address `&daddr=` (destination address)—put together from the latitude (`BackLatLabel.Text`) and longitude (`BackLonLabel.Text`) of the saved parking location. The resulting text string is inserted as a URI into the property field `ActivityStarterMaps.DataUri`. Now we can easily invoke the desired activity through the method `ActivityStarterMaps.StartActivity`, which then starts Google Maps with the appropriate navigation query, as shown in Figure 13.32 (third picture from left).

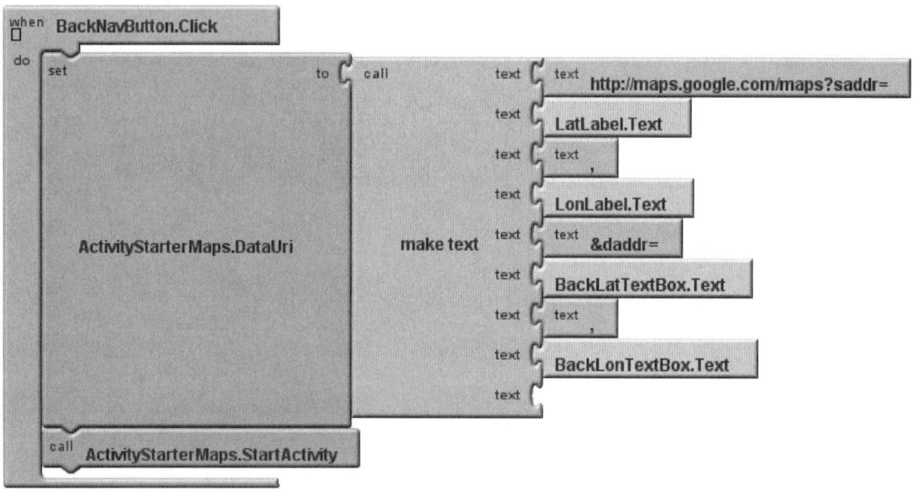

Figure 13.37 Navigation query to Google Maps via URI

As you can see, dealing with an activity starter can be considerably easier than the theoretical explanations might have led you to suspect. Perhaps you are still wondering how you are supposed to know how to formulate a URI, like the one shown in Figure 13.37. For example, in a navigation query about going from Frankfurt to Berlin, the URI could look like this:

```
http://maps.google.com/maps?saddr=Frankfurt&daddr=Berlin
```

You can find out the correct way of formulating this URI by consulting the online documentation for Google Maps (`http://mapki.com/wiki/Google_Map_Parameters`). In the "Directions" section on that webpage, you will find explanations and notes on using the two parameters `saddr` and `daddr`. To make matters even easier, just go to Google Maps in your web browser, specify a start address "A" and destination address "B", tell Google Maps to "Get Directions," and then copy the link location via the Link button (chain icon) in the upper-right corner. The result will look something like this: `http://maps.google.com/maps?saddr=Frankfurt&daddr=Berlin&ie=UTF8&t=h&z=7`. You can copy this address over more or less unchanged to the URI of your activity starter. As querying Google Maps is a rather robust and flexible process, you can also pass the geocoordinates in the parameters `saddr` and `daddr` instead of the address, as we did in Figure 13.37:

```
http://maps.google.com/maps?saddr=50.111464,8.681145&daddr=52.526499,13.414078
```

In case of the "walking" navigation back to the location of the parked car, we deliberately used the geocoordinates, as not every parking space has a street address associated with it, but all locations definitely have geocoordinates. Moreover, the geocoordinates are available on your smartphone even when mobile data reception is not available, so you do not have to worry about not getting a signal when you have parked your car somewhere in the woods. We also want to leave it up to the user to decide prior to the navigation in Google Maps how to travel back to the car—whether by walking, bicycling, taking the bus, or in another car.

Car Navigation with Integrated Google Navigation

For reaching your own home or workplace, the selection of the method of transport is no longer relevant, as we assume that the user will use his or her car to get there. We also want to keep the amount of distractions for the driver to a minimum, by starting the navigation to these fixed destinations with just a single press of a button in the driver assistance system's switchboard. For these reasons, we will implement this navigation functionality via an additional Activity Starter with which we invoke the Google Navigation activity directly. We create the Activity Starter in AI Designer by dragging a new ActivityStarter component object `ActivityStarterNavi` into the Viewer and entering the properties of Table 13.6 as default settings.

Table 13.6 **Default Settings of the ActivityStarterNavi Activity Starter**

Property	Default Settings for Object ActivityStarterNavi
"Action"	android.intent.action.VIEW
"ActivityClass"	com.google.android.maps.driveabout.app.NavigationActivity
"ActivityPackage"	com.google.android.apps.maps

As we have already created the other components for the Home and Work function keys, in the Navi Setup of Table 13.4 and the original design of the switchboard in Table 13.1, we can now turn right to the implementation of the navigation functionality in AI Editor. The required block structures are even easier and more manageable than those involved in the pedestrian navigation and are built on the same principle. The current address from the NaviAddressLabel, which is determined by the geosensor, can be conveniently copied in the Navi Setup under Home by the Current button—or rather the underlying event handler `HomeCurrentButton.Click` (Figure 13.38, top)—and inserted as the home address into the HomeTextBox; it can also be entered by hand. As we can assume that both the home and work addresses are regular street addresses, we do not need the geocoordinates this time; thus we will work exclusively on the basis of the street address information. This data is also used as the query parameter when we invoke the Google Navigation activity. When the user presses the Home function key in the switchboard, that action triggers the associated event handler `HomeButton.Click` (Figure 13.38, bottom), and the URI is assembled by the text method `make text`.

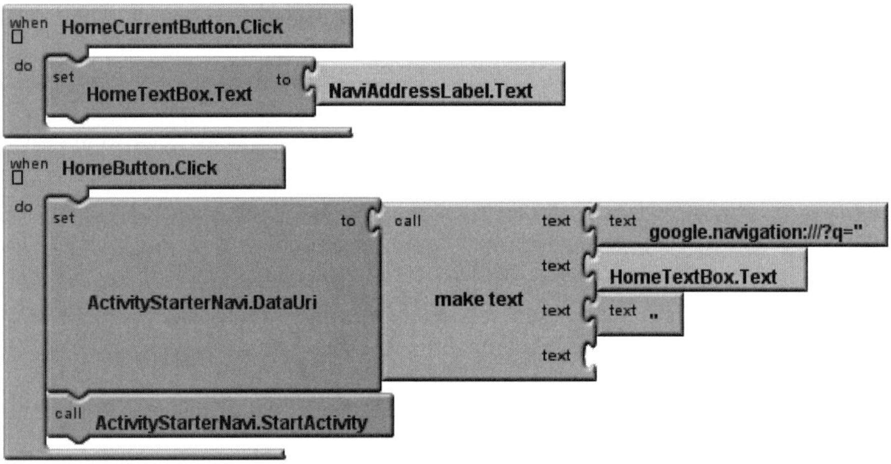

Figure 13.38 Starting the navigation to the home address via Google Navigation

In exactly the same way, we implement the Work function key; the only difference is the address used. Normally we would have constructed a generic structure to invoke the Google Navigation activity, with the same block structure being used to start the navigation to any kind of address. In the case of our driver assistance system, however, one-button control while driving is our main priority, even at the expense of an efficient block structure. As a consequence, the same block structures appear in Figure 13.39 as in Figure 13.38, but this time are applied to the Work function key. Entering the address in the Navi Setup under Work also takes place in the same way as before, and for invoking the activity we use the same `ActivityStarterNavi`.

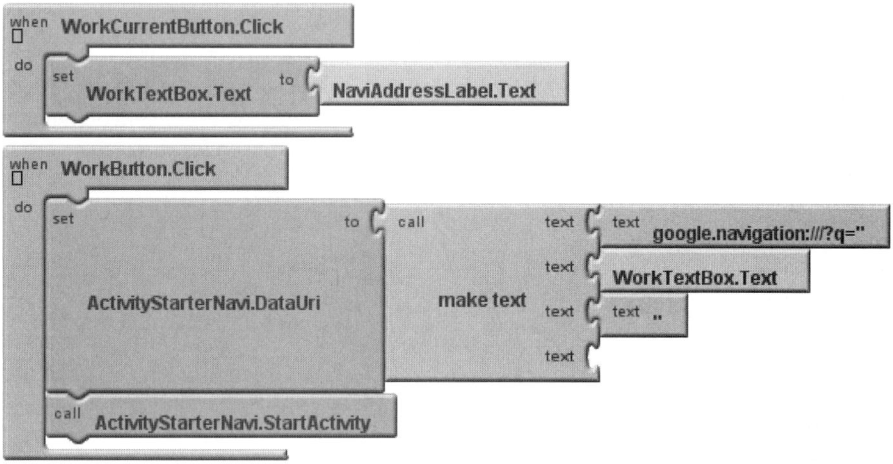

Figure 13.39 Starting the navigation to the work address via Google Navigation

As you saw in the event handlers `HomeButton.Click` and `WorkButton.Click`, the URI when invoking the activity of Google Navigation is shorter than the URI when invoking the web service of Google Maps. We invoke the local navigation application Google Navigation directly via the local directory address on the smartphone under `google.navigation:///` and simply pass it the desired destination address with the general query parameter `?q=` (*query*; corresponds to manually entering the destination address in the app Google Navigation), enclosed by quotation marks. The enclosing quotation marks are used so that we can enter special characters such as spaces as part of the address, without having to use the special URI encoding (such as `%20` for a space). For example, when starting the navigation to Berlin, the URI would look like this:

```
google.navigation:///?q="Berlin"
```

URI Encoding

An overview of encoding special characters in URLs or URIs can be found at:

`http://www.w3schools.com/TAGS/ref_urlencode.asp`

As we are not launching a web service from our app with this activity (*app-to-Web*), but instead starting another local app on the smartphone (*app-to-app*), we do not specify an Internet address (`http`), but instead provide the local directory address of the application we are accessing. The activity Google Navigation expects only a destination address, as it automatically uses the current location as the start address, just like any other navigation device.

Identifying and Using Activities with ADB

This time, to determine the syntax for formulating a navigation query to the Google Navigation activity, we used the *Android Debug Bridge* (*ADB*), an analysis tool that was installed automatically on your computer when you installed AI, and that you have encountered in Chapter 1 in the section on installing the App Inventor Setup Software. Connect your smartphone to the computer via a USB cable, go to (for example) Windows Start > Run, and enter the command `cmd` to open the Windows command line. There, enter the command `adb logcat` and press the **Enter** key. Usually you will see a number of text lines racing by in the command line, which you can safely ignore. Now, however, we want to find out which system calls take place on your smartphone when you start the app Google Navigation manually, enter the destination address `Berlin`, and start the navigation, so that we can start this process (activity) also from within our driver assistance system. To do so, follow the same steps on your smartphone as shown in Figure 13.40 and keep an eye on the protocol data in the command line.

Figure 13.40 Manually starting navigation to Berlin with Google Navigation

As soon as you enter the place name `Berlin` into the input field of Google Navigation and press the magnifying glass icon on the right to start the navigation, the data in the command line will become interesting. Now you need to look for an entry starting with the word "ActivityManager." You may need to scroll a bit through the many protocol data items before you find the right entry. In Figure 13.41, you can see all of the data that we require for starting the desired activity with AI. For example, in the line that begins with `I/ActivityManager(1364): Starting activity` in the data on the `Intent` under the parameter `act`, you will find the complete identifier of the "activity" `android.intent.action.VIEW`; under the parameter `cmp`, you will see the ActivityPackage `com.google.android.apps.maps` and the ActivityClass `com.google.android.maps.driveabout.app.NavigationActivity`; and under the parameter `dat`, you can see the DataUri `google.navigation:///?q=Berlin` (see also Table 13.6).

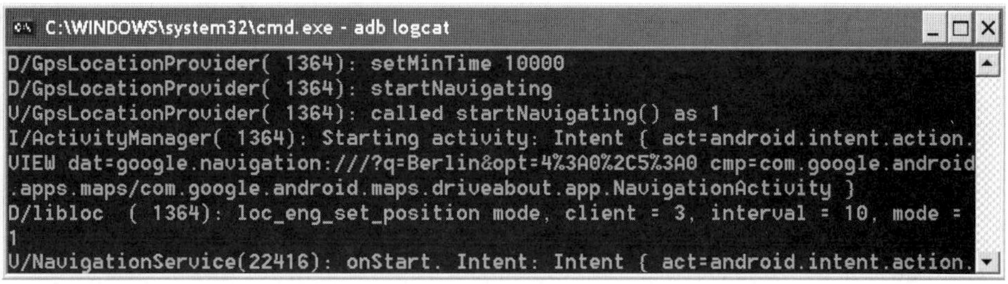

C:\WINDOWS\system32\cmd.exe - adb logcat
D/GpsLocationProvider(1364): setMinTime 10000
D/GpsLocationProvider(1364): startNavigating
V/GpsLocationProvider(1364): called startNavigating() as 1
I/ActivityManager(1364): Starting activity: Intent { act=android.intent.action.
VIEW dat=google.navigation:///?q=Berlin&opt=4%3A0%2C5%3A0 cmp=com.google.android
.apps.maps/com.google.android.maps.driveabout.app.NavigationActivity }
D/libloc (1364): loc_eng_set_position mode, client = 3, interval = 10, mode =
1
V/NavigationService(22416): onStart. Intent: Intent { act=android.intent.action.

Figure 13.41 Tracking activity in ADB Logcat and inserting data into AI

You can use this example of how to invoke Google Navigation as a pattern for generically determining any intents with whose configuration data you can, in principle, access any app on your smartphone via the ActivityStarter component and integrate it in your apps. Using the URI shown in Figure 13.38, the activity of Google Navigation can be invoked directly from the driver assistance system via the Home or Work function key, and the navigation to the home or work address launched accordingly, as shown in Figure 13.42.

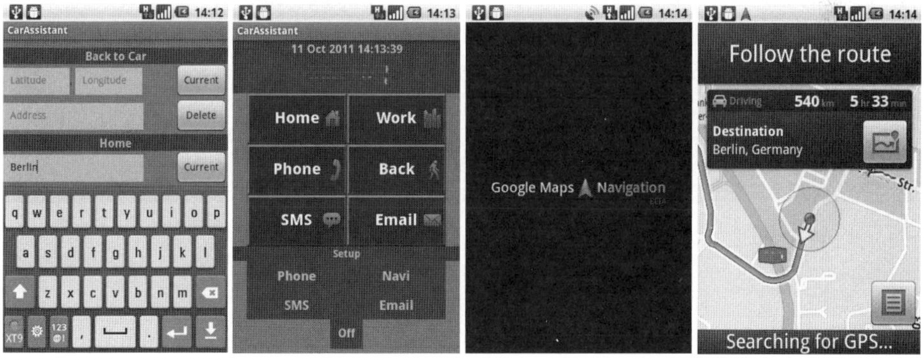

Figure 13.42 Starting the navigation from within the driver assistance system via the Home button

Now take a deep breath and take a moment to think about the many possibilities and the whole world of apps, web services, and other options that this fundamental and generic interface for developing your own apps opens up for you. Next, we want to demonstrate one more possibility within the context of our driver assistance system, providing you with even more inspiration for your own projects.

Selecting Contacts with the EmailPicker and ContactPicker Components

This discussion brings us to the last remaining function key in the switchboard of our driver assistance system, Email. As the text on this button indicates, the user can use it to send an e-mail with just one press of the button—for example, to inform a passenger who car-shares with the user that the user is now leaving the office and will pick the passenger shortly, giving the latter a chance to shut down his or her PC and get ready for the moment when the driver arrives. Similar to the fully automated reply SMS function, the user should have the option with the semi-automated e-mail message to change the message text and subject within an Email Setup, optionally adding the location data and either selecting the e-mail recipient from a list or entering his or her address manually. Both for selecting and manually entering an e-mail address, we want the user to be able to use the contact data present in the smartphone's address book, so that he or she can conveniently insert this data into the Email Setup via a menu selection or autocompletion feature. In Figure 13.43, you can see how pressing the Search button (first from the left) in the Recipient area accesses the address book, selects a contact from it (second from the left), and inserts it into the Setup menu (third from the left). Pressing the Email function button launches the default or preferred e-mail account, from which the automatically generated e-mail text can then be sent by pressing the Send button (right).

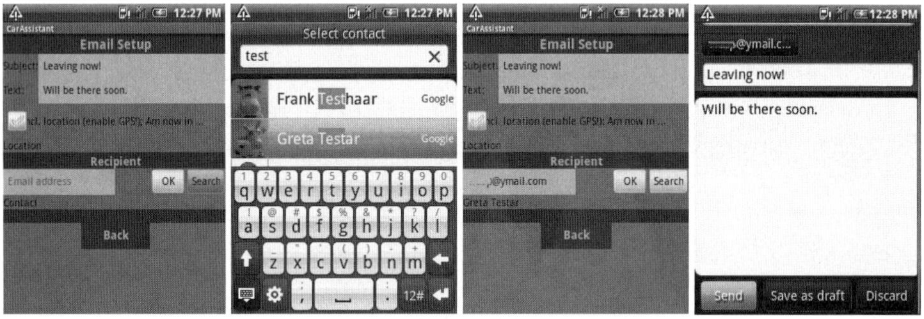

Figure 13.43 Selecting an e-mail address via ContactPicker from the system address book

In addition to directly selecting and copying existing e-mail addresses from the smartphone's address book, the user can start entering the desired contact name in the text box under Recipient. While the user is typing, suggestions consisting of contact names from the address book are displayed automatically that match the existing input, similar to the suggestions that appear when you start typing a search term into a search field such as on `www.google.com`. Figure 13.44 depicts this autocompletion process: When the first two letters "gr" are input, the name "Greta Testar" is displayed (left). You can select this name by tapping it with a finger, thereby inserting the name into the text box. In the text box, you can then see the complete name together with the e-mail address (center), which you can accept by tapping OK to reduce it to the e-mail address itself. The Email function key is now configured in the same way as the process for selecting names via the address book. If no matching entry is found in the address book, the user can enter an entirely new e-mail address in the text box.

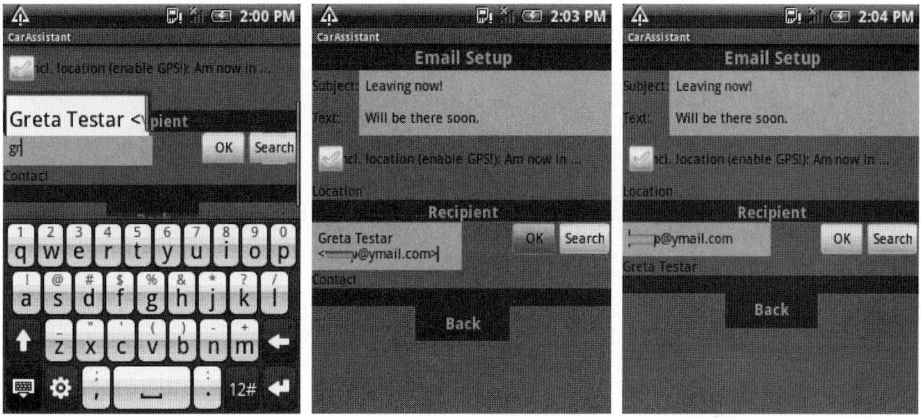

Figure 13.44 Inserting the e-mail address suggested by EmailPicker

To implement the two alternatives for selecting e-mail addresses from the address book, AI offers two components, ContactPicker and EmailPicker, in the Social group. The component ContactPicker has almost the same characteristics as the component PhoneNumberPicker (see Figure 13.7), with the exception that the latter collects the phone number of the selected contact and makes it available for further processing. Correspondingly, the specification of the ContactPicker component (Figure 13.45) is almost identical to the PhoneNumberPicker specification. The visual design and many of the properties correspond to those of a button. After calling the ContactPicker and selecting a contact from the address book, that contact's name, e-mail address, and (if applicable) photo are available for further processing in the corresponding property fields ContactName, EmailAddress, and Picture.

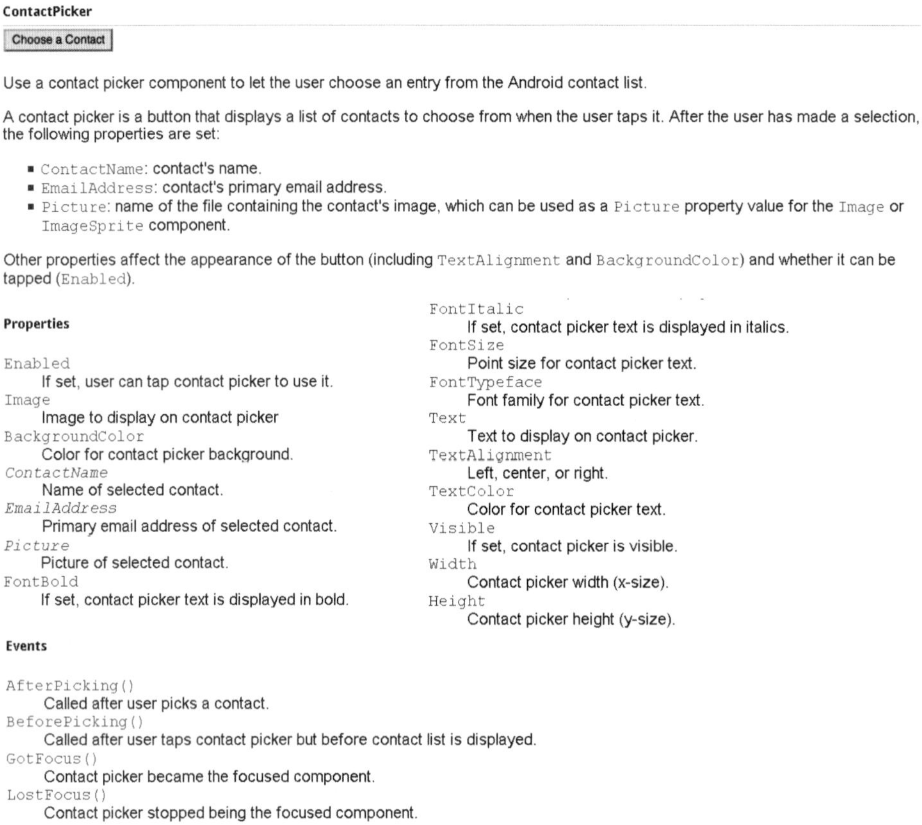
ContactPicker

Choose a Contact

Use a contact picker component to let the user choose an entry from the Android contact list.

A contact picker is a button that displays a list of contacts to choose from when the user taps it. After the user has made a selection, the following properties are set:

- `ContactName`: contact's name.
- `EmailAddress`: contact's primary email address.
- `Picture`: name of the file containing the contact's image, which can be used as a `Picture` property value for the `Image` or `ImageSprite` component.

Other properties affect the appearance of the button (including `TextAlignment` and `BackgroundColor`) and whether it can be tapped (`Enabled`).

Properties

`Enabled`
If set, user can tap contact picker to use it.
`Image`
Image to display on contact picker
`BackgroundColor`
Color for contact picker background.
`ContactName`
Name of selected contact.
`EmailAddress`
Primary email address of selected contact.
`Picture`
Picture of selected contact.
`FontBold`
If set, contact picker text is displayed in bold.
`FontItalic`
If set, contact picker text is displayed in italics.
`FontSize`
Point size for contact picker text.
`FontTypeface`
Font family for contact picker text.
`Text`
Text to display on contact picker.
`TextAlignment`
Left, center, or right.
`TextColor`
Color for contact picker text.
`Visible`
If set, contact picker is visible.
`Width`
Contact picker width (x-size).
`Height`
Contact picker height (y-size).

Events

`AfterPicking()`
Called after user picks a contact.
`BeforePicking()`
Called after user taps contact picker but before contact list is displayed.
`GotFocus()`
Contact picker became the focused component.
`LostFocus()`
Contact picker stopped being the focused component.

Figure 13.45 Specification of the ContactPicker component in AI References

The EmailPicker component also strongly resembles a familiar GUI component, the TextBox. Almost all the property fields are identical to this component, as you can see from the specification of the component EmailPicker in Figure 13.46. The only major difference relates to the additional functionality behind the Text property field. When the user selects the input field and starts entering text, the autocomplete suggestions described earlier will appear. If the user selects a suggestion, it will be entered in the EmailPicker input field just like a normal text input and can be processed exactly as if the input was made through a text box. We will see later how this process works.

EmailPicker

Select email

Use an email picker component to let the user enter a user's email address from the Android contact list.

An email picker is a text box in which a user can begin entering an email address of a contact and be offered auto-completion. The initial value of the box and the value after user entry is in the `Text` property. If the `Text` property is initially empty, the contents of the `Hint` property will be faintly shown in the text box as a hint to the user.

Other properties affect the appearance of the email picker (including `TextAlignment` and `BackgroundColor`) and whether it can be used (`Enabled`).

Email pickers are usually used with a button. The user taps the button when text entry is complete.

Properties

`Enabled`
  If set, user can tap email picker to use it.
`BackgroundColor`
  Color for email picker background.
`FontBold`
  If set, email picker text is displayed in bold.
`FontItalic`
  If set, email picker text is displayed in italics.
`FontSize`
  Point size for email picker text.
`FontTypeface`
  Font family for email picker text.
`Text`
  Initial text to display in email picker.
`TextAlignment`
  Left, center, or right.
`TextColor`
  Color for email picker text.
`Hint`
  If Text property is empty, Hint is shown in gray.
`Visible`
  If set, email picker is visible.
`Width`
  Email picker width (x-size).
`Height`
  Email picker height (y-size).

Events

`GotFocus()`
  Email picker became the focused component.
`LostFocus()`
  Email picker stopped being the focused component.

Figure 13.46 Specification of the EmailPicker component in AI References

You may have noticed that we used a different smartphone (HTC Tattoo) for the screenshots of the Email Setup in Figure 13.43 than was used previously in this project (LG P500). Different smartphones behave differently when fetching e-mail addresses from the address book, and these differences are even more pronounced than those seen with the other Picker component, PhoneNumberPicker (see Figure 13.7). For example, e-mail addresses are inserted without any problems into the input field on the HTC Tattoo via both the ContactPicker and the EmailPicker, whereas the selected entry does not appear at all on the LG P500.

Differences in Accessing Contact Data II

Different smartphones also behave differently when it comes to the use of the ContactPicker and EmailPicker components. Moreover, error messages may occasionally be generated. These irregularities have been investigated under AI Issue 1462, which now has the status "fixed." On smartphones that do not support the two Picker components, AI now displays an informative message.

Try out the behavior of the two Picker components on your own smartphone. As a third alternative, the user of our driver assistance system can enter the desired e-mail address manually, which is a little more challenging for the user.

Now that we have introduced the other two new components, it's time to add another still missing module to our CarAssistant project.

Sending E-Mails with Integrated Android Mailer

In this section we will slot the last module into our driver assistance system, combine the Email function with the Email Setup and the input options described earlier, and implement the *Android Mailer* as an activity for conveniently sending e-mails that have been predefined by the user. The Android Mailer manages the e-mail accounts on your smartphone and, by default, your *Googlemail* account and any other e-mail accounts you may be using. As we have already created the Email function key in the switchboard of our driver assistance system, we can now start designing the Email Setup in AI Designer. As usual, you can set the label texts, font sizes and colors, DivisionLabels, BufferLabels, SpacerLabels, and Arrangements yourself, as shown in Figures 13.44 and 13.47. The components of Table 13.7 then need to be added in AI Designer below the existing components, encapsulated as an independent module within the VerticalArrangement component object `EMAILvArr`.

Table 13.7 **Adding the Components for the Email Module**

Component	Object Name	Adapted Properties
VerticalArrangement	EMAILvArr	"Visible" disable "Width": Fill parent
ActivityStarter	ActivityStarterEmail	"Activity": see Table 13.8
TextBox	EmailSubjTextBox	"Text": Leaving now!
TextBox	EmailBodyTextBox	"Text": Will be there soon.
CheckBox	EmailGPSCheckBox	"Text": incl. location (enable GPS!): Am now in ...
Label	EmailLocationLabel	"Text": Location
EmailPicker	EmailPicker	"Hint": E-mail address
ContactPicker	EmailContactPicker	"Text": Search
Button	EmailOkButton	"Text": OK
Label	ContactLabel	"Text": Contact
Button	EmailBackButton	"Text": Back

With the components and default settings shown in Table 13.7, the CarAssistant project should now appear in AI Designer as shown in Figure 13.47.

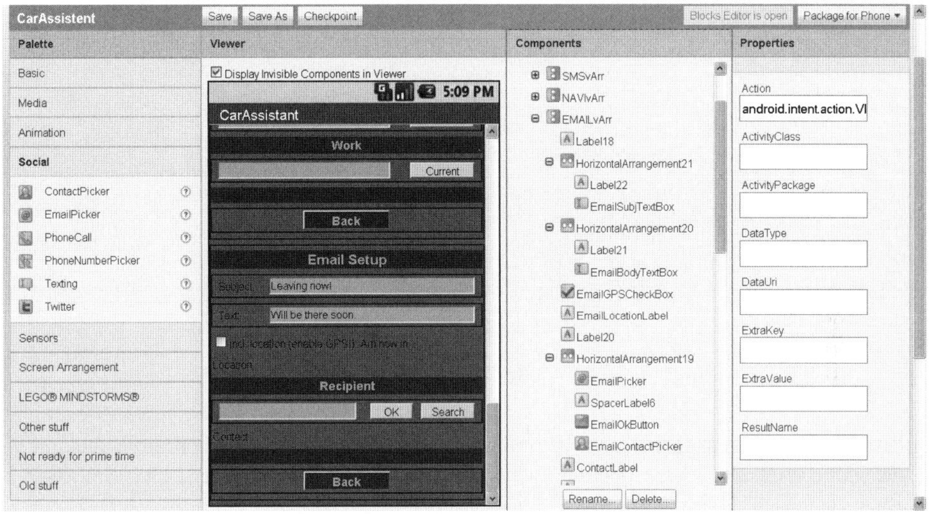

Figure 13.47 The added module Email in AI Designer

As you can see in Figure 13.47, the default settings for the additional activity starter `ActivityStarterEmail` this time include only the specification of the property Action, which means Table 13.8 is also correspondingly short.

Table 13.8 **Default Settings of the ActivityStarterEmail Activity Starter**

Property	Default Setting for Object ActivityStarterEmail
"Action"	android.intent.action.VIEW

Now that we have created the Email module and added the components of the Email Setup, we can turn to the implementation of the various functionalities in AI Editor. As with the other modules, we use the event handlers `EmailSetupButton.Click` for starting the Email Setup and `EmailBackButton.Click` for closing it, as shown in Figure 13.48. In the latter event handler, we automatically save the last used e-mail data from the three text boxes (EmailPicker, EmailSubjTextBox, and EmailBodyTextBox) when the Email Setup is closed under the corresponding identifiers (`emailAdr`, `emailSubj`, and `emailBody`) in the local app memory, so that they will be available automatically the next time the driver assistance system is opened.

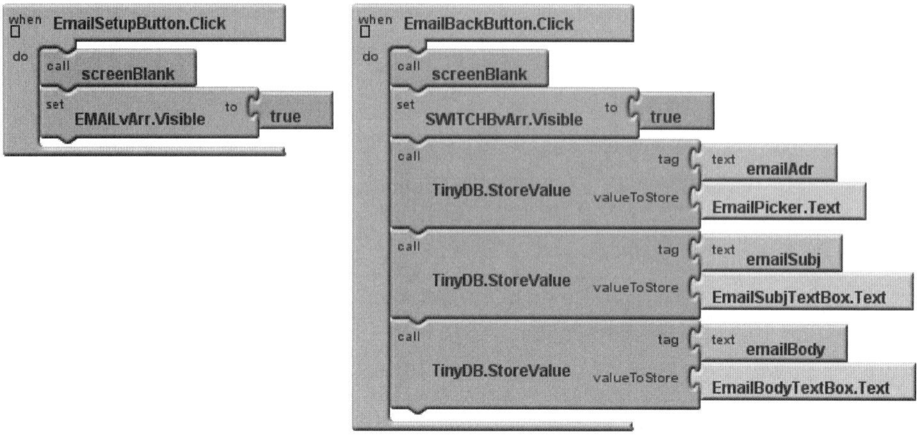

Figure 13.48 Starting and closing the Email Setup

For the Search button, behind which lurks the ContactPicker component object `EmailContactPicker`, we implement—instead of a Click event handler (which is not available for the Picker)—the event handler `EmailContactPicker.AfterPicking` (Figure 13.49). In this event handler, we pass only the e-mail address `EmailContactPicker.EmailAddress` and the name `EmailContactPicker.ContactName` of the contact selected via the ContactPicker to the corresponding fields in the Email Setup, `EmailPicker.Text` and `ContactLabel.Text`, to display them. The question mark icon seen on the black background in the event handler of Figures 13.49 and 13.50 conceals a comment pointing out the different implementation of the Picker component in different smartphones (see also the project file `CarAssistant` on the companion website).

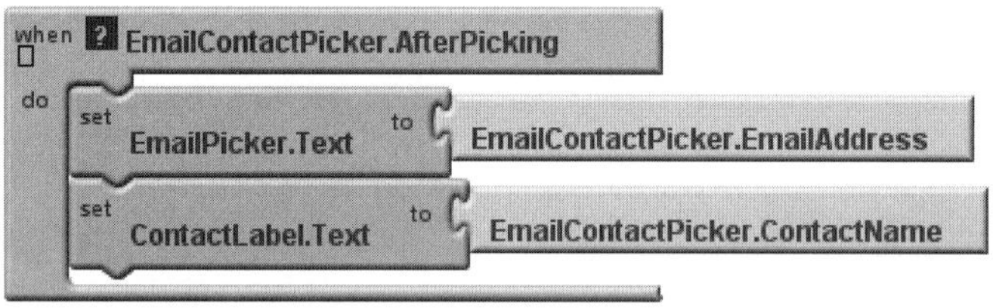

Figure 13.49 Retrieving selected contact data from the ContactPicker component

The alternative method of selecting the contact data via the EmailPicker component is a bit more complex. The EmailPicker component deals with selecting the contact just as comfortably in the first step, but does not just return the e-mail address as the result in the property field `EmailPicker.Text` (for example, `greta.testar@ymail.com`);

instead, it returns this e-mail address as a text string in pointed brackets together with the contact name (for example, `Greta Testar <greta.testar@ymail.com>`). In this case, before we can use the e-mail address for sending the message, we need to extract it from the text string. This happens in the event handler `EmailOkButton.Click` (Figure 13.50), which has to be explicitly triggered by the user after selecting the contact via the Email-Picker in a second step—that is, by pressing the OK button. (Otherwise, the attempt to send the e-mail will fail later due to an invalid e-mail address.) After the initial check in a conditional `if` statement to see whether a text string was inserted into the property field `EmailPicker.Text`, the index positions of the opening (<) and closing (>) brackets are determined via the text method `starts at` in the text string and recorded in the two auxiliary variables `a` and `b`. With these two index positions, we can then cut out the contact name (position `1` to `a-2`; in our example, `Greta Testar`) from the text string and insert it into the ContactLabel; we can also extract the e-mail address itself (position `a` to `b-a`; in our example, `greta.testar@ymail.com`) and display it in the EmailPicker.

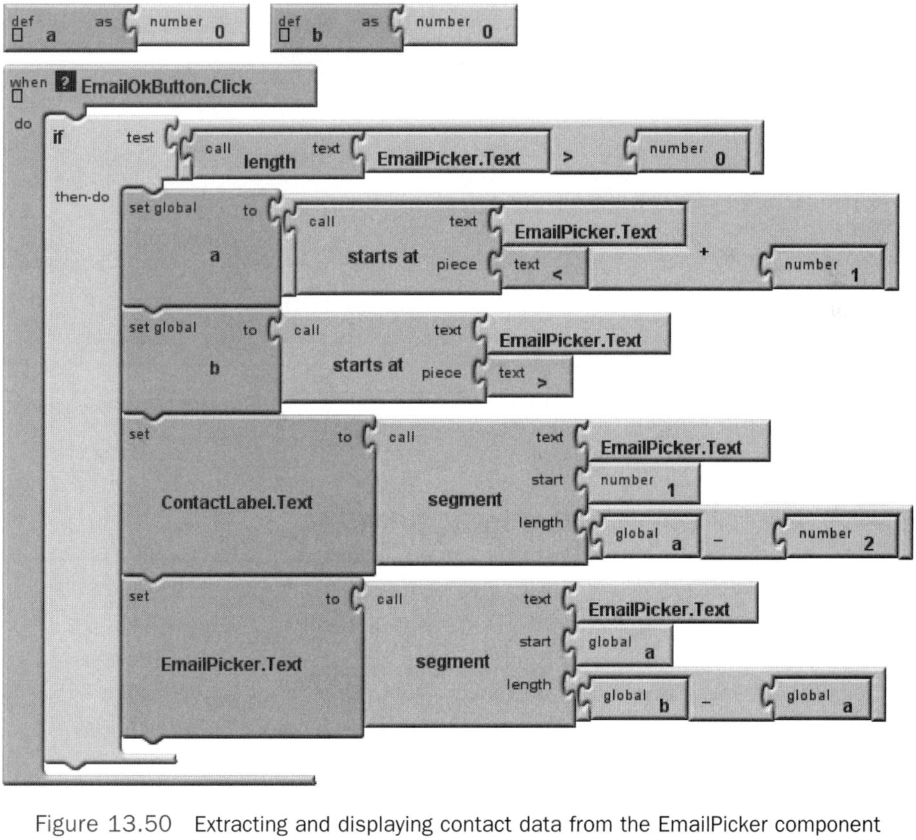

Figure 13.50 Extracting and displaying contact data from the EmailPicker component

After executing the statements of Figure 13.50 (and thereby using the second method for selecting an e-mail address from the address book), we now have an e-mail address in our Email Setup that can be used for sending the e-mail. To send the now fully user-defined e-mail via the Email function key from within the switchboard of our driver assistance system, we need to compose a corresponding instruction as the URI for the `ActivityStarterEmail` we previously created in AI Designer and pass it to the activity starter. This happens in the familiar way within the event handler `EmailButton.Click` (Figure 13.51), in which we create the URI as text string using the method `make text`.

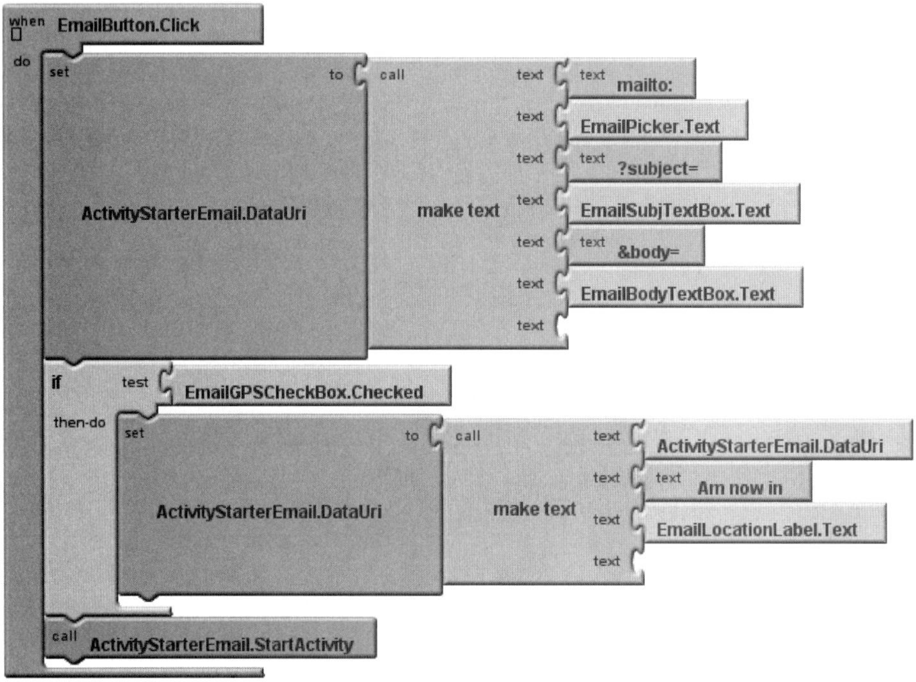

Figure 13.51 Passing an e-mail as a URI to the e-mail client and sending it

The complete URI starts with the specification of the URI scheme `mailto:`, followed by the e-mail address from EmailPicker, the query parameter `?subject=` with the appropriate e-mail subject line from EmailSubjTextBox, plus the second parameter `&body=` and the appropriate e-mail text from EmailBodyTextBox. With the example used earlier, the URI would look like this:

```
mailto:greta.testar@ymail.com?subject=Leaving%20now!&body=Will%20be%20there%20
soon.
```

Again, you do not need to take care of the URI encoding of the spaces (`%20`), as AI will handle that task for you. In the event handler `EmailButton.Click` shown in Figure 13.51, the e-mail text can optionally have the location data added to it. The conditional `if` statement verifies that the user has checked the `EmailGPSCheckBox` in the Email Setup. If this is the case, the text `Am now in`, together with the current address from EmailLocationLabel, is appended to the URI (for inserting the geoposition into the Email Setup, see also Figure 13.34). Once the URI is complete, the Android Mailer can be started as an external application via the method `ActivityStarterEmail.StartActivity`. If several e-mail accounts should be available on your smartphone, the Android Mailer will ask automatically which one should be used for sending the e-mail. You can also specify a default account permanently.

> **Summary of Encoding Options in the URI Scheme *mailto***
>
> A summary of the possible details in the URI scheme *mailto* is available at the following site:
>
> `http://www.ianr.unl.edu/internet/mailto.html`
>
> An overview of the other URI schemes and their encodings can be found at this site:
>
> `http://en.wikipedia.org/wiki/URI_scheme`

Mobile Mashups with Web Services

The driver assistance system should really be complete with the functions we have added up to now. With the AI update of June 2011, however, the Google App Inventor Team added yet another powerful function to the development environment, which we would not want to deprive you of. For that reason we will add one more button to the control center of the driver assistance system, labeled "Ticker." By pressing this button, the driver can get information on the current stock prices and the latest headlines on a specified topic. Of course, this button should be used only if the circumstances allow it—for example, during a traffic jam or once the driver has reached his or her destination.

In contrast to the buttons previously placed on the switchboard, the Ticker button corresponds to both a function key and a configuration key, as the resulting subscreen combines the functions and settings of both. Pressing the new Ticker button in Figure 13.52 (left) displays the Ticker subscreen (center). In the top configuration area, the user can set the automatic update cycle (Reload) of the stock market and news ticker in seconds. In the "Stock quotes" section, the user can enter and save any number of stocks under "Your stocks" by inserting their official abbreviations (such as GOOG for Google Inc.); the user will then receive continuous information on these stocks' current prices in the area below. In the "News" section, the user can specify the category of the news he or she wants to see by entering the appropriate number (for example, 22 for "Business"); the three most current headlines from that category will then be displayed and updated continuously. By tapping a headline, the user can go to the corresponding website to read the complete article directly below the headlines (see Figure 13.52, right).

Figure 13.52 Stocks and news ticker in action

To integrate this mobile information service providing current data such as stock information and news headlines into our app, we use a technical principle that is referred to as a "mashup." In the context of the Internet and, above all, Web 2.0, the term "mashup" refers to the enhancement or creation of your own websites by dynamically integrating and combining content (e.g., text, images, videos) from other websites and web services, which are then made available via open interfaces (application programming interface, or API). Apart from chargeable services and those you need to register for, there are a large number of freely accessible Web APIs, two of which we will use for our ticker.

Information and Overviews on Mashups and Web APIs

General information and an overview of existing mashups and Web APIs can be found on these websites, among others:

`http://en.wikipedia.org/wiki/Mashup_(web_application_hybrid)`

`http://www.programmableweb.com/`

Using Web APIs with the Web Component

Since the AI update of June 2011, AI has offered the non-visible component known as "Web" in the group "Other stuff," with which AI developers can access Web APIs with the usual ease and combine their apps into impressive mashups containing current data from numerous online sources. In the specification of the Web component shown in Figure 13.53, a number of properties, events, and methods are defined that require a certain basic knowledge of the transfer protocol HTTP (Hypertext Transfer Protocol)—the basis on which most of the data on the Web is exchanged between servers and clients (for example, when accessing a website via the browser). For our driver assistance system and for many other application purposes, only a small selection of the functional elements of the Web component are needed; you can easily use them even without any previous knowledge of HTTP.

Information on HTTP and the Request Methods POST and GET

You can find further information on the HTTP protocol and the two central request methods `POST` and `GET` online at this website:

`http://en.wikipedia.org/wiki/Hypertext_Transfer_Protocol`

Generally, you can distinguish elements for the two basic HTTP methods `GET` and `POST`, with which data can be exchanged in different ways with a web service via its API. With the `POST` method, the service request must be encoded together with the sometimes considerable amount of data to be processed in a special way in the HTTP body. In the simpler `GET` method, short requests can be appended to the web address (URL) of the API. The latter method is reminiscent of starting a web service via ActivityStarter, where you also pass parameters in addition to the called URL. Whereas the external service is started within an additional app and takes control in the case of the ActivityStarter, the control stays entirely with the requesting app when the Web component is used, and the requesting app has to process the returned data itself. In looking at the web specification shown in Figure 13.53, we want to concentrate on those elements required for calling and processing data via the HTTP `GET` method.

Web

Non-visible component that provides functions for HTTP GET and POST requests.

Properties

`AllowCookies`
Whether the cookies from a response should be saved and used in subsequent requests. Cookies are only supported on Android version 2.3 or greater.

`RequestHeaders`
The request headers, as a list of two-element sublists. The first element of each sublist represents the request header field name. The second element of each sublist represents the request header field values, either a single value or a list containing multiple values.

`ResponseFileName`
The name of the file where the response should be saved. If SaveResponse is true and ResponseFileName is empty, then a new file name will be generated.

`SaveResponse`
Whether the response should be saved in a file.

`Url`
The URL for the web request.

Events

`GotFile(text url, number responseCode, text responseType, text fileName)`
Event indicating that a request has finished.

`GotText(text url, number responseCode, text responseType, text responseContent)`
Event indicating that a request has finished.

Methods

`text BuildPostData(list list)`
Converts a list of two-element sublists, representing name and value pairs, to a string formatted as application/x-www-form-urlencoded media type, suitable to pass to PostText.

`ClearCookies()`
Clears all cookies for this Web component.

`Get()`
Performs an HTTP GET request using the Url property and retrieves the response.
If the SaveResponse property is true, the response will be saved in a file and the GotFile event will be triggered. The ResponseFileName property can be used to specify the name of the file.
If the SaveResponse property is false, the GotText event will be triggered.

`text HtmlTextDecode(text htmlText)`
Decodes the given HTML text value. HTML character entities such as &, <, >, ', and " are changed to &, <, >, ', and ". Entities such as &#xhhhh, and &#nnnn are changed to the appropriate characters.

`text JsonTextDecode(text jsonText)`
Decodes the given JSON text value. If the given JSON text is surrounded by quotes, the quotes will be removed.

`PostFile(text path)`
Performs an HTTP POST request using the Url property and data from the specified file.
If the SaveResponse property is true, the response will be saved in a file and the GotFile event will be triggered. The ResponseFileName property can be used to specify the name of the file.
If the SaveResponse property is false, the GotText event will be triggered.

`PostText(text text)`
Performs an HTTP POST request using the Url property and the specified text.
The characters of the text are encoded using UTF-8 encoding.
If the SaveResponse property is true, the response will be saved in a file and the GotFile event will be triggered. The responseFileName property can be used to specify the name of the file.
If the SaveResponse property is false, the GotText event will be triggered.

`PostTextWithEncoding(text text, text encoding)`
Performs an HTTP POST request using the Url property and the specified text.
The characters of the text are encoded using the given encoding.
If the SaveResponse property is true, the response will be saved in a file and the GotFile event will be triggered. The ResponseFileName property can be used to specify the name of the file.
If the SaveResponse property is false, the GotText event will be triggered.

`text UriEncode(text text)`
Encodes the given text value so that it can be used in a URL.

Figure 13.53 Specification of the Web component in AI References

In the `GET` request, the property field "Url" plays a central role, as the entire request to the web service must be specified here and needs to be converted into a valid URI format via the `UriEncode` method before the corresponding `Get` method can be called to send the `GET` request. Depending on the API contacted and the initial settings of the

SaveResponse and ResponseFileName properties, the data returned by the web service can be received either via the event block GotFile as a file or via the event block GotText as text, and then further processed. Depending on the data formats supported by the API, the text data is returned in a format-specific encoding. Answers in HTML (Hypertext Markup Language), for example, can be conveniently decoded into the corresponding plain text via the method HtmlTextDecode (for example, & is decoded as an ampersand, &) before being displayed; similarly, answers in JSON (JavaScript Object Notation) can be decoded via the method JsonTextDecode (for example, eliminating surplus brackets). During the implementation of our ticker for the driver assistance system, we will introduce this procedure in more detail and even show you how to process JSON responses.

Before turning to the program logic, we first need to equip our driver assistance system with the new module for the ticker. Open the CarAssistant project in AI Designer and add the components shown in Table 13.9. Do not forget to add the additional Ticker button to the left of the Off button in the switchboard. As with the other modules you have created previously, you can insert the required labels, color and font size settings, buffer and division labels, and arrangements shown in Figure 13.54 on your own. We then encapsulate the entire module for the multiple screens in a VerticalArrangement component object TICKERvArr.

Table 13.9 **Additional Components for the Ticker Module**

Component	Object Name	Adapted Properties
Button	TickerButton	"Text": Ticker
VerticalArrangement	TICKERvArr	"Visible" disable "Width": Fill parent
Web	WebYahoo	
Web	WebFeedzilla	
Clock	TickerClock	"Timer enabled": disable "TimerInterval": 1000
Button	TickerReloadButton	"Text": Reload
TextBox	TickerReloadTextBox	"Text": 30
Label	TickerUpdateLabel	"Text": –
TextBox	TickerStocksTextBox	"Text": AMZN, GOOG, YHOO
Label	TickerQuotesLabel	"Text": Stock quotes ... "Background": Black "TextColor": White
TextBox	TickerNewsCategoryTextBox	"Text": 26
Button (3x)	News1Button, News2Button, News3Button	"Text": News1, News2, News3 "Background": Black "TextColor": White
Button	TickerBackButton	"Text": Back

With the components and initial settings shown in Table 13.9, the CarAssistant project should now be displayed in AI Designer as shown in Figure 13.54.

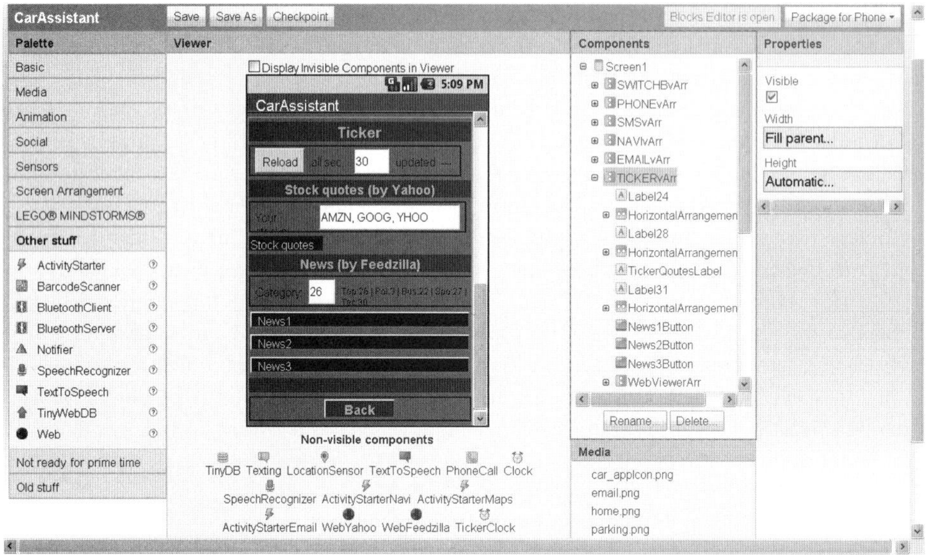

Figure 13.54 The additional Ticker module in AI Designer

Now we have created the Ticker module in the CarAssistant project and can move on to implementing the two ticker functions, along with the configuration options.

Stock Market Ticker with Data from Yahoo

Before implementing the functions of the stock market ticker, we want to realize the central configuration area above the tickers, through which different update methods for both tickers can be controlled. For example, the current stock prices and headlines should be updated whenever the ticker subscreen is activated, the Reload button is pressed, or the specified upload cycle has elapsed. These three triggers for the ticker update are implemented in a corresponding number of event handlers, as shown in Figure 13.55. Pressing the Ticker button to call the ticker in the switchboard causes the event handler `TickerButton.Click` to display the corresponding subscreen `TICKERvArr` as usual. The timer of the previously disabled `TickerClock` is then activated, and an immediate update is triggered by calling the home-grown procedure `tickerUpdate`. The same procedure `tickerUpdate` is also called within the corresponding event handler `TickerReloadButton` when the Reload button is pressed on the ticker screen. If the timer in `TickerButton.Click` was enabled, the event handler `TickerClock.Timer` is called for the first time once the preset time interval (1000 ms

= 1 sec) has elapsed. In it, the value of the update cycle entered by the user in seconds is read from the TickerReloadTextBox, converted to milliseconds, and set as the new `TickerClock.TimerInterval`. The user can easily customize the update cycle for the ticker at any time. Once the current interval has elapsed, the procedure `tickerUpdate` is called again.

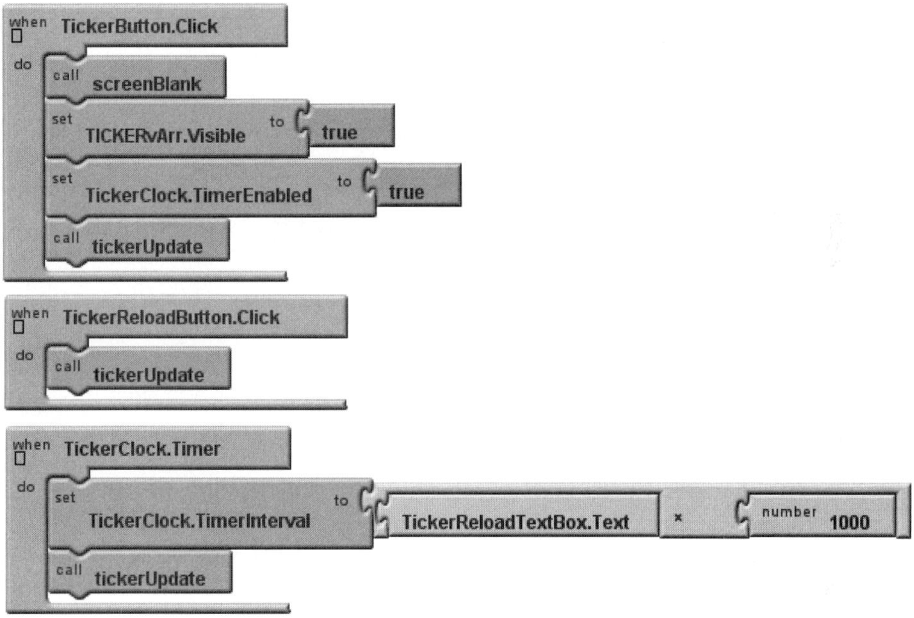

Figure 13.55 Triggering ticker updates with three events

The descriptions of Figure 13.55 should have made it clear why we put the statements required for the ticker updates in a separate procedure. This strategy ensures that the three triggers can all initiate the same action—an update of the tickers—which needs to be implemented only once. In Figure 13.56, you can see the procedure `tickerUpdate` with the statements for requesting data from the Web API of the Yahoo stock service (the statements for requesting the News API will be added later). The first statement verifies the time `Clock.Now` of the current request and displays it as the latest update time in the TickerUpdateLabel on the ticker subscreen. In the next statement, the stock codes entered by the user in the TickerStocksTextBox (for example, AMZN, GOOG, and YHOO) are entered into the variable `stocksString`. We take into consideration that several stock codes are usually entered by the user separated by a comma with space, and replace these separators where necessary, using the method `replace all`, with a plus symbol (+). We require this notation for the correct `GET` request (for example, `AMZN+GOOG+YHOO`) to the Yahoo API.

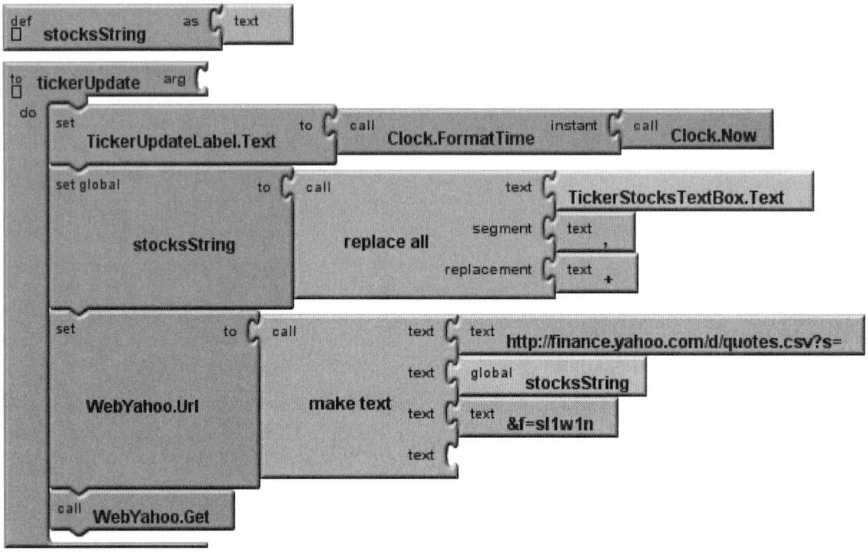

Figure 13.56: Procedure for a data request to the Yahoo web API

We prepare the `GET` request in the next statement within the procedure `tickerUpdate` shown in Figure 13.56, in which we assemble the URL for our request via the method `make text`. We proceed in a similar way as we used to create the `ActivityStarter.DataUri` in the previous section on pedestrian navigation with Google Maps. The `WebYahoo.Url` for retrieving the stock data is also put together from the base URL of the Yahoo API (`http://finance.yahoo.com`), the desired data format (`/d/quotes.csv`), and the parameter area introduced by a question mark (`?`) plus the value pairs it contains, which are joined via ampersand symbols (`&`). In our case, we tell the Yahoo API via the parameters `s` and `f` which information we require for which stocks. As the value for the parameter `s`, we enter the string saved in the variable `stocksString`, which is put together from stock codes (such as `AMZN+GOOG+YHOO`). With the value pair `f=sl1w1n`, we request for each stock its symbol (`s`), its current price (`l1`), the difference between the current price and the issue price at the beginning of the trading day formatted as a percentage (`w1`), and the name of the relevant company (`n`).

Overview of Request Parameters in Yahoo API

An overview of the abbreviations for specifying the desired information on the requested stocks through the Web API of the Yahoo finance service can be found at this site:

`http://www.gummy-stuff.org/Yahoo-data.htm`

Depending on the stock quotes entered, the complete request URL for the Yahoo API could look like this:

```
http://finance.yahoo.com/d/quotes.csv?s=AMZN+GOOG+YHOO&f=sl1w1n
```

Feel free to enter this URL directly into the address field of your web browser. The Yahoo web service will then send you a file named `quotes.csv`, which you can open directly in a text editor or a spreadsheet application. The data in this file, which is displayed in the CSV (Comma-Separated Values) format, corresponds largely to the data we want to use in our stock ticker, as you can see in Figure 13.57 by comparing the raw version in the text editor (left) to the final version in the stock ticker (right).

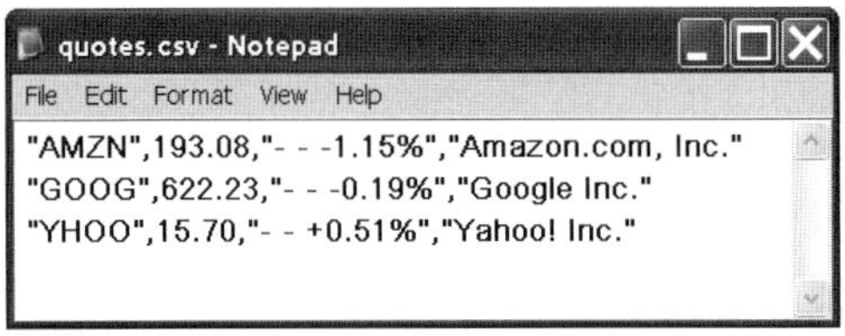

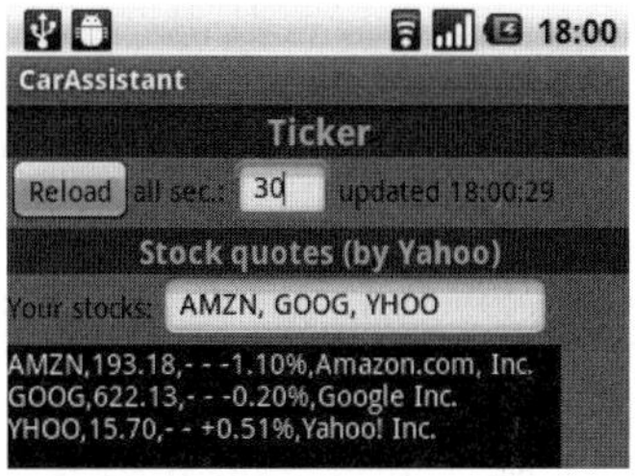

Figure 13.57: Stock data in raw CSV format and in the ticker

In our procedure `tickerUpdate` (Figure 13.56), we assign the generated request URL to the Web component object `WebYahoo.Url`. We then call the web method `WebYahoo.Get` to send the corresponding `GET` request to the Yahoo API. Once the Yahoo finance service has successfully processed our request, the Yahoo API returns a result that we receive in the event handler `WebYahoo.GotText` (Figure 15.58). The reply always consists of four returned values that are available for further processing in four local variables within the event handler: the URL of the answering API (`url`), the HTTP status message (`responseCode`), the data type (MIME type such as "text/csv" or "image.jpeg") of the returned data (`responseType`), and the actual data itself (`responseContent`).

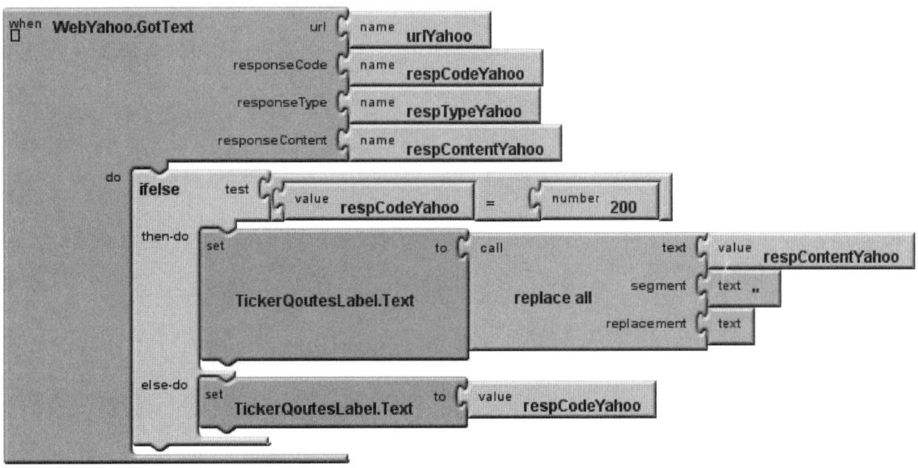

Figure 13.58 Receiving and processing the stock data from the Yahoo API

In the event handler `WebYahoo.GotText` (Figure 13.58), we process only two of the values returned by the Yahoo API. Only when the HTTP status message indicates a successful data exchange (`respCodeYahoo=200`) do we take the stock data returned in `respContentYahoo`, eliminate the quotation marks surrounding each individual value in the data, and display the result in the TickerQuotesLabel. If the data exchange fails, we simply display the appropriate error code (e.g., `responseCode` = `400` [Bad request], `404` [Not found], `503` [Service unavailable]). This approach makes it easy to process the stock data, because we can take the CSV-formatted data, which are by default formatted with the values of one stock per line, and insert them almost without further editing into the display of the stock ticker. Unfortunately, the corresponding process for the news ticker will be a little more complicated.

News Ticker with Data from Feedzilla

For the news ticker, we use the Web API of the newsfeed provider Feedzilla, which collects current news headlines on various topics from a multitude of online sources and makes them available for downloading. The Feedzilla API is thoroughly documented and easy to use even for beginners, thanks to the many example requests provided by its developer. A further advantage is that the Feedzilla API supports different data exchange formats, such as XML, JSON, RSS, and Atom.

> **Documentation on Feedzilla API**
>
> Detailed documentation for the Feedzilla API with many examples can be found at:
>
> `http://code.google.com/p/feedzilla-api/wiki/RestApi`
>
> An overview of the various topics with their associated category numbers can retrieved directly via the Feedzilla API from the following URL (the returned file `categories.json` can be opened in a text editor such as Notepad):
>
> `http://api.feedzilla.com/v1/categories.json`

Just as with the Yahoo API, we send an HTTP `GET` request to the Feedzilla API, to retrieve the desired news data. We also make use of the previously implemented program structures: the three update triggers from Figure 13.55 and the procedure `tickerUpdate` from Figure 13.56, which we expand by adding two more statements for the Feedzilla API (see the bottom of Figure 13.59).

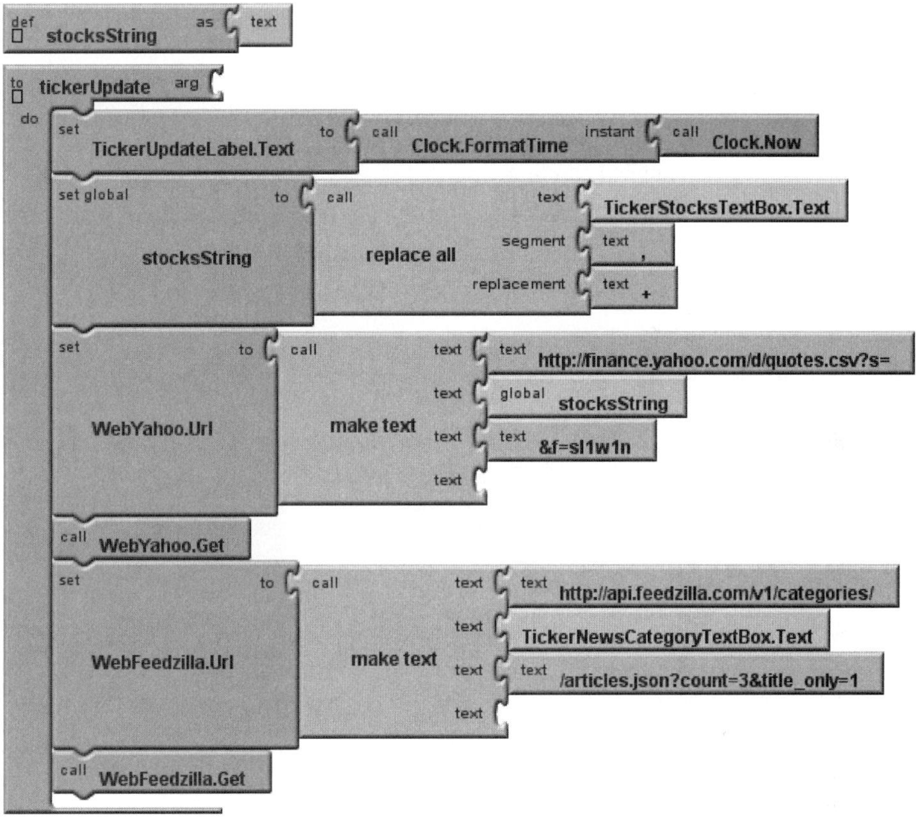

Figure 13.59 Adding statements for the Feedzilla API

When putting together the `WebFeedzilla.Url`, we follow the familiar principle. The URL for the Feedzilla API is composed from a base URL with the appropriate version number (`http://api.feedzilla.com/v1`), an optional category number (e.g., `/categories/22` for Business News), the desired data exchange format (e.g., `/articles.json`), and the parameter range introduced with `?`. In our case, we instruct the Feedzilla API from which category we require news data, how many news items we require (the most current one first), in which format, and whether to include a text summary (the answer to the last question is no—we will just use the item title); to indicate these choices, we specify the category number and the desired data exchange format as well as the parameters `count` and `title_only`. Thus, to retrieve the three most current pieces of Business News in JSON format, the request URL to the Feedzilla API would look like this:

```
http://api.feedzilla.com/v1/categories/22/articles.json?count=3&title_only=1
```

We generate this URL in the procedure `tickerUpdate` from Figure 13.56 with the relevant category number from the TickerNewsCategoryTextBox and assign the URL to the `WebFeedzilla.Url`. Then, just as we did with the stock ticker, we use the method `WebFeedzilla.Get` to send the `GET` request to the Feedzilla API. The design of the event handler `GotText` for receiving and processing the API reply is bulkier in this case, however. The reason is simple: There is a clear discrepancy between the format of the returned data and the desired display in the news ticker. You can clearly see the difference between the raw version of the JSON data and the filtered display in the news ticker in Figure 13.60.

{"articles":[{"publish_date":"Thu, 08 Dec 2011 19:27:00 +0100","source":"Knoxville News Sentinel","source_url":"http:\/\/www.knoxnews.com\/rss\/headlines\/archives\/","title":"Va. Tech alerts: Police officer shot, gunman at large (Knoxville News Sentinel)","url":"http:\/\/news.feedzilla.com\/en_us\/stories\/top-news\/172063671?count=3&client_source=api&format=json"},{"publish_date":"Thu, 08 Dec 2011 19:26:00 +0100","source":"Minneapolis Star Tribune","source_url":"http:\/\/www.startribune.com\/rss\/?sf=1&s=\/","title":"DNA from invasive Asian Carp found north of Twin Cities (Minneapolis Star Tribune)","url":"http:\/\/news.feedzilla.com\/en_us\/stories\/top-news\/172063944?count=3&client_source=api&format=json"},{"author":"Daily News Wire Services","publish_date":"Thu, 08 Dec 2011 19:24:00 +0100","source":"Los Angeles Daily News","source_url":"http:\/\/feeds.dailynews.com\/mngi\/rss\/CustomRssServlet\/200\/202971.xml","title":"Gas prices keep on falling -- click for lowest prices in the Valley (Los Angeles Daily News)","url":"http:\/\/news.feedzilla.com\/en_us\/stories\/top-news\/172063738?count=3&client_source=api&format=json"}],"description":"Top News","syndication_url":"http:\/\/news.feedzilla.com\/en_us\/news\/top-news.rss?count=3&client_source=api","title":"Feedzilla: Top News"}

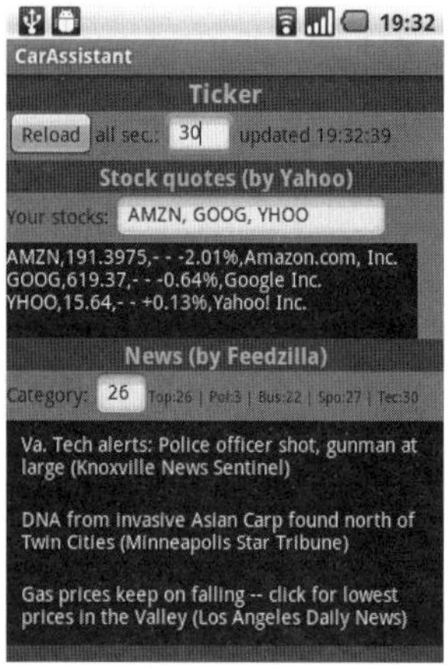

Figure 13.60 News data in raw JSON format and in the news ticker

The data in JSON format shown in Figure 13.60 (left) contains not just the news item, but also a tag that describes the semantic type of the news data. The tag and the data are enclosed by quotation marks and linked into a value pair via a colon. We cannot present this confusing and cumbersome data display in the news ticker as is; instead, we need to extract the relevant news data from the raw JSON data. We are interested in presenting just the title and the URL of the complete news text. In the raw data, we can see that the text strings we want start immediately after the corresponding tags for the title (tag `"title":"`) and the URL (tag `"url":"`). The end of the desired text string can also be determined from the symbol patterns: a `",` following the title string and a `"}` following the URL string. This tells us clearly at which starting and ending points we need to cut the text strings (see the highlighted text sections in Figure 13.60) out of the raw data to extract all three titles and URLs. The procedure `parseFeedzilla` shown in Figure 13.61 takes care of *parsing* the raw data for our news ticker.

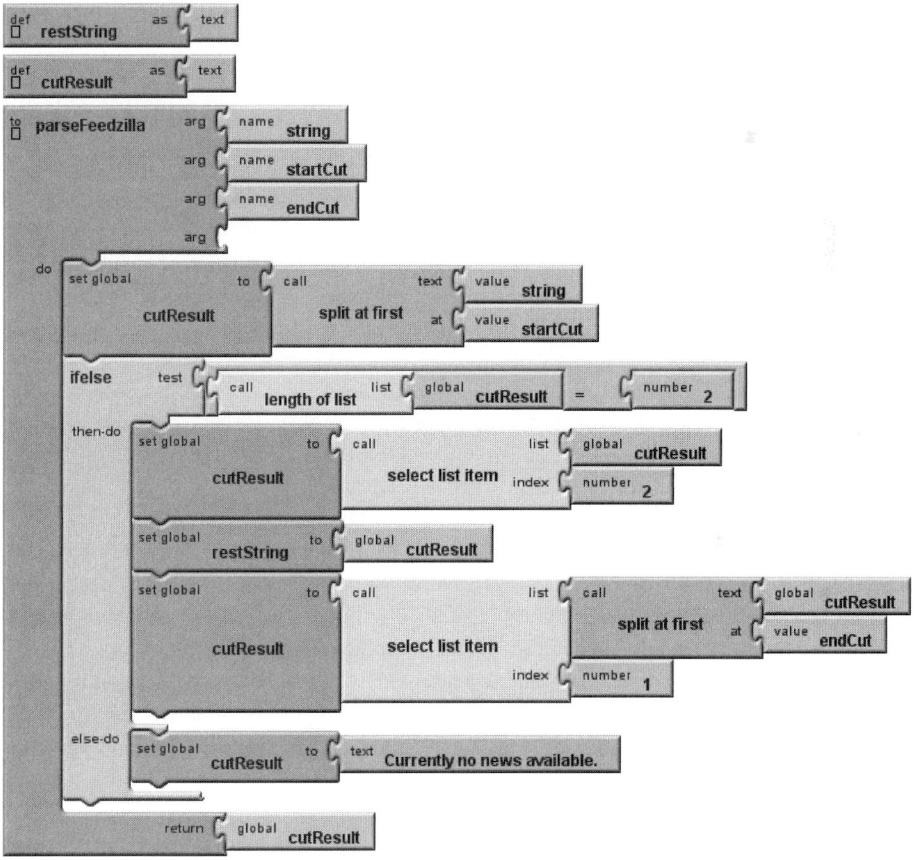

Figure 13.61 Generic procedure for extracting text passages

The procedure `parseFeedzilla` is generically designed, so it can receive any raw texts in JSON format via the variable string, plus the starting and ending tags via the variables `startCut` and `endCut`, respectively. In the isolation of the desired target string, we separate the raw text, including the starting tag in the first step with the text method `split at first` before the target text, and record the remaining raw text in the second list element—if any is present—in the variable `cutResult`. At this point, we also save the remaining raw text from `cutResult` in the global variable `restString`. As we are looking three times for the same starting and ending tags for the three different news items in the generic procedure, the already edited text passages must not be passed to the procedure again. Thus, in the next call of the procedure, the entire raw text is not passed to the method, but rather just the remaining text from the global variable `restString` is passed to the local variable `string`, which allows us to avoid endless loops. After the remaining raw text is saved, it can be processed further with the next statement of the procedure `parseFeedzilla`, and the raw text, including the ending tag that follows the target text, can be separated via the `split at first` method. At that point, the target text remaining as the first list element is fully extracted and is returned in the variable `cutResult` as the return value to the procedure. If no more starting tags are found, the procedure instead returns a corresponding error message.

Now let's take a look at the event handler `WebFeedzilla.GotText` shown in Figure 13.62, through which the Feedzilla API sends the JSON raw data as the answer to your `GET` request. As was the case with the reply sent by the Yahoo API, we use only two of the values received from the Feedzilla API—namely, the values in the local variables `respCodeFeedzilla` and `respContentFeedzilla`. The latter contains the raw text in JSON format, which we have already discussed in depth. After checking the HTTP status message, the event handler extracts all three titles successively and the associated web addresses via the procedure `parseFeedzilla`. While the first call still passes the complete raw text from `respContentFeedzilla` to the procedure, it contains the successively shortened raw text string from `restString` after the second call for the reasons mentioned earlier. The passed starting and ending tags are the same for all three titles and web addresses.

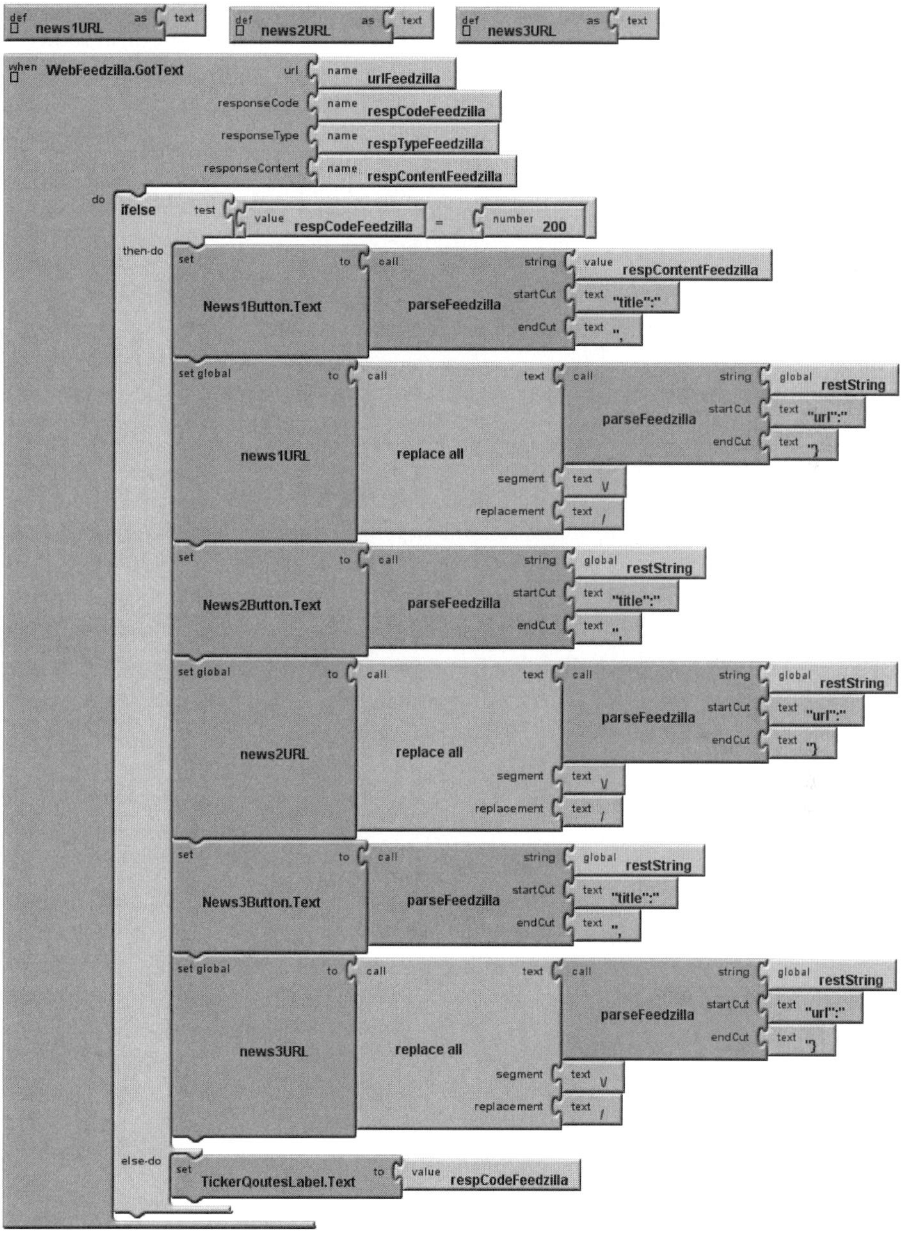

Figure 13.62 Reading out the three headlines and web addresses for the news ticker

The titles returned by the procedure `parseFeedzilla` are allocated as text properties to the three news buttons (News1Button, News2Button, and News3Button), as shown in Figure 13.62, and are displayed appropriately in the ticker subscreen. One particular point needs to be observed with the returned URLs. The Feedzilla API precedes the slash sign (/) with a backslash (\) in its JSON reply, as you can see in the raw text shown in Figure 13.60. To ensure that the extracted web addresses can be used later for fetching the original news, the symbols `\/` must be replaced with a simple slash `/` via the `replace all` method before they are allocated to the three global variables (`news1URL`, `news2URL`, and `new3URL`). With the previously described functions, each update of the news ticker then sends a `GET` request and the headline titles received from the Feedzilla API are displayed in the ticker subscreen.

Integrating Websites in Your App with the WebViewer Component

To complete our news ticker, we need to implement the call to the websites for displaying the complete news text. We could do so by starting a separate web browser on the smartphone via the ActivityStarter component and passing it the web address to display. With the AI update of July 2011, however, the development environment offers a more elegant solution, through which we can display the website directly within our own app. The group "Not ready for prime time" offers the WebViewer component, whose specification (shown in Figure 13.63) lists properties and methods that should already be largely familiar to you from working with any kind of web browser.

WebViewer

Component for viewing Web pages. The Home URL can be specified in the Designer or in the Blocks Editor. The view can be set to follow links when they are tapped, and users can fill in Web forms. Warning: This is not a full browser. For example, pressing the phone's hardware Back key will exit the app, rather than move back in the browser history.

Properties

`CurrentPageTitle`
Title of the page currently viewed
`CurrentUrl`
URL of the page currently viewed. This could be different from the Home URL if new pages were visited by following links.
`FollowLinks`
Determines whether to follow links when they are tapped in the WebViewer. If you follow links, you can use GoBack and GoForward to navigate the browser history.
`Height`
`HomeUrl`
URL of the page the WebViewer should initially open to. Setting this will load the page.
`Visible`
Whether the component is visible
`Width`

Events

none

Methods

`boolean CanGoBack()`
Returns true if the WebViewer can go back in the history list.
`boolean CanGoForward()`
Returns true if the WebViewer can go forward in the history list.
`GoBack()`
Go back to the previous page in the history list. Does nothing if there is no previous page.
`GoForward()`
Go forward to the next page in the history list. Does nothing if there is no next page.
`GoHome()`
Loads the home URL page. This happens automatically when the home URL is changed.
`GoToUrl(text url)`
Load the page at the given URL.

Figure 13.63 Specification of the WebViewer component in AI References

For our news ticker, we use the WebViewer component so that when the user presses the button for one of the three headlines displayed in the ticker subscreen, our app will display the associated website with the complete news item directly below the headlines. If several web pages are accessed in succession, the user can also switch between them using a backward key (<<<) and a forward key (>>>). The user can then hide the web viewer and its user elements again by pressing a Close button. To provide this functionality, we need to add the components shown in Table 13.10 to the ticker subscreen, or rather to the corresponding module of the CarAssistant project. We position them below the headlines and above the Back button, encapsulated in the VerticalArrangement `WebViewerArr`.

Table 13.10 **Additional Components for the WebViewer**

Component	Object Name	Adapted Properties
VerticalArrangement	WebViewerArr	"Visible" disable "Width": Fill parent
WebViewer	WebViewer	
Button (3x)	WebBackButton, CloseWebsiteButton, WebForwardButton	"Text": <<<, Close, >>>

With the additional components, the ticker module should now look as shown in Figure 13.64. The encapsulation within `WebViewerArr` ensures that the WebViewer and its control elements become visible only when a headline has been selected by the user.

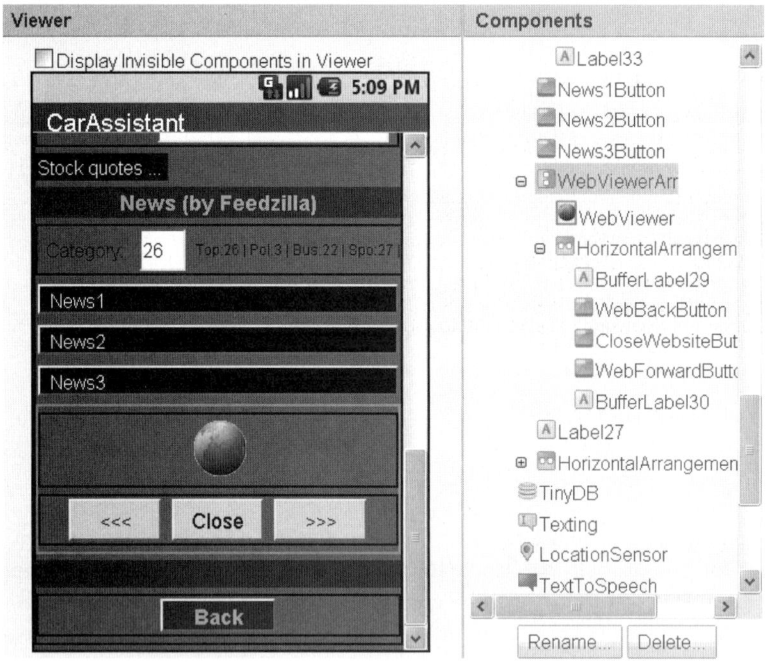

Figure 13.64 Arrangement of the additional components for the WebViewer

The implementation of these functionalities is very simple due to the web addresses extracted in the previous analysis of the JSON raw text. When the user presses one of the three News buttons, the associated event handler shown in Figure 13.65 (left) is called and the `WebViewerArr` is displayed along with the web viewer and its control elements. Calling the selected web address is done via the WebViewer method `WebViewer.GoToUrl`. To switch between the web pages in the web viewer, the user can press the backward or forward button, which triggers either the web method `WebViewer.GoBack` or the web method `WebViewer.GoForward`, respectively. Pressing the Close button then hides the `WebViewerArr` again.

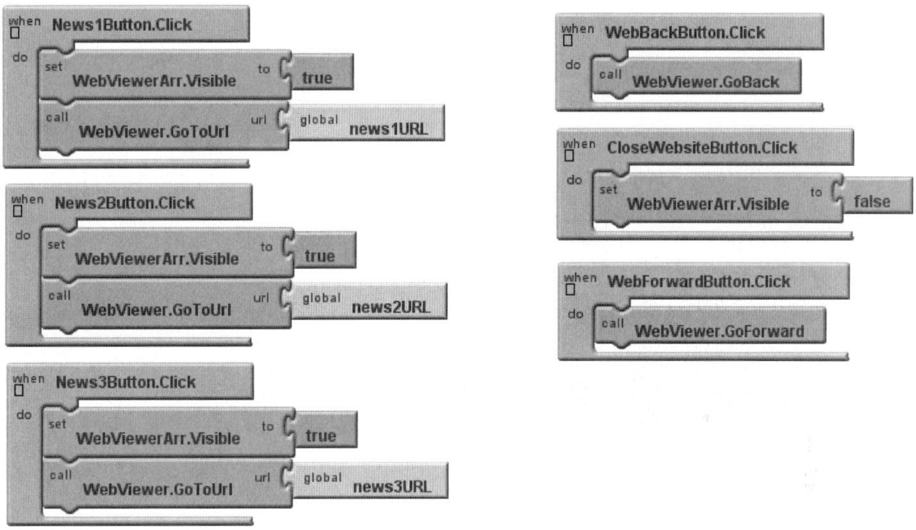

Figure 13.65 Calling news websites and surfing via the WebViewer

Of course, we also want our ticker module to be just as user friendly as the other modules, so we want the user input to persist in the app for the next use. Thus, when the Back button is pressed, we need to save all user input locally via the corresponding statements in the event handler `TickerBackButton` (Figure 13.66). It is also important that we disable the `TickerClock` timer upon leaving the ticker subscreen, thereby ensuring that no updates are loaded in the background through the mobile data connection.

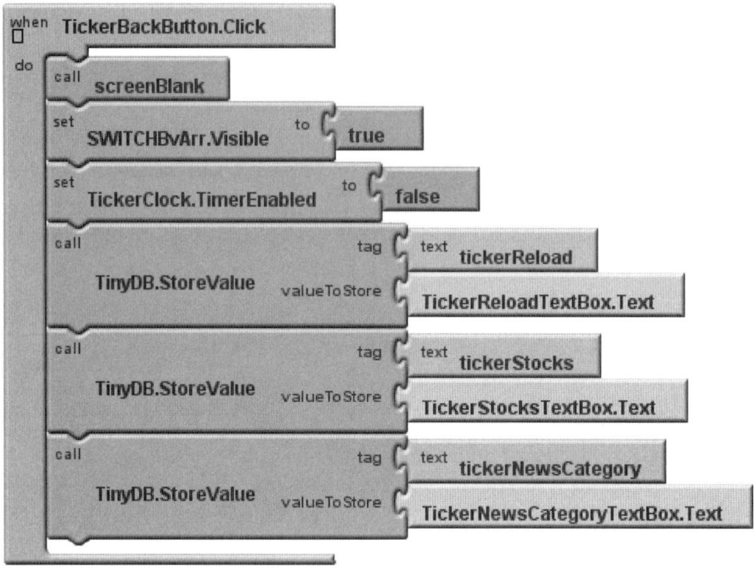

Figure 13.66 Closing the ticker, ending the timer, and saving the user's data

The implementation of the ticker module is now complete. You should be able to readily envisage the huge possibilities offered by the Web component and potentially by the web services of the Internet—they open up boundless design options for your own apps. Indeed, more and more web services are now offering web APIs, including social networks such as Google+ and Facebook.

Now we just need to discuss the implementation of the event handler `Screen1.Initialize` (Figure 13.67), which we have mentioned previously in the context of saving the input data locally. When starting the CarAssistant app, this event handler loads all of the data from the local app memory that the user had entered and configured in the various modules and setup areas, and that the user will expect to find available the next time he or she starts the driver assistance system. In this way, the user can reuse his or her personal settings without having to reenter them. Each one of the numerous loading processes follows the familiar procedure, in which the memory content is first checked to see whether it exists, and then (if it does) entered into the corresponding property field in the many different setup areas. At that point, the data is available for use again, just as when it was originally entered by the user.

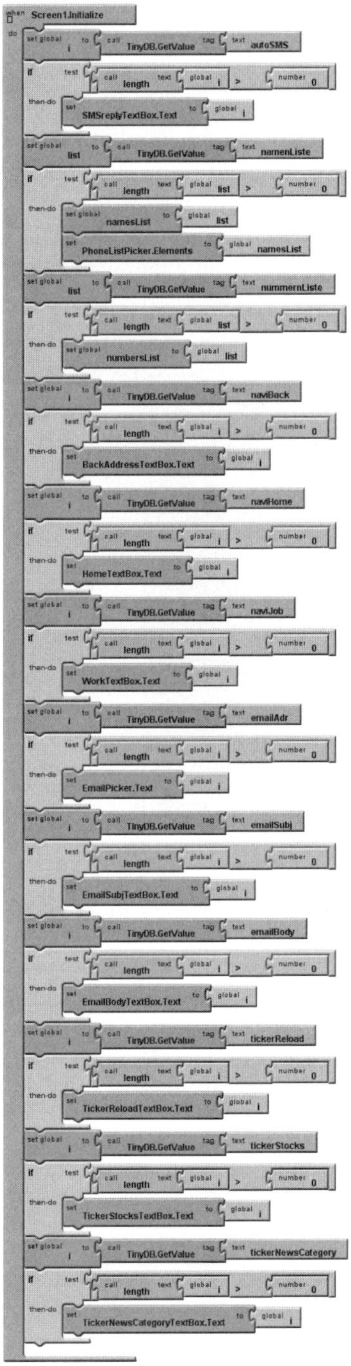

Figure 13.67 Loading saved data when launching the driver assistance system

Surely you now want to test out the entire range of functions found in the driver assistance system on your own smartphone. Before you transfer the CarAssistant app to your smartphone, however, don't forget to switch the multiple screens of the various setup areas from visible editing mode (`Visible=true`) to non-visible working mode (`Visible=false`). You just need to uncheck the Visible property in AI Designer for all corresponding VerticalArrangement component objects except the switchboard `SWITCHBvArr`, which should be the only screen visible when the app is launched (see Figure 13.68). If you have the correct setting and disable the check box "Display Invisible Components in Viewer," you should see only the switchboard in the Viewer.

Figure 13.68 Set all multiple screens to non-visible, except for "SWITCHBvArr"

Now you can install the CarAssistant app on your smartphone. The confirmation prompt for the installation shown in Figure 13.69 indicates the wide range of functions covered by our project. Here you need to confirm more system access prompts than in any other app you have developed yourself in the course of this book.

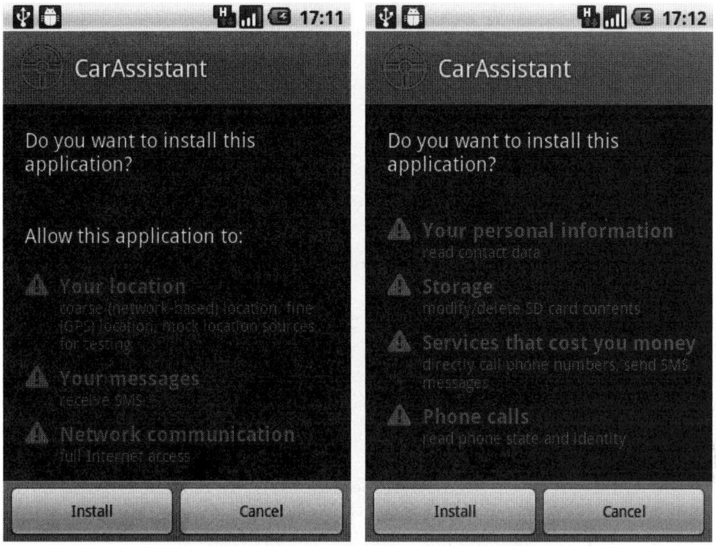

Figure 13.69 The numerous functions evident in the installation prompts

The long list of installation prompts in Figure 13.69 and the length of the event handler in Figure 13.67 for initializing our driver assistance system indicate the huge range of functions and wealth of data that our final project utilizes. As you can see, this project is clearly different from the beginners' projects we undertook in the earlier chapters of this book—and it suggests the immense development of your own skills throughout the course of this book, from a beginner to a full-fledged developer of Android apps with App Inventor. The overview of start icons shown in Figure 13.70, which represent the many apps we have developed throughout this book, also reflects this development.

Figure 13.70 Start icons for all of the example apps developed in this book

By focusing on the content-related tasks and requirements for a driver assistance system, we divided our last large overall project into manageable modules, designed these pieces in a progressive fashion under a user-friendly and stringent user interface, and successively implemented the many different functionalities by using synergies. To do so, we used familiar specific and generic components almost without thinking about it, and we looked up new components in the AI specification to use them in the project when necessary. In the process, we discovered a very wide range of areas in the context of a project and a widely defined communication concept, though this breadth hardly influenced the development process itself. That is, multiple screens, telephony, geodata, SMS, speech synthesis and analysis, a universal concept for activating and integrating a wide range of external applications for navigation or sending e-mail, and even a standardized interface for data exchange with Web APIs were readily fit together to form a cohesive whole. The importance of this step-by-step development approach cannot be emphasized enough, and goes far beyond the here-and-now task of learning more and more new components and functions. If you are now ready to develop interesting, attractive, useful, entertaining, small or even large apps with AI even without this book, and if you discover future smartphone functions and new components on your own and integrate them naturally—then this book has fulfilled its purpose.

Part V

Useful Things for the Developer

As a developer of apps, you will make use of many additional tools and sources of information in your work, more frequently especially at the beginning and in a more targeted way with growing experience. This final part of the book presents brief explanations of special functional areas of AI, together with useful tools and helpful tips. The appendix contains additional sources for tutorials, websites, and developer forums dealing with App Inventor, Android, and app development. You should regularly consult the developer forums in particular because there is always something new to discover that can help you in many respects in your work as developer.

Chapter 14

Special Functional Areas

In addition to the many functional areas, components, and component groups that we have encountered and used in the course of the chapters and projects in this book, other special elements are available in the context of the development environment and language of App Inventor. These elements have a less generic character, but rather are geared toward special areas of use or even require the presence of special services, memberships, or systems. We quickly mention them here for the sake of completeness and will take the opportunity in this chapter to briefly point out these special functional areas. After completing the projects in the preceding chapters, you now know how you can gain access to additional components on your own, get information on how to use them and what their properties are, and combine them with other block structures to create run-capable apps. The descriptions of the components and functional areas in this chapter are intended as an incentive to tap into these elements on your own if you need to, and as encouragement to prepare yourself for dealing with the new and additional components and functional areas that App Inventor will surely continue to make available in the future. With the introduction to the components in this chapter, you will have encountered all elements of App Inventor that were available at the time this chapter was written and that are mostly ready for use. Perhaps some others will have been created since this book's publication—have a look for yourself.

Application-Specific Components

Under the special components heading, we include all of the as-yet-unmentioned options available under the many component groups from which we have been using other components in the course of this book. The number of components that we have not yet discussed is manageable, but these items could certainly be of interest for some special area of use or another.

Tweeting with the Twitter Component

In the Social group, AI offers the Twitter component, with which you can access the *Twitter* service to send brief text messages resembling SMS messages (currently up to 140 characters) via the Internet ("tweeting") or can follow ("followers") other authors ("twitterers") and their contributions ("tweets"). As the Twitter-specific terminology indicates, this typical representative of a *Web 2.0* service is, in fact, a special application for *microblogging*—in other words, a highly abbreviated, spontaneous, and often very individual form of *blogging*—and a special variation of a social network in which you as user have to register first before you can use all its functions. The AI component Twitter assumes that you have a corresponding Twitter account, which makes its classification as a *special* component seem justified.

Perhaps while you were reading the brief summary of the features of this web service, you suddenly had lots of ideas about how you could generically implement a similar functionality for automatically distributing messages to subscribers—for example, based on the familiar TinyWebDB or Texting component—and even add geodata or similar data. However, if you are using Twitter and want to be able to access this service from within the apps you have developed yourself, you can do so by using the AI component Twitter. A small extract from its rather large specification appears in Figure 14.1.

Twitter

Twitter1

This component allows users to interact with Twitter.

This non-visible component enables communication with Twitter. Methods are included to enable searching (`SearchTwitter`) and logging in to Twitter (`Authorize`). Once a user has logged in and the login has been confirmed successful by the `IsAuthorized` event, you can use the following methods:

- Set the status of the logged-in user (`SetStatus`).
- Send a direct message to a specific user (`DirectMessage`).
- Receive the most recent direct messages (`RequestDirectMessages`).
- Follow a user (`Follow`).
- Unfollow a user (`StopFollowing`.)
- Get the list of users who follow the logged-in user (`RequestFollowers`).
- Get the most recent messages of followed users (`RequestFriendTimeline`).
- Get the most recent mentions of the logged-in user (`RequestMentions`).

Properties

ConsumerKey
The consumer key identifying this app, obtained from twitter.com/oauth_clients/new as described above.

ConsumerSecret
The consumer secret identifying this app, obtained from twitter.com/oauth_clients/new as described above.

DirectMessages
User's direct messages on Twitter.

Followers
User's list of Twitter followers.

FriendTimeline
User's Twitter message timeline.

Figure 14.1 Extract from the specification of the Twitter component in AI References

As you might guess from the references in the specification of Figure 14.1, the communication of the Twitter component with the Twitter service takes place on a relatively high level of abstraction via its specific interface, the *Twitter API* (application programming interface), with the open protocol *OAuth* being used for API authentication. In the specification, you can find more background information on dealing with the many property fields, event handlers, and methods of this special component, plus information about the specific authentication, registration, and communication processes with the Twitter API. In principle, the communication with the Twitter online service takes place in a manner similar to the familiar data transfer between your app and an external web service using the generic AI component Web, except that the specialized Twitter component is dedicated and designed for this service and the instructions are not carried out via a common HTTP `GET` request. Perhaps you will want to try out this alternative yourself one day, if you are interested in this topic.

Reading Barcodes with the BarcodeScanner Component

The next special component, BarcodeScanner, from the group "Other stuff," is strongly reminiscent of the general principle of starting another app via the generic component ActivityStarter. The BarcodeScanner component makes the explicit assumption that the barcode scanner developed by ZXing is available as a pre-installed app, as noted in the specification shown in Figure 14.2. This barcode scanner is started via the method `DoScan`, and its decoded text result is returned as the event `AfterScan` in the Result property.

BarcodeScanner

This non-visible component uses the phone's camera to read a 1-dimensional barcode or 2-dimensional barcode (QR code). In order for this component to work, the Barcode scanner app from ZXing must be installed on the phone. This app is available for free in the Android Market.

Properties

Result
The text result of the last successful scan. This becomes available after `AfterScan` has been signaled. This value is also returned as the `result` value.

Methods

`DoScan()`
Start a scan

Events

`AfterScan(text result)`
Called after scanning ends.

Figure 14.2 Specification of the BarcodeScanner component in AI References

The BarcodeScanner component is an example of the great potential inherent in the open interface component ActivityStarter. By integrating external applications, you can not only expand the functions of an app you have developed yourself, but also expand the function range or component inventory of the AI developer language. You could easily have assembled a BarcodeScanner component yourself, just by invoking an appropriate external app via an activity starter. Perhaps you can think of other useful components that you would like to construct yourself in a similar way and use in your own apps.

Online Elections with the Voting Component

Another specialized component that could be represented by a corresponding construct with a Web or ActivityStarter component is the Voting component, which is found in the group "Not ready for prime time." With this component, you can retrieve virtual ballots via the method `RequestBallot` from an appropriate web service for online elections or votes. These ballots can then be filled in by the user in the app and sent back via the method `SendBallot`, perhaps accompanied by the e-mail address (`UserEmailAddress`) and identification of the user who is voting (`UserId`). Figure 14.3 shows part of the specification of this special component.

Voting

Voting1

The Voting component communicates with a Web service to retrieve a ballot and send back users' votes.

The application should call the method `RequestBallot`, usually in the `Initialize` event handler, in order to get the ballot question and options from the Web service (specified by the `ServiceURL` property). Depending on the response from the Web service, the system will raise one of the following three events:

After getting the ballot, the application should allow the user to make a choice from among `BallotOptions` and set the property `UserChoice` to that choice. The application should also set `UserId` to specify which user is voting. Often, this will be set to the property `UserEmailAddress`, which specifies the email address associated with the phone.

Once the application has set `UserChoice` and `UserId`, the application can call `SendBallot` to send this information to the Web service. If the service successfully receives the vote, the event `GotBallotConfirmation` will be raised. Otherwise, the event `WebServiceError` will be raised with the appropriate error message.

Properties

`BallotOptions`
The list of ballot options.
`BallotQuestion`
The question to be voted on.
`ServiceURL`
The URL of the Voting service
`UserChoice`
The ballot choice to send to the server, which must
`UserEmailAddress`
The email address associated with this device.
`UserId`
A text identifying the voter that is sent to the Voting

Events

`GotBallot()`
Event indicating that a ballot was retrieved from the Web service and that the prop
`BallotOptions` have been set. This is always preceded by a call to the method
`GotBallotConfirmation()`
Event confirming that the Voting service received the ballot.
`NoOpenPoll()`
Event indicating that the service has no open poll.
`WebServiceError(text message)`
Event indicating that the communication with the Web service resulted in an error.

Methods

`RequestBallot()`
Send a request for a ballot to the Web service specified by the property `ServiceURL`. When the completes, one of the following events will be raised: `GotBallot`, `NoOpenPoll`, or `WebServiceError`.
`SendBallot()`
Send a completed ballot to the Web service. This should not be called until the properties `UserId` and `UserChoice` have been set by the application.

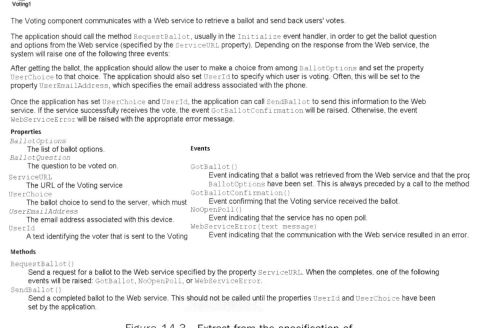

Figure 14.3 Extract from the specification of the Voting component in AI References

Of course, the Voting component shown in Figure 14.3 requires a corresponding web service at the other end that works under the same principle as the voting process intended in the specification. The topics of "e-voting" and "e-government" are certain to become increasingly important in future, and with AI you are prepared to develop these types of applications in the best possible way.

Data Tables with the FusiontablesControl Component

With the FusiontablesControl component in the group "Not ready for prime time," you can use Google's web service known as Fusion Tables. With this service, users can upload their gathered data at `http://www.google.com/fusiontables/Home/`, publish it, combine it with the data of other users, and visualize it expressively in the context of maps, time graphs, and other typical chart graphics. With the AI component known as FusiontablesControl (Figure 14.4), you can also use this online database from within your app by creating new tables and querying or changing the content of existing tables with appropriate search requests (queries).

FusiontablesControl

Google Fusion Tables lets you store, share, query and visualize data tables; this component lets you query, create, and modify these tables, using the Fusion Tables SQL API.

To use the component, define a query, call DoQuery to execute the query, and GotResult will hand you the result when it is ready.

Note that you do not need to worry about encoding the query, but you do have to make sure it follows the syntax described in the reference manual, which means that things like capitalization for names of columns matter, and that single quotes must be used around column names if there are spaces in them.

The results of the query will generally be returned in CSV format, and can be converted to list format using the "list from csv table" or "list from csv row" blocks.

Properties

`Query`: text (read-only)
The query to send to the Fusion Tables API.

For legal query formats and examples, see the Fusion Tables SQL API reference manual.

Note that you do not need to worry about encoding the query, but you do have to make sure it follows the syntax described in the reference manual, which means that things like capitalization for names of columns matters, and that single quotes need to be used around column names that contain.

Events

`GotResult(text result)`
Indicates that the Fusion Tables query has finished processing, with a result. The result of the query will generally be returned in CSV format, and can be converted to list format using the "list from csv table" or "list from csv row" blocks.

Methods

`DoQuery()`
Send the query to the Fusion Tables server.

Figure 14.4 Specification of the FusiontablesControl component in AI References

For accessing the online data tables, the AI component uses the so-called Fusion Tables API, an interface (application programming interface [API]) to the Fusion Tables web service, through which tables can be created or deleted; individual rows can be inserted, changed, or deleted; and data entries can be selected and retrieved in Standard Query Language (SQL). Each query must be formulated in the correct syntax of an SQL statement (see `http://code.google.com/apis/fusiontables/docs/developers_guide.html`) in the component property `Query` as a text string and then sent to the online database via the method `DoQuery` (see the specification in Figure 14.4). After the web service has processed the search query and sent the result back, the resulting data entries are received via the event block `GotResult` and can then be processed further in the app. The entire data exchange takes place in the data format known as CSV (Comma-Separated Values), which means that the CSV data can be comfortably converted between list and table formats via the generic list methods (in AI Editor, go to Built-In > Lists > `list to csv row` [or some other option]). With the Fusiontables-Control component, AI offers you a professional and scalable online database plus structured access to a lot of additional data in the cloud.

Dedicated Component Groups

In our previous discussions, we omitted an entire component group, as well as components that involve more comprehensive concepts, but we did so for the same reasons as arose with the individual components with a very special background or area of application. That is, these components, groups, and concepts—which we introduce in the following section—require special systems and deeper knowledge for their use.

Online Multiplayer Games with the GameClient Component

A somewhat more manageable representative of this subgroup is the GameClient component, which is found in the AI group "Not ready for prime time." It has only a single component, but behind it lies a complex concept—namely, the very demanding topic of *online multiplayer games*. PC-based online games have already proved fascinating for millions of users worldwide in the form of *MMOG* (massive multiplayer online games) and *MMORPG* (massive multiplayer online role-playing games). Such games are only in their infancy on smartphones now, but will probably get a strong boost from the widespread adoption of tablets and other mobile devices. AI's GameClient component remains somewhat experimental for this reason, and at the time of writing it really did belong into the group "Not ready for prime time." If you are interested in developing mobile online multiplayer games and have the required knowledge, you should have a closer look at the specification of this component, an extract of which is shown in Figure 14.5.

GameClient

GameClient1

GameClient communicates with online game servers to support the implementation of multiplayer games. For information on the clients and servers and examples of games, see the MIT Master's Thesis by Bill Magnuson, *Building Blocks for Mobile Games* available at http://people.csail.mit.edu/misc/magnuson-meng-eecs-2010.pdf. There is an experimental game server running at appinvgameserver.appspot.com, but this may be up only intermittently. For serious work, you will probably want to deploy your own game server on Google Appengine. The implementation is described in the thesis, and the code is available at http://code.google.com /p/app-inventor-for-android/source/browse/#svn/trunk/app_inv_game_server

Properties

InstanceId: text (read-only)
The game instance id. Taken together,the game ID and the instance ID uniquely identify the game.

InvitedInstances: list (read-only)
The set of game instances to which this player has been invited but has not yet joined. To ensure current values are returned, first invoke GetInstanceLists.

JoinedInstances: list (read-only)
The set of game instances in which this player is participating. To ensure current values are returned, first invoke GetInstanceLists.

Leader: text (read-only)
The game's leader. At any time, each game instance has only one leader, but the leader may change with time. Initially, the leader is the game instance creator. Application writers determine special properties of the leader. The leader value is updated each time a successful communication is made with the server.

Players: list (read-only)
The current set of players for this game instance. Each player is designated by an email address, which is a string. The list of players is updated each time a successful communication is made with the game server.

Figure 14.5 Extract from the specification of the GameClient component in AI References

Similar to the test server for the TinyWebDB component, which is also currently delegated to the group "Not ready for prime time," there is a multiplayer game server available online for testing the GameClient component. You can use this server to test your own mobile game app. For further details on the use of the server, its configuration, and the creation of your own game server, please refer to the specification and the references listed there.

Exchange of Data with the BluetoothClient and BluetoothServer Components

Using the two components BluetoothClient and BluetoothServer from the "Other stuff" group also requires deeper knowledge of data communication in general and of the industry standard *Bluetooth* (IEEE 802.15.1) for data exchange over short distances in particular. The documentation of data communication via Bluetooth was still being prepared at the time of this book's publication (it was announced as "Coming soon" in the AI Concepts Reference), so you can use the specifications of the two components and your own urge to experiment if you want to know more about it. Figure 14.6 shows part of the specification of the BluetoothClient component, in which the introductory explanations were missing at the time of this book's writing.

BluetoothClient

Bluetooth client component

Properties

AddressesAndNames
A list of the addresses and names of paired Bluetooth devices.
Available
Tell whether Bluetooth is available on the Android device.
CharacterEncoding
The character encoding to use when sending and receiving text.
DelimiterByte
The delimiter byte to use when passing a negative number for the numberOfBytes parameter when calling ReceiveText, ReceiveSignedBytes, or ReceiveUnsignedBytes.
Enabled
Tell whether Bluetooth is enabled.
HighByteFirst
Whether 2 and 4 byte numbers should be sent and received with the high (or most significant) byte first. Check the documentation for the device with which your app will be communicating for the appropriate setting. This is also known as big-endian.

Figure 14.6 Extract from the specification of the BluetoothClient component in AI References

Despite the fact that this component has a high degree of abstraction for communicating via Bluetooth, the property fields described in Figure 14.6 indicate that the data exchange takes place based on bytes and requires in-depth knowledge of how to use them. Of course, this same caveat applies to the BluetoothServer component—the counterpart of the BluetoothClient component—as you can see from the specification extract in Figure 14.7.

BluetoothServer

Bluetooth server component

Properties

Available: boolean
Tell whether Bluetooth is available on the Android device.
CharacterEncoding: text
The character encoding to use when sending and receiving text.
DelimiterByte: number
The delimiter byte to use when passing a negative number for the numberOfBytes parameter when calling ReceiveText, ReceiveSignedBytes, or ReceiveUnsignedBytes.
Enabled: boolean
Tell whether Bluetooth is enabled.
HighByteFirst: boolean
Whether 2 and 4 byte numbers should be sent and received with the high (or most significant) byte first. Check the documentation for the device with which your app will be communicating for the appropriate setting. This is also known as big-endian.
IsAccepting: boolean
Tell whether this BluetoothServer component is accepting an incoming connection.
IsConnected: boolean
Tell whether a Bluetooth connection has been made.

Figure 14.7 Extract from the specification of the BluetoothServer component in AI References

Feel free to experiment with the properties and, above all, the many methods of the two Bluetooth components, and perhaps visit the AI Forum to find useful hints and tips on their use. You should also consult the AI References, as perhaps the announced documentation will have been added by the time you read these words.

Controlling Robots with the Lego Mindstorms Group

With the AI update of December 9, 2010, the entire component group Lego Mindstorms was added to App Inventor. It currently includes seven components that an AI app can use to communicate, via Bluetooth, with a programmable "Lego brick" (*Intelligent Brick*) named *NXT*—the successor of the original *RCX* (*Robotics Command System*). This forms the central unit for managing and controlling up to four sensors and three motors—for example, on a robot or another autonomous Lego system that can be constructed from Lego Technic or Mindstorms electronic motors, sensor elements, and other building parts, and programmed accordingly.

> **Further Information on Lego Mindstorms and NXT**
>
> If you have not already experienced this really impressive technical "toy" created by Lego, you can find a good description and summary of it on the Internet. For example, helpful information can be found on *Wikipedia*:
>
> `http://en.wikipedia.org/wiki/Lego_Mindstorms`
>
> `http://en.wikipedia.org/wiki/Lego_Mindstorms_NXT`

The motivation to include such a specialized component group in AI is certainly based on the common—in terms of both history and didactics—approach of imparting knowledge by programming robots and developing mobile devices with relatively simple methods and connecting them with one another. It is certainly no coincidence that Massachusetts Institute of Technology (MIT; Cambridge, Massachusetts), which is legendary for its innovation efforts, is taking part in the development of both Lego Mindstorms and App Inventor. In Figure 14.8, you can see an extract from the component group Lego Mindstorms, whose introductory description explains the use of the BluetoothClient component in great detail; this component serves as the basis of the communication between an AI app on the smartphone and the NXT on the Lego system.

Learn > Reference > LEGO MINDSTORMS > About Learn Forum My Projects

LEGO® MINDSTORMS®

These components provide control of LEGO® MINDSTORMS® NXT robots using Bluetooth.

LEGO and MINDSTORMS are registered trademarks of the LEGO Group.

IMPORTANT: All of these components have a **BluetoothClient *property*** that must be set in the App Inventor designer (in the browser). The property cannot be set in the blocks editor. The property tells which **BluetoothClient *component*** to use for communication with the robot. You will need to explicitly add a BluetoothClient component to your project. If you have one robot, you should have one BluetoothClient component. If you are lucky enough to have two robots and you want to control both of them simultaneously from one application, you'll need two BluetoothClient components in your project. The BluetoothClient component is available from the "Not ready for prime time" section of the palette.

Here's a list of the initial steps you'll need to perform to use one or more of the NXT components:

1. Go to the *Palette* and click on "Not ready for prime time".
2. Drag a *BluetoothClient* component and drop it on to the *Viewer*.
3. The component will automatically be named *BluetoothClient1*.
4. In the *Palette*, click on "LEGO MINDSTORMS".
5. Drag one of the components, for example *NxtDirectCommands*, and drop it on to the *Viewer*.
6. In the *Properties box*, click on the area after *BluetoothClient* (currently "None...").
7. A box appears with a list of all the BluetoothClient components in your project.
8. Click on *BluetoothClient1* and click *OK*.
9. If desired, add another component, for example *NxtColorSensor*, and repeat steps 6-8 to set its *BluetoothClient* property.

Table of Contents

NxtDirectCommands

A component that provides a low-level interface to a LEGO MINDSTORMS NXT robot, with functions to send NXT Direct Commands

Properties

`BluetoothClient`
The BluetoothClient component that should be used for communication. **Must be set in the Designer**

Methods

`DeleteFile`(text fileName)
Delete a file on the robot.
`DownloadFile`(text source, text destination)
Download a file to the robot.
`GetBatteryLevel`()
Get the battery level for the robot. Returns the voltage in millivolts.

Figure 14.8 Extract from the Lego Mindstorms component group

The table of contents of the Lego Mindstorms component group shown in Figure 14.8 lists the seven components it contains. Their names all start with the identifier NXT, as the components communicate with this central Lego element when exchanging data via Bluetooth. The NxtDirectCommands component is used for exchanging general control instructions. The NxtColorSensor, NxtLightSensor, NxtSoundSensor, NxtTouchSensor, and NxtUltrasonicSensor components read and process the measured values of color, light, sound, touch, and ultrasonic sensors, respectively, provided these sensors are present on the Lego robot. With the component NxtDrive, the Lego robot's movements can be remotely controlled by the smartphone via the AI app.

As use of the entire component group identified in Figure 14.8 requires the presence of a corresponding Lego Mindstorms system, we have included this group in the special functional areas. If you have such a Lego system available, you should definitely try out the components of this group. They will not only provide a lot of fun but also give you an intensive taste of all that's yet to come in the future for mobile, embedded, and ubiquitous computing plus robotics.

Java Interface with the AI Java Bridge

With the Java interface, we are addressing a very special area of functions that goes beyond the familiar terrain of visual app development with AI. Against the backdrop of the didactic intention of AI, the Google App Inventor Team was also interested in making smartphone users familiar with developing apps in general, independent of the specific development tool. They also took into account that the majority of Android apps are still being developed with Java and the Android SDK (Software Development Kit). To make this option available to AI users as well and lead them toward it, they introduced an alpha version of the so-called Java Bridge in May 2011 (see Figure 14.9).

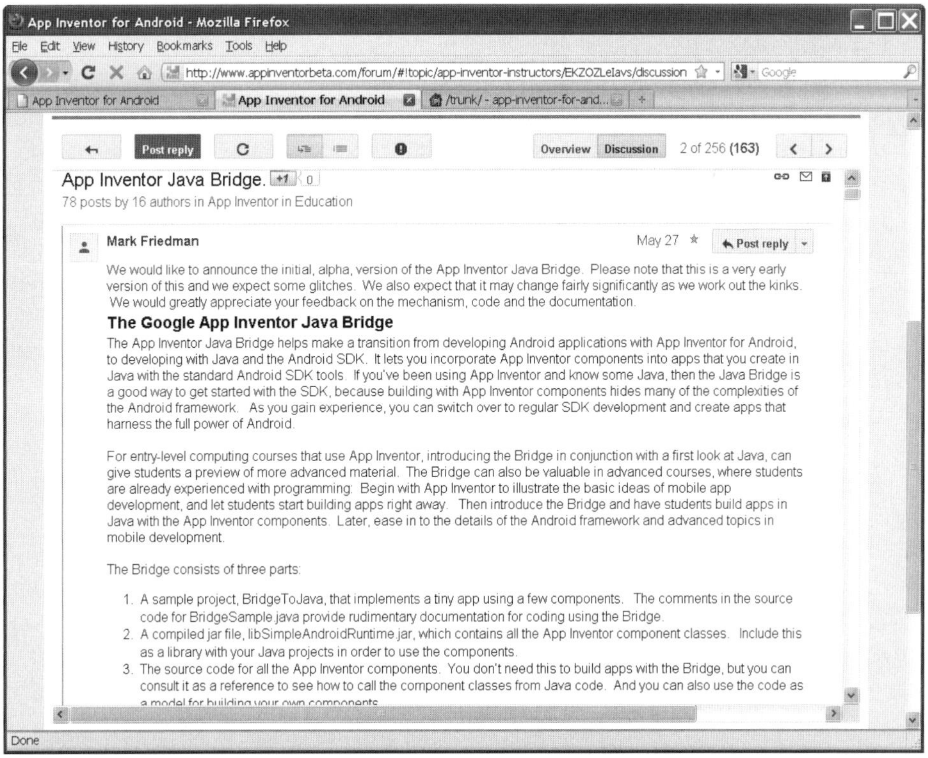

Figure 14.9 Introduction and discussion of the AI Java Bridge in AI Forum

In the wider sense, the Java Bridge is a Java class library with which the familiar AI components, along with their properties, event handlers, and methods, can be integrated into programming with Java and, therefore, used in the source code. A developer who is familiar with the process of visual app development with AI is supposed to be able to work with these familiar components and concepts if he or she chooses to switch to Java development, thereby making it easier for the app developer to find his or her way around the new development environment of the Android SDK. As the Java Bridge is not another component of AI, it is not documented in the usual way in AI; that is, it is currently introduced and discussed in entries in the AI Forum, as you can see in Figure 14.9.

Documentation and Downloading the AI Java Bridge

Information on installation and using the Java Bridge can be found at these sites:

`http://experimental.appinventor.mit.edu/forum/#!topic/app-inventor-instructors/EKZOZLeIavs/discussion`

`http://app-inventor-for-android.googlecode.com/svn/trunk/samples/BridgeToJava/README`

Links for downloading the Java Bridge package can be found at this site:

`http://code.google.com/p/app-inventor-for-android/source/browse/trunk`

Tips and examples for using the AI Java Bridge are available at this site:

`http://experimental.appinventor.mit.edu/forum/#!topic/app-inventor-instructors/mM-pIRmRn3M/discussion`

The AI Java Bridge currently comprises the three subsections shown in Figure 14.10. These can be selected under the link listed for downloading the Java Bridge package, in the section "Directories," and can be downloaded in the section "Filename": the Java class library itself (`libSimpleAndroidRuntime.jar`) including all AI component classes (in the directory `../trunk/jars`), several example projects (`../trunk/samples`), and even source code for the individual AI component classes (`../trunk/src`).

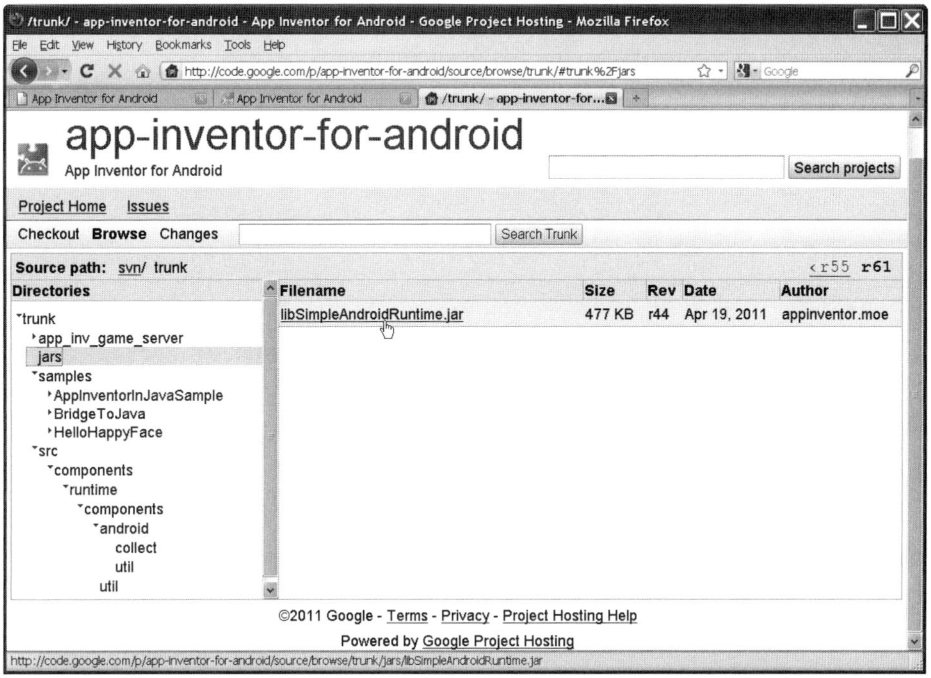

Figure 14.10 Elements of AI Java Bridge available for downloading

To work with the Java Bridge, you need to have installed a Java development environment (for example, *Eclipse*) and the Android SDK on your computer, and you need to have basic knowledge of how to program a Java application. You can find further information and helpful links to the corresponding online resources at the links given earlier for using the AI Java Bridge.

If you believe that you have gained enough experience with developing apps under AI and are now curious about programming with Java, AI offers you (very unselfishly) the option of making a smooth transition into the world of programming Android apps with Java. Have a go and get to know the strengths and weaknesses of the two development approaches—Java versus App Inventor. Perhaps you will decide to switch completely to Java, or perhaps you will quickly return to AI. You might also decide to develop certain apps in Java and others in AI, using the advantages of each method depending on the different app projects involved. And if you find it really difficult to choose between the two, you can even use both approaches in combination and make the most of them within one app project, thanks to the AI Java Bridge.

Chapter 15

Tips and Tools

In this chapter, you will find tips, tools, and other hints that may be important for your work as an app developer with App Inventor. These topics were relegated to a separate chapter so as to make the previous chapters easier to read—long explanatory notes and asides would have detracted from the flow of the text and distracted you as reader too much from the focal issues. For that reason, the preceding chapters contain brief references to the items covered here in more detail. If you have not yet followed the prompts for referring to this chapter where appropriate, you may still find this chapter a helpful source of further information and hints.

Supported Media Formats

If you design your own apps that use media files, you need to make sure that these files are available in the media formats supported by AI or Android. The following tables list the various media formats that are (or should be) supported by all Android devices. Some Android devices might support other formats as well. Nevertheless, if you want to ensure that your apps, including the media files they use, can run on all or as many Android devices as possible, you should take care to use the formats listed here. Please note that the tables list playback formats (decoders), rather than recording formats (encoders).

Audio Formats

Table 15.1 lists the audio formats supported by Android.

Table 15.1 **Android-Supported Audio Formats According to http://developer.android.com/guide/appendix/media-formats.html as of September 22, 2011**

Format	Details	File Types
AAC LC/LTP, HE-AACv1 (AAC+), HE-AACv2 (enhanced AAC+)	Mono/stereo content in any combination of standard bit rates up to 160 kbps and sampling rates from 8 to 48 kHz.	3GPP (.3gp), and MPEG-4 (.mp4, .m4a). ADTS raw AAC (.aac, decode only, ADIF not supported, Android 3.1+).
AMR-NB	4.75 to 12.2 kbps sampled at 8 kHz.	3GPP (.3gp)
AMR-WB	9 rates from 6.60 kbit/s to 23.85 kbit/s sampled at 16 kHz.	3GPP (.3gp)
FLAC	Mono/stereo (no multichannel). Sample rates up to 48 kHz (but up to 44.1 kHz is recommended on devices with 44.1 kHz output, as the 48 to 44.1 kHz downsampler does not include a low-pass filter). 16-bit recommended; no dither applied for 24-bit.	FLAC (.flac) only
MP3	Mono/stereo 8 to 320 Kbps constant (CBR) or variable bit-rate (VBR).	MP3 (.mp3)
MIDI	MIDI Type 0 and 1. DLS Version 1 and 2. XMF and Mobile XMF. Support for ringtone formats RTTTL/RTX, OTA, and iMelody	Type 0 and 1 (.mid, .xmf, .mxmf); also RTTTL/RTX (.rtttl, .rtx), OTA (.ota), and iMelody (.imy)
Ogg Vorbis		Ogg (.ogg)
PCM/WAVE	8- and 16-bit linear PCM (rates up to the limit of the hardware).	WAVE (.wav)

Image Formats

Table 15.2 lists the image formats supported by Android.

Table 15.2 **Android-Supported Image Formats According to http://developer.android.com/guide/appendix/media-formats.html as of September 22, 2011**

Format	Details	File Types
JPEG	Base+progressive	JPEG (.jpg)
GIF		GIF (.gif)
PNG		PNG (.png)
BMP		BMP (.bmp)

Video Formats

Table 15.3 lists the video formats supported by Android.

Table 15.3 **Android-Supported Video Formats According to http://developer.android.com/guide/appendix/media-formats.html as of September 22, 2011**

Format	Details	File Types
H.263		3GPP (.3gp) and MPEG-4 (.mp4)
H.264 AVC	Baseline Profile (BP)	3GPP (.3gp) and MPEG-4 (.mp4); MPEG-TS (.ts, AAC audio only, not seekable, Android 3.0+)
MPEG-4 SP		3GPP (.3gp)
VP8		WebM (.webm)

Supported Decoder and Encoder Formats

The most up-to-date list of Android-supported media formats is available at the following site:

`http://developer.android.com/guide/appendix/media-formats.html`

News from the Developer Forum

From the supported media formats, you can tell how close the various developer languages for Android apps are to one another. Regardless of whether you are developing apps for Android in the visual IDE of AI, with the Android SDK (Software Development Kit) in the programming language Java, or in the web browser based on HTML5, up to a certain point the underlying properties and functions are identical. The details on the supported media formats listed in Tables 15.1, 15.2, and 15.3 were taken directly from the developer forum known as "Android Developers," which is used mainly by Java developers. Of course, this forum contains other interesting information that may prove helpful for your work with AI.

The "Android Developers" Developer Forum

The link to the "Android Developers" developer forum can be found at `http://developer.android.com`.

Go ahead and explore the "Android Developers" forum from time to time. The App Inventor forum, which is geared toward those individuals who are working with AI, also refers to the relevant pages of the developer forum when certain topics are discussed.

Control with the Java Console

Another useful tool that will help you in your work as an Android app developer with AI is the *Java console*. Using the Java console, you can track all of the processes that happen "behind the scenes" of the AI IDE, as it were. For example, you can see on the Java console how AI loads your current project data from the remote AI server or saves it there, how your smartphone logs in and is registered in the AI IDE, and how your app is packaged and downloaded to the smartphone. This information is interesting especially if the AI IDE suddenly starts behaving differently than you expected—for example, as described in the section on start-up problems (Chapter 2). Without this additional information, you would have only a very slim chance of finding the cause of the problem or adequately communicating it. The more precisely you can identify a problem and describe it, the better your chances of being able to fix it yourself or finding help on the AI forum. For that reason, it's worth having a closer look at this helpful tool.

Enabling the Console

The Java console is very easy to start on your computer, as long as you have installed and configured the Java environment as described in Chapter 1, "Preparation and Installation." Depending on the operating system and web browser you are using, the Java console can be started via a simple menu item. *Oracle* provides the necessary online instructions for the different system environments.

> **The Java Console: Documentation**
>
> Online instructions for enabling and viewing the Java console:
>
> `http://www.java.com/en/download/help/javaconsole.xml`

To enable the Java console generally for Java—or more precisely, the JRE (Java Runtime Environment)—on your computer, you can do so, for example, in Windows, by going to the Java Control Panel, selecting the Advanced tab, enabling "Show console" under "Java Console," and then clicking the Apply and OK buttons, as shown in Figure 15.1.

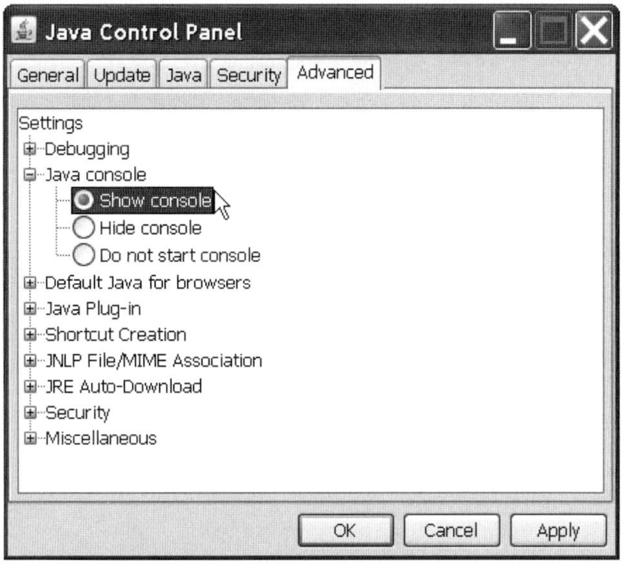

Figure 15.1 Permanently enabling display of the Java console

Alternatively, you can enable the Java console directly in the web browser if required. In the browser Mozilla Firefox, for example, you will find the item "Java Console" in the Tools menu (see Figure 15.2).

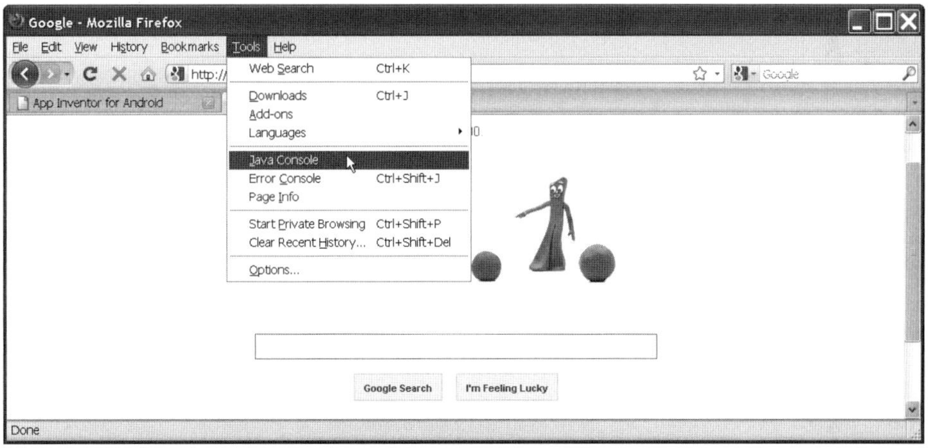

Figure 15.2 Starting the Java console directly from within the Mozilla Firefox browser

Monitoring Loading Processes in AI

If you have enabled the Java console, it will become active as soon as you start a Java application. As you know from reading Chapter 1, the AI Blocks Editor is designed as a *Java Web Start* application. Thus, if you open the Blocks Editor from within AI Designer by clicking the "Open the Blocks Editor" button, the Java console will also open, as shown in Figure 15.3.

Figure 15.3 Java console when starting the Web Start application AI Blocks Editor

Once you have confirmed (if necessary) that you want to start the AI Blocks Editor without verifying the certificate, you can monitor its loading process on the console. In Figure 15.4, you can see clearly in which steps the loading and launch of the Blocks Editor takes place. Directly below the start menu, you will see that the Web Start application Blocks Editor is being downloaded and can see the directory in which it is saved temporarily locally under your Home directory. Once the language settings have been read, the graphical user interface of the AI Blocks Editor is created ("Creating GUI ...").

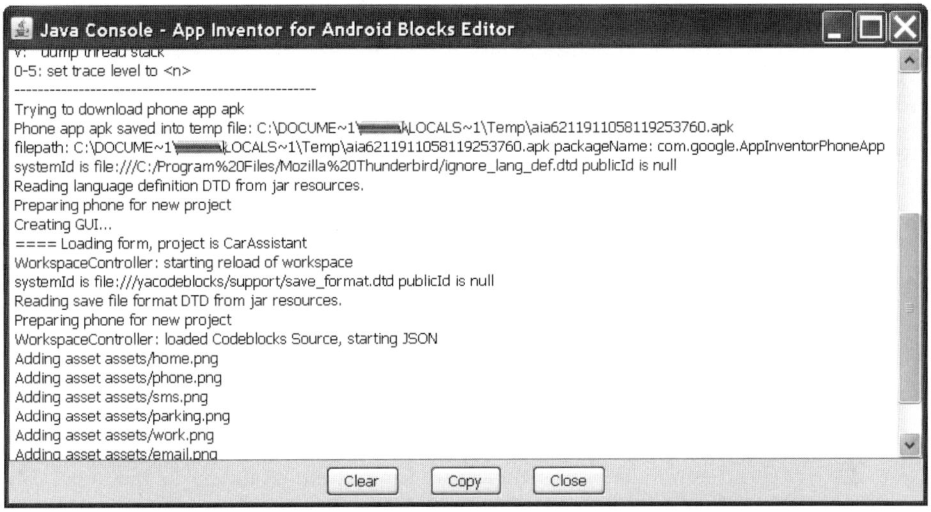

Figure 15.4 Status messages in the console when loading the AI Blocks Editor

As soon as the generic user interface of AI Blocks Editor has been successfully started, your specific project files are loaded. In Figure 15.4, notice the line "==== Loading form, project is CarAssistant"; from this point forward, the files relate to our CarAssistant project from Chapter 13. By examining the details, you can determine which media files are being loaded as assets into your local working environment. Finally, the successful reloading of your work interface in the current project is confirmed ("workspace reload done"). You should be able to confirm that this operation was successful by glancing at your local AI Blocks Editor.

Using Status Information

As mentioned earlier, you can use the status information in the Java console during your work with AI. For example, if the AI Blocks Editor should happen to start with errors, or not start at all, the messages in the console will generally give you important clues as to the possible cause. Although you may not be able to use this information to fix the problem yourself if you are a beginner, the messages will be helpful error analysis tools for other developers—including those whom you can ask for help in the AI forum. In such a case, you can highlight and copy the messages in the Java console just as in any other editor, and paste them into your forum post if required.

The information in the console can also provide important hints for beginners in terms of your daily work with AI. For example, you can check whether your smartphone has been detected properly and integrated for USB debugging, as shown in Figure 15.5 after connecting an LG P500 smartphone to the computer via USB cable ("Device connected").

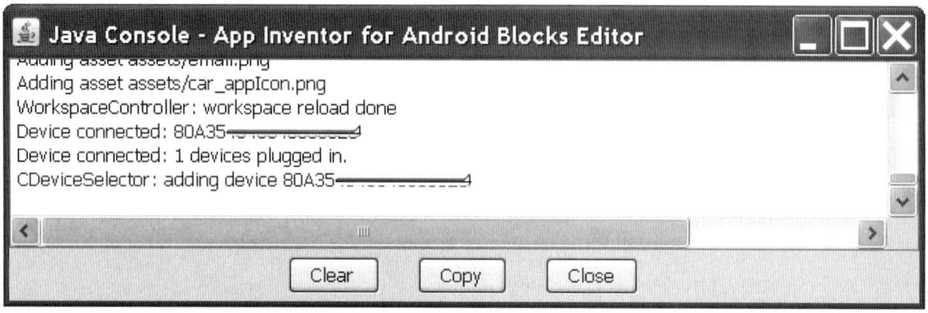

Figure 15.5 Display when connecting a smartphone via USB

If you now click the "Connect to phone" button in the AI Blocks Editor, you will be able to monitor the communication of the Blocks Editor with the connected smartphone live in the Java console. In Figure 15.6, you can see how AI pushes the media files mentioned previously—that is, the assets—to the smartphone ("Trying to push asset ..."). The receipt is then confirmed ("Asset pushed to phone ...") as are the facts that the current app project was successfully loaded ("Project loading: Success") and that the connection to the Blocks Editor was successfully established ("The blocks editor is connected to the phone.").

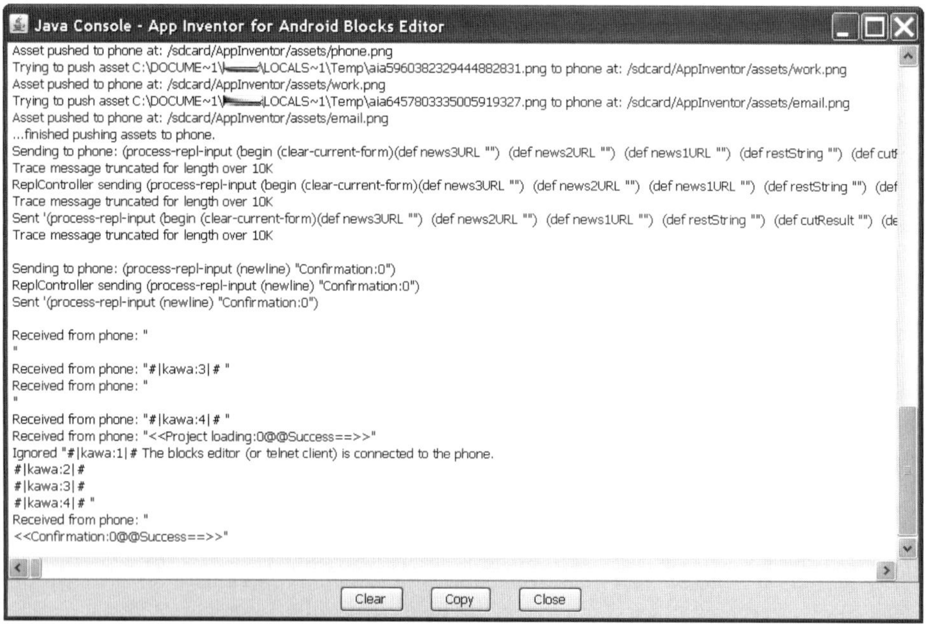

Figure 15.6 Creating the connection between the Blocks Editor and the smartphone

As these examples are meant to suggest, the Java console can help you find out a lot more about the processes taking place behind the scenes of the AI IDE, both on the remote AI servers of the provider and on your own computer, as well as between the individual elements of the development environment, such as AI Designer, the Blocks Editor, and your smartphone or the emulator. Even if you do not want to use the Java console permanently, you should keep it in mind as an option for cases where you may need this background knowledge.

Setting Up the Speech Module

The development or use of apps that read text aloud requires a corresponding module for speech synthesis on the smartphones you are using. This module is not always installed and enabled on all smartphones, and in some cases you may want to adapt the language. Have a look in the application overview of your smartphone or in a settings index for speech synthesis or output to see if setting options for *text-to-speech* (*TTS*) are available. If you find them, test the speech synthesis by listening to an example (preview). If the speech output works, your smartphone should be sufficiently ready for developing and using apps with speech output. If not, this section will give you a quick guide on how to prepare your smartphone for speech synthesis.

Installing Text-to-Speech

In case your smartphone does not have any TTS module installed at all, you can download a speech module from the Android Market. If you enter the search term "TTS," you will, for example, find the free speech module eSpeak for Android by Eyes-Free Project.

> **Speech Synthesis App: eSpeak for Android by Eyes-Free Project**
>
> To download the speech module and install it on your smartphone, simply enter the search term "eSpeak" or "TTS" on the Android Market.

The installation is initiated just as with any other app—that is, by pressing the Download button. The "Description" gives you a quick overview of the app and tells you how to enable it, as shown in Figure 15.7.

Figure 15.7 Downloading and enabling the speech module "eSpeak for Android"

Once the installation has been successfully completed, follow the instructions for setting up and testing eSpeak on your smartphone. Ensure that the speech output is working correctly to rule it out as a potential source of errors in your later app development. Perhaps you would like to change other settings for speech synthesis. Read the following section to find out how to do so.

Speech Synthesis Settings

Although speech synthesis is supposedly included with Android 1.6 and subsequent versions of the operating system, the country-specific speech modules required for input and output in the languages of different countries are often missing on smartphones. You can check whether your smartphone has an output language installed by default by going to the application overview, selecting the Settings tab, and choosing the menu item "Speech Synthesis" or "Voice input & output" (depending on your smartphone), as shown in Figure 15.8.

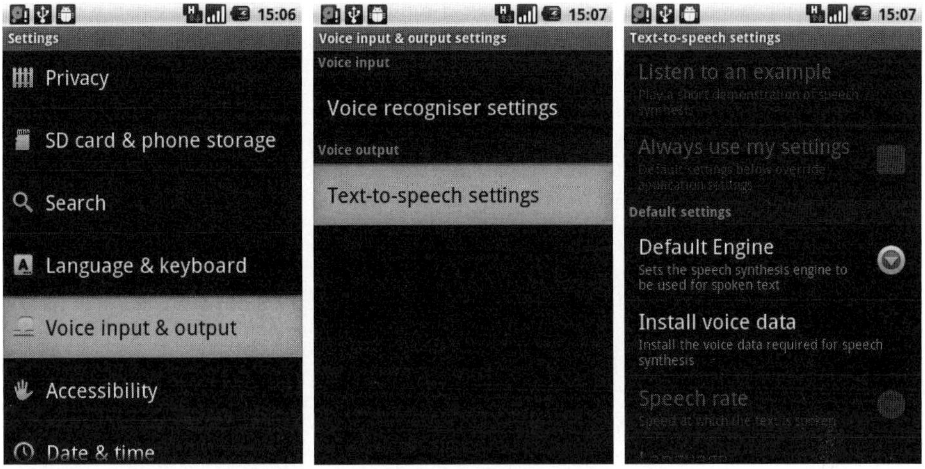

Figure 15.8 Checking the settings for speech synthesis on the smartphone

If your smartphone shows the menu item "Listen to an example" as grayed out (as in Figure 15.8) or not selectable, this is usually an indication that the speech synthesis either is not configured or is incompletely configured. Incomplete configuration is apparent when the menu item "Default Engine" is selectable, such that a corresponding module for speech synthesis does seem to be present on the smartphone. This is confirmed when you scroll down the menu and find, for example, "Pico TTS" (or "eSpeak") in the category "Engines" as an installed speech synthesis module, as shown in Figure 15.9 on the left.

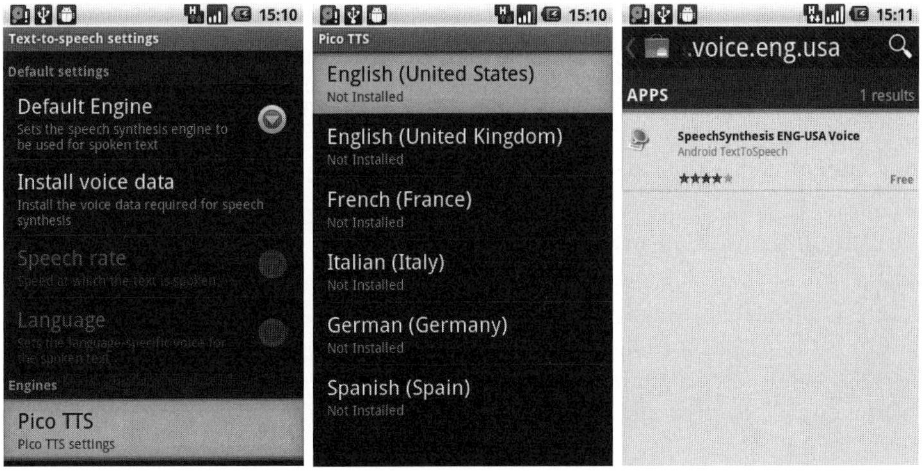

Figure 15.9 Installation of a speech module for speech synthesis in English

If you select the Pico TTS speech synthesis module, another menu for selecting the desired language will open. As you can see in Figure 15.9, all languages still have the comment "Not Installed." To select a language, you must first download and install the corresponding language package. Press the menu item "English (United States)" to go to the Android Market and start the search. The appropriate language package is then shown as a result. You can install it on your smartphone just like any other app by pressing the Download button, as shown in Figure 15.10 on the left.

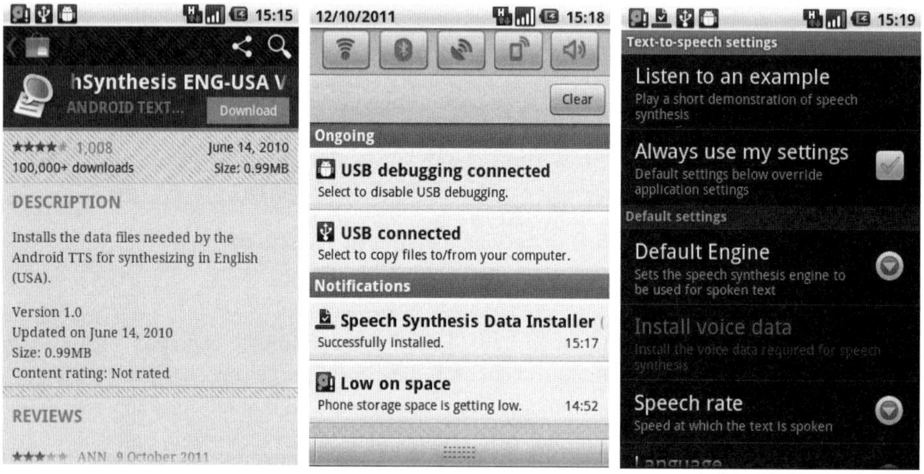

Figure 15.10 Speech synthesis settings after successful installation

After successful installation of the speech package for English, the many other setting options in the "Text-to-speech settings" menu become available. In Figure 15.10 (right), you can test the speech synthesis by tapping "Listen to an example"; you can also change more settings, if you like. With this step, you have successfully implemented the preparations necessary for developing and using AI apps with speech synthesis functions via text-to-speech. If you run into other problems with speech output during your development work with AI, you can always come back to this chapter and read the next section.

Troubleshooting Speech Output

Even if the speech module on your smartphone has been configured properly, sometimes problems may crop up when you are developing AI apps that make use of the TextToSpeech component. For example, executing the block statement `TextToSpeech1.Speak` can result in a serious runtime error (Figure 15.11), after which you can do no more than end the app.

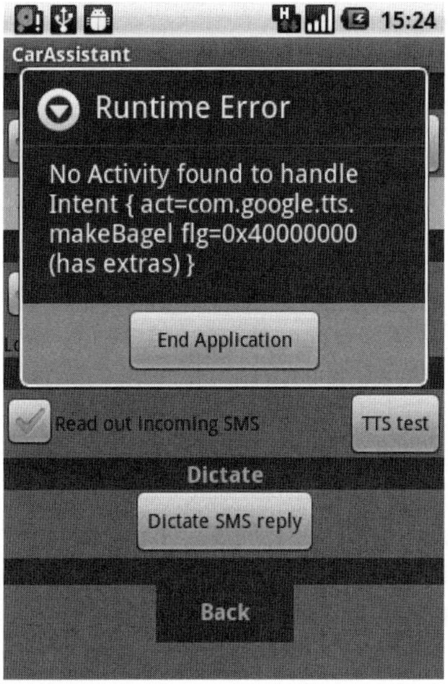

Figure 15.11 Runtime error in an AI app using the TextToSpeech component

The error message shown in Figure 15.11 indicates that a request action—in this case, a request started internally by the block statement `TextToSpeech1.Speak` to the Android system via the intent `act=com.google.tts.makeBagel` for speech output of a text block—has not been received by any TTS module on the smartphone and has, therefore, failed. At the time of writing, the apps generated with AI could only start this special intent to launch a TTS activity; that is, another TTS module on your smartphone was required to react to this intent with a suitable activity. You will find this module under the name *TTS Extended Service* (from Eyes-Free Project) on the Android Market, where you can also download it free of charge.

TTS Extended Service by Eyes-Free Project

If the error message shown in Figure 15.11 should occur when you are developing AI apps with text-to-speech functionality on your smartphone, installing the module TTS Extended Service is the only thing that is likely to help. Search for this module on the Android market, or download the APK file `tts_3.1_market.apk` from the website for the Eyes-Free Project:

`http://code.google.com/p/eyes-free/`

`http://code.google.com/p/eyes-free/downloads/list`

A barcode for directly installing the TTS Extended Service onto your smartphone via a barcode scanner can be found at the following address (see also Figure 15.12):

`http://code.google.com/p/eyes-free/downloads/detail?name=tts_3.1_market.apk&can=2&q=`

Figure 15.12 Barcode and link for downloading the TTS Extended Service

Download the TTS Extended Service to your smartphone and install it like any other app or TTS module. For automatically downloading the required language files, launch the app via the app menu. Set up TTS Extended if necessary, and test the speech output by pressing the "Listen to an example" button. Now you can test your AI app again as an independent app on your smartphone with the previously problematic TextToSpeech component and (we hope) enjoy the speech output of your app.

If you are the owner of a smartphone with the Android version "Froyo" or a later version, you may face an additional challenge. With Android 2.2 onward, the TTS functions have been integrated into the operating system—except, sadly, those functions that process the intent `com.google.tts.makeBagel`. Thus the problem described earlier may also surface in the Android smartphones of the newest generation. In addition, you will not find the TTS Extended Service for such a smartphone on the Android Market, so you cannot download this module from there, either. During your search request, the Android Market registers that you are sending the request from a smartphone equipped with Android 2.2 (e.g., the LG P500), which includes the preinstalled TTS module, and automatically filters out all superfluous apps in the search results. In this case, the only solution is downloading the APK file from another source, such as the website of the Eyes-Free Project mentioned earlier.

Appendix

Additional Resources

On the Companion Website

On the companion website for this book, you will find all demo and example projects from the book, as well as all media files such as the pictures or sounds needed for the projects. With the latter files, you can recreate all projects described in the book from scratch by yourself, which will help you better understand the individual learning steps described in the book. The complete project files, which are provided in ZIP format, allow you to comfortably upload the entire project to AI Designer; you can then take a closer look at the components in AI Designer and the block structures in AI Editor, and experiment with them if you want. All projects are also provided as finished apps in APK format so that you can install and try them straight away on your smartphone before re-creating the projects yourself or modifying them for your own purposes and new projects. In detail, the companion website contains the following directories:

- `\APK`: Finished apps as APK files, ready for installation on your smartphone. Connect your smartphone via a USB cable to the computer, mount it as a drive, and copy the desired APK files from the companion website to your smartphone (or rather its SD card). You can then open the APK file on your smartphone via a file manager—for example, AndExplorer by Lysesoft (see Android Market)—which starts the usual installation process. At that point, the relevant app will be available on your smartphone with its start icon.
- `\MEDIA`: Individual media files, such as pictures in PNG and JPG format and audio files in WAV format, that are used in the demo and example projects throughout this book. Load them in AI Designer as part of the project you are working on, via the property fields of the components that should have images (e.g., Picture, Image, Icon) or audio files (e.g., Source) associated with them. Of course, you can also create and use your own media files, if you prefer.
- `\PROJECT`: The entire project files as ZIP archives for all demo and example projects of this book. You can upload the complete ZIP files (do not extract or unzip them) conveniently as follows: My Projects > More Options > Upload Source to AI

Designer; you can then view and edit the files in AI Designer as necessary. In the section "Save Project Locally" in Chapter 3, you will find further details on the directories and files contained in an app project developed in the AI IDE.

> **Downloading Files from the Companion Website Locally First**
>
> It is best if you download all directories and files from the companion website (www.informit.com/title/9780321812704) to your computer at one time, as you can only use locally saved files for direct uploading to the AI development environment. For the projects described in this book, you can then simply use the local copies of the files.

Online Sources and Interesting Links

A book is printed and permanent—unlike websites, which are constantly changing and adapting to the most recent developments. For that reason, you should refer to the online resources when developing Android apps with App Inventor, both while you are reading this book and after you have finished it and begun to work on your own. That strategy will ensure that you get the most out of your experience as a developer, that your apps are cutting edge, and, above all, that the users of your apps perceive them as up-to-date. In the next section, you will find a collection of important and useful web addresses that can serve as a starting point for your further projects and research.

Official Resources

Here are the links for the official start pages, resources, and documentations of the App Inventor and Android Developers platforms:

- App Inventor at MIT: Official website from Massachusetts Institute of Technology and the associated Center for Mobile Learning (CML), which hosts and develops AI with support from Google, and provides AI as a free service to the public. This is the central starting point for working with AI, and it includes all kinds of background information, download and access addresses, official documents, tutorials, the official user forum, the issues list, and the cloud-based development environment itself.
    - Direct link to the public MIT AI system, open to all users:
      `http://beta.appinventor.mit.edu`
    - Direct link to the AI Experimental system (formerly closed user group):
      `http://experimental.appinventor.mit.edu`
    - The central AI information and start website at MIT:
      `http://appinventor.mit.edu`
    - The official website of the CML at the MIT Media Lab:
      `http://mitmobilelearning.org`

- The teacher's website for MIT AI in education:

  `http://appinventoredu.mit.edu`

- App Inventor at Google (historic): Former official website from Google, which was officially supported until December 31, 2011, and the central starting point for working with the development environment AI until then. It includes all kinds of background information, download and access addresses, official documents, tutorials, the official user forum, the issues list, and the cloud-based development environment itself:
  - The public service:

    `http://appinventorbeta.com`
  - Tutorials, documentation, and the AI Forum:

    `http://appinventorbeta.com/learn`

    `http://appinventorbeta.com/forum`
- Android Developers: Official website for all aspects of developing Android apps. The main focus is on development with Java, but much useful information and tools for development with AI are provided as well:

  `http://developer.android.com`

Initiatives, Tutorials, and Collections of Examples

The following sites represent just some of the constantly growing number of private and semi-official resources and websites focusing on app development with App Inventor. Visit them to find very useful tips as well as further examples and ideas for your own projects.

- App Inventor Blog: Blog on current topics related to App Inventor by the AI pioneer Professor David Wolber (University of San Francisco):

  `http://appinventorblog.com/`
- Blocks123: Collection of demos and example implementations with the most varied components and functions, which you can certainly make use of in your own apps:

  `https://sites.google.com/site/blocks123/`
- Collection of video tutorials by J. W. Tyler on different AI topics with tips and tricks:

  `http://android.jwtyler.com/Tutorials.html`
- App Inventor Extender: A kind of functions library for extending the AI function range by Pete Matt, which you can integrate via the activity starter to implement online data exchange via GET and POST (UrlFetch), display websites in AI (Webframes), and create and use shared data banks for different apps locally on the smartphone (TinySharedDB):

  `https://sites.google.com/site/appinventorextender/home`
- App Inventor Repository (tAIR): Comprehensive collection of examples, tips, and tricks for app development with AI:

http://www.tair.info/home

http://sites.google.com/site/theairepository/

http://code.google.com/p/the-ai-repository/

Background, History, and Outlook

The following sources provide background information on App Inventor, which can give you a better understanding of the approach used by this visual development language.

- The beginnings of App Inventor as a teaching and learning instrument for colleges and universities:

  http://googleresearch.blogspot.com/2009/07/app-inventor-for-android.html

  http://web.mit.edu/newsoffice/2010/android-abelson-0819.html

- Information and background on the work done by Hal Abelson, a professor at MIT and the co-founder of App Inventor:

  http://en.wikipedia.org/wiki/Hal_Abelson

- Official positions of Google and MIT regarding the open-source version of App Inventor, and the new MIT-based center seeking to enhance App Inventor:

  http://googleresearch.blogspot.com/2011/08/new-mit-center-for-mobile-learning-with.html

  http://web.mit.edu/press/2011/mit-launches-new-center-for-mobile-learning.html

Running Your Own Service with App Inventor Open Source

Since the setup and operation of the open-source version of AI is beyond this book's scope, the following sources provide background information on how to set up and run your own App Inventor service on Google's App Engine.

- Information about the open-source version of AI:

  http://appinventor.mit.edu/explore/content/running-your-own-app-inventor-service.html

- Official JAR testing forum:

  http://groups.google.com/group/mit-appinventor-jars

Index

Essential Resources for Android Developers

Android™ for Programmers
Paul Deitel, Harvey Deitel, Abby Deitel, and Michael Morgano
ISBN-13: 978-0-13-212136-1

Sams Teach Yourself Android™ Application Development in 24 Hours, Second Edition
Lauren Darcey and Shane Conder
ISBN-13: 978-0-672-33569-3

The Android Developer's Cookbook
James Steele and Nelson To
ISBN-13: 978-0-321-74123-3

Learning Android Game Programming
Rick Rogers
ISBN-13: 978-0-321-76962-6

Android App Development Fundamentals I and II LiveLessons Downloadable Video
Paul J. Deitel
ISBN-13: 978-0-13-216062-9

Android™ Wireless Application Development: Volume I, Third Edition
Lauren Darcey and Shane Conder
ISBN-13: 978-0-321-81383-1

Android Apps with App Inventor
Jörg H. Kloss
ISBN-13: 978-0-321-81270-4

Addison Wesley · PRENTICE HALL · SAMS

Titles are available in print and eBook formats.

informIT — For more information and to read sample material, please visit informit.com.

Safari Books Online — Titles are also available at safari.informit.com.

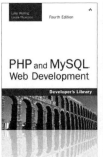

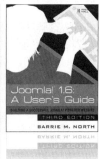